THE OXFORD HISTORY OF

WESTERN MUSIC

THE OXFORD HISTORY OF WESTERN MUSIC

VOLUME 1

The Earliest Notations to the Sixteenth Century

VOLUME 2

The Seventeenth and Eighteenth Centuries

VOLUME 3

The Nineteenth Century

VOLUME 4

The Early Twentieth Century

VOLUME 5

The Late Twentieth Century

VOLUME 6

Resources: Chronology, Bibliography, Master Index

THE OXFORD HISTORY OF

WESTERN

MUSIC

Richard Taruskin

Volume 6

RESOURCES: CHRONOLOGY, BIBLIOGRAPHY,
MASTER INDEX

OXFORD

UNIVERSITY PRESS

2005

OXFORD
UNIVERSITY PRESS

Oxford   New York

Auckland   Bangkok   Buenos Aires   Cape Town   Chennai
Dar es Salaam   Delhi   Hong Kong   Istanbul   Karachi   Kolkata
Kuala Lumpur   Madrid   Melbourne   Mexico City   Mumbai   Nairobi
São Paulo   Shanghai   Taipei   Tokyo   Toronto

Copyright © 2005 by Oxford University Press, Inc.

Published by Oxford University Press, Inc.
198 Madison Avenue, New York, New York 10016
http://www.oup.com/us

Oxford is a registered trademark of Oxford University Press

Library of Congress Cataloging-in-Publication Data
Taruskin, Richard.
The Oxford history of western music / by Richard Taruskin.
p. cm.
Includes bibliographical references and index.
ISBN 0-19-516979-4
1. Music — History and criticism. I. Title.
ML160.T18 2004
780′.9 — dc22
2004017897
ISBN Vol. 1   0-19-522270-9
ISBN Vol. 2   0-19-522271-7
ISBN Vol. 3   0-19-522272-5
ISBN Vol. 4   0-19-522273-3
ISBN Vol. 5   0-19-522274-1
ISBN Vol. 6   0-19-522275-X
1   3   5   7   9   8   6   4   2
Printed in the United States of America

Editorial and Production Staff

Editorial Directors
Maribeth Anderson Payne
Nancy Toff

Development Editors
Tanya Laplante
Jonathan Wiener

Editorial Assistant and Music Editor
Timothy Sachs

Editorial Assistant
Ryan Sullivan

Copy Editors, Fact Checkers, Proofreaders
Beth Adelman
Dorothy Bauhoff
Frances Barulich
Sylvia J. Cannizzaro
Wesley Chinn
Melissa A. Dobson
Mary Flower
Susan Gamer
James Adams Holman
Steve Holtje
Mark Laiosa
Alexa Nieschlag
Linda Sanders
Andrea Saposnik
Paul E. Schlotthauer
Peter E. Stone
Mary L. Sutherland
Matthew Zay

Music Engravers
A-R Editions, Inc.
André Cormier
Burt Fenner
Don Giller
Kenneth Godel
Dana Haynes
Ernie Mansfield
Brian Robinson
Woytek Rynczak
Bernard Allen Schulz

Dennis Stafira
Philip Thomas
Robert E. Thomas

Music Proofreaders
Stephen Black
Donna M. Di Grazia
J. Stephen Dydo
Brenda Fairaday
Steve Holtje
Jacqueline Horner
Orly L. Krasner
Marc Mellits
Johanna Maria Rose
Patrick Sharpe

Picture Researchers
Maria Vincenza Aloisi
Martin Baldessari
Gabriel Caplan
Ann Deborah Levy

Cartographer
William L. Nelson

Line Artist
A Good Thing, Inc.

Indexers
Cynthia Crippen, AEIOU, Inc.
Margaret Dengler
Joan Wolk Editorial Services, LLC

Designer
Lisa Chovnick

Compositor
Laserwords, Inc.

Manufacturing Controller
Christine Critelli

Director of Editing, Design, and Production
John Sollami

Director of Editorial Development and Production
Timothy J. DeWerff

Contents

VOLUME 1: The Earliest Notations to the Sixteenth Century

Introduction   xxi

Acknowledgments   xxxi

Chapter 1 The Curtain Goes Up   I
"Gregorian" Chant, the First Literate Repertory, and How It Got That Way

Literacy • The Romans and the Franks • The Carolingian Renaissance • The chant comes north • The legend of St. Gregory • The origins of Gregorian chant • Monastic psalmody • The development of the liturgy • The Mass and its music • Neumes • Persistence of oral tradition • Psalmody in practice: The Office • Psalmody in practice: The Mass • Evidence of "oral composition" • Why we will never know how it all began • Beginnings, as far as we know them

Chapter 2 New Styles and Forms   37
Frankish Additions to the Original Chant Repertory

Longissimae melodiae • *Prosa* • Sequences • How they were performed • Hymns • Tropes • The Mass Ordinary • Kyries • The full Franko-Roman Mass • "Old Roman" and other chant dialects • What is art?

Chapter 3 Retheorizing Music   69
New Frankish Concepts of Musical Organization and Their Effect on Composition

Musica • Tonaries • A new concept of mode • Mode classification in practice • Mode as a guide to composition • *Versus* • Liturgical drama • Marian antiphons • Theory and the art of teaching

Chapter 4 Music of Feudalism and *Fin' Amors*   105
The Earliest Literate Secular Repertories: Aquitaine, France, Iberia, Italy, Germany
Binarisms
AQUITAINE
Troubadours • Minstrels • High (Latinate) and low ("popular") style • Rhythm and Meter • *Trobar clus*
FRANCE
Trouvères • Social transformation • Adam de la Halle and the *formes fixes* • The first opera?

GEOGRAPHICAL DIFFUSION

Cantigas • A note on instruments • *Laude* and related genres • *Minnesang* • Popularization, then and since • *Meistersinger* • Peoples and nations • What is an anachronism? • Philosophy of History

Chapter 5 Polyphony in Practice And Theory   147
Early Polyphonic Performance Practices and the Twelfth-Century Blossoming of Polyphonic Composition

Another renaissance • "Symphonia" and its modifications • Guido, John, and discant • Polyphony in aquitanian monastic centers • The Codex Calixtinus

Chapter 6 Notre Dame de Paris   169
Parisian Cathedral Music in the Twelfth and Thirteenth Centuries and Its Makers

The cathedral-university complex • Piecing the evidence together • Measured music • Whys and wherefores • *Organum cum alio* • Theory or practice? • *Conductus* at Notre Dame

Chapter 7 Music for an Intellectual and Political Elite   207
The Thirteenth-Century Motet

A new class • The nascent motet • "Franconian" notation • Confluence of traditions • A new *trobar clus?* • Tenor "families" • Color and *talea* • The art of mélange • The "Petronian" motet

Chapter 8 Business Math, Politics, and Paradise: The *Ars Nova*   247
Notational and Stylistic Change in Fourteenth-Century France: Isorhythmic Motets from Machaut to Du Fay

A "new art of music"? • Music from mathematics • Putting it into practice • Representing it • Backlash • Establishing the prototype: The *Roman de Fauvel* • Taking a closer look • More elaborate patterning • Isorhythm • Music about music • Machaut: The occult and the sensuous • *Musica ficta* • Cadences • Ciconia: The motet as political show • Du Fay: The motet as mystical *summa* • A final word from Dante

Chapter 9 Machaut and His Progeny   289
Machaut's Songs and Mass; Music at the Papal Court of Avignon; Ars Subtilior

Maintaining the art of courtly song • Redefining (and re-refining) a genre • The top-down style • Cantilena • Functionally differentiated counterpoint • The luxuriant style • What instrumentalists did • Machaut's Mass and its background • Avignon • Votive formularies • *Ci commence la messe de nostre dame* • Kyrie • Gloria • Dismissal • *Subtilitas* • Canon • *Ars Subtilior* • Berry and Foix • Outposts • Faux-naïveté

Chapter 10 "A Pleasant Place": Music of the Trecento   351
Italian Music of the Fourteenth Century

CONTENTS

Vulgar eloquence • Madrigal culture • A new discant style • The "wild bird" songs •
Ballata culture • Landini • Late-century fusion • An important side issue:
Periodization

Chapter 11 Island and Mainland   387
Music in the British Isles through the Early Fifteenth Century and Its Influence on the Continent

The first masterpiece? • Viking harmony • Insular fauna? • *Pes* motets and *rondellus* •
The Worcester fragments • Nationalism? • "English descant" • The beginnings of
"functional" harmony? • Old Hall and Roy Henry • Fortunes of war • Dunstable and
the *"contenance angloise"* • Voluptuousness and how to acquire it • *Fauxbourdon* and
faburden • Du Fay and Binchois

Chapter 12 Emblems and Dynasties   453
The Cyclic Mass Ordinary Setting

The internationalism of the upper crust • The "Tinctoris generation" • The cyclic
Mass • Cantus firmus as trope of glory • "Caput" and the beginnings of four-part
harmony • How controversies arise (and what they reveal) • Patterns of emulation •
The composer as virtuoso • Farther along the emulation chain • The Man at Arms •
"Pervading imitation" • An esthetic paradox (or, The paradox of "esthetics") • Old and
young alike pay tribute

Chapter 13 Middle and Low   501
The Fifteenth-Century Motet and Chanson; Early Instrumental Music; Music Printing

Hailing Mary • Personal prayer • The English keep things high • The Milanese go
lower still • Fun in church? • Love songs • Instrumental music becomes literate at last
• Music becomes a business • "Songs" without words

Chapter 14 Josquin and the Humanists   547
Josquin des Prez in Fact and Legend; Parody Masses

What legends do • A poet born, not made • Josquin as the spirit of a (later) age •
Recycling the legend back into music • What Josquin was really like • A model
masterpiece • Parodies • Facts and myths

Chapter 15 A Perfected Art   585
Sixteenth-Century Church Music; New Instrumental Genres

All is known • The triad comes of age • "Il eccelentissimo Adriano" and his
contemporaries • Gombert • Clemens • Willaert and the art of transition • The
progress of a method • Academic art • Spatialized form • Alternatives to perfection •
Peeking behind the curtain • Dances old and new

IX

Chapter 16 The End of Perfection

629

Palestrina, Byrd, and the Final Flowering of Imitative Polyphony

Palestrina and the ecumenical tradition • Besting the Flemings; or, the last of the *tenoristas* • Parody pairs • Palestrina and the bishops • Freedom and constraint • Cryogenics • Byrd • Church and state • The first English cosmopolite • The music of defiance • Musical hermeneutics • The peak (and limit) of stylistic refinement

Chapter 17 Commercial and Literary Music

691

Vernacular Song Genres in Italy, Germany, and France; Lasso's Cosmopolitan Career

Music printers and their audience • Vernacular song genres: Italy • Germany: The *Tenorlied* • The "Parisian" chanson • Music as description • Lasso: The cosmopolite supreme • The literary revolution and the return of the madrigal • "Madrigalism" in practice • Paradox and contradiction • Exterior "nature" and interior "affect" • Postscript: The English madrigal

Chapter 18 Reformations and Counter-Reformations

753

Music of the Lutheran Church; Venetian Cathedral Music

The challenge • The Lutheran chorale • The response • *Augenmusik* • "Concerted" music • The art of orchestration is born • "Songs" for instruments

Chapter 19 Pressure of Radical Humanism

797

The "Representational" Style and the Basso Continuo; Intermedii; Favole in Musica

The technical, the esthetic, and the ideological • Academies • The representational style • Intermedii • The "monodic revolution" • Madrigals and arias redux • Favole in musica • Oratorio

Notes

835

Art Credits

849

VOLUME 2: The Seventeenth and Eighteenth Centuries

Chapter 20 Opera from Monteverdi to Monteverdi

1

Princely and Public Theaters; Monteverdi's Contributions to Both

Court and commerce • From Mantua to Venice • Poetics and esthesics • Opera and its politics • Sex objects, sexed and unsexed • The quintessential princely spectacle • The carnival show

Chapter 21 Fat Times and Lean

35

Organ Music from Frescobaldi to Scheidt; Schütz's Career; Oratorio and Cantata

Some organists • The toccata • Sweelinck—His patrimony and his progeny •
Lutheran adaptations: The chorale partita • The chorale concerto • Ruin • A creative
microcosm • Luxuriance • Shriveled down to the expressive nub • Carissimi: Oratorio
and cantata • Women in music: A historians' dilemma

Chapter 22 Courts Resplendent, Overthrown, Restored   85
Tragédie Lyrique from Lully to Rameau; English Music in the Seventeenth Century

Sense and sensuousness • The politics of patronage • Drama as court ritual • *Atys*, the
king's opera • Art and politics: Some caveats • Jacobean England • Masque and consort
• Ayres and suites: Harmonically determined form • Distracted times • Restoration •
Purcell • *Dido and Aeneas* and the question of "English opera" • The making of a classic

Chapter 23 Class and Classicism   139
Opera Seria and Its Makers

Naples • Scarlatti • Neoclassicism • Metastasio • Metastasio's musicians • The
fortunes of *Artaserse* • Opera seria in (and as) practice • "Performance practice"

Chapter 24 The Italian Concerto Style and the Rise of Tonality-Driven   177
Form
Corelli, Vivaldi, and Their German Imitators

Standardized genres and tonal practices • What, exactly, is "tonality"? • The spread of
"tonal form" • The fugal style • Handel and "defamiliarization" • Bach and
"dramatized" tonality • Vivaldi's five hundred • "Concerti madrigaleschi"

Chapter 25 Class of 1685 (I)   233
Careers of J. S. Bach and G. F. Handel Compared; Bach's Instrumental Music

Contexts and canons • Careers and lifestyles • Roots (domestic) • Roots (imported) •
Bach's suites • A close-up • "Agrémens" and "doubles" • Stylistic hybrids • The
"Brandenburg" Concertos • "Obbligato" writing and/or arranging • What does it
all mean?

Chapter 26 Class of 1685 (II)   305
Handel's Operas and Oratorios; Bach's Cantatas and Passions; Domenico Scarlatti

Handel on the Strand • Lofty entertainments • Messiah • "Borrowing" • Back to
Bach: The cantatas • The old style • The new style • Musical symbolism, musical
idealism • What music is for • Bach's "testaments" • The Bach revival • Cursed
questions • Scarlatti, at last

Chapter 27 The Comic Style   399
*Mid-Eighteenth-Century Stylistic Change Traced to Its Sources in the 1720s; Empfindsamkeit;
Galanterie; "War of the Buffoons"*

You can't get there from here • The younger Bachs • Sensibility • The London Bach • Sociability music • "Nature" • Intermission plays • The "War of the Buffoons"

Chapter 28 Enlightenment and Reform   445
The Operas of Piccinni, Gluck, and Mozart

Novels sung on stage • Noble simplicity • Another *querelle* • What was Enlightenment? • Mozart • *Idomeneo* • *Die Entführung aus dem Serail* • The "Da Ponte" operas • Late works • *Don Giovanni* close up • Music as a social mirror • Music and (or as) morality

Chapter 29 Instrumental Music Lifts Off   497
The Eighteenth-Century Symphony; Haydn

Party music goes public • Concert life is born • An army of generals • The Bach sons as "symphonists" • Haydn • The perfect career • The Esterházy years • Norms and deviations: Creating musical meaning • Sign systems • Anatomy of a joke • The London tours • Addressing throngs • Variation and development • More surprises • The culminating work

Chapter 30 The Composer's Voice   589
Mozart's Piano Concertos; His Last Symphonies; the Fantasia as Style and as Metaphor

Art for art's sake? • Psychoanalyzing music • The "symphonic" concerto is born • Mozart in the marketplace • Composing and performing • Performance as self-dramatization • The tip of the iceberg • Fantasia as metaphor • The coming of museum culture

Chapter 31 The First Romantics   641
Late Eighteenth-century Music Esthetics; Beethoven's Career and His Posthumous Legend

The beautiful and the sublime • Classic or Romantic? • Beethoven and "Beethoven" • *Kampf und Sieg* • The *Eroica* • Crisis and reaction • The "Ninth" • Inwardness

Chapter 32 C-Minor Moods   691
The "Struggle and Victory" Narrative and Its Relationship to Four C-Minor Works of Beethoven

Devotion and derision • Transgression • *Morti di Eroi* • Germination and growth • Letting go • The music century

Notes   741

Art Credits   755

VOLUME 3: The Nineteenth Century

Chapter 33 Real Worlds, and Better Ones   I
Beethoven vs. Rossini; Bel Canto Romanticism

Deeds of music • The dialectical antithesis • The Code Rossini • Imbroglio • Heart
Throbs • "Realism" • Bel canto • Utopia

Chapter 34 The Music Trance   61
Romantic Characterstücke; Schubert's Career

The I and the we • Private music • Altered consciousness • Salon culture • Schubert:
A life in art • Privatizing the public sphere • Crossing the edge • Only connect • New
cycles • B-minor moods • Constructions of identity

Chapter 35 *Volkstümlichkeit*   119
The Romantic Lied; Mendelssohn's Career; the Two Nationalisms

The lied is born • The discovery of the folk • *Kultur* • Lyrics and narratives • The lied
grows up: Haydn, Mozart, Beethoven • Schubert and romantic irony •
Representations of consciousness • Romantic nationalism • The liturgy of nationhood
• The oratorio reborn • Mendelssohn and civic nationalism • Nationalism takes a turn
• Epilogue: Two prodigies

Chapter 36 Nations, States, and Peoples   187
*Romantic Opera in Germany (Mozart, Weber), France (Auber, Meyerbeer), and
Russia (Glinka)*
I. PEASANTS (GERMANY)
Mr. Natural • Der Freischütz
II. HISTORY (FRANCE)
Opera and revolution • Bourgeois kings • Grandest of the grand • Vagaries
of reception
III. PEASANTS AND HISTORY (RUSSIA)
A newcomer to the tradition

Chapter 37 Virtuosos   251
Paganini and Liszt

Stimulus • Response • The concerto transformed • A divided culture

Chapter 38 Critics   289
Schumann and Berlioz

The public sphere • What is a philistine? • Literary music • How music poses
questions • Anxiety and recoil • Instrumental drama • The limits of music • Varieties
of representation • Discriminating romanticisms

Chapter 39 Self and Other   343
Chopin and Gottschalk as Exotics; Orientalism

Genius and stranger • National or universal? • Or exotic? • The pinnacle of salon
music • The Chopinesque miniature • Nationalism as a medium • Harmonic
dissolution • Playing "romantically" • The Chopinesque sublime • Sonata later on •
Nationalism as a message • America joins in • Art and democracy • Stereotyping the
other: "Orientalism" • Sex à la russe • The other in the self

Chapter 40 Midcentury   411
The New German School; Liszt's Symphonic Poems; Harmonic Explorations

Historicism • The new German school • The symphony later on • But what does it
really mean? • The new madrigalism • Art and truth • Art for art's sake

Chapter 41 Slavs as Subjects and Citizens   443
Smetana, Glinka, and Balakirev

Progressive vs. popular • The nationalist compact • Fluidity • Folk and nation • How
the acorn took root • National becomes nationalist • The politics of interpretation

Chapter 42 Deeds of Music Made Visible (Class of 1813, I)   479
Wagner

The problem • Art and revolution • The artwork of the future, modeled (as always)
on the imagined past • From theory into practice: The *Ring* • Form and content • The
texture of tenseless time • The sea of harmony • Desire and how to channel it • The
ultimate experience • How far can you stretch a dominant? • When resolution
comes. . . • The problem revisited

Chapter 43 Artist, Politician, Farmer (Class of 1813, II)   563
Verdi

Spooked • The galley years • The popular style • Tragicomedy • Opera as modern
drama • A job becomes a calling • Compression and expansion • Comedization

Chapter 44 Cutting Things Down to Size   617
Russian Realism (Musorgsky, Chaikovsky); Opéra Lyrique; Operetta; Verismo

Going too far • Art and autocracy • Stalemate and subversion • Crisis • Codes • Lyric
drama • Satyr plays • Operetta and its discontents • Verismo • Truth or sadism?

Chapter 45 The Return of the Symphony   675
Brahms

The dry decades • Museum culture • New paths • Three "Firsts" • Struggle (with whom?) • A choral (and a nationalistic) interlude • Inventing tradition • Victory through critique • Reconciliation and backlash • Brahminism • Developing variation

Chapter 46 The Symphony Goes (Inter)National   745
Bruckner, Dvořák, Beach, Franck, Saint-Saëns, Borodin, Chaikovsky

Germany recedes • Symphony as sacrament • A Bohemian prescription for America • An American response • War brings it to France • Symphonist as virtuoso • The epic style • Symphonies of Suffering

Notes   803

Art Credits   825

VOLUME 4: The Early Twentieth Century

Chapter 47 Reaching (for) Limits   I
Modernism: Mahler, Strauss, Schoenberg

Modernism • Maximalism • Mahler: Maximalizing the symphony • Is there or isn't there? (Not even the composer knows for sure) • High tension composing • Half-steps over fifths • *Lyrisches intermezzo* • Folklore for city folk • What then? • Decadence • Strauss: Maximalizing opera • Consummation • Another madwoman • Hysteria

Chapter 48 Getting Rid of Glue   59
Satie, Debussy, Fauré, Ravel, Lili Boulanger

Denaturing desire • Halfsteplessness • Impressionism • Symbolism • *Mélodie* • "Essentially" (and intolerantly) French • The exoticized self • The sensual surface • Russian fantasy • Female competition

Chapter 49 Aristocratic Maximalism   131
Ballet from Sixteenth-Century France to Nineteenth-Century Russia; Stravinsky

A missing genre • *Ballet d'action* • Off to Russia • Chaikovsky's ballets • Ballet finds its theorist • Back to France • Stravinsky • *Petrushka* • *The Rite of Spring* • The *ne plus ultra* • The reaction

Chapter 50 Extinguishing the "Petty 'I'" (Transcendentalism, I)   191
Scriabin; Messiaen

Maximalism reaches the max • Rush-to-the-patent-office modernism • From expression to revelation • Extinguishing the "I" • Approaching the ultimate • Ecstasy, and after • Atonality? • The final burst • A maximalist against the tide • "The charm of impossibilities" • So old it's new • The *summa summarum*

Chapter 51 Containing Multitudes (Transcendentalism, II) 243
Ives, Ruggles, Crawford; Microtonality

Maximalism, American style • Two American careers • Sexual—and stylistic—politics • Terms of reception • Manner and substance • Nostalgia • Reaching—and transcending—the limit • Accepting boundaries • More patent-office modernism • Transcendentalism vs. Futurism

Chapter 52 Inner Occurrences (Transcendentalism, III) 303
Schoenberg, Webern, and Expressionism; Atonality

Rejecting success • Expression becomes an "ism" • Art and the unconscious • "Emancipation of dissonance" • Theory and practice • Atonality? • "Contextuality" • Tonal or atonal? • A little "set theory" • *Grundgestalt* • Psychological realism • Atonal triads • Crossing the cusp • Musical space • "Brahminism" revisited • Maxing out • At the opposite extreme • The ivory tower
EPILOGUE: HOW MYTHS BECOME HISTORY
Schoenberg's Brahms • Ontogeny becomes phylogeny • "Motivicization" in practice

Chapter 53 Socially Validated Maximalism 365
Bartók, Janáček

What is Hungarian? • A change of course • A precarious symbiosis • A bit of theory • Symmetrical fugue, symmetrical sonata • A new tonal system? • Retreat? • The oldest twentieth-century composer? • Speech-tunelets • A musico-dramatic laboratory • Research *vs.* communication

Chapter 54 Pathos Is Banned 447
Stravinsky and Neoclassicism

The "real" twentieth century begins • Pastiche as metaphor • Cracking (jokes) under stress • Breaking with tradition • The end of the "long nineteenth century" • Vital vs. geometrical • Some more troubling politics • And now the music • Plus some famous words about it

Chapter 55 Lost—or Rejected—Illusions 495
Prokofieff; Satie Again; Berg's Wozzeck; *Neue Sachlichkeit, Zeitoper, Gebrauchsmusik (Hindemith, Krenek, Weill); Korngold, Rachmaninoff, and a New* Stile Antico

Breaching the fourth wall • Art as plaything • A new attitude toward the "classics"? • "How" vs. "what" • Putting things "in quotes" • Irony and social reality • "Americanism" and media technology • Music for political action • Righteous renunciation, or what? • New-morality plays • The death of opera? • From Vienna to Hollywood • A new *stile antico?*

Chapter 56 The Cult of The Commonplace 561
Satie, the French "Six," and Surrealism; Thomson and the "Lost Generation"

The Anti-*Petrushka* • "Lifestyle modernism" • Nakedness • Gender bending • From subject to style: Surrealist "classicism" • Groups • Finding oneself

Chapter 57 In Search of the "Real" America   599
European "Jazz"; Gershwin; Copland; the American "Symphonists"

Americans in Paris, Parisians in America • Transgression • Redemption • "Sociostylistics" • The Great American Symphony • Ferment on the left • "Twentieth-century Americanism" • Prairie neonationalism

Chapter 58 In Search of Utopia   675
Schoenberg, Webern, and Twelve-Tone Technique

Progress vs. restoration • Discovery or invention? • *Nomos* (the law) • Giving music an axiomatic basis • Irony claims its due • Back again to Bach • Consolidation • Spread • Clarification • Epitome

Chapter 59 Music and Totalitarian Society   743
Casella and Respighi (Fascist Italy); Orff, Hindemith, Hartmann (Nazi Germany); Prokofieff and Shostakovich (Soviet Russia)

Mass politics • Music and music-making in the new Italy • Degeneracy • Youth culture • Varieties of emigration • Shades of gray • Socialist realism and the Soviet avant-garde • Protagonist or victim? • Readings

Notes   797

Art Credits   823

VOLUME 5: The Late Twentieth Century

Chapter 60 Starting from Scratch   I
Music in the Aftermath of World War II; Zhdanovshchina, Darmstadt

A new age • Cold war • Denunciation and contrition • Breaking ranks • Zero hour • Polarization • Darmstadt • Fixations • "Total serialism" • Disquieting questions • Disquieting answers • Solace in ritual • Poster boy

Chapter 61 Indeterminacy   55
Cage and the "New York School"

Means and ends • Whose liberation? • *Ne plus ultra* (going as far as you can go) • Purification and its discontents • Permission • Music and politics revisited • Internalized conflict • Conflicts denied • New notations • Preserving the sacrosanct

Chapter 62 The Apex   103
Babbitt and Cold War Serialism

Conversions • "Mainstream" dodecaphony • The grand prize • The path to the new/old music • Requiem for a heavyweight • Academicism, American style • An integrated musical time/space • Full realization • Another cold war • Logical positivism • The new patronage and its fruits • Elites and their discontents • Life within the enclave • But can you *hear* it? • Ultimate realization or reductio ad absurdum?

Chapter 63 The Third Revolution 175
Music and Electronic Media; Varèse's Career

Tape • An old dream come true • Generating synthetic sounds • A maximalist out of season • "Real" vs. "pure" • The new technology spreads • The big science phase • A happy ending • Big questions reopened • Reciprocity • Renaissance or co-option?

Chapter 64 Standoff (I) 221
Music in Society: Britten

History or society? • Some facts and figures • A modern hero • Social themes and leitmotives • Allegory (but of what?) • Exotic/erotic • To serve by challenging

Chapter 65 Standoff (II) 261
Music in History: Carter

Explain nothing • From populism to problem-solving: An American career • Theory: The Time Screen • Practice: The First Quartet • Reception • A wholly disinterested art? • At the pinnacle

Chapter 66 The Sixties 307
Changing Patterns of Consumption and the Challenge of Pop

What were they? • The music of youth • The British "invasion" • Defection • Rock'n'roll becomes rock • Fusion • Integration without prejudice? • Radical chic

Chapter 67 A Harmonious Avant-Garde? 351
Minimalism: Young, Riley, Reich, Glass; Their European Emulators

New sites of innovation • Legendary beginnings • Music as spiritual discipline • A contradiction in terms? • "Classical" minimalism • Secrets of structure • "All music is folk music" • A postmodernist masterwork? • "Crossover": Who's on top? • Disco at the Met • Americanization • Closing the spiritual circle

Chapter 68 After Everything 411
Postmodernism: Rochberg, Crumb, Lerdahl, Schnittke

Postmodernism? • Its beginnings for music • A parenthesis on collage • Collage as theater • Apostasy • Esthetics of pastiche • Accessibility • Cognitive constraints? • Where to go from here? • One proposal • The end of Soviet music • Polystylistics

Chapter 69 Millennium's End   473
The Advent of Postliteracy: Partch, Monk, Anderson, Zorn; New Patterns of Patronage

Grand old men • Terminal complexity • "Big science" eclipsed • Twentieth-century
"orality" • Hobo origins • Imaginary folklore • A feminine redoubt • Music and
computers • The elite phase • Spectralism • "Then along came MIDI!" • First fruits •
Modernists in postmodernist clothing? • A glimpse of the future? • Back to nature •
Paying the piper, calling the tune • A new topicality • A new spirituality

Notes   529

Art Credits   555

VOLUME 6: Resources: Chronology, Bibliography, Master Index

Chronology   I

Further Reading: A Checklist of Books in English   67

List of Musical Examples in Order of Appearance   121

Index of Musical Examples by Composer   171

Master Index   183

THE OXFORD HISTORY OF

WESTERN MUSIC

CHRONOLOGY

MUSIC, OTHER ARTS AND PHILOSOPHY, HISTORY

1200 B.C.E. – 2003

Compiled by

Frances M. Barulich

Paul E. Schlotthauer

Date	Music	Other Arts and Philosophy	History
ca. 1200 B.C.E.	Musical notation on a cuneiform tablet in ancient Babylonian city of Ugarit		20th Dynasty in Egypt
8th century B.C.E.		Homer, *Iliad* and *Odyssey*	Rise of Greek city-states Traditional founding of Rome (753) First Olympic games (776)
6th century B.C.E.	Pythagoras (ca. 580–ca. 500)	Sappho (fl. ca. 610–580), *Odes* Anacreon (ca. 582–ca. 485) Theater at Syracuse built	Roman republic established (509–27)
5th century B.C.E.		Aeschylus (525–456), *Oresteia, Prometheus Bound* Pindar (ca. 522–ca. 438), *Odes* Sophocles (ca. 496–406), *Antigone, Oedipus Rex, Electra* Euripides (ca. 484–406), *Medea, Electra* Socrates (469–399) Aristophanes (ca. 450–ca. 388), *The Clouds, The Birds, Lysistrata* Parthenon built on the Acropolis in Athens	Herodotus (484–432), *History* Thucydides (ca. 460–ca. 401), *History of the Peloponnesian War* Twelve Tables codifying Roman law (ca. 450)
4th century B.C.E.	Aristoxenus (b. ca. 375–360), *Harmonic Elements; Rhythmic Elements*	Aristotle (384–322), *Poetics;* founds Lyceum in Athens (335) Plato (ca. 429–347) founds the Academy ca. 385; *Timaeus* Euclid (fl. ca. 300), *Elements*	Construction of Appian Way begins (312)
3rd century B.C.E.		Lighthouse at Pharos, Alexandria, completed (ca. 280) Colossus of Rhodes completed (ca. 280)	Library at Alexandria begun Hannibal (247–ca. 183–181) crosses the Alps (217)
2nd century B.C.E.	Delphic hymn noted on stone tablet (ca. 130)	Terence (ca. 195–159), comedies	
1st century B.C.E.		Cicero (106–43), *De republica, De legibus* Lucretius (ca. 96–ca. 55), *On the Nature of Things* Catullus (84–54), *Odes* Virgil (70–19) begins the *Aeneid* (ca. 30) Horace (65–8), *Satires, Odes*	Julius Caesar (100–44) assassinated Roman empire founded (27 B.C.E.–476 C.E.)
1st century C.E.	Temple destroyed by Romans, bringing an end to pre-Christian Jewish psalmody (70)	Seneca (ca. 4 B.C.E.–65 C.E.), plays Ovid (43 B.C.E.–17 C.E.), *Metamorphoses* (7) Roman Colosseum dedicated (80)	Mount Vesuvius erupts, destroying Roman cities of Pompeii and Herculaneum (79) Fire in Rome destroys much of Emperor Nero's city (64)

Date	Music	Other Arts and Philosophy	History
2nd century	Nicomachus (fl. late 1st–early 2nd century), *Harmonikon encheiridion* (Manual of Harmonics) Ptolemy (after 83–161), *Harmonics*		Cornelius Tacitus (ca. 55–ca. 117), *Histories* and *Annals* Hadrian's Wall built
3rd century		Baths of Caracalla completed in Rome (216)	
4th century	Fragment of Christian service music notated on papyrus strip preserving Greek-texted music of Orthodox church of Eastern Roman empire St. Ambrose (ca. 340–397), hymnographer St. Augustine (354–430), *De musica* (391)	Constantine (280?–337) builds St. Peter's basilica in Rome (320–327) St. Augustine, *Confessions* (ca. 400)	Rise of Christian monasticism Vulgate, standard Latin translation of the Bible, prepared by St. Jerome Edict of Milan establishes toleration of Christianity (313) Council of Nicaea (325) Constantine establishes Constantinople as the capital of the Roman empire (330)
5th century			Fall of the Roman empire (476) Rise of feudalism Clovis I (ca. 466–511), king of the Franks, converts to Christianity (496)
6th century	Boethius (ca. 480–ca. 524), *De institutione musica* (probably from first decade of 6th century) Venantius Fortunatus (530–540 to ca. 600), *Pange lingua gloriosi*	Academy founded by Plato closed by Emperor Justinian (529) Gregory of Tours (538/539–594/595), *Historia francorum*	St. Benedict (ca. 480–543) founds monastery at Monte Cassino (*Regula monachorum*, 529)
8th century	Paul the Deacon (ca. 720–ca. 799), hymn text *Ut queant laxis*		
ca. 715		Lindisfarne Gospels (–720)	
731			Venerable Bede (673–735), *Historia ecclesiastica gentis Anglorum*
754			Pope Stephen II (r. 752–757) appeals to Pepin III (715–758), king of the Franks, for help against the Lombards who are threatening Rome
773			Charlemagne (742–814) defeats Lomabards in Italy, incorporating their kingdom into his own
ca. 781			Alcuin (ca. 735–804) invited by Charlemagne to set up a cathedral school
789	*Admonitio generalis* issued by Charlemagne		
ca. 800		*Book of Kells* *Hildebrandslied*	

Date	Music	Other Arts and Philosophy	History
800			Pope Leo III (r. 795–816) crowns Charlemagne as temporal ruler (with Leo as spiritual ruler) of Western Roman empire, inaugurating the Holy Roman Empire
9th century	Pope Gregory (r. 590–604) credited by the Carolingian kings as composer-codifier of Roman chant through divine inspiration *Alia musica* Amalar of Metz (ca. 775–ca. 850), *Liber officialis* *Musica enchiriadis* (between 860 and 900) uses Daseian notation *Scolica enchiriadis*		
814			Louis the Pious (b. 778; r. to 840) succeeds his father, Charlemagne, as emperor
ca. 840	*born:* Notker Balbulus		
ca. 843	Aurelian of Réôme (fl. ?840–50), *Musica disciplina*		
843			Treaty of Verdun divides Carolingian empire among Charlemagne's three grandsons
ca. 870		Otfrid (fl. 9th century), *Evangelienbuch*	
ca. 880	Hucbald (ca. 850–930), *De harmonica institutione* Notker, *Liber hymnorum*		
10th century	Carolingian neumes St. Martial tropers		
ca. 901	Tonary of Regino of Prüm (ca. 842–915)		
910			Abbey of Cluny, Roman Catholic monastic congregation, founded in Burgundy
912	*died:* Notker		
973		*Regularis concordia*	
ca. 975		Old English poetry collected in the Exeter Book	
997	Winchester Tropers (to 1006)		
ca. 1000	*Dialogus de musica*		

Date	Music	Other Arts and Philosophy	History
11th century	Structure of Mass Ordinary solidified Chartres fragment (late 11th century)	*Beowulf* written down Extensive church construction	
1013	*born*: Hermannus Contractus		
ca. 1028	Guido of Arezzo (b. ca. 991–992, d. after 1033), *Micrologus*		
1054	*died*: Hermannus (treatise *Musica*)		Schism between Eastern and Western Christian churches
1066			Norman conquest
1071		Basilica of St. Mark's completed	
1077		Bayeux tapestry, portraying scenes from the Norman conquests	
1079	*born*: Pierre Abelard		
1084			Carthusian order founded by Bruno of Cologne
1085			William the Conqueror commissions the Domesday Book
1088			University of Bologna founded
1098	*born*: Hildegard of Bingen *died*: Adhemar, bishop of LePuy (Marian antiphon *Salve regina*)		Cistercian monastic order founded
1099			"Latin Kingdom of Jerusalem" established by the First Crusades
ca. 1100	John Afflighem (fl. ca. 1100), *De musica* "St. Martial" manuscripts (to ca. 1150) compiled *Ad organum faciendum*	*Chanson de Roland*	
12th century	Square notation becomes prevalent Marcabru (fl. ca. 1129–ca. 1150), pastorela *L'autrier jost' una sebissa* Arnaut Daniel (1150–1160 to ca. 1200) *A l'entrada del tens clar* (balada) Magnus Liber (second half of 12th century to early 13th century) of Leonin (fl. 1150s–ca. 1201) and Perotin (fl. ca. 1200) Beatriz, countess of Dia (late 12th century), *A chantar*	Abelard, *Sic et non* John of Salisbury (1115–1120 to 1180), *Metalogicus* and *Policraticus*	

Date	Music	Other Arts and Philosophy	History
12th century	Chrétien de Troyes (fl. ca. 1160–1190), *Lancelot* and *Perceval* Audefroi le Bastart (fl. 1190–1230), chanson de toile *Bele Ydoine* Founding of the Confrérie des Jongleurs et des Bourgeois (late 12th century–ca. mid-14th century) Fleury Playbook, including *Play of Daniel*		
1115			St. Bernard (1090–1153) founds Abbey of Clairvaux
1122			Spiritual versus temporal supremacy settled by Concordat of Worms; Guelfs support pope, Ghibellines support German emperor
ca. 1127	*died:* William IX of Aquitaine		
1128		Cathedral of Santiago de Compostela consecrated	
ca. 1130	*born:* Bernart de Ventadorn (–1195?)		
1137			Eleanor of Aquitaine (ca. 1122–1204) marries future King Louis VII (ca. 1121–1180) of France
ca. 1140	*born:* Guiraut de Bornelh		
1140		Abbey and basilica of St. Denis constructed (–1144)	
1142	*died:* Abelard		
1146	*died:* Adam of St. Victor (sequence *Laudes crucis attolamus*)		
ca. 1147	John of Salisbury (ca. 1110–1180), *Polycraticus*		
ca. 1150	Hildegard, *Symphonia armonie celestium revelationum*	Heinrich von Melk (fl. 1150), *Von des Tôdes gehügede* (–1160)	
1152			Eleanor of Aquitaine marries future King Henry II (1133–1189) of England
ca. 1155			Carmelite order founded in Palestine
1156			Frederick I (1125–1190), Holy Roman emperor and German king, marries duchess Beatrice of Burgundy (ca. 1145–1184)

Date	Music	Other Arts and Philosophy	History
1157	*born*: Richard Lion-Heart		
ca. 1160	*born*: Conon de Béthune; Gace Brulé	*König Rother*	
1163			Cornerstone of Notre Dame in Paris laid by Pope Alexander III (r. 1159–1181)
ca. 1167			University of Oxford founded
ca. 1170	Codex Calixtinus, containing *Congaudeant catholici* by Magister Albertus Parisiensis (fl. 1146–1177)	Eilhart von Oberg (fl. 1170–1180), *Tristrant*	
1170			Thomas à Becket (1118–1170) murdered in Canterbury cathedral
1173		Tower of Pisa begun	
1179	*died*: Hildegard (*Symphonia armonie celestium revelationum*, late 1150s; and liturgical drama *Ordo vurtutum*)		
1189			Richard Lion-Heart becomes king of England (—1199)
1192	Richard Lion-Heart, *Ja nun hons pris* (—1194)		
1199	Alexandre de Villedieu (ca. 1175–1250), *Doctrinale* Gaucelm Faidit (ca. 1150–ca. 1220), planh *Fortz causa es* *died*: Richard Lion-Heart		John Lackland (1167–1216), succeeds his brother as king of England
ca. 1200	*died*: Guiraut de Bornelh (alba *Reis glorios*); Bernart de Ventadorn (canso *Can vei la lauzeta mover*)	Jean Bodel (ca. 1165–ca. 1210), *Jeu de Saint Nicolas* *Nibelungenlied* Wolfram von Eschenbach (fl. ca 1170–1220), *Parzival* Nicholas of Verdun (fl. 1181–1205), Three Kings' shrine in Cologne cathedral;	
13th century	"Carmina burana" Moniot d'Arras (fl. 1213–1239), pastourelle *Ce fut en mai* Ernoul Caupain (fl. mid-13th century), chanson avec des refrains *Ier mains pensis chevauchai* Widespread use of *formes fixes* (ballade, virelai, rondeau) Italian vernacular song, *lauda spirituale* Minnelieder Twinsong *Nobilis, humilis* (late 13th century)	*Huon de Bordeaux*, chanson de geste Guido Cavalcanti (ca. 1255–1300), *Donna mi prega* Rutebeuf (fl. 1245–1285), *Miracle de Théophile*	Francis of Assisi (1181/1182–1226) founds Franciscan order, and Dominic (ca. 1170–1221) founds Dominican order (early 13th century)

Date	Music	Other Arts and Philosophy	History
1201	*born:* Thibaut IV		
1208			Albigensian Crusade (−1229)
1209			University of Cambridge founded
ca. 1210	*born:* Jehan Bretel		
1213	*died:* Gace (after 1213)		
1214	Plantus *Rex obiit et labitur*		
ca. 1215	*died:* Raimon de Miraval		
1215			Magna Carta signed
1220	*died:* Conon	Salisbury Cathedral begun	University of Montpellier founded
1222			University of Padua founded
1224	Walther von der Vogelweide (d. ca. 1230), *Palästinalied* (or 1225)		
ca. 1225		Francis of Assisi, *Laudes creaturarum*	
1226			Louis IX (1214–1270) succeeds his father as king of France
ca. 1230	*born:* Guiraut Riquier; Jacopone da Todi	Freidank (fl. 13th century), *Bescheidenheit* Guillaume de Lorris (fl. 13th century), *Roman de la Rose*	
1239		Master of Naumburg (fl. 13th century), sculptures at Mainz cathedral completed	
ca. 1240	Johannes de Garlandia (fl. ca. 1270–1320), *De mensurabili musica* and *De plana musica*		
1240	Sources of Notre Dame polyphony (−1280s) compiled: Florence manuscript (*Flo* or *F*); Wolfenbüttel 1 (W1); Wolfenbüttel 2 (W2); Madrid manuscript (Ma)		
1245	*born:* Adam de la Halle (−1250)		
1246	Manuscrit du Roi (−1254) compiled	Sainte Chapelle in Paris, commissioned by King Louis IX, built (−1248)	
1248		Foundation stone laid for the rebuilding of Cologne cathedral (consecrated 1322)	

Date	Music	Other Arts and Philosophy	History
ca. 1250	*Sumer is icumen in* *died*: Neidhardt von Reuenthal	Master of Naumburg, sculptures at Naumburg cathedral (—1260)	
1250	*Cantigas de Santa María* of Alfonso X (*El Sabio*) compiled (—1280)		
1253	*died*: Thibaut IV (*De bone amour*)		Sorbonne (University of Paris) founded
ca. 1260	*born*: Frauenlob	Cimabue (fl. 1272; d. 1302), *Madonna and Child* (—1280)	
1260	Bamberg Codex (—1290)	Burgos cathedral consecrated Chartres cathedral consecrated	
1265		Thomas Aquinas (ca. 1225–1274), *Summa theologiae* (—1273)	
ca. 1268		Master of Naumburg, sculptures at Meissen cathedral (—1280)	
ca. 1270	Worcester fragments (–ca. 1330) include *Balaam* motet, conductus-rondellus *Flors regalis*; conductus-motet *Beatus viscera* Magister Lambertus (fl. ca. 1270), *Tractatus de musica* Anonymous IV, *De mensuris et discantu* (–ca. 1280)		
1272	*died*: Jehan (jeu-parti with Adam de la Halle *Adan a moi respondés*)		
1274		Bonvesin de la Riva (ca. 1240–ca. 1315), *Libro delle tre scritture*	
1277		Cimabue, frescoes at Assisi (—1280)	
ca. 1280	Franco of Cologne (fl. mid- to late 13th century), *Ars cantus mensurabilis* Montpellier Codex (–ca. 1300)		
1282			Sicilian Vespers, the massacre of the French in Sicily
1283	Adam de la Halle, *Le jeu de Robin et Marion*		
1291	*born*: Philippe de Vitry		
1293		Dante (1265–1321), *Vita nuova*	City of Florence adopts Ordinances of Justice as a constitution
1296		Building of cathedral of Florence	

Date	Music	Other Arts and Philosophy	History
1297		Giotto (1267/75–1337), *Life of St. Francis*, frescoes in upper church of San Francesco, Assisi (–1305)	
ca. 1299		Marco Polo (ca. 1254–1324), *Il milione*	
ca. 1300	*born:* Guillaume de Machaut Walter Odington (fl. 1298–1316), *Summa de speculatione musicae* Johannes de Grocheio (fl. ca. 1300), *De musica* *died:* Riquier		
1301		Giovanni Pisano (ca. 1245–50—1319), Pistoia pulpit completed	
1304		Dante, *De vulgari eloquentia* (–1306)	
ca. 1305		Giotto frescoes in the Arena Chapel, Padua	
1306	*died:* Jacopone		
ca. 1307	*died:* Adam		
1307		Dante begins *The Divine Comedy*	
1309			Pope Clement V moves papal seat to Avignon
ca. 1316	Roman de Fauvel		
1318	*died:* Frauenlob		
1319	Marchetto of Padua (d. 1326), *Pomerium* Jehan des Murs (ca. 1290–1295 to after 1344), *Ars novae musicae* (–1321)		
1322	*Ars nova*, based on the teachings of Philippe de Vitry (–1323)		
1323			Pope John XXII (r. 1316–1334), *Docta sanctorum*
1326	*Rosula primula* in Robert de Handlo (fl. 1326), *Regule*		
ca. 1330	Jacobus de Liège (ca. 1260–after 1330), *Speculum musicae*	St. Gall Passion	
1330		Guillaume de Deguileville (fl. 14th century), *Le pèlerinage de la vie humaine* and *Le pèlerinage de l'âme* (–1358)	

Date	Music	Other Arts and Philosophy	History
1337			Hundred Years' War begins between England and France
1343		Gersonides (1288–1342), *De numeris harmonicis*	
1347			Black Death spreads through Europe (–1351)
1349	Hugo Spechtshart von Reutlingen (ca. 1285–1359 or 1360) transcribes *Geisslerlieder* Machaut, *Le remède de Fortune*		
1353		Giovanni Boccaccio (1313–1375) finishes the *Decameron*	
1356		Nicole d'Oresme (ca. 1320–1382), *Algorismus proportionum* (–1361)	
ca. 1360	Machaut, hoquetus "David" Machaut, *Messe de Nostre Dame*	William Langland (ca. 1330–ca. 1400), *Piers Plowman*	
1361	*died*: Vitry		
1363		Machaut, *Le voir dit* (–1365)	
1366		Petrarch (1304–1374), *Canzoniere* Andrea da Firenze (fl. 1346; d. 1379), frescoes in Spanish Chapel of Santa Maria Novella, Florence (–1367)	
1369			Philip the Bold (1342–1404), duke of Burgundy, marries Margaret of Flanders
ca. 1370	*born*: Johannes Ciconia Ivrea manuscript includes virelai *Or sus, vous cormez trop, Madame Joliete*		
ca. 1375	*born*: Leonel Power	*Sir Gawain and the Green Knight*	
1376	*born*: Oswald von Wolkenstein		
1377	*died*: Machaut		
1378			Great Schism begins: Urban VI (r. 1378–1389) at Rome and Clement VII (r. 1378–1394) at Avignon
1381			Peasants' Revolt in England
1385		Construction of Milan cathedral begins	
ca. 1386		John Gower (1330?–1408), *Confessio amantis*	

Date	Music	Other Arts and Philosophy	History
1387		Chaucer (ca. 1342–1400) begins *The Canterbury Tales*	
ca. 1390	*born:* John Dunstable	Franco Sacchetti (1330–1335 to 1400), *Trecentonovelle*	
1392	Eustache Deschamps (ca. 1346–ca. 1407), *Art de dictier et de fere chançons*		
1395		Estoire de Griseldis	
1397	*born:* Guillaume Du Fay		
ca. 1400	*born:* Gilles Binchois Apt manuscript Aegidius of Murino (fl. mid-14th century), *De motettis componendis*	Johannes von Tepl (ca. 1350–ca. 1415), *Ackermann aus Böhmen*	Jean Froissart (1333?–1400?), *Chronicles*
1405		Christine de Pisan (1364–ca. 1430), *La cité des dames*	
ca. 1409	Ciconia, isorhythmic motet *Doctorum principem super ethera/Melodia suavissima*		
ca. 1410	*born:* Johannes Ockeghem Old Hall Manuscript (–1450), includes Pycard, *Gloria;* Power, *Gloria;* and Roy Henry, *Sanctus* Faenza Codex (–1420)		
1411		Donatello (1386 or 1387–1466), marble statue of *St. Mark* (–1413)	
1412	*died:* Ciconia	John Lydgate (ca. 1370–ca. 1450), *Troy Book* (–1421)	
ca. 1415	Squarcialupi Codex, includes works by Jacopo da Bologna (fl. 1340–?1386), Giovanni da Cascia (fl. 1340–1350), Ghirardello da Firenze (ca. 1320–1325 to 1362 or 1363), Lorenzo da Firenze (d. 1372 or 1373), and Francesco Landini (1325–1397) Faenza Codex		
1415			King Henry V (1387–1422) of England defeats French at Agincourt
ca. 1416		Donatello, marble statue of *St. George*	
1417			Council of Constance ends the Great Schism

Date	Music	Other Arts and Philosophy	History
1418		Thomas à Kempis (1379–1380 to 1471), *De imitatione Christi*	
1420		Filippo Brunelleschi (1377–1446), dome of Florence cathedral (—1436)	Treaty of Troyes Marriage of Henry V of England and Catherine of Valois (1401–1437), daughter of King Charles VI of France (1368–1422)
1422			Henry VI (1421–1471) becomes king of England (and king of France); his uncles the duke of Bedford and the duke of Gloucester become regents
ca. 1423		Donatello, bronze statue of *David*	
1429			Joan of Arc (1412?–1431) liberates Orléans Charles VII (1403–1461) crowned king of France in Paris during the English occupation
ca. 1430	*born:* Antoine Busnoys Power, Mass on *Alma redemptoris Mater* (cyclic Mass) appears in manuscripts (—1435)		
1430			Philip of Burgundy (1396–1467) creates the Order of the Golden Fleece
1431		Luca Della Robbia (1399–1400 to 1482), work begins on *Cantoria* for cathedral of Florence	Joan of Arc burned at the stake
1432		Jan van Eyck (ca. 1395–1441), completes Ghent altarpiece	
1434		Jan van Eyck, *The Marriage of Giovanni Arnolfini and Giovanna Cenami*	Medici family comes to power in Florence
1436	Du Fay, motet *Nuper rosarum flores*	Filippo Brunelleschi's dome of Santa Maria del Fiore (Florence) completed	
1437		Fra Filippo Lippi (ca. 1406–1469), Tarquinia *Virgin and Child*	
1439		Lippi, Barbadori altarpiece	
ca. 1440		Martin le Franc, *Le champion des dames* Fra Angelico (ca. 1400–1445), murals for the monastery of San Marco (—1445)	

Date	Music	Other Arts and Philosophy	History
ca. 1440		Lippi, *Portrait of a Man and a Woman at a Casement* Book of Hours of Catherine of Cleves (—1145)	
1440			Eton College founded by King Henry VI
ca. 1445	*born*: Alexander Agricola; Loyset Compère; Hayne van Ghizeghem		Johannes Gutenberg (ca. 1400–1468) develops first printing press with movable type
1445	*died*: Oswald; Power		
ca. 1448		Fra Angelico, series of frescos for Vatican palace	
ca. 1450	*born*: Henricus Isaac (—1455); Josquin des Prez (—1455) Ockeghem, *Missa Caput*		
1450			Francesco Sforza (1401–1466) becomes duke of Milan
1451	*born*: Franchino Gafori *The Sight of Faburdon*		
1453	*died*: Dunstable	Arnoul Gréban (1420–1471), *Mystère de la Passion*	Fall of Constantinople Hundred Years' War between England and France ends
ca. 1455		Rogier van der Weyden (ca. 1399–1464), *Adoration of the Magi*	
1455			War of the Roses (—1485)
1456			Gutenberg prints the Mazarin (Gutenberg) Bible
ca. 1457	*born*: Jacobus Obrecht		
ca. 1459	*born*: Jean Mouton		
1460	*died*: Binchois		
ca. 1460	Ockeghem, déploration on the death of Binchois (chanson-lament) Busnoys, cantus-firmus Mass *Missa L'homme armé*		
ca. 1461		François Villon (1431–after 1463), *Le grand testament*	
ca. 1463		Andrea Della Robbia (1435–1525), roundels on facade of the Ospedale degli Innocenti in Florence	
ca. 1465	*born*: Marchetto Cara	*La farce de maistre Pierre Pathelin*	

Date	Music	Other Arts and Philosophy	History
1465	Du Fay, motet *Ave Regina coelorum* (copied into Cambrai choirbook)	Andrea Mantegna (1430–1431 to 1506), frescoes for Camera Picta, Gonzaga ducal palace in Mantua (—1474)	
1466		Lippi, Prato frescoes completed	
1467	Busnoys, motet *In hydraulis*		Charles the Bold (1433–1477) succeeds his father, Philip the Good (1396–1467), as duke of Burgundy
1469			Isabella of Aragon (1451–1504) and Ferdinand of Castile (1452–1516) wed
ca. 1470	*born*: Antoine de Févin	Thomas Malory (ca. 1405–1471), *Le mort d'Arthur*	
1470		Accademia Platonica led by Marsilio Ficino (1433–1499) meets at the palace of Lorenzo de' Medici	
1474	*died*: Du Fay		
ca. 1475	*born*: Philippe Verdelot	Hugo van der Goes (ca. 1440–1482), Portinari Altarpiece	
1476	*died*: Hayne (—1497)		
1477		William Caxton (ca. 1422–1491), *Dictes and Sayings of the Philosophers*	Death of Charles the Bold, last of the Burgundian dukes
ca. 1478		Sandro Botticelli (1444/45–1510), *Primavera*	
1478			Lorenzo de' Medici (Il Magnifico, 1449–1492) sole ruler of Florence Beginning of the Spanish Inquisition
ca. 1479		Hans Memling (1430/40–1494), *Virgin and Child with Saints and Donors*	
ca. 1480	Glogauer Liederbuch		
1483	*born*: Jacquet of Mantua	Matteo Maria Boiardo (1440/41–1494), *Orlando innamorato*	Tomás de Torquemada (1420–1498) becomes Spain's first grand inquisitor
ca. 1484		Botticelli, *Birth of Venus*	
ca. 1485	*born*: Clément Janequin		
1485		*Everyman*	

Date	Music	Other Arts and Philosophy	History
ca. 1486	*born*: Ludwig Sennfl		
1486	*born*: Martin Agricola	Domenico Ghirlandaio (ca. 1448–1494), *Life of the Virgin* and *Life of St. John the Baptist* (—1490) Pico della Mirandola (1463–1494), *Oration on the Dignity of Man*	
1488			Bartolomeu Dias rounds the Cape of Good Hope
ca. 1490	*born*: Marco Antonio Cavazzoni; Claudin de Sermisy; Adrian Willaert		
1490	*born*: John Taverner Eton Choirbook (—1502) compiled		Girolamo Savonarola (1452–1498) preaches reform in Florence
1492	*born*: Sylvestro Ganassi dal Fontego *died*: Busnoys		Columbus (1451–1506) discovers New World
1493			Maximilian I (1459–1519) becomes Holy Roman emperor
ca. 1494	*born*: Matthias Greiter		
1494	*born*: Hans Sachs	Sebastian Brant (ca. 1458–1521), *Narrenschiff*	Italian wars (—1559) Medici expelled from Florence
ca. 1495	*born*: Nicolas Gombert		
1495		Leonardo da Vinci (1452–1519), *Last Supper* (—1498)	
1496	*born*: Johann Walther		
ca. 1497		Michelangelo (1475–1564), *Pietà*	
1497	*died*: Ockeghem		Savonarola's "burning of the vanities" in the Piazza della Signoria
1498	Chigi Codex commissioned	Albrecht Dürer (1471–1528), *Self-Portrait with a Landscape* and *Apocalypse*	Louis XII (1462–1515) becomes king of France Savonarola burned at the stake Vasco da Gama (ca. 1460–1524) discovers route to India
ca. 1500	*born*: Jacques Buus; Cristóbal de Morales; Philip van Wilder	Mantegna, *Dead Christ*	
1501	*Odhecaton* (Venice: Petrucci)	Pietro Bembo (1470–1547) edits complete works of Petrarch	

Date	Music	Other Arts and Philosophy	History
1502	*Canti B* (Venice: Petrucci) *Motetti A* (Venice: Petrucci) *Liber primus missarum Josquin* (Venice: Petrucci)		
ca. 1503		Leonardo, *Mona Lisa* (—1506)	
ca. 1504		Hieronymus Bosch (ca. 1450–1516), *The Garden of Earthly Delights*	
1504	*Canti C* (Venice: Petrucci) *Frottole libro primo* (Venice: Petrucci)	Michelangelo, *David* Jacopo Sannazzaro (1456–1530), *Arcadia* Dürer, *Adam and Eve*	
ca. 1505	*born:* Christopher Tye		
1505	*born:* Thomas Tallis Petrucci prints second volume of Josquin masses *Modo di cantar sonetti* from Strambotti, ode, frattole, sonetti . . . , *Libro quatro* (Venice: Petrucci) *died:* Obrecht	Giovanni Bellini (?1431–1436 to 1516), *Madonna with Saints* Raphael (1483–1520), *Madonna of the Meadows*	
1506	*died:* A. Agricola	Donato Bramante (1444–1514), new St. Peter's basilica begun	
?1507	*born:* Jacques Arcadelt		
1507	Francesco Spinacino, *Intabolatura de lauto* (Venice: Petrucci) Petrus Tritonius's setting of Latin odes by Horace (Augsburg: Öglin) Cara, barzelleta *Mal unmuta per effecto* from seventh book of frottole (Venice: Petrucci)	Antonio da Tempo's treatise of 1332, *Summa artis rithimici vulgaris dictaminis*, published	
ca. 1508	*born:* Vincenzo Ruffo		
ca. 1509		Raphael (1483–1520), *The School of Athens*	
1509		Desiderius Erasmus (1469–1536), *The Praise of Folly*	Henry VIII (1491–1547) becomes king of England
ca. 1510	*born:* Jacobus Clemens non Papa (—1515); Diego Ortiz		
1510	*born:* Juan de Cabezón (—1519) *Canzoni nove* (Rome: Andrea Antico)		
1511	*born:* Nicola Vicentino		
1512	*died:* Févin	Michelangelo completes painting the ceiling of the Sistine Chapel	Medici return to Florence Copernicus (1473–1543), *Commentariolus*

Date	Music	Other Arts and Philosophy	History
1513	Jörg Schönfelder, *Von elder Art* from *Liederbuch* (Mainz: Schöffer) Sachs, *Silberweise*	Michelangelo, statue of Moses (—1515)	Niccolò Machiavelli (1469–1527), *The Prince*
ca. 1514	*born:* Claude Goudimel	Raphael, *Baldassare Castiglione* (—1515)	
1514	Petrucci prints third volume of Josquin's masses, eleventh Italian songbook (frottole)	Dürer, *St. Jerome in His Study* Raphael, *Fire in the Borgo* (—1517) Gian Giorgio Trissino (1478–1550), *Sofonisba* (—1515) Antonio da Sangallo (1484–1546), Farnese Palace for Cardinal Alessandro Farnese (1468–1549), later Pope Paul III	
ca. 1515	*born:* Cipriano de Rore		
1515	Antoine de Févin, *Ave Maria . . . Virgo serena* published by Petrucci		Francis I (r. 1515–1547), king of France, conquers Milan
1516		Thomas More (1478–1535), *Utopia* Ludovico Ariosto (1474–1533), *Orlando furioso* Titian (1485–1490—1576), *Assumption of the Virgin* (—1518)	
1517	*born:* Gioseffo Zarlino *died:* Isaac	Teofilo Folengo (1491–1544), *Baldus*	Martin Luther (1483–1546) nails his 95 "theses" to door of Wittenberg castle church
1518	*died:* Compère	Fugger chapel	
1519	*LXXV. hubsher Lieder* (Cologne: Arnt von Aich)		Charles I, king of Spain (1500–1558), becomes Holy Roman emperor (r. —1556) Ferdinand Magellan (ca. 1480–1521) leaves Spain with five ships to find spices from the Orient
1521	*died:* Josquin		
1522	*died:* Gafori; Mouton		Magellan's expedition returns to Spain, thus circumnavigating the globe
1523	Marco Antonio Cavazzoni, *Ricercari, motetti, canzoni* (Venice: Vercelensis) Pietro Aaron (ca. 1480–d. after 1545), *Thoscanello de la musica*	Hans Holbein the Younger (1497/98–1543), *Portrait of Erasmus* Michelangelo, Laurentian Library	
1524	Walther, *Geystliches gesangk Buchleyn*		

Date	Music	Other Arts and Philosophy	History
ca. 1525	*born:* John Blitheman; Giovanni Pierluigi da Palestrina *died:* Cara		
1525		Pietro Bembo, *Prose della volgar lingua*	Peasants' Revolt in Germany Ulrich Zwingli (1484–1531), *Action or Use of the Lord's Supper*, leader of Swiss-German Reformation
1526		Titian, *Death of Saint Peter Martyr* (−1530)	
1527		Holbein the Younger, *Sir Thomas More*	Henry VIII (1491–1547) of England requests permission from Rome to divorce Catherine of Aragon
ca. 1528	Taverner, *Missa Gloria tibi Trinitas*	Lucas Cranach the Elder (1472–1553), *Judgment of Paris*	
1528	Claudin, *Tant que vivray* from *Chansons nouvelles* (Paris: Attaingnant) Clément Janequin, *La guerre* from *Chansons de Maistre Clement Janequin* (Paris: Arraignant)	Castiglione (1478–1529), *Il cortegiano* (The Book of the Courtier)	
1529		Guillaume Budé (1467–1540), *Commentaries on the Greek Language*	
ca. 1530	*born:* Vincenzo Galilei	Holbein the Younger, *Virgin and Child with Burgomaster Jakob Meyer zum Hasen and His Family*	
1530	*XX. Songes* appears in England	Correggio (ca. 1494–1534), *Assumption of the Virgin* Collège de France founded in Paris by Francis I	Augsburg Confession
ca.1532	*born:* Andrea Gabrieli		
1532	*born:* Orlando di Lasso	François Rabelais (ca. 1494–1553), *Pantagruel*	
1533	*born:* Claudio Merulo Luther, chorale *Ein' feste Burg ist unser Gott* published in Joseph Klug's *Geistliche Lieder auffs new gebessert* Verdelot, first book of madrigals		Excommunication of Henry VIII of England by pope
1534		Rabelais, *Gargantua*	Act of Supremacy, Henry VIII becomes head of the Church of England
1535	*born:* Marc'Antonio Ingegneri (−1536); Giaches de Wert Sylvestro Ganassi dal Fontego, *Fontegara* (Venice: Ganassi)		Thomas More beheaded for refusal to recognize Henry VIII's religious authority

Date	Music	Other Arts and Philosophy	History
1536		The reformer John Calvin (1509–1564) of Geneva, *Christianae religionis institutio*	Thomas Cromwell (ca. 1485–1540) seizes monastic property (–1539)
ca. 1537		Jacopo Sansovino (1486–1570), Marciana Libreria	
1537	Nikolaus Listenius (b. ca. 1510), *Musica* (Wittenberg: Rhau) Seybald Heyden (1499–1561), *Artis canendi* (Nürnberg: Johann Petreius) Sennfl, *Ave Maria . . . Virgo serena* (Nürnberg: Fromschneider) Lampadius of Lüneburg (ca. 1500–1559), *Compendium musices* (Bern: Mathias Apiarius)		
1538	Georg Rhau, *Symphoniae jucundae*, with preface by Luther "Longueval" Passion (composed first decade of 16th century) published Luis de Narváez (fl. 1526–1549), *Los seys libros del delphín*, contains *diferencias*		
1539	Arcadelt, *Il bianco e dolce cigno* from his first book of madrigals		
ca. 1540	*born*: Florentio Maschera		
1540	*Musica nova*	Accademia degli Umidi (later Accademia Fiorentina) founded Holbein the Younger, *Henry VIII*	Establishment of the Society of Jesus (Jesuits): founded by St. Ignatius of Loyola (1491–1556), approved by Pope Paul III
1541		Michelangelo, *Last Judgment* completed Farnese Palace in Rome begun	
1542	Sylvestro Ganassi dal Fontego, *Regola rubertina* (–1543)	Clément Marot (1496?–1544), *Trente pseaulmes de David*	
ca. 1543	*died*: Sennfl		
1543	*born*: William Byrd; Alphonso Ferrabosco (the Elder) Geneva Psalter	Benvenuto Cellini (1500–1571), saltcellar for King Francis I of France Lucas Cranach the Elder, *Portrait of Martin Luther*	
1544	*born*: Ascanio Trombetti Georg Rhau, *Newe duedsche geistliche Gesenge*		

Date	Music	Other Arts and Philosophy	History
1545	Gombert, *Musae Jovis* commissioned Willaert, *Benedicta es coelorum regina* Georg Rhau (1488–1548) publishes *bicinia* Greiter, motet *Passibus ambiguis* *died:* Taverner		Pope Paul III (r. 1534–1549) convenes the Council of Trent to undertake church reform
1547	*born:* Cristofano Malvezzi Buus, *Recercari da cantare, et sonare* (Venice: Gardano) Glareanus (1488–1563), *Dodekachordon*		Edward VI (1537–1553) succeeds his father, Henry VIII of England
1548	*born:* Tomás Luis de Victoria		Sarum rite abolished St. Ignatius of Loyola, *Spiritual Exercises* published
1549		Joachim du Bellay (ca. 1522–1560), *L'Olive* and *Défense et illustration de la langue française* Andrea Palladio (1508–1580), basilica in Vicenza begun	Archbishop of Canterbury Thomas Cranmer (1489–1556), *The Book of Common Prayer*
ca. 1550	*born:* Emilio de' Cavalieri *died:* Ganassi; Philippe Verdelot		
1550	*born:* Jakob Handl Willaert, Vespers Psalms Isaac, *Choralis Constantinus* (−1555) *died:* Greiter	Pierre de Ronsard (1524–1585), *Odes* (−1552) Giorgio Vasari (1511–1574), *Lives of the Painters*	
1551	*born:* Giulio Caccini		
1552		Ronsard, *Les amours* (−1553)	
ca. 1553	*born:* Giovanni Gabrieli		
1553	*born:* Luca Marenzio (or 1554) Ortiz, *Trattado de glosas* Clemens non Papa, motet *Musica dei donum* (Antwerp: Susato) *died:* Morales; van Wilder	Cellini, *Perseus with the Head of Medusa* completed	Mary I (1516–1558) becomes queen, returns Catholicism to England
1554	Clemens, motet *Qui consolabatur me* Palestrina, first book of masses, dedicated to Pope Julius III Philip van Wilder, *Pater noster* published		
1555	Lasso, chanson *Je l'ayme bien* from *D'Orlando di Lassus il primo libro . . .* (Antwerp: Susato)	Ronsard, *Les hymnes* (−1556)	Pope Marcellus II (r. 20 days) Peace of Augsburg
1556	*born:* Sethus Calvisius Gombert, motet *In illo tempore loquente Jesu ad turbas* Clemens, *Souterliedekens* (−1557) *died:* M. Agricola; Clemens		

Date	Music	Other Arts and Philosophy	History
1557	*born:* Thomas Morley		
1558	Zarlino, *Le Istitutioni harmoniche* *died:* Janequin	Du Bellay, *Les Regrets*	Elizabeth I (1533–1603) becomes queen of England; Elizabethan Settlement
1559	*died:* Jacquet of Mantua	Palladio, Villa Emo in Treviso Titian, *Rape of Europa* (—1560)	
ca. 1560	*born:* Ludovico Viadana Vicentino builds archigravicembalo *died:* Cavazzoni; Gombert		
1560	*born:* Carlo Gesualdo *died:* Peter Philips		
1561	*born:* Jacopo Corsi; Jacopo Peri		
1562	*born:* John Bull; Jan Pieterszoon Sweelinck *died:* Claudin; Willaert		Council of Trent addresses music reform
1563	*born:* John Dowland; Giles Farnaby	Pieter Bruegel the Elder (ca. 1525–1569), *The Tower of Babel*	Church of England established Council of Trent ends
1564	*born:* Hans Leo Hassler		
ca. 1565		Giambologna (1529–1608), *Mercury*	
1565	Ruffo, *Missae quatuor concinnate ad ritum concilii mediolani* (published 1570) *died:* Buus; Rore	Palladio, Villa Rotunda in Vicenza Tintoretto (1518–1594), series of sacred paintings for the Scuola di San Rocco, Venice (—1587)	St. Teresa of Ávila (1515–1582), *Vida*
1566	Rore, *Dalle belle contrade d'oriente* from his fifth book of madrigals *died:* Cabezón	Palladio, S. Giorgio Maggiore, Venice	
1567	*born:* Thomas Campion; Girolamo Giacobbi; Claudio Monteverdi Palestrina's second book of masses, including *Missa Papae Marcelli*	Cosimo Bartoli (1503–1572), *Ragionamenti Accademici* Federico Barocci (ca. 1535–1612), *Deposition* for chapel of San Bernardino in Perugia	
1568	*born:* Adriano Banchieri; Christian Erbach Maddalena Casulana (fl. 1566–1583), three books of madrigals (—1583) *died:* Arcadelt		
1569	Palestrina, motet *O magnum mysterium*		
ca. 1570	*born:* John Coprario (—1580) *died:* Ortiz		

Date	Music	Other Arts and Philosophy	History
1570	Palestrina, third book of masses, including *Missa L' homme armé, Missa Ut re mi fa sol la,* and *Missa Repleatur os meum laude* *died:* Walther		
1571	*born:* Michael Praetorius; John Ward A. Gabrieli, *Canzoni alla francese per sonar sopra stromenti da tasti*		
ca. 1572	*died:* Tye	Santi di Tito (1536–1602), altarpiece *Resurrection*	
1572	*born:* Thomas Tomkins *died:* Goudimel	Nicholas Hilliard (ca. 1547–1619), miniature of Elizabeth I	Saint Bartholomew's Day massacre, Paris: Protestants slaughtered
1573	Tallis, motet *Spem in alium* Lasso, *Audite nova* (Munich) Girolamo Mei (1519–1594), *De modis musicis antiquorum*	Titian, *Pietà* (−1576)	
1574	*born:* John Wilbye		
1575	Tallis, hymn *O nata lux de lumine* (published) *Cantiones,* published by Byrd and Tallis		
1576	*born:* Thomas Weelkes *died:* Sachs; Vicentino		
1578	*born:* Alfonso Ferrabosco II Cabezón, diferencias *Guárdame las vacas* published		
1580	Marenzio, first book of madrigals	Michel de Montaigne (1533–1592), *Essays* Angelo Poliziano (1454–1491), *Fabula di Orfeo*	Sir Francis Drake (ca. 1540/43–1596) completes circumnavigation of the globe
1581	Lasso, villanella *Matona mia casa* from *Libro de villanelle* Wert, *A un giro sol* from his seventh book of madrigals V. Galilei, *Dialogo della musica antica e della moderna*	Torquato Tasso (1544–1595), *Gerusalemme liberata* published	
1582	*born:* Marco de Gagliano; Sigismondo d'India Palestrina, *Missa O magnum mysterium* Monteverdi, book of three-voice motets published	Giambologna, *Rape of a Sabine* Paolo Veronese (1528–1588), *Triumph of Venice* Giordano Bruno (1548–1600), *Il candelaio*	
ca. 1583	*born:* Robert Johnson		
1583	*born:* Girolamo Frescobaldi	Federico Barocci, *Visitation* (−1586)	
ca. 1584	*died:* Maschera		

Date	Music	Other Arts and Philosophy	History
1584	Maschera, *Libro primo de canzoni da sonare*		
1585	*born*: Heinrich Schütz A. Gabrieli, music for Sophocles's *Oedipus tyrannis* A. Gabrieli, Mass for 16 voices (in "concerted" style) performed *died*: A. Gabrieli; Tallis		
1586	*born*: Claudio Saracini; Johann Hermann Schein Jakob Handl, *Opus musicum* (—1591) Lucas Osiander, *Funfftzig geistliche Lieder und Psalmen*	El Greco (ca. 1541–1614), *The Burial of Count Orgaz* (—1588)	
ca. 1587		Christopher Marlowe (1564–1593), *Tamburlaine the Great*	
1587	*born*: Francesca Caccini; Samuel Scheidt *died*: Ruffo	*Historia von Dr. Johann Fausten* Tasso, *Re Torrismondo*	
ca. 1588		Marlowe, *Dr. Faustus*	
1588	*born*: Nicholas Lanier *Psalmes, Sonets, and Songs* *Musica Transalpina*, edited by Nicholas Yonge Zarlino, *Sopplimenti musicali* *died*: Ferrabosco (the Elder)		English defeat of the Spanish Armada
ca. 1589		Marlowe, *The Jew of Malta*	
1589	Palestrina, book of Vespers hymns Byrd, first book of *Cantiones sacrae* Byrd, *Songs of Sundrie Natures* Trombetti, *Il primo libro de motetti accomodati per cantare e far concerti*	Giovanni Battista Guarini (1538–1612), *Il pastor fido* Edmund Spenser (1552–1599), *The Faerie Queene*	Wedding of Grand Duke Ferdinando de' Medici to Princess Christine of Lorraine
1590	Vecchi, *So ben mec'ha bon tempo* from his *Selva di varia ricreatione* *died*: Trombetti; Zarlino		
1591	Byrd, second book of *Cantiones sacrae* *died*: Blitheman; V. Galilei; Handl		
1592	*died*: Ingegneri		
1593	Palestrina, *Tu sunt coeli*, from complete cycle of Mass Offertories Byrd, Mass in Four Parts	Tasso, *Gerusalemme conquistata*	

Date	Music	Other Arts and Philosophy	History
1594	Byrd, Mass in Three Parts *died*: Lasso; Palestrina	Shakespeare (1564–1616), *Two Gentlemen of Verona*	
ca. 1595		Michelangelo Merisi da Caravaggio (1571–1610), *The Lute Player* (–1597)	
1595	Byrd, Mass in Five Parts Banchieri, *Concerti ecclesiastici a otto voci*	Shakespeare, *Romeo and Juliet* (–1596); *A Midsummer Night's Dream* (–1596)	
1596	*died*: Wert	Shakespeare, *The Merchant of Venice* (–1597), *Henry IV, Part 1* (–1597)	
ca. 1597	*born*: Luigi Rossi	Shakespeare, *Henry IV, Part 2*	
1597	Morley, *Plaine and Easie Introduction to Practicall Musicke* *Canzonets or Little Short Songs to Four Voices*, edited by Morley G. Gabrieli, *Sacrae symphoniae* (Venice: Gardano)	Shakespeare, *Merry Wives of Windsor* Annibale Carracci (1560–1609), frescos in Farnese Palace in Rome (–1601)	
1598	*Madrigals to Five Voices* edited by Morley Peri and Corsi, *La Dafne*	Ben Jonson (1572–1637), *Every Man in His Humour*	Edict of Nantes: Henry IV of France (r. 1589–1610) grants Protestants religious freedom
1599	*died*: Malvezzi; Marenzio	Opening of London's Globe Theatre Shakespeare, *Julius Caesar*	
ca. 1600		Shakespeare, *Hamlet* (–1601)	
1600	Lasso, *Prophetiae Sibyllarum* Giovanni Maria Artusi (1540–1613), *L'Artusi, overo delle imperfettioni della moderna musica* Victoria, *Missa pro Victoria* Cavalieri, *Rappresentatione di Anima, et di Corpo* Peri, *Euridice* performed		Marriage of Maria de' Medici (1573–1642) to king of France, Henri IV
1601	*The Triumphes of Oriana*, anthology of English madrigals, published by Morley Peri, *Euridice* (play by Rinuccini) printed G. Caccini, *Euridice* (play by Rinuccini) printed		
ca. 1602	*born*: Christopher Simpson (–1606)		
1602	*born*: Francesco Cavalli; William Lawes; Michelangelo Rossi; Jacques Champion de Chambonnières Viadana, *Cento concerti ecclesiastici* G. Caccini, *Nuove musiche* *died*: Cavalieri; Corsi; Morley	Tommaso Campanella (1568–1639), *La città del sole*	

Date	Music	Other Arts and Philosophy	History
1603	*born:* Denis Gaultier Monteverdi, *A un giro sol* from his fourth book of madrigals Sethus Calvisius, *Ein feste Burg*		
1604	Dowland, *The Lachrymae Pavan* *died:* Merulo	Shakespeare, *Othello*	
1605	*born:* Giacomo Carissimi Byrd, Gradualia containing the motet *Ave verum corpus* Monteverdi, *Cruda Amarilli* from his fifth book of madrigals Praetorius, *Musae Sioniae* (—1610)	Miguel de Cervantes (1547–1616), *Don Quixote* (Part 1) Francis Bacon (1561–1626), *Advancement of Learning*	
1606		Jonson, *Volpone* Shakespeare, *King Lear*	
1607	Agostino Agazzari (ca. 1580–1642), *Del sonare sopra'l basso con tutti li stromenti . . .* Byrd, second book of Gradualia, containing the Vespers antiphon *Nos vos relinquam* Monteverdi, *Orfeo* (first performed; published 1609), *Scherzi musicali*	Shakespeare, *Coriolanus* (—1608)	
1608	Gagliano, *La Dafne*		
1609	Giacobbi, *Prima parte dei salmi concertati* d'India, madrigal *Piange madonna* from his *Primo libro di musiche* Fitzwilliam *Virginal Book* compiled (—1619), containing Farnaby's *Daphne* divisions	Johannes Kepler (1571–1630), first two laws of planetary motion Shakespeare, *Sonnets*	
ca. 1610		El Greco, *View of Toledo*	
1610	Monteverdi, *Vespers*	Jonson, *The Alchemist*	
1611	Gesualdo, *Moro, lasso* from his sixth book of madrigals Schütz, book of Italian madrigals *died:* Victoria	Shakespeare, *The Tempest*	Authorized (King James) Version of the Bible
1612	*born:* Thomas Mace (or 1613) Praetorius, *Terpsichore* *died:* G. Gabrieli; Hassler		
1613	Ward, *Upon a Bank* *died:* Gesualdo		
1614	Felice Anerio and Francesco Soriano, *Editio Medicaea* Monteverdi, *Sixth Book of Madrigals*, containing *Lagrime d'amante al sepolcro dell'amata* (composed in 1610)	Jonson, *Bartholomew Fair*	

Date	Music	Other Arts and Philosophy	History
1614	Praetorius, treatise *Syntagma musicum* (−1618)		
1615	Frescobaldi, *Primo libro d'intavolatura* G. Gabrieli, *In ecclesiis* from his second book of *Sacrae symphoniae* G. Gabrieli, *Canzoni et sonate* Gagliano, monody *Valli profonde* *died*: Calvisius	Cervantes, *Don Quixote* (Part 2)	
1616	*born*: Johann Jakob Froberger	Théodore-Agrippa d'Aubigné (1552−1630), *Les Tragiques*	
ca. 1617		Peter Paul Rubens (1577−1640), *Rape of the Daughters of Leucippus*	
1617	Schein, Suite No. 8 from *Banchetto musicale* Lanier, masque *Lovers Made Men*	Inigo Jones (1573−1652), stage designs for *The Vision of Delight*	
1618	Schein, *Christ lag in Todesbanden* from *Opella nova* F. Caccini, book of monodies *died*: G. Caccini	Kepler, third law of planetary motion	Thirty Years' War (−1648)
1619	*born*: Barbara Strozzi Monteverdi, *Seventh Book of Madrigals*, containing monody *Lettera amorosa* Praetorius, *Christ lag in Todesbanden* from *Polyhymnia caduceatrix et panegyrica* (−1621) Schütz, *Psalmen Davids*	Jones, Banqueting Hall in Whitehall (−1622)	
1620	Saracini, hermit song *Da te parto* from his *Seconde musiche* *died*: Campion	Bacon, *Novum organum*	
1621	*died*: Praetorius; Sweelinck		
ca. 1622	*born*: Matthew Locke		
1623	*died*: Byrd; Weelkes	Giambattista Marino (1569−1625), *Adone* Shakespeare's collected plays (First Folio) published Giovanni Bernini (1598−1680), *baldacchino* in St. Peter's basilica (−1634)	
1624	Scheidt, partita *Christ lag in Todesbanden* from second book of *Tabulatura nova*	Rubens, *Adoration of the Magi*	Richelieu (1585−1642) becomes chief minister of state to Louis XIII of France
ca. 1625	Ferrabosco II, *In nomine a 6*		

Date	Music	Other Arts and Philosophy	History
1625	Schütz, *Cantiones sacrae* F. Caccini, opera *La liberazione di Ruggiero dall'isola d'Alcina*		
ca. 1626	*born:* Louis Couperin		
1626	*died:* Coprario; Dowland	Basilica of St. Peter's consecrated	
1627	*died:* Viadana	Nicolas Poussin (1594–1665), *Death of Germanicus* (−1628)	
1628	Schütz, *Psalmen Davids* *died:* Bull; Ferrabosco II; Giacobbi; Philips		
1629	*born:* Lelio Colista Schütz, *O quam tu pulchra es* from *Symphoniae sacrae* *died:* d'India		
1630	Frescobaldi, *Arie musicale* *died:* Schein	Rubens, *St. Ildefonso* triptych (−1632)	
1632	*born:* Jean-Baptiste Lully	Galileo Galilei (1564–1642), *Dialogo dei massimi sistemi del mondo*, defense of Copernican system Rembrandt van Rijn (1606–1669), *The Anatomy Lesson of Dr. Tulp*	
ca. 1633		Franz Hals (1581/85–1666), *Assembly of Officers and Subalterns of the Civic Guards of St. Hadrian at Haarlem*	
1633	*died:* Johnson; Peri		
1634	*died:* Banchieri	Académie Française established	
1635	Frescobaldi, *Fiori musicali,* containing organ masses	Pedro Calderón de la Barca (1600–1681), *La vida es sueño* Jones, stage designs for *Florimène* Diego Velázquez (1599–1660), *Philip IV on Horseback*	
1636	Schütz, *Eile mich, Gott, zu erretten* from *Kleine geistliche Concerte* *died:* Erbach	Rembrandt, *Danaë*	
ca. 1637	*born:* Dietrich Buxtehude		
1637	Teatro San Cassiano of Venice opens Frescobaldi, *Toccate d'intavolatura di cembalo et organo*	Pierre Corneille (1606–1684), *Le Cid* René Descartes (1596–1650), *Discourse on Method*	

Date	Music	Other Arts and Philosophy	History
1638	Monteverdi, *Eighth Book of Madrigals*, containing *Combattimento di Tancredi e Clorinda* and *Lamento della ninfa* *died:* Ward, Wilbye		
1639	*born:* Johann Pezel; Alessandro Stradella		
ca. 1640	Rossi, *Toccata VII* from his first *Libro d'intavolatura* *died:* F. Caccini		
1640	*died:* Farnaby		
1641	Monteverdi, *Selva morale et spirituale*		
1642		Rembrandt, *Night Watch*	English Civil War (−1648)
1643	*born:* Marc-Antoine Charpentier; Johann Adam Reinken Monteverdi, *L'incoronazione di Poppea* *died:* Frescobaldi; Gagliano; Monteverdi		Louis XIV (1638–1715) becomes king of France
1644	*born:* Antonio Stradivari		
1645	*died:* Lawes		
1647	Schütz, second book of *Symphoniae sacrae* Rossi, *Orfeo*		
1648	Schütz, polyphonic motets *Geistliche Chor-Music*		Peace of Westphalia
ca. 1649	*died:* Claudio Saracini		
1649	*born:* John Blow Tomkins, *A Sad Pavan for These Distracted Times*		Beheading of King Charles I (b. 1600) of England Puritans close theaters in England (−1660)
ca. 1650		Velázquez, *Pope Innocent X*	
1650	Descartes's *Compendium musicae* published (written 1618) Athanasius Kircher (1601–1680), *Musurgia universalis* Schütz, *Saul, Saul, was verfolgst du mich* from third book of *Symphoniae sacrae*	Corneille, *Andromède*	
1652	Giovan Domenico Ottonelli, treatise, *Delle cristiana moderazione del teatro*	Bernini, *Ecstasy of St. Teresa* completed	
1653	*born:* Arcangelo Corelli *died:* Rossi	Rembrandt, *Aristotle Contemplating the Bust of Homer*	Oliver Cromwell (1599–1658) becomes Lord Protector

Date	Music	Other Arts and Philosophy	History
1654	*born:* Agostino Steffani Renovated Teatro di Santo Bartolomeo, first Neapolitan opera house, opens *died:* Scheidt	Rembrandt, *Woman Bathing in a Stream*	
1656	*born:* Johann Caspar Ferdinand Fischer; Marin Marais *died:* Tomkins	Velázquez, *Las meninas*	
1657		Bernini, *Cathedra Petri* (—1666) Blaise Pascal (1623–1662) assembles notes for a work published after his death as *Pensées* (—1658)	
1658	*born:* Giuseppe Torelli		Christiaan Huygens (1629–1695), *Horologium*
1659	*born:* Henry Purcell Strozzi, cantata *Lagrime mie* from *Diporti di Euterpe* Christopher Simpson, *The Division-Violist*		
1660	*born:* André Campra; Johann Joseph Fux; Johann Kuhnau; Johann Sigismund Kusser; Alessandro Scarlatti Schütz, oratorio *Weihnachtsgeschichte*		Stuart Restoration, Charles II (1630–1685) crowned king of Great Britain
1661	*died:* L. Couperin		
ca. 1662		Jan Vermeer (1632–1675), *Woman with a Water Jug* (—1665)	
1664		Molière (1622–1673), *Tartuffe*	
ca. 1665		Vermeer, *Head of a Girl with a Pearl Earring* and *The Concert* (—1666)	
1665		Molière, *Dom Juan*	
1666	*died:* Lanier	Molière, *Le Misanthrope*	Great Fire of London
1667	*born:* Gottfried Reiche *died:* Froberger	John Milton (1608–1674), *Paradise Lost*	
1668	*born:* François Couperin	Jean de La Fontaine (1621–1695), *Fables* (—1694)	
1669	Founding of the Académie Royale de Musique *died:* Simpson	Hans Jacob Christoph von Grimmelshausen (ca. 1621–1676), *Abenteuerlicher simplicissimus*	

Date	Music	Other Arts and Philosophy	History
1670	*born:* Giovanni Bononcini	Molière, *Le bourgeois gentilhomme* Jean Nocret (1615–1672), *Louis XIV and His Family as Olympian Gods*	
1671	*born:* Antonio Caldara		
ca. 1672		Vermeer, *Guitar Player*	
1672	*died:* Chambonnières; Gaultier; Schütz		
1673	Locke, *Masque of Orpheus* in *The Empress of Morocco* (play by Elkanah Settle)		
1674	Lully, *Alceste* *died:* Carissimi	Jean Racine (1639–1699), *Iphigénie en Aulide*	
1675	Nikolai Diletsky's music treatise *Grammatika musikiyskaya*	Sir Christopher Wren (1632–1723), St. Paul's cathedral (begun) William Wycherley (1640–1716), *The Country Wife*	
1676	*born:* Giuseppe Maria Orlandini Lully, *Atys* Mace, *Musick's Monument* *died:* Cavalli		
1677	*died:* Strozzi; Matthew Locke	Racine, *Phèdre* John Dryden (1631–1700), *All for Love*	
1678	*born:* Antonio Vivaldi	John Bunyan (1628–1688), *Pilgrim's Progress*	
1679	Nikolai Diletsky (d. after 1680), treatise *Grammatika*		
1680	Purcell, set of consort "fantazias" *died:* Colista	Comédie-Française founded	
1681	*born:* Georg Philipp Telemann Corelli, 48 trio sonatas in four collections (–1695)		
1682	Purcell, Overture in D minor *died:* Stradella		Peter the Great (d. 1725) becomes tsar of Russia and begins westernization
1683	*born:* Christoph Graupner; Jean-Philippe Rameau Blow, *Venus and Adonis* A. Scarlatti, *S'empia man* from *L'Aldimiro* Purcell, *Sonnatas of III Parts*		
1685	*born:* Johann Sebastian Bach; George Frideric Handel; Domenico Scarlatti Luis Grabu (fl. 1665–1694), *Albion and Albanius*		Revocation of the Edict of Nantes: Protestantism banned

31

Date	Music	Other Arts and Philosophy	History
1686	*born:* Nicola Porpora Lully, tragédie lyrique *Armide*		
1687	*born:* Francesco Geminiani *died:* Lully	Isaac Newton (1642–1727), *Principia*	
1688			"Glorious Revolution" dislodges the Stuart dynasty in England
1689	Purcell, *Dido and Aeneas* Kuhnau, *Neuer Clavier-Übung*, I	John Locke (1632–1704), *Toleration*	
1690	*born:* Gottlieb Muffat Arcadian Academy founded in Rome	Locke, *On Civil Government*	
1692	Purcell, semi-opera, *The Fairy-Queen*		
1693		William Congreve (1670–1729), *The Old Bachelour* and *The Double-Dealer*	
1694	*died:* Pezel	Johann Bernhard Fischer von Erlach (1656–1723), *Dreifaltigkeitskirche*	
1695	Fischer, dance suites *Le journal de printemps*, op. 1 *died:* Purcell	Congreve, *Love for Love*	
1696	*born:* Leonardo Vinci Fischer, suite *Musicalisches Blumen-Büschlein*	Wren, Royal Hospital, Greenwich (−1716)	
ca. 1697	Froberger, *Dix suittes de clavessin* published		
1697	*born:* Jean-Marie Leclair; Johann Joachim Quantz A. Scarlatti, "Sinfonia" from the opera *La caduta de' Decemviri*		
1699	*born:* Johann Adolf Hasse		
1700	*born:* Giovanni Battista Sammartini Kuhnau, *Musicalische Vorstellung einiger biblischer Historien* A. Scarlatti, opera *L'Eraclea* Corelli, "La Folia," op. 5, no. 12	Congreve, *The Way of the World*	
1701	Joseph Sauveur (1653–1716) publishes first theoretical account of the overtone series	Hyacinthe Rigaud (1659–1743), *Portrait of Louis IV*	
1702	Fischer, *Ariadne musica*		
1704	*died:* Charpentier		
1705	*born:* Louis-Gabriel Guillemain		

Date	Music	Other Arts and Philosophy	History
1706	*born:* Baldassare Galuppi Marais, *Alcyone* Anon., Intermezzo *Frappolone e Florinetta*		
1707	J. S. Bach, Cantata BWV 4: *Christ lag in Todesbanden* *died:* Buxtehude		
1708	J. S. Bach, Toccata in F, BWV 540 (−1717) *died:* Blow		
1709	*died:* Torelli		
ca. 1710	*born:* Domenico Alberti		
1710	*born:* Wilhelm Friedemann Bach; Giovanni Battista Pergolesi Apostolo Zeno (1668–1750), libretto *Scipione nelle Spagne*		
1711	*born:* Jean-Joseph Cassanéa de Mondonville Vivaldi, Concerto for Four Violins, op. 3, no. 10, in *L'Estro armonico* First music criticism by Joseph Addison in *The Spectator*		
1712	*born:* Jean-Jacques Rousseau Campra, *Idoménée* A. Scarlatti, cantata *Andate, o miei sospiri*	Alexander Pope (1688–1744), *The Rape of the Lock*	
1713	J. S. Bach, *Orgelbüchlein* (−1715) F. Couperin, *Pièces de clavecin*, includes explanation of ornaments *died:* Corelli		Treaty of Utrecht
1714	*born:* Carl Philipp Emanuel Bach; Christoph Willibald Gluck Corelli, Concerto Grosso ("Christmas Concerto"), op. 6, no. 8, published J. S. Bach, Cantata BWV 61: *Nun komm, der Heiden Heiland*		George Louis (1660–1727), Elector of Hanover, becomes King George I of Great Britain
ca. 1715	J. S. Bach, *English Suites*		
1715	Orlandini, *Bajocco e Serpilla* Balthasar Sartori, motet *O magnum mysterium*		
1717	*born:* Johann Stamitz Handel, *Water Music*		
ca. 1718		Antoine Watteau (1684–1721), *Pierrot* (−1719)	
1718		Watteau, *Mezzetin* (−1720)	

Date	Music	Other Arts and Philosophy	History
1719		Daniel Defoe (1660–1731), *Robinson Crusoe*	
1721	A. Scarlatti, *Griselda* J. S. Bach, Brandenburg Concertos	Watteau, *L'Enseigne de Gersaint* Fischer von Erlach, *Entwurf einer historischen Architektur*	
1722	Rameau, *Traité de l'harmonie* J. S. Bach, *Das wohltemperirte Clavier*, I F. Couperin, *Le rossignol-en-amour* First appearance of *Critica musica*, the first specialized music journal, by Johann Mattheson *died*: Kuhnau; Reinken		
1723	*born*: Carl Friedrich Abel J. S. Bach, Cantata BWV 179: *Siehe zu, dass deine Gottesfurcht*		
1724	Metastasio (1698–1782), libretto *Didone abbandonata* J. S. Bach, Cantata BWV 80, *Ein' feste Burg*; Cantata BWV 101, *Nimm von uns, Herr, du treuer Gott*; Cantata BWV 178, *Wo Gott der Herr nicht bei uns hält*; Cantata BWV 104, *Du Hirte Israel, höre*; St. John Passion		
1725	Concert Spirituel founded in Paris by Anne Danican Philidor (1681–1728) Fux, *Gradus ad Parnassum* Vivaldi, *Il cimento dell'harmonia e dell'invenzione*, op. 8, includes the *Four Seasons* Handel, *Rodelinda* *died*: A. Scarlatti		
1726	J. S. Bach, *Clavier-Übung*, I; Cantata BWV 13, *Meine Seufzer, meine Tränen*	Jonathan Swift (1667–1745), *Gulliver's Travels*	
1727	*died*: Kusser		
1728	*born*: Johann Adam Hiller; Niccolò Piccinni Pier Francesco Tosi (1654–1732), *Observations on the Florid Song* John Gay, *Beggar's Opera* *died*: Marais; Steffani		
1729	*born*: Giuseppe Sarti	William Hogarth (1697–1764), *The Beggar's Opera* (—1731)	
1730	Vinci, *Artaserse* Hasse, *Artaserse* *died*: Vinci		
1731	*born*: Christian Cannabich		

Date	Music	Other Arts and Philosophy	History
1732	*born*: Franz Joseph Haydn		
ca. 1733		Jean-Baptiste-Siméon Chardin (1699–1779), *Soap Bubbles*	
1733	Rameau, *Hyppolite et Aricie* Pergolesi, intermezzo *La serva padrona* *died*: F. Couperin; Stradivari		
1734	Farinelli (1705–1782), *Son qual nave* Mondonville, *Pièces de clavecin en sonates avec accompagnement de violon* *died*: Reiche		
1735	*born*: Johann Christian Bach J. S. Bach, Italian Concerto Rameau, *Les Indes galantes* Empress Anna Ivanovna (r. 1730–1740) imports troupe of Italian opera singers to Russia J. S. Bach, St. Matthew Passion	Hogarth, *A Rake's Progress*	John Harrison (1693–1776) completes his first ship's chronometer for measuring longitude
1736	*died*: Caldara; Pergolesi		
1737	*born*: Johann Michael Haydn Rameau, *Castor et Pollux*		
1738	J. S. Bach, *Das wohltemperirte Clavier*, II (−1742) D. Scarlatti, *Essercizi* published		Unearthing of Herculaneum
ca. 1739	Muffat, *Componimenti musicali*		
1739	Handel, *Saul* and *Israel in Egypt*		
1740	*born*: Giovanni Paisiello Handel, Twelve Grand Concertos C. P. E. Bach, Sonata No. 1 in F ("Prussian," −1742) Guillemain, *Premier amusement à la mode*, op. 8	Samuel Richardson (1689–1761), *Pamela*	War of Austrian Succession (−1748) Maria Theresa (1717–1780), archduchess of Austria and queen of Hungary and Bohemia, succeeds her father, Charles VI (1685–1740) Frederick II (1712–1786) succeeds his father, Frederick William I, as king of Prussia
1741	*born*: André Grétry Rameau, *Pièces de clavecin en concerts* *died*: Fux; Vivaldi		
1742	Handel, *Messiah*	François Boucher (1703–1770), *Lady Tying Her Garter*	
1743	*born*: Luigi Boccherini Guillemain, *Conversations galantes et amusantes*, op. 12	Canaletto (1697–1768), *Capriccio: The Horses of S. Marco in the Piazzetta* Hogarth, *Marriage à la Mode*	

Date	Music	Other Arts and Philosophy	History
1744	*born*: Georg Joseph Vogler ("Abbé Vogler") *died*: Campra		
ca. 1745	W. F. Bach, Sonata in F		
1745	*born*: Carl Stamitz		
1746	*born*: Johann Friedrich Peter *died*: Alberti; Fischer		
1747	*born*: Johann Abram Peter Schulz J. S. Bach, *Musikalisches Opfer* *died*: Bononcini		
ca. 1748		Giovanni Battista Piranesi (1720–1778), *Vedute di Roma*	
1748	Alberti, Sonata in C, op. 1, no. 3		Unearthing of Pompeii
1749	*born*: Domenico Cimarosa Handel, *Music for the Royal Fireworks* Geminiani, *A Treatise of Good Taste in the Art of Musick*	Henry Fielding (1707–1754), *Tom Jones*	
1750	*born*: Antonio Salieri Hasse, *Attilio Regolo* *died*: J. S. Bach	Alexander Gottlieb Baumgarten, treatise *Aesthetica*	
1751	Geminiani, treatise *The Art of Playing on the Violin* J. S. Bach, *Die Kunst der Fuge* published	*Le jugement de Paris*, ballet d'action by Jean-Georges Noverre (1727–1810), produced	Denis Diderot (1713–1784) and Jean d'Alembert (1717–1783), *Encyclopédie* (–1780)
1752	*born*: Muzio Clementi; Johann Friedrich Reichardt Christian Gottfried Krause (1719–1790), *Von der musikalischen Poesie* Quantz, *Versuch einer Anweisung die Flöte traversiere zu spielen* Rousseau, *Le devin du village*		
1753	Krause, *Oden mit Melodien*, including C. P. E. Bach's *Amint* C. P. E. Bach, *Versuch über die wahre Art das Clavier zu spielen* (and 1762), including Fantasia in C minor Rousseau, *Letter on French Music*	Sir Joshua Reynolds (1723–1792), *Commodore Keppel*	
1754	*born*: Vicente Martín y Soler		
1755		Johann Joachim Winckelmann (1717–1768), *Thoughts on the Imitation of Greek Works*	

Date	Music	Other Arts and Philosophy	History
1756	*born:* Wolfgang Amadeus Mozart Galuppi, Sonate, op. 1	Piranesi, *Le antichità Romane*	Seven Years' War (—1763)
1757	*died:* D. Scarlatti; J. Stamitz	Giambattista Tiepolo (1696–1770), *Sacrifice of Iphigenia*	
1758	*born:* Carl Friedrich Zelter J. Stamitz, Trio in C minor, op. 4, no. 3	Boucher, *Madame de Pompadour*	
1759	*died:* Handel	Voltaire (1694–1778), *Candide*	
1760	*born:* Luigi Cherubini; Jan Ladislav Dussek; Pierre Gaveaux Piccinni, *La buona figliuola* Abel, *Six Sonatas for the Harpsichord with Accompanyments for a Violin or German Flute and Violoncello* *died:* Graupner; Orlandini	Voltaire, *Tancredi* Diderot, *Rameau's Nephew* Laurence Sterne (1713–1768), *Tristram Shandy* (—1767) Reynolds, *Laurence Sterne*	
1761		Carlo Gozzi (1720–1806), *L'amore delle tre melarance*	
1762	Gluck, reform opera *Orfeo ed Euridice* Rosseau, *Pygmalion*, first important melodrama; *Le Roi et le fermier* *died:* Geminiani	Gozzi, *Turandot*	Jean-Jacques Rousseau, *Social Contract* Catherine the Great becomes tsarina of Russia
1763	*born:* Simon Mayr; Étienne-Nicolas Méhul		
1764	*died:* Lecalir; Rameau		
1766	*born:* Rudolphe Kreutzer J. C. Bach, Six Sonatas, op. 5	Thomas Gainsborough (1727–1788), *Johann Christian Bach* George Stubbs (1724–1806), *The Anatomy of the Horse*	Reign of Emperor Joseph II (d. 1790) begins, initiating reforms in Austria
1767	Gluck, reform opera *Alceste* *died:* Telemann	Jean-Honoré Fragonard (1732–1806), *The Swing*	
1768	Mozart, singspiel *Bastien und Bastienne* (possibly as early as 1768) *died:* Porpora		
1769	Mozart, opera buffa *La finta semplice*		James Watt (1736–1819) patents steam engine
1770	*born:* Ludwig van Beethoven Mozart, opera seria *Mitridate* *died:* Guillemain; Muffat	Gainsborough, *The Blue Boy*	Louis (1754–1793) marries Marie Antoinette (1755–1793)
1771	*born:* Ferdinando Paer		

Date	Music	Other Arts and Philosophy	History
1772	F. J. Haydn, Symphony No. 45 ("Farewell") *died:* Mondonville	Johann Gottfried von Herder (1744–1803), *Über der Ursprung der Sprache*	
1773	C. P. E. Bach, Six Symphonies *died:* Quantz	Johann Wolfgang von Goethe (1749–1832), *Heidenröslein* Oliver Goldsmith (1728–1774), *She Stoops to Conquer*	
1774	*born:* Václav Jan Tomášek J. C. Bach, Sinfonia, op. 18, no. 2 Gluck, *Orfeo ed Euridice* Meistersinger guild officially disbanded		Louis XVI succeeds his grandfather, Louis XV, as king of France
1775	Mozart, Violin Concerto no. 5, K. 219 *died:* Sammartini	Franz Anton Mesmer (1734–1832), *Sendschreiben an einen auswärtigen Arzt* Pierre-Augustin Caron de Beaumarchais (1732–1799), *Le barbier de Séville* Richard Sheridan (1751–1816), *The Rivals* Adam Smith (1723–1790), *The Wealth of Nations*	American Revolution (—1783)
1776		F. M. von Klinger (1752–1831), *Die Wirrwarr*	Thomas Paine (1737–1809), *Common Sense* American Declaration of Independence
ca. 1777		Jean-Baptiste Greuze (1725–1805), *A Father's Curse*	
1777		Gainsborough, *Carl Friedrich Abel* (exhibited)	
1778	Herder, *Stimmen der Völker* (—1779) *died:* Rousseau	Greuze, *Punished Son*	War of Bavarian Succession (—1779)
1779	Pascal Boyé (1743–1794), treatise *L'expression musicale mise au rang des chimères*		
1780	C. P. E. Bach, *Orchester-Sinfonien* (composed 1776)		
1781	Mozart, opera seria *Idomeneo* Leipzig Gewandhaus built, first of the large concert halls	Immanuel Kant (1724–1804), *The Critique of Pure Reason* Vincenzo Monti (1754–1828), *La bellezza dell'universo* Friedrich von Schiller (1759–1805), *Die Räuber* Henry Fuseli (1741–1825), *The Nightmare*	
1782	*born:* John Field; Niccolò Paganini F. J. Haydn, "Russian" Quartets, op. 33 Mozart, *Die Entführung aus dem Serail*	Rousseau, *Confessions* Goethe, *Erlkönig* Vittorio Alfieri (1749–1803), *Saul*	

Date	Music	Other Arts and Philosophy	History
1782	Grétry, rescue opera *Richard Coeur-de-Lion* Paisiello, *Il barbiere di Siviglia* Sarti, *Fra i due litiganti il terzo gode* *died*: J. C. Bach		
1783	*died*: Hasse		Joseph-Michel (1740–1810) and Jacques-Étienne (1745–1799) Montgolfier, first flight of a hot-air balloon
1784	Mozart, Piano Concerto no. 17, K.453 *died*: W. F. Bach	Immanuel Kant (1724–1804), *Was ist Aufklärung?* Beaumarchais, *Le mariage de Figaro* Jacques-Louis David (1748–1825), *Oath of the Horatii* Thomas Rowlandson (1756 or 1757–1827), *Vauxhall Gardens* Johann Gottfried von Herder (1744–1803), *Outlines of a Philosophy of the History of Man* (–1791)	
1785	Mozart, Six Quartets, op. 10 (including "Dissonance"); Piano Concerto no. 20, K.466; Fantasia, K. 475; *Das Veilchen* *died*: Galuppi	Schiller, *An die Freude*	
1786	*born*: Carl Maria von Weber Rousseau, *Dictionnaire de musique* Mozart, *Le Nozze di Figaro*; Piano Concerto no. 24, K.491	Alfieri, *Mirra*	
1787	Mozart, *Don Giovanni* *died*: Abel; Gluck		
1788	Mozart, Symphonies nos. 39, 40, 41 ("Jupiter") *died*: C. P. E. Bach	Goethe, *Egmont* David, *Antoine-Laurent de Lavoisier and His Wife Marie-Anne Pierette*	Constitution of the United States
1789	*born*: Maria Agata Szymanowska Peter, String Quintets	William Blake (1757–1827), *Songs of Innocence*	Storming of the Bastille, beginning of the French Revolution
1790	Mozart, *Così fan tutte* Méhul, rescue opera *Euphrosine* First collection of Russian folk songs published		Edmund Burke (1729–1797), *Reflections on the Revolution in France*
1791	*born*: Giacomo Meyerbeer Francesco Galeazzi (1758–1819), treatise *Elementi teorico-pratici di musica* (vol. 2 in 1796) Mozart, *Die Zauberflöte*; *La Clemenza di Tito* Kreutzer, rescue opera *Lodoïska* Cherubini, rescue opera *Lodoïska* *died*: Mozart		

Date	Music	Other Arts and Philosophy	History
1792	*born:* Gioacchino Rossini F. J. Haydn, Symphony no. 94 ("Surprise")	Mary Wollstonecraft (1759–1797), *A Vindication of the Rights of Women*	
1793	Heinrich Christoph Koch (1749–1816), *An Essay in Composition Instruction* Dussek, *The Sufferings of the Queen of France*	David, *Death of Marat* William Godwin (1756–1836), *The Enquiry Concerning Political Justice*	Louis XVI of France and Marie Antoinette beheaded Reign of Terror in France (–1794)
1794	Reichardt, *Lyrischen Gedichten*	Blake, *Songs of Experience*	
1795	*born:* Heinrich August Marschner F. J. Haydn, Symphony no. 104 ("London") Beethoven, Piano Trios, op. 1 Paris Conservatory founded	Giuseppe Parini (1729–1799), *Odi* Gilbert Stuart (1755–1828), portraits of Washington	
1796	*born:* Carl Loewe	Pierre Simon Laplace (1749–1827), *Exposition du système du monde*	Edward Jenner (1749–1823), vaccination for smallpox Catherine the Great dies
1797	*born:* Gaetano Donizetti; Franz Schubert Haydn, String Quartet, op. 76, no. 3, includes variations on "Gott, erhalte Franz den Kaiser!"	Friedrich Hölderlin (1770–1843), *Hyperion*	Charles-Maurice de Talleyrand (1754–1838) appointed French foreign minister
1798	Haydn, *The Creation* Beethoven, Piano Sonata no. 8, op. 13 ("Pathétique") Gaveaux, rescue opera *Léonore* *died:* Cannabich	William Wordsworth (1770–1850), *Lyrical Ballads* Samuel Taylor Coleridge (1772–1834), *Rime of the Ancient Mariner* First phantasmagoria First issue of journal *Athenäum*	Aloys Senefelder (1771–1834) invents lithography Poland absorbed by Russia, Prussia, and Austria Napoleon (1769–1821) begins Egyptian campaigns
1799	*born:* Jacques Fromental Halévy	Francisco Goya (1746–1828), *Caprichos*	Rosetta Stone found, eventually enabling deciphering of hieroglyphic writing French Revolution ends Napoleonic wars begin
1800	*died:* Piccinni; Schulz	Schiller, *Wallenstein* trilogy (–1801) Goya, *The Family of Charles IV* Johann Paul Friedrich Richter ("Jean Paul") (1763–1825), *Titan* Madame de Staël (Germaine de Staël, 1766–1817), *De la littérature*	Britain annexes Ireland in Act of Union Manufacturing with interchangeable parts begins
1801	*born:* Vincenzo Bellini Haydn, *The Seasons* *died:* Cimarosa; C. Stamitz	Schiller, *Maria Stuart*	United States at war with Tripoli
1802	*died:* Sarti	Ugo Foscolo (1778–1827), *Ultime lettere di Jacopo Ortis* François-René de Chateaubriand (1768–1848), *The Genius of Christianity*	

Date	Music	Other Arts and Philosophy	History
1802		Jakob Ludwig Karl Grimm (1785–1863) and Wilhelm Karl Grimm (1786–1859), *Household Tales* Friedrich von Hardenberg ("Novalis"), *Heinrich von Offerdingen*	
1803	*born:* Hector Berlioz	Bertel Thorvaldsen (1770–1844), *Jason*	Louisiana Purchase *Marbury v. Madison*
1804	*born:* Mikhail Glinka; Solomon Sulzer Beethoven, Symphony no. 3, op. 55 ("Eroica"); Piano Sonata, op. 53 ("Waldstein") Paer, rescue opera *Leonora* *died:* Hiller	Schiller, *Wilhelm Tell* Benjamin Latrobe (1764–1820) begins Cathedral of the Assumption in Baltimore	Napoleon (1769–1821) crowns himself emperor of the French Lewis and Clark's expedition begins
1805	*born:* Fanny Mendelssohn Beethoven, Piano Sonata, op. 57 ("Appassionata") Mayr, rescue opera *L'amor coniugale* *died:* Boccherini	Achim von Arnim (1781–1831) and Clemens Brentano (1778–1842), *Des Knaben Wunderhorn* (—1808) François René de Chateaubriand (1768–1848), *René* François Gérard (1770–1837), *Napoleon in His Imperial Robes* Louise-Elisabeth Vigée-Le Brun (1755–1842), *Portrait of Viotti*	Battle of Trafalgar Giuseppe Mazzini born
1806	Beethoven, Razumovsky Quartets, op. 59 *died:* J. M. Haydn; Martín y Soler	David, *Coronation of Napoleon in Notre-Dame* (—1807) J. M. W. Turner (1775–1851), *The Battle of Trafalgar* (—1808)	Napoleon's brother Joseph (1768–1844) becomes king of Naples (r. —1808) Holy Roman Empire dissolved Lewis and Clark's expedition ends
1807	Beethoven, Coriolan Overture Tomášek, *Eclogues* (—1819)	Foscolo, *Dei sepolcri* G. W. F. Hegel (1770–1831), *The Phenomenology of Mind*	Robert Fulton (1765–1815), steamboat
1808	Beethoven, Symphony no. 5, op. 67	Goethe, *Faust Part 1* Heinrich von Kleist (1777–1811), *Penthesilea* William Rush (1756–1833), *Comedy and Tragedy* Friedrich von Schlegel (1772–1845), *Über die Sprache and Weisheit der Indier*	Joseph Bonaparte becomes king of Spain (r. –1813)
1809	*born:* Felix Mendelssohn Beethoven, Piano Concerto no. 5, op. 73 ("Emperor") *died:* F. J. Haydn	Washington Irving (1783–1859), *History of New York* August Wilhelm von Schlegel (1809–1811), *Lectures on Dramatic Art and Literature*	Metternich (1773–1859) appointed Austria's minister of foreign affairs (—1848)
1810	*born:* Robert Schumann; Frédéric Chopin Beethoven, Egmont Overture, op. 84	E. T. A. Hoffmann (1776–1822), essay on Beethoven's Fifth Symphony in *Allgemeine musikalische Zeitung* Walter Scott (1771–1832), *The Lady of the Lake*	

Date	Music	Other Arts and Philosophy	History
1811	*born*: Franz Liszt Beethoven, "Archduke" Trio, op. 97	Jane Austen (1775–1817), *Sense and Sensibility* Caspar David Friedrich (1774–1840), *Winter Landscape with Church*	
1812	Beethoven, Symphony no. 8, op. 93 Gesellschaft der Musikfreunde founded in Vienna *died*: Dussek	Jacob (1785–1863) and Wilhelm (1786–1859) Grimm, *Kinder- und Hausmärchen* (and 1815) George Gordon, Lord Byron (1788–1824), *Childe Harold's Pilgrimage* Théodore Géricault (1791–1824), *Charging Chasseur*	Napoleon invades Russia United States declares war on Britain Mexico achieves independence
1813	*born*: Richard Wagner; Giuseppe Verdi Rossini, *Di tanti palpiti* from *Tancredi*; *L'Italiana in Algeri* Field, Nocturne, no. 1 *died*: Grétry; Peter	Ernst Moritz Arndt (1769–1860), *Was ist des Deutschen Vaterland* Austen, *Pride and Prejudice*	Battle of Vittoria
1814	Beethoven, rescue opera *Fidelio*, oratorio *Der glorreiche Augenblick* Rossini, *Il Turco in Italia* Schubert, *Gretchen am Spinnrade* (published 1821) *died*: J. F. Reichardt; Abbé Vogler	Goya, *The Third of May, 1808* E. T. A. Hoffman (1776–1822), *Phantasiestücke in Callots Manier*	Congress of Vienna (–1815) Treaty of Ghent formally ends War of 1812 Congress of Vienna restructures Europe George Stephenson develops steam locomotive
1815	Schubert, *Erlkönig* (published 1821); *Heidenröslein*	Goya, *Self-Portrait*	Treaty of Vienna Napoleon defeated at Waterloo
1816	Beethoven, song cycle *An die ferne Geliebte*, op. 93; Piano Sonata, op. 101 Rossini, *Il barbiere di Siviglia* Schubert, Symphony no. 4 ("Tragic," published 1884); Symphony no. 5 (published 1885) *died*: Paisiello	Jacob and Wilhelm Grimm, *Deutsche Sagen* (–1818)	
1817	*died*: Méhul	Sergey Nikolayevich Glinka, *Russian History for Purposes of Upbringing* John Keats (1795–1821), *Endymion*	Seminole War
1818	*born*: Charles Gounod Beethoven, Piano Sonata, op. 106 ("Hammerklavier") Tomášek, *Dithyrambs*, op. 65 Schubert, Symphony no. 6 (published 1885) Loewe, *Erlkönig*	Mary Shelley (1797–1851), *Frankenstein*	
1819	*born*: Clara Wieck; Jacques Offenbach Schubert, Quintet in A ("Trout")	Sir Walter Scott (1771–1832), *The Bride of Lammermoor* Géricault, *The Raft of the Medusa* Jean-Auguste-Dominique Ingres (1780–1867), *Niccolò Paganini*	

Date	Music	Other Arts and Philosophy	History
1819		Arthur Schopenhauer (1788–1860), *Die Welt als Wille und Vorstellung* (*The World as Will and Representation*)	
1820	Paganini, 24 *Caprices* for violin	Percy Bysshe Shelley (1722–1822), *Prometheus Unbound* Francisco Goya (1746–1828), *Black Paintings* Hudson River school of painting begins	Missouri Compromise created
1822	*born*: César Franck Beethoven, Piano Sonata no. 31, op. 110; Piano Sonata no. 32, op. 111 Schubert, "Wanderer" Fantasy, op. 15 (published 1823); Symphony No. 8 ("Unfinished," published 1867) Weber, *Der Freischütz*	Eugène Delacroix (1798–1863), *Dante and Virgil* William Cullen Bryant (1794–1878), *Thanatopsis* Thomas de Quincey, *Confessions of an English Opium-Eater* Friedrich Ernst Schleiermacher (1768–1834), *The Christian Faith* Heinrich Heine (1797–1856), *Gedichte*	Congress of Verona Greek War of Independence Brazil achieves independence
1823	Beethoven, *Missa solemnis*, op. 123 Schubert, *Die schöne Müllerin* and *Lachen und Weinen*	John Constable (1776–1837), *Salisbury Cathedral from the Bishop's Grounds* James Fenimore Cooper (1789–1851), *The Leatherstocking Tales* (–1841) Aleksandr Pushkin (1799–1837), *Eugene Onegin* (–1831)	
1824	*born*: Bedřich Smetana; Anton Bruckner Anton Reicha's *Traité de haute composition musicale* describes sonata-allegro form Beethoven, Symphony no. 9, op. 125 Schubert, String Quartet in D minor ("Death and the Maiden"); Octet		
1825	*born*: Johann Strauss II Beethoven, String Quartet in A minor, op. 132 Szymanowska, Nocturne Schubert, Moment musical no. 6 published, *Die Allmacht* Gustav Reichardt, *Des deutschen Vaterland* Mendelssohn, Octet, op. 20 *died*: Gaveaux; Salieri	William Hazlitt (1778–1830), *The Spirit of the Age* Alessandro Manzoni (1785–1873), *I promessi sposi* (–1827) Aleksandr Pushkin (1799–1837), *Eugene Onegin* (–1832)	Nikolai I becomes tsar of Russia Decembrist uprising in St. Petersburg Erie Canal opens
1826	*born*: Stephen Foster Beethoven, String Quartet, no. 13, op. 130; Grosse Fuge, op. 133; String Quartet in F, op. 135		

Date	Music	Other Arts and Philosophy	History
1826	Schubert, String Quartet in G Major (D887) Mendelssohn, *Midsummer Night's Dream* *died*: Weber		
1827	Schubert, *Die Winterreise*; Impromptus, op. 90 *died*: Beethoven	Victor Hugo (1802–1885), *Cromwell* Heinrich Heine (1797–1856), *Buch der Lieder* Delacroix, *Death of Sardanapalus* Ingres, *Oedipus Solving the Riddle of the Sphinx*	
1828	Schubert, Symphony no. 9 ("Great," published 1840); *Schwanengesang*; Piano Sonata in B-Flat (D960); Mass in E-Flat (published 1865); String Quintet Marschner, *Der Vampyr* *La musette de Portici*, which Daniel-François-Esprit Auber (1782–1871) took as a model for *grand opéra* *died*: Schubert	Delacroix, *Mephistopheles in Flight* Noah Webster (1758–1843), *American Dictionary of the English Language*	
1829	*born*: Louis Moreau Gottschalk; Anton Rubinstein Rossini, *Guillaume Tell* Mendelssohn conducts J. S. Bach's *St. Matthew Passion*		Baltimore and Ohio Railroad begun
1830	*born*: Hans von Bülow Bellini, *I Capuleti ed i Montecchi* Berlioz, *Symphonie fantastique* Mendelssohn, Symphony no. 5 ("Reformation"); *Die Hebriden*	Hugo, *Hernani* Stendhal (1783–1842), *Le rouge et le noir* Delacroix, *Liberty Leading the People* Friedrich, *Evening in the Baltic* Adalbert von Chamisso (1781–1838), *Frauenliebe und Leben* Barbizon school begins ca. 1830	July Revolution in France Belgian insurrection Polish revolt Indian Removal Act in United States
1831	*born*: Joseph Joachim Rossini, *Stabat Mater* (–1841) Bellini, *La Sonnambula*; cavatina *Casta diva* from *Norma* F. Mendelssohn, *Oratorium nach den Bildern der Bibel* Meyerbeer, *Robert le diable* *died*: Kreutzer; Szymanowska	Giacomo Leopardi (1798–1837), *I canti* John Constable (1776–1837), *Salisbury Cathedral from the Meadows*	Leopold of Saxe-Coburg-Gotha elected king of independent Belgium William Lloyd Garrison (1805–1879) publishes first issue of *The Liberator*
1832	Donizetti, *L'Elisir d'amore* Loewe, oratorio *Die Zerstörung Jerusalems* Mendelssohn, *Paulus* (–1836) *died*: Clementi; Zelter	Delacroix, *Portrait of Paganini*	Cholera epidemic in Paris First Reform Act passed in Britain
1833	*born*: Alexander Borodin; Johannes Brahms Mendelssohn, Symphony no. 4 ("Italian")	Goethe, *Faust*, Part 2 George Sand (1804–1876), *Lélia* Charles Lamb (1775–1834), *Essays of Elia*	

Date	Music	Other Arts and Philosophy	History
1834	First issue of *Neue Zeitschrift für Musik*		Grain reaper patented by Cyrus McCormick (1809–1884)
1835	born: César Cui; Camille Saint-Saëns Bellini, *I Puritani* Donizetti, *Lucia di Lammermoor* died: Bellini	Georg Büchner (1813–1837), *Dantons Tod* *Kalevala*, compiled by Elias Lönnrot (1802–1884) Turner, *Burning of the Houses of Lords and Commons, 16th October, 1834* First fairy tales of Hans Christian Andersen (1805–1875) published Alexis de Tocqueville (1805–1859), *Democracy in America*	Boers found republics of Natal, Transvaal, and Orange Free States
1836	Amadeus Wendt (1783–1836), *Über den gegenwärtigen Zustand der Musik besonders in Deutschland und wie er geworden* Loewe, *Gutenberg* Meyerbeer, *Les Huguenots* Glinka, *A Life for the Tsar*	Alfred de Musset (1810–1857), *Confession d'un enfant du siècle* Thomas Cole (1801–1848), *The Course of Empire* Ralph Waldo Emerson (1803–1882), *Nature* A. W. N. Pugin (1812–1852) begins new houses of Parliament in London	Texas becomes independent
1837	born: Miliy Balakirev Adolf Bernhard Marx, *Die Lehre von der musikalischen Composition* died: Field	Charles Dickens (1812–1870), *Oliver Twist* (—1839)	Queen Victoria ascends British throne Georg Wilhelm Friedrich Hegel (1770–1831), in *Lectures on the Philosophy of History*, postulates theory of dialectic Steel plow invented by John Deere
1838	born: Georges Bizet First publication of Liszt's *Études d'Exécution Transcendante d'après Paganini*	Delacroix, *Frédéric Chopin*	Underground Railroad begins
1839	born: Modest Musorgsky died: Paer	L. J. M. Daguerre (1789–1851) invents daguerreotype William Henry Fox Talbot (1800–1877) invents paper photography	Opium War in China *Amistad* affair
1840	born: Pyotr Ilyich Chaikovsky Schumann's "song year" Donizetti, *La fille du régiment* died: Paganini	Josef Danhauser (1805–1845), *Liszt at the Piano* Mikhail Lermontov (1814–1841), *A Hero of Our Time* Transcendentalist periodical *The Dial* founded	
1841	born: Antonín Dvořák Loewe, *Palestrina*		
1842	born: Jules Massenet New York Philharmonic and Vienna Philharmonic founded Glinka, *Ruslan and Lyudmila* Loewe, *Johann Hus*	Nicolai Gogol (1809–1852), *Dead Souls* Honoré de Balzac (1799–1850), *La comédie humaine* (—1848) Joseph Turner (1775–1851), *Snow Storm*	

Date	Music	Other Arts and Philosophy	History
1842	Mendelssohn, Symphony no. 3 ("Scottish") *died:* Cherubini		
1843	Donizetti, *Don Pasquale* Berlioz, *Treatise on Instrumentation*	Søren Kierkegaard (1813–1855), *Either/Or* Edgar Allan Poe (1809–1849), *The Gold Bug;* Thomas Babington Macaulay (1800–1859), *Critical and Historical Essays* Hiram Powers (1805–1873), *The Greek Slave*	Oregon Trail opens
1844	*born:* Nikolai Rimsky–Korsakov	Turner, *Rain, Stream, and Speed: The Great Western Railway* Mathew Brady (1823?–1896) opens photography studio in New York	First telegraph set up
1845	*born:* Gabriel Fauré Brendel becomes editor of *Neue Zeitschrift für Musik* and spokesman for the "new German school" *died:* Mayr	Prosper Merimée (1803–1870), *Carmen* Alexandre Dumas *père* (1802–1870) *Le Comte de Monte-Cristo* Frederick Douglass (1817–1895), *Narrative of the Life of Frederick Douglass* Margaret Fuller (1810–1850), *Woman in the Nineteenth Century*	Pius IX becomes pope Texas annexed to United States
1846	Mendelssohn, *Elijah*	George Sand, *Lucrezia Floriani* Thomas Carlyle (1795–1881), *On Heroes* Søren Kierkegaard (1813–1855), *Fear and Trembling*	Mexican War begins Oregon Treaty between Britain and United States settles border dispute at 49th parallel
1847	*died:* Fanny Mendelssohn; Felix Mendelssohn	Henry Wadsworth Longfellow (1807–1882), *Evangeline* Charlotte Brontë (1816–1855), *Jane Eyre* Emily Brontë (1818–1848), *Wuthering Heights* Camillo Benso di Cavour (1810–1861) helps found newspaper *Il Risorgimento* William Makepeace Thackeray (1811–1863), *Vanity Fair* (−1848)	Mormons settle at Salt Lake City Liberia independent
1848	*died:* Donizetti	Alexandre Dumas *fils* (1824–1895), *La Dame aux Camélias* Karl Marx (1818–1883), *Communist Manifesto*	Revolutions in France, Prussia, Austria-Hungary, and Italian states July Monarchy in France ends Mexican War ends
1849	Wagner's article "Die Kunst und die Revolution" sets forth his theory of music drama *died:* Chopin	Dickens, *David Copperfield* (−1850) John Ruskin (1819–1900), *The Seven Lamps of Architecture*	Lajos Kossuth (1802–1894) declares Magyar republic in Hungary California gold rush begins

Date	Music	Other Arts and Philosophy	History
1850	died: Tomášek	Elizabeth Barrett Browning (1806–1861), *Sonnets from the Portuguese* Nathaniel Hawthorne (1804–1864), *The Scarlet Letter* Alfred, Lord Tennyson (1809–1892), *In Memoriam*	Taiping Rebellion First National Women's Convention in Worcester, Massachusetts Compromise of 1850
1851		Herman Melville (1819–1891), *Moby-Dick* Crystal Palace begun in London	Christiana Revolt, Pennsylvania, first violent uprising in response to the Fugitive Slave Act of 1850. Erie Railroad reaches Great Lakes
1852	Théâtre Lyrique opens in Paris Karl Franz Brendel (1811–1868), *Geschichte der Musik*	Harriet Beecher Stowe (1811–1896), *Uncle Tom's Cabin*	Napoleon III (1808–1873) becomes emperor of France
1853		William Wells Brown, *Clotel* (first novel by an African American)	
1854	born: Leoš Janáček Eduard Hanslick (1825–1904), in "On the Musically Beautiful," opposes the "new German school"	Theodor Mommsen (1817–1903), *Roman History* (—1856) Henry David Thoreau (1817–1862), *Walden*	Commodore Perry opens Japan to the West Crimean War begins Kansas-Nebraska Act
1855		Gustave Courbet (1819–1877), *The Artist's Studio* Henry Wadsworth Longfellow (1807–1882), *The Song of Hiawatha* Anthony Trollope (1815–1882), *The Barsetshire Chronicles* (—1867) Walt Whitman (1891–1892), *Leaves of Grass*	Sigmund Freud born David Livingstone discovers Victoria Falls Battle of Sevastopol
1856	died: Schumann		
1857	Rossini, *Péchés de vieillesse* (—1868) died: Glinka	Charles Pierre Baudelaire (1821–1867), *Les fleurs du mal* Gustave Flaubert (1821–1880), *Madame Bovary* Hippolyte Adolphe Taine (1828–1893), *Les philosophes classiques du XIXᵉ siècle en France*	Sepoy Mutiny in India
1858	born: Giacomo Puccini	Théophile Gautier (1811–1872), *Histoire de l'art dramatique depuis vingt-cinqans* (—1859)	First successful laying of transatlantic cable
1859	born: Victor Herbert Russian Musical Society founded Allgemeiner Deutscher Musikverein founded	Frederick E. Church (1826–1900), *The Heart of the Andes* Harriet E. Wilson, *Our Nig* (first novel by an African-American woman)	John Brown leads revolt against slavery in Harpers Ferry, Virginia Charles Darwin publishes *Origin of the Species*

Date	Music	Other Arts and Philosophy	History
1859			Italian War First oil well started in United States
1860	*born:* Edward MacDowell; Gustav Mahler; Ignacy Jan Paderewski; Hugo Wolf	Jakob Burckhardt (1818–1897), *Kultur der Renaissance in Italien*	
1861	Ferenc Erkel (1810–1893), *Bánk Bán* *died:* Marschner	Charles Dickens (1812–1870), *Great Expectations* George Eliot (1819–1880), *Silas Marner*	Kingdom of Italy proclaimed Serfdom abolished in Russia by Tsar Alexander II American Civil War begins Pasteurization introduced
1862	*born:* Claude Debussy St. Petersburg Conservatory founded *died:* Halévy	Alexander Herzen (1812–1870), in the article "The Giant Wakes," supports student demonstrations in Russia Victor Hugo (1802–1885), *Les Misérables* Ivan Turgenev (1818–1883), *Fathers and Sons*	
1863	*born:* Horatio Parker	Édouard Manet (1832–1883), *Le déjeuner sur l'herbe*	Emancipation Proclamation issued by President Abraham Lincoln Battle of Gettysburg
1864	*born:* Richard Strauss *died:* Foster; Meyerbeer	Camille Corot (1796–1875), *Memory of Mortefontaine*	
1865	*born:* Jean Sibelius Wagner, *Tristan und Isolde*	Leo Tolstoy (1828–1910), *War and Peace* (—1869)	American Civil War ends Abraham Lincoln assassinated Thirteenth Amendment is passed, forbidding slavery in the United States
1866	*born:* Ferruccio Busoni; Erik Satie	John Greenleaf Whittier (1807–1892), *Snow-Bound*	Austro-Prussian War Reconstruction begins in the American South
1867	*born:* Amy Marcy Beach; Arturo Toscanini Vladimir Stasov refers to Russian nationalist composers Balakirev, Cui, Borodin, Musorgsky, and Rimsky-Korsakov as "mighty little band"		Dominion of Canada formed First volume of Marx's *Das Kapital* Dual monarchy of Austria-Hungary begins (*Ausgleich*) United States purchases Alaska from Russia
1868	*died:* Rossini	Louisa May Alcott (1832–1888), *Little Women* Robert Browning (1812–1889), *The Ring and the Book* (—1869)	President Andrew Johnson impeached Meiji Restoration in Japan
1869	*born:* Hans Pfitzner *died:* Berlioz; Gottschalk; Lowe		Fifteenth Amendment grants suffrage to black men in the United States Suez Canal opens Transcontinental rail service begins in United States

Date	Music	Other Arts and Philosophy	History
1870	Orchestral subscription series becomes standard in Europe		Franco-Prussian War Lenin (Vladimir Ilyich Ulyanov) born Standard Oil Company formed by John D. Rockefeller
1871	*born:* Alexander Scriabin; Alexander Zemlinsky Société Nationale de Musique founded Louis Lewandowski (1821–1894), 3 vols. of collected synagogue music (–1882)	Francesco De Sanctis (1817–1883), *Storia della letteratura italiana* Claude Monet (1840–1926), *Impression: Sunrise* James Whistler (1834–1903), *Portrait of the Artist's Mother* Émile Zola (1840–1902), *Les Rougon-Macquart* (–1893)	German Empire (Second Reich) formed Unification of Italy Paris Commune Third Republic begins in France Chicago fire
1872	*born:* Ralph Vaughan Williams Alexander Dargomïzhky (1813–1869), *The Stone Guest*	Alphonse Daudet (1840–1897), *L'arlésienne* Friedrich Engels (1820–1895), *Dialectics of Nature* First exhibition of Monet's *Impression: Sunrise*	
1873	*born:* Sergei Rachmaninoff First volume of Philipp Spitta's biography of J. S. Bach	Walter Pater (1839–1894), *Studies in the History of the Renaissance*	
1874	*born:* Gustav Holst; Charles Ives; Serge Koussevitsky; Arnold Schoenberg Musorgsky, *Boris Gudunov*	Paul Verlaine (1844–1896), *Romances sans paroles*	
1875	*born:* Maurice Ravel Gilbert and Sullivan, *Trial by Jury* *died:* Bizet	Thomas Eakins (1844–1916), *The Gross Clinic* Mikhail Saltykov (1826–1889), *The Golovlyov Family* (–1880)	Theosophical movement founded by Helena Blavatsky (1831–1891)
1876	*born:* Manuel de Falla First performance of Wagner's complete *Ring* cycle at Bayreuth Brahms, First Symphony	Edgar Degas (1834–1917), *Ballet Rehearsal* Stéphane Mallarmé (1842–1898), *L'après-midi d'un faune* Pierre August Renoir (1841–1919), *Le bal au Moulin de la Galette*	Telephone invented by Alexander Graham Bell (1847–1922) Centennial Exposition in Philadelphia Battle of Little Big Horn
1877			Germ theory of disease promulgated by Louis Pasteur Phonograph invented by Thomas Edison
1879	*born:* Ottorino Respighi	Fyodor Dostoevsky (1821–1881), *The Brothers Karamazov* (–1880) Henrik Ibsen (1828–1906), *A Doll's House* Büchner, *Woyzeck* published	Albert Einstein born Joseph Stalin born Electric light invented by Thomas Edison Zulu War
1880	*born:* Ernest Bloch Cui's *La musique en Russie* *died:* Offenbach	August Rodin (1840–1917), *The Thinker* Giovanni Verga (1840–1922), *Cavalleria rusticana*	

Date	Music	Other Arts and Philosophy	History
1881	*born*: Béla Bartók; Nikolai Myaskovsky *died*: Musorgsky	Henry James (1843–1916), *Washington Square*	Tsar Alexander II and President James Garfield assassinated
1882	*born*: Percy Grainger; Zoltán Kodály; Igor Stravinsky; Karol Syzmanowski	Henri Becque (1837–1899), *Les corbeaux* Vladimir Stasov, "Twenty–Five Years of Russian Art"	Britain invades Egypt Triple Alliance between Russia, Germany, and Austria-Hungary
1883	*born*: Edgard Varèse; Anton von Webern *died*: Wagner	Friedrich Wilhelm Nietzsche (1844–1900), *Also sprach Zarathustra* (–1885) Robert Louis Stevenson (1850–1894), *Treasure Island* Henri Amiel (1821–1881), *Journal intime* published	General Charles George Gordon executed by Sudanese Brooklyn Bridge opens Modern American navy begun Victoria Claflin Woodhull (1838–1927) is first woman to run for U.S. presidency
1884	Bruckner, Seventh Symphony	Joris Karl Huysmans (1848–1907), *À rebours* John Singer Sargent (1856–1925), *Madame X* Georges Seurat (1859–1891), *Sunday Afternoon on the Island of Le Grande Jatte* Mark Twain (Samuel Clemens; 1835–1910), *The Adventures of Huckleberry Finn*	
1885	*born*: Alban Berg; Jerome Kern Guido Adler's *Umfang, Methode und Ziel der Musikwissenschaft* published, charting the course of musicology as a discipline	William Dean Howells (1837–1920), *The Rise of Silas Lapham* William Le Baron Jenney designs Home Insurance Company Building in Chicago	
1886	*born*: Al Jolson; Wilhelm Furtwängler *died*: Liszt	Benito Pérez Galdós (1843–1920), *Fortunata y Jacinta* (–1887) Augustus Saint–Gaudens (1848–1907), Adams Memorial in Washington, D.C. (–1891) Arthur Rimbaud (1854–1891), *Illuminations*	Richard von Krafft-Ebing (1840–1902), *Psychopathia sexualis*
1887	*born*: Nadia Boulanger; Arthur Rubinstein Verdi, *Otello* *died*: Borodin	Giuseppe Garibaldi (1807–1882), *Autobiography*	Ethiopian-Italian War begins Interstate Commerce Act regulates U.S railroads
1888	*born*: Irving Berlin	Guy de Maupassant (1850–1893), *Pierre et Jean* August Strindberg (1849–1912), *Miss Julie* Kodak camera perfected by George Eastman (1854–1932)	George Eastman patents handheld camera
1889	Franck, Symphony in D minor	Gerhart Hauptmann (1862–1946), *Vor Sonnenaufgang* Eiffel Tower completed	Oklahoma land rush Japan receives first written constitution

Date	Music	Other Arts and Philosophy	History
1890	*died:* Franck; Sulzer	Emily Dickinson (1830–1886), *Poems of Emily Dickinson* published William James (1842–1910), *Principles of Psychology* Vincent van Gogh (1853–1890), *Cows in the Wheatfields* Jacob Riis (1849–1914), *How the Other Half Lives*	Otto von Bismarck dismissed as chancellor of Germany Eiffel Tower completed National American Women's Suffrage Association formed
1891	*born:* Sergei Prokofieff	Henri Toulouse-Lautrec (1864–1901), *Moulin Rouge, La Goulue*	Yellowstone becomes first national park
1892	*born:* Arthur Honegger; Darius Milhaud	Maurice Maeterlinck (1862–1949), *Pelléas et Mélisande*	Ellis Island opens
1893	*born:* Lili Boulanger *died:* Chaikovsky; Gounod	Edvard Munch (1863–1944), *The Scream* Max Nordau (1849–1923), in *Entartung,* applies theories of "degeneracy," proposed by Cesare Lombroso (1836–1909), to art and literature	Panic of 1893 causes economic depression Revolt in Hawaii
1894	*born:* Walter Piston; Bessie Smith *died:* Anton Rubinstein; Smetana; von Bülow	Rudyard Kipling (1865–1936), *The Jungle Book*	Alfred Dreyfus found guilty of treason and transported to Devil's Island
1895	*born:* Paul Hindemith; Carl Orff *Liber responsorialis* edited by monks of Solesmes *died:* Bruckner	Stephen Crane (1871–1900), *The Red Badge of Courage* Thomas Hardy (1840–1928), *Jude the Obscure* Camille Pissarro (1830–1903), *Bather in the Woods* Richard Morris Hunt (1827–1895) builds Great Hall of the Metropolitan Museum of Art in New York (—1902) Firm of McKim, Mead, and White builds Boston Public Library First moving pictures shown to general public in Paris	Final volume of Marx's *Das Kapital* Pullman rail strike French West Africa organized First Sino-Japanese War Sun Yat-sen's revolt in China fails Italian invasion of Ethiopia ends
1896	*born:* Howard Hanson; Roger Sessions; Virgil Thomson *died:* Clara (Wieck) Schumann	Antonio Fogazzaro (1842–1911), *Piccolo mondo antico* A. E. Housman (1859–1936), *A Shropshire Lad* William Morris (1834–1896), *The Kelmscott Chaucer*	
1897	*born:* Henry Cowell; Erich Wolfgang Korngold *died:* Brahms	Paul Gauguin (1848–1903), *Where Do We Come From?*	
1898	*born:* George Gershwin; Roy Harris Satie, *Gymnopédies*	Tolstoy, *What Is Art?* Otto Wagner (1841–1918) builds Majolika House in Vienna	Spanish-American War

Date	Music	Other Arts and Philosophy	History
1898		H. G. Wells (1866–1946), *The War of the Worlds* Oscar Wilde (1854–1900), *The Ballad of Reading Gaol* Zola, "J'accuse"	
1899	*born*: Francis Poulenc; Gustave Reese *died*: J. Strauss (the Younger)	Giosuè Carducci (1835–1907), *Lyrics and Rhythms* Paul Cézanne (1839–1906), *The Large Bathers* (–1906) Kate Chopin (1850–1904), *The Awakening* Winslow Homer (1836–1910), *Gulf Stream* Frank Norris (1870–1902), *McTeague*	Dreyfus pardoned
1900	*born*: Aaron Copland; Ernst Křenek; Otto Luening; Kurt Weill	Mary Cassatt (1844–1926), *The Mirror* Sigmund Freud (1856–1939), *The Interpretation of Dreams* Charles Rennie Mackintosh shows at the Seccessionist Exhibit in Vienna	Boxer Rebellion in China Boer War begins Freud publishes *The Interpretation of Dreams*
1901	*born*: Paul Henry Lang; Oliver Strunk *died*: Verdi	Thomas Mann (1875–1955), *Buddenbrooks* Arthur Schnitzler (1862–1931), *Leutnant Gustl*	Queen Victoria dies President William McKinley assassinated Boxer Rebellion ends Australia created Trans-Siberian Railroad completed Mosquitos found to transmit yellow fever
1902	*born*: Stefan Wolpe Debussy, *Pelléas et Mélisande*	Benedetto Croce (1866–1952), *Filosofia come scienza dello spinto* (–1917)	South African peace agreement
1903	*born*: Aram Khachaturian; Theodor Wiesengrund Adorno Restoration of Gregorian chant to active church use *died*: Wolf	Gabriele D'Annunzio (1863–1938), *Laudi* (–1912) W. E. B. Du Bois (1868–1963), *The Souls of Black Folk* Hugo von Hofmannsthal (1874–1929), *Elektra* Alfred Stieglitz (1864–1946) launches the journal *Work*	Entente Cordiale between Britain and France Kishnev pogrom in Russia Construction begins on Panama Canal Henry Ford's first Model A automobile Wright brothers fly first airplane First message sent over Pacific cable
1904	*Born*: Bing Crosby; Luigi Dallapiccola; Glenn Miller *died*: Dvořák	Anton Chekhov (1860–1904), *The Cherry Orchard* Joseph Conrad (1857–1924), *Nostromo* Frank Wedekind (1864–1918), *Die Büchse der Pandora* Abbey Theatre opens in Dublin	B. F. Skinner born Russo-Japanese War begins New York subway opens
1905	*Born*: Marc Blitzstein	Antonio Gaudi (1852–1926) builds Casa Milá (–1907) Edward Steichen (1879–1973) opens 291 Gallery with Alfred Stieglitz	Sinn Fein organized as Irish nationalist party Revolution in Russia Russo-Japanese War ends

Date	Music	Other Arts and Philosophy	History
1905			Einstein publishes special theory of relativity
1906	*Born:* Josephine Baker; Dmitry Shostakovich Kodály and Bartók issue Hungarian folk song anthology *Magyar népdalok* R. Strauss's opera *Salome*	Ruth St. Denis (1878?–1968), *Radha* Upton Sinclair (1878–1968), *The Jungle*	Battleship *Dreadnaught* launched by Britain Dreyfus affair ends All India League organized San Francisco earthquake Finland is first country in Europe to give vote to women U.S. troops occupy Cuba Wasserman test for syphilis developed
1907	Busoni's *Sketch of a New Esthetic of Music* *died:* Joachim	Jacinto Benavente y Martinez (1866–1954), *Los intereses creados* Gustav Klimt (1862–1917), *The Kiss*	Hague Peace Conference Montessori schools introduced First helicopter flies Luxury liner *Mauritania* launched
1908	*born:* Elliott Carter; Olivier Messiaen; Edward Lowinsky Schoenberg, Second String Quartet *died:* MacDowell; Rimsky-Korsakov	Adolf Loos (1870–1933), *Ornament and Crime*	Congo Free State becomes Belgian Congo Robert Peary becomes first man to reach North Pole Singer Building, first skyscraper, is constructed Oil discovered in Persia
1909	*born:* Benny Goodman R. Strauss, *Elektra*	Filippo Marinetti (1876–1944), *Futurist Manifesto* Ferenc Molnár (1878–1952), *Liliom*	Revolution in Persia Prince Ito assassinated in Japan First newsreel shown in theaters Louis Bleriot becomes first person to fly across English Channel
1910	*born:* William Schuman Stravinsky, *Firebird* *died:* Balakirev	Paul Claudel (1868–1955), *Five Great Odes*	Japan annexes Korea Union of South Africa founded National Association for the Advancement of Colored People (NAACP) founded
1911	*born:* Mahalia Jackson; Gian Carlo Menotti Satie, *Trois Sarabandes* Schoenberg, *Harmonielehre* *died:* Mahler	Michel Fokine (1880–1942), *Petrushka*	Chinese Revolution First aircraft landing on ship Standard Oil trust broken up First U.S. coast-to-coast flight
1912	*born:* John Cage Schoenberg, *Pierrot Lunaire* *died:* Massenet	Maksim Gorky (1868–1936), *The Lower Depths* Zane Grey (1875–1939), *Riders of the Purple Sage* James Weldon Johnson (1871–1938), *The Autobiography of an Ex-Colored Man* Wassily Kandinsky (1866–1944), *Concerning the Spiritual in Art* Carl Gustav Jung (1875–1961), *Psychology of the Unconscious*	War in the Balkans Libya ceded to Italy Sun Yat-sen founds Kuomintang Party

Date	Music	Other Arts and Philosophy	History
1913	*born:* Benjamin Britten Berg's *Fünf Orchesterlieder* premiered Stravinsky, *The Rite of Spring*	Pio Baroja y Nessi (1872–1956), *Memorias de un hombre de acción* Willa Cather (1873–1947), *O Pioneers!* Marcel Proust (1871–1922), *Swann's Way* Rainer Maria Rilke (1875–1926), *Das Marienleben* George Bernard Shaw (1856–1950), *Pygmalion* Armory Show (international art exhibition)	Suffragists march on Washington, D.C. Federal Reserve Act First home electric refrigerator Ford Motor Company begins first moving assembly line
1914	Luigi Russolo (1885–1947), *L'arte dei rumori,* includes first designs for futurist instruments		Assassination of Archduke Franz Ferdinand of Austria-Hungary World War I begins Panama Canal opens United States intervenes in Mexican Civil War Clayton Antitrust Act
1915	*born:* George Perle; Vincent Persichetti; Frank Sinatra Founding of Institute Jacques-Dalcroze to teach eurhythmics *died:* Scriabin	Marcel Duchamp (1887–1968), *The Large Glass* (—1923) Somerset Maugham (1874–1915), *Of Human Bondage* Founding of Provincetown Players in Provincetown, Massachusetts	Armenian genocide by Turks Gallipoli campaign Zeppelin bombing of England *Lusitania* sunk First transcontinental telephone conversation
1916	*born:* Milton Babbitt	Hilda Doolittle (1886–1961), *Sea Garden* Juan Ramón Jiménez (1881–1958), *Sonetos espirituales 1914–1915*	General John Pershing raids Mexico in pursuit of Pancho Villa Child Labor Law passed Easter Uprising in Ireland
1917	*born:* Ella Fitzgerald Hans Pfitzner, *Palestrina* (composed 1915)	Duchamp, *Fountain* Heinrich Mann (1871–1950), *Kaiserreich* trilogy (—1925) *Parade, ballet réaliste,* produced by Diaghilev Miguel de Unamuno y Jugo (1864–1936), *Abel Sánchez*	Russian Revolution begins Britain captures Palestine United States enters World War I
1918	*born:* Leonard Bernstein; George Rochberg *died:* Lili Boulanger; Cui; Debussy	Aleksandr Blok (1880–1921), *The Twelve* Mary Wigman (1886–1973), *The Seven Dances of Life* Apollinaire's play *Les mamelles de Tirésias,* first explicitly designated "surrealist drama"	World War I ends Poland and Czechoslovakia achieve independence Flu epidemic
1919	*died:* Horatio Parker	Bauhaus school begins H. L. Mencken (1880–1956), *The American Language*	Treaty of Versailles League of Nations created White Russians defeated by Bolsheviks British massacre demonstrators at Amritsar Mohandas Gandhi (1869–1948) begins policy of passive resistance in India

Date	Music	Other Arts and Philosophy	History
1919			U.S. seaplanes cross Atlantic for the first time
1920	*born:* Ravi Shankar Korngold, *Die tote Stadt* "Les Six" (Honegger, Milhaud, Poulenc, Auric, Tailleferre, and Durey) first designated by Henri Collet Theremin invented	Colette (Sidonie Gabrielle Claudine Colette, 1873–1954), *Chéri* Sigrid Unset (1882–1949), *Kristin Lavransdatter* (—1922) Edith Wharton (1862–1937), *The Age of Innocence*	Ireland granted home rule Finland gains independence from Russia Gandhi leads Indian independence movement Palestine becomes British mandate Prohibition begins in United States Women gain right to vote in United States
1921	*died:* Saint-Saëns	Luigi Pirandello (1867–1936), *Sei personaggi in cerca d'autore* Man Ray (1890–1976), *The Gift*	Modern Turkey founded U.S. immigration quota passed
1922	*born:* Iannis Xenakis	T. S. Eliot (1888–1965), *The Waste Land* John Galsworthy (1867–1933), *The Forsyte Saga* James Joyce (1882–1941), *Ulysses* Sinclair Lewis (1885–1951), *Babbitt* Marcel Proust (1871–1922), *À la recherche du temps perdu* (—1931) Edith Sitwell (1887–1964), *Façade*	Benito Mussolini (1883–1945) seizes power in Italy Irish Free State established First U.S. aircraft carriers launched
1923	*born:* György Ligeti; Ned Rorem		Munich "beer-hall putsch" suppressed Tokyo earthquake First nonstop flight across United States Ku Klux Klan exposed
1924	*born:* Luigi Nono; Joseph Kerman Gershwin, *Rhapsody in Blue* Poulenc, *Les biches*, one of the first ballets typifying "lifestyle modernism" *died:* Busoni; Fauré; Herbert; Puccini	E. M. Forster (1879–1970), *A Passage to India* André Breton (1896–1966), "Surrealist Manifesto"	Teapot Dome scandal First around-the-world flight
1925	*born:* Pierre Boulez Berg, *Wozzeck* *died:* Satie	Theodore Dreiser (1871–1945), *An American Tragedy* F. Scott Fitzgerald (1896–1940), *The Great Gatsby* André Gide (1869–1951), *Les faux-monnayeurs* Franz Kafka (1883–1924), *The Trial* Virginia Woolf (1882–1941), *Mrs. Dalloway*	Scopes "monkey trial"
1926	*born:* Miles Davis; Morton Feldman; Hans Werner Henze; Seymour Shifrin Shostakovich, Symphony no. 1	Paul Élouard (1895–1952), *Capitale de la douleur* Sean O'Casey (1880–1964), *The Plough and the Stars* First talkies	Stalin seizes control of U.S.S.R.

Date	Music	Other Arts and Philosophy	History
1927	Oscar Hammerstein II (1895–1960) and Jerome Kern (1885–1945), *Show Boat*	Ansel Adams (1902–1984), *Monolith, the Face of Half Dome, Yosemite National Park* Herman Hesse's novel *Steppenwolf* Paul Klee (1879–1940), *Pastoral*	AT&T inaugurates transatlantic radio-telephone service Television invented First solo transatlantic flight by Charles Lindbergh (1902–1974)
1928	*born*: Karlheinz Stockhausen; Carl Dahlhaus Schoenberg, *Variations for Orchestra* Stravinsky, *Oedipus Rex* Weill, *Die Dreigroschenoper*, with Bertolt Brecht (1898–1956) *died*: Janáček	André Breton (1896–1966), *Nadja* Stefan George (1868–1933), *Das neue Reich* D. H. Lawrence (1885–1930), *Lady Chatterley's Lover* William Butler Yeats (1865–1939), *The Tower*	Rudolf Carnap (1891–1970), *Der logische Aufbau der Welt*, discussing logical positivism Amelia Earhart becomes first woman to fly across Atlantic First flight from San Francisco to Australia
1929	*born*: George Crumb	Hart Crane (1899–1932), *The Bridge* William Faulkner (1897–1962), *The Sound and the Fury* Ernest Hemingway (1899–1961), *A Farewell to Arms*	Stock market crashes and Great Depression begins Stalin begins forced collectivization of farms in U.S.S.R.
1930	Knud Jeppesen (1892–1974), *Kontrapunkt*	Noël Coward (1899–1973), *Private Lives* José Ortega y Gasset (1883–1955), *The Revolt of the Masses* Carl Zuckmayer (1896–1977), *Der blaue Engel*	General Electric introduces camera flashbulb
1931			Second Spanish Republic Japanese attack Manchuria Empire State Building opens
1932		Louis-Ferdinand Céline (1894–1961), *Voyage au bout de la nuit* Aldous Huxley (1894–1963), *Brave New World* François Mauriac (1885–1970), *Le Noeud de vipères* Theory of "socialist realism" enunciated at first Congress of the Union of Soviet Writers	U.S. army veterans march on Washington, D.C.
1933	*born*: Krzysztof Penderecki	Federico García Lorca (1898–1936), *Blood Wedding* André Malraux (1901–1976), *La condition humaine* Gertrude Stein (1874–1946), *The Autobiography of Alice B. Toklas*	Hitler becomes chancellor of Germany and Nazi regime begins First Nazi concentration camp opens at Dachau New Deal begins under President Franklin Delano Roosevelt Tennessee Valley Authority created Prohibition repealed Hoover Dam completed

Date	Music	Other Arts and Philosophy	History
1934	*born:* Peter Maxwell Davies Virgil Thomson, *Four Saints in Three Acts* Cole Porter (1893–1964), *Anything Goes* *died:* Holst	Robert Graves (1895–1985), *I, Claudius* Lillian Hellman (1905–1984), *The Children's Hour*	Stalin begins purges
1935	*born:* Arvo Pärt; Elvis Presley; Terry Riley; La Monte Young Gershwin, *Porgy and Bess*	Jean Giraudoux (1882–1944), *La guerre de Troie n'aura pas lieu* Clifford Odets (1906–1963), *Waiting for Lefty*	German firm AEG exhibits the Magnetophone, forerunner of the tape recorder Social Security Act passed Works Progress Administration created Amelia Earhart becomes first woman to fly across the Pacific DC-3 airplane introduced Commonwealth of Philippines declared
1936	*born:* Steve Reich *Pravda* editorial, "Muddle instead of Music," initiates period of heavy Soviet arts censorship *died:* Respighi	Miguel Hernández (1910–1942), *El rayo que no cesa* Margaret Mitchell (1900–1949), *Gone with the Wind* Carl Sandburg (1878–1967), *The People, Yes* Robert Sherwood (1896–1955), *Idiot's Delight* Frank Lloyd Wright (1867–1959) builds Fallingwater	Italy invades Ethiopia Spanish Civil War begins Oil found in Saudi Arabia Arab revolt in Palestine
1937	*born:* David Del Tredici; Philip Glass Blitzstein, *The Cradle Will Rock* Orff, *Carmina burana* Shostakovich, Symphony no. 5 First part of Hindemith's *Unterweisung in Tonsatz* *died:* Gershwin; Ravel; Bessie Smith; Szymanowski	Piet Mondrian (1872–1944), *Composition with Red, Yellow, and Blue* (–1942) Pablo Picasso (1881–1973), *Guernica*	U.S. army gets first B-17 bomber *Hindenburg* disaster Sino-Japanese War resumes Italian-German Axis formed
1938	*born:* William Bolcom; John Corigliano; Jean-Claude Risset; Joan Tower; Charles Wuorinen	John Dos Passos (1896–1970), *U.S.A* Thornton Wilder (1897–1975), *Our Town*	Austria incorporated into Third Reich (*Anschluss*) Munich agreement
1939	*born:* Judy Collins Cage, *Imaginary Landscape No. 1*	Berenice Abbott (1898–1991), *Changing New York* Clement Greenberg's essay "Avant-Garde and Kitsch" John Steinbeck (1902–1968), *The Grapes of Wrath*	Freud dies World War II begins Spanish Civil War ends Pan Am begins regularly scheduled air service across Atlantic DDT discovered as insecticide
1940	Cage, *Bacchanale* for prepared piano Richard Rodgers (1902–1979) and Lorenz Hart (1895–1943), *Pal Joey*	Carson McCullers (1917–1967), *The Heart Is a Lonely Hunter* Jaroslav Seifert (1901–1986), *Clothed in Light*	Dunkirk evacuated France surrenders Battle of Britain begins First xerographic machine invented

Date	Music	Other Arts and Philosophy	History
1941	*born:* Joan Baez; Bob Dylan First volume of *The Schillinger System of Musical Composition* by Joseph Schillinger (1895–1943) *died:* Paderewski		Lend-Lease passed Japanese attack Pearl Harbor Penicillin used on a human patient
1942	*born:* Charles Dodge; Meredith Monk Britten, *Ceremony of Carols* composed *died:* Zemlinsky	Jean Anouilh (1910–1987), *Antigone* Agnes de Mille (1909–1993), *Rodeo* (Aaron Copland) Edward Hopper (1882–1967), *Nighthawks* Wallace Stevens (1879–1955), *Notes toward a Supreme Fiction*	Manhattan Project established to create first atomic bomb Philippines surrender to Japan Battles of Midway and El-Alamein Japanese-Americans interned
1943	*born:* Joni Mitchell Richard Rodgers and Oscar Hammerstein II (1895–1960), *Oklahoma!* *died:* Rachmaninoff	Jean Genet (1910–1986), *Notre Dame des fleurs* Hermann Hesse (1877–1962), *Das Glasperlenspiel* Jean-Paul Sartre (1905–1980), *Being and Nothingness*	Casablanca, Quebec, and Teheran conferences Warsaw ghetto uprising
1944	*born:* John Tavener; Paul Lansky Messiaen, *Technique de mon langage musical* *died:* Amy Beach; Glenn Miller	Jerome Robbins (1918–1998), *Fancy Free*	Battle of the Bulge Monte Cassino falls to Allies Rome, Paris, and Philippines liberated by Allies Normandy invasion by Allies
1945	*born:* Richard Taruskin Britten, *Peter Grimes* *died:* Bartók; Kern; Webern	Margaret Bourke-White (1904–1971) photographs the liberation of Buchenwald Jean Cocteau (1889–1963), *La belle et la bête* Evelyn Waugh (1903–1966), *Brideshead Revisited*	Concentration camps liberated Fire-bombing of Dresden Yalta and Potsdam conferences U.S. forces land on Iwo Jima First atomic bombs dropped on Hiroshima and Nagasaki World War II ends Hitler dies United Nations established
1946	*born:* Gérard Grisey; Susan McClary Irving Berlin (1888–1989), *Annie Get Your Gun* International Summer Courses for New Music (Darmstadt school) founded *died:* de Falla	Walter Gropius (1883–1969) forms Architects Collaborative Christopher Isherwood (1904–1986), *The Berlin Stories* Robert Penn Warren (1905–1989), *All the King's Men*	League of Nations disbanded First meeting of U.N. General Assembly Iron Curtain descends on Europe Juan Perón becomes dictator of Argentina Nuremburg trials First electronic computer Philippines become independent Atomic test at Bikini Atoll Benjamin Spock publishes *The Common Sense Book of Baby and Child Care*
1947	*born:* John Adams; Laurie Anderson; Tristan Murail	W. H. Auden (1907–1973), *The Age of Anxiety* Countee Cullen (1903–1946), *On These I Stand* Robert Frost (1874–1963), *Steeple Bush* Carlo Levi (1902–1975), *Cristo si è fermato a Eboli*	House Committee on Un-American Activities creates blacklist in the entertainment industry Truman Doctrine Marshall Plan

Date	Music	Other Arts and Philosophy	History
1947		Henri Matisse (1869–1954), Chapel of Saint-Marie du Rosaire at Vence (—1951) James Michener (1907–1997), *Tales of the South Pacific* Jean-Paul Sartre (1905–1980), *L'existentialisme* Tennessee Williams (1911–1983), *A Streetcar Named Desire*	Taft-Hartley Act India and Pakistan gain independence Charles Yeager breaks sound barrier
1948	The term "musique concrète" coined by Pierre Schaeffer (1910–1995) *Resolution on Music* of Soviet Communist Party: official disgrace of Khachaturian, Myaskovsky, Prokofieff, and Shostakovich Folk group The Weavers formed	Andrew Wyeth (b. 1917), *Christina's World*	Gandhi assassinated State of Israel founded Berlin blockade Organization of American States (OAS) created South Africa establishes apartheid First Polaroid camera Improved quantum dynamics theory developed by Richard Feynman
1949	Henry Partch (1901–1974), in *Genesis of a Music*, explains his theories of performance art *died*: Pfitzner; Richard Strauss	Simone de Beauvoir (1908–1986), *Le deuxième sexe* Gwendolyn Brooks (b. 1917), *Annie Allen* Willem de Kooning (1904–1997), *Attic* Aldo Leopold (1886–1948), *A Sand County Almanac* Arthur Miller (b. 1915), *Death of a Salesman* George Orwell (1903–1950), *Nineteen Eighty-Four*	U.S.S.R. becomes a nuclear power China becomes a Communist republic under Mao Zedong North Atlantic Treaty Organization (NATO) established Ireland achieves independence Federal Republic of Germany created First commercial jet plane Nuclear arms race begins Communists take over China
1950	Messiaen, *Mode de valeurs et d'intensités* *died*: Jolson; Myaskovsky; Weill	William Inge (1913–1973), *Come Back, Little Sheba* Eugène Ionesco (1904–1994), *La cantatrice chauve* Jackson Pollock (1912–1956), *Autumn Rhythm* Lionel Trilling (1905–1975), *The Liberal Imagination* Congress for Cultural Freedom established in Berlin	Korean War begins
1951	Cage, *Music of Changes* Studio set up in Cologne for electronic music *died*: Koussevitzky; Schoenberg	Camilo José Cela (b. 1916), *La colmena* James Jones (1921–1977), *From Here to Eternity* Pär Lagerkvist (1891–1974), *Barabbas* Marianne Moore (1887–1972), *Collected Poems* J. D. Salinger (b. 1919), *The Catcher in the Rye*	UNIVAC computer developed Color television introduced
1952	*born*: John Zorn	Samuel Beckett (1906–1989), *Waiting for Godot* Merce Cunningham (b. 1919), *Suite by Chance*	First hydrogen bomb exploded on Enewetak Atoll Mau Mau terrorism begins in Kenya

Date	Music	Other Arts and Philosophy	History
1952		Ralph Ellison (1914–1994), *The Invisible Man*	Polio vaccine developed by Jonas Salk (1914–1995)
1953	Boulez, *Le Marteau sans Maître* Henry Brant (b. 1913), *Antiphony One* died: Prokofieff	James Baldwin (1924–1987), *Go Tell It on the Mountain*	Korean War ends Julius and Ethel Rosenberg executed DC-7 introduced Stalin dies
1954	died: Berg; Furtwängler; Ives	Kingsley Amis (1922–1995), *Lucky Jim* Brendan Behan (1923–1964), *The Quare Fellow* Salvador Dali (1904–1989), *Crucifixion* Dylan Thomas (1914–1953), *Under Milk Wood*	U.S. Supreme Court rules segregated schools unconstitutional in *Brown v. Board of Education* South East Asia Treaty Organization (SEATO) formed Senator Joseph McCarthy censured Boeing unveils 707, first commercially successful jet aircraft First kidney transplant *Nautilus*, first atomic-powered submarine, is launched
1955	George Rochberg, *The Hexachord and Its Relation to the Twelve-Tone Row* Xenakis, *Metastasis* died: Honegger	Elizabeth Bishop (1911–1979), *North and South — A Cold Spring* Allen Ginsberg (1926–1997), *Howl* Graham Greene (1904–1991), *The Quiet American* Vladimir Nabokov (1899–1977), *Lolita* Flannery O'Connor (1925–1964), *A Good Man Is Hard to Find* Robert Rauschenberg (b. 1925), *Monogram* (—1959)	Warsaw Pact signed Boycott of segregated buses by African Americans in Montgomery, Alabama Geneva Summit First McDonald's restaurant opens Military coup ousts Juan Perón as president of Argentina
1956		Eugene O'Neill (1888–1953), *Long Day's Journey into Night* Mark Rothko (1903–1920), *Green and Tangerine on Red* Paul Taylor (b. 1930), *Three Epitaphs* Yevgeny Yevtushenko (b. 1933), *Zima Junction*	Soviet troops march into Hungary Suez War First transatlantic telephone cable
1957	Max V. Mathews (b. 1926) produces computer-generated musical sounds with a transducer died: Korngold; Sibelius; Toscanini	Albert Camus (1913–1960), *La chute* Langston Hughes (1902–1967), *I Wonder as I Wander* Jack Kerouac (1922–1969), *On the Road* Alberto Moravia (1907–1990), *La ciociàra*	U.S.S.R. launches Sputnik Common Market established Federal troops integrate schools in Little Rock, Arkansas United States and U.S.S.R. launch intercontinental ballistic missiles
1958	Babbitt, "Who Cares If You Listen?" Noah Greenberg's New York Pro Musica revives the Play of Daniel	Francisco Ayala (b. 1906), *Muertes de perro* Eugenio Montale (1896–1981), *Poésie*	Explorer I launched F-4 Phantom fighter planes unveiled 707 transatlantic jet service introduced

Date	Music	Other Arts and Philosophy	History
1958	Performance association Fluxus formed *died*: Vaughan Williams	Boris Pasternak (1890–1960), *Dr. Zhivago* Ludwig Mies van der Rohe (1886–1969) designs Seagram Building in New York Giuseppe Ungaretti (1888–1970), *Vita di un nomo*	
1959	*died*: Bloch	Heinrich Böll (1917–1985), *Billard um halb zehn* William S. Burroughs (1914–1997), *Naked Lunch* Marguerite Duras (1914–1996), *Hiroshima mon amour* Günter Grass (b. 1927), *Die Blechtrommel* Lorraine Hansberry (1930–1965), *A Raisin in the Sun* Philip Roth (b. 1933), *Goodbye, Columbus*	Cuban Revolution Vietnam War begins Uprising in Tibet St. Lawrence Seaway opens Alaska and Hawaii become states Fidel Castro seizes power in Cuba
1960		Pier Luigi Nervi (1891–1979) builds the Palazetto dello Sport in Rome Harold Pinter (b. 1930), *The Caretaker* Eero Saarinen (1910–1961) builds Dulles Airport in Washington, D.C. John Updike (b. 1932), *Rabbit, Run*	Belgian Congo becomes independent U-2 spy plane shot down over Soviet Union Polaris missile test-fired USS *Enterprise* becomes first aircraft carrier powered by nuclear reactors
1961	Ligeti, *Atmosphères* Penderecki, *Threnody for the Victims of Hiroshima* Folk group Peter, Paul, and Mary formed *died*: Grainger	Joseph Heller (b. 1923), *Catch-22* Max Rudolf Frisch (1911–1991), *Andorra*	Berlin Wall built Peace Corps founded Bay of Pigs invasion
1962		Edward Albee (b. 1928), *Who's Afraid of Virginia Woolf?* Anthony Burgess (1917–1993), *A Clockwork Orange* Doris Lessing (b. 1919), *The Golden Notebook* Roy Lichtenstein (1923–1997) exhibits comic-strip paintings in New York	Cuban missile crisis Border war between China and India Rachel Carson's *Silent Spring* launches environmental movement Prayer in schools ruled unconstitutional First African American admitted to University of Mississippi Telstar allows first international satellite television broadcast Alan Shepard becomes first American in space Pope John XXIII convenes the Second Vatican Council
1963	*died*: Hindemith; Poulenc	Betty Friedan (b. 1921), *The Feminine Mystique* John Le Carré (b. 1931), *The Spy Who Came In from the Cold*	President John F. Kennedy assassinated Organization of African Unity (OAU) founded

Date	Music	Other Arts and Philosophy	History
1963		Aleksandr Solzhenitsyn (b. 1918), *A Day in the Life of Ivan Denisovich* Christa Wolf (b. 1929), *Der geteilte Himmel*	Betty Friedan's *The Feminine Mystique* published, launching women's movement University of Alabama forcibly integrated by National Guard Civil rights march on Washington, D.C. Measles vaccine developed
1964	Terry Riley, *In C* Britten, *War Requiem* The Beatles first perform in United States *died:* Marc Blitzstein	John Berryman (1914–1972), *77 Dream Songs* Rachel Carson (1907–1964), *Silent Spring*	Civil Rights Act passed in United States Surgeon General reports on dangers of smoking
1965	Rochberg's *Contra Mortem et Tempus* experiments with collage techniques Bernd Alois Zimmerman (1918–1970), *Die Soldaten* *died:* Cowell; Varèse	Malcolm X (1925–1965), *The Autobiography of Malcolm X* Georgia O'Keeffe (1887–1986), *Sky Above Clouds IV* Neil Simon (b. 1927), *The Odd Couple* Andy Warhol (1928–1987), *Campbell's Soup Can* Richard Wollheim coins the term "minimalism" in art	Malcolm X assassinated War escalates in Vietnam War on Poverty launched Voting Rights Act passed Great blackout in Northeast Violence in Selma, Alabama, and in Watts section of Los Angeles
1966	First course in computer-music technology offered at Princeton University by Godfrey Winham (1934–1975)	Truman Capote (1924–1984), *In Cold Blood* Bernard Malamud (1914–1986), *The Fixer* Sylvia Plath (1932–1963), *Ariel* Robert Venturi (b. 1925), *Complexity and Contradiction in Architecture*	National Organization for Women (NOW) founded Black Panther Party founded
1967	*died:* Kodály	Jacques Derrida (b. 1930), *Speech and Phenomena* David Hockney (b. 1937), *A Bigger Splash*	Tet Offensive begins Six-Day War Che Guevara killed in Bolivia First heart transplant
1968		Henri Cartier-Bresson (b. 1908), *The World of Henri Cartier-Bresson* N. Scott Momaday (b. 1934), *House Made of Dawn*	Martin Luther King assassinated Robert F. Kennedy assassinated Student demonstrations at Columbia University and the Sorbonne Violence at the Democratic National Convention in Chicago Soviet troops invade Czechoslovakia
1969	Cage, *HPSCHD* Woodstock Music and Art Festival *died:* Adorno	Maya Angelou (b. 1928), *I Know Why the Caged Bird Sings* Joyce Carol Oates (b. 1938), *Them* Kurt Vonnegut, Jr. (b. 1922), *Slaughterhouse-Five*	Stonewall riot in New York Nuclear Non-Proliferation Treaty Violence erupts in Northern Ireland First 747 flight Apollo 11 moon landing
1970		Ezra Pound (1885–1972), *Cantos*	Kent State shootings War in Vietnam spreads to Cambodia Aswan Dam finished

Date	Music	Other Arts and Philosophy	History
1971	Reich, *Drumming* *died:* Stravinsky	Alvin Ailey (1931–1989), *Mass* (Leonard Bernstein) Christo (b. 1935), *Wrapped Reichstag* (–1995)	Communist China admitted to United Nations
1972	Rochberg, String Quartet no. 3 *died:* Mahalia Jackson; Wolpe	Diane Arbus (1923–1971), *Diane Arbus* Louis I. Kahn (1901–1974) builds Kimbell Art Museum in Fort Worth, Texas Eudora Welty (b. 1909), *The Optimist's Daughter*	Strategic Arms Limitation Treaty (SALT I) signed by United States and U.S.S.R. Arab terrorists murder Israeli athletes at Munich Olympic games President Nixon visits China Watergate scandal begins
1973		Anna Akhmatova (1886–1966), *Poem without a Hero*	Paris Peace Accords Yom Kippur War CAT scan developed
1974	*died:* Milhaud	Adrienne Rich (b. 1929), *Driving into the Wreck*	Nixon resigns Soyuz-Apollo mission is first cooperative space venture between United States and U.S.S.R.
1975	*died:* Dallapiccola; Shostakovich	Saul Bellow (b. 1915), *Humboldt's Gift*	Vietnam War ends Pol Pot regime takes over Cambodia Franco dies King Juan Carlos restores democracy to Spain
1976	Glass, *Einstein of the Beach* Reich, *Music for Eighteen Musicians* *died:* Britten; Piston	Alex Haley (1921–1992), *Roots* I. M. Pei (b. 1917) builds John Hancock Tower in Boston Twyla Tharp (b. 1941), *Push Comes to Shove*	U.S. bicentennial Raid on Entebbe Apple II desktop computer introduced
1977	IRCAM, electroacoustical research institute, set up under Boulez's directorship *died:* Bing Crosby; Elvis Presley; Gustave Reese		United States agrees to return the Panama Canal by 2000
1978		John Cheever (1912–1982), *The Stories of John Cheever* Iris Murdoch (1919–1999), *The Sea, the Sea* Sam Shepard (b. 1943), *Buried Child*	Smallpox eradicated Election of Pope John Paul II, first Polish pope First in vitro birth
1979	*died:* Josephine Baker; Nadia Boulanger; Harris	Norman Mailer (b. 1923), *The Executioner's Song* Stephen Spender (1909–1995), *The Thirties and After*	SALT II signed Soviets invade Afghanistan Sandinistas force Somoza out of Nicaragua United States and China establish full diplomatic relations Nuclear accident at Three Mile Island Iranian Revolution and seizure of U.S. embassy by militant Iranian students

Date	Music	Other Arts and Philosophy	History
1980		Bob Fosse (1927–1987), *All That Jazz* Umberto Eco (b. 1932), *The Name of the Rose*	Solidarity trade union formed in Poland Iran-Iraq War begins
1981	*died:* Hanson		Anwar Sadat assassinated Sandra Day O'Connor becomes first woman appointed to U.S. Supreme Court
1982	*died:* Orff; Arthur Rubinstein	Primo Levi (1919–1987), *Se non ora, quando?* Alice Walker (b. 1944), *The Color Purple*	Falkland Islands War
1983	Fred Lerdahl and Ray Jackendorff, *A Generative Theory of Tonal Music*	Václav Havel (b. 1936), *Letters to Olga* David Mamet (b. 1947), *Glengarry Glen Ross* August Wilson (b. 1945), *Fences*	Korean Air flight 747 shot down by Soviets U.S. marines killed in Lebanon United States invades Grenada
1984		Milan Kundera (b. 1929), *The Unbearable Lightness of Being*	AIDS virus identified
1985	*died:* Lowinsky; Sessions		Palestinian terrorists seize cruise ship *Achille Lauro* Mikhail Gorbachev initiates reforms in U.S.S.R.
1986	Zorn, *Spillane* *died:* Benny Goodman		Nuclear accident at Chernobyl Space shuttle *Challenger* explodes Iran-Contra scandal
1987	John Adams, *Nixon in China* Stephen Sondheim (b. 1930), *Into the Woods* *died:* Feldman; Persichetti	Toni Morrison (b. 1931), *Beloved*	INF treaty signed, beginning the end of the Cold War Intifada begins in Palestine
1988	Reich, *Trains* *died:* Grisey	Wendy Wasserstein (b. 1950), *The Heidi Chronicles*	Soviets pull out of Afghanistan First free elections held in Soviet Union
1989	*died:* Irving Berlin; Dahlhaus; Thomson	Court-ordered destruction of *Tilted Arc*, sculpture by Richard Serra (b. 1939) Amy Tan (b. 1952), *The Joy Luck Club*	Berlin Wall falls Solidarity wins elections in Poland Communism defeated in East Germany, Poland, Romania, and Czechoslovakia First liver transplant U.S. troops invade Panama Exxon *Valdez* oil spill Pro-democracy rallies in Beijing
1990	*died:* Bernstein; Copland; Lang; Nono		East and West Germany reunited Boris Yeltsin elected president of Russian Federation Nelson Mandela freed from prison Gulf War begins Free elections held in Nicaragua

Date	Music	Other Arts and Philosophy	History
1991	*died*: Miles Davis; Křenek	Tony Kushner (b. 1956), *Angels in America* (−1993)	U.S.S.R. formally comes to an end Failed Kremlin coup Cold War ends Hubble telescope launched
1992	*died*: Cage; Messiaen; William Schuman		Civil war begins in former Yugoslavia
1993			Terrorists attack World Trade Center Israel and PLO reach accord American soldiers killed in Somalia
1994			Nelson Mandela elected president of South Africa
1995		Joseph Brodsky (1940–1996), *On Grief and Reason*	Murrah Federal Building destroyed by truck bomb in Oklahoma City
1996	*died*: Ella Fitzgerald; Luening	Amiri Bakara (b. 1934), *Eulogies*	Taliban takes control of Afghanistan
1997	*died*: Frank Sinatra		Britain turns Hong Kong over to China Mars Pathfinder lands
1998			Northern Ireland peace accord Simultaneous bombings of U.S. embassies in Kenya and Tanzania
1999			Serbs initiate ethnic cleansing in Kosovo President Bill Clinton impeached
2000			Millennium celebrated
2001	*died*: Xenakis		September 11 terrorist attacks United States invades Afghanistan
2003	*died*: Berio		United States–led coalition invades Iraq and ousts Saddam Hussein

Further Reading: A Checklist of Books in English

This listing of recommended further reading in English is a supplement to the literature cited in the Notes sections in Volumes 1 through 5. It is largely confined to books, rather than journal articles where the cutting edge of research is often found (and which are favored in the citations).

General Companions

Lang, Paul Henry. *Music in Western Civilization*. New York: Norton, 1941.

Lippman, Edward A. *Musical Aesthetics: A Historical Reader*. Three vols. Stuyvesant, N.Y.: Pendragon Press, 1986–90.

New Grove Dictionary of Music and Musicians. Rev. ed., New York: Grove, 2000.

New Grove Dictionary of Opera. New York: Oxford University Press, 1992.

Treitler, Leo, ed. *Strunk's Source Readings in Music History*. Rev. ed., New York: Norton, 1998.

Weiss, Piero, and Richard Taruskin. *Music in the Western World: A History in Documents*. New York: Schirmer, 1984.

Volume 1: The Earliest Notations to the Sixteenth Century

General Sources

Atlas, Allan. *Renaissance Music: Music in Western Europe, 1400–1600*. New York: Norton, 1998.

Brown, Howard Mayer, and Stanley Sadie. *Performance Practice: Music before 1600*. New York: Norton, 1989.

Cattin, Giulio. *Music of the Middle Ages*. Vol. I, trans. Steven Botterill. Cambridge: Cambridge University Press, 1984.

Fenlon, Iain, ed. *Man and Music: The Renaissance*. Englewood Cliffs, N.J.: Prentice Hall, 1989.

_____. *Music in Medieval and Early Modern Europe: Patronage, Sources, and Text*. Cambridge: Cambridge University Press, 1981.

Gallo, F. Alberto. *Music of the Middle Ages*. Vol. II. Cambridge: Cambridge University Press, 1985.

Hoppin, Richard H. *Medieval Music*. New York: Norton, 1978.

Knighton, Tess, and David Fallows. *Companion to Medieval and Renaissance Music*. New York: Schirmer, 1992.

McKinnon, James, ed. *Music and Society: Antiquity and the Middle Ages*. Englewood Cliffs, N.J.: Prentice Hall, 1991.

Perkins, Leeman L. *Music in the Age of the Renaissance*. New York: Norton, 1999.

Reese, Gustave. *Music in the Middle Ages*. 1940. Rev. ed., New York: Norton, 1964.

_____. *Music in the Renaissance*. 1954. Rev. ed., New York: Norton, 1958.

Sternfeld, Frederick W., ed. *Music from the Middle Ages to the Renaissance*. New York: Praeger, 1973.

Strohm, Reinhard. *The Rise of European Music, 1380–1500*. Cambridge: Cambridge University Press, 1993.

Wilson, David Fenwick. *Music of the Middle Ages: Style and Structure*. New York: Schirmer, 1990.

Yudkin, Jeremy. *Music in Medieval Europe*. Englewood Cliffs, N.J.: Prentice Hall, 1989.

Chapter 1   The Curtain Goes Up

Apel, Willi. *Gregorian Chant*. Bloomington: Indiana University Press, 1958.

Crocker, Richard L. *An Introduction to Gregorian Chant*. New Haven: Yale University Press, 2000.

Hiley, David. *Western Plainchant: A Handbook*. Oxford: Clarendon Paperbacks, 1995.

Jeffery, Peter. *Re-Envisioning Past Musical Cultures: Ethnomusicology in the Study of Gregorian Chant*. Chicago: University of Chicago Press, 1995.

Jones, Cheslyn, Geoffrey Wainwright, and Edward Yarnold, eds. *The Study of Liturgy*. New York: Oxford University Press, 1978.

Jungmann, Josef. *The Mass of the Roman Rite*, trans. Francis A. Brunner. 2 vols. New York: Benziger, 1951–55.

Karp, Theodore C. *Aspects of Orality and Formularity in Gregorian Chant*. Evanston, Ill.: Northwestern University Press, 1998.

McKinnon, James C. *The Advent Project: The Later Seventh-Century Creation of the Roman Mass Proper*. Berkeley and Los Angeles: University of California Press, 2000.

Ong, Walter J. *Orality and Literacy (New Accents)*. New York: Routledge, 2002.

Rayburn, John. *Gregorian Chant: A History of the Controversy Concerning Its Rhythm*. 1964. Reprint, Westport, Conn.: Greenwood Press, 1981.

Treitler, Leo. *With Voice and Pen: Coming to Know Medieval Song and How It Was Made*. New York: Oxford University Press, 2003.

Vogel, Cyrille. *Medieval Liturgy: An Introduction to the Sources*. Rev. and ed. by W. G. Storey and N. K. Rasmussen. Washington, D.C.: Pastoral Press, 1986.

Wagner, Peter. *Introduction to the Gregorian Melodies*, trans. Agnes Orme and E. G. P. Wyatt. 2nd ed., New York: Da Capo Press, 1986.

Werf, Hendrik van der. *The Emergence of Gregorian Chant*. Rochester, N.Y.: privately printed by the author, 1983.

Chapter 2   New Styles and Forms

Crocker, Richard L. *Studies in Medieval Music Theory and the Early Sequence*. Aldershot: Variorum, 1997.

Evans, Paul. *The Early Trope Repertory of Saint Martial de Limoges*. Princeton, N.J.: Princeton University Press, 1970.

Planchart, Alejandro Enrique. *The Repertory of Tropes at Winchester*. Princeton, N.J.: Princeton University Press, 1977.

Chapter 3   Retheorizing Music

Babb, Warren, trans., and Claude V. Palisca, ed. *Hucbald, Guido and John on Music*. New Haven: Yale University Press, 1978.

Campbell, Thomas P., and Clifford Davidson, eds. *The Fleury Playbook*. Kalamazoo: Western Michigan University Press, 1985.

Carpenter, Nan Cooke. *Music in the Medieval and Renaissance Universities*. Norman: University of Oklahoma Press, 1958; Reprint, New York: Da Capo, 1972.

Christensen, Thomas, ed. *The Cambridge History of Western Music Theory*. Cambridge: Cambridge University Press, 2002.

Hardison, O. B., Jr. *Christian Rite and Christian Drama in the Middle Ages*. 1965. Reprint, Westport, Conn.: Greenwood Press, 1983.

Pesce, Dolores. *The Affinities and Medieval Transposition*. Bloomington: Indiana University Press, 1987.

Rankin, Susan. *The Music of the Medieval Liturgical Drama in France and in England*. New York: Garland Publishing, 1989.

Smoldon, William L. *The Music of the Medieval Church Dramas*. London: Oxford University Press, 1980.

Chapter 4   Music of Feudalism and *Fin' Amors*

Bergin, Thomas G., ed. *Anthology of the Provcençal Troubadours*. 2nd ed., New Haven: Yale University Press, 1974.

Chickering, Howell, and Margaret Switten, eds. *The Medieval Lyric: Commentary Volume*. South Hadley, Mass.: Mount Holyoke College Press, 1988.

Crane, Frederick. *Extant Medieval Musical Instruments*. Iowa City: University of Iowa Press, 1972.

Dronke, Peter. *The Medieval Lyric*. London: Hutchinson & Co., 1968.

Page, Christopher. *Voices and Instruments of the Middle Ages: Instrumental Practice and Songs in France, 1100–1300*. Berkeley and Los Angeles: University of California Press, 1986.

Stevens, John. *Words and Music in the Middle Ages: Song, Narrative, Dance and Drama, 1050–1350*. Cambridge: Cambridge University Press, 1986.

Werf, Hendrik van der. *The Chansons of the Troubadours and Trouvères: A Study of the Melodies and Their Relation to the Poems*. Utrecht: A. Oosthoek, 1972.

Chapter 5   Polyphony in Practice and Theory

Bonderup, Jens. *The Saint Martial Polyphony: Texture and Tonality*. Copenhagen: Dan Fog, 1982.

Karp, Theodore C. *The Polyphony of Saint Martial and Santiago de Compostela*. Berkeley and Los Angeles: University of California Press, 1992.

Chapter 6 Notre Dame de Paris

Falck, Robert. *The Notre Dame Conductus: A Study of the Repertory.* Henryville, Pa.: Institute of Medieval Music, 1981.

Johannes de Garlandia, Concerning Measured Music, trans. Stanley H. Birnbaum. Colorado Springs: Colorado College Music Press, 1979.

Wright, Craig. *Music and Ceremony at Notre Dame of Paris, 500–1500.* Cambridge: Cambridge University Press, 1990.

Yudkin, Jeremy. *The Music Treatise of Anonymous I: A New Translation.* Rome: American Institute of Musicology, 1985.

Chapter 7 Music for an Intellectual and Political Elite

Boorman, Stanley, ed. *Studies in the Performance of Late Mediaeval Music.* Cambridge: Cambridge University Press, 1984.

Chapter 8 Business Math, Politics, and Paradise: The Ars Nova

Berger, Karol. *Musica Ficta: Theories of Accidental Inflections in Vocal Polyphony from Marchetto of Padova to Gioseffo Zarlino.* Cambridge: Cambridge University Press, 1987.

Ellsworth, Oliver B. *The Berkeley Manuscript: A New Critical Text and Translation.* Lincoln: University of Nebraska Press, 1984.

Chapter 9 Machaut and His Progeny

Apel, Willi. *French Secular Music of the Late Fourteenth Century.* Cambridge, Mass.: Mediaeval Academy of America, 1950.

Leech-Wilkinson, Daniel. *Machaut's Mass: An Introduction.* Oxford: Oxford University Press, 1990.

Reaney, Gilbert. *Guillaume de Machaut.* London: Oxford University Press, 1971.

Tomasello, Andrew. *Music and Ritual at Papal Avignon, 1309–1403.* Ann Arbor, Mich.: UMI Research Press, 1983.

Wilkins, Nigel. *Music in the Age of Chaucer.* Cambridge: Brewer, 1979.

Chapter 10 "A Pleasant Place": Music of the Trecento

Pirrotta, Nino. *Music and Culture in Italy from the Middle Ages to the Baroque.* Cambridge: Harvard University Press, 1984.

Chapter 11 Island and Mainland

Bent, Margaret. *Dunstaple.* London: Oxford University Press, 1981.

Fallows, David. *Dufay.* London: J. M. Dent, 1982.

Kaye, Philip. *The Sacred Music of Gilles Binchois.* London: Oxford University Press, 1992.

Kemp, Walter H. *Burgundian Court Song in the Time of Binchois: The Anonymous Chansons of El Escorial, MS V.III.24.* Oxford: Clarendon Press, 1990.

Kenney, Sylvia. *Walter Frye and the Contenance Angloise*. New Haven: Yale University Press, 1964.

Kirkman, Andrew, and Dennis Slavin. *Binchois Studies*. New York: Oxford University Press, 2001.

Lefferts, Peter. *The Motet in England in the Fourteenth Century*. Ann Arbor, Mich.: UMI Research Press, 1986.

Rankin, Susan, and David Hiley. *Music in the Medieval English Liturgy: Plainsong & Medieval Music Society Centennial Essays*. Oxford: Clarendon Press, 1993.

Chapter 12 Emblems and Dynasties

Aaron, Pietro. *Toscanello in musica*, trans. Peter Bergquist. Colorado Springs: Colorado College Music Press, 1970.

Atlas, Allan. *Music at the Aragonese Court of Naples*. Cambridge: Cambridge University Press, 1985.

Cohen, Judith. *The Six Anonymous L'homme armé Masses in Naples, Biblioteca Nazionale, MS VI E 40*. Stuttgart: American Institute of Musicology, 1981.

D'Accone, Frank A. *The Civic Muse: Music and Musicians in Siena during the Middle Ages and the Renaissance*. Chicago: University of Chicago Press, 1997.

Hamm, Charles. *A Chronology of the Works of Guillaume Dufay Based on a Study of Mensural Practice*. Princeton: Princeton University Press, 1964.

Higgins, Paula, ed. *Antoine Busnoys: Methods, Meaning, and Context in Late Medieval Music*. Oxford: Clarendon Press, 1997.

Lockwood, Lewis. *Music in Renaissance Ferrara, 1400–1505*. Cambridge: Harvard University Press, 1985.

Reynolds, Christopher. *Papal Patronage and the Music of St. Peter's, 1380–1513*. Berkeley and Los Angeles: University of California Press, 1995.

Sparks, Edgar H. *Cantus Firmus in Mass and Motet, 1420–1520*. Berkeley and Los Angeles: University of California Press, 1963.

Strohm, Reinhard. *Music in Late Medieval Bruges*. Rev. ed., Oxford: Clarendon Press, 1990.

Tinctoris, Johannes. *The Art of Counterpoint*, trans. and ed. Albert Seay. Rome: American Institute of Musicology, 1961.

Wegman, Rob. *Born for the Muses: The Life and Masses of Jacob Obrecht*. Oxford: Clarendon Press, 1994.

Wright, Craig. *The Maze and the Warrior: Symbols in Architecture, Theology, and Music*. Cambridge: Harvard University Press, 2004.

_____. *Music at the Court of Burgundy, 1364–1419*. Henryville, Pa.: Institute of Medieval Music, 1979.

Chapter 13 Middle and Low

Brown, Howard Mayer. *A Florentine Chansonnier from the Time of Lorenzo the Magnificent: Florence, Biblioteca Nazionale Centrale, MS Banco Rari 229*. Chicago: University of Chicago Press, 1983.

Cumming, Julie E. *The Motet in the Age of Du Fay*. Cambridge: Cambridge University Press, 1999.

Finscher, Ludwig. *Loyset Compère (c. 1450–1518): Life and Works*. Rome: American Institute of Musicology, 1964.

Harrán, Don. *Word-Tone Relations in Musical Thought from Antiquity to the Seventeenth Century*. Stuttgart: American Institute of Musicology, 1986.

Krummel, Donald W., and Stanley Sadie, eds. *Music Printing and Publishing*. New York: Norton, 1990.

Pesce, Dolores, ed. *Hearing the Motet: Essays on the Motet of the Middle Ages and Renaissance*. London: Oxford University Press, 1996.

Polk, Keith. *German Instrumental Music of the Late Middle Ages: Players, Patrons, and Performance Practice*. Cambridge: Cambridge University Press, 1992.

Woodfield, Ian. *The Early History of the Viol*. Cambridge: Cambridge University Press, 1984.

Chapter 14 Josquin and the Humanists

Elders, Willem, and Frits De Haen, eds. *Proceedings of the International Josquin Symposium, Utrecht 1986*. Amsterdam: Vereiniging voor Nederlandse Muziekgeschiedenis, 1991.

Glareanus. *Dodecachordon*, trans. Clement Miller. Rome: American Institute of Musicology, 1965.

Lowinsky, Edward, and Bonnie J. Blackburn, eds. *Josquin des Prez: Proceedings of the International Festival-Conference Held at The Juilliard School at Lincoln Center in New York City, 22–25 June 1971*. London: Oxford University Press, 1976.

Sherr, Richard, ed. *The Josquin Companion*. New York: Oxford University Press, 2001.

Chapter 15 A Perfected Art

Benham, Hugh. *Latin Church Music in England, c. 1460–1575*. London: Barrie & Barrie, 1975.

Blackburn, Bonnie J., Clement Miller, and Edward Lowinsky. *A Correspondence of Renaissance Musicians*. Oxford: Oxford University Press, 1991.

Brown, Howard Mayer. *Embellishing Sixteenth-Century Music*. London: Oxford University Press, 1976.

Carver, Anthony F. *"Cori spezzati": The Development of Sacred Polychoral Music to the Time of Schütz*. Cambridge: Cambridge University Press, 1988.

Crane, Frederick. *Materials for the Study of the Fifteenth-Century Basse Danse*. Brooklyn: Institute of Mediaeval Music, 1968.

Josephson, David S. *John Taverner: Tudor Composer*. Ann Arbor, Mich.: UMI Research Press, 1979.

Lowinsky, Edward. *Secret Chromatic Art of the Netherlands Motet*. New York: Columbia University Press, 1946.

Meier, Bernhard. *The Modes of Classical Vocal Polyphony*, trans. Ellen S. Beebe. New York: Broude Bros., 1988.

Owens, Jessie Ann. *Composers at Work: The Craft of Musical Composition, 1450–1600.* Oxford: Clarendon Press, 1996.

Slim, H. Colin. *Musica Nova.* Chicago: University of Chicago Press, 1964.

Stevens, Denis. *Tudor Church Music.* New York: Merlin Press, 1955; Reprint, New York: Norton, 1966.

Warren, Edward B. *Life and Works of Robert Fayrfax, 1464–1521.* Rome: American Institute of Musicology, 1969.

Wulstan, David. *Tudor Music.* Iowa City: University of Iowa Press, 1986.

Zarlino, Gioseffo. *The Art of Counterpoint,* trans. Guy A. Marco and Claude V. Palisca. New Haven: Yale University Press, 1968.

Chapter 16   The End of Perfection

Andrews, H. K. *Technique of Byrd's Vocal Polyphony.* London: Oxford University Press, 1964.

Brown, Alan, and Richard Turbet. *Byrd Studies.* Cambridge: Cambridge University Press, 1992.

Doe, Paul. *Tallis.* London: Oxford University Press, 1968.

Fellowes, Edmund H. *William Byrd.* London: Oxford University Press, 1948.

Holst, Imogen. *Byrd.* London: Faber and Faber, 1972.

Jeppesen, Knud. *Counterpoint: The Polyphonic Vocal Style of the Sixteenth Century,* trans. Glen Haydon. New York: Prentice-Hall, 1939; Reprint, New York: Dover, 1992.

——— . *The Style of Palestrina and the Dissonance.* Oxford: Oxford University Press, 1927.

Kerman, Joseph. *The Masses and Motets of William Byrd.* Berkeley and Los Angeles: University of California Press, 1981.

Le Huray, Peter. *Music and the Reformation in England: 1549–1660.* New York: Oxford University Press, 1967.

Lockwood, Lewis. *The Counter Reformation and the Masses of Vincenzo Ruffo.* Vienna: Universal Edition, 1970.

——— . *Palestrina: Pope Marcellus Mass.* New York: Norton, 1975.

Phillips, Peter. *English Sacred Music: 1549–1649.* Oxford: Gimell, 1991.

Roche, Jerome. *Palestrina.* Oxford: Oxford University Press, 1971.

Stevenson, Robert. *Spanish Cathedral Music in the Golden Age.* Berkeley and Los Angeles: University of California Press, 1961.

Temperley, Nicholas. *The Music of the English Parish Church.* Cambridge: Cambridge University Press, 1979.

Woodfill, Walter. *Musicians in English Society from Elizabeth to Charles I.* Rev. ed., Princeton: Princeton University Press, 1969.

Chapter 17   Commercial and Literary Music

Arnold, Denis. *Marenzio.* London: Oxford University Press, 1965.

——— . *Monteverdi Madrigals.* London: British Broadcasting Corporation, 1967.

Bernstein, Jane A. *Music Printing in Renaissance Venice: The Scotto Press (1539–1572)*. New York: Oxford University Press, 1998.

Brown, David. *Thomas Weelkes: A Biographical and Critical Study*. New York: Praeger, 1969.

_____. *Wilbye*. London: Oxford University Press, 1974.

Brown, Howard Mayer. *Music in the French Secular Theater, 1400–1550*. Cambridge: Harvard University Press, 1963.

Cardamone, Donna G. *The Canzone villanesca alla napolitana and Related Forms, 1537–1570*. Ann Arbor, Mich.: UMI Research Press, 1981.

Carter, Tim. *Music in Late Renaissance and Early Baroque Italy*. Portland, Oreg.: Amadeus Press, 1992.

Cazeaux, Isabelle. *French Music in the Fifteenth and Sixteenth Centuries*. New York: Praeger, 1975.

Cusick, Suzanne. *Valerio Dorico: Music Printer in Sixteenth-Century Italy*. Ann Arbor, Mich.: UMI Research Press, 1981.

Cuyler, Louise. *The Emperor Maximilian I and Music*. London: Oxford University Press, 1973.

Einstein, Alfred. *The Italian Madrigal*. Three vols., trans. Alexander H. Kruppe, Roger H. Sessions, and Oliver Strunk. Princeton: Princeton University Press, 1949; Reprint, 1971.

Feldman, Martha. *City Culture and the Madrigal at Venice*. Berkeley and Los Angeles: University of California Press, 1995.

Fenlon, Iain. *Music and Patronage in Sixteenth-Century Mantua*. Two vols. Cambridge: Cambridge University Press, 1980–82.

Haar, James. *Essays on Italian Poetry and Music in the Renaissance, 1350–1600*. Berkeley and Los Angeles: University of California Press, 1986.

Haar, James, ed. *Chanson and Madrigal, 1480–1530*. Cambridge: Harvard University Press, 1964.

Heartz, Daniel. *Pierre Attaingnant, Royal Printer of Music*. Berkeley and Los Angeles: University of California Press, 1969.

Kerman, Joseph. *The Elizabethan Madrigal: A Comparative Study*. New York: American Musicological Society, 1962.

Lesure, François. *Musicians and Poets of the French Renaissance*, trans. Elia Gianturco and Hans Rosenwald. New York: Merlin Press, 1955.

Lewis, Mary S. *Antonio Gardano, Venetian Music Printer, 1538–1569: A Descriptive Bibliography and Historical Study*. New York: Garland Publishing, 1988.

Lowinsky, Edward. *Tonality and Atonality in Sixteenth-Century Music*. Berkeley and Los Angeles: University of California Press, 1962.

MacClintock, Carol. *Giaches de Wert (1535–1596): Life and Works*. Rome: American Institute of Musicology, 1966.

Maniates, Maria Rika. *Mannerism in Italian Music and Culture, 1530–1630*. Durham: Duke University Press, 1979.

Morley, Thomas. *A Plain and Easy Introduction to Practical Music*, ed. R. Alec Harman. New York: Norton, 1973.

Neighbour, Oliver. *The Consort and Keyboard Music of William Byrd*. Berkeley and Los Angeles: University of California Press, 1979.

Newcomb, Anthony. *The Madrigal at Ferrara, 1579–1597*. Princeton: Princeton University Press, 1980.

Pogue, Samuel. *Jacques Moderne*. Lyons: Droz, 1969.

Poulton, Diana. *John Dowland: His Life and Works*. Berkeley and Los Angeles: University of California Press, 1972.

Prizer, William F. *Courtly Pastimes: The Frottole of Marchetto Cara*. Ann Arbor, Mich.: UMI Research Press, 1980.

Roche, Jerome. *Lassus*. London: Oxford University Press, 1982.

———. *The Madrigal*. 2nd ed., New York: Scribner's, 1990.

Rubsamen, Walter. *Literary Sources of Secular Music in Italy (c. 1500)*. Berkeley and Los Angeles: University of California Press, 1943.

Spinks, Ian. *English Song: Dowland to Purcell*. Rev. ed., London: Batsford, 1986.

Stevenson, Robert. *Spanish Music in the Age of Columbus*. The Hague: Martinus Nijhoff, 1960.

Watkins, Glenn. *Gesualdo: The Man and His Music*. Chapel Hill: University of North Carolina Press, 1973.

Chapter 18   Reformations and Counter-Reformations

Arnold, Denis. *Giovanni Gabrieli*. Oxford: Oxford University Press, 1974.

———. *Giovanni Gabrieli and the Music of the Venetian High Renaissance*. Oxford: Oxford University Press, 1979.

Blume, Friedrich, *Protestant Church Music: A History*. New York: Norton, 1974.

Daniel-Rops, Henri. *The Catholic Reformation*, trans. John Warrington. London: J. M. Dent, 1962.

Garside, Charles, Jr. *Zwingli and the Arts*. New Haven: Yale University Press, 1966.

Nettl, Paul. *Luther and Music*. Philadelphia: Muhlenberg Press, 1948.

Schalk, Carl. *Luther on Music: Paradigms of Praise*. St. Louis, Mo.: Concordia, 1988.

Scribner, Bob, Roy Parker, and Mikuláš Teich, *The Reformation in National Context*. Cambrdige: Cambridge University Press, 1994.

Stevenson, Robert. *Patterns of Protestant Church Music*. Durham: Duke University Press, 1953.

Chapter 19   Pressure of Radical Humanism

Berger, Karol. *Theories of Chromatic and Enharmonic Music in Late Sixteenth-Century Italy*. Ann Arbor, Mich.: UMI Research Press, 1980.

Hanning, Barbara Russano. *Of Poetry and Musics Power: Humanism and the Creation of Opera*. Ann Arbor, Mich.: UMI Research Press, 1980.

Joyce, John J. *The Monodies of Sigismondo d'India*. Ann Arbor, Mich.: UMI Research Press, 1981.

Nagler, Alois Maria. *Theatre Festivals of the Medici, 1539–1637*. New Haven: Yale University Press, 1964.

Palisca, Claude V. *Humanism in Italian Renaissance Musical Thought*. New Haven: Yale University Press, 1985.

Strong, R. *Art and Power: Renaissance Festivals, 1450–1650*. Rev. ed., Woodbridge, Suffolk: Boydell Press, 1999.

Vicentino, Nicola. *Ancient Music Adapted to Modern Practice*, trans. Maria Rika Maniates. New Haven: Yale University Press, 1996.

Volume 2: The Seventeenth and Eighteenth Centuries

General Sources

Bianconi, Lorenzo. *Music in the Seventeenth Century*, trans. D. Bryant. Cambridge: Cambridge University Press, 1987.

Boyden, David. *The History of Violin Playing from Its Origins to 1761 and Its Relationship to the Violin and Violin Music*. London: Oxford University Press, 1965.

Brown, Howard Mayer, and Stanley Sadie. *Performance Practice: Music after 1600*. New York: Norton, 1989.

Carse, Adam. *The Orchestra in the Eighteenth Century*. New York: Broude Bros., 1969.

Cowart, Georgia. *The Origins of Modern Music Criticism: French and Italian Music, 1600–1750*. Ann Arbor, Mich.: UMI Research Press, 1981.

Downs, Philip G. *Classical Music: The Era of Haydn, Mozart, and Beethoven*. New York: Norton, 1992.

Fubini, Enrico. *Music and Culture in Eighteenth-Century Europe: A Source Book*. Chicago: University of Chicago Press, 1994.

Heartz, Daniel. *Haydn, Mozart and the Viennese School, 1740–1780*. New York: Norton, 1995.

_____ . *Music in European Capitals: The Galant Style, 1720–1780*. New York: Norton, 2003.

Hutchings, Arthur J. B. *The Baroque Concerto*. 3rd ed., London: Faber and Faber, 1973.

Le Huray, Peter, and James Day, eds. *Music and Aesthetics in the Eighteenth and Early-Nineteenth Centuries*. Cambridge: Cambridge University Press, 1981.

Montagu, Jeremy. *The World of Baroque and Classical Musical Instruments*. London: Overlook Press, 1979.

Newman, William S. *The Sonata in the Baroque Era*. 4th ed., New York: Norton, 1983.

_____ . *The Sonata in the Classic Era*. 3rd ed., New York: Norton, 1983.

Palisca, Claude V. *Baroque Music*. 2nd ed., Englewood Cliffs, N.J.: Prentice Hall, 1979.

Pauly, Reinhard. *Music in the Classic Period*. 3rd ed., Englewood Cliffs, N.J.: Prentice Hall, 1988.

Pestelli, Giorgio. *The Age of Mozart and Beethoven*, trans. Eric Cross. Cambridge: Cambridge University Press, 1984.

Price, Curtis, ed. *Music and Society: The Early Baroque Era*. Englewood Cliffs, N.J.: Prentice Hall, 1994.

Quantz, Joseph Joachim. *On Playing the Flute* (1752), trans. and ed. E. Reilly. 2nd ed., Boston: Northeastern University Press, 2001.

Ratner, Leonard G. *Classic Music: Expression, Form, and Style.* New York: Schirmer, 1980.

Rosen, Charles. *The Classical Style: Haydn, Mozart, Beethoven.* New York: Norton, 1972.

Sadie, Julie Anne, ed. *Companion to Baroque Music.* New York: Schirmer, 1991.

Selfridge-Field, Eleanor. *Venetian Instrumental Music from Gabrieli to Vivaldi.* Oxford: Oxford University Press, 1975.

Smither, Howard E. *A History of the Oratorio, Vol. I.* Chapel Hill: University of North Carolina Press, 1977.

Smithers, Don L. *The Music and History of the Baroque Trumpet before 1721.* London: J. M. Dent, 1973.

Zaslaw, Neal. *Man and Music: The Classical Era.* Englewood Cliffs, N.J.: Prentice Hall, 1989.

Chapter 20   Opera from Monteverdi to Monteverdi

Arnold, Denis. *Monteverdi.* 3rd ed., Revised by Tim Carter. London: J. M. Dent, 1990.

_____ . *Monteverdi Church Music.* London: British Broadcasting Corporation, 1982.

Arnold, Denis, and Nigel Fortune, *The New Monteverdi Companion.* Oxford: Clarendon Press, 1985.

Carter, Tim. *Monteverdi's Musical Theatre.* New Haven: Yale University Press, 2002.

Leopold, Silke. *Monteverdi: Music in Transition,* trans. Anne Smith. Oxford: Oxford University Press, 1991.

Pirrotta, Nino, and Elena Povoledo. *Music and Theatre from Poliziano to Monteverdi.* trans. K. Eales. Cambridge: Cambridge University Press, 1982.

Roche, Jerome. *North Italian Church Music in the Age of Monteverdi.* Oxford: Oxford University Press, 1984.

Rosand, Ellen. *Opera in Seventeenth-Century Venice.* Berkeley and Los Angeles: University of California Press, 1991.

Stevens, Denis, trans. and ed. *The Letters of Claudio Monteverdi.* New York: Columbia University Press, 1980.

Tomlinson, Gary. *Monteverdi and the End of the Renaissance.* Berkeley and Los Angeles: University of California Press, 1987.

Whenham, John, ed. *Claudio Monteverdi: "Orfeo."* Cambridge: Cambridge University Press, 1986.

Chapter 21   Fat Times and Lean

Apel, Willi. *The History of Keyboard Music to 1700.* Rev. ed., Bloomington: Indiana University Press, 1972.

Bowers, Jane, and Judith Tick, eds. *Women Making Music: The Western Art Tradition, 1150–1950.* Urbana: University of Illinois Press, 1986.

Bradshaw, Murray C. *The Origin of the Toccata.* Rome: American Institute of Musicology, 1972.

Culley, Thomas. D., S. J. *Jesuits and Music, Vol. I: A Study of the Musicians Connected with the German College in Rome during the Seventeenth Century and of Their Activities in Northern Europe.* Rome: Jesuit Historical Institute/St. Louis University, 1970.

Curtis, Alan. *Sweelinck's Keyboard Music: A Study of English Elements in Seventeenth-Century Dutch Composition.* 2nd ed., London: Kluwer Academic Publishers, 1972.

Dixon, Graham. *Carissimi.* Oxford: Oxford University Press, 1986.

Glover, Jane. *Cavalli.* London: Batsford, 1978.

Moore, James H. *Vespers at St. Mark's: Music of Alessandro Grandi, Giovanni Rovetta and Francesco Cavalli.* Ann Arbor, Mich.: UMI Research Press, 1981.

Moser, Hans Joachim. *Heinrich Schütz: His Life and Work,* trans. C. F. Pfatteicher. St. Louis, Mo.: Concordia, 1959.

Pendle, Karin: *Women and Music: A History.* Bloomington: Indiana University Press, 1991.

Silbiger, Alexander, ed. *Frescobaldi Studies.* Durham: Duke University Press, 1987.

——. *Keyboard Music before 1700.* New York: Schirmer, 1995.

Smallman, Basil. *Schütz.* Oxford: Oxford University Press, 2000.

Spagnoli, Gina. *Letters and Documents of Heinrich Schütz: An Annotated Translation.* 2nd ed., Rochester, N.Y.: University of Rochester Press, 1992.

Chapter 22 Courts Resplendent, Overthrown, Restored

Adams, Martin. *Henry Purcell: The Origins and Development of His Musical Style.* Cambridge: Cambridge University Press, 1995.

Anthony, James R. *French Baroque Music from Beaujoyeulx to Rameau.* Rev. ed., New York: Norton, 1978.

Auld, Louis E. *The Lyric Art of Pierre Perrin, Founder of French Opera.* Henryville, PA: Institute of Mediaeval Music, 1986.

Burden, Michael, ed. *Performing the Music of Henry Purcell.* Oxford: Clarendon Press, 1996.

Dill, Charles W. *Monstrous Opera: Rameau and the Tragic Tradition.* Princeton: Princeton University Press, 1998.

Girdlestone, Cuthbert. *Jean-Philippe Rameau, His Life and Work.* Rev. ed., New York: Dover, 1969.

Gustafson, Bruce. *French Harpsichord Music in the XVIIth Century.* Ann Arbor, Mich.: UMI Research Press, 1978.

Hajdu Heyer, John, ed. *Jean-Baptiste Lully and the Music of the French Baroque.* Cambridge: Cambridge University Press, 1989.

Harris, Ellen. *Henry Purcell's "Dido and Aeneas."* Oxford: Oxford University Press, 1987.

Hitchcock, H. Wiley. *Marc-Antoine Charpentier.* Oxford: Oxford University Press, 1990.

Holman, Peter: *Four and Twenty Fiddlers: The Violin at the English Court, 1540–1690.* Oxford: Oxford University Press, 1993.

Isherwood, Robert M. *Music in the Service of the King: France in the Seventeenth Century.* Ithaca: Cornell University Press, 1973.

Lefkowitz, Murray. *William Lawes.* London: Kegan Paul, 1960.

Meyer, Ernst H. *English Chamber Music: The History of a Great Art.* 1946. Reprint, New York: Da Capo Press, 1971.

Newman, Joyce E. W. *Jean-Baptiste de Lully and his Tragédies Lyriques.* Ann Arbor, Mich.: UMI Research Press, 1979.

Price, Curtis A. *Henry Purcell and the London Stage.* Cambridge: Cambridge University Press, 1984.

_____. *Music in the Restoration Theatre.* Ann Arbor, Mich.: UMI Research Press, 1979.

Scott, R. H. F. *Jean-Baptiste Lully: the Founder of French Opera.* London: Peter Owen, 1973.

Spink, Ian. *Blackwell History of Music in Britain.* Vol. III: *The Seventeenth Century.* Oxford: Basil Blackwell, 1992.

Sternfeld, Frederick W. *Music in Shakespearean Tragedy.* London: Routledge and Kegan Paul, 1963.

Stevens, Denis. *Thomas Tomkins.* 2nd ed., New York: Dover, 1967.

Zimmerman, Franklin B. *Henry Purcell, 1659–1695.* 2nd ed., Philadelphia: University of Pennsylvania Press, 1983.

Chapter 23   Class and Classicism

Barbier, Patrick. *The World of the Castrati: The History of an Extraordinary Operatic Phenomenon,* trans. Margaret Crosland. London: Souvenir Press, 1996.

D'Accone, Frank A. *The History of a Baroque Opera: Alessandro Scarlatti's "Gli equivoci nel sembiante."* Hillsdale, N.Y.: Pendragon Press, 1985.

Grout, Donald J. *Alessandro Scarlatti: An Introduction to his Operas.* Berkeley and Los Angeles: University of California Press, 1979.

Heriot, Angus. *The Castrati in Opera.* London: Secker and Warburg, 1956.

Holmes William C. *Opera Observed: Views of a Florentine Impresario in the Early Eighteenth Century.* Chicago: University of Chicago Press, 1993.

Neville, Don, ed. *Metastasio at Home and Abroad* (Papers from the International Symposium, Faculty of Music, The University of Western Ontario, 1996).

Special issue of *Studies in Music from the University of Western Ontario,* Vol. 16.

Robinson, Michael F. *Naples and Neapolitan Opera.* Oxford: Clarendon Press, 1972.

Tosi, Pier Francesco. *Observations on the Florid Song.* 1723. Reprint, London: Stainer and Bell, 1973.

Chapter 24   The Italian Concerto Style and the Rise of Tonality-Driven Form

Everett, Paul. *Vivaldi: "The Four Seasons" and Other Concertos, Op. 8.* Cambridge: Cambridge University Press, 1996.

Pincherle, Marc. *Corelli: His Life, His Work,* trans. Hubert E. M. Russell. New York: Norton, 1956.

_____. *Vivaldi: Genius of the Baroque,* trans. Christopher Hatch. New York: Norton, 1957.

Sadie, Stanley. *Handel's Concertos*. London: British Broadcasting Corporation, 1972.

Talbot, Michael. *Vivaldi*. Rev. ed., London: J. M. Dent, 1984.

Chapter 25   Class of 1685 (I)

Boyd, Malcolm. *Bach*. 3rd ed., Oxford: Oxford University Press, 2000.

———. *Bach: The Brandenburg Concertos*. Cambridge: Cambridge University Press, 1993.

Butt, John, ed. *The Cambridge Companion to Bach*. Cambridge: Cambridge University Press, 1997.

David, Hans T., and Arthur Mendel. *The Bach Reader: A Life of Johann Sebastian Bach in Letters and Documents*. Rev. ed., New York: Norton, 1966.

Dreyfus, Laurence. *Bach and the Patterns of Invention*. Cambridge: Harvard University Press, 1996.

Geiringer, Karl. *The Bach Family: Seven Generations of Creative Genius*. 2nd ed., London: Oxford University Press, 1977.

Marissen, Michael. *Social and Religious Designs of J. S. Bach's Brandenburg Concertos*. Princeton: Princeton University Press, 1995.

Marshall, Robert L. *The Music of Johann Sebastian Bach: The Sources, the Style, the Significance*. New York: Schirmer, 1989.

Mellers, Wilfrid. *François Couperin ad the French Classical Tradition*. Rev. ed., New York: Farrar Straus and Giroux, 1987.

Schulenberg, David. *The Keyboard Music of J. S. Bach*. New York: Gala Group, 1992.

Stauffer, George, and Ernest May. *J. S. Bach as Organist: His Instruments, Music, and Performance Practices*. Bloomington: Indiana University Press, 1986.

Stinson, Russell. *Bach: The Orgelbüchlein*. New York: Schirmer, 1996.

Snyder, Kerala. *Dietrich Buxtehude: Organist in Lübeck*. New York: Schirmer, 1987.

Williams, Peter. *The Organ Music of J. S. Bach*. Three vols. Cambridge: Cambridge University Press, 1980–84.

Wolff, Christoph. *Bach: Essays on His Life and Music*. Cambridge: Harvard University Press, 1991.

———. *Johann Sebastian Bach: The Learned Musician*. New York: Norton, 2000.

Yearsley, David. *Bach and the Meanings of Counterpoint*. Cambridge: Cambridge University Press, 2002.

Chapter 26   Class of 1685 (II)

Boyd, Malcolm. *Domenico Scarlatti: Master of Music*. New York: Schirmer, 1987.

Butt, John. *Bach: Mass in B Minor*. Cambridge: Cambridge University Press, 1991.

Chafe, Eric. *Analyzing Bach Cantatas*. Rev. ed., New York: Oxford University Press, 2003.

———. *Tonal Allegory in the Vocal Music of J. S. Bach*. Berkeley and Los Angeles: University of California Press, 1991.

Dean, Winton. *Handel and the Opera Seria*. Berkeley and Los Angeles: University of California Press, 1969.

_____ . *Handel's Dramatic Oratorios and Masques*. London: Oxford University Press, 1959.

Dean, Winton, and J. Merrill Knapp. *Handel's Operas, 1704–1726*. Oxford: Clarendon Press, 1987.

Deutsch, Otto Erich. *Handel: A Documentary Biography*. New York: Norton, 1955; Reprint, New York: Da Capo Press, 1974.

Harris, Ellen. *Handel and the Pastoral Tradition*. London: Oxford University Press, 1980.

_____ . *Handel as Orpheus: Voice and Desire in the Chamber Cantatas*. Cambrdige: Harvard University Press, 2001.

Hogwood, Christopher. *Handel*. London: Thames and Hudson, 1984.

Kirkpatrick, Ralph. *Domenico Scarlatti*. Rev. ed., Princeton: Princeton University Press, 1983.

Leaver, Robin A.: *Music as Preaching: Bach, Passions and Music in Worship*. Oxford: Latimer House, 1982.

Marissen, Michael. *Lutheranism, Anti-Judaism, and Bach's St. John Passion: With an Annotated Literal Translation of the Libretto*. New York: Oxford University Press, 1998.

Marshall, Robert L. *The Compositional Process of J. S. Bach: A Study of the Autograph Scores of the Vocal Works*. Princeton: Princeton University Press, 1972.

Smallman, Basil. *The Background of Passion Music: J. S. Bach and His Predecessors*. 2nd ed., New York: Dover, 1970.

Smith, Ruth. *Handel's Oratorios and Eighteenth-Century Thought*. Cambridge: Cambridge University Press, 1995.

Stauffer, George. *Bach: The Mass in B Minor*. New Haven: Yale University Press, 2003.

Strohm, Reinhard. *Essays on Handel and Italian Opera*. Cambridge: Cambridge University Press, 1985.

Chapter 27   The Comic Style

Barford, Philip. *The Keyboard Music of C. P. E. Bach, Considered in Relation to His Musical Aesthetic and the Rise of the Sonata Principle*. New York: October House, 1966.

Bach, Carl Philipp Emanuel. *Essay on the True Art of Keyboard Playing*, trans. and ed. William J. Mitchell. New York: Norton, 1948.

Clark, Stephen L., ed. *C. P. E. Bach Studies*. Oxford: Oxford University Press, 1988.

Helm, E. Eugene. *Music at the Court of Frederick the Great*. Norman: University of Oklahoma Press, 1960.

Oliver, Alfred R. *The Encyclopedists as Critics of Music*. New York: Columbia University Press, 1947.

Ottenberg, Hans-Gunter. *Carl Philipp Emanuel Bach*. Oxford: Oxford University Press, 1988.

Schulenberg, David. *The Instrumental Music of Carl Philipp Emanuel Bach*. Ann Arbor, Mich.: UMI Research Press, 1984.

Terry, Charles Sanford. *John Christian Bach*. 2nd ed., London: Oxford University Press, 1967.

Troy, Charles E. *The Comic Intermezzo: A Study in the History of Eighteenth-Century Opera*. Ann Arbor, Mich.: UMI Research Press, 1979.

Chapter 28   Enlightenment and Reform

Allanbrook, Wye J. *Rhythmic Gesture in Mozart: Le nozze di Figaro and Don Giovanni.* Chicago: University of Chicago Press, 1983.

Anderson, Emily, ed. *The Letters of Mozart and His Family.* 3rd ed., London: Palgrave Macmillan, 1989.

Bauman, Thomas. *W. A. Mozart: Die Entführung aus dem Serail.* Cambridge: Cambridge University Press, 1987.

Branscombe, Peter. *W. A. Mozart: Die Zauberflöte.* Cambridge: Cambridge University Press, 1991.

Brown, Bruce Alan. *W. A. Mozart: Così fan tutte.* Cambridge: Cambridge University Press, 1995.

Bauman, Thomas. *North German Opera in the Age of Goethe.* Cambridge: Cambridge University Press, 1985.

Carter, Tim. *W. A. Mozart: Le nozze di Figaro.* Cambridge: Cambridge University Press, 1987.

Charlton, David. *Grétry and the Growth of Opéra Comique.* Cambridge: Cambridge University Press, 1986.

Dent, Edward J. *Mozart's Operas: A Critical Study.* 2nd ed., London: Oxford University Press, 1947.

Deutsch, Otto Erich. *Mozart: A Documentary Biography*, trans. Jeremy Noble and Peter Branscombe. Stanford: Stanford University Press, 1965.

Einstein, Alfred. *Gluck*, trans. Eric Blom. New York: Collier Books, 1962.

_____ . *Mozart: His Character, His Work*, trans. Arthur Mendel and Nathan Broder. 6th ed., New York: Norton, 1945.

Flaherty, Gloria. *Opera in the Development of German Critical Thought.* Princeton: Princeton University Press, 1978.

Heartz, Daniel, and Thomas Bauman. *Mozart's Operas.* Berkeley and Los Angeles: University of California Press, 1990.

Howard, Patricia. *Gluck and the Birth of Modern Opera.* London: Barrie & Rockliff, 1963.

Hunter, Mary. *The Culture of Opera Buffa in Mozart's Vienna: A Poetics of Entertainment.* Princeton: Princeton University Press, 1999.

Landon, H. C. Robbins, and Donald Mitchell, eds. *The Mozart Companion.* New York: Norton, 1969.

Liebner, Janos. *Mozart on the Stage.* New York: Praeger, 1972.

Rice, John A. *W. A. Mozart: La clemenza di Tito.* Cambridge: Cambridge University Press, 1991.

Rushton, Julian. *W. A. Mozart: Don Giovanni.* Cambridge: Cambridge University Press, 1981.

_____ . *W. A. Mozart: Idomeneo.* Cambridge: Cambridge University Press, 1993.

Sadie, Stanley. *The New Grove Mozart.* New York: Norton, 1983.

Solomon, Maynard. *Mozart: A Life.* New York: HarperCollins, 1995.

Steptoe, Andrew. *The Mozart-Da Ponte Operas: Cultural and Musical Background to Le nozze di Figaro, Don Giovanni, and Così fan Tutte.* Oxford: Clarendon Press, 1988.

Till, Nicholas. *Mozart and the Enlightenment: Truth, Virtue and Beauty in Mozart's Operas.* London: Faber and Faber, 1992.

Weimer, Eric. *Opera Seria and the Evolution of Classical Style, 1755–1772.* Ann Arbor, Mich: UMI Research Press, 1984.

Chapter 29 Instrumental Music Lifts Off

Barrett-Ayres, Reginald. *Joseph Haydn and the String Quartet.* London: Barrie and Jenkins, 1974.

Burney, Charles. *The Present State of Music in Germany, the Netherlands, and United Provinces.* London, 1771; Reprint, New York: Broude Bros., 1969.

Carse, Adam. *Eighteenth Century Symphonies.* London: Augener, 1951.

Churgin, Bathia. *The Symphonies of G. B. Sammartini.* Vol. I, *The Early Symphonies.* Cambridge: Harvard University Press, 1968.

Geiringer, Karl. *Haydn: A Creative Life in Music.* 3rd ed., Berkeley and Los Angeles: University of California Press, 1982.

Gotwals, Vernon. *Haydn: Two Contemporary Portraits.* Madison: University of Wisconsin Press, 1968.

Kirkendale, Warren. *Fugue and Fugato in Rococo and Classical Chamber Music,* trans. Margaret Bent and the author. Durham: Duke University Press, 1979.

Landon, H. C. Robbins. *Haydn: Chronicle and Works.* 5 vols. Bloomington: Indiana University Press, 1976–80.

_____ . *The Symphonies of Joseph Haydn.* London: Barrie and Rockliff, 1961.

Morrow, Mary Sue. *Concert Life in Haydn's Vienna: Aspects of a Developing Musical and Social Institution.* Stuyvesant, N.Y: Pendragon Press, 1988.

Rosen, Charles. *Sonata Forms.* New York: Norton, 1980.

Schroeder, David. *Haydn and the Enlightenment: The Late Symphonies and Their Audience.* Oxford: Clarendon Press, 1990.

Sisman, Elaine R. *Haydn and the Classical Variation.* Cambridge: Harvard University Press, 1993.

_____ . ed. *Haydn and His World.* Princeton: Princeton University Press, 1997.

Somfai, László. *Joseph Haydn: His Life in Pictures.* New York: Taplinger, 1969.

Webster, James C. *Haydn's "Farewell" Symphony and the Idea of Classical Style.* Cambridge: Cambridge University Press, 1991.

Wheelock, Gretchen A. *Haydn's Ingenious Jesting with Art: Contexts of Musical Wit and Humor.* New York: Schirmer, 1992.

Will, Richard. *The Characteristic Symphony in the Age of Haydn and Beethoven.* Cambridge: Cambridge University Press, 2002.

Wolf, Eugene K. *The Symphonies of Johann Stamitz: A Study in the Formation of the Classic Style.* Utrecht: Kluwer Academic Publishers, 1981.

Chapter 30 The Composer's Voice

Girdlestone, Cuthbert. *Mozart and His Piano Concertos.* 3rd ed., New York: Dover, 1978.

Hutchings, Arthur. *A Companion to Mozart's Piano Concertos.* London: Oxford University Press, 1948.

Irving, John. *Mozart: The "Haydn" Quartets.* Cambridge: Cambridge University Press, 1998.

Kerman, Joseph, ed. *W. A. Mozart:* Piano *Concerto in C Major, K. 503.* New York: Norton, 1970.

King, Alec Hyatt. *Mozart String and Wind Concertos.* London: Granite Impex, 1978.

Landon, H. C. Robbins. *Mozart and Vienna.* London: Thames and Hudson, 1991.

_____. *Mozart: The Golden Years, 1781–1791.* London: Thames and Hudson, 1989.

MacIntyre, Bruce A. *Haydn: The Creation.* New York: Thomson Learning, 1998.

Neumann, Frederick. *Ornamentation and Improvisation in Mozart.* Princeton: Princeton University Press, 1986.

Richards, Annette. *The Free Fantasia and the Musical Picturesque.* Cambridge: Cambridge University Press, 2001.

Sisman, Elaine R. *Mozart: The "Jupiter" Symphony.* Cambridge: Cambridge University Press, 1993.

Temperley, Nicholas. *Haydn: "The Creation."* Cambridge: Cambridge University Press, 1991.

Zaslaw, Neal. *Mozart's Symphonies: Context, Performance Practice, Reception.* Oxford: Oxford University Press, 1989.

_____. ed. *Mozart's Piano Concertos: Text, Context, Interpretation.* Ann Arbor, Mich: University of Michigan Press, 1996.

Chapter 31 The First Romantics

Anderson, Emily, ed. *The Letters of Beethoven.* New York: Norton, 1985.

Arnold, Denis, and Nigel Fortune, eds. *The Beethoven Reader.* New York: Norton, 1971.

Cook, Nicholas. *Beethoven: Symphony No. 9.* Cambridge: Cambridge University Press, 1993.

Cooper, Barry, ed. *The Beethoven Compendium: A Guide to Beethoven's Life and Music.* London: Thames and Hudson, 1991.

Kerman, Joseph. *The Beethoven Quartets.* New York: Norton, 1979.

Kinderman, William. *Beethoven.* Berkeley and Los Angeles: University of California Press, 1995.

Lockwood, Lewis. *Beethoven: The Music and the Life.* New York: Norton, 2003.

Nottebohm, Gustav. *Two Beethoven Sketchbooks,* trans. Jonathan Katz. London: Victor Gollancz, 1979.

Plantinga, Leon. *Beethoven's Concertos: History, Stile, Performance.* New York: Norton, 1999.

Ratner, Leonard G. *The Beethoven String Quartets: Compositional Strategies and Rhetoric.* Stanford: Stanford University Bookstore, 1995.

Schindler, Anton Felix. *Beethoven as I Knew Him*, ed. D. W. MacArdle, trans. Constance S. Jolly. New York: Norton, 1972.

Solomon, Maynard. *Beethoven*. New York: Schirmer, 1977.

_____ . *Beethoven Essays*. Cambridge: Harvard University Press, 1988.

Sonneck, Oscar George, ed. *Beethoven: Impressions of Contemporaries*. New York: Schirmer, 1967.

Spohr, Louis. *Autobiography*. New York: Da Capo Press, 1969.

Thayer, Alexander Wheelock. *Thayer's Life of Beethoven*, Revised by Elliott Forbes. Princeton: Princeton University Press, 1967.

Wallace, Robin. *Beethoven's Critics: Aesthetic Dilemmas and Resolutions during the Composer's Lifetime*. Cambridge: Cambridge University Press, 1986.

Wegeler, Franz Gerhard. *Beethoven Remembered: The Biographical Notes of Franz Wegeler and Ferdinand Ries*. Arlington, Va.: Great Ocean Publishers, 1987.

Chapter 32   C-Minor Moods

Burnham, Scott. *Beethoven Hero*. Princeton: Princeton University Press, 1995.

Cooper, Martin. *Beethoven: The Last Decade, 1817–1827*. London: Oxford University Press, 1970.

Rosen, Charles. *Beethoven's Piano Sonatas: A Short Companion*. New Haven: Yale University Press, 2002.

Rumph, Stephen. *Beethoven after Napoleon: Political Romanticism in the Late Works*. Berkeley and Los Angeles: University of California Press, 2004.

Solomon, Maynard. *Late Beethoven: Music, Thought, Imagination*. Berkeley and Los Angeles: University of California Press, 2003.

Sterba, Editha, and Richard Sterba. *Beethoven and His Nephew: A Psychoanalytical Study of Their Relationship*, trans. Willard Trask. New York: Schocken Books, 1971.

Sullivan, J. W. N. *Beethoven: His Spiritual Development*. New York: Knopf, 1964.

Volume 3: The Nineteenth Century

General Sources

Abraham, Gerald. *A Hundred Years of Music*. 4th ed., London: Duckworth, 1974.

Bent, Ian, ed. *Music Theory in the Age of Romanticism*. Cambridge: Cambridge University Press, 1996.

Bujić, Bojan, ed. *Music in European Thought, 1851–1912*. Cambridge: Cambridge University Press, 1988.

Dahlhaus, Carl. *Nineteenth-Century Music*, trans. J. Bradford Robinson. Berkeley and Los Angeles: University of California Press, 1989.

Dale, Kathleen. *Nineteenth-Century Piano Music*. London: Oxford University Press, 1954.

Daverio, John. *Nineteenth-Century Music and the German Romantic Ideology*. New York: Schirmer, 1993.

Donakowski, Conrad. *A Muse for the Masses: Ritual and Music in an Age of Democratic Revolution, 1770–1870*. Chicago: University of Chicago Press, 1977.

Einstein, Alfred. *Music in the Romantic Era*. New York: Norton, 1947.

Holoman, D. Kern, ed. *The Nineteenth-Century Symphony*. New York: Schirmer Books, 1997.

Lippman, Edward, ed. *Musical Aesthetics: A Historical Reader*, Vol. II: *The Nineteenth Century*. Stuyvesant, N.Y.: Pendragon Press, 1986.

Longyear, Rey M. *Nineteenth-Century Romanticism in Music*. 2nd ed., Englewood Cliffs, N.J.: Prentice Hall, 1973.

Newman, William S. *The Sonata Since Beethoven*. 3rd ed., New York: Norton, 1983.

Plantinga, Leon. *Romantic Music: A History of Musical Style in Nineteenth-Century Europe*. New York: Norton, 1984.

Ratner, Leonard G. *Romantic Music: Sound and Syntax*. New York: Gale Group, 1992.

Ringer, Alexander, ed. *Music and Society: The Early Romantic Era*. Englewood Cliffs, N.J.: Prentice Hall, 1991.

Rosen, Charles. *The Romantic Generation*. Cambridge: Harvard University Press, 1995.

Samson, Jim, ed. *The Cambridge History of Nineteenth-Century Music*. Cambridge: Cambridge University Press, 2002.

_____. *Music and Society: The Late Romantic Era*. Englewood Cliffs, N.J.: Prentice Hall, 1991.

Todd, R. Larry. *Nineteenth-Century Piano Music*. New York: Routledge, 1990.

Weber, William. *Music and the Middle Class: The Social Structure of Concert Life in London, Paris, and Vienna*. London: Croom Helm, 1975.

Young, Percy M. *The Concert Tradition*. London: Routledge and Kegan Paul, 1965.

Chapter 33   Real Worlds, and Better Ones

Ashbrook, William. *Donizetti and His Operas*. Cambridge: Cambridge University Press, 1982.

Bushnell, Howard. *Maria Malibran: A Biography of the Singer*. University Park: Pennsylvania State University Press, 1979.

Dent, Edward J. *The Rise of Romantic Opera*, ed. Winton Dean. Cambridge: Cambridge University Press, 1976.

FitzLyon, April. *The Price of Genius: A Life of Pauline Viardot*. London: J. Calder, 1964.

Gossett, Philip. *Anna Bolena and the Artistic Maturity of Gaetano Donizetti*. Oxford: Oxford University Press, 1985.

_____. *The Tragic Finale of [Rossini's] 'Tancredi.'* Pesaro: Fondazione Rossini, 1977.

Orrey, Leslie. *Bellini*. London: J. M. Dent, 1969.

Osborne, Richard. *Rossini*. London: J. M. Dent, 1987.

Rosselli, John. *The Life of Bellini*. Cambridge: Cambridge University Press, 1996.

_____. *The Opera Industry in Italy from Cimarosa to Verdi: The Role of the Impresario*. Cambridge: Cambridge University Press, 1984.

Stendhal. *Life of Rossini*, trans. R. N. Coe. London: Calder and Boyars, 1956. Reprint, Seattle: University of Washington Press, 1972.

Till, Nicholas. *Rossini: His Life and Times*. London: Hippocrene Books, 1983.

Weinstock, Herbert. *Donizetti and the World of Opera in Italy, Paris, and Vienna in the First Half of the Nineteenth Century*. New York: Random House, 1963.

_____ . *Rossini: A Biography*. New York: Knopf, 1968.

_____ . *Vincenzo Bellini: His Life and His Operas*. New York: Knopf, 1971.

Chapter 34   The Music Trance

Bloom, Peter, ed. *Music in Paris in the 1830s*. Stuyvesant, N.Y.: Pendragon Press, 1987.

Chusid, Martin. *Schubert: Symphony in B minor ("Unfinished")*. Norton Critical Scores. New York: Norton, 1968.

Deutsch, Otto Erich. *The Schubert Reader: A Life of Franz Schubert in Letters and Documents*, trans. Eric Blom. New York: Norton, 1947.

Deutsch, Otto Erich, ed. *Schubert: Memoirs by Family and Friends*. London: A. and C. Black, 1958.

Gibbs, Christopher. *The Life of Schubert*. Cambridge: Cambridge University Press, 2000.

Gibbs, Christopher, ed. *The Cambridge Companion to Schubert*. Cambridge: Cambridge University Press, 1997.

Hanson, Alice M. *Musical Life in Biedermeier Vienna*. Cambridge: Cambridge University Press, 1985.

Johnson, James H. *Listening in Paris: A Cultural History*. Berkeley and Los Angeles: University of California Press, 1995.

Loesser, Arthur. *Men, Women, and Pianos: A Social History*. New York: Simon and Schuster, 1954.

McKay, Elizabeth Norman. *Franz Schubert: A Biography*. Oxford: Oxford University Press, 1996.

Newbould, Brian. *Schubert and the Symphony: A New Perspective*. London: Toccata Press, 1993.

_____ . *Schubert: The Music and the Man*. Berkeley and Los Angeles: University of California Press, 1997.

Piggot, Patrick. *The Life and Music of John Field*. Berkeley and Los Angeles: University of California Press, 1973.

Chapter 35   *Volkstümlichkeit*

Citron, Marcia J., ed. *The Letters of Fanny Hensel to Felix Mendelssohn*. Stuyvesant, N.Y.: Pendragon Press, 1987.

Elvers, Rudolf, ed. *Felix Mendelssohn: A Life in Letters*, trans. Craig Tomlinson. New York: Fromm International, 1986.

Hensel, Sebastian, ed. *The Mendelssohn Family (1729–1847)*, trans. Carl Klingemann. New York: Harper, 1882.

Kramer, Richard. *Distant Cycles: Schubert and the Conceiving of Song*. Chicago: University of Chicago Press, 1994.

Mendelssohn, Felix. *Letters*, trans. G. Selden-Goth. New York: Pantheon, 1945. Reprint, New York: Vienna House, 1973.

Mercer-Taylor, Peter. *The Life of Mendelssohn*. Cambridge: Cambridge University Press, 2000.

Nichols, Roger, ed. *Mendelssohn Remembered*. London: Faber and Faber, 1997.

Porter, Cecelia Hopkins. *The Rhine as Musical Metaphor: Cultural Identity in German Romantic Music*. Boston: Northeastern University Press, 1996.

Sposato, Jeffrey S. "The Price of Assimilation: The Oratorios of Felix Mendelssohn and Nineteenth-Century Anti-Semitic Tradition." Ph.D. diss., Brandeis University, 2000. New York: Oxford University Press, forthcoming.

Stein, Jack M. *Poem and Music in the German Lied from Gluck to Hugo Wolf*. Cambridge: Harvard University Press, 1971.

Tillard, Françoise. *Fanny Mendelssohn*. Portland, Ore.: Amadeus Press, 1996.

Todd, R. Larry. *Mendelssohn: A Life in Music*. New York: Oxford University Press, 2004.

_____. *Mendelssohn: "The Hebrides" and Other Overtures*. Cambridge: Cambridge University Press, 1993.

Todd, R. Larry, ed. *Mendelssohn and His World*. Princeton: Princeton University Press, 1991.

Werner, Eric. *Mendelssohn: A New Image of the Composer and His Age*. New York: Free Press of Glencoe, 1963.

Youens, Susan. *Retracing a Winter's Journey: Schubert's Winterreise*. Ithaca: Cornell University Press, 1991.

_____. *Schubert: Die schöne Müllerin*. Cambridge: Cambridge University Press, 1992.

_____. *Schubert's Late Lieder: Beyond the Song-Cycles*. Cambridge: Cambridge University Press, 2002.

_____. *Schubert, Müller, and Die schöne Müllerin*. Cambridge: Cambridge University Press, 1997.

_____. *Schubert's Poets and the Making of Lieder*. Cambridge: Cambridge University Press, 1996.

Chapter 36   Nations, States, and Peoples

Abraham, Gerald. *The Tradition of Western Music*. Berkeley and Los Angeles: University of California Press, 1974.

Becker, Heinz, and Gudrun Becker. *Meyerbeer: A Life in Letters*. London: A. & C. Black, 1989.

Brown, David. *Glinka: A Biographical and Critical Study*. London: Oxford University Press, 1974.

Charlton, David, ed. *The Cambridge Companion to Grand Opera*. Cambridge: Cambridge University Press, 2003.

Crosten, William. *French Grand Opera: An Art and a Business*. New York: Columbia University Press, 1948.

Fulcher, Jane. *The Nation's Image: French Grand Opera as Politics and Politicized Art*. Cambridge: Cambridge University Press, 1987.

Gerhard, Anselm. *The Urbanization of Opera: Music Theater in Paris in the Nineteenth Century*, trans. Mary Whittall. Chicago: University of Chicago Press, 1998.

Glinka, Mikhail Ivanovich. *Memoirs*, trans. Richard B. Mudge. Norman: University of Oklahoma Press, 1963.

Hallman, Diana R. *Opera, Liberalism, and Antisemitism in Nineteenth-Century France: The Politics of Halévy's "La Juive."* Cambridge: Cambridge University Press, 2002.

Kemp, Ian. *Hector Berlioz: Les Troyens*. Cambridge: Cambridge University Press, 1988.

Pendle, Karin. *Eugène Scribe and French Grand Opera of the Nineteenth Century*. Ann Arbor, Mich.: UMI Research Press, 1979.

Ridenour, Robert C. *Nationalism, Modernism and Personal Rivalry in Nineteenth-Century Russian Music*. Ann Arbor, Mich.: UMI Research Press, 1977.

Swan, Alfred J. *Russian Music and Its Sources in Chant and Folk Song*. New York: Norton, 1973.

Taruskin, Richard. *Opera and Drama in Russia*. Ann Arbor, Mich.: UMI Research Press, 1981.

Warrack, John. *Carl Maria von Weber*. 2nd ed., Cambridge: Cambridge University Press, 1976.

Chapter 37   Virtuosos

Allsobrook, David Ian. *Liszt: My Travelling Circus Life*. Carbondale: Southern Illinois University Press, 1991.

Burger, Ernst. *Franz Liszt: A Chronicle of His Life in Pictures and Documents*. Princeton: Princeton University Press, 1989.

Courcy, Geraldine I. C. de. *Paganini, the Genoese*. Norman: University of Oklahoma Press, 1957.

La Mara [Ida Marie Lipsius], ed. *Letters of Franz Liszt*. 2 vols. New York: Haskell House, 1968.

Merrick, Paul. *Revolution and Religion in the Music of Liszt*. Cambridge: Cambridge University Press, 1987.

Metzner, Paul. *Crescendo of the Virtuoso: Spectacle, Skill, and Self-Promotion in Paris during the Age of Revolution*. Berkeley and Los Angeles: University of California Press, 1998.

Pulver, Jeffrey. *Paganini, the Romantic Virtuoso*. London: H. Joseph, 1936.

Walker, Alan. *Franz Liszt: The Virtuoso Years, 1811–1847*. New York: Random House, 1983.

Watson, Derek. *Liszt*. London: J. M. Dent, 1983.

Williams, Adrian, ed. *Portrait of Liszt by Himself and His Contemporaries*. London: Oxford University Press, 1990.

Williams, Adrian, ed. and trans. *Franz Liszt: Selected Letters*. Oxford: Oxford University Press, 1999.

Chapter 38   Critics

Barzun, Jacques. *Hector Berlioz and the Romantic Century*. 3rd ed., New York: Columbia University Press, 1969.

Berlioz, Hector. *The Art of Music and Other Essays (A Travers Chants)*, trans. Elizabeth Csicsery-Rónay. Bloomington: Indiana University Press, 1994.

_____ . *The Conductor: The Theory of His Art* (anonymous translation). Temecula, Calif.: Best Books, 2001.

_____ . *Evenings in the Orchestra*, trans. C. R. Fortescue. Baltimore: Penguin Books, 1963.

_____ . *Memoirs*, trans. David Cairns. 3rd ed., New York: Random House, 2002.

_____ . *A Selection from His Letters*, ed. Humphrey Searle. New York: Vienna House, 1973.

Cairns, David. *Berlioz.* 2 vols. Berkeley and Los Angeles: University of California Press, 2000.

Carse, Adam. *The Orchestra from Beethoven to Berlioz.* Cambridge: Cambridge University Press, 1948.

Chissell, Joan. *Clara Schumann: A Dedicated Spirit.* New York: Taplinger, 1983.

Cone, Edward T. *Hector Berlioz: Fantastic Symphony.* Norton Critical Scores. New York: Norton, 1971.

Daverio, John. *Robert Schumann: Herald of a "New Poetic Age."* New York: Oxford University Press, 1997.

Holoman, D. Kern. *Berlioz.* Cambridge: Harvard University Press, 1989.

Komar, Arthur, ed. *Schumann: Dichterliebe.* Norton Critical Scores. New York: Norton, 1971.

Macdonald, Hugh. *Berlioz Orchestral Music.* London: British Broadcasting Corporation, 1969.

Macdonald, Hugh, ed. *Selected Letters of Berlioz.* London: Faber and Faber, 1995.

Marston, Nicholas. *Schumann: Fantasie, op. 17.* Cambridge: Cambridge University Press, 1992.

Murphy, Kerry: *Hector Berlioz and the Development of French Music Criticism.* Ann Arbor, Mich.: UMI Research Press, 1988.

Ostwald, Peter. *Schumann: The Inner Voices of a Musical Genius.* Boston: Northeastern University Press, 1985.

Plantinga, Leon. *Schumann as Critic.* New Haven: Yale University Press, 1967.

Pleasants, Henry, ed. *The Musical World of Robert Schumann.* New York: St. Martin's Press, 1965.

Reich, Nancy B. *Clara Schumann.* Rev. ed., Ithaca: Cornell University Press, 2001.

Rushton, Julian. *Berlioz: Roméo et Juliette.* Cambridge: Cambridge University Press, 1994.

_____ . *The Musical Language of Berlioz.* Cambridge: Cambridge University Press, 1983.

Sams, Eric. *The Songs of Robert Schumann.* 2nd ed., London: Methuen, 1975.

Schumann, Robert. *On Music and Musicians*, ed. Konrad Wolff. New York: McGraw Hill, 1964.

Todd, R. Larry, ed. *Schumann and His World.* Princeton: Princeton University Press, 1994.

Walker, Alan, ed. *Robert Schumann: The Man and His Music.* London: Barrie & Jenkins, 1972.

Chapter 39   Self and Other

Branson, David. *John Field and Chopin.* New York: St. Martin's Press, 1972.

Curtiss, Mina. *Bizet and His World.* New York: Vienna House, 1974.

Dean, Winton. *Bizet*. 3rd ed., London: J. M. Dent, 1975.

Dianin, Sergei Alexandrovich. *Borodin*, trans. Robert Lord. Oxford: Oxford University Press, 1963.

Eigeldinger, Jean-Jacques. *Chopin: Pianist and Teacher*, trans. N. Shohet, K. Osostrowicz, and R. Howat. 3rd ed., Cambridge: Cambridge University Press, 1986.

Gottschalk, Louis Moreau. *Notes of a Pianist*, ed. Jeanne Behrend. New York: Da Capo Press, 1979.

Hagan, Dorothy Veinus. *Félicien David, 1810–1876: A Composer and a Cause*. Syracuse, N.Y.: Syracuse University Press, 1985.

Higgins, Thomas. *Frederic Chopin: Preludes, opus 28: An Authoritative Score, Historical Background, Analysis, Views and Comments*. Norton Critical Scores. New York: Norton, 1973.

John, Nicholas. *Georges Bizet: Carmen*. English National Opera Guide. London, 1982.

Kallberg, Jeffrey. *Chopin at the Boundaries: Sex, History, and Musical Genre*. Cambridge: Harvard University Press, 1996.

Locke, Ralph P. *Music, Musicians, and the Saint-Simonians*. Chicago: University of Chicago Press, 1986.

Long, E. R. *A History of the Therapy of Tuberculosis and the Case of Frederic Chopin*. Lawrence: University of Kansas Press, 1956.

McClary, Susan. *Georges Bizet: Carmen*. Cambridge: Cambridge University Press, 1992.

Parakilas, James. *Ballads without Words: Chopin and the Tradition of the Instrumental Ballade*. Portland, Ore.: Amadeus Press, 1992.

Rink, John. *Chopin: The Piano Concertos*. Cambridge: Cambridge University Press, 1997.

Samson, Jim. *Chopin*. Oxford and New York: Oxford University Press, 1996.

_____. *Chopin: The Four Ballades*. Cambridge: Cambridge University Press, 1992.

Samson, Jim, ed. *The Cambridge Companion to Chopin*. Cambridge: Cambridge University Press, 1992.

Starr, S. Frederick. *Bamboula! The Life and Times of Louis Moreau Gottschalk*. New York: Oxford University Press, 1994.

Walker, Alan. *The Chopin Companion*. London: Barrie and Rockliff, 1973.

Chapter 40   Midcentury

Dahlhaus, Carl. *The Idea of Absolute Music*, trans. Roger Lustig. Chicago: University of Chicago Press, 1989.

_____. *Realism in Nineteenth-Century Music*, trans. Mary Whittall. Cambridge: Cambridge University Press, 1982.

Hamilton, Kenneth. *Liszt: Sonata in B Minor*. Cambridge: Cambridge University Press, 1996.

Hanslick, Eduard. *On the Musically Beautiful*, trans. Geoffrey Payzant. Indianapolis: Hackett Publishing, 1986.

Hueffer, Francis, ed. and trans. *Correspondence of Wagner and Liszt*. 2 vols. New York: Vienna House, 1973.

Johns, Kathryn. *The Symphonic Poems of Franz Liszt.* Stuyvesant, N.Y.: Pendragon Press, 1997.

Saffle, Michael. *Liszt in Germany, 1840–1845: A Study in Sources, Documents, and the History of Reception.* Stuyvesant, N.Y.: Pendragon Press, 1994.

Walker, Alan. *Franz Liszt: The Final Years, 1861–1886.* Ithaca: Cornell University Press, 1997.

_____. *Franz Liszt: The Weimar Years, 1848–1861.* Ithaca: Cornell University Press, 1993.

Chapter 41   Slavs as Subjects and Citizens

Abraham, Gerald. *Essays on Russian and East European Music.* Oxford: Oxford University Press, 1985.

_____. *On Russian Music.* London: William Reeves, 1939.

_____. *Slavonic and Romantic Music.* New York: St. Martin's Press, 1968.

_____. *Studies in Russian Music.* London: William Reeves, 1936.

Asafyev, Boris. *Russian Music from the Beginning of the Nineteenth Century,* trans. Alfred J. Swan. Ann Arbor: University of Michigan Press, 1953.

Bowen, Catherine Drinker. *Free Artist: The Story of Anton and Nicholas Rubinstein.* Boston: Little, Brown and Co., 1939.

Calvocoressi, Michel D. and Gerald Abraham. *Masters of Russian Music.* New York: Tudor Publishing Co., 1944.

Clapham, John. *Smetana.* London: J. M. Dent, 1972.

Garden, Edward. *Balakirev: A Critical Study of His Life and Music.* London: Faber and Faber, 1967.

Large, Brian. *Smetana.* London: Duckworth, 1970.

Rimsky-Korsakov, Nikolai. *My Musical Life* (1909), trans. Judah A. Joffe. London: Eulenburg Books, 1974.

Stasov, Vladimir Vasilievich. *Selected Essays on Music,* trans. Florence Jonas. New York: Praeger, 1968.

Taruskin, Richard. *Defining Russia Musically: Historical and Hermeneutical Essays.* Princeton: Princeton University Press, 1997.

Tyrrell, John. *Czech Opera.* Cambridge: Cambridge University Press, 1988.

Chapter 42   Deeds of Music Made Visible (Class of 1813, I)

Abbate, Carolyn. *Unsung Voices: Opera and Musical Narrative in the Nineteenth Century.* Princeton: Princeton University Press, 1991.

Bailey, Robert, ed. *Richard Wagner: Prelude and Transfiguration from "Tristan und Isolde."* Norton Critical Scores. New York: Norton, 1985.

Barth, Herbert, Dietrich Mack, and Egon Voss. *Wagner: A Documentary Study.* New York: Oxford University Press, 1975.

Barzun, Jacques. *Darwin, Marx, Wagner.* Boston: Little, Brown, 1941.

Beckett, Lucy. *Richard Wagner: Parsifal.* Cambridge: Cambridge University Press, 1981.

Dahlhaus, Carl. *Richard Wagner's Music Dramas*, trans. Mary Whittall. Cambridge: Cambridge University Press, 1979.

Deathridge, John, P. Wapnewski, and U. Müller, eds. *The Wagner Handbook*. Cambridge: Harvard University Press, 1991.

Donington, Robert. *Wagner's 'Ring' and Its Symbols: The Music and the Myth*. Rev. ed., New York: St. Martin's Press, 1974.

Grey, Thomas S. *Wagner's Musical Prose: Texts and Contexts*. Cambridge: Cambridge University Press, 1995.

Hartford, Robert, ed. *Bayreuth: The Early Years*. Cambridge: Cambridge University Press, 1980.

Large, David C., and William Weber, eds. *Wagnerism in European Culture and Politics*. Ithaca: Cornell University Press, 1984.

Laudon, Robert T. *Sources of the Wagnerian Synthesis: A Study of the Franco-German Tradition in the Nineteenth Century Opera*. Munich and Salzburg: Katzbichler, 1979.

Magee, Bryan. *Aspects of Wagner*. New York: Stein and Day, 1969.

Millington, Barry. *Wagner*. Rev. ed., Princeton: Princeton University Press, 1992.

———. *The Wagner Compendium: A Guide to Wagner's Life and Music*. London: Thames and Hudson, 2001.

Nietzsche, Friedrich. *The Birth of Tragedy* and *The Case of Wagner*, trans. Walter Kaufmann. New York: Vintage Books, 1967.

Sabor, Rudolph. *Richard Wagner, Der Ring des Nibelungen: A Companion*. 5 vols. London: Phaidon Press, 1997.

Shaw, George Bernard. *The Perfect Wagnerite: A Commentary on the Nibelung's Ring* (1898); in Shaw, *Major Critical Essays*. London: Penguin, 1986.

Spencer, Stewart, and Barry Millington, ed. *Selected Letters of Richard Wagner*. New York: Norton, 1988.

Spotts, Frederic. *Bayreuth: A History of the Wagner Festival*. New Haven: Yale University Press, 1994.

Wagner, Richard. *My Life*, trans. Andrew Gray, ed. Mary Whittall. New York: Cambridge University Press, 1983.

———. *Wagner on Music and Drama: A Compendium of Richard Wagner's Prose Works*, ed. Albert Goldman and Evert Sprinchorn, trans. William Ashton Ellis. New York: Dutton, 1964. Reprint, New York: Da Capo Press, 1981.

Warrack, John. *Richard Wagner: Die Meistersinger von Nürnberg*. Cambridge: Cambridge University Press, 1994.

Weiner, Marc A. *Richard Wagner and the Anti-Semitic Imagination*. Lincoln: University of Nebraska Press, 1995.

Westernhagen, Curt. *The Forging of the 'Ring': Richard Wagner's Composition Sketches for Der Ring des Nibelungen*, trans. Arnold and Mary Whittall. Cambridge: Cambridge University Press, 1976.

Zimmerman, Elliott. *The First Hundred Years of Wagner's Tristan*. New York: Columbia University Press, 1964.

Chapter 43 Artist, Politician, Farmer (Class of 1813, II)

Budden, Julian. *The Operas of Verdi*. 3 vols. London: Oxford University Press, 1973–81.

Busch, Hans. *Verdi's Aida: The History of an Opera in Letters and Documents*. Minneapolis: University of Minnesota Press, 1978.

_____. *Verdi's Falstaff in Letters and Contemporary Reviews*. Bloomington: Indiana University Press, 1997.

_____. *Verdi's 'Otello' and 'Simon Boccanegra' (revised version) in Letters and Documents*. Oxford: Oxford University Press, 1988.

Conati, Marcello, ed. *Encounters with Verdi*, trans. Richard Stokes. Ithaca: Cornell University Press, 1984.

Hepokoski, James. *Giuseppe Verdi: Falstaff*. Cambridge: Cambridge University Press, 1983.

_____. *Giuseppe Verdi: Otello*. Cambridge: Cambridge University Press, 1987.

John, Nicholas, ed. *Falstaff*. English National Opera Guides. New York: Riverrun Press, 1982.

_____. *Otello*. English National Opera Guides. New York: Riverrun Press, 1981.

_____. *Rigoletto*. English National Opera Guides. New York: Riverrun Press, 1982.

_____. *La Traviata*. English National Opera Guides. New York: Riverrun Press, 1981.

_____. *Il Trovatore*. English National Opera Guides. New York: Riverrun Press, 1983.

Kimbell, David. *Verdi in the Age of Italian Romanticism*. Cambridge: Cambridge University Press, 1981.

Medici, M., and M. Conati. *The Verdi-Boito Correspondence*, ed. William Weaver. Chicago: University of Chicago Press, 1994

Osborne, Charles. *Verdi: A Life in the Theatre*. New York: Knopf, 1987.

Osborne, Charles, ed. *Letters of Giuseppe Verdi*. London: Victor Gollancz, 1971.

Parker, Roger. *'Arpa d'or': The Verdian Patriotic Chorus in the 1840s*. Parma: Istituto Nazionale di Studi Verdiani, 1998.

_____. *Leonora's Last Act: Essays in Verdian Discourse*. Princeton: Princeton University Press, 1997.

Phillips-Matz, Mary Jane. *Verdi: A Biography*. Oxford: Oxford University Press, 1993.

Weaver, William. *Verdi: A Documentary Study*. London: Thames and Hudson, 1977.

Weaver, William, and Martin Chusid, eds. *The Verdi Companion*. New York: Norton, 1979.

Werfel, Franz, and Paul Stefan. *Verdi: The Man in His Letters*, trans. Edward Downes. New York: Vienna House, 1973.

Chapter 44 Cutting Things Down to Size

Ashbrook, William. *The Complete Operas of Puccini*. Rev. ed., Oxford: Oxford University Press, 1985.

Ashbrook, William, and Harold Powers. *Puccini's Turandot: The End of the Great Tradition*. Princeton: Princeton University Press, 1991.

Brown, Malcolm H., ed. *Musorgsky: In Memoriam, 1881–1981*. Ann Arbor, Mich.: UMI Research Press, 1982.

Budden, Julian. *Puccini: His Life and Works*. New York: Oxford University Press, 2002.

Carner, Mosco. *Giacomo Puccini: Tosca*. Cambridge: Cambridge University Press, 1985.

_____. *Puccini: A Critical Biography*. 3rd ed., London: Holmes & Meier, 1992.

Crittenden, Camille. *Johann Strauss and Vienna: Operetta and the Politics of Popular Culture*. Cambridge: Cambridge University Press, 2000.

Emerson, Caryl. *The Life of Musorgsky*. Cambridge: Cambridge University Press, 1999.

Emerson, Caryl, and Robert W. Oldani. *Modest Musorgsky and Boris Godunov: Myths, Realities, Reconsiderations*. Cambridge: Cambridge University Press, 1994.

Faris, Alex. *Jacques Offenbach*. Boston: Faber and Faber, 1980.

Gartenberg, Egon. *Johann Strauss: The End of an Era*. University Park: Pennsylvania State University Press, 1974.

Girardi, Michele. *Puccini: His International Art*, trans. Laura Basini. Chicago: University of Chicago Press, 2000.

Groos, Arhur, and Roger Parker, eds. *Giacomo Puccini: La Bohème*. Cambridge: Cambridge University Press, 1986.

Harding, James. *Folies de Paris: The Rise and Fall of French Operetta*. London: Chappell, 1979.

_____. *Gounod*. New York: Stein and Day, 1973.

_____. *Jacques Offenbach: A Biography*. New York: Riverrun Press, 1980.

_____. *Massenet*. London: J. M. Dent, 1970.

Huebner, Steven. *The Operas of Charles Gounod*. Oxford: Oxford University Press, 1990.

Hughes, Gervase. *Composers of Operetta*. London: Macmillan, 1962.

Jacobs, Arthur. *Arthur Sullivan: A Victorian Musician*. Oxford: Oxford University Press, 1984.

John, Nicholas, ed. *Puccini: Madama Butterfly*. English National Opera Guides. New York: Riverrun Press, 1984.

_____. *Tchaikovsky: Eugene Onegin*. English National Opera Guides. New York: Riverrun Press, 1988.

Kemp, Peter. *The Strauss Family: Portrait of a Musical Dynasty*. 2nd ed., Tunbridge Wells: Seven Hills Books, 1989.

Leyda, Jay, and Sergei Bertensson, eds. *The Musorgsky Reader: A Life of M. P. Musorgsky in Letters and Documents*. New York: Norton, 1947.

Nicolaisen, Jay R. *Italian Opera in Transition, 1871–1893*. Ann Arbor, Mich.: UMI Research Press, 1980.

Orlova, Alexandra, ed. *Musorgsky Remembered*. Bloomington: Indiana University Press, 1991.

Phillips-Matz, Mary Jane. *Puccini: A Biography*. Boston: Northeastern University Press, 2002.

Puccini, Simonetta, and William Weaver. *The Puccini Companion*. Rev. ed., New York: Norton, 2000.

Taruskin, Richard. *Musorgsky: Eight Essays and an Epilogue*. Princeton: Princeton University Press, 1993.

Walsh, Thomas J. *Second-Empire Opera: The Théâtre-Lyrique, Paris, 1851–1870*. London: John Calder, 1981.

Wilson, Conrad. *Puccini*. London: Phaidon Press, 1997.

Chapter 45   The Return of the Symphony

Avins, Styra, ed. *Johannes Brahms: Life and Letters*. New York: Oxford University Press, 1997.

Bonds, Mark Evan. *After Beethoven: Imperatives of Originality in the Symphony*. Cambridge: Harvard University Press, 1996.

Brodbeck, David. *Brahms: Symphony No. 1*. Cambridge: Cambridge University Press, 1997.

Frisch, Walter. *Brahms and the Principle of Developing Variation*. Berkeley and Los Angeles: University of California Press, 1984.

_____ . *Brahms: The Four Symphonies*. New York: Schirmer, 1996.

Frisch, Walter, ed. *Brahms and His World*. Princeton: Princeton University Press, 1990.

Gál, Hans. *Schumann Orchestral Music*. BBC Music Guides. Seattle: University of Washington Press, 1979.

Geiringer, Karl. *Brahms: His Life and Work*. 3rd ed., New York: Da Capo Press, 1984.

Hancock, Virginia L. *Brahms's Choral Compositions and His Library of Early Music*. Ann Arbor, Mich.: UMI Research Press, 1983.

Hull, Kenneth, ed. *Johannes Brahms Symphony No. 4 in E Minor, op. 98*. Norton Critical Scores. New York: Norton, 2000.

Keys, Ivor. *Brahms Chamber Music*. Seattle: University of Washington Press, 1974.

Knapp, Raymond. *Brahms and the Challenge of the Symphony*. Stuyvesant, N.Y.: Pendragon, 1997.

Musgrave, Michael. *Brahms: A German Requiem*. Cambridge: Cambridge University Press, 1996.

_____ . *A Brahms Reader*. New Haven: Yale University Press, 2000.

Swafford, Jan. *Johannes Brahms*. New York: Knopf, 1997.

Chapter 46   The Symphony Goes (Inter)National

Abraham, Gerald, ed. *The Music of Tchaikovsky*. 2nd ed., New York: Norton, 1974.

Beckerman, Michael. *New Worlds of Dvořák*. New York: Norton, 2003.

Beckerman, Michael, ed. *Dvořák and His World*. Princeton: Princeton University Press, 1993.

Beveridge, David. *Rethinking Dvořák: Views from Five Countries*. Oxford: Oxford University Press, 1996.

Clapham, John. *Antonín Dvořák: Musician and Craftsman*. New York: St. Martin's Press, 1969.

_____ . *Dvořák*. New York: Norton, 1979.

Davies, Laurence. *César Franck and His Circle*. London: Barrie & Jenkins, 1970.

_____ . *Franck*. London: J. M. Dent, 1973.

D'Indy, Vincent. *César Franck* (1914). Reprint, New York: Dover Publications, 1965.

Doernberg, Erwin. *The Life and Symphonies of Anton Bruckner*. London: Barrie and Rockliff, 1960.

Garden, Edward, and Nigel Gotteri, eds. *"To My Best Friend": Correspondence between Tchaikovsky and Nadezhda von Meck, 1876–1878*. Oxford: Clarendon Press, 1993.

Gilman, Lawrence. *Edward MacDowell: A Study* (1908). Reprint, Boulder, Colo.: Perseus Books, 1969.

Harding, James. *Saint-Saëns and His Circle*. London: Chapman and Hall, 1965.

Jackson, Timothy L., and Paul Hawkshaw, eds. *Bruckner Studies*. Cambridge: Cambridge University Press, 1997.

Kearney, Leslie, ed. *Tchaikovsky and His World*. Princeton: Princeton University Press, 1998.

Layton, Robert. *Dvořák Symphonies and Concertos*. London: British Broadcasting Corporation, 1978.

Poznansky, Alexander. *Tchaikovsky: The Quest for the Inner Man*. New York: Schirmer, 1991.

Redlich, Hans. *Bruckner and Mahler*. Rev. ed., London: J. M. Dent, 1955.

Rees, Brian. *Camille Saint-Saëns: A Life*. London: Chatto and Windus, 1999.

Schönzeler, Hans Hubert. *Bruckner*. London: Calder and Boyars, 1970.

Simpson, Robert. *The Essence of Bruckner: An Essay towards the Understanding of His Music*. London: Victor Gollancz, 1967.

Smaczny, Jan. *Dvořák: Cello Concerto*. Cambridge: Cambridge University Press, 1999.

Šourek, Otakar. *Antonín Dvořák: Letters and Reminiscences*, trans. Roberta Samsour. Prague: Artaria, 1954. Reprint, New York: Da Capo Press, 1983.

Tchaikovsky, Modeste. *The Life and Letters of Peter Ilich Tchaikovsky*, ed. Rosa Newmarch. New York: Vienna House, 1973.

Tibbetts, J. C., ed. *Dvořák in America, 1892–1895*. Portland, Ore.: Amadeus Press, 1993.

Warrack, John. *Tchaikovsky*. London: Hamish Hamilton, 1973.

Watson, Derek. *Bruckner*. London: J. M. Dent, 1975.

Volumes 4–5: The Twentieth Century

General Sources

Adorno, Theodor W. *Quasi una Fantasia: Essays on Modern Music*, trans. Rodney Livingstone. New York: Norton, 1994.

Albright, Daniel. *Untwisting the Serpent: Modernism in Music, Literature, and Other Arts*. Chicago: University of Chicago Press, 2000.

Antokoletz, Elliott. *Twentieth-Century Music*. Englewood Cliffs, N.J.: Prentice Hall, 1992.

Austin, William W. *Music in the Twentieth Century*. New York: Norton, 1966.

Battcock, Gregory, ed. *Breaking the Sound Barrier: A Critical Anthology of the New Music*. New York: E. P. Dutton, 1981.

Burbank, Richard. *Twentieth-Century Music: A Chronology*. London: Thames and Hudson, 1984.

Cope, David H. *New Directions in Music.* 5th ed., Dubuque, Iowa: William C. Brown, 1989.

Gann, Kyle. *American Music in the Twentieth Century.* New York: Schirmer, 1997.

Hitchcock, H. Wiley. *Music in the United States.* 4th ed., Englewood Cliffs, N.J.: Prentice Hall, 1999.

Kallin, Anna, and Nicolas Nabokov, eds. *Twentieth-Century Composers.* 3 vols. Vol. I: Virgil Thomson, *American Music since 1910*; Vol. II: Hans Heinz Stuckenschmidt, *Germany and Central Europe*; Vol. III: Humphrey Searle and Robert Layton, *Britain, Scandinavia and the Netherlands.* New York: Holt, Rinehart and Winston, 1971–72.

Mitchell, Donald. *The Language of Modern Music.* London: Faber and Faber, 1963.

Morgan, Robert P. *Twentieth-Century Music.* New York: Norton, 1991.

Salzman, Eric. *Twentieth-Century Music: An Introduction.* 4th ed., Englewood Cliffs, N.J.: Prentice Hall, 2001.

Schwartz, Elliott, and Barney Childs, eds. *Contemporary Composers on Contemporary Music.* New York: Holt, Rinehart and Winston, 1967. Expanded ed., New York: Da Capo, 1998.

Schwartz, Elliot, and Daniel Godfrey, eds. *Music since 1945: Issues, Materials, and Literature.* New York: Schirmer, 1993.

Sheppard, W. Anthony. *Revealing Masks: Exotic Influences and Ritualized Performance in Modernist Music Theater.* Berkeley and Los Angeles: University of California Press, 2001.

Simms, Bryan R. *Music of the Twentieth Century: Style and Structure.* New York: Schirmer, 1986.

Simms, Bryan R., ed. *Composers on Modern Musical Culture.* New York: Schirmer, 1999.

Slonimsky, Nicolas. *Music since 1900.* 4th ed., New York: Scribners, 1971.

——. *Supplement to Music since 1900.* New York: Scribners, 1986.

Vinton, John, ed. *Dictionary of Contemporary Music.* New York: E. P. Dutton, 1971.

Watkins, Glenn. *Pyramids at the Louvre: Music, Culture, and Collage from Stravinsky to the Postmodernists.* Cambridge: Harvard University Press, 1994.

——. *Soundings: Music in the Twentieth Century.* New York: Schirmer, 1988.

Whittall, Arnold. *Exploring Twentieth-Century Music: Tradition and Innovation.* Cambridge: Cambridge University Press, 2003.

——. *Musical Composition in the Twentieth Century.* Oxford: Oxford University Press, 1999.

Yates, Peter. *Twentieth-Century Music.* New York: Pantheon Books, 1967.

Chapter 47   Reaching (for) Limits

Adorno, Theodor W. *Mahler: A Musical Physiognomy*, trans. Edmund Jephcott. Chicago: University of Chicago Press, 1992.

Bauer-Lechner, Natalie. *Recollections of Gustav Mahler*, ed. Peter Franklin, trans. Dika Newlin. Cambridge: Cambridge University Press, 1980.

Blaukopf, Herta, ed. *Gustav Mahler, Richard Strauss: Correspondence, 1888–1911*, trans. Edmund Jephcott. Chicago: University of Chicago Press, 1984.

Blaukopf, Kurt, ed. *Mahler: A Documentary Study*. New York: Oxford University Press, 1976.

Butler, Christopher. *Early Modernism: Literature, Music and Painting in Europe, 1900–1914*. Oxford: Clarendon Press, 1994.

Dahlhaus, Carl. *Between Romanticism and Modernism*, trans. Mary Whittall. Berkeley and Los Angeles: University of California Press, 1980.

De la Grange, Henri-Louis. *Gustav Mahler: Vienna: The Years of Challenge (1897–1904)*. Oxford: Oxford University Press, 1995.

_____. *Gustav Mahler: Vienna, Triumph and Disillusion (1904–1907)*. Oxford: Oxford University Press, 2000.

Del Mar, Norman. *Richard Strauss: A Critical Commentary on His Life and Works*. 3 vols. Ithaca: Cornell University Press, 1986.

Floros, Constantin. *Gustav Mahler: The Symphonies*, trans. Vernon Wicker. Portland, Ore.: Amadeus Press, 1993.

Franklin, Peter R. *The Life of Mahler*. Cambridge: Cambridge University Press, 1997.

_____. *Mahler: Symphony No. 3*. Cambridge: Cambridge University Press, 1991.

Frisch, Walter. *The Early Works of Arnold Schoenberg, 1893–1908*. Berkeley and Los Angeles: University of California Press, 1993.

Gilliam, Brian. *The Life of Richard Strauss*. Cambridge: Cambridge University Press, 1999.

_____. *Richard Strauss's 'Elektra.'* Oxford: Oxford University Press, 1991.

_____. *Richard Strauss: New Perspectives on the Composer and His Work*. Chapel Hill: University of North Carolina Press, 1992.

Gilliam, Brian, ed. *Richard Strauss and His World*. Princeton: Princeton University Press, 1992.

Hartmann, Rudolf. *Richard Strauss: The Staging of His Operas and Bellets*. New York: Oxford University Press, 1981.

Jefferson, Alan. *Richard Strauss: Der Rosenkavalier*. Cambridge: Cambridge University Press, 1986.

Kennedy, Michael. *Mahler*. London: J. M. Dent, 1974.

_____. *Richard Strauss: Man, Musician, Enigma*. Cambridge: Cambridge University Press, 1999.

_____. *Strauss Tone Poems*. London: British Broadcasting Corporation, 1984.

Kravitt, Edward F. *The Lied: Mirror of Late Romanticism*. New Haven: Yale University Press, 1996.

Lebrecht, Norman, ed. *Mahler Remembered*. New York: Norton, 1987.

Mahler, Alma. *Gustav Mahler: Memories and Letters*, trans. Basil Creighton, ed. Donald Mitchell. London: J. Murray, 1973.

Mann, William. *Richard Strauss: A Critical Study of the Operas*. London: Cassell, 1964.

Martner, Knud, ed. *Selected Letters of Gustav Mahler*, trans. Eithne Wilkins, Ernest Kaiser, and Bill Hopkins. New York: Farrar, Straus and Giroux, 1979.

Mitchell, Donald. *Gustav Mahler: The Early Years*. Rev. ed., London: Boydell Press, 2003.

_____. *Gustav Mahler: Songs and Symphonies of Life and Death. Interpretations and Annotations*. Rev. ed., London: Boydell Press, 2002.

_____ . *Gustav Mahler: The Wunderhorn Years*. 3rd ed., London: Boydell Press, 2004.

Myers, Rollo, ed. *Richard Strauss and Romain Rolland: Correspondence*. Berkeley and Los Angeles: University of California Press, 1968.

Painter, Karen, ed. *Gustav Mahler and His World*. Princeton: Princeton University Press, 2002.

Puffett, Derrick. ed. *Richard Strauss: Elektra*. Cambridge: Cambridge University Press, 1990.

_____ . *Richard Strauss: Salome*. Cambridge: Cambridge University Press, 1989.

Roman, Zoltan. *Gustav Mahler's American Years, 1907–1911: A Documentary History*. Stuyvesant, N.Y.: Pendragon Press, 1989.

Samson, Jim. *Music in Transition*. London: J. M. Dent, 1977.

Samuels, Robert. *Mahler's Sixth Symphony: A Study in Musical Semiotics*. Cambridge: Cambridge University Press, 1995.

Schorske, Carl. *Fin-de-siècle Vienna: Politics and Culture*. New York: Random House, 1980.

Strauss, Richard. *The Correspondence between Richard Strauss and Hugo von Hoffmansthal*, trans. Hanns Hammelmann and Ewald Osers. London: Collins, 1961.

_____ . *Recollections and Reflections*, ed. Willi Schuh, trans. L. J. Lawrence. London: Boosey & Hawkes, 1953.

Wilhelm, Kurt. *Richard Strauss: An Intimate Portrait*. London: Thames & Hudson, 1989.

Williamson, John. *Strauss: 'Also Sprach Zarathustra.'* Cambridge: Cambridge University Press, 1993.

Chapter 48   Getting Rid of Glue

Austin, William W., ed. *Debussy: Prelude to "The Afternoon of a Faun."* Norton Critical Scores. New York: Norton, 1970.

Brody, Elaine. *Paris: The Musical Kaleidoscope, 1870–1925*. New York: George Braziller, 1987.

Debussy, Claude-Achille. *Letters*, ed. François Lesure and Roger Nichols, trans. Roger Nichols. Cambridge: Harvard University Press, 1987.

Fulcher, Jane. *Debussy and His World*. Princeton: Princeton University Press, 2001.

_____ . *French Cultural Politics and Music from the Dreyfus Affair to the First World War*. New York: Oxford University Press, 1999.

Gillmor, Alan M. *Erik Satie*. Boston: Twayne, 1988.

Grayson, David. *The Genesis of Debussy's Pelléas et Mélisande*. Ann Arbor, Mich.: UMI Research Press, 1986.

Harding, James. *Erik Satie*. London: Secker and Warburg, 1975.

Holloway, Robin. *Debussy and Wagner*. London: Eulenburg Books, 1979.

Huebner, Steven. *French Opera at the 'Fin de Siècle': Wagnerism, Nationalism, and Style*. Oxford: Oxford University Press, 1999.

Jarocinski, Stefan. *Debussy, Impressionism and Symbolism*, trans. Rollo Myers. London: Eulenburg Books, 1976.

Koechlin, Charles. *Gabriel Fauré*, trans. L. Orrey (1946). New York: AMS Press, 1976.

Lesure, François, ed. *Debussy on Music*, trans. Richard Langham Smith. Ithaca: Cornell University Press, 1988.

Lockspeiser, Edward. *Debussy: His Life and Mind*. 2 vols. Cambridge: Cambridge University Press, 1962.

Mawer, Deborah. *The Cambridge Companion to Ravel*. Cambridge: Cambridge University Press, 2000.

Meister, Barbara. *Nineteenth-Century French Song: Fauré, Chausson, Duparc, and Debussy*. Bloomington: Indiana University Press, 1980.

Myers, Rollo. *Emmanuel Chabrier and His Circle*. London: J. M. Dent, 1969.

_____. *Erik Satie*. London: Dobson, 1948.

_____. *Modern French Music: Its Evolution and Cultural Background from 1900 to the Present Day*. Oxford: Oxford University Press, 1971.

Nectoux, Jean-Michel. *Gabriel Fauré: A Musical Life*, trans. Roger Nichols. Cambridge: Cambridge University Press, 1991.

Nectoux, Jean-Michel, ed. *Gabriel Fauré: His Life through His Letters*, trans. J. A. Underwood. St. Paul, Minn.: Consortium Book Sales, 1984.

Nichols, Roger, ed. *Claude Debussy: Pelléas et Mélisande*. Cambridge: Cambridge University Press, 1989.

_____. *Debussy Remembered*. Portland, Oreg.: Amadeus Press, 1992.

_____. *The Life of Debussy*. Cambridge: Cambridge University Press, 1998.

_____. *Ravel Remembered*. New York: Norton, 1988.

Noske, Frits. *French Song from Berlioz to Duparc*, revised by Frits Noske and Rita Benton, trans. Rita Benton. 2nd ed., New York: Dover Publications, 1970.

Orledge, Robert. *Debussy and the Theatre*. Cambridge: Cambridge University Press, 1982.

_____. *Gabriel Fauré*. London: Eulenberg Books, 1979.

_____. *Satie the Composer*. Cambridge: Cambridge University Press, 1990.

Orledge, Robert, ed. *Satie Remembered*. Portland, Ore.: Amadeus Press, 1995.

Ornstein, Arbie. *Ravel: Man and Musician*. New York: Columbia University Press, 1975.

Ornstein, Arbie, ed. *A Ravel Reader: Correspondence, Articles, Interviews*. New York: Columbia University Press, 1990.

Roland-Manuel, Alexis. *Maurice Ravel*, trans. C. Jolly. London: Dennis Dobson, 1947.

Shattuck, Roger. *The Banquet Years*. New York: Random House, 1955.

Stuckenschmidt, Hans Heinz. *Maurice Ravel: Variations on His Life*, trans. Samuel R. Rosenbaum. Philadelphia: Chilton Books, 1968.

Trezise, Simon. *The Cambridge Companion to Debussy*. Cambridge: Cambridge University Press, 2003.

Volta, Ornella. *Satie: His World through His Letters*, trans. Michael Bullock. London: Marion Boyars, 1989.

Vuillermoz, Émile. *Gabriel Fauré*. Philadelphia: Chilton Books, 1969.

Whiting, Steven Moore. *Satie the Bohemian: From Cabaret to Concert Hall*. Oxford: Oxford University Press, 1999.

Wilkins, Nigel, ed. *The Writings of Erik Satie*. London: Eulenburg Books, 1980.

Chapter 49   Aristocratic Maximalism

Asafiev, Boris. *A Book about Stravinsky* (1929), trans. Richard F. French. Ann Arbor, Mich.: UMI Research Press, 1982.

Cross, Jonathan, ed. *The Cambridge Companion to Stravinsky*. Cambridge: Cambridge University Press, 2003.

Druskin, Mikhail. *Igor Stravinsky: His Personality, Works, and Views* (1974), trans. Martin Cooper. Cambridge: Cambridge University Press, 1983.

Garafola, Lynn. *Diaghilev's Ballets Russes*. New York: Oxford University Press, 1989.

Guest, Ivor. *The Romantic Ballet in Paris*. Middletown, Conn.: Wesleyan University Press, 1966.

Hill, Peter. *Stravinsky: The Rite of Spring*. Cambridge: Cambridge University Press, 2000.

Kochno, Boris. *Diaghilev and the Ballets Russes*. New York: Harper & Row, 1970.

Lederman, Minna, ed. *Stravinsky in the Theatre*. New York: Pellegrini and Cudahy, 1949.

Press, Stephen D. *Prokofiev's Ballets for Diaghilev*. Aldershot: Ashgate, 2004.

Roslavleva, Natalia Petrovna. *Era of the Russian Ballet*. New York: Da Capo Press, 1979.

Schouvaloff, Alexander, and Victor Borovsky. *Stravinsky on Stage*. London: Stainer and Bell, 1982.

Searle, Humphrey. *Ballet Music*. 2nd ed., New York: Dover Publications, 1973.

Smith, Marian. *Ballet and Opera in the Age of Giselle*. Princeton: Princeton University Press, 2000.

Stravinsky, Igor, and Robert Craft. *Dialogues and a Diary*. Garden City, N.Y.: Doubleday, 1963.

———. *Expositions and Developments*. Garden City, N.Y.: Doubleday, 1962.

———. *Memories and Commentaries*. Garden City, N.Y.: Doubleday, 1960.

———. *Retrospectives and Conclusions*. New York: Knopf, 1969.

———. *Themes and Episodes*. New York: Knopf, 1966.

Stravinsky, Vera, and Robert Craft. *Stravinsky in Pictures and Documents*. New York: Simon and Schuster, 1978.

Taruskin, Richard. *Stravinsky and the Russian Traditions*. Berkeley and Los Angeles: University of California Press, 1996.

Van den Toorn, Pieter. *The Music of Igor Stravinsky*. New Haven: Yale University Press, 1983.

———. *Stravinsky and "The Rite of Spring": The Beginnings of a Musical Language*. Berkeley and Los Angeles: University of California Press, 1987.

Vershinina, Irina. *Stravinsky's Early Ballets*, trans. L. G. Heien. Ann Arbor, Mich.: UMI Research Press, 1989.

Walsh, Stephen. *The Music of Stravinsky*. London: Routledge and Kegan Paul, 1988.

———. *Stravinsky: A Creative Spring: Russia and France, 1882–1934*. New York: Knopf, 1999.

White, Eric Walter. *Stravinsky: The Composer and His Works*. 2nd ed., Berkeley and Los Angeles: University of California Press, 1979.

Wiley, Roland John. *Tchaikovsky's Ballets*. Rev. ed., Oxford: Clarendon Press, 1991.

Chapter 50   Extinguishing the "Petty 'I'" (Transcendentalism, I)

Baker, James. *The Music of Alexander Scriabin*. New Haven: Yale University Press, 1986.

Bowers, Faubion. *Scriabin: a Biography of the Russian Composer, 1871–1915*. Tokyo and Palo Alto, Calif.: Kodansha International, 1969.

Griffiths, Paul. *Olivier Messiaen and the Music of Time*. Ithaca, N.Y.: Cornell University Press, 1985.

Hill, Peter, ed. *The Messiaen Companion*. London: Faber & Faber, 1995.

Johnson, Robert Sherlaw. *Messiaen*. London: J. M. Dent, 1975.

Messiaen, Olivier. *Music and Color: Conversations with Claude Samuel*, trans. E. T. Glasgow. Portland, Oreg.: Amadeus Press, 1994.

_____. *The Technique of My Musical Language*, trans. John Satterfield. Paris: Leduc, 1957.

Morrison, Simon. *Russian Opera and the Symbolist Movement*. Berkeley and Los Angeles: University of California Press, 2002.

Nichols, Roger. *Messiaen*. London: Oxford University Press, 1975.

Pople, Anthony. *Messiaen: Quatuor pour la fin du temps*. Cambridge: Cambridge University Press, 1998.

Rischin, Rebecca. *For the End of Time: The Story of the Messiaen Quartet*. Ithaca, N.Y.: Cornell University Press, 2003.

Roberts, Peter D. *Modernism in Russian Piano Music: Skriabin, Prokofiev and Their Contemporaries*. Bloomington: Indiana University Press, 1993.

Schloezer, Boris de. *Skryabin: Artist and Mystic*, trans. Nicolas Slonimsky. Berkeley and Los Angeles: University of California Press, 1987.

Scott, Cyril. *Music: Its Secret Influence throughout the Ages* (1933). Rev. ed., New York: Samuel Weiser, 1976.

Chapter 51   Containing Multitudes (Transcendentalism, II)

Block, Geoffrey. *Ives: Concord Sonata*. Cambridge: Cambridge University Press, 1996.

Burkholder, J. Peter. *All Made of Tunes: Charles Ives and the Uses of Musical Borrowing*. New Haven: Yale University Press, 1965.

_____. *Charles Ives: The Ideas behind the Music*. New Haven: Yale University Press, 1985.

Burkholder, J. Peter, ed. *Charles Ives and His World*. Princeton: Princeton University Press, 1996.

Cowell, Henry. *New Musical Resources*. New York: Knopf, 1930.

Feder, Stuart. *Charles Ives: "My Father's Song": A Psychoanalytic Biography*. New Haven: Yale University Press, 1992.

_____. *The Life of Charles Ives*. Cambridge: Cambridge University Press, 1999.

Hicks, Michael. *Henry Cowell: Bohemian*. Urbana: University of Illinois Press, 2002.

Higgins, Dick, ed. *Essential Cowell: Selected Writings on Music by Henry Cowell, 1921–1964*. Kingston, N.Y.: McPherson, 2002.

Hisama, Ellie M. *Gendering Musical Modernism: The Music of Ruth Crawford, Marion Bauer, and Miriam Gideon*. Cambridge: Cambridge University Press, 2001.

Hitchcock, H. Wiley. *Ives*. London: Oxford University Press, 1977.

Ives, Charles. *Essays before a Sonata, The Majority, and Other Writings*, ed. Howard Boatwright. New York: Norton, 1970.

———. *Memos*, ed. John Kirkpatrick. New York: Norton, 1972.

Mead, Rita H. *Henry Cowell's New Music, 1925–1936: The Society, the Music Edition, and the Recordings*. Ann Arbor, Mich.: UMI Research Press, 1981.

Miller, Leta E., and Fredric Lieberman. *Lou Harrison: Composing a World*. New York: Oxford University Press, 1998.

Nicholls, David. *American Experimental Music, 1890–1940*. Cambridge: Cambridge University Press, 1990.

Nicholls, David, ed. *The Whole World of Music: A Henry Cowell Symposium*. Amsterdam: Harwood Academic Publishers, 1997.

Oja, Carol. *Making Music Modern: New York in the 1920s*. New York: Oxford University Press, 2000.

Perlis, Vivian, ed. *Charles Ives Remembered: An Oral History*. New York: Norton, 1976.

Rich, Alan. *American Pioneers: Ives to Cage and Beyond*. London: Phaidon Press, 1995.

Rossiter, Frank. *Charles Ives and His America*. New York: Liveright, 1975.

Saylor, Bruce, and William Lichtenwanger, eds. *The Writings of Henry Cowell*. Brooklyn, N.Y.: Institute for Studies in American Music, 1986.

Swafford, Jan. *Charles Ives: A Life with Music*. New York: Norton, 1996.

Tick, Judith. *Ruth Crawford Seeger, a Composer's Search for American Music*. New York: Oxford University Press, 1997.

Ziffrin, Marilyn J. *Carl Ruggles: Composer, Painter and Storyteller*. Urbana: University of Illinois Press, 1994.

Chapter 52   Inner Occurrences (Transcendentalism, III)

Auner, Joseph. *A Schoenberg Reader: Documents of a Life*. New Haven: Yale University Press, 2003.

Behr, Shulamith, David Fanning, and Douglas Jarman, eds. *Expressionism Reassessed*. Manchester: Palgrave-Macmillan, 1994.

Brand, Juliane, and Christopher Hailey, eds. *Constructive Dissonance: Arnold Schoenberg and the Transformations of Twentieth-Century Culture*. Berkeley and Los Angeles: University of California Press, 1997.

Crawford, John C., and Dorothy L. Crawford. *Expressionism in Twentieth-Century Music*. Bloomington: Indiana University Press, 1993.

Dahlhaus, Carl. *Schoenberg and the New Music*, trans. Derrick Puffett and Alfred Clayton. Cambridge: Cambridge University Press, 1987.

Dale, Catherine. *Tonality and Structure in Schoenberg's Second String Quartet, op. 10*. New York: Garland Publishing, 1993.

Forte, Allen. *The Atonal Music of Anton Webern*. New Haven: Yale University Press, 1998.

Hahl-Koch, Jelena. *Arnold Schoenberg and Wassily Kandinsky: Letters, Pictures and Documents*. London: Faber & Faber, 1984.

Hicken, Kenneth L. *Aspects of Harmony in Schoenberg's Six Little Piano Pieces, op. 19*. Winnipeg: Robert P. Frye and Co., 1984.

Lessem, Alan Philip. *Music and Text in the Works of Arnold Schoenberg: The Critical Years, 1908–1922.* Ann Arbor, Mich.: UMI Research Press, 1982.

Newlin, Dika. *Bruckner, Mahler, Schoenberg.* Rev. ed., New York: Norton, 1978.

Reich, Willi. *Arnold Schoenberg: A Critical Biography,* trans. Leo Black. London: Longman, 1971.

Reti, Rudolf. *Tonality, Atonality, Pantonality: A Study of Some Trends in Twentieth-Century Music.* New York: Macmillan, 1958.

Ringer, Alexander. *Arnold Schoenberg: The Composer as Jew.* Oxford: Oxford University Press, 1990.

Rosen, Charles. *Arnold Schoenberg.* Baltimore, Md.: Penguin USA, 1975.

Schoenberg, Arnold. *Letters,* ed. Erwin Stein, trans. Eithne Wilkins and Ernst Kaiser. London: Faber & Faber, 1964.

_____. *Style and Idea,* trans. Leo Black. 2nd ed., Berkeley and Los Angeles: University of California Press, 1975.

_____. *Style and Idea: Selected Writings of Arnold Schoenberg,* ed. Leonard Stein, trans. Leo Black. Expanded ed., Berkeley and Los Angeles: University of California Press, 1984.

_____. *Theory of Harmony (Harmonielehre, 1911),* trans. Roy E. Carter. Berkeley and Los Angeles: University of California Press, 1978.

Shawn, Allen. *Arnold Schoenberg's Journey.* New York: Farrar Straus & Giroux, 2002.

Simms, Bryan. *The Atonal Music of Arnold Schoenberg.* New York: Oxford University Press, 2000.

Smith, Joan Allen. *Schoenberg and His Circle: A Viennese Portrait.* New York: Schirmer, 1986.

Stuckenschmidt, Hans Heinz. *Arnold Schoenberg: His Life, World, and Work,* trans. Humphrey Searle. London: Calder, 1977.

Chapter 53   Socially Validated Maximalism

Antokoletz, Elliot, *The Music of Béla Bartók: A Study of Tonality and Progression in Twentieth-Century Music.* Berkeley and Los Angeles: University of California Press, 1984.

Beckerman, Michael. *Janáček as Theorist.* Stuyvesant, N.Y.: Pendragon Press, 1994.

Beckerman, Michael, ed. *Janáček and His World.* Princeton: Princeton University Press, 2003.

Bellman, Jonathan. *The Style Hongrois in the Music of Western Europe.* Boston: Northeastern University Press, 1993.

Eösze, László. *Zoltán Kodály: His Life and Work,* trans. Istvan Farkas and Gyula Gulyas. London: Collet's, 1962.

Evans, Michael. *Janáček's Tragic Operas.* London: Faber and Faber, 1977.

Frigyesi, Judit. *Béla Bartók and Turn-of-the-Century Budapest.* Berkeley and Los Angeles: University of California Press, 1998.

Gillies, Malcolm, ed. *The Bartók Companion.* London: Faber & Faber, 1994.

_____. *Bartók Remembered.* London: Faber & Faber, 1990.

Horsbrugh, Ian. *Leoš Janáček: The Field That Prospered.* Newton Abbot and London: David & Charles, 1981.

Janáček, Leoš. *Leaves from His Life*, ed. and trans. Vilem and Margaret Tausky. London: Kahn and Averill, 1982.

_____. *Letters and Reminiscences*, ed. Bohumir Stedron, trans. Geraldine Thomsen. Prague: Artia, 1955.

Kodály, Zoltán. *Folk Music of Hungary*, trans. Ronald Tempest and Cynthia Jolly. 2nd ed., London: Barrie & Jenkins, 1971.

Laki, Peter. *Bartók and His World*. Princeton: Princeton University Press, 1995.

Leafstedt, Carl S. *Inside Bluebeard's Castle: Music and Drama in Béla Bartók's Opera*. New York: Oxford University Press, 1999.

Legány, Dezso. *Liszt and His Country*, trans. G. Gulyas. Budapest: Corvina Press, 1976.

Lendvai, Ernő. *Béla Bartók: An Analysis of His Music*. London: Kahn and Averill, 1971.

_____. *Symmetries of Music*, ed. M. Szábo and M. Mohay. Kecskemét, 1993.

_____. *The Workshop of Bartók and Kodály*. Budapest: Editio Musica, 1983.

Sárosi, Bálint. *Gypsy Music*, trans. F. Macnicol. Budapest: Corvina Press, 1971.

Somfai, László. *Béla Bartók: Composition, Concepts, and Autograph Sources*. Berkeley and Los Angeles: University of California Press, 1996.

Stevens, Halsey. *The Life and Music of Béla Bartók*, ed. Malcolm Gillies. 3rd ed., Oxford: Oxford University Press, 1993.

Suchoff, Benjamin, ed. *Béla Bartók's Essays*. New York: St. Martin's Press, 1976.

Szabolcsi, Bence. *A Concise History of Hungarian Music*, trans. Sára Karig. Rev. ed., Budapest: Corvina Press, 1974.

Tallián, Tibor. *Béla Bartók: The Man and His Work*. Budapest: Corvina, 1981.

Tyrrell, John. *Janáček's Operas: A Documentary Account*. London: Faber & Faber, 1992.

Tyrrell, John, ed. *Janáček: Kat'a Kabanova*. Cambridge: Cambridge University Press, 1982.

Walsh, Stephen. *Bartók's Chamber Music*. London: British Broadcasting Corporation, 1982.

Chapter 54   Pathos Is Banned

Andriessen, Louis, and Elmer Schönberger. *The Apollonian Clockwork: On Stravinsky*, trans. Jeff Hamburg. Oxford: Oxford University Press, 1989.

Boehm, Gottfried, Ulrich Mosch, and Katharina Schmidt, eds. *Canto d'Amore: Classicism in Modern Art and Music, 1914–1935*. London: Merrell Holberton, 1996.

Carr, Maureen A. *Multiple Masks: Neoclassicism in Stravinsky's Works on Greek Subjects*. Lincoln: University of Nebraska Press, 2002.

Cocteau, Jean. *A Call to Order*, trans. Rollo H. Myers. London: Faber and Gwyer, 1926.

Daviau, Donald G., and George J. Buelow. *The "Ariadne auf Naxos" of Hugo von Hofmannsthal and Richard Strauss*. Chapel Hill: University of North Carolina Press, 1975.

Dunsby, Jonathan. *Schoenberg: Pierrot Lunaire*. Cambridge: Cambridge University Press, 1992.

Forsyth, Karen. *'Ariadne auf Naxos' by Hugo von Hofmannsthal and Richard Strauss: Its Genesis and Meaning*. London: Oxford University Press, 1982.

Lambert, Constant. *Music Ho!* London: Faber and Faber, 1934.

Levitz, Tamara. *Teaching New Classicality: Ferruccio Busoni's Master Class in Composition.* Frankfurt: Peter Lang, 1996.

Messing, Scott. *Neoclassicism in Music from the Genesis of the Concept through the Schoenberg/Stravinsky Polemic.* Ann Arbor, Mich.: UMI Research Press, 1988.

Oja, Carol J. ed. *Stravinsky in "Modern Music," 1924–1946.* New York: Da Capo Press, 1982.

Stravinsky, Igor. *An Autobiography (Chroniques de ma vie, 1935–36).* New York: Norton, 1962.

——. *Poetics of Music in the Form of Six Lessons* (1939), trans. Arthur Knodel and Ingolf Dahl. New York: Knopf, 1960.

Watkins, Glenn. *Proof through the Night: Music and the Great War.* Berkeley and Los Angeles: University of California Press, 2003.

Chapter 55   Lost—or Rejected—Illusions

Appel, David H., ed. *Prokofiev by Prokofiev,* trans. Guy Daniels. New York: Doubleday, 1979.

Bazelon, Irwin. *Knowing the Score: Notes on Film Music.* New York: Van Nostrand Reinhold, 1975.

Bertensson, Sergei, and Jay Leyda. *Sergei Rachmaninoff.* New York: New York University Press, 1956.

Betz, Albrecht. *Hanns Eisler: Political Musician,* trans. Bill Hopkins. Cambridge: Cambridge University Press, 1982.

Cook, Susan. *Opera during the Weimar Republic: The "Zeitopern" of Ernst Krenek, Kurt Weill, and Paul Hindemith.* Ann Arbor, Mich.: UMI Research Press, 1989.

Culshaw, John. *Sergei Rachmaninov.* London: Dobson, 1949.

Drew, David. *Kurt Weill: A Handbook.* Berkeley and Los Angeles: University of California Press, 1987.

Eisler, Hanns. *A Rebel in Music: Selected Writings,* ed. Manfred Grabs, trans. Marjorie Meyer. New York: International Publishers, 1978.

Eisler, Hanns, and Theodor W. Adorno. *Composing for the Films* (1947). London: Athlone Press, 1994.

Flinn, Caryl. *Strains of Utopia: Gender, Nostalgia, and Hollywood Film Music.* Princeton: Princeton University Press, 1992.

Gorbman, Claudia. *Unheard Melodies: Narrative Film Music.* Bloomington: Indiana University Press, 1987.

Hinton, Stephen. *The Idea of Gebrauchsmusik: A Study of Musical Aesthetics in the Weimar Republic (1919–1933) with Particular Reference to the Works of Paul Hindemith.* New York: Garland Publishing, Inc., 1989.

——. *Kurt Weill: The Threepenny Opera.* Cambridge: Cambridge University Press, 1990.

Jarman, Douglas. *Alban Berg: Wozzeck.* Cambridge: Cambridge University Press, 1989.

——. *Kurt Weill: An Illustrated Biography.* Bloomington: Indiana University Press, 1982.

Kemp, Ian. *Paul Hindemith.* London: Oxford University Press, 1970.

Kowalke, Kim H. *Kurt Weill in Europe.* Ann Arbor, Mich.: UMI Research Press, 1979.

Neumeyer, David. *The Music of Paul Hindemith*. New Haven: Yale University Press, 1986.

Nice, David. *Prokofiev — A Biography: From Russia to the West, 1891–1935*. New Haven: Yale University Press, 2003.

Norris, Geoffrey. *Rakhmaninov*. 2nd ed., revised, New York: Oxford University Press, 2001.

Palmer, Christopher. *The Composer in Hollywood*. London: Marion Boyars, 1990.

Perle, George. *The Operas of Alban Berg*, Vol. I: *Wozzeck*. Berkeley and Los Angeles: University of California Press, 1980.

Prendergast, Roy M. *Film Music: A Neglected Art*. New York: Norton, 1977.

Schmalfeldt, Janet. *Berg's "Wozzeck."* New Haven: Yale University Press, 1983.

Skelton, Geoffrey. *Paul Hindemith: The Man behind the Music*. New York: Crescendo, 1975.

Stewart, John L. *Ernst Krenek: The Man and His Music*. Berkeley and Los Angeles: University of California Press, 1991.

Thomas, Tony. *Music for the Movies*. Cranbury, N.J.: A. S. Barnes, 1973.

Chapter 56   The Cult of the Commonplace

Axsom, Richard H. *Parade: Cubism as Theatre*. New York: Garland Publishing, 1979.

Buckland, Sidney, and Myriam Chimènes, eds. *Francis Poulenc: Music, Art, and Literature*. Aldershot: Ashgate, 1999.

Clair, René. *A nous la liberté and Entr'acte: Classic Film Scripts*. London: Lorimer, 1970.

Collaer, Paul. *Darius Milhaud*. San Francisco: San Francisco Press, 1988.

Daniel, Keith W. *Francis Poulenc: His Artistic Development and Musical Style*. Ann Arbor, Mich.: UMI Research Press, 1982.

Drake, Jeremy. *The Operas of Darius Milhaud*. New York: Garland Publishing, 1989.

Harding, James. *The Ox on the Roof: Scenes from Musical Life in Paris in the Twenties*. London: Macdonald, 1972.

Mellers, Wilfrid. *Poulenc*. Oxford: Oxford University Press, 1993.

Milhaud, Darius. *Notes without Music*, trans. Donald Evans. London: Dobson, 1952. Rev. ed. (titled *My Happy Life*), ed. Rollo H. Myers. London: Calder & Boyers, 1967.

Perloff, Nancy. *Art and the Everyday: Popular Entertainment and the Circle of Erik Satie*. Oxford: Oxford University Press, 1991.

Poulenc, Francis. *Diary of My Songs*, trans. Winifred Radford. London: Gollancz, 1985.

_____ . *Echo and Source: Selected Correspondence 1918–1963*, ed. Sidney Buckland. London: Trafalgar Square, 1991.

_____ . *My Friends and Myself*, trans. James Harding. London: Dobson, 1978.

Rostand, Claude. *French Music Today* [*La Musique française contemporaine*, 1952], trans. Henry Marx. New York: Merlin Press, 1955.

Shead, Richard. *Music in the 1920s*. New York: St. Martin's Press, 1976.

Thomson, Virgil. *Virgil Thomson by Virgil Thomson*. New York: Knopf, 1966.

Watson, Steven. *Prepare for Saints: Gertrude Stein, Virgil Thomson, and the Mainstreaming of American Modernism*. New York: Random House, 1998.

Chapter 57 In Search of the "Real" America

Alpert, Hollis. *The Life and Times of Porgy and Bess: The Story of an American Classic*. New York: Random House, 1990.

Berger, Arthur. *Aaron Copland: This Work and Contribution to American Music*. New York: Oxford University Press, 1955.

Copland, Aaron, and Vivian Perlis. *Copland: 1900 through 1942*. New York: St. Martin's Press, 1984.

Cowell, Henry. *American Composers on American Music: A Symposium*. New York: Ungar, 1933. Reprint, Palo Alto: Stanford University Press, 1962.

Gordon, Eric A. *Mark the Music: The Life and Work of Marc Blitzstein*, New York: St. Martin's Press, 1989.

Heyman, Barbara. *Samuel Barber: The Composer and His Music*. New York: Oxford University Pres, 1992.

Jablonski, Edward. *Gershwin: A Biography*. Rev. ed., New York: Da Capo Press, 1998.

_____. *Gershwin Remembered*. Portland, Ore.: Amadeus Press, 1992.

Jablonski, Edward, and Lawrence D. Stewart. *The Gershwin Years: George and Ira*. Rev. ed., New York: Da Capo Press, 1996.

Levy, Alan Howard. *Musical Nationalism: American Composers' Search for Identity*. Westport, Conn.: Greenwood Press, 1983.

Mason, Daniel Gregory. *Tune In, America: A Study of Our Coming Musical Independence* (1931). Freeport, N.Y.: Books for Libraries Press, 1969.

Moore, Macdonald Smith. *Yankee Blues: Musical Culture and American Identity*. Bloomington: Indiana University Press, 1985.

Pollack, Howard. *Aaron Copland: The Life and Work of an Uncommon Man*. New York: Henry Holt & Co., 1999.

Saminsky, Lazar. *Living Music of the Americas*. New York: Howell, Soskin and Crown, 1949.

Schiff, David. *Gershwin: Rhapsody in Blue*. Cambridge: Cambridge University Press, 1997.

Schneider, Wayne J., ed. *The Gershwin Style: New Looks at the Music of George Gershwin*. New York: Oxford University Press, 1999.

Stehman, Dan. *Roy Harris: An American Musical Pioneer*. Boston: Twayne, 1984.

Tawa, Nicholas E. *Serenading the Reluctant Eagle: American Musical Life, 1925–1945*. New York: Schirmer, 1984.

Tischler, Barbara L. *An American Music: The Search for an American Musical Identity*. Oxford: Oxford University Press, 1986.

Zuck, Barbara A. *A History of Musical Americanism*. Ann Arbor, Mich.: UMI Research Press, 1980.

Chapter 58 In Search of Utopia

Adorno, Theodor W. *Alban Berg: Master of the Smallest Link*, trans. Juliane Brand and Christopher Hailey. Cambridge: Cambridge University Press, 1991.

Bailey, Kathryn. *The Life of Webern*. Cambridge: Cambridge University Press, 1998.

_____ . *The Twelve-Note Music of Anton Webern: Old Forms in a New Language*. Cambridge: Cambridge University Press, 1991.

Brande, Juliane, Christopher Hailey, and Donald Harris, eds. *The Berg-Schoenberg Correspondence*. New York: Norton, 1986.

Carner, Mosco. *Alban Berg: The Man and His Work*. 2nd ed., London: Holmes and Meier, 1983.

Doctor, Jennifer. *The BBC and Ultra-Modern Music, 1922–1936: Shaping a Nation's Tastes*. Cambridge: Cambridge University Press, 1999.

Haimo, Ethan. *Schoenberg's Serial Odyssey: The Evolution of His Twelve-Tone Method*. Oxford: Oxford University Press, 1990.

Headlam, Dave. *The Music of Alban Berg*. New Haven: Yale University Press, 1996.

Hyde, Martha M. *Schoenberg's Twelve-Tone Harmony: The Suite Op. 29 and the Compositional Sketches*. Ann Arbor, Mich.: UMI Research Press, 1982.

Jarman, Douglas. *The Music of Alban Berg*. Berkeley and Los Angeles: University of California Press, 1979.

Jarman, Douglas, ed. *The Berg Companion*. Boston: Northeastern University Press, 1990.

John, Nicholas. *Igor Stravinsky: Oedipus Rex, The Rake's Progress*. English National Opera Guides. New York: Riverrun Press, 1991.

Kolneder, Walter. *Anton Webern: An Introduction to His Work*, trans. Humphrey Searle. Berkeley and Los Angeles: University of California Press, 1968.

Milstein, Silvina. *Arnold Schoenberg: Notes, Sets, Forms*. Cambridge: Cambridge University Press, 1992.

Moldenhauer, Hans, and Rosaleen Moldenhauer. *Anton von Webern: A Chronicle of His Life and Work*. New York: Knopf, 1979.

Perle, George. *The Operas of Alban Berg*, Vol. II: *Lulu*. Berkeley and Los Angeles: University of California Press, 1985.

_____ . *Serial Music and Atonality*. 6th ed., Berkeley and Los Angeles: University of California Press, 1991.

Pople, Anthony. *Berg: Violin Concerto*. Cambridge: Cambridge University Press, 1991.

Pople, Anthony, ed. *The Cambridge Companion to Berg*. Cambridge: Cambridge University Press, 1997.

Redlich, Hans. *Alban Berg: The Man and His Music*. London: John Calder, 1957.

Reich, Willi. *Alban Berg*, trans. Cornelius Cardew. London: Thames and Hudson, 1965.

Rufer, Joseph. *Composition with Twelve Notes*, trans. Humphrey Searle. London: Rockliff, 1954.

Rognoni, Luigi. *The Second Vienna School: Expressionism and Dodecaphony*, trans. Robert W. Mann. London: John Calder, 1977.

Shreffler, Anne C. *Webern and the Lyric Impulse: Songs and Fragments on Poems of Georg Trakl*. Oxford: Oxford University Press, 1994.

Walsh, Stephen. *Stravinsky: Oedipus Rex*. Cambridge: Cambridge University Press, 1993.

Webern, Anton. *The Path to the New Music*, trans. Leo Black. Bryn Mawr: Theodore Presser, 1963.

Whittall, Arnold. *Schoenberg Chamber Music*. London: British Broadcasting Corporation, 1972.

Chapter 59   Music and Totalitarian Society

Applegate, Celia, and Pamela Potter, eds. *Music and German National Identity*. Chicago: University of Chicago Press, 2002.

Bartlett, Rosamund, ed. *Shostakovich in Context*. Oxford: Oxford University Press, 2000.

Blokker, Roy, and Robert Dearling. *The Music of Dimitri Shostakovich: The Symphonies*. London: Tantivy Press, 1979.

Brinkmann, Reinhold, and Christoph Wolff. *Driven into Paradise: The Musical Migration from Nazi Germany to the United States*. Berkeley and Los Angeles: University of California Press, 1999.

Brown, Malcolm H., ed. *A Shostakovich Casebook*. Bloomington: Indiana University Press, 2004.

Bruhn, Siglind. *The Temptation of Paul Hindemith: Mathis Der Maler As a Spiritual Testimony*. Stuyvesant, N.Y.: Pendragon Press, 1998.

Cooper, David. *Bartók: Concerto for Orchestra*. Cambridge: Cambridge University Press, 1996.

Fanning, David. *The Breath of the Symphonist: Shostakovich's Tenth*. London: Royal Musical Association, 1988.

_____. *Shostakovich: String Quartet No. 8*. Aldershot: Ashgate, 2004.

_____. *Shostakovich Studies*. Cambridge: Cambridge University Press, 1995.

Fay, Laurel E. *Shostakovich: A Life*. New York: Oxford University Press, 1999.

_____. *Shostakovich and His World*. Princeton: Princeton University Press, 2004.

Grigoryev, Lev, and Yakov Platek, eds. *Dimitry Shostakovich about Himself and His Times*. Moscow: Progress Publishers, 1981.

Hakobian, Levon. *Music of the Soviet Age, 1917–1987*. Stockholm: Melos, 1998.

Kater, Michael H. *Composers of the Nazi Era: Eight Portraits*. New York: Oxford University Press, 2000.

_____. *The Twisted Muse: Musicians and Their Music in the Third Reich*. New York: Oxford University Press, 1997.

Levi, Erik. *Music in the Third Reich*. London: Macmillan, 1994.

Meyer, Michael. *The Politics of Music in the Third Reich*. New York: Peter Lang, 1991.

Nestyev, Israel. *Prokofiev*, trans. Florence Jonas. Palo Alto, Calif.: Stanford University Press, 1960.

Norris, Christopher, ed. *Shostakovich: The Man and His Music*. London: Laurence & Wishart, 1982.

Olkhovsky, Andrey. *Music under the Soviets*. London: Routledge and Kegan Paul, 1955.

Potter, Pamela M. *Most German of the Arts: Musicology and Society from the Weimar Republic to the End of Hitler's Reich*. New Haven: Yale University Press, 1998.

Prokofieff, Sergei. *Autobiography, Aricles, Reminiscences*. Moscow: Foreign Languages Publishing House, n.d. Reprint, University Press of the Pacific, 2000.

_____. *Selected Letters*, ed. Harlow Robinson. Boston: Northeastern University Press, 1998.

_____. *Soviet Diary 1927 and Other Writings*, ed. Oleg Prokofiev. Boston: Northeastern University Press, 1992.

Russolo, Luigi. *The Art of Noises*, trans. Barclay Brown. New York: Pendragon, 1986.

Sachs, Harvey. *Music in Fascist Italy*. New York: Norton, 1987.

Schuh, Willi, ed. *A Confidential Matter: The Letters of Richard Strauss and Stefan Zweig, 1931–1935*, trans. Max Knight. Berkeley and Los Angeles: University of California Press, 1977.

Schwarz, Boris. *Music and Musical Life in Soviet Russia*. 2nd ed., Bloomington: Indiana University Press, 1983.

Sollertinsky, Dimitri, and Ludmilla Sollertinsky. *Pages from the Life of Dimitri Shostakovich*. London: Hale, 1981.

Steinberg, Michael P. *The Meaning of the Salzburg Festival: Austria as Theater and Ideology, 1890–1938*. Ithaca, N.Y.: Cornell University Press, 1990.

Steinweis, Alan E. *Art, Ideology, and Economics in Nazi Germany: The Reich Chambers of Music, Theater, and the Visual Arts*. Chapel Hill: University of North Carolina Press, 1993.

Volkov, Solomon. *Shostakovich and Stalin: The Extraordinary Relationship between the Great Composer and the Brutal Dictator*. New York: Knopf, 2004.

_____. *Testimony: The Memoirs of Dmitri Shostakovich as Related to and Edited by Solomon Volkov*. New York: Harper & Row, 1979.

Wilson, Elizabeth. *Shostakovich: A Life Remembered*. Princeton: Princeton University Press, 1994.

Chapter 60   Starting from Scratch

Adorno, Theodor W. *Philosophy of Modern Music*, trans. Anne G. Mitchel and Wesley V. Blomster. New York: Seabury Press, 1973.

Bandur, Markus. *Aesthetics of Total Serialism*. Basel: Birkhäuser, 2001.

Boulez, Pierre. *Boulez on Music Today*, trans. Susan Bradshaw and Richard Rodney Bennet. Cambridge: Harvard University Press, 1971.

_____. *Orientations: Collected Writings*, ed. Jean-Jacques Nattiez, trans. Martin Cooper. Cambridge: Harvard University Press, 1986.

_____. *Stocktakings from an Apprenticeship*, trans. Stephen Walsh. Oxford: Clarendon Press, 1991.

Brindle, Reginald Smith. *The New Music*. Oxford: Oxford University Press, 1974.

_____. *Serial Composition*. New York: Oxford University Press, 1966.

Carroll, Mark. *Music and Ideology in Cold War Europe*. Cambridge: Cambridge University Press, 2003.

Cott, Jonathan. *Stockhausen: Conversations with the Composer*. New York: Simon and Schuster, 1975.

Glock, William, ed. *Pierre Boulez: A Symposium*. London: Eulenburg Books, 1986.

Grant, M. J. *Serial Music, Serial Aesthetics: Compositional Theory in Postwar Europe.* Cambridge: Cambridge University Press, 2001.

Griffiths, Paul. *Boulez.* London: Oxford University Press, 1978.

_____ . *Modern Music: The Avant-Garde since 1945.* London: J. M. Dent, 1981.

Harvey, Jonathan. *The Music of Stockhausen.* Berkeley and Los Angeles: University of California Press, 1975.

Henze, Hans Werner. *Bohemian Fifths: An Autobiography,* trans. Stewart Spencer. London: Faber & Faber, 1998.

_____ . *Music and Politics: Collected Writings, 1953–81,* trans. P. Labanyi. London: Faber & Faber, 1982.

Hodeir, André. *Since Debussy: A View of Contemporary Music,* trans. Noel Burch. New York: Grove Press, 1961.

Koblyakov, Lev. *Pierre Boulez: A World of Harmony.* Milton Park: Taylor & Francis, 1990.

Kurtz, Michael. *Stockhausen: A Biography,* trans. Richard Toop. New York: Farrar Straus & Giroux, 1993.

Leibowitz, René. *Schoenberg and His School: The Contemporary Stage of the Language of Music,* trans. Dika Newlin. New York: Philosophical Library, 1949. Reprint, New York, Da Capo, 1975.

Maconie, Robin. *Stockhausen on Music: Lectures and Interviews.* London: Marion Boyars, 1989.

_____ . *The Works of Karlheinz Stockhausen.* London: Oxford University Press, 1976.

Stacy, Peter F. *Boulez and the Modern Concept.* Lincoln: University of Nebraska Press, 1987.

Tannenbaum, Mya. *Conversations with Stockhausen.* Oxford: Oxford University Press, 1987.

Williams, Alastair. *New Music and the Claims of Modernity.* Aldershot, U.K.: Ashgate, 1997.

Wörner, Karl Heinrich. *Stockhausen: Life and Work,* trans. G. W. Hopkins. London: Faber & Faber, 1973.

Chapter 61   Indeterminacy

Bailey, Derek. *Improvisation: Its Nature and Practice in Music.* Ashebourne, Derbyshire: Moorland, 1980.

Bois, Mario. *Iannis Xenakis, the Man and His Music: A Conversation wth the Composer and a Description of His Works.* London: Boosey & Hawkes, 1967.

Cage, John. *A Year from Monday.* Middletown, Conn.: Wesleyan University Press, 1967.

_____ . *Empty Words: Writings, 1973–78.* Middletown, Conn.: Wesleyan University Press, 1979.

_____ . *For the Birds: In Conversation with Daniel Charles.* London: Boyars, 1981.

_____ . *M: Writings, 1967–73.* Middletown, Conn.: Wesleyan University Press, 1973.

_____ . *Silence.* Middletown, Conn.: Wesleyan University Press, 1961.

Cage, John, ed. *Notations.* New York: Something Else Press, 1969.

Cardew, Cornelius. *Stockhausen Serves Imperialism and Other Essays.* London: Latimer, 1974.

Cardew, Cornelius, ed. *Scratch Music*. Cambridge, Mass.: MIT Press, 1974.

Cole, Hugo. *Sounds and Signs: Aspects of Musical Notation*. Oxford: Oxford University Press, 1974.

DeLio, Thomas. *Circumscribing the Open Universe: Essays on Cage, Feldman, Wolff, Ashley and Lucier*. Washington, D.C.: Rowman and Littlefield, 1984.

DeLio, Thomas, ed. *The Music of Morton Feldman*. Westport, Conn.: Greenwood Press, 1996.

Feldman, Morton. *Essays*, ed. Walter Zimmerman. Kerpen: Beginner Press, 1985.

Gena, Peter, ed. *A John Cage Reader*. New York: C. F. Peters, 1982.

Kaprow, Allan. *Assemblage, Environments, and Happenings*. New York: Abrams, 1966.

Karkoschka, Erhard. *Notation in New Music*. New York: Praeger, 1972.

Kostelanetz, Richard, ed. *Conversing with Cage*. New York: Limelight Editions, 1987.

———. *John Cage*. New York: Praeger, 1970.

———. *John Cage: Writer*. New York: Limelight Editions, 1993.

Nattiez, Jean-Jacques, ed. *The Boulez-Cage Correspondence*, trans. R. Samuels. Cambridge: Cambridge University Press, 1993.

Pritchett, James. *The Music of John Cage*. Cambridge: Cambridge University Press, 1993.

Revill, David. *The Roaring Silence: John Cage, A Life*. New York: Arcade, 1992.

Stone, Kurt. *Music Notation in the Twentieth Century*. New York: Norton, 1980.

Varga, Bálint András. *Conversations with Iannis Xenakis*. New York: Farrar, Straus and Giroux, 1996.

Xenakis, Iannis. *Arts, Sciences: Alloys*, trans. Sharon Kanach. New York: Pendragon Press, 1985.

———. *Formalized Music: Thought and Mathematics in Composition*. Bloomington: Indiana University Press, 1971.

Chapter 62   The Apex

Babbitt, Milton. *Words about Music*, ed. Stephen Dembski and Joseph N. Straus. Madison: University of Wisconsin Press, 1987.

Boretz, Benjamin, and Edward T. Cone. *Perspectives on American Composers*. Princeton: Princeton University Press, 1971.

———. *Perspectives on Contemporary Music Theory*. New York: Norton, 1972.

———. *Perspectives on Notation and Performance*. New York: Norton, 1976.

———. *Perspectives on Schoenberg and Stravinsky*. Princeton: Princeton University Press, 1968.

Copland, Aaron, and Vivian Perlis. *Copland: Since 1943*. New York: St. Martin's Press, 1989.

Craft, Robert. *Stravinsky: Chronicle of a Friendship, 1948–1971*. Rev. ed., Nashville: Vanderbilt University Press, 1994.

Forte, Allen. *The Structure of Atonal Music*. New Haven: Yale University Press, 1973.

Krenek, Ernst. *Horizons Circled: Reflections on My Life in Music*. Berkeley and Los Angeles: University of California Press, 1974.

Lang, Paul Henry, ed. *Problems of Modern Music*. New York: Norton, 1962.

Mead, Andrew W. *An Introduction to the Music of Milton Babbitt*. Princeton: Princeton University Press, 1994.

Nabokov, Nicolas. *Bagazh: Memoirs of a Russian Cosmopolitan*. New York: Atheneum, 1975.

Peles, Stephen, et al., eds. *The Collected Essays of Milton Babbitt*. Princeton: Princeton University Press, 2003.

Perspectives of New Music, Vol. XIV/2 and XV/1 (1976), special issue.

Straus, Joseph N. *Stravinsky's Late Music*. Cambridge: Cambridge University Press, 2001.

Sravinsky, Igor, and Robert Craft. *Conversations with Igor Stravinsky*. Garden City, N.Y.: Doubleday, 1959.

Werth, Alexander, ed. *Musical Uproar in Moscow*. London: Turnstile Press, 1949. Reprint, Westport, Conn.: Greenwood Press, 1973.

Wuorinen, Charles. *Simple Composition*. New York: Longman, 1979.

Chapter 63   The Third Revolution

Appleton, Jon, and Ronald Perera, eds. *The Development and Practice of Electronic Music*. Englewood Cliffs, N.J.: Prentice Hall, 1974.

Chadabe, Joel. *Electric Sound: The Past and Promise of Electronic Music*. Upper Saddle River, N.J.: Prentice Hall, 1997.

Ernst, David. *The Evolution of Electronic Music*. New York: Schirmer, 1977.

Heikinheimo, Seppo. *The Electronic Music of Karlheinz Stockhausen: Studies of the Esthetical and Formal Problems of Its First Phase*, trans. Brad Absetz. Helsinki: Suomen Musikkitieteellinin Seura, 1972.

Howe, Hubert S., Jr. *Electronic Music Synthesis*. New York: Norton, 1975.

Jacobson, Bernard. *A Polish Renaissance*. London: Phaidon Press, 1996.

Mirka, Danuta. *The Sonoristic Structuralism of Krzysztof Penderecki*. Katowice: Akademia Muzyczna, 1997.

Ouellette, Fernand. *A Biography of Edgard Varèse*, trans. D. Coltman. New York: Orion Press, 1966.

Robinson, Ray. *Krzysztof Penderecki: A Guide to His Work*. Princeton: Prestige, 1983.

Robinson, Ray, and Allen Winold. *A Study of the Penderecki St Luke Passion*. Celle, N.J.: Warner Bros., 1983.

Steinitz, R. *György Ligeti: Music of the Imagination*. Boston: Northeastern University Press, 2003.

Schwartz, Elliott. *Electronic Music: A Listener's Guide*. New York: Praeger, 1972.

Stucky, Steven. *Lutoslawski and His Music*. Cambridge: Cambridge University Press, 1981.

Thomas, Adrian. *Górecki*. Oxford: Oxford University Press, 1997.

Toop, Richard. *György Ligeti*. London: Phaidon Press, 1999.

Van Solkema, Sherman, ed. *The New Worlds of Edgard Varèse: A Symposium*. Brooklyn, N.Y.: Institute for Studies in American Music, 1979.

Chapter 64 Standoff (I)

Banks, Paul, ed. *The Making of Peter Grimes*. Woodbridge: Boydell Press/Britten-Pears Library, 1995.

Brett, Philip, ed. *Benjamin Britten: Peter Grimes*. Cambridge: Cambridge University Press, 1983.

Britten, Benjamin. *On Receiving the First Aspen Award*. London: Faber & Faber, 1964.

Carpenter, Humphrey. *Benjamin Britten: A Biography*. New York: Simon and Schuster, 1993.

Cooke, Mervyn. *Britten and the Far East: Asian Influences in the Music of Benjamin Britten*. Woodbridge: Boydell Press/Britten-Pears Library, 1998.

————. *Britten: War Requiem*. Cambridge: Cambridge University Press, 1996.

Cooke, Mervyn, ed. *The Cambridge Companion to Benjamin Britten*. Cambridge: Cambridge University Press, 1999.

Cooke, Mervyn, and Philip Reed, eds. *Benjamin Britten: Billy Budd*. Cambridge: Cambridge University Press, 1993.

Evans, Peter. *The Music of Benjamin Britten*. Rev. ed., Oxford: Oxford University Press, 1995.

Howard, Patricia, ed. *Benjamin Britten: The Turn of the Screw*. Cambridge: Cambridge University Press, 1985.

Howes, Frank. *The English Musical Renaissance*. London: Secker and Warburg, 1966.

Hughes, Meirion, and Robert Stradling. *The English Musical Renaissance, 1840–1940: Constructing a National Music*. 2nd ed., Manchester: Manchester University Press, 2001.

Kennedy, Michael. *Britten*. London: J. M. Dent, 1981.

Kildea, Paul. *Selling Britten: Music and the Market Place*. Oxford: Oxford University Press, 2002.

Mitchell, Donald. *Benjamin Britten: Death in Venice*. Cambridge: Cambridge University Press, 1987.

————. *Britten and Auden in the Thirties: The Year 1936*. Seattle: University of Washington Press, 1981.

Mitchell, Donald, and Hans Keller, eds. *Benjamin Britten: A Commentary on His Works from a Group of Specialists*. London: Rockliff, 1952.

Mitchell, Donald, and Philip Reed, eds. *Letters from a Life: Selected Letters and Diaries of Benjamin Britten*. Berkeley and Los Angeles: University of California Press, 1991.

Palmer, Christopher, ed. *The Britten Companion*. London: Faber and Faber, 1984.

Pirie, Peter J. *The English Musical Renaissance*. London: Victor Gollancz, 1979.

White, Eric Walter. *Benjamin Britten: His Life and Operas*. 3rd ed., London: Faber and Faber, 1983.

Wilcox, Michael. *Benjamin Britten's Operas*. Bath: Absolute Press, 1997.

Chapter 65 Standoff (II)

Carter, Elliott. *Collected Essays and Lectures, 1937–1995*, ed. Jonathan W. Bernard. Rochester, N.Y.: University of Rochester Press, 1997.

Edwards, Allen. *Flawed Words and Stubborn Sounds: A Conversation with Elliott Carter.* New York: Norton, 1971.

Pollack, Howard. *Harvard Composers: Walter Piston and His Students, from Elliott Carter to Frederic Rzewski.* Metuchen, N.J.: Scarecrow Press, 1992.

Rosen, Charles. *The Musical Languages of Elliott Carter.* Washington, D.C.: United States Government Printing Office, 1984.

Schiff, David. *The Music of Elliott Carter.* London: Eulenburg Books, 1983. 2nd ed., Ithaca, N.Y.: Cornell University Press, 1998.

Stone, Kurt, and Else Stone, eds. *The Writings of Elliott Carter: An American Composer Looks at Modern Music.* Bloomington: Indiana University Press, 1977.

Chapter 66　The Sixties

Berio, Luciano. *Two Interviews,* ed. and trans. David Osmond-Smith. London: Marion Boyars, 1985.

Davis, Edward E., ed. *The Beatles Book.* New York: Cowles, 1968.

Davis, Jerome. *Talking Heads.* New York: Vintage Books, 1986.

DeLio, Thomas, ed. *Contiguous Lines: Issues and Ideas in the Music of the Sixties and Seventies.* Lanham, N.Y.: University Press of America, 1985.

Eisen, Jonathan, ed. *The Age of Rock: Sounds of the American Cultural Revolution.* New York: Vintage Books, 1969.

Friedlander, Paul. *Rock and Roll: A Social History.* Boulder: Westview Press, 1996.

Frith, Simon. *Sound Effects: Youth, Leisure and the Politics of Rock 'n' Roll.* New York: Random House, 1981.

Frith, Simon, and Andrew Goodwin, eds. *On Record: Rock, Pop, and the Written Word.* New York: Random House, 1990.

Gitlin, Todd. *The Sixties: Years of Hope, Days of Rage.* New York: Bantam Books, 1987.

Hamm, Charles, Bruno Nettl, and Ronald Byrneside. *Contemporary Music and Music Cultures.* Englewood Cliffs, N.J.: Prentice Hall, 1975.

Haskell, Barbara. *Blam! The Explosion of Pop, Minimalism, and Performance, 1958–1964.* New York: Norton, 1984.

Kozinn, Allan. *The Beatles.* London: Phaidon Press, 1995.

Macdonald, Ian. *Revolution in the Head: The Beatles' Records and the Sixties.* Rev. ed., London: Fourth Estate, 1994.

Marcus, Greil. *Mystery Train: Images of American Rock 'n' Roll Music.* New York: E. P. Dutton, 1975.

Moore, A. F. *The Beatles: Sgt. Pepper's Lonely Hearts Club Band.* Cambridge: Cambridge University Press, 1997.

Osmond-Smith, David. *Berio.* Oxford: Oxford University Press, 1991.

———. *Playing with Words: A Guide to Luciano Berio's Sinfonia.* London: Royal Musical Association, 1985.

Rockwell, John. *All American Music: Composition in the Late Twentieth Century.* New York: Knopf, 1983.

Tamm, Eric. *Brian Eno: His Music and the Vertical Color of Sound*. New York: Farrar Straus & Giroux, 1989.

Thomson, Elizabeth, and David Gutman, eds. *The Lennon Companion*. Rev. ed., New York: Da Capo Press, 2004.

Chapter 67   A Harmonious Avant-Garde?

Battcock, Gregory, ed. *Minimal Art: A Critical Anthology*. New York: E. P. Dutton, 1968.

Haydon, Geoffrey. *John Tavener: Glimpses of Paradise*. London: Victor Gollancz, 1994.

Hillier, Paul. *Arvo Pärt*. Oxford: Oxford University Press, 1997.

Jones, Robert T., ed. *Music by Philip Glass*. New York: Harper & Row, 1987.

Kostelanetz, Richard, ed. *Writings on Glass: Essays, Interviews, Criticism*. New York: Schirmer, 1998.

Mertens, Wem. *American Minimal Music*. New York: Alexander Broude, 1983.

Potter, Keith. *Four Musical Minimalists*. Cambridge: Cambridge University Press, 2000.

Reich, Steve. *Writings about Music*. New York: Oxford University Press. 2002.

Schwarz, K. Robert. *Minimalists*. London: Phaidon, 1996.

Strickland, Edward. *Minimalism: Origins*. Bloomington: Indiana University Press, 1993.

Tavener, John, with Mother Thekla, and Ivan Moody. *Ikons: Meditations in Words and Music*. London: HarperCollins, 1995.

_____ . *The Music of Silence: A Composer's Testament*, ed. Brian Keeble. London: Faber & Faber, 1999.

Young, La Monte, and Marian Zazeela. *Selected Writings*. Munich: Heiner Friedrich, 1969.

Chapter 68   After Everything

Attali, Jacques. *Noise: The Political Economy of Music*, trans. Brian Massumi. Minneapolis: University of Minnesota Press, 1985.

Gillespie, Don, ed. *George Crumb: Profile of a Composer*. New York: C. F. Peters, 1985.

Griffiths, Paul. *Modern Music and After: Directions since 1945*. Oxford: Oxford University Press, 1995.

_____ . *Peter Maxwell Davies*. London: Robson, 1982.

Ivashkin, Alexander. *Alfred Schnittke*. London: Phaidon, 1996.

Kaczynski, Tadeusz. *Conversations with Witold Lutoslawski*, trans. Yolanta May. London: J. & W. Chester, 1984.

Lochhead, Judy, and Joseph Auner, eds. *Postmodern Music/Postmodern Thought*. New York: Routledge, 2002.

Meyer, Leonard B. *Music, the Arts, and Ideas*. 2nd ed., Chicago: University of Chicago Press, 1994.

Nyman, Michael. *Experimental Music: Cage and Beyond*. New York: Schirmer, 1974.

Penderecki, Krzysztof. *Labyrinth of Time: Five Addresses for the End of the Millennium*, ed. Ray Robinson, trans. William Brand. Chapel Hill, N.C.: Hinshaw Music, 1998.

Pruslin, Stephen, ed. *Peter Maxwell Davies: Studies from Two Decades*. London: Boosey & Hawkes, 1970.

Reynolds, Roger. *Mind Models: New Forms of Music Experience*. New York: Praeger, 1975.

Rochberg, George. *The Aesthetics of Survival: A Composer's View of Twentieth-Century Music*, ed. William Bolcom. Ann Arbor: University of Michigan Press, 1984.

Seabrook, Mike. *Max: The Life and Music of Peter Maxwell Davies*. London: Trafalgar Square, 1994.

Shepherd, John, Phil Virden, Graham Vulliamy, and Trevor Wishart. *Whose Music? A Sociology of Musical Languages*. London: Latimer New Dimensions, 1977.

Slobin, Mark. *Subcultural Sounds: Micromusics of the West*. Middletown, Conn.: Wesleyan University Press, 1993.

Small, Christopher. *Musicking*. Middletown, Conn.: Wesleyan University Press, 1998.

Willis, Brian. *Art after Modernism: Rethinking Representation*. Boston: Godine, 1984.

Chapter 69   Millennium's End

Anderton, Craig. *MIDI for Musicians*. New York: Amsco, 1986.

Biggs, Hayes, and Susan Orzel, eds. *Musically Incorrect: Conversations about Music at the End of the Twentieth Century*. New York: C. F. Peters, 1998.

Boom, Michael. *Music through MIDI*. Redmond, Wash.: Microsoft Press, 1987.

Born, Georgina. *Rationalizing Culture: IRCAM, Boulez, and the Institutionalization of the Avant-Garde*. Berkeley and Los Angeles: University of California Press, 1995.

Brentano, Robyn. *Outside the Frame: Performance and the Object: A Survey History of Performance Art in the USA since 1950*. Cleveland: Cleveland Center for Contemporary Art, 1994.

DeFuria, Steve. *The MIDI Book*. Milwaukee: Hal Leonard Books, 1988.

Dodge, Charles, and Thomas A. Jerse. *Computer Music: Synthesis, Composition, and Performance*. New York: Schirmer, 1985.

Ferneyhough, Brian. *Collected Writings*, ed. James Boros and Richard Toop. London: Routledge, 1995.

Gilmore, Bob. *Harry Partch: A Biography*. New Haven: Yale University Press, 1998.

Goldberg, Roselee. *Performance Art: From Futurism to the Present*. Rev. ed., New York: Thames & Hudson, 2001.

Howell, John. *Laurie Anderson*. New York: Thunder's Mouth Press, 1992.

Jabobson, Linda, ed. *Cyberarts: Exploring Art and Technology*. San Francisco: Backbeat Books, 1992.

Kornick, Rebecca H. *Recent American Opera*. New York: Columbia University Press, 1991.

Manning, Peter. *Electronic and Computer Music*. Oxford: Clarendon Press, 1985.

Mathews, Max. *The Technology of Computer Music*. Cambridge, Mass.: MIT Press, 1985.

Partch, Harry. *"Bitter Music": Collected Journals, Essays, Introductions, and Librettos*, ed. Thomas McGeary. Urbana: University of Illinois Press, 1991.

_____. *Genesis of a Music.* 2nd ed., Madison: University of Wisconsin Press, 1974.

Roads, Curtis, ed. *The Music Machine.* Cambridge, Mass.: MIT Press, 1989.

Roads, Curtis, and John Strawn, eds. *Foundations of Computer Music.* Cambridge, Mass.: MIT Press, 1985.

Roth, Moira. *Amazing Decade: Women and Performance Art, 1970–1980.* Hollywood, Calif.: Astro Artz, 1984.

List of Musical Examples
in Order of Appearance

VOLUME 1

Chapter 1

Ex. 1-1	*Justus ut palma* as antiphon to Psalm 91
Ex. 1-2	*Justus ut palma* as a Vespers antiphon
Ex. 1-3	*Justus ut palma* as a versicle
Ex. 1-4	*Justus ut palma* as Introit
Ex. 1-5	*Justus ut palma* as Offertory
Ex. 1-6	*Justus ut palma* as Alleluia
Ex. 1-7a	*Justus ut palma* as Gradual
Ex. 1-7b	*Haec dies* (Easter Gradual)
Ex. 1-8	*Differentiae* of the first psalm tone
Ex. 1-9a	Deduction of the diatonic pitch set from the Pythagorean consonances
Ex. 1-9b	Deduction of the diatonic pitch set by fifths
Ex. 1-10	First phrase of Hurrian cult song from ancient Ugarit, transcribed by Anne Draffkorn Kilmer
Ex. 1-11a	Second stanza of the First Delphic Hymn, transcribed by Egert Pöhlmann and Martin L. West
Ex. 1-11b	Fourth verse of a proto-Byzantine Hymn to the Trinity, transcribed by E. Pöhlmann and M. West
Ex. 1-12	Beginning of "Credo I"

Chapter 2

Ex. 2-1	*Neuma triplex*
Ex. 2-2	*Prosulae* to the *neuma triplex*: (a) *Facture tue*; (b) *Rex regum*
Ex. 2-3	Prosulated version of Alleluia, *Justus ut palma*
Ex. 2-4a	Sequence by Notker Balbulus:, *Angelorum ordo*
Ex. 2-4b	Sequence by Notker Balbulus, *Rex regum*
Ex. 2-5	*Rex caeli Domine* (Fig. 2-2a) transcribed
Ex. 2-6	Polyphonic example from *Musica enchiriadis* (Fig. 2-2b) transcribed
Ex. 2-7	Three Frankish hymns: (a) *Ave maris stella*; (b) *Pange lingua gloriosi*; (c) *Veni creator spiritus*
Ex. 2-8a	Prefatory trope to the Easter Introit, *Resurrexi*

Ex. 2-8b   The Easter Introit, larded with two sets of tropes from the monastery of St. Martial

Ex. 2-9   Easter dialogue trope (*Quem quaeritis in sepulchro*)

Ex. 2-10   Gloria IV

Ex. 2-11   Sanctus I

Ex. 2-12a   Agnus XVIII

Ex. 2-12b   Agnus II

Ex. 2-13   A *prosula* within a *neuma* within a *laus* within a Gloria

Ex. 2-14a   Kyrie IV

Ex. 2-14b   Kyrie, *Cunctipotens Genitor Deus*

Ex. 2-15   Incipit of the *Gaudeamus* Introit and the climactic phrase of the *Haec dies* gradual in West Frankish and East Frankish versions

Chapter 3

Ex. 3-1   The four species of fifth and the "four finals"

Ex. 3-2   The eight medieval modes

Ex. 3-3   Disjunct and conjunct replication of the T-S-T tetrachord (the tetrachord of the four finals) as described by Hucbald

Ex. 3-4   Gloria in mode 6, with laudes by Hucbald of St. Amand (texted in italics)

Ex. 3-5   Kyrie IX, *Cum jubilo*

Ex. 3-6   *Ite/deo gratias* from Mass IX

Ex. 3-7   Two sequences in modern use: (a) *Victimae paschali laudes* (Easter); (b) *Dies irae* (Requiem)

Ex. 3-8   *Libera me* (responsory verse)

Ex. 3-9   *Lauda Sion Salvatorem/Laudes crucis attolamus*

Ex. 3-10   Hildegard of Bingen, *Columba aspexit*

Ex. 3-11   The Play of Daniel: (a) *Astra tenenti* (conductus); (b) *Heu heu* (Daniel's lament)

Ex. 3-12a   Marian antiphon, *Regina caeli, laetare*

Ex. 3-12b   Marian antiphon, *Salve, Regina*

Ex. 3-13   Raimon de Miraval, *Aissi cum es genser pascors*

Ex. 3-14   Hymn, *Ut queant laxis*; words by Paul the Deacon, music possibly by Guido d'Arezzo

Ex. 3-15   The gamut, or full range of pitches represented on the Guidonian hand, together with the seven hexachords that are required for its solmization.

Chapter 4

Ex. 4-1   Guiraut de Bornelh, *Reis glorios* (first verse)

Ex. 4-2   *A l'entrada del tens clar* (balada)

Ex. 4-3   Richard Coeur-de-Lion (Lion-Heart), *Ja nun hons pris* (first verse)

Ex. 4-4   Thibaut IV de Champagne, *De bone amour vient seance et bonté* (first verse)

Ex. 4-5   Moniot d'Arras, *Ce fut en mai* (pastourelle)

Ex. 4-6   Adam de la Halle, *Bone amourete*

Ex. 4-7   Adam de la Halle, *Dieus soit en cheste maison* (ballade)

Ex. 4-8   Adam de la Halle, *Fines amouretes ai:* (a) virelai, (b) rondeau

Ex. 4-9   Adam de la Halle, *Robins m'aime* (from *Le jeu de Robin et de Marion*)

Ex. 4-10   *Porque trobar* (canso)

Ex. 4-11   Flagellants' song: *Nu ist diu Betfart so here* (Geisslerlied, transcribed by Hugo Spechtshart von Reutlingen)

Ex. 4-12   Guyot de Provins, *Ma joie premeraine*, with German text (*Ich denke under wilen*) by Friedrich von Hausen

Ex. 4-13   Walther von der Vogelweide, *Palästinalied*

Ex. 4-14   Anon. ("Pseudo-Neidhardt"), *Meienzit*

Ex. 4-15   Hans Sachs, *Silberweise*

Chapter 5

Ex. 5-1   Transcriptions of *Scolica enchiriadis* examples (Fig. 5-1): (a) Double diapason. (b) Diapente. (c) Diatessaron. (d) Composite.

Ex. 5-2a   Disjunct tetrachord scale from *Musica enchiriadis*

Ex. 5-2b   Hypothetical conjunct tetrachord scale

Ex. 5-3   Guido d'Arezzo, *Micrologus*: Two counterpoints to *Jherusalem*

Ex. 5-4   Guido d'Arezzo, *Micrologus*: Counterpoint to *Sexta hora*

Ex. 5-5   From the Chartres fragment: (a) "Dicant nunc judei"; (b) "Angelus Domini"

Ex. 5-6   Transcription of the beginning of *Jubilemus, exultemus* (Fig. 5-2)

Ex. 5-7   Versus sung as a prosulated *Benedicamus Domino* response at St. Martial and elsewhere (Paris, BN, LAT. 1139)

Ex. 5-8a   *Cunctipotens genitor* setting, from *Ad organum faciendum*

Ex. 5-8b   *Cunctipotens genitor* setting, from Codex Calixtinus

Ex. 5-9   *Congaudeant catholici* transcribed as two separate two-part pieces, but aligned

Ex. 5-10   *Verbum patris humanatur* (twelfth-century conductus setting in three parts)

Chapter 6

Ex. 6-1a   Trochaic pattern notated with "modal" ligatures

Ex. 6-1b   Iambic pattern notated with "modal" ligatures

Ex. 6-2   Transcription of *-derunt* from organum setting shown in Fig. 6-3b

Ex. 6-3a   "Do-" clausulae transcribed from **Flo**, f. 99′, with barring following the tractus in the tenor

Ex. 6-3b   "Do-" clausulae transcribed from **W₂**, f. 63–63′, in 6/8 meter

Ex. 6-3c   "Do-" clausulae transcribed from **Flo**, f. 150′ (with double cursus)

Ex. 6-3d   "Do-" clausulae transcribed from **Flo**, f. 149′ (both parts in iambic patterns)

Ex. 6-4   *Viderunt omnes* a 4 (attributed to Perotin), first syllable of setting

Ex. 6-5   *Alleluia Nativitas* (attributed to Perotin): (a) mm. 1–63; (b) mm. 72–104; (c) mm. 168–89

Ex. 6-6   *Vetus abit littera*: (a) transcribed in first mode; (b) transcribed in fifth mode

Ex. 6-7   Final cauda from *Dic, Christi veritas* (text by Philip the Chancellor), transcribed from **Flo**, f. 204

Ex. 6-8   Transcription of *Veste nuptiali* (Fig. 6-7b) in rhythm of Fig. 6-7a

Chapter 7

Ex. 7-1   Double motet on *Ex semine* (transcription of Fig. 7-3)

Ex. 7-2   Principles of Franconian notation

Ex. 7-3   Paris, BN 844 ("Manuscrit du Roi"), interpolation no. 8, transcribed by Judith Peraino

Ex. 7-4   Transcription of Fig. 7-5 (*L'autre jour/Au tens pascour/IN SECULUM*)

Ex. 7-5   *J'ai les maus d'amours/que ferai/IN SECULUM* (Montpellier, Faculté de médicines H196 (**Mo**), f. 188′)

Ex. 7-6a   "Instrumental" (textless) motet, *In seculum longum*

Ex. 7-6b   "Instrumental" (textless) motet, *In seculum breve*

Ex. 7-7   Transcription of Fig. 7-7 (*Mout me fu grief*)

Ex. 7-8   Transcription of Fig. 7-8 (*El mois de mai/De se debent bigami/KYRIE*)

Ex. 7-9   Transcription of Fig. 7-9 (*On parole/A Paris/FRESE NOUVELE*)

Ex. 7-10   Transcription of Fig. 7-10 (*Aucun/Lonc tans/ANNUN*)

Chapter 8

Ex. 8-1   Philippe de Vitry, *Tribum/Quoniam/MERITO*, mm. 1–40

Ex. 8-2   The two alternatives and their equivalents in modern notatation: (a) Major prolation. (b) Minor prolation

Ex. 8-3   Philippe de Vitry, *Tuba sacre/In Arboris/VIRGO SUM*

Ex. 8-4   *Musicalis Sciencia/Sciencie Laudabili*, mm. 121–67 (Paris, BN, Coll. de Picardie 67, f. 67′)

Ex. 8-5   Guillaume de Machaut, *Felix virgo/Inviolata/AD TE SUSPIRAMUS*, tenor talea

Ex. 8-6   Guillaume de Machaut, *Felix virgo/Inviolata/AD TE SUSPIRAMUS*, mm. 1–33

Ex. 8-7   Johannes Ciconia, *Doctorum principem super ethera/Melodia suavissima cantemus*: (a) mm. 1–14; (b) mm. 45–58; (c) mm. 89–100

Ex. 8-8   Guillaume Du Fay, *Nuper rosarum flores*, mm. 141–70

Ex. 8-9   Proportional numbers in *Nuper rosarum flores* represented as pitch intervals

Chapter 9

Ex. 9-1   Guillaume de Machaut, hoquetus "DAVID," color and taleae

Ex. 9-2   Guillaume de Machaut, *Pourquoy me bat mes maris*, tenor

Ex. 9-3   Guillaume de Machaut, *Lasse/Se j'aime/POURQUOY*, mm. 1 – 42

Ex. 9-4   Guillaume de Machaut, *Douce dame jolie* (monophonic virelai)

Ex. 9-5   Guillaume de Machaut, *En mon cuer* (virelai a 2)

Ex. 9-6   Guillaume de Machaut, *Tres bonne et belle* (virelai a 3)

Ex. 9-7   Guillaume de Machaut, Rondeau no. 10, *Rose, liz, printemps*, mm. 1 – 11

Ex. 9-8   Guillaume de Machaut, Ballade no. 31, *De toutes flours*

Ex. 9-9   *Cunctipotens genitor* from Faenza Codex

Ex. 9-10   Guillaume de Machaut, *De toutes flours* as arranged in the Faenza Codex

Ex. 9-11   Guymont, Kyrie

Ex. 9-12   Original incipits and opening phrases in transcription: (a) Ivrea 26 (Gloria). (b) Ivrea 52 (Credo)

Ex. 9-13   Incipit and beginning of A siglum. Apt 27 (Sanctus)

Ex. 9-14   Agnus Dei from Cambrai, 1328 (Fascicle IV, no. 1), mm. 1 – 18

Ex. 9-15   Guillaume de Machaut, *La messe de Nostre Dame*, Kyrie, mm. 1 – 27

Ex. 9-16   Guillaume de Machaut, *La messe de Nostre Dame*, Gloria: (a) mm. 1 – 29; (b) final Amen

Ex. 9-17   Guillaume de Machaut, *La messe de Nostre Dame: Ite, missa est*

Ex. 9-18   Guillaume de Machaut, *Ma fin est mon commencement* in transcription

Ex. 9-19   *Se je chant mains*, middle section

Ex. 9-20   Guillaume de Machaut, Chace 4 from *Lai de la fonteinne*

Ex. 9-21   Philippus de Caserta, *En remirant* (ballade)

Ex. 9-22   Philippus de Caserta, quotation from *En remirant* in Ciconia's ballade *Sus un fontayne*

Ex. 9-23   Solage, *Fumeux fume* (rondeau)

Ex. 9-24   Pan-isorhythm in a French-Cypriot Gloria-Credo pair (MS. Torino, f. 32 – 33, 34 – 35)

Ex. 9-25   Nicolaus de Radom, Gloria, mm. 1 – 20

Ex. 9-26   Anon., *Or sus, vous dormez trop* (virelai), mm. 22 – 30

Chapter 10

Ex. 10-1   Giovanni de Cascia, *Appress' un fiume* (madrigal)

Ex. 10-2a   Jacopo da Bologna, *Oselleto salvagio*, set as madrigal, mm. 1 – 30

Ex. 10-2b   Jacopo da Bologna, *Oselleto salvagio*, set as caccia, mm. 1 – 12

Ex. 10-3   Gherardello da Firenze, *Tosto che l'alba* (caccia)

Ex. 10-4   Lorenzo Masini, *Non so qual i' mi voglia* (ballata; text by Boccaccio)

Ex. 10-5   Francesco Landini, *Non avrà ma' pietà* (ballata)

Ex. 10-6   Gherardello da Firenze, *Donna l'altrui mirar* (monophonic ballata), cadences embellished with "Landini sixth"

Ex. 10-7   Faenza version of *Non avrà ma' pietà*

Ex. 10-8   Landini, *Sy dolce non sonò* (madrigal in motet style)

Ex. 10-9   Johannes Carmen, *Pontifici decora speculi* (motet in caccia style)

Chapter 11

Ex. 11-1   Sumer Canon, as realized by Frank Llewellyn Harrison

Ex. 11-2   Benjamin Britten, *A Ceremony of Carols*, opening of *Wolcum yole!*

Ex. 11-3   *Nobilis, humilis* in transcription

Ex. 11-4a   *Edi beo thu, hevene Quene*

Ex. 11-4b   *Foweles in the frith*, beginning

Ex. 11-5   *Jesu Cristes milde moder*, beginning

Ex. 11-6   *Veris ad imperia* (conductus)

Ex. 11-7a   *Balaam inquit, vaticinans*

Ex. 11-7b   "Balaam" verse from sequence *Epiphanium Domino*

Ex. 11-8   *Flos regalis* (conductus/rondellus), mm. 87–117

Ex. 11-9   *Beata viscera* (conductus/motet), mm. 1–13

Ex. 11-10   *Sancta Maria virgo, intercede* (Marian antiphon)

Ex. 11-11   *Thomas gemma Cantuariae/Thomas caesus in Doveria*, mm. 1–32

Ex. 11-12   Pycard, Gloria, mm. 25–48

Ex. 11-13   Leonel Power, Gloria, mm. 1–14

Ex. 11-14   Roy Henry, Sanctus, mm. 1–25

Ex. 11-15   *Deo gratias anglia* ("Agincourt Carol")

Ex. 11-16   *Nova, nova, ave fit ex Eva*

Ex. 11-17   Jean de Noyers (Tapissier), *Eya dulcis/Vale placens*, mm. 77–115

Ex. 11-18   John Dunstable, *Salve scema/Salve salus*, mm. 145–80

Ex. 11-19   John Dunstable, *Quam pulchra es*

Ex. 11-20   Guillaume Du Fay, *Vos qui secuti estis me* (Communion from *Missa Sancti Jacobi*): (a) original chant; (b) as notated (chant notes denoted by +); (c) first phrase as realized in performance

Ex. 11-21   *Salvator mundi Domine* in faburden

Ex. 11-22   *Heir beginnis countering*: (a) presumed cantus firmus; (b) final example, mm. 1–6

Ex. 11-23   Gilles Binchois, *Veni Creator Spiritus*

Ex. 11-24a Guillaume Du Fay, *Ave maris stella* in fauxbourdon

Ex. 11-24b *Ave maris stella* with "contratenor sine faulx bourdon"

Ex. 11-25   Guillaume Du Fay, *Craindre vous vueil*

Ex. 11-26   Cadential motion in superius/tenor pair accompanied by three different contratenors: (a) doubled leading tone; (b) octave leap; (c) "V–I"

Ex. 11-27   Gilles Binchois, *Deuil angoisseux*

Chapter 12

Ex. 12-1a   Antoine Busnoys, *In hydraulis*, tenor layout

Ex. 12-1b   Antoine Busnoys, *In hydraulis*, beginning of *secunda pars* (point of imitation on "haec Ockeghem")

Ex. 12-1c   Johannes Ockeghem returns the compliment to Busnoys in *Ut heremita solus*

Ex. 12-2a   *Alma Redemptoris Mater* (eleventh-century Marian antiphon)

Ex. 12-2b   Tenor of Leonel Power's Mass on *Alma Redemptoris Mater*

Ex. 12-3   Leonel Power, *Missa Alma Redemptoris Mater*: (a) Gloria, beginning; (b) Sanctus, beginning

Ex. 12-4a   *Missa Caput*, Kyrie (sung with prosulas), mm. 11–25

Ex. 12-4b   The *Caput* melisma

Ex. 12-4c   *Missa Caput*, Kyrie (sung with prosulas), mm. 50–52

Ex. 12-5   *Missa Caput*: (a) middle of Gloria; (b) end of Gloria; (c) middle of Credo; (d) end of Credo; (e) middle of Sanctus; (f) end of Sanctus; (g) middle of Agnus Dei; (h) end of Agnus Dei.

Ex. 12-6   Johannes Ockeghem, *Missa Caput*, first Kyrie, mm. 1–8

Ex. 12-7   *Missa Prolationum*, Agnus II: (a) in the original notation as a single voice; (b) realized as a mensuration canon in two parts

Ex. 12-8   Johannes Ockeghem, *Missa cuiusvis toni*, Kyrie I: (a) pitched on D (Dorian); (b) pitched on E (Phrygian); (c) pitched on F (Lydian); (d) pitched on G (Mixolydian)

Ex. 12-9a   Jacobus Obrecht, *Missa Caput*, Gloria, mm. 1–5

Ex. 12-9b   Original *Missa Caput*, opening phrase

Ex. 12-9c   Jacobus Obrecht, *Missa Caput*, Gloria, mm. 17–23

Ex. 12-9d   Jacobus Obrecht, *Missa Caput*, Gloria, mm. 213–end

Ex. 12-10   Transcription of *L'Homme Armé*

Ex. 12-11   Antoine Busnoys, *Missa L'Homme Armé*, first Kyrie, mm. 1–19

Ex. 12-12   Antoine Busnoys, *Missa L'Homme Armé*, last Agnus Dei, mm. 14–22

Ex. 12-13   Antoine Busnoys, *Missa L'Homme Armé*, Gloria, "Tu solus altissimus"

Ex. 12-14   Antoine Busnoys, *Missa L'Homme Armé*, Christe

Ex. 12-15a   Antoine Busnoys, *Missa L'Homme Armé*, Sanctus, mm. 26–29

Ex. 12-15b   Philippe Basiron, *Missa L'Homme Armé*, Agnus I, mm. 8–23

Ex. 12-16   Guillaume Du Fay, *Missa L'Homme Armé*, Credo, "Et exspecto"

Ex. 12-17   Josquin des Prez, *Missa L'Homme Armé super voces musicales*, Kyrie

Chapter 13

Ex. 13-1   Philippe Basiron, *Salve Regina*: (a) mm. 1–25; (b) mm. 98–end

Ex. 13-2   Johannes Ockeghem, *Salve Regina*, "O clemens, O pia, O dulcis"

Ex. 13-3   Guillaume Du Fay, *Ave Regina coelorum* III: (a) mm. 1–29; (b) "Miserere supplicanti Dufaÿ"

Ex. 13-4   Guillaume Du Fay, *Missa Ave Regina coelorum*, Agnus II

Ex. 13-5   Guillaume Du Fay, *Hélas mon deuil*, mm. 1–8

Ex. 13-6   William Cornysh, *Salve Regina*: (a) beginning; (b) end

Ex. 13-7   Gaspar van Weerbeke, *Mater, Patris Filia*, mm. 1–11

Ex. 13-8   Gaspar van Weerbeke, *Quem terra pontus aethera*, mm. 1–23

Ex. 13-9   Loyset Compère, *Ave Maria*, mm. 1–18

Ex. 13-10   Johannes Ockeghem, *Ma bouche rit*

Ex. 13-11   Josquin des Prez, *Missa L'Homme Armé super voces musicales*, Credo, mm. 1–13

Ex. 13-12   Josquin des Prez, *Missa L'Homme Armé super voces musicales*, Agnus II, realized in three parts

Ex. 13-13   Josquin des Prez, *Christe, Fili Dei* (*loco Agnus Dei* in cycle *Vultum Tuum deprecabuntur*): (a) mm. 1–11; (b) mm. 28–end

Ex. 13-14   *J'ay pris amours* (anonymous rondeau)

Ex. 13-15   Instrumental duo on *J'ay pris amours*

Ex. 13-16a   Henricus Isaac, *J'ay pris amours*, mm. 1–13

Ex. 13-16b   Johannes Martini, *J'ay pris amours*, mm. 1–4

Ex. 13-17   *Gross senen* (*J'ay pris amours*) settings from the Glogauer Liederbuch:
(a) Original superius and tenor beneath a new cantus part.
(b) Original tenor with two new voices (c) Superius and tenor of the preceding with a new contratenor. (d) Superius of the preceding with two new voices.

Ex. 13-18   Henricus Isaac, Benedictus from *Missa Quant j'ay au cuer*, as it appears (without text) in Petrucci's *Odhecaton*

Ex. 13-19a   Johannes Ghiselin, *La Alfonsina*, mm. 1–19

Ex. 13-19b   Josquin des Prez, *Ile fantazies de Joskin*, mm. 1–12

Chapter 14

Ex. 14-1   Josquin des Prez, *Memor esto*, mm. 1–14

Ex. 14-2   Josquin des Prez, *Missa Pange lingua*, Kyrie I

Ex. 14-3   "Hercules, Dux Ferrari(a)e" in musical notation

Ex. 14-4   Josquin des Prez, *Missa Hercules Dux Ferrariae*, Hosanna

Ex. 14-5   Josquin des Prez, *Pater noster*, mm. 1–17

Ex. 14-6   Josquin des Prez, *Ave Maria. . . Virgo serena*: (a) mm. 1–8; (b) mm. 9–14; (c) mm. 20–28; (d) mm. 28–35; (e) mm. 36–end

Ex. 14-7   Ludwig Sennfl, *Ave Maria. . . Virgo serena*, mm. 76–80

Ex. 14-8   Antoine de Févin, *Missa super Ave Maria*, Kyrie, first section

Ex. 14-9   Josquin des Prez, *Benedicta es, coelorum regina*, mm. 1–10

Chapter 15

Ex. 15-1   Gioseffo Zarlino's *senaria* (chord of six), based on C

Ex. 15-2   Nicolas Gombert, *In illo tempore*, mm. 1–23

Ex. 15-3   Jacobus Clemens, *Qui consolabatur me recessit a me*: (a) mm. 1–24; (b) mm. 78–end

Ex. 15-4   Jacobus Clemens, *Souterliedekens*, Psalm 71 (*In te, Domine, speravi*)

Ex. 15-5   Adrian Willaert, *Benedicta es, coelorum regina*: (a) mm. 1–15, (b) mm. 24–31, (c) mm. 144–50

Ex. 15-6   Gioseffo Zarlino, *Il modo di fugir le cadenze* (*Istitutione harmoniche*, Book III)

Ex. 15-7   Jacques Buus, Ricercare no. 4: (a) mm. 1–15, (b) mm. 98–110

Ex. 15-8   John Taverner, *Missa Gloria Tibi Trinitas*, Benedictus: (a) mm. 7–21; (b) mm. 26–end

Ex. 15-9a   Jacques Buus, Ricercare no. 1 from *Il secondo libro di recercari* (Venice: Gardane, 1549), opening point, scored from partbooks

Ex. 15-9b   Jacques Buus, Ricercare no. 1, opening point, as it appears in *Intabolatura d'organo di recercari* (Venice: Gardane, 1549)

Ex. 15-10   Henricus Isaac, *Missa super La Spagna*, Agnus II

Ex. 15-11   Diego Ortiz, *Tratado de glosas* (1553), six recercadas on *La Spagna*

Ex. 15-12   Traditional ground-bass tenors: (a) *Passamezzo antico*; (b) *Romanesca*; (c) *Folia*; (d) *Passamezzo moderno*; (e) *Ruggiero*

Ex. 15-13   Diego Ortiz, *Recercada segunda* (on the *passamezzo moderno*)

Chapter 16

Ex. 16-1   Responsory *Angelus Domini*, in Medicean and Solesmes (Roman) versions

Ex. 16-2a   Giovanni Pierluigi da Palestrina, *Missarum liber tertius* (1570): *Missa L'Homme Armé*, final Agnus Dei

Ex. 16-2b   *Missa super Ut re mi fa sol la*, final Agnus Dei

Ex. 16-3a   Jacquet of Mantua, *Repleatur os meum laude*, opening point

Ex. 16-3b   Giovanni Pierluigi da Palestrina, *Missa Repleatur os meum laude*, Kyrie I

Ex. 16-3c   Giovanni Pierluigi da Palestrina, *Missa Repleatur os meum laude*, Christe

Ex. 16-3d   Giovanni Pierluigi da Palestrina, *Missa Repleatur os meum laude*, Kyrie II

Ex. 16-4   Giovanni Pierluigi da Palestrina, *O magnum mysterium*, opening phrase

Ex. 16-5   Giovanni Pierluigi da Palestrina, *Missa O magnum mysterium*: (a) Kyrie, beginning; (b) Gloria ("Et in terra. . ."), beginning; (c) Credo ("Patrem omnipotentem. . ."), beginning; (d) Sanctus, beginning; (e) Agnus Dei, beginning

Ex. 16-6   Vincenzo Ruffo, *Missae Quatuor concinate ad ritum Concilii Mediolani*

Ex. 16-7   Giovanni Pierluigi da Palestrina, *Missa Papae Marcelli*, opening Kyrie

Ex. 16-8   Giovanni Pierluigi da Palestrina, *Missa Papae Marcelli*, Credo, mm. 1–8

Ex. 16-9   Giovanni Pierluigi da Palestrina, *Missa Papae Marcelli*, Sanctus, mm. 1–16

Ex. 16-10   Giovanni Pierluigi da Palestrina, *Missa Papae Marcelli*, Credo, mm. 186–97

Ex. 16-11   Giovanni Pierluigi da Palestrina, *Missa Papae Marcelli*, Agnus Dei, mm. 1–15

Ex. 16-12   Giovanni Pierluigi da Palestrina, *Missa Papae Marcelli*, Agnus II: (a) mm. 1–10; (b) mm. 40–53

Ex. 16-13   Giovanni Pierluigi da Palestrina, *Tui sunt coeli* (Offertory), mm. 1–22

Ex. 16-14   Balthasar Sartori, *O magnum mysterium*, mm. 1–10

Ex. 16-15   Thomas Tallis, *O nata lux de lumine*, mm. 1–9

Ex. 16-16   Philip van Wilder, *Pater noster*, beginning

Ex. 16-17   William Byrd, Mass in Four Parts, Agnus Dei, mm. 40–56

Ex. 16-18   William Byrd, Mass in Five Parts, Agnus Dei, mm. 33–42

Ex. 16-19a   Giovanni Pierluigi da Palestrina, *Missa Papae Marcelli*, Credo, mm. 145–53

Ex. 16-19b   William Byrd, Mass in Five Parts, Credo, mm. 157–68

Ex. 16-20   William Byrd, *Ave verum corpus*, mm. 36–43

Ex. 16-21   William Byrd, *Non vos relinquam* (*Gradualia*, Book II)

Chapter 17

Ex. 17-1   Marco Cara, *Mal un muta per effecto*

Ex. 17-2   "Modo di cantar sonetti" from Ottaviano Petrucci, *Strambotti, ode, frottole, sonetti. Et modo de cantar versi latini e capituli. Libro quarto* (1505)

Ex. 17-3   "Josquin Dascanio," *El Grillo*, mm. 1–21

Ex. 17-4   Jörg Schönfelder, *Von edler Art* (1513)

Ex. 17-5   Johannes Brahms, *Von edler Art* (1864), mm. 1–10

Ex. 17-6   Ludwig Sennfl, *Lust hab ich ghabt zuer Musica*, mm. 1–15

Ex. 17-7   Claudin de Sermisy, *Tant que vivray*, mm. 1–16

Ex. 17-8a   Hypothetical beginning for *Tant que vivray*

Ex. 17-8b   Clemens non Papa, beginning of motet *Musica dei donum*

Ex. 17-9   Clément Janequin, *La guerre*, a 5, with Verdelot's extra voice (secunda pars, mm. 1–6)

Ex. 17-10   Orlando di Lasso, *Je l'ayme bien*

Ex. 17-11   Orlando di Lasso, *Matona mia cara*

Ex. 17-12   Orlando di Lasso, *Audite nova*

Ex. 17-13   Orlando di Lasso, *Prophetiae Sibyllarum*: (a) Prologue; (b) *Sibylla cimmeria*, mm. 35–46

Ex. 17-14   Jacques Arcadelt, *Il bianco e dolce cigno*: (a) mm. 1–10; (b) mm. 34–46

Ex. 17-15   Cipriano de Rore, *Dalle belle contrade d'oriente*, mm. 26–48

Ex. 17-16   Luca Marenzio, *Solo e pensoso*, mm. 1–24

Ex. 17-17   Giaches de Wert, *Solo e pensoso*, opening point

Ex. 17-18   Claudio Monteverdi, *A un giro sol*: (a) mm. 16–27; (b) mm. 43–55

Ex. 17-19   Claudio Monteverdi, *Cruda Amarilli*, mm. 1–14, encompassing the first of Artusi's "spots"

Ex. 17-20   Carlo Gesualdo, *Moro, lasso*, mm. 1–12

Ex. 17-21   John Dowland, "Flow My Tears," first strain

Ex. 17-22   John Dowland, "The Lachrymae Pavan," opening

Ex. 17-23   John Dowland, *Can shee excuse my wrongs*: (a) first strain; (b) voice part rebarred to show hemiola scansions

Ex. 17-24a   Thomas Morley, "Now is the month of Maying"

Ex. 17-24b   Orazio Vecchi, *So ben mi c'ha bon tempo*

Ex. 17-25   John Ward, *Upon a Bank*, mm. 12–27

Chapter 18

Ex. 18-1   Claudio Monteverdi, *A un giro sol*: (a) as set by Martin Luther; (b) as set by Ludwig Sennfl

Ex. 18-2   *Christ lag in Todesbanden* compared with *Victimae paschali* and *Christ ist erstanden*

Ex. 18-3   Heinrich Isaac, *Innsbruck, ich muss dich lassen*, underlaid both with original text and with Lutheran *contrafactum*, mm. 1–9

Ex. 18-4   Johann Walther, *Christ lag in Todesbanden*

Ex. 18-5   *Ein' feste Burg ist unser Gott*: (a) as set by Martin Agricola; (b) as set by Stephan Mahu

Ex. 18-6   *Christ lag in Todesbanden*: (a) from Lucas Osiander, *Funfftzig geistliche Lieder* (1586); (b) from Michael Praetorius, *Musae sioniae* (1609-10)

Ex. 18-7   Sethus Calvisius, *Ein' feste Burg* (1603)

Ex. 18-8   Benedictus Ducis, *Ein Lämmlein geht*

Ex. 18-9   Jacobus Gallus, *Mirabile mysterium*: (a) mm. 1–11; (b) mm. 16–28; (c) mm. 43–47

Ex. 18-10   From the "Longueval" Passion, mm. 10–21

Ex. 18-11   Jacobus Gallus, St. John Passion, tertia pars, end

Ex. 18-12   Jacobus Gallus, St. John Passion, tertia pars, mm. 1–7, high voices only

Ex. 18-13   Giovanni Gabrieli, *In ecclesiis* (*Sacrae Symphoniae*, Book II) mm. 1–12

Ex. 18-14a   Canzona incipit by Andrea Gabrieli

Ex. 18-14b   Canzona incipit by Claudio Merulo

Ex. 18-15   Andrea Gabrieli, *Aria della battaglia*, secunda pars, mm. 1–4

Ex. 18-16   Tomás Luis de Victoria, *Missa pro Victoria*, Benedictus, mm. 7–13

Ex. 18-17   Giovanni Gabrieli, *Sonata pian'e forte*, end

Ex. 18-18   Giovanni Gabrieli, *Sonata per tre violini*, end

Chapter 19

Ex. 19-1   From the *intermedii* of 1589: (a) opening aria, mm. 5–9; (b) main ritornello of closing *ballo* (*Aria di Fiorenza*); (c) Giulio Caccini, *Io che dal ciel cader*, beginning; (d) Jacopo Peri, *Dunque fra torbid' onde*, beginning

Ex. 19-2   Giuliu Caccini, *Amarilli mia bella*, first couplet in transcription, mm. 1–10

Ex. 19-3   Marco da Gagliano, *Valli profonde*: (a) mm. 1–8, (b) mm. 38–45, (c) mm. 51–54

Ex. 19-4   Sigismondo d'India, *Piange, madonna*: (a) mm. 1–4, (b) mm. 8–17

Ex. 19-5   Claudio Saracini, *Da te parto*: (a) mm. 1–4, (b) end

Ex. 19-6   Romanesca tenor, with Caccini's and Frescobaldi's variants

Ex. 19-7   Girolamo Frescobaldi, *Dunque dovro* (*Aria di romanesca*): (a) mm. 1–6,
(b) mm. 19–24, (c) mm. 37–42, (d) mm. 55–60

Ex. 19-8   Jacopo Peri, *La Dafne*: "Qual' nova meraviglia"

Ex. 19-9   Jacopo Peri, *Euridice*: (a) scene 2, mm. 39–51; (b) Orfeo's closing
monologue

Ex. 19-10   *Anima mia che pensi*: (a) the original lauda (pub. 1577); (b) beginning
of Emilio de' Cavalieri's dialogue setting

VOLUME 2

Chapter 20

Ex. 20-1   Claudio Monteverdi, *Scherzi musicali: O rosetta*

Ex. 20-2   Claudio Monteverdi, *Sestina* (Madrigals, Book VI), no. 1 (*Incenerite
spoglie*), mm. 1–9

Ex. 20-3   Claudio Monteverdi, *Concerto* (Madrigals, Book VII), *Lettera amorosa*
(*Se i languidi miei sguardi*), mm. 1–22

Ex. 20-4   Claudio Monteverdi, *Combattimento*, fifth stanza, *L'onta irrita lo sdegno
a la vendetta*

Ex. 20-5   Claudio Monteverdi, Madrigals, Book VIII, *Non havea febo* (*Lamento
della ninfa*), mm 1–12

Ex. 20-6   Claudio Monteverdi, *Vespro della beata virgine* (1610), *Deus in
adiutorium meum intende* (doxology), mm. 14–18

Ex. 20-7   Claudio Monteverdi, *Orfeo*, Act II, messenger breaks in on song and
dance

Ex. 20-8   Claudio Monteverdi, *Orfeo*, Orfeo gets the horrifying news from the
messenger

Ex. 20-9   Claudio Monteverdi, *Orfeo*, Orfeo's recitative ("Tu se' morta")

Ex. 20-10   Claudio Monteverdi, *Orfeo*, Chorus ("Ahi caso acerbo")

Ex. 20-11   Claudio Monteverdi, *L'incoronazione di Poppea*, Act III, scene 6
(Octavia), mm. 1–18

Ex. 20-12   Claudio Monteverdi, *L'incoronazione di Poppea*, Act III, scene 7
(Arnalta), mm. 1–28

Ex. 20-13   Claudio Monteverdi, *L'incoronazione di Poppea*, Act I, scene 6,
mm. 113–41

Ex. 20-14   Claudio Monteverdi, *L'incoronazione di Poppea*, Act I, scene 10,
mm. 1–38

Ex. 20-15   Claudio Monteverdi, *L'incoronazione di Poppea*, final scene, no. 24
(ciaccona: *Pur ti miro*), end

Chapter 21

Ex. 21-1   Claudio Monteverdi, *Zefiro torna*, beginning

Ex. 21-2   Girolamo Frescobaldi, *Cento partite sopra passacagli*, conclusion

Ex. 21-3   Girolamo Frescobaldi, Toccata IX (*Toccata nona*), mm. 11–22

Ex. 21-4   Michelangelo Rossi, Toccata VII (*Toccata settima*), mm. 9–16

Ex. 21-5   Girolamo Frescobaldi, *Messa della Madonna* (in *Fiori musicali*), opening section of Kyrie, mm. 13–23

Ex. 21-6   Jan Pieterszoon Sweelinck, *Fantasia chromatica*, mm. 1–16

Ex. 21-7   Giles Farnaby, *Daphne*, mm. 1–13

Ex. 21-8   Samuel Scheidt, *Christ lag in Todesbunden*: (a) first versus, mm. 1–7; (b) second versus, mm. 1–5; (c) third versus, mm. 1–19; (d) fourth versus, mm. 39–44; (e) fifth versus, mm. 65–end

Ex. 21-9   Johann Hermann Schein, *Christ lag in Todesbanden* from *Opella nova* (1618), mm. 20–25

Ex. 21-10   Michael Praetorius, *Christ lag in Todesbanden* from *Polyhymnia caduceatrix et panegyrica*, vol. II (Cantus I)

Ex. 21-11a First line of Heinrich Schütz's *O quam tu pulchra es* rhetorically parsed

Ex. 21-11b Christoph Bernhard, example of *Quaesitio notae*

Ex. 21-12   Heinrich Schütz, *O quam tu pulchra es* (*Symphoniae sacrae I*): (a) mm. 56–58, mm. 66–68; (b) mm. 91–95; (c) mm. 100–111; (d) mm. 112–end

Ex. 21-13   Heinrich Schütz, *Eile mich, Gott, zu erretten* (*Kleine geistliche Concerte I*), mm. 1–16

Ex. 21-14   Heinrich Schütz, *Saul, Saul, was verfolgst du mich* (*Symphoniae sacrae III*), mm. 67–74

Ex. 21-15   Barbara Strozzi, Cantata: *Lagrime mie*: (a) mm. 1–13; (b) mm. 49–55; (c) mm. 88–108

Chapter 22

Ex. 22-1   Jean-Baptiste Lully, Overture to *Atys* (1676): (a) opening section; (b) beginning of middle section

Ex. 22-2   Jean-Philippe Rameau, *Castor et Pollux*, Prologue

Ex. 22-3   Jean-Baptiste Lully, *Armide*, Passacaille, beginning

Ex. 22-4a   Jean-Baptiste Lully, *Atys*, Act III, Atys's opening *air* (sarabande)

Ex. 22-4b   Jean-Baptiste Lully, *Atys*, Act III, *Air à trois* (allemande)

Ex. 22-4c   Jean-Baptise Lully, *Atys*, Act III, *Sommeil*

Ex. 22-4d   Jean-Baptiste Lully, *Atys*, *Choeur des Songes Funestes*

Ex. 22-4e   Jean-Baptiste Lully, *Atys*, Act III, Cybele's complaint

Ex. 22-4f   Jean-Baptiste Lully, *Atys*, Act III, Melissa's *petit air* (gavotte)

Ex. 22-4g   Claudio Monteverdi, *Lamento d'Arianna*, refrain

Ex. 22-4h   Jean-Baptiste Lully, *Atys*, Act III, Cybele's lament (sarabande)

Ex. 22-5   André Campra, *Idoménée*, from the final mad scene

Ex. 22-6   Jean-Philippe Rameau, *Castor et Pollux*, Act V, ariette, *Brillez, brillez astres nouveaux*

Ex. 22-7   Christopher Tye, *In Nomines*: (a) "Crye" (opening); (b) "Howld Fast" (opening); (c) "Trust" (opening)

Ex. 22-8   Alfonso Ferrabosco II, *In Nomine a 6*

Ex. 22-9   William Lawes, Ayre in six parts
Ex. 22-10   William Lawes, fantazia themes: (a) Suite in G Minor; (b) Suite in C
                Minor in five parts; (c) Suite in C Major (two variants); (d) Suite in
                C Minor in six parts
Ex. 22-11   Thomas Tomkins, "A Sad Pavan for These Distracted Times"
Ex. 22-12   Henry Purcell, Overture in D Minor: (a) beginning; (b) end
Ex. 22-13   Henry Purcell, *The Fairy Queen*, Act II masque, Secrecy's song
Ex. 22-14   Henry Purcell, *Dido and Aeneas*, recitative and dance song
Ex. 22-15   Henry Purcell, *Dido and Aeneas*, Act III, scene 2, Dido's lament

Chapter 23
Ex. 23-1   Alessandro Scarlatti, Cantata: *Andate, oh miei sospiri*: (a) opening
                recitative; (b) third recitative, harmonic "aside"
Ex. 23-2   Alessandro Scarlatti, Cantata: *Andate, oh miei sospiri*, second aria (in
                siciliana style): (a) setting of opening line; (b) section break; (c) end of
                middle section
Ex. 23-3   Alessandro Scarlatti, L'Eraclea, "Ricordati ch'io t'amo," mm. 1–6
Ex. 23-4   Alessandro Scarlatti, *La caduta de' decemviri*, Sinfonia: (a) mm. 1–7,
                (b) Sinfonia, mm. 29–36, (c) mm. 55–end
Ex. 23-5   Leonardo Vinci, "L'onda dal mare divisa" (*Artaserse*, Act III, scene 1):
                (a) mm. 1–24, (b) mm. 39–55, (c) mm. 136–56
Ex. 23-6   Johann Adolf Hasse, *Artaserse* (1730), recitativo obligato ("Ch'io
                parta?") and aria ("Parto qual pastorello prima che rompa il fiume"):
                (a) mm. 1–9, (b) mm. 37–45, (c) mm. 49–57
Ex. 23-7   Riccardo Broschi, "Son qual nave ch'agitata"

Chapter 24
Ex. 24-1a   Arcangelo Corelli, *Sonata da chiesa*, Op. 3, no. 11, final Allegro,
                mm. 1–12
Ex. 24-1b   Arcangelo Corelli, *Sonata da camera*, Op. 4, no. 2, final Corrente,
                mm. 1–25
Ex. 24-2   Johann Joseph Fux, Canonic Sonata in G minor, I, 1–8
Ex. 24-3   Arcangelo Corelli, *Sonata da chiesa*, Op. 3, no. 11, second movement
                (Presto)
Ex. 24-4   Diatonic circles of fifths on C major and G minor
Ex. 24-5   Alessandro Scarlatti, *L'Aldimiro* (1683), "S'empia man" (Act III, scene
                12)
Ex. 24-6a   Circle of fifths in Corelli, Op. 3, no.11, II (Presto)
Ex. 24-6b   Circle of fifths in G minor with interlocking sevenths
Ex. 24-7a   Arcangelo Corelli, Op. 3, no. 11, II (Presto), mm. 34–36, analyzed to
                show *basse fondamentale*
Ex. 24-7b   Arcangelo Corelli, Op. 4, no. 2, I, mm. 1–5, analyzed to show *basse
                fondamentale*

Ex. 24-8a   Arcangelo Corelli, *Pastorale ad libitum* from the "Christmas Concerto", Op. 6, no. 8

Ex. 24-8b   Arcangelo Corelli, *Pastorale ad libitum*, mm. 8–11, analyzed to show *basse fondamentale*

Ex. 24-9a   Alessandro Marcello, Oboe Concerto in D minor, III, beginning

Ex. 24-9b   Alessandro Marcello, Concerto in D minor, III, mm. 22–25 and mm. 32–52, analyzed to show *basse fondamentale*

Ex. 24-10   Henry Purcell, "Fantazia 7" a 4, mm. 1–26

Ex. 24-11   Henry Purcell, *Sonnatas of III Parts*, no. 3 in D minor, mm. 25–62

Ex. 24-12   Henry Purcell, *Sonnatas of III Parts*, no. 3 in D minor, m. 98–110

Ex. 24-13   G. F. Handel, Concerto grosso in B-flat major, Op. 6, no. 7

Ex. 24-14   G. F. Handel, Concerto grosso in B-flat major, Op. 6, no. 7, Allegro, mm. 1–22

Ex. 24-15   J. S. Bach, Toccata in F, BWV 540: (a) mm. 1–82; (b) mm. 169–76; (c) mm. 188–219. (d) Ordinary deceptive cadences in D major and D minor.

Ex. 24-16   Antonio Vivaldi, Concerto for Bassoon in C major, F VIII/13, mm. 1–12

Ex. 24-17   Antonio Vivaldi, Concerto for Bassoon in C major, F VIII/13: (a) mm. 12–14; (b) mm. 30–25; (c) mm. 44–48; (d) mm. 162–165; (e) mm. 74–78

Ex. 24-18   Antonio Vivaldi, Concerto for Four Violins Op. 3, no. 10, I: (a) mm. 37–39, (b) mm. 68–72

Ex. 24-19   Antonio Vivaldi, *La primavera* (Op. 8, no. 1), I: (a) mm. 1–3; (b) mm. 15–18; (c) mm. 37–41; (d) 45–46; (e) 60–65

Chapter 25

Ex. 25-1a   J. A. Reincken, *Hortus musicus*, Sonata no. 1, Gigue, mm. 1–21

Ex. 25-1b   J. S. Bach, A. Reincken's *Hortus musicus*, Sonata no. 1, Gigue, arranged as a keyboard sonata, mm. 1–34

Ex. 25-2a   J. C. F. Fischer, *Ariadne musica*, subject of the E-major Fugue

Ex. 25-2b   J. S. Bach, *Das wohltemperirte Clavier*, Book II, subject of the E-major Fugue

Ex. 25-3   J. S. Bach, *Das wohltemperirte Clavier*, Book I: (a) Prelude no. 1 (C major); (b) Fugue no. 24 (B minor), mm. 1–19

Ex. 25-4   Louis Couperin, unmeasured prelude

Ex. 25-5   J. S. Bach, Prelude no. 1, mm. 5–11, analyzed for voice leading

Ex. 25-6a   Dietrich Buxtehude, *Durch Adams Fall*, mm. 1–23

Ex. 25-6b   J. S. Bach, *Durch Adams Fall* (*Orgelbüchlein*, no. 38)

Ex. 25-7a   J. S. Bach, French Suite no. 5 in G major, Allemande

Ex. 25-7b   Johann Jakob Froberger, Suite in E minor, Allemande

Ex. 25-7c   J. S. Bach, Concerto in C for Two Harpsichords, BWV 1061, I, mm. 1–4

Ex. 25-7d   J. S. Bach, Concerto in C for Two Harpsichords, BWV 1061, I, mm. 28–32

Ex. 25-8a   J. S. Bach, French Suite no. 5 in G major, Courante

Ex. 25-8b   J. S. Bach, French Suite no. 3 in B minor, Courante

Ex. 25-9   J. S. Bach, French Suite no. 5 in G major, Sarabande

Ex. 25-10   J. S. Bach, French Suite no. 5 in G major: (a) Gavotte; (b) Bourée; (c) Loure

Ex. 25-11   J. S. Bach, French Suite no. 5 in G major, Gigue

Ex. 25-12   François Couperin, *Le Rossignol en amour* (14th Ordre, no. 1): (a) beginning; (b) "Double de Rossignol"

Ex. 25-13   Arcangelo Corelli, Sonata in D major, Op. 5, no. 1

Ex. 25-14   J. S. Bach, slow movement from the "Italian Concerto" with the Incipit of a hypothetical "original"

Ex. 25-15   J. S. Bach, Ouverture (Orchestral Suite) no. 3, I: (a) beginning; (b) end of fugal exposition and beginning of episode

Ex. 25-16   J. S. Bach, Brandenburg Concerto no. 5, I: (a) opening; (b) mm. 47–51; (c) mm. 71–74; (d) mm. 95–99; (e) mm. 151–59

Chapter 26

Ex. 26-1   George Frideric Handel, "Vivi, tiranno!" from *Rodelinda*, Act III, scene 8: (a) mm. 1–18; (b) mm. 68–81

Ex. 26-2   George Frideric Handel, *Israel in Egypt*: (a) no. 2, recitative, "Now there arose a new king"; (b) no. 4, chorus, "They loathed to drink of the river," mm. 1–13; (c) no. 5, aria, "Their land brought forth frogs," mm. 1–11; (d) no. 6, chorus, "He spake the word," mm. 1–3; (e) no. 7, chorus, "He gave them hailstones," mm. 22–26; (f) no. 8, chorus, "He sent a thick darkness," mm. 1–13; (g) no. 9, chorus, "He smote all the first-born of Egypt," mm. 1–4

Ex. 26-3   Alessandro Stradella, *Qual prodigio e ch'io miri*, plundered for *Israel in Egypt*

Ex. 26-4a   Gottlieb Muffat, *Componimenti musicali*, Suite no. 4

Ex. 26-4b   George Frideric Handel, *Ode for St. Cecilia's Day*

Ex. 26-5a   George Frideric Handel, duetto, *No, di voi non vo' fidarmi*

Ex. 26-5b   *Messiah*, no. 12 ("For unto us a child is born"), mm. 1–14

Ex. 26-6   *Messiah*, no. 6 ("But who may abide"): (a) 1741 version, mm. 1–18; (b) 1750 version, m. 139–end

Ex. 26-7a   Gregorian hymn, *Veni redemptor gentium*

Ex. 26-7b   Chorale: *Nun komm, der Heiden Heiland*

Ex. 26-8   J. S. Bach, *Christ lag in Todesbanden*, BWV 4: (a) Sinfonia; (b) Verse II, mm. 1–8; (c) Verse V, mm. 1–12; (d) Verse V, 64–74; (e) Verse VI, mm. 1–5

Ex. 26-9   J. S. Bach, *Nun komm, der Heiden Heiland*, BWV 61: (a) Overture, mm. 1–7; (b) no. 2, recitativo; (c) no. 3, aria, mm. 1–5, 17–21; (d) no. 4, recitativo, mm. 1–4; (e) no. 5, aria, mm. 1–16

Ex. 26-10   J. S. Bach, *Ein' feste Burg*, BWV 80, the four chorale movements: (a) the concluding *Cantionalsatz*; (b) no. 5, chorus, "Und wenn die Welt voll Teufel wär," beginning of ritornello; (c) no. 5, end of ritornello; (d) no. 2, Aria con Choral, "Mit unser Macht," mm. 9–13; (e) no. 1, Choral Fantasia, "Ein' feste Burg," mm. 23–30; (f) no. 1, harmonic "Far-Out Point"

Ex. 26-11   J. S. Bach, Cantata: *Meine Seufzer, meine Tränen*, BWV 13, bass aria, "Ächzen und erbärmlich Weinen" (ritornello and voice incipit), mm. 1–10

Ex. 26-12   J. S. Bach, *Nimm von uns, Herr, du treuer Gott*, BWV 101, opening chorus

Ex. 26-13   J. S. Bach, Cantata: *Wo Gott der Herr nicht bei uns hält*, BWV 178, tenor aria, "Schweig nur, taumelnde Vernunft!", mm. 11–17

Ex. 26-14a   Cantata: *Siehe zu, daß deine Gottesfurcht*, BWV 179, soprano aria "Liebster Gott," mm. 34–71

Ex. 26-14b   Cantata: *Du Hirte Israel, höre*, BWV 104, bass aria "Beglückte Heerde," middle section

Ex. 26-15   J. S. Bach, *St. John Passion*, turba, "Weg! Weg!," mm. 40–51

Ex. 26-16   J. S. Bach, *St. Matthew Passion*, opening chorus, mm. 34–36

Ex. 26-17a   Goldberg bass

Ex. 26-17b   Canon no. 14 as written by Bach

Ex. 26-17c   Canon no. 14 as realized by Christoph Wolff

Ex. 26-18   (a) The B-A-C-H cipher; (b) B-A-C-H cipher at end of *The Art of Fugue*

Ex. 26-19   Domenico Scarlatti, Sonata in G, K. 105, mm. 39–54

Ex. 26-20   Domenico Scarlatti, Sonata in E major, K. 264, mm. 127–46

Ex. 26-21   Domenico Scarlatti, Sonata in F minor, K. 481: (a) mm. 9–12; (b) mm. 36–44

Ex. 26-22   Domenico Scarlatti, Sonata in C, K. 159: (a) mm. 1–6; (b) mm. 38–47

Chapter 27

Ex. 27-1   W. F. Bach, Sonata in F (Falck catalogue no. 6), first movement

Ex. 27-2   W. F. Bach, Sonata in F (Falck catalogue no. 6), second movement (Minuet and Trio)

Ex. 27-3   C. P. E. Bach, "Prussian" Sonata no. 1 in F (Wotquenne catalogue no. 48/1): (a) first movement, mm. 1–4, 32–37; (b) second movement

Ex. 27-4   C. P. E. Bach, Fantasia in C minor

Ex. 27-5   C. P. E. Bach, Fantasia in C minor with Shakespeare text overlaid by Gerstenberg

Ex. 27-6   J. C. Bach, Sonata in D, Op. 5, no. 2: (a) first page; (b) second page

Ex. 27-7   Jean-Joseph Cassanéa de Mondonville, Accompanied Sonata in C, Op. 3, no. 4

Ex. 27-8   Carl Friedrich Abel, Sonata in B-flat, Op. 2, no. 4: (a) first
               movement, mm. 1–11; (b) end of second movement
Ex. 27-9a   Domenico Alberti, Sonata in C, Op. 1, no. 3 (London, 1748),
               mm. 1–4
Ex. 27-9b   Baldassare Galuppi, Sonata no. 2 (London, 1756), I, mm. 69–79
Ex. 27-10   Bajocco's aria from Giuseppe Maria Orlandini's *Il giocatore*
Ex. 27-11   Giovanni Pergolesi, *La serva padrona*, Act II: (a) Serpina's aria,
               mm. 8–18; (b) Uberto's aria, mm. 12–15, 31–39
Ex. 27-12   Jean-Jacques Rousseau, *Le devin du village*, no. 1, "J'ai perdu mon
               serviteur"

Chapter 28
Ex. 28-1   Niccolò Piccinni, *La buona figliuola*: (a) "Una povera ragazza" (Act I,
               scene 12), mm. 5–9; (b) "Furie di donna irata" (Act I, scene 14),
               mm. 21–31
Ex. 28-2   Niccolò Piccinni, *La buona figliuola*, Act II finale
Ex. 28-3   Christoph Willibald Gluck, *Orfeo ed Euridice*, Act I, scene 1, chorus,
               recitative and pantomime
Ex. 28-4   Christoph Willibald Gluck, *Orfeo ed Euridice*, Act III, scene 1: "Che
               faro senza Euridice?" refrain, mm. 7–16
Ex. 28-5a   Christoph Willibald Gluck, *Alceste*, Act I, scene 4, High Priest's
               exhortation, mm. 1–18
Ex. 28-5b   W. A. Mozart, *Idomeneo*, no. 23, mm. 2–23
Ex. 28-6   W. A. Mozart, *Die Entführung aus dem Serail*, Belmonte's aria, "O wie
               ängstlich": (a) mm. 1–8; (b) mm. 29–37
Ex. 28-7   W. A. Mozart, *Magic Flute*: (a) "Der Hölle Rache" (The Queen of the
               Night), mm. 21–47; (b) "In diesen heil'gen Hallen" (Sarastro),
               mm. 16–26

Chapter 29
Ex. 29-1   Giovanni Battista Sammartini, Sinfonia in G, from Fonds
               Blancheton: (a) mm. 1–17; (b) mm. 23–34
Ex. 29-2   J. C. Bach, Sinfonia, Op. 18, no. 2: (a) mm. 1–7; (b) mm. 81–87
Ex. 29-3   C. P. E. Bach, first Orchestral Symphony (Wotquenne. 183; 1776):
               (a) mm. 1–19; (b) mm. 35–48; (c) mm. 206–17
Ex. 29-4   Franz Joseph Haydn, Symphony "A," I: (a) mm. 43–79;
               (b) mm. 1–4; (c) mm. 31–37; (d) mm. 23–27
Ex. 29-5   Franz Joseph Haydn, Symphony no. 45 in F-sharp minor
               ("Farewell"): (a) I, mm. 1–16; (b) I, mm. 108–15; (c) III, mm. 1–12;
               (d) end of the symphony
Ex. 29-6   Franz Joseph Haydn, Quartet in E-flat, Op. 33, no. 2 ("The Joke"):
               (a) I, mm. 1–32; (b) II, mm. 1–10, 21–26; (c) II, mm. 35–42 (first
               strain of the Trio); (d) III, mm. 1–8; (e) IV, mm. 1–8; (f) IV,
               mm. 133–140; (g) IV, mm. 145–152; (h) IV, end

Ex. 29-7a   Franz Joseph Haydn, Symphony no. 94 in G ("Surprise"), I, slow introduction

Ex. 29-7b   Franz Joseph Haydn, Symphony no. 94 in G ("Surprise"), I, Vivace assai, mm. 1–5

Ex. 29-7c.   Franz Joseph Haydn, Symphony no. 94 in G ("Surprise"), hypothetical "symmetrical" version of Ex. 29-7b

Ex. 29-7d   Franz Joseph Haydn, Symphony no. 96, I, mm. 18–26

Ex. 29-7e   Franz Joseph Haydn, Symphony no. 94 in G ("Surprise"), I, mm. 30–38

Ex. 29-7f   Franz Joseph Haydn, Symphony no. 94 in G ("Surprise"), I, mm. 101–107

Ex. 29-7g   Franz Joseph Haydn, Symphony no. 94 in G ("Surprise"), I, mm. 218–228

Ex. 29-8a   Franz Joseph Haydn, Symphony no. 94 in G ("Surprise"), II, mm. 1–16

Ex. 29-8b   Comparison of the opening of Ex. 29-8a with its "development" in the minor variation

Ex. 29-9   Franz Joseph Haydn, Symphony no. 94 in G ("Surprise"), IV: (a) mm. 1–8; (b) mm. 138–48

Ex. 29-10   Franz Joseph Haydn, Symphony no. 104 ("London"), I: (a) slow introduction; (b) beginning of the Allegro; (c) mm. 32–7; (d) mm. 50–53; (e) mm. 58–60; (f) mm. 124–35; (g) mm. 146–55

Chapter 30

Ex. 30-1   W. A. Mozart, Symphony no. 39 in E-flat, II: (a) opening; (b) mm. 33–38; (c) mm. 48–53; (d) mm. 91–97; (e) mm. 103–108; (f) mm. 121–125; (g) end

Ex. 30-2   W. A. Mozart, Violin Concerto no. 5, K. 219, I: (a) mm. 1–9; (b) mm. 37–41; (c) mm. 61–73

Ex. 30-3   W. A. Mozart, Concerto in G major, K. 453, I: beginnings of two different cadenzas

Ex. 30-4   W. A. Mozart, Concerto in G major, K. 453, II: (a) mm. 1–5; (b) mm. 35–38

Ex. 30-5   W. A. Mozart, Concerto no. 17 in G major, K. 453, II: (a) mm. 35–41; (b) mm. 69–86; (c) mm. 86–94

Ex. 30-6   W. A. Mozart, Concerto no. 17 in G major, K. 453, III, mm. 218–29

Ex. 30-7   W. A. Mozart, Fantasia in D minor, K. 397: (a) mm. 1–22; (b) m. 34

Ex. 30-8   W. A. Mozart, Fantasia in C minor, K. 475: (a) mm. 1–22; (b) mm. 10–6 in harmonic reduction; (c) mm. 167–182

Ex. 30-9   François-Joseph Fétis, rewrite of slow introduction to K. 465, I, mm. 1–5

Ex. 30-10   Franz Joseph Haydn, *Creation, Vorstellung des Chaos* in piano reduction: (a) mm. 1–10; (b) mm. 37–44; (c) mm. 48–59

Ex. 30-11   Franz Joseph Haydn, *Creation*, recitative with chorus in full score

Chapter 31

Ex. 31-1a   W. A. Mozart, *Bastien und Bastienne*, first theme of intrada, mm. 1–8

Ex. 31-1b   W. A. Mozart, *Bastien und Bastienne*, intrada, whole first period

Ex. 31-1c   Ludwig van Beethoven, Symphony no. 3, Op. 55 (*Eroica*), I, mm. 1–44 in thematic outline

Ex. 31-2   Ludwig van Beethoven, Symphony no. 3, Op. 55 (*Eroica*), I, mm. 248–65

Ex. 31-3   Ludwig van Beethoven, Symphony no. 3, Op. 55 (*Eroica*), I, mm. 276–288

Ex. 31-4   Ludwig van Beethoven, Symphony no. 3, Op. 55 (*Eroica*), I, the relationship between the E minor theme at mm. 284 ff and the main theme of the first movement

Ex. 31-5   Ludwig van Beethoven, Symphony no. 3, Op. 55 (*Eroica*), I, mm. 378–405

Ex. 31-6   Ludwig van Beethoven, Symphony no. 3, Op. 55 (*Eroica*), I, mm. 631–639

Ex. 31-7   Ludwig van Beethoven, Symphony no. 9, Op. 125, IV, *"Schreckensfanfare"* (arr. Franz Liszt)

Ex. 31-8a   Ludwig van Beethoven, Symphony no. 9, IV, "Ode to Joy" theme

Ex. 31-8b   Ludwig van Beethoven, beginning of "Turkish" variation on the "Ode to Joy" (arr. Liszt)

Ex. 31-9   Ludwig van Beethoven, Symphony no. 9, foreshadowing the "Ode to Joy" in earlier movements: (a) I, mm. 74–77; (b) II, Trio; (c) mm. 127-30

Ex. 31-10   Ludwig van Beethoven, Quartet no. 13 in B-flat, Op. 130, V ("Cavatina")

Ex. 31-11   Ludwig van Beethoven, Symphony no. 3, II ("Marcia funebre"), first violin: (a) mm. 1–8; (b) mm. 238–47

Ex. 31-12   Ludwig van Beethoven, Quartet no. 15 in A minor ("chorale" tune), Op. 132, III ("Heiliger Dankgesang"), reconstructed from mm. 3–7, 9–13, 15–19, 21–25

Ex. 31-13   Ludwig van Beethoven, Quartet no. 15 in A minor, Op. 132, III, Last variation on the "Heiliger Dankgesang"

Chapter 32

Ex. 32-1a   Ludwig van Beethoven, Piano Trio in C minor, Op. 1, no. 3, I, mm. 1–10

Ex. 32-1b   W. A. Mozart, Piano Concerto in C minor, K. 491, opening theme

Ex. 32-2   Ludwig van Beethoven, Piano Trio in C minor (Op. 1, no. 3), I:
             (a) mm. 29–36; (b) mm. 138–49; (c) mm. 224–35

Ex. 32-3   Ludwig van Beethoven, Piano Trio in C minor (Op. 1, no. 3), Finale:
             (a) mm. 1–8; (b) end

Ex. 32-4   Ludwig van Beethoven, *Coriolan* Overture: (a) mm. 1–21;
             (b) mm. 52–75; (c) end

Ex. 32-5   Ludwig van Beethoven, Symphony no. 5 in C minor, Op. 67, I:
             (a) mm. 1–24; (b) mm. 62–65 (strings only); (c) mm. 109–21

Ex. 32-6   Ludwig van Beethoven, Symphony no. 5 in C minor, Op. 67: (a) II,
             mm. 76–77; (b) II, mm. 88–96; (c) III, mm. 19–26.

Ex. 32-7   Ludwig van Beethoven, Symphony no. 5 in C minor, Op. 67, IV:
             (a) mm. 1–12, piccolo; (b) mm. 45–48, first violins; (c) mm. 64–70,
             violas

Ex. 32-8   Ludwig van Beethoven, Symphony no. 5 in C minor, Op. 67, IV:
             (a) mm. 402–404; (b) Presto, outer string parts

Ex. 32-9   Ludwig van Beethoven, Symphony no. 5, in C minor, Op. 67, I:
             (a) opening unisons (mm. 1–5); (b) horn call (mm. 59–63);
             (c) mm. 195–231

Ex. 32-10   Ludwig van Beethoven, Symphony no. 5 in C minor, Op. 67, first
             movement coda

Ex. 32-11   Ludwig van Beethoven, Symphony no. 5 in C minor, Op. 67, II:
             (a) mm. 1–8; (b) mm. 23–31

Ex. 32-12a   Carl Stamitz, Trio, Op. 4, no. 3, IV, mm. 141–164

Ex. 32-12b   Ludwig van Beethoven, Symphony no. 5 in C minor, Op. 67, III,
             mm. 1–20

Ex. 32-13   Ludwig van Beethoven, *Der glorreiche Augenblick*, final Presto,
             beginning of fugal exposition

Ex. 32-14   Ludwig van Beethoven, late fugue subjects: (a) Cello Sonata in D,
             Op. 102, no. 2 (Finale); (b) Piano Sonata in A, Op. 101 (Finale);
             (c) "Hammerklavier" Sonata in B-flat, Op. 106 (Finale)

Ex. 32-15a   Ludwig van Beethoven, Piano Sonata no. 8, Op. 13 ("Pathétique"),
             beginning of the slow introduction

Ex. 32-15b   Ludwig van Beethoven, Piano Sonata no. 32, Op. 111, beginning of
             slow introduction

Ex. 32-16   Ludwig van Beethoven, Piano Sonata no. 32 in C minor, Op. 111, I:
             (a) mm. 17–31; (b) mm. 146–end

Ex. 32-17   Ludwig van Beethoven, Piano Sonata no. 32 in C minor, Op. 111, II:
             (a) *Arietta* (mm. 1–18); (b) mm. 72–80; (c) mm. 106–20;
             (d) mm. 160–69

Ex. 32-18   Ludwig van Beethoven, Piano Sonata no. 32 in C minor, Op. 111, I,
             mm. 48–49, 114–116

Ex. 32-19   Ludwig van Beethoven, Piano Sonata no. 32 in C minor, Op. 111, II,
             mm. 89–92

VOLUME 3

Chapter 33

Ex. 33-1   Ludwig van Beethoven, *Fidelio* in vocal score: (a) no. 11 (Florestan, introduction and aria, mm. 14–20); (b) mm. 33–41

Ex. 33-2   Ludwig van Beethoven, *Fidelio*, Act II finale

Ex. 33-3   Giovanni Paisiello, *Il barbiere di Siviglia*, Overture (beginning)

Ex. 33-4   Gioacchino Rossini, *Il barbiere di Siviglia*, Overture: (a) slow introduction; (b) Allegro, Codetta ("Rossini crescendo")

Ex. 33-5   Giovanni Paisiello, *Il barbiere di Siviglia*, Act II, *Terzetto buffo* (yawning and sneezing)

Ex. 33-6   Gioacchino Rossini, *Il barbiere di Siviglia*, "Largo al factotum," coda

Ex. 33-7   Gioacchino Rossini, *L'Italiana in Algeri*, from the Act I Finale

Ex. 33-8   Richard Wagner, *Die Meistersinger*, Act III, Tailors' Chorus (*"mit Bockstriller"*)

Ex. 33-9   Gioacchino Rossini, *Tancredi*, Act II, "Tu che accendi/Di tanti palpiti": (a) orchestral introdution; (b) cantabile; (c) cabaletta; (d) coda

Ex. 33-10   Vincenzo Bellini, *Norma*, Scene e cavatina (Act I, scene 5): (a) *Parlante*: "In pagine di morte"; (b) Cavatina con coro ("Casta diva," beginning); (c) Cabaletta ("Ah! bello a me ritorna," beginning)

Ex. 33-11   Gaetano Donizetti, *Lucia di Lammermoor*, Act II finale: (a) beginning of sextet ("Chi mi frena"); (b) climax of cantabile

Ex. 33-12   Gaetano Donizetti, *Lucia di Lammermoor*: (a) Aria: "Regnava nel silenzio" (Act I). (b) Act III, scene 2, introductory flute solo. (c) Duet: "Verrano a te" (Act I). (d) Act III, scene 2, flute and clarinet. (e) Cello motif from Act II finale. (f) Act III, scene 2, violin motif.

Ex. 33-13   Gaetano Donizetti, *Lucia di Lammermoor*, Act III, scene 2 ("mad scene"): (a) Cantabile: "Del ciel clemente." (b) Cabaletta, "Spargi d'amaro pianto."

Chapter 34

Ex. 34-1a   Johann Jakob Froberger, end of *Tombeau de M. Blancheroche*

Ex. 34-1b   Jan Ladislav Dussek, *The Sufferings of the Queen of France*, no. 9

Ex. 34-2   Václav Jan Tomášek, *Eclogue*, Op. 35, no. 1, beginning

Ex. 34-3   Use of flat submediant in Václav Jan Tomášek, *Dithyramb*, Op. 65, no. 2, mm. 36–58

Ex. 34-4   John Field, Nocturne no. 4 in A major: (a) mm. 24–37; (b) mm. 41–45

Ex. 34-5   Franz Schubert, Impromptu in E-flat, Op. 90, no. 2: (a) mm. 77–106; (b) mm. 155–70

Ex. 34-6   Franz Schubert, *Moment musical* no. 6 (D. 780)

Ex. 34-7   Harmonic abstract of Franz Schubert, Symphony no. 9 ("Great"), I, mm. 181–240

Ex. 34-8   Franz Schubert, Sonata in B-flat, D. 960, I, beginning

Ex. 34-9   Cyclic resolutions of diminished-seventh chords: (a) leading tone to tonic; (b) single appoggiatura to dominant; (c) triple appoggiatura to dominant; (d) neighbors to a triad

Ex. 34-10   Franz Schubert, Quartet in G major, IV, modulatory sequence

Ex. 34-11   Franz Schubert, Mass in E-flat, Sanctus, beginning

Ex. 34-12   Giovanni Maria Nanino, "Ascendit in celum" canon (1605)

Ex. 34-13   Franz Schubert, Octet, VI, mm. 172–77

Ex. 34-14   Franz Schubert, Quartet in G major, IV: (a) another modulatory sequence; (b) demonstration of the scale that emerges from the interpolated passing tones

Ex. 34-15   Franz Schubert, Symphony no. 8 ("Unfinished"), mm. 1–8

Ex. 34-16a   Franz Schubert, Symphony no. 8 ("Unfinished"), I, second theme

Ex. 34-16b   A possible source for the second theme of Schubert's Symphony no. 8 ("Unfinished")

Ex. 34-16c   Franz Schubert, Impromptu, Op. 142, no. 2, beginning

Ex. 34-17   Franz Schubert, Symphony no. 8 ("Unfinished"), II, mm. 280–300

Chapter 35

Ex. 35-1   C. P. E. Bach, *Amint* (Wotquenne.199, no. 11)

Ex. 35-2   J. F. Reichardt, *Heidenröslein*

Ex. 35-3   J. F. Reichardt, *Erlkönig*, ending

Ex. 35-4   Joseph Haydn, "Kaiserhymne" (*Gott erhalte Franz den Kaiser!*)

Ex. 35-5   Ludwig van Beethoven, *An die ferne Geliebte*: (a) no. 1, mm. 1–9; (b) no. 2, middle stanza; (c) no. 6, mm. 1–16; (d) cyclic return; (e) the motivic relationship between the first and last songs

Ex. 35-6   Franz Schubert, *Lachen und Weinen*, D. 777

Ex. 35-7   Franz Schubert, Quartet in G, D. 887, I: (a) mm. 1–10; (b) analogous spot in recap

Ex. 35-8a   Franz Schubert, *Schwanengesang*, opening of *Am Meer*

Ex. 35-8b   Franz Schubert, opening of *Die Allmacht*

Ex. 35-8c   Franz Schubert, opening of Quintet in C

Ex. 35-9   Franz Schubert, *Wasserfluth* (from *Die Winterreise*, no. 5), mm. 1–14

Ex. 35-10   Franz Schubert, *Die schöne Müllerin*, "Der Müller und der Bach": (a) mm. 1–10; (b) mm. 29–40; (c) mm. 71–82

Ex. 35-11   Franz Schubert, *Heidenröslein*, model stanza

Ex. 35-12   Franz Schubert, *Erlkönig*, mm. 66–85

Ex. 35-13   Franz Schubert, *Gretchen am Spinnrade*: (a) mm. 1–17; (b) mm. 63–75

Ex. 35-14   Franz Schubert, *Der Doppelgänger*

Ex. 35-15   Carl Loewe, *Erlkönig*: (a) mm. 27–34; (b) ending

Ex. 35-16   Felix Mendelssohn, *Paulus*, Chorale (no. 16), beginning

Ex. 35-17   Felix Mendelssohn, *Paulus*, Chorale (no. 2), beginning

Ex. 35-18   Felix Mendelssohn, *Paulus*, last part of no. 36, *con molto di moto*, mm. 122–49

Ex. 35-19   Louis Lewandowski, *Ma towu oholecho Jaakow* ("How goodly are thy tents, O Jacob"), opening psalm for sabbath morning service (*Todah w'simrah*, I, no. 1)

Ex. 35-20   Felix Mendelssohn's "elfin" style: (a) opening of *Midsummer Night's Dream* Overture, Op. 21 (1826), mm. 8–15; (b) opening of Rondo capriccioso, Op. 14 (1827), mm. 1–4; (c) Violin Concerto, Op. 64 (1844), beginning of last movement, mm. 3–10

Ex. 35-21   Felix Mendelssohn, Octet, Op. 20, IV, mm. 22–33

Ex. 35-22a   *Ferne* (text by J. G. Droysen), Op. 9, no. 9, mm. 1–12

Ex. 35-22b   *Verlust* (text by H. Heine), Op. 9, no. 10, mm. 1–19

Chapter 36

Ex. 36-1a   W. A. Mozart, *Die Zauberflöte*, no. 2, Papageno's aria ("Der Vogelfänger bin ich ja")

Ex. 36-1b   W. A. Mozart, *Die Zauberflöte*, Act II finale, Papageno/Papagena duet

Ex. 36-2   Carl Maria von Weber, beginning of Overture to *Turandot*

Ex. 36-3   Carl Maria von Weber, *Der Freischütz*, no. 14, "Volkslied"

Ex. 36-4   Carl Maria von Weber, *Der Freischütz*: (a) no. 3, Allegro con fuoco; (b) no. 8, Vivace con fuoco, mm. 2–11

Ex. 36-5   Carl Maria von Weber, *Der Freischütz*, Overture, mm. 9–36

Ex. 36-6   Daniel-François-Esprit Auber, *La muette de Portici*, no. 8, duo, "Amour sacrée de la patrie," mm. 48–56

Ex. 36-7   Ludwig van Beethoven's *Egmont* Overture, second theme

Ex. 36-8   Giacomo Meyerbeer, *Les Huguenots*, "Pour cette cause sainte," compared with "La Marseillaise"

Ex. 36-9   Giacomo Meyerbeer, *Les Huguenots*, Act IV (blessing scene)

Ex. 36-10   Giacomo Meyerbeer, *Les Huguenots*, Act IV ("Cavatine," *andante amoroso*)

Ex. 36-11   *Ein' feste Burg* in *Les Huguenots*: (a) Overture, mm. 1–13; (b) Act I, "Choral"; (c) Act V, height of the massacre

Ex. 36-12   Yevstigney Fomin, *Yamshchiki na podstave*, no. 8

Ex. 36-13   Alexey Nikolayevich Verstovsky, *Askold's Grave*, no. 10

Ex. 36-14   Folklore in Mikhail Ivanovich Glinka's *A Life for the Tsar*: (a) Susanin's "Chto gadat' o svad'be." (b) Susanin's "Tuda zavyol ya vas.; (c) "Vniz po matushke po Volge." (d) Girls' chorus: "Razgulyalasya, razlivalasya."

Ex. 36-15   Mikhail Ivanovich Glinka, *A Life for the Tsar*, Act III, montage of "Russian" and "Polish" styles

Ex. 36-16   Mikhail Ivanovich Glinka, *A Life for the Tsar*, Epilogue, mm. 1–16

Ex. 36-17   Prefigurings of the *Slav'sya* theme in *A Life for the Tsar*: (a) Epilogue, "Hymn-March," mm. 1–4. (b) Act I, opening chorus. (c) Beginning of Overture.

Ex. 36-18   More prefigurings of the *Slav'sya* theme in *A Life for the Tsar*: (a) Act I, no. 1 (voices only). (b) Act III, no. 11 (quartet).

Chapter 37

Ex. 37-1   Niccolò Paganini, Caprice, Op. 1: (a) no. 13 ("Rire du diable"); (b) no. 17 (Andante); (c) no. 17, middle section; (d) no. 24, Tema; (e) no. 24, Variation 9

Ex. 37-2   Niccolò Paganini, *I palpiti*: (a) Recitativo; (b) Theme; (c) Variation II, mm. 1–12; (d) Variation II as edited

Ex. 37-3   Franz Liszt's "Diabelli Variation" (Variation 24 from Diabelli's "Patriotic Anthology")

Ex. 37-4   "Variation à la Paganini" from Franz Liszt, *Grande fantaisie de bravoure sur La Clochette de Paganini*

Ex. 37-5   Franz Liszt, *Paganini Études* (1851 ed.): (a) no. 2, mm. 6–11; (b) no. 2, mm. 24–28; (c) no. 6, mm. 1–16; (d) no. 6, var. 11, mm. 1–4; (e) no. 6, var. 10, mm. 1–8

Ex. 37-6   Franz Liszt, *Réminiscences de Don Juan*: (a) transition to "Duetto" ("Là ci darem la mano"); (b) juxtaposition of Seduction and Perdition; (c) "Champagne" aria accompanied by "Statue's tread"

Ex. 37-7   Ludwig van Beethoven, Piano Concerto no. 3, I: (a) opening theme (mm. 1–8); (b) first solo entrance

Ex. 37-8   Ludwig van Beethoven, Piano Concerto no. 4, I, mm. 1–14

Ex. 37-9   Franz Liszt, Piano Concerto no. 1: (a) mm. 1–4; (b) mm. 14–23; (c) no. 1, mm. 25–37; (d) mm. 61–70

Ex. 37-10   Franz Liszt, Piano Concerto no. 1: (a) Adagio, mm. 108–112; (b) Finale, mm. 352–56; (c) Finale, mm. 368–72

Chapter 38

Ex. 38-1   Robert Schumann, *Dichterliebe*, Op. 47: (a) no. 1 ("Im wunderschönen Monat Mai"); (b) no. 2 ("Aus meinen Thränen"); (c) no. 7 ("Ich grolle nicht"), mm. 16–end; (d) no. 12 ("Am leuchtenden Sommermorgen"), mm. 1–9; (e) no. 16 ("Die alten, bösen Lieder"), mm. 53–67

Ex. 38-2   Robert Schumann, *Phantasiestücke*, Op. 12, no. 3

Ex. 38-3   Francesco Morlacchi, *Tebaldo ed Isolina* (1822), Act II, Scena e romanza: "Caro suono lusinghier"

Ex. 38-4   Robert Schumann, *Phantasie*, Op. 17, I: (a) mm. 295–end; (b) mm. 1–19; (c) mm. 77–81

Ex. 38-5   Thematic transformations in Robert Schumann's *Fantaisie* for Piano and Orchestra

Ex. 38-6   Hector Berlioz, *Symphonie fantastique*, the idée fixe in Liszt's transcription

Ex. 38-7a   Ludwig van Beethoven, Symphony no. 3, I, mm. 182–90

Ex. 38-7b   Hector Berlioz, *Symphonie fantastique*, I, mm. 168–81

Ex. 38-8   Hector Berlioz, *Symphonie fantastique*, III, mm. 87–92

Ex. 38-9   Hector Berlioz, *Symphonie fantastique*, IV, mm. 174–end

Ex. 38-10   Ludwig van Beethoven, *Fidelio*, Act II, no. 12 ("Es ist nicht leicht!" "Nur etwas noch!"), mm. 1–4

Ex. 38-11   Hector Berlioz, *Symphonie fantastique*, V, mm. 7–11

Ex. 38-12   Hector Berlioz, *Symphonie fantastique*, V, mm. 40–54

Ex. 38-13   Hector Berlioz, *Symphonie fantastique*, V, mm. 121–146

Ex. 38-14   Camille Saint-Saëns, Dies Irae in *Danse macabre*

Chapter 39

Ex. 39-1   Frédéric Chopin, Prelude, Op. 28, no. 1

Ex. 39-2   Frédéric Chopin, Prelude, Op. 28, no. 2

Ex. 39-3   Frédéric Chopin, Prelude, Op. 28, no. 4

Ex. 39-4   *Mazurek Dlbrowskiego*

Ex. 39-5   Frédéric Chopin, Mazurka, Op. 17, no. 2

Ex. 39-6   Frédéric Chopin, Mazurka, Op. 17, no. 3, mm. 1–4

Ex. 39-7   Frédéric Chopin, Mazurka, Op. 17, no. 4: (a) mm. 1–20; (b) end

Ex. 39-8   Robert Schumann, *Kinderscenen*, end of no. 12 and beginning of no. 13

Ex. 39-9   Stephen Heller, *Spaziergänge eines Einsamen*, Op. 78, end of no. 6

Ex. 39-10   Franz Liszt, *Bagatelle ohne Tonart*, mm. 169–end

Ex. 39-11   Frédéric Chopin, Sonata in B-flat minor, IV

Ex. 39-12   Frédéric Chopin, Ballade no. 1 in G minor: (a) mm. 1–17; (b) mm. 40–44; (c) mm. 206–212; (d) mm. 216–22; (e) mm. 257–end; (f) mm. 68–82; (g) mm. 98–109

Ex. 39-13   Louis Moreau Gottschalk, *Bamboula*, mm. 1–24

Ex. 39-14   Louis Moreau Gottschalk, *Souvenir de Porto Rico, Marche des Gibaros*

Ex. 39-15a   Louis Moreau Gottschalk, the Foster-quoting section of *The Banjo*

Ex. 39-15b   The corresponding snatch of Foster's *Camptown Races*

Ex. 39-16a   Louis Moreau Gottschalk, *Union*, mm. 11–24

Ex. 39-16b   Chorus from *Home on the Range*, arranged for barbershop quartet by Ozzie Westley, mm. 17–end

Ex. 39-17   Félicien David, *Le Désert*: (a) *Danse des almées*; (b) Muezzin's call

Ex. 39-18   Camille Saint-Saëns, *Samson et Dalila*, Act III, *Bacchanale*

Ex. 39-19   *Ne poy, krasavitsa* (Pushkin): (a) Glinka's setting, mm. 1–12; (b) Miliy Alexeyevich Balakirev's setting, mm. 1–8; (c) Sergei Rachmaninoff's setting, mm. 1–12; (d) Sergei Rachmaninoff's setting, mm. 5–8

Ex. 39-20   Georges Bizet, *Carmen*, Act I, "Habañera", mm. 1–12

Ex. 39-21   Alexander Borodin, *Arabskaya melodiya*, second strophe, mm. 1–8

Ex. 39-22a   Alexander Borodin, *Prince Igor*, Chorus of Polovtsian Maidens

Ex. 39-22b   Alexander Borodin, *Prince Igor*, Polovtsian Dance
Ex. 39-22c   Alexander Borodin, *In Central Asia*, mm. 175–92
Ex. 39-23   Alexander Borodin, from *Prince Igor*, Act II, Love Duet
Ex. 39-24   Pyotr Ilyich Chaikovsky, *Romeo and Juliet* ("Overture-Fantasia"): (a) main love theme (Romeo?); (b) subsidiary love theme (Juliet?); (c) climax
Ex. 39-25   Robert Schumann, *The Bride of Messina*, Overture, second theme

Chapter 40

Ex. 40-1   Table of themes derived from the main motive in Liszt's *Les Préludes* (Symphonic Poem no. 3)
Ex. 40-2   Ludwig van Beethoven, *Der schwer gefasste Entschluss*, Op. 135
Ex. 40-3a   Normal resolutions of diminished-seventh and augmented triads
Ex. 40-3b   Ludwig van Beethoven, "Pathétique" Sonata, I, "Tempo I"
Ex. 40-3c   Franz Schubert, Quintet in C, I, mm. 11–24
Ex. 40-4   Franz Liszt, Symphonic Poem no. 1, *Ce qu'on entend sur la montagne*
Ex. 40-5   Glinka, Overture to *Ruslan and Lyudmila*
Ex. 40-6   Franz Liszt, climax of *Sursum corda* (last number in *Années de pèlerinage*)
Ex. 40-7   Franz Liszt, Sonata in B minor: (a) mm. 1–17; (b) transformations of diminished-seventh motive (mm. 18–21, 55–59, 125–30, 385–88)
Ex. 40-8   Franz Liszt, *Faust-Symphonie*: (a) opening; (b) Allegro agitato ed appassionato (mm. 71–74); (c) Grandioso (mm. 223–28)

Chapter 41

Ex. 41-1   Bedřich Smetana, *Braniboři v Čechách*, two recitatives for Oldoich
Ex. 41-2   Hussite hymn: *Ktož jsú Boži bojovnici* ("Ye Warriors of God")
Ex. 41-3   Harp solo at the outset of Smetana's *Vyšehrad*
Ex. 41-4a   Bedřich Smetana, *Moldau* theme
Ex. 41-4b   Swedish folk song: *Ack, Värmaland, du sköna*
Ex. 41-4c   Zionist hymn, *Hatikvah* ("The Hope")
Ex. 41-5   Bedřich Smetana, *Vltava*, mm. 359–62
Ex. 41-6   Culmination of Bedřich Smetana's *Blaník* with its combination of emblematic themes
Ex. 41-7   Bedřich Smetana, *Libuše*, Act III, "Můj drahý národ český neskoná!"
Ex. 41-8a   Furiant: "Sedlák, sedlák," from K. J. Erben, *Napevy prostonarodnich pisni ceskych* ("The Tunes of Czech Peasant Songs"), no. 588
Ex. 41-8b   Bedřich Smetana, *The Bartered Bride*, II, Furiant, mm. 7–14
Ex. 41-9   Folk themes in Glinka's *Kamarinskaya*
Ex. 41-10a   Motivic derivations in Glinka's *Kamarinskaya*, mm. 35–48
Ex. 41-10b   Glinka, *Kamarinskaya*, mm. 155–169
Ex. 41-10c   Glinka, *Kamarinskaya*, mm. 202–209
Ex. 41-11   Folk songs in Miliy Balakirev's *Overture on Russian Themes* (1858)

Ex. 41-12   Protyazhnaya pesnya (melismatic folk song) from the
        Nizhny-Novgorod District, as harmonized in Miliy Balakirev,
        Sbornik russkikh narodnïkh pesen (St. Petersburg, 1866).

Ex. 41-13   Themes from Miliy Balakirev's second *Overture on Russian Themes*
        (1864), as printed in his anthology *Sbornik Russkikh narodnïkh
        pesen*

Ex. 41-14   Miliy Balakirev, second *Overture on Russian Themes*: (a) mm. 5–25;
        (b) mm. 169–74

Chapter 42

Ex. 42-1   Norns' refrain and First Norn's first speech from Wagner's sketches
        for *Siegfrieds Tod*

Ex. 42-2   Richard Wagner, Prologue to *Götterdämmerung*: (a) "Revival"
        leitmotif; (b) "Rhine" leitmotif; (c) "Erda" leitmotif; (d) "Fate"
        leitmotif; (e) "Death" leitmotif; (f) "Loge" leitmotif; (g) Norns' ballad
        refrain; (h) "Genesis" leitmotif' (i) "Valhalla" leitmotif; (j) "Treaty"
        leitmotif; (k) "Götterdämmerung" leitmotif; (l) "Ring" leitmotif;
        (m) "Authority" leitmotif; (n) "Omen" leitmotif; (o) "Oblivion"
        leitmotif; (p) "Grief" leitmotif; (q) "Liebe-Tragik" leitmotif;
        (r) "Rhine gold" leitmotif; (s) "Joy" leitmotif; (t) "Gold's Dominion"
        leitmotif;; (u) "Sword" leitmotif; (v) Siegfried's horn call; (w) "Curse"
        leitmotif

Ex. 42-3   Richard Wagner, Prologue to *Götterdämmerung* in vocal score,
        leitmotives labeled (on first occurrence only) as in Ex. 42-2:
        (a) mm. 105–111; (b) mm. 27–29; (c) mm. 1–26

Ex. 42-5   Dmitri Shostakovich, Symphony no. 15, beginning of fourth
        movement

Ex. 42-6   Richard Wagner, Prologue to *Götterdämmerung* in vocal score,
        leitmotives labeled as in Ex. 42-2, mm. 175–83

Ex. 42-7   Richard Wagner, Prologue to *Götterdämmerung* in vocal score,
        leitmotives labeled as in Ex. 42-2, mm. 255–72

Ex. 42-8a   Richard Wagner, Prologue to *Götterdämmerung* in vocal score,
        leitmotives labeled as in Ex. 42-2, mm. 635–39.

Ex. 42-8b   Richard Wagner, *Götterdämmerung*, Act I, scene 1, mm. 1–11

Ex. 42-9   Richard Wagner, Prologue to *Götterdämmerung* in vocal score,
        leitmotives labeled as in Ex. 42-2, mm. 158–175

Ex. 42-10   Richard Wagner, Prologue to *Götterdämmerung* in vocal score,
        leitmotives labeled (on first occurrence only) as in Ex. 42-2,
        mm. 245–54

Ex. 42-11   Richard Wagner, Prologue to *Götterdämmerung* in vocal score,
        mm. 315–34

Ex. 42-12   Richard Wagner, Prologue to *Götterdämmerung* in vocal score,
        mm. 375–381

Ex. 42-13   Richard Wagner, Prologue to *Götterdämmerung* in vocal score, leitmotives labeled as in Ex. 42-2, mm. 588–635

Ex. 42-14   Richard Wagner, The Valkyries' Song as sketched in 1850

Ex. 42-15   Richard Wagner, Prologue to *Götterdämmerung* in vocal score, mm. 876–92

Ex. 42-16   Richard Wagner, Prelude to *Tristan und Isolde*, mm. 1–11

Ex. 42-17   *Tristan*-chord conflated with Mozart Fantasia theme

Ex. 42-18a   Franz Liszt, *Die Lorelei*, mm. 1–7

Ex. 42-18b   *Tristan*-chord in Carl Maria von Weber, *Euryanthe* Overture

Ex. 42-19   "Lisztian" variant of Richard Wagner's Prelude to *Tristan und Isolde* (opening)

Ex. 42-20   Modest Musorgsky, coronation bells in *Boris Godunov* (Prologue, scene 2)

Ex. 42-21   Richard Wagner, Prelude to *Tristan und Isolde*: (a) mm. 16–23; (b) mm. 55–63

Ex. 42-22   Richard Wagner, *Tristan und Isolde*, Act II, Love Duet (*Tagelied*), mm. 261–284

Ex. 42-23   Richard Wagner, *Tristan und Isolde*, Act II, climax of Love Duet (*Tagelied*), mm. 487–515

Ex. 42-24   Richard Wagner, *Tristan und Isolde*, Isolde's *Verklärung*

Chapter 43

Ex. 43-1   Giuseppe Verdi, *Nabucco*, "Va, pensiero"

Ex. 43-2a   Giuseppe Verdi, *I Lombardi*, "O signore, dal tetto natio"

Ex. 43-2b   Giuseppe Verdi, *Ernani*, "Si ridesti il Leon di Castiglia"

Ex. 43-3   Giuseppe Verdi, *Il trovatore*, "Di quella pira"

Ex. 43-4   Giuseppe Verdi, *La traviata*: (a) "Ah, fors'è lui"; (b) "Sempre libera"; (c) "Addio del passato"; (d) "Parigi, o cara"

Ex. 43-5   Giuseppe Verdi, *Rigoletto*, Act III, "La donna è mobile"

Ex. 43-6   Giuseppe Verdi, *Rigoletto*, Act III, Quartet, "Bella figlia dell'amore"

Ex. 43-7   Giuseppe Verdi, *Rigoletto*, Act III, Rigoletto conspires with Sparafucile

Ex. 43-8   Giuseppe Verdi, *Rigoletto*, Act III, beginning of storm

Ex. 43-9   Giuseppe Verdi, *Otello*, Act I, scene 1: (a) mm. 1–16; (b) lyrical climax of chorus, mm. 1–8

Ex. 43-10   Giuseppe Verdi, *Otello*, Act I, scene 3, end

Ex. 43-11   Giuseppe Verdi's "*Tristan*-chords" compared with Wagner's

Ex. 43-12   Giuseppe Verdi, *Otello*: (a) Act IV, mm. 1–11; (b) Act IV, scene 3 (Otello enters Desdemona's bedchamber)

Ex. 43-13   Giuseppe Verdi, *Otello*, Act IV, scene 4: (a) Otello's remorse; (b) death of Otello

Ex. 43-14   Alexander Dargomïzhsky, *Stone Guest*: Act II, Don Juan's Arioso

Ex. 43-15   Giuseppe Verdi, *Falstaff*, "Quand'ero paggio"

Chapter 44

Ex. 44-1   Modest Musorgsky, *Marriage*, opening speech

Ex. 44-2   *Slava*, original folk melody (from Nikolai Lvov and Johann Pratsch, *Russkiye narodnïye pesni*, 1790)

Ex. 44-3   Modest Musorgsky, *Boris Godunov*, Coronation Scene, Boris's monologue

Ex. 44-4   Franz Liszt, *Orpheus*, opening

Ex. 44-5   Modest Musorgsky, *Boris Godunov*, scene at St. Basil's Shrine

Ex. 44-6a   Alexander Varlamov, *Krasnïy sarafan* (romance)

Ex. 44-6b   Alexander Varlamov, *Na zarye tï eyo ne budi* (romance)

Ex. 44-7   Pyotr Ilyich Chaikovsky, *Eugene Onegin*: (a) beginning of Act I (first verse of "Slïkhal li vï" with sixths labeled; (b) Tatyana's leitmotif

Ex. 44-8   Pyotr Ilyich Chaikovsky, *Eugene Onegin*, sixths in Tatyana's letter scene: (a) beginning of first romance; (b) second romance, beginning of second strophe; (c) beginning of third romance; (d) introduction to fourth romance

Ex. 44-9   Pyotr Ilyich Chaikovsky, *Eugene Onegin*, letter scene, "writing music"

Ex. 44-10   Georges Bizet, *Carmen*, Don José's last line

Ex. 44-11   Jacques Offenbach, *Orphée aux enfers*, Finale

Ex. 44-12   Johann Strauss, opening strain of the "Blue Danube" Waltz

Ex. 44-13   Johann Strauss, *Die Fledermaus*, Act II, Waltz Finale: (a) ritornello; (b) "What a party!"; (c) the chiming clock is heard

Ex. 44-14a   Giuseppe Verdi, "Anvil Chorus" (*Il trovatore*, Act II)/Sir Arthur Sullivan, *The Pirates of Penzance*, "Come, friends who plow the sea"

Ex. 44-14b   Charles Gounod, "Faites lui mes aveux" (*Faust*, Act II)/Sir Arthur Sullivan, *The Pirates of Penzance* "Poor wand'ring one"

Ex. 44-15   Sir Arthur Sullivan, *Ruddigore*, Act II, "Matter" Trio ("My eyes are fully open")

Ex. 44-16   Pietro Mascagni, *Cavalleria rusticana*, Turiddu's arioso

Ex. 44-17   Ruggero Leoncavallo, *I pagliacci*, "Vesti la giubba"

Ex. 44-18   Giacomo Puccini, *Madama Butterfly*, "Un bel di": (a) mm. 1–8; (b) mm. 149–56; (c) mm. 159–70. (d) Reminiscence of "Un bel di" at end of Act II.

Chapter 45

Ex. 45-1   Johannes Brahms, Piano Concerto in D minor, Op. 15, beginning

Ex. 45-2   Robert Schumann, Symphony no. 4, I: (a) slow introduction, mm. 1–7; (b) *Lebhaft* (Allegro) theme, mm. 1–11

Ex. 45-3a   Johannes Brahms, D-major Serenade, V (second scherzo)

Ex. 45-3b   Ludwig van Beethoven, Symphony no. 2, Trio of Scherzo

Ex. 45-3c   Joseph Haydn, "London" Symphony, Finale, mm. 1–8

Ex. 45-4   Motivic interweaving in Johannes Brahms, Symphony no. 1, I: (a) beginning of Allegro; (b) transition to second theme; (c) slow introduction; (d) closing theme of exposition

Ex. 45-5   Johannes Brahms, Symphony no. 1, II: (a) mm. 1–7;
             (b) mm. 114–24

Ex. 45-6   Johannes Brahms, Symphony no. 1, I, mm. 243–52

Ex. 45-7   Johannes Brahms, Symphony no. 1, I: (a) mm. 185–91;
             (b) mm. 331–43

Ex. 45-8a   Johann Hermann Schein, *Die mit Tränen säen*, the two opening points

Ex. 45-8b   Johannes Brahms, *Ein deutsches Requiem*, I ("Die mit Tränen säen. . .")

Ex. 45-9   Johannes Brahms, *Triumphlied*, I

Ex. 45-10   Johannes Brahms, "Haydn Variations": (a) mm. 1–10; (b) beginning
             of Finale ("St. Anthony's Hymn")

Ex. 45-11   Johannes Brahms, Symphony No. 1, IV: (a) alphorn theme;
             (b) chorale theme

Ex. 45-12a   Johannes Brahms, Symphony No. 1, IV, main theme

Ex. 45-12b   Ludwig van Beethoven, Symphony No. 9, IV, choral theme
             (transposed)

Ex. 45-13a   J. S. Bach, ground bass from Cantata no. 106, "Gottes Zeit ist die
             allerbeste Zeit"

Ex. 45-13b   Johannes Brahms, Symphony no. 1, IV, beginning of main finale
             theme

Ex. 45-13c   Johannes Brahms, Symphony no. 1, slow introduction of finale,
             mm. 1–15

Ex. 45-14   Johannes Brahms, Symphony no. 1, IV, mm. 118–124 (strings only)

Ex. 45-15   Johannes Brahms, Symphony no. 1, IV, mm. 156–159

Ex. 45-16   Johannes Brahms, Symphony no. 1, IV: (a) mm. 391–395;
             (b) mm. 407–416

Ex. 45-17   Johannes Brahms, Quartet no. 1 in C minor, Op. 51, no. 1: (a) I,
             mm. 1–10; (b) IV, end; (c) IV, beginning; (d) I, beginning of
             development section

Ex. 45-18   Johannes Brahms, Quartet no. 1 in C minor, Op. 51, no. 1, II,
             beginning

Ex. 45-19   Johannes Brahms, Quartet no. 1 in C minor, Op. 51, no. 1, III:
             (a) beginning; (b) "charming" melody; (c) contrapuntal montage

Ex. 45-20   Johannes Brahms, Quartet no. 1 in C minor, Op. 51, no. 1, I,
             mm. 11–27

Ex. 45-21   Johannes Brahms, Quartet no. 1 in C minor, Op. 51, no. 1, I,
             mm. 143–50

Chapter 46

Ex. 46-1   Anton Bruckner, Symphony no. 7, II (Adagio), mm. 1–9

Ex. 46-2   Anton Bruckner, Symphony no. 7, II, mm. 114–33

Ex. 46-3   Anton Bruckner, Symphony no. 7: (a) I, mm. 1–5; (b) IV, mm. 1–2

Ex. 46-4   Antonín Dvořák, "New World" Symphony, II, 5 measures before
             fig. 5

Ex. 46-5   Antonin Dvořák, "New World" Symphony, I: (a) first theme; (b) second theme

Ex. 46-6   Antonin Dvooak, "New World" Symphony, IV, coda (motivic montage)

Ex. 46-7   Antonin Dvořák, "New World" Symphony, III, mm. 13–21 (woodwinds)

Ex. 46-8   Spiritual, *Swing Low, Sweet Chariot*

Ex. 46-9   Antonin Dvořák, Symphony no. 8 in G: (a) I, flute solo, mm. 18–22 (pentatonic); (b) II, eight measures after fig. F (woodwinds)

Ex. 46-10   Antonin Dvořák, "New World" Symphony, I, "Indian" theme

Ex. 46-11a   Mrs. H. H. A. Beach, "Gaelic" Symphony, IV, one measure before F

Ex. 46-11b   Antonin Dvořák, "New World" Symphony, I, mm. 1–4

Ex. 46-12   César Franck, Symphony in D minor, thematic conspectus

Ex. 46-13   César Franck, Symphony in D minor, I, mm. 17–28

Ex. 46-14   César Franck, Symphony in D minor, I, mm. 298–304

Ex. 46-15   Camille Saint-Saëns, Symphony no. 3, thematic résumé

Ex. 46-16   Alexander Borodin, Symphony no. 1, III, cello theme

Ex. 46-17   Alexander Borodin, Symphony no. 2, II (Scherzo), mm. 370–77

Ex. 46-18   Alexander Borodin, Symphony no. 2, I, mm. 1–7

Ex. 46-19   Pyotr Ilyich Chaikovsky, Symphony no. 4, I, beginning

Ex. 46-20   Pyotr Ilyich Chaikovsky, Symphony no. 4, I, the three collisions

Ex. 46-21a   Frédéric Chopin, beginning of Polonaise, Op. 40, no. 1

Ex. 46-21b   Pyotr Ilyich Chaikovsky, *Eugene Onegin*, Act III, scene 1, Polonaise

Ex. 46-22   Pyotr Ilyich Chaikovsky, Symphony no. 4, I, m. 404

VOLUME 4

Chapter 47

Ex. 47-1   Gustav Mahler, Symphony no. 2, I, first page of the score

Ex. 47-2   Gustav Mahler, sketch for *Todtenfeier*

Ex. 47-3   Gustav Mahler, *Todtenfeier*, modulatory progression to secondary theme area

Ex. 47-4   Gustav Mahler, Symphony no. 2, I: (a) mm. 107–108; (b) mm. 381–386

Ex. 47-5   Gustav Mahler, Symphony no. 2, V: (a) trombone solo at fig. 21; (b) alto solo at fig. 39

Ex. 47-6   Gustav Mahler, Symphony no. 10, Adagio: (a) fig. 27 to fig. 29; (b) fig. 27 to fig. 29, analytical reduction

Ex. 47-7   Gustav Mahler, Symphony no. 10, Adagio, mm. 1–24

Ex. 47-8   Richard Strauss, *Rêverie*, Op. 9, no. 4

Ex. 47-9   Arnold Schoenberg, *Erwartung*, Op. 2, no. 1, mm. 1–23

Ex. 47-10   Richard Strauss, *Salome*: (a) mm. 1–16; (b) mm. 24–26

Ex. 47-11   Richard Strauss, *Salome*: (a) Salome's first entrance (fig. 20);
             (b) Salome teases Narraboth (two before fig. 57)

Ex. 47-12   Richard Strauss, *Salome*: (a) Herod flirts with Salome (4 before
             fig. 179); (b) harmonic abstract of semitonal chiasmus (the "master
             array")

Ex. 47-13   Richard Strauss, *Salome*, Salome's dance: (a) beginning; (b) first
             violins at 3 before L ; (c) first violins at 3 after R

Ex. 47-14   Richard Strauss, *Salome*, final scene: (a) adaptation of organ part at
             "Auf deinen Lippen"; (b) "Was tut's?"

Ex. 47-15   Richard Strauss, *Salome*, ending: (a) in full score; (b) in piano
             reduction

Ex. 47-16   Richard Strauss, *Elektra*, mm. 1–18 in vocal score

Ex. 47-17   Richard Strauss, *Elektra*: (a) Elektra's first lines; (b) Chrysothemis
             calls Elektra

Ex. 47-18   Richard Strauss, *Elektra*: (a) another intervallic "array"; (b) Elektra
             tells Chrysothemis to "Shut up and dance!"

Ex. 47-19   Richard Strauss, *Elektra*, end

Ex. 47-20   Richard Strauss, *Also sprach Zarathustra*, ending (with harmonic
             reduction)

Chapter 48

Ex. 48-1a   Emmanuel Chabrier, *Le roi malgré lui*, III (Entr'acte)

Ex. 48-1b   Emmanuel Chabrier, *Souvenirs de Munich*, refrain (*Ecstasies*)

Ex. 48-1c   Emmanuel Chabrier, *Souvenirs de Munich*, "Death Song"

Ex. 48-2   Erik Satie, first *Sarabande* for Piano: (a) mm. 1–21; (b) mm. 100–
             end

Ex. 48-3   Camille Saint-Saëns, Septet for trumpet, string quintet, and piano,
             "Gavotte en final"

Ex. 48-4   Emmanuel Chabrier, *Le roi malgré lui*, Prelude

Ex. 48-5   Erik Satie, *Trois gymnopédies*; (a) no.1, mm. 1–8; (b) no. 2, mm. 1–8;
             (c) no. 3, mm. 1–8

Ex. 48-6   "Debussy at the piano strikes these chords"(comment by Maurice
             Emmanuel, the stenographer)

Ex. 48-7   Claude Debussy, Sarabande from *Pour le piano*: (a) mm. 1–22;
             (b) mm. 67–72; (c) mm. 54–57

Ex. 48-8   Claude Debussy, "Voiles" (*Préludes*, Book I): (a) mm. 1–13; (b) m. 31;
             (c) mm. 41–48

Ex. 48-9   Whole-tone and pentatonic collections represented as symmetrical
             scales

Ex. 48-10   Claude Debussy, *Nuages*: (a) mm. 1–3; (b) mm. 5–10; (c) mm.64–68;
             (d) mm. 82–83 (third horn), mm. 86–87 (oboe)

Ex. 48-11   Zeroing in on the tone center in Claude Debussy, *Nuages*

Ex. 48-12   From the sketches to *Pelléas et Mélisande*, Act IV, scene 4

Ex. 48-13   Claude Debussy, *Pelléas et Mélisande*, Mélisande, "Si, si, je suis heureuse. . ."

Ex. 48-14   Claude Debussy, *Pelléas et Mélisande*, Act IV, scene 4, mm. 81–87

Ex. 48-15   Claude Debussy, *Pelléas et Mélisande*, Act IV, scene 4, mm. 266–271

Ex. 48-16   Claude Debussy, *Pelléas et Mélisande*, Act IV, scene 4, mm. 96–98

Ex. 48-17   Claude Debussy, *Pelléas et Mélisande*, Act IV, scene 4, mm. 176–201

Ex. 48-18   Claude Debussy, *Pelléas et Mélisande*, Act IV, scene 4:
(a) mm. 133–135; (b) mm. 154–156

Ex. 48-19   Gabriel Fauré, *Le parfum impérissable*, Op. 76. no. 1, mm. 1–17

Ex. 48-20   Gabriel Fauré, Requiem, *In paradisum*: (a) mm. 17–20;
(b) mm. 25–29

Ex. 48-21   "Artificially" harmonized folk tune from Paul Dukas, *Ariane et Barbe-Bleue*

Ex. 48-22a   Maurice Ravel, *Deux mélodies hébraïques* (1914), no. 2, *L'énigme éternelle*, mm. 1–26

Ex. 48-22b   Alexander Zhitomirsky's harmonization in "Ahavoh-rabboh" mode

Ex. 48-23   Octatonic analysis of Maurice Ravel's *L'énigme éternelle*

Ex. 48-24   Maurice Ravel, *Jeux d'eau*: (a) first page; (b) mm. 4–5, reduced

Ex. 48-25   Maurice Ravel, *Jeux d'eau*: (a) mm. 19–21; (b) mm. 75–82

Ex. 48-26   Maurice Ravel, *Jeux d'eau*, m. 72

Ex. 48-27   Triadic harmonies referable to an octatonic collection

Ex. 48-28   Nikolai Rimsky-Korsakov, *Sadko*, Act I, scene 2, mm. 51–55

Ex. 48-29a   Nikolai Rimsky-Korsakov, *Sadko*, Act I, scene 2

Ex. 48-29b   The symmetrical scales and their points of intersection

Ex. 48-30   Nikolai Rimsky-Korsakov, sketch for *Heaven and Earth* (1908)

Ex. 48-31   Nikolai Rimsky-Korsakov, *Sheherazade*, II

Ex. 48-32   Maurice Ravel, *Rapsodie espagnole*, I: (a) Cadenza at fig. 6 ;
(b) Cadenza at fig. 8

Ex. 48-33   Lili Boulanger, *Pie Jesu*: (a) mm. 3–9; (b) last seven measures;
(c) block representation of last harmony

Chapter 49

Ex. 49-1   Adolphe Adam, *Giselle*, Act II, apparition of the wilis

Ex. 49-2   Adolphe Adam, *Giselle*: (a) Act I, fig. 9 ; (b) Act II Finale, Valse

Ex. 49-3   Leo Delibes, *Coppélia*, from the Act I Finale

Ex. 49-4   Pyotr Ilyich Chaikovsky, *Swan Lake*: (a) beginning of Act II;
(b) climax of Act IV

Ex. 49-5   Pyotr Ilyich Chaikovsky, *Nutcracker*, Sugarplum Fairy Variation, mm. 1–12

Ex. 49-6   "Omnibus progression"

Ex. 49-7   Pyotr Ilyich Chaikovsky, *The Sleeping Beauty*, Carabosse music: (a) no. 1, mm. 1–2; (b) no. 4 (finale), mm. 37 ff; (c) no. 5 (scène), mm. 202–14

Ex. 49-8   Nikolai Rimsky-Korsakov, *Kashchey the Deathless*, scene 2, mm. 171–75

Ex. 49-9   Igor Stravinsky, *Firebird*, "ladder of thirds"

Ex. 49-10   Igor Stravinsky, *Firebird*, "Dawn"

Ex. 49 11   Igor Stravinsky's analytical example from piano roll notes

Ex. 49-12   Igor Stravinsky, *Firebird*, Kashchey music: (a) opening theme; (b) "In the Darkness, Kashchey Watches for Victims"; (c) "Arrival of Kashchey the Deathless"; (d) "Dialogue of Kashchey and Ivan Tsarevich"; (e) Death of Kashchey"; (f) end

Ex. 49-13   Igor Stravinsky, *Firebird*, "Apparition de l'Oiseau de feu"

Ex. 49-14   Igor Stravinsky, *Petrushka*, opening of first tableau, street-vendors' cries against a steady hum of accordion music

Ex. 49-15   Igor Stravinsky, remnants of the piano "Konzertstück" in *Petrushka*, "Danse Russe," fig. 43

Ex. 49-16   Octatonic derivation of the *Petrushka*-chord

Ex. 49-17   Igor Stravinsky, *Petrushka*, second tableau ("Chez Pétrouchka"), mm. 1–8

Ex. 49-18   Igor Stravinsky, *Petrushka*, "Malédictions de Pétrouchka"

Ex. 49-19   Igor Stravinsky, remnants of the piano "Konzertstück" in *Petrushka*, "Chez Pétrouchka," fig. 50

Ex. 49-20   Igor Stravinsky, *Petrushka*, cadence establishing F-sharp as tonic at end of second tableau

Ex. 49-21   Igor Stravinsky, remnants of the piano "Konzertstück" in *Petrushka*, "Chez Pétrouchka," 4 after fig. 58 , "Petrushka's despair"

Ex. 49-22a   "Ai, vo polye lipin'ka" compared with main tune of "Danse russe"

Ex. 49-22b   *Ivanovskaya* (F. M. Istomin and S. M. Lyapunov, *Pesni russkogo naroda* [1899], p. 167)

Ex. 49-23   *Tevuseli manu!* (Anton Juszkiewicz, *Melodje ludowe litewskie* [Cracow, 1900], no. 142)

Ex. 49-24   Igor Stravinsky, *The Rite of Spring* (piano four-hands arrangement), "Ritual of Abduction," mm. 1–10

Ex. 49-25   Igor Stravinsky, *The Rite of Spring* (piano four-hands arrangement), "Ritual of Abduction," mm. 23–28

Ex. 49-26   Tetrachordal partition of an octatonic scale

Ex. 49-27a   *Oy vir vir kolodez*, vesnyanka recorded ca. 1965 from the singing of Agrafena Glinkina, Smolensk, Russia

Ex. 49-27b   Igor Stravinsky, *The Rite of Spring*, from "Ritual Action of the Ancestors"

Ex. 49-28   The *Rite*-chord: (a) "Dance of the Adolescent Girls" (Part I); (b) "Sacrificial Dance" (Part II); (c) sketch for the "Glorification of the Chosen One" (Part II); (d) preparatory measure before "Glorification of the Chosen One"; (e) "Spring Rounds" (Part I); (f) "Mystic Circles" (Part II)

Ex. 50-21a–b   Aggregate harmonies from Alexander Scriabin's sketches for the *Acte préalable*

Ex. 50-22   Nikolai Obouhov, *Berceuse d'un bienheureux*, beginning

Ex. 50-23   The modes of limited transposition

Ex. 50-24   Olivier Messiaen, *Les corps glorieux*, no. 2 (*Les eaux de la grace*), mm. 1–8

Ex. 50-25   Olivier Messiaen, *Technique de mon langage musical*, example 33

Ex. 50-26   Olivier Messiaen, *Quatuor pour la fin du temps*, I ("Liturgie de cristal"), mm. 1–12

Ex. 50-27   Analysis of Olivier Messiaen's rhythmic palindromes

Chapter 51

Ex. 51-1   Charles Ives, *The Celestial Country*, no. 3, mm. 50–57

Ex. 51-2   Horatio Parker, *Hora novissima*, no. 3, mm. 33–47

Ex. 51-3a   Charles Ives, *The Celestial Country*, no. 7, mm. 107–115

Ex. 51-3b   Horatio Parker, *Hora novissima*, no. 1, mm. 138–146

Ex. 51-4   Horatio Parker, *Hora novissima*, no. 4, mm. 128–134

Ex. 51-5   Charles Ives, String Quartet no. 2, II: (a) mm. 31–42; (b) mm. 65–69

Ex. 51-6   Charles Ives, "Nov. 2, 1920" (a.k.a. "An Election"), mm. 12–17

Ex. 51-7   Charles Ives, "From 'Paracelsus'": (a) mm. 1–6; (b) *Andante molto*, end

Ex. 51-8   Charles Ives, "Concord" Sonata, I ("Emerson"), beginning

Ex. 51-9   Charles Ives, "Concord" Sonata, end of IV ("Thoreau")

Ex. 51-10   Charles Ives, "Concord" Sonata, beginning of III ("The Alcotts")

Ex. 51-11a   Simeon B. Marsh, *Martyn*

Ex. 51-11b   Charles Zeuner, *The Missionary Chant*

Ex. 51-12   March: *The British Grenadiers*

Ex. 51-13   Charles Ives, "Putnam's Camp" (*Three Places in New England*, II): (a) mm. 91 ff; (b) mm. 14 ff

Ex. 51-14   Charles Ives, "Putnam's Camp," (*Three Places in New England*, II), mm. 27–30 in full score

Ex. 51-15   Charles Ives, "Putnam's Camp," (*Three Places in New England*, II), fig. H

Ex. 51-16   Charles Ives, "Putnam's Camp," (*Three Places in New England*, II), 2 before fig. N

Ex. 51-17   Charles Ives, *Three Quarter-Tone Pieces*: (a) first piece, mm. 18–28; (b) second piece, mm. 53–56; (c) third piece, end

Ex. 51-18   Charles Ives, *In Flanders Fields*, end

Ex. 51-19   Julián Carrillo, *Preludio a Colón*

Ex. 51-20   Ruth Crawford, Prelude no. 6 (Andante mystico), beginning

Ex. 51-21   Carl Ruggles, *Sun-Treader*, opening theme

Ex. 51-22a   Leo Ornstein, *Danse sauvage*

Ex. 51-22b   Leo Ornstein, *Suicide in an Airplane*

Ex. 51-23   Henry Cowell, *Dynamic Motion*, mm. 1–18

Chapter 52

Ex. 52-1	Offending passage from Arnold Schoenberg, *Verklärte Nacht*
Ex. 52-2	Arnold Schoenberg, *Der Wanderer*, Op. 6, no. 8, mm. 9–11
Ex. 52-3	Arnold Schoenberg, *Harmonielehre*, examples 232 and 233
Ex. 52-4	Alban Berg, motto from the *Kammerkonzert*
Ex. 52-5	Arnold Schoenberg, *Mädchenlied*, Op. 6, no. 3, beginning
Ex. 52-6	Arnold Schoenberg, Quartet no. 2, IV (*Entrückung*), arr. Berg, m. 1
Ex. 52-7	Transposition of the "Eschbeg" set in Arnold Schoenberg, Quartet no. 2, IV (*Entrückung*)
Ex. 52-8	Arnold Schoenberg, Quartet no. 2, IV (*Entrückung*), arr. Berg, mm. 21–26
Ex. 52-9	Arnold Schoenberg, Quartet no. 2, IV (*Entrückung*), arr. Berg, mm. 3–6
Ex. 52-10	Arnold Schoenberg, Quartet no. 2, IV (*Entrückung*), arr. Berg, mm. 9–15
Ex. 52-11	Arnold Schoenberg, Quartet no. 2, IV (*Entrückung*), arr. Berg: (a) mm. 38–40; (b) mm. 51–55
Ex. 52-12	Arnold Schoenberg, Quartet no. 2, IV (*Entrückung*), arr. Berg, mm. 100–105
Ex. 52-13	Arnold Schoenberg, *Sechs kleine Klavierstücke*, Op. 19, no. 1
Ex. 52-14	"Aschbeg" set in Arnold Schoenberg, *Sechs kleine Klavierstücke*, Op. 19, no. 1, m. 5
Ex. 52-15a	Richard Strauss, *Salome*, mm. 319–320
Ex. 52-15b	Arnold Schoenberg, *Erwartung*, mm. 263–264
Ex. 52-16a	Arnold Schoenberg, *Erwartung*, mm. 190–195
Ex. 52-16b	Richard Wagner, *Parsifal*, Act II, "Lachte!"
Ex. 52-17	Arnold Schoenberg, *Erwartung*, Op. 17, mm. 1–7
Ex. 52-18a–c	Atonal triads and extensions in Arnold Schoenberg, *Erwartung*
Ex. 52-19a–c	Melodic motif in Arnold Schoenberg, *Erwartung*
Ex. 52-20a	Arnold Schoenberg, *Am Wegrand*, mm. 3–4
Ex. 52-20b	Arnold Schoenberg, *Am Wegrand*, mm. 22–24
Ex. 52-20c	Arnold Schoenberg, *Erwartung*, mm. 411–412
Ex. 52-21	/0 1 4/motif in Arnold Schoenberg, *Erwartung*, m. 411: (a) voice part; (b) figuration; (c) bass
Ex. 52-22	A "tonal" cadence inverted
Ex. 52-23	Joseph Schillinger's inversion of the subject of Bach's F-major Invention
Ex. 52-24	Reduction of Arnold Schoenberg's *Vorgefühle*, mm. 1–3
Ex. 52-25	Arnold Schoenberg, *Die Jakobsleiter*: (a) mm. 1–8; (b) complementary hexachord and derivative harmonies
Ex. 52-26a	Arnold Schoenberg, *Kleine Klavierstücke*, Op. 19, no. 6
Ex. 52-26b	Anton Webern, *Sechs Bagatellen* Op. 9, no. 5
Ex. 52-26c	Anton Webern, *Fünf Stücke* Op. 10, no. 4

Ex. 52-27   Johannes Brahms, Cello Sonata no. 2, Op. 99, first theme, as cited by
             Schoenberg
Ex. 52-28   Arnold Schoenberg's diagram of Brahms's Op. 51, no. 2 theme
Ex. 52-29   Arnold Schoenberg, analysis of "O Tod" from *Brahms the Progressive*
Ex. 52-30   Theme from Bach's Six-Part Ricercar as segmented by Anton
             Webern

Chapter 53

Ex. 53-1   *Magyar nóta* and *style hongrois*: (a) Ignác Ruzitska, *Búcsuzó és friss
             magyar* (Farewell and Fast Hungarian); (b) Franz Joseph Haydn,
             Rondo all'ongarese, the last minore (piano right hand); (c) Franz
             Schubert, "Great" Symphony in C, II, mm. 160–166 (oboe);
             (d) Johannes Brahms, Hungarian Dance no. 5 (1869), mm. 33–48
             (Primo right hand)
Ex. 53-2   Franz Erkel, *Bánk bán*, Act II, scene 1, duet
Ex. 53-3   Franz Liszt, *Hungarian Coronation Mass*, violin solo from Benedictus
Ex. 53-4   Béla Bartók, *Kossuth*, opening theme
Ex. 53-5   Two versions of no. 1 from Bartók/Kodály, *Magyar népdalok*
Ex. 53-6   (a) Béla Bartók, Bagatelle, Op. 6, no. 4; (b) song model for this
             Bagatelle
Ex. 53-7   (a) Béla Bartók, Bagatelle, Op. 6, no. 5, mm. 1–19; (b) song model for
             this Bagatelle
Ex. 53-8a   Dorian inversional symmetry
Ex. 53-8b   Dorian/octatonic interaction
Ex. 53-9   Béla Bartók, *Four Dirges*, Op. 9a (1912), no. 2: (a) mm. 1–29;
             (b) mm. 1–14, compared with folk tune in Ex. 53-6b; (c) mm. 31–37
Ex. 53-10   Béla Bartók, Bagatelle, Op. 6, no. 7, mm. 49–70
Ex. 53-11a   Béla Bartók, Bagatelle, Op. 6, no. 11, mm. 1–18
Ex. 53-11b   Béla Bartók, Bagatelle, Op. 6, no. 11, mm. 55–60
Ex. 53-11c   Béla Bartók, Bagatelle, Op. 6, no. 8, end
Ex. 53-12   "Z-tetrachords" in Béla Bartók, Bagatelles, Op. 6, nos. 8 and 11
Ex. 53-13   Béla Bartók, Bagatelle, Op. 6, no. 2
Ex. 53-14   Axial symmetry in Béla Bartók, Bagatelle, Op. 6, no. 2
Ex. 53-15   A representative "odd" array (sum 7)
Ex. 53-16a   Béla Bartók, *Music for Strings, Percussion and Celesta*, III, mm. 1–10
Ex. 53-16b   Béla Bartók, Bagatelle, Op. 6, no. 12, mm. 1–8
Ex. 53-16c   Béla Bartók, *Music for Strings, Percussion and Celesta*, III, 1 after letter B
Ex. 53-17   Béla Bartók, *Music for Strings, Percussion and Celesta*, I: (a) mm. 1–15;
             (b) mm. 56–64; (c) mm. 86–88
Ex. 53-18   Béla Bartók, Quartet no. 4: (a) I, end; (b) V, end
Ex. 53-19   Béla Bartók, Quartet no. 4, V: (a) m. 1; (b) m. 11; (c) mm. 31–53;
             (d) mm. 90–101
Ex. 53-20   Permutations of the Z-tetrachord

Ex. 53-21   Symmetrical arrays for Béla Bartók, Quartet no. 4, I

Ex. 53-22   Béla Bartók, Quartet no. 4, I, mm. 1–22

Ex. 53-23   X- and Y-tetrachords

Ex. 53-24   Béla Bartók, Quartet no. 4, I: (a) mm. 48–57; (b) mm. 75–82

Ex. 53-25   Béla Bartok, Quartet no. 4, I, octatonic complementation ("Z to Z progressions") in mm. 75–82

Ex. 53-26   Béla Bartók, Quartet no. 4, I, mm. 93–104

Ex. 53-27   Béla Bartók, Quartet no. 4, I, re-introduction of Z-tetrachords after reprise (mm. 112–114)

Ex. 53-28   Bedřich Smetana's speech melody as recalled by his daughter and notated by Leoš Janáček

Ex. 53-29   "Janáček" as a speech tunelet

Ex. 53-30   Comparative settings from Janáček's *Šárka*

Ex. 53-31   Leoš Janáček, *A Blown-Away Leaf* (from *On an Overgrown Path*, no. 2), mm. 1–17

Ex. 53-32   Leoš Janáček, *Kát'a Kabanová*, motifs: (a) timpani motif; (b) Allegro theme; (c) "Katérino!" with its accompaniment; (d) chromatic transformation and ensuing ostinato; (e) Curtain (*Opona/Vorhang*) Music

Ex. 53-33   Leoš Janáček, *Kát'a Kabanová*, Act III, scene 2: (a) obsessive reverberations of speech tunelet; (b) transformation of speech tunelet into love music

Ex. 53-34   Leoš Janáček, *Kát'a Kabanová*. Act III, scene 2: (a) "Sighing of the Volga"; (b) end

Ex. 53-35   Leoš Janáček, *Kát'a Kabanová*, Act III, scene 2, Katerina's suicide

Ex. 53-36   Leoš Janáček, *From the House of the Dead*, Act III: (a) 6 before fig. 15 ; (b) ostinato at fig. 26

Chapter 54

Ex. 54-1   Claude Le Jeune, *Qu'est devenue ce bel oeil* (Le printemps, no. XXX)

Ex. 54-2   W. A. Mozart, Gigue for piano, K. 574

Ex. 54-3   Ambroise Thomas, *Mignon*, Entr'acte to Act II, mm. 9–25

Ex. 54-4   Pyotr Ilyich Chaikovsky, Gavotte from Suite no. 1, mm. 35–54

Ex. 54-5   Engelbert Humperdinck, *Die Königskinder*, from Act I

Ex. 54-6   Arnold Schoenberg, *Pierrot lunaire*, no. 1, *Mondestrunken*, mm. 1–18

Ex. 54-7   Arnold Schoenberg, *Pierrot lunaire*, no. 18, *Der Mondfleck*, mm. 8–12

Ex. 54-8   Igor Stravinsky, *Symphonies d'instruments à vent*, final section as published in *Revue Musicale*

Ex. 54-9   Igor Stravinsky, *Octet for Winds* in Arthur Lourié's piano transcription, I, mm. 1–4

Ex. 54-10   Igor Stravinsky, *Octet for Winds* in Arthur Lourié's piano transcription, I, mm. 5–32

Ex. 54-11 Igor Stravinsky, *Octet for Winds* in Arthur Lourié's piano
transcription, I: (a) mm. 42–48; (b) mm. 71–74; (c) mm. 88–91;
(d) mm. 137–151

Ex. 54-12 Igor Stravinsky, *Octet for Winds* in Arthur Lourié's piano
transcription, II ("Tema con variazioni"), mm. 1–14

Ex. 54-13 Igor Stravinsky, *Octet for Winds* in Arthur Lourié's piano
transcription, II, variation B, final cadence

Ex. 54-14 Igor Stravinsky, *Octet for Winds* in Arthur Lourié's piano
transcription, II, variation E (fugato), mm. 1–7

Ex. 54-15 Igor Stravinsky, *Octet for Winds* in Arthur Lourié's piano
transcription, III (Finale), mm. 1–33

Ex. 54-16 Igor Stravinsky, *Octet for Winds* in Arthur Lourié's piano
transcription, III, end

Ex. 54-17 Igor Stravinsky, *Sérénade en la*, "Rondoletto," mm. 1–27

Chapter 55

Ex. 55-1 Serge Prokofieff, "Classical Symphony," III (Gavotte), in the
composer's piano arrangement

Ex. 55-2 Serge Prokofieff, *Love for Three Oranges*, Act III, scene 3: (a) fig. 384
(the first princess begs for water); (b) fig. 391 (the second princess
begs for water); (c) fig. 415 (Ninetta, the third princess, begs for
water)

Ex. 55-3 Serge Prokofieff, *Love for Three Oranges*, Act III, scene 3, fig. 418
(Princess Ninetta gets her drink)

Ex. 55-4 Caricatures of Beethoven's Fifth: (a) Serge Prokofieff, *Love for Three
Oranges*, Act I, scene 1; (b) Igor Stravinsky, *Souvenir d'un marche boche*;
(c) Manuel da Falla, *El sombrero de tres picos*; (d) Erik Satie, "De
podophthalma" (from *Embryons desséchées*, no. 3)

Ex. 55-5 Alban Berg, *Wozzeck*, Act I, scene 1, "Air" ("Wir arme Leut")

Ex. 55-6 Alban Berg, *Wozzeck*, "Wir arme Leut" leitmotif

Ex. 55-7 Alban Berg, *Wozzeck*, Act I, scene 1, "Quasi Gavotte," transition from
"Double I" to "Double II"

Ex. 55-8 Alban Berg, *Wozzeck*, Act III, scene 2, the murder

Ex. 55-9 Alban Berg, *Wozzeck*, Act III, Entr'acte between scenes 2 and 3

Ex. 55-10 "Leitharmony" in Alban Berg, *Wozzeck*, Act III, scene 4

Ex. 55-11 Alban Berg, *Wozzeck*, Act III, scene 5, end

Ex. 55-12 Alban Berg, *Wozzeck*, Act III, Entr'acte between scenes 4 and 5
("Invention on a Key"), climax

Ex. 55-13a Alban Berg's "master array"

Ex. 55-13b Alban Berg, *Wozzeck*, Act II, scene 3, incorporation of the "master
array"

Ex. 55-14 Paul Hindemith, Sonata for solo viola, Op. 25, no. 1, IV

Ex. 55-15 Ernst Krenek, *Jonny spielt auf*, "Leb' wohl, mein Schatz"

Ex. 55-16   Paul Hindemith, *Neues vom Tage*, Bathtub Aria

Ex. 55-17   Kurt Weill, "No. 16"

Ex. 55-18   Kurt Weill, *Die Dreigroschenoper*, "Zweites Dreigroschenfinale," mm. 18–31

Ex. 55-19   Hanns Eisler, *Die Massnahme*, "Ändere die Welt, sie braucht es," mm. 19–38

Ex. 55-20   Kurt Weill, *Der Jasager*: (a) no. 1 (chorus); (b) no. 10 (concluding scene)

Ex. 55-21   Erich Korngold, Violin Concerto, beginning of first movement

Ex. 55-22   Serge Rachmaninoff, *Rhapsody on a Theme of Paganini*, 18th variation

Ex. 55-23   Nikolai Medtner, *Skazka*, Op. 26, no. 3: (a) mm. 1–16; (b) recapitulation

Ex. 55-24   Richard Addinsell, second theme from "Warsaw Concerto"

Chapter 56

Ex. 56-1a   Erik Satie, *Parade*, *Rag-time du paquebot* episode in piano score

Ex. 56-1b   Irving Berlin, *That Mysterious Rag*

Ex. 56-2   Francis Poulenc, *Les biches*, opening bars of *Rag mazurka*

Ex. 56-3   Erik Satie, *Vexations*

Ex. 56-4   Erik Satie, *Relâche*, two "Entrées"

Ex. 56-5   Erik Satie, *Socrate*, III, end

Ex. 56-6   Francis Poulenc, *Cocardes*, no. 3, end

Ex. 56-7   Francis Poulenc, *Les mamelles de Tirésias*, Prologue, 4 to 6

Ex. 56-8   Darius Milhaud, *Saudades do Brasil*, V (*Ipanema*): (a) mm. 1–9; (b) mm. 33–55

Ex. 56-9   Darius Milhaud, String Quartet no. 4, I, mm. 1–15

Ex. 56-10   Darius Milhaud, Symphony no. 3 (*Sérénade*): (a) mm. 1–4; (b) mm. 9–16

Ex. 56-11   Virgil Thomson, *Susie Asado*, beginning

Ex. 56-12   Virgil Thomson, *Capital Capitals*: (a) "Cannot express can express tenderness"; (b) opening baritone solo

Ex. 56-13   Virgil Thomson, *Four Saints in Three Acts*, IV, intermezzo

Chapter 57

Ex. 57-1   Claude Debussy, "Golliwog's Cakewalk": (a) mm. 1–17; (b) mm. 61–73

Ex. 57-2   Darius Milhaud, *La création du monde*, jazz fugue, beginning

Ex. 57-3   Riff figure from Milhaud's *La création du monde* compared with *12th Street Rag*

Ex. 57-4   W. C. Handy, *St. Louis Blues*, first stanza

Ex. 57-5   Maurice Ravel, Violin Sonata, II ("Blues"): (a) mm. 1–27; (b) mm. 95–100; (c) end

Ex. 57-6   Aaron Copland, "Jazzy" (1920)

Ex. 57-7   Aaron Copland *Music for the Theatre*, I: (a) trumpet solo; (b) Molto moderato (harmonic "planing"); (c) oboe solo; (d) Molto meno mosso

Ex. 57-8   Aaron Copland, *Music for the Theatre*, IV ("Burlesque"), mm. 128–147

Ex. 57-9   George Gershwin, *Lady, Be Good!* "You Don't Know the Half of It, Dearie"

Ex. 57-10   George Gershwin, *Rhapsody in Blue* themes: (a) I (mm. 225–240); (b) II (mm. 91–106); (c) III (mm. 179–194); (d) IV (mm. 138–153); (e) V (mm. 300 ff).

Ex. 57-11   George Gershwin, *Rhapsody in Blue*, mm. 1–27

Ex. 57-12   George Gershwin, *Rhapsody in Blue*, end

Ex. 57-13   Roy Harris, "autogenetic" melodies: (a) *Symphony 1933*, I, second theme; (b) from *A Farewell to Pioneers* (1935); (c) *A Farewell to Pioneers*, opening melody

Ex. 57-14   Roy Harris, Symphony no. 3, excerpts demonstrating the main themes: I, Tragic. II, Lyric. III, Pastoral. IV, Fugue

Ex. 57-15   Roy Harris, Symphony no. 3, 6 after fig. 56

Ex. 57-16   Howard Hanson, Symphony no. 2, motto theme

Ex. 57-17   Aaron Copland, *Piano Variations* (theme)

Ex. 57-18   Aaron Copland, "Into the Streets, May First!"

Ex. 57-19   Virgil Thomson, *Symphony on a Hymn Tune*

Ex. 57-20   Aaron Copland, *Prairie Journal*, clarinet solo

Ex. 57-21   "Git Along, Little Dogies": (a) as transcribed by John Lomax; (b) as arranged by White and Shackley in *The Lonesome Cowboy*; (c) as harmonized by Oscar J. Fox; (d) as adapted by Aaron Copland in *Billy the Kid*

Ex. 57-22   Aaron Copland, *Rodeo*, "Corral nocturne" in the composer's piano score, beginning

Ex. 57-23   Aaron Copland, *Rodeo*, "Corral nocturne" in the composer's piano score, mm. 33–37

Ex. 57-24   Aaron Copland, *Fanfare for the Common Man*, mm. 1–21

Ex. 57-25   Aaron Copland, *A Lincoln Portrait*, mm. 257–264

Chapter 58

Ex. 58-1   Josef Matthias Hauer, *Nomos*, Op. 19, beginning

Ex. 58-2   Arnold Schoenberg, Op. 23, no. 5 (*Walzer*), mm. 1–60

Ex. 58-3   Arnold Schoenberg, Op. 23, no. 5 (*Walzer*), mm. 104–end

Ex. 58-4   Arnold Schoenberg, Op. 23, no. 1 (*Sehr langsam*), mm. 1–5

Ex. 58-5   Row complex from Arnold Schoenberg, Suite, Op. 25

Ex. 58-6   Arnold Schoenberg, *Serenade*, Op. 24, IV (*Sonett No. 217 von Petrarch*), voice part

Ex. 58-7   Arnold Schoenberg, Suite, Op. 25, Gigue, mm. 1–13

Ex. 58-8   Arnold Schoenberg, Suite, Op. 25, Trio, mm. 34–44

Ex. 58-9   Arnold Schoenberg, Suite, Op. 25, Musette, beginning

Ex. 58-10   Arnold Schoenberg, Suite, Op. 25, Präludium, beginning

Ex. 58-11   Arnold Schoenberg, Suite, Op. 25, Menuett, beginning

Ex. 58-12   Arnold Schoenberg, Suite, Op. 25, Menuett, mm. 31–33

Ex. 58-13   Arnold Schoenberg, Suite, Op. 25, Gavotte, beginning

Ex. 58-14   Arnold Schoenberg, Variations for Orchestra, Op. 31: (a) the theme; (b) theme as harmonized over Radio Frankfurt in 1931; (c) prime and inverted row forms; (d) mm. 24–25; (e) the row forms in Ex. 58-14c transposed to reveal additional BACH ciphers. (f) J. S. Bach, main subject from *The Art of Fugue*.

Ex. 58-15   Combinatorial row forms in Arnold Schoenberg, Variations for Orchestra, Op. 31

Ex. 58-16   Opening of Arnold Schoenberg, *Klavierstück*, Op. 33a and 33b, with a summary of its combinatorial row forms

Ex. 58-17a   All-interval row in Alban Berg, *Schliesse mir die Augen beide*

Ex. 58-27b   All-interval row in Alban Berg, *Lyric Suite*

Ex. 58-18   Permutations of *Lyric Suite* row

Ex. 58-19   *Largo desolato* from *Lyric Suite*, with Baudelaire-George text underlaid, end

Ex. 58-20   Alban Berg, Violin Concerto: (a) entrance of solo violin (mm. 15–18) and (b) mm. 11–15. (c) J. S. Bach, harmonized chorale, "Es ist genug!" Alban Berg, Violin Concerto: (d) mm. 24–27 (solo violin); (e) symmetrical pitch circle formed by prime and inverted row forms; (f) symmetrical circle laid out as a melodic palindrome; and (g) intervallic palindrome condensed.

Ex. 58-21   Alban Berg, Violin Concerto: (a) mm. 1–8; (b) analytical sketch for Violin Concerto, mm. 1–8

Ex. 58-22   Alban Berg, Violin Concerto, coda

Ex. 58-23   Jacob Obrecht, *Missa Graecorum*, cantus firmi from Gloria, Agnus I and Agnus III

Ex. 58-24   Anton Webern, rows and their properties: (a) Variations for Piano, Op. 27 (1936); (b) Symphony, Op. 21 (1928); (c) Quartet, Op. 28 (1938); (d) Concerto, Op. 24 (1934). (e) Anton Webern, row forms arranged in magic square: Concerto, Op. 24.

Ex. 58-25   Anton Webern, Variations for Piano, Op. 27, I, mm. 1–7

Ex. 58-26   Anton Webern, Variations for Piano, Op. 27, II

Ex. 58-27   Anton Webern, Variations for Piano, Op. 27, III, mm. 1–12

Ex. 58-28   Anton Webern, Variations for Piano, Op. 27, III, mm. 56–end

Ex. 58-29   Anton Webern, Symphony, Op. 21, I, mm. 1–25

Ex. 58-30   Anton Webern, Symphony, Op. 21, I, mm. 27–42 (the pitch-rhythm palindrome minus the ends, which overlap with other material)

Ex. 58-31   Anton Webern, String Quartet, Op. 28, I, mm. 1–15

Ex. 58-32   Anton Webern, Concerto, Op. 24, I, mm. 1–5

Chapter 59

Ex. 59-1   Carl Orff, *Carmina burana*: (a) no. 1, "O fortuna," mm. 5–28; (b) no. 22, "Tempus est iocundum"; (c) no. 23, "Dulcissime"

Ex. 59-2   Carl Orff, *Catulli carmina*, "mammae molliculae"

Ex. 59-3   Paul Hindemith, "Series I" from *Unterweisung in Tonsatz*

Ex. 59-4   Paul Hindemith, *Ludus tonalis*, Interlude and Fugue no. 5 (in E)

Ex. 59-5   Paul Hindemith, *Das Marienleben*, "Vom Tode Mariä III": (a) 1923 version, end; (b) 1948 version, end

Ex. 59-6   Dmitriy Shostakovich, *The Nose* in vocal score, end of Act I, scene 2

Ex. 59-7   Dmitriy Shostakovich, *The Nose* in vocal score, Act I, scene 3, Kovalyov's "cavatina"

Ex. 59-8   Dmitriy Shostakovich, *The Lady Macbeth of the Mtsensk District*, Act I, scene 5

Ex. 59-9   Dmitriy Shostakovich, Symphony no. 5, IV, coda

VOLUME 5

Chapter 60

Ex. 60-1   Aaron Copland, Symphony no. 3, IV, climax (original version)

Ex. 60-2   Stefan Wolpe, Quartet (1950), II, mm. 1–5

Ex. 60-3   Olivier Messiaen, *Mode de valeurs et d'intensités*, prefatory table

Ex. 60-4   Olivier Messiaen, *Mode de valeurs et d'intensités*, mm. 1–10

Ex. 60-5   Olivier Messiaen's scheme reduced to a single succession (after R. S. Johnson)

Ex. 60-6   Olivier Messiaen, *Mode de valeurs et d'intensités*, mm. 54–56

Ex. 60-7   Transformation of Pierre Boulez's *Structures*: (a) row; (b) durational "scale"

Ex. 60-8   Pierre Boulez, *Structures Ia*, "O" and "I" matrices

Ex. 60-9   Pierre Boulez, *Structures Ia*, mm. 1–15

Ex. 60-10   Pierre Boulez, *Structures Ia*, mm. 65–81

Ex. 60-11   Cyclic permutation in Ernst Krenek, *Sestina*

Ex. 60-12   Karlheinz Stockhausen, *Kreuzspiel*, mm. 1–13, tumbas

Ex. 60-13   Karlheinz Stockhausen, *Kreuzspiel*: (a) mm. 14–20; (b) mm. 85–91

Chapter 61

Ex. 61-1   John Cage, *Imaginary Landscape No. 1*, beginning

Ex. 61-2   John Cage, *Bacchanale*, "piano preparation" chart and first page of musical notation

Ex. 61-3   John Cage, *Music of Changes*, II, fourth page of score (diamond note-heads indicate keys silently depressed)

Ex. 61-4   Frederic Rzewski, "The People United Will Never Be Defeated!": (a) theme; (b) f-First variation

Ex. 61-5   Morton Feldman, *Piece for Four Pianos*

Chapter 62

Ex. 62-1   Paul Hindemith, Tuba Sonata: (a, b, c, d) twelve-tone theme, sketches; (e) opening theme as eventually worked out

Ex. 62-2   Dmitriy Shostakovich, Quartet no. 12, Op. 133, I, opening

Ex. 62-3   Aaron Copland, Piano Quartet, development of twelve-tone themes: (a) complementary whole-tone scales; (b) main theme of first movement; (c) main theme as first heard; (d) second theme (pitch content of Example 62-3c transposed and reversed); (e) opening of second movement (violin); (f) third movement, viola and cello in mm. 103–105

Ex. 62-4   Aaron Copland, Piano Quartet, I: (a) mm. 55–61; (b) mm. 98–end

Ex. 62-5   Aaron Copland, *Piano Fantasy*, mm. 1–22

Ex. 62-6   Aaron Copland, *Connotations*: (a) opening ("three harsh chords" and their immediate consequences); (b) ending

Ex. 62-7   Igor Stravinsky, *Cantata*, Ricercar II ("Tomorrow Shall Be My Dancing Day"): (a) derivation of the subject; (b) Stravinsky's table of serial permutations; (c) beginning of the tenor part

Ex. 62-8   Igor Stravinsky *Cantata*, Ricercar II, fourth canon

Ex. 62-9   "Rotation" (cyclic permutation and transposition) in Ernst Krenek, *Lamentatio Jeremiae prophetae*

Ex. 62-10   Ernst Krenek, *Lamentatio Jeremiae prophetae*, full tabulation of "verticals" from the hexachord rotated in Fig. 62-4

Ex. 62-11   Igor Stravinsky, *Variations*, mm. 73–85

Ex. 62-12   Igor Stravinsky, *Requiem Canticles*, Lacrimosa

Ex. 62-13   Igor Stravinsky, *Requiem Canticles*, source array for Lacrimosa

Ex. 62-14   Igor Stravinsky, *Requiem Canticles*, Libera me

Ex. 62-15   Igor Stravinsky, *Requiem Canticles*, Postlude

Ex. 62-16   Igor Stravinsky, *Requiem Canticles*, the two series as deployed in the Postlude

Ex. 62-17   Symmetrical harmonies in Igor Stravinsky, *The Firebird*

Ex. 62-18   George Perle's analytical table summarizing the "set complex" of Milton Babbitt's *Three Compositions for Piano*, no. 1

Ex. 62-19   Milton Babbitt, *Three Compositions for Piano*, no. 1: (a) mm. 1–8; (b) last two measures; (c) mm. 9–17

Ex. 62-20   Milton Babbitt, *Composition for Four Instruments*: (a) end; (b) three forms of the basic set, P_0, P_6, and I_5

Ex. 62-21   The four derived sets in Milton Babbitt, *Composition for Four Instruments*

Ex. 62-22a   J. S. Bach, Fugue from Cello Suite no. 5

Ex. 62-22b   Milton Babbitt, *Composition for Four Instruments*, mm. 1–15, with registers delineated

Ex. 62-23   Milton Babbitt, *Composition for Four Instruments*, mm. 36–59

Ex. 62-24   Milton Babbitt, *Composition for Four Instruments*, superimposed rhythmic series

Ex. 62-25   P₆ and I₇ from Milton Babbitt's *Composition for Twelve Instruments* (pitched on F), with order and pitch numbers

Ex. 62-26   Durational series derived from P₆ (Milton Babbitt, *Composition for Twelve Instruments*)

Ex. 62-27   Milton Babbitt, *Composition for Twelve Instruments*, mm. 1–18

Ex. 62-28   The "time-point system" as expounded in Milton Babbbitt's "Twelve-tone Rhythmic Structure and the Electronic Medium" (*Perspectives of New Music*, I:1 [fall 1962]): (a) The hypothetical chromatic pitch/duration scale. (b) A pitch/time-point series. (c) A pitch/time-point series translated into actual pitches. (d) A pitch/time-point series translated into actual durations. (e) All of the above, combined into a string-quartet texture.

Chapter 63

Ex. 63-1   Milton Babbitt, *Philomel*, opening

Ex. 63-2   Magic square (prime-inversion matrix) for Milton Babbitt, *Philomel*

Ex. 63-3   Milton Babbitt, *Philomel*, end (voice only)

Ex. 63-4   Opening up of symmetrical pitch space in Edgard Varèse's *Déserts*

Ex. 63-5   Mario Davidovsky, *Synchronisms No. 1*, end

Ex. 63-6   Krzysztof Penderecki, *Threnody for the Victims of Hiroshima*, beginning

Chapter 64

Ex. 64-1   Benjamin Britten, *Peter Grimes*, Act I, scene 1, "What Harbour Shelters Peace?"

Ex. 64-2   Benjamin Britten, *Peter Grimes*, unaccompanied duet at end of Prologue

Ex. 64-3   Benjamin Britten, *Peter Grimes*, Act II, scene 1: (a) "Wrong to plan!" (b) Peter, we've failed!"

Ex. 64-4   Benjamin Babbitt, *Peter Grimes*, Act II, scene 1, "Grimes is at his exercise"

Ex. 64-5   Benjamin Britten, *Peter Grimes*, Act II, scene 1, "Murder!"

Ex. 64-6   Benjamin Britten, *Peter Grimes*, Passacaglia (Interlude IV), beginning

Ex. 64-7   Benjamin Britten, *Peter Grimes*, Act III, scene 2 (Grimes's mad scene)

Ex. 64-8   Benjamin Britten, *Peter Grimes*: (a) Prologue, "When women gossip. . . "; (b) Grimes's replique in Act I, scene 1

Ex. 64-9   Benjamin Britten, *Peter Grimes*, Act III, scene 2, choral epilogue

Ex. 64-10   Benjamin Britten, *A Midsummer Night's Dream*: (a) beginning of Act I; (b) the passacaglia ground

Ex. 64-11   Benjamin Britten, *The Turn of the Screw*: (a) tonal plan (analytical chart by Peter Evans); (b) theme with pitches numbered; (c) Variation I with pitches numbered

Ex. 64-12   Benjamin Britten, *Death in Venice*, gamelan stylization in Tadzio music

Chapter 65

Ex. 65-1   Elliott Carter, Double Concerto, p. 101 of the score
Ex. 65-2   Elliott Carter, Double Concerto, Adagio, mm. 360–374
Ex. 65-3   Elliott Carter, *Eight Etudes and a Fantasy*: (a) Etude no. 3; (b) Etude no. 7 (beginning)
Ex. 65-4   Elliott Carter, *Eight Etudes and a Fantasy*, Fantasy, mm. 108–111
Ex. 65-5   Elliott Carter, *Eight Pieces for Four Timpani*, "Canaries," middle section
Ex. 65-6   Elliott Carter, Cello Sonata, I, opening
Ex. 65-7   Elliott Carter, String Quartet no. 1, I, mm. 1–23
Ex. 65-8a   Renotations from Elliott Carter, String Quartet no. 1, I, first violin at m. 22
Ex. 65-8b   Renotations from Elliott Carter, String Quartet no. 1, I, cello at m. 27
Ex. 65-8c   Charles Ives, Violin Sonata no. 1, mm. 1–2 (piano)
Ex. 65-9   Elliott Carter, String Quartet no. 1, I, mm. 197–204
Ex. 65-10   Guillaume Du Fay, *Missa L'homme armé*, Credo, "Genitum non factum est"
Ex. 65-11   Elliott Carter, String Quartet no. 1, I, mm. 312–23
Ex. 65-12   Elliott Carter, String Quartet no. 1: (a) violins at mm. 356–7; (b) II, all-interval tetrachords in basic motive; (c) II, all-interval tetrachords as harmonies; (d) IV, all-interval tetrachord as contrapuntal regulator
Ex. 65-13   Progress of "passacaglia" theme in Elliott Carter, String Quartet no. 1, IV
Ex. 65-14   Elliott Carter, String Quartet no. 2: (a) first score page (all-interval tetrachords circled); (b) last score page (all-interval tetrachords circled)

Chapter 66

Ex. 66-1a   Progression from John Lennon/Paul McCartney, "Not a Second Time"
Ex. 66-1b   Gustav Mahler, *Das Lied von der Erde*, end
Ex. 66-2   John Lennon/Paul McCartney, "Tommorow Never Knows," opening
Ex. 66-3   John Lennon/Paul McCartney, "A Day in the Life," end
Ex. 66-4   Freddie Mercury, *Bohemian Rhapsody*, A-major section
Ex. 66-5   Gunther Schuller, *Transformation*, fig. $\boxed{J}$ to fig. $\boxed{L}$
Ex. 66-6   John Lewis, *Sketch*, end
Ex. 66-7   Hans Werner Henze, *Musen Siziliens*, III (Silenus), mm. 108–11
Ex. 66-8   Luciano Berio, *Sinfonia*, II ("O King")

Chapter 67

Ex. 67-1   La Monte Young, String Trio, mm. 1–159

Ex. 67-2   La Monte Young, *31 VII 69 10:26–10:49 pm*, transcribed from "Black LP"

Ex. 67-3   Terry Riley, *In C*, full score

Ex. 67-4   Steve Reich, *Piano Phase*, first "basic unit"

Ex. 67-5   Steve Reich, *Clapping Music*

Ex. 67-6   Steve Reich, *Four Organs*, beginning (figs. 1-10) and end (last two figures)

Ex. 67-7   Steve Reich, *Music for 18 Musicians*, "cycle of chords"

Ex. 67-8   Steve Reich, *Music for 18 Musicians*, introduction and first "small piece"

Ex. 67-9   Philip Glass, *Einstein on the Beach*: (a) "Night Train" module ("first theme" in Glass's analysis); (b) "Spaceship" module ("third theme")

Ex. 67-10   Louis Andriessen, *De Staat*, mm. 719–734

Ex. 67-11   Two themes from Arvo Pärt, Symphony no. 3: "Doubled leading-tone" cadence, and chantlike cantus firmus

Ex. 67-12   Arvo Pärt, "tintinnabulation": (a) 1st position, superior; (b) 1st position, inferior; (c) 2nd position, superior; (d) 2nd position, inferior; (e) T-voice from Ex. 67-12b transposed up an octave; (f) M-voice accompanied by "alternating" T-voice

Ex. 67-13   Arvo Pärt, St. John Passion, *Conclusio*

Ex. 67-14   Arvo Pärt, *Tabula rasa*, II (*Silentium*): (a) mm. 1–8; (b) end

Ex. 67-15   John Tavener, *Ikon of Light*, opening section in analytical reduction

Chapter 68

Ex. 68-1   George Rochberg, *Music for the Magic Theater*: (a) II, end; (b) III, resumption and completion of the cadence

Ex. 68-2   Peter Maxwell Davies, *Eight Songs for a Mad King*, VII ("Country Dance")

Ex. 68-3   George Rochberg, Quartet no. 3: (a) I, beginning; (b) III, mm. 1–32

Ex. 68-4   David Del Tredici, *Syzygy*: (a) the midpoint of the palindrome in I; (b) the canon by inversion in II

Ex. 68-5a   David Del Tredici, *Final Alice*, main tune

Ex. 68-5b   David Del Tredici, *In Memory of a Summer Day*, main tune

Ex. 68-6   Fred Lerdahl, String Quartet no. 1, sections I–XIV

Ex. 68-7   Fred Lerdahl, String Quartet no. 1, analytical sketches: (a) inversional matrices on D and G superimposed; (b) inversional matrix that includes reference dyad G-D; (c) matrix that includes E-flat–B-flat and A-E

Ex. 68-8   Fred Lerdahl, String Quartet no. 1, section (C_4)

Ex. 68-9   Andrey Volkonsky, *Musica stricta*, II, mm. 1–9

Ex. 68-10a   Alfred Schnittke, Concerto for Piano and Strings, fig. 6

Ex. 68-10b   Pyotr Ilyich Chaikovsky, *1812* Overture, beginning

Ex. 68-11   Alfred Schnittke, Concerto for Piano and Strings, reprise of chorale

Chapter 69

Ex. 69-1   Harry Partch, *Bitter Music*, speech melodies

Ex. 69-2   Beginning of Harry Partch's *Barstow*: (a) Partch's tablature; (b) as transcribed by the musicologist Richard Kassel

Ex. 69-3   Meredith Monk, *Atlas*, ostinato from "Travel Dream Song"

Ex. 69-4   John Adams, *Nixon in China*, Act I: (a) Chou En-lai's toast; (b) choral response

Index of Musical Examples by Composer

References in *italics* indicate either an analytical treatment of a composer's work or a cross-reference to a related musical example (as in a folk melody quoted by the composer).

Breakdown of Volumes by Chapter:
Volume 1 Chapters 1–19
Volume 2 Chapters 20–32
Volume 3 Chapters 33–46
Volume 4 Chapters 47–59
Volume 5 Chapters 60–69

Composer	Example nos. (chapter number followed by example number)
Abel, Carl Friedrich	27-8a–b
Adam de la Halle	4-6, 4-7, 4-8, 4-9
Adam, Adolphe	49-1, 49-2a–b
Adams, John	69-4a–b
Addinsell, Richard	55-24
Agricola, Martin	18-5a
Alberti, Domenico	27-9a
Albertus Parisiensis	5-9 *(attrib.)*
Analytical Examples	1-8, 1-9a–b, 3-1, 3-2, 3-3, 3-15, 5-2a–b, 6-1a–b, 7-2, 8-2a–b, 8-5, 8-9, 9-1, 9-24, 11-26a–c, 15-1, 17-8a, 17-23b, 18-2, 19-6, 21-11b, 24-4, 24-6a–b, 24-7a–b, 24-8b, 24-15d, 26-17c, 30-8b, 34-14b, 34-9a–d, 35-5e, 38-5, 40-1, 40-3a, 40-7b, 41-10a, 42-17, 42-18b, 42-19, 43-11, 47-6b, 47-12b, 47-18a, 47-20, 48-6, 48-9, 48-11, 48-23, 48-27, 48-29b, 48-33c, 49-6, 49-9, 49-11, 49-16, 49-22a, 49-26, 49-29a–b, 49-29d, 50-1, 50-9, 50-10, 50-11, 50-12b, 50-14, 50-17, 50-18, 50-19, 50-21a–b, 50-23, 50-27, 52-1, 52-14, 52-18a–c, 52-3, 52-4, 52-7, 52-22, 52-23, 52-25b, 52-27, 52-28, 52-29, 52-30, 53-8a–b, 53-15, 53-20, 53-21, 53-23, 55-13a, 58-5, 58-14b–c, 58-14e, 58-15, 58-18, 58-21b, 58-24a–e, 60-5, 60-7a–b, 60-8, 60-11, 62-7a–b, 62-9, 62-10, 62-16, 62-18, 62-26, 62-28a–e, 64-11a, 64-12, 67-2, 67-12a–f, 67-15, 68-7a–c

Composer	Example nos. (chapter number followed by example number)
Andriessen, Louis	67-10
Anonymous	1-10, 4-2, 4-10, 4-11, 5-1a–d, 5-5a–b, 5-6, 5-7, 5-8a–b, 5-10, 6-7, 6-8, 7-1, 7-3, 7-4, 7-5, 7-6a–b, 7-7, 7-8, 7-9, 7-10, 8-4, 9-9, 9-12a–b, 9-13, 9-14, 9-19, 9-26, 10-7, 11-1, 11-3, 11-4a, 11-5, 11-6, 11-7a–b, 11-8, 11-9, 11-10, 11-11, 11-15, 11-16, 11-21, 11-22a–b, 12-2a, 12-4a–c, 12-5a–h, 12-10, 13-14, 13-15, 13-17a–d, 15-12a–e, 19-10a, 26-7b, 51-12
Arcadelt, Jacques	17-14a–b
Auber, Daniel-François-Esprit	36-6
Babbitt, Milton	62-18, 62-19a–c, 62-20a–b, 62-21, 62-22b, 62-23, 62-24, 62-25, 62-26, 62-27, 62-28a–e, 63-1, 63-2, 63-3
Bach, Carl Philipp Emanuel	27-3a–b, 27-4, 27-5, 29-3a–c, 35-1
Bach, Johann Christian	27-6a–b, 29-2a–b
Bach, Johann Sebastian	24-15a–c, 25-1b, 25-2b, 25-3a–b, 25-5, 25-6b, 25-7a, 25-7c–d, 25-8a–b, 25-9, 25-10a–c, 25-11, 25-14, 25-15a–b, 25-16a–e, 26-8a–e, 26-9a–e, 26-10a–f, 26-11, 26-12, 26-13, 26-14a–b, 26-15, 26-16, 26-17a–b, 26-17c, 26-18a–b, 45-13a, 52-23, 52-30, 58-14f, 58-20c, 62-22a
Bach, Wilhelm Friedemann	27-1, 27-2
Balakirev, Miliy	39-19b, 41-11, 41-12, 41-13, 41-14a–b
Balbulus, Notker	See Notker Balbulus
Bartók, Béla	53-4, 53-5, 53-6a, 53-6b, 53-7a–b, 53-9a–c, 53-10, 53-11a–c, 53-12, 53-13, 53-14, 53-16a–c, 53-17a–c, 53-18a–b, 53-19a–d, 53-20, 53-21, 53-23, 53-22, 53-24a–b, 53-25, 53-26, 53-27
Basiron, Philippe	12-15b, 13-1a–b
Beach, Amy	46-11a
Beethoven, Ludwig van	31-1c, 31-2, 31-3, 31-4, 31-5, 31-6, 31-7, 31-8a–b, 31-9a–c, 31-10, 31-11a–b, 31-12, 31-13, 32-1a, 32-2a–c, 32-3a–b, 32-4a–c, 32-5a–c, 32-6a–c, 32-7a–c, 32-8a–b, 32-9a–c, 32-10, 32-11a–b, 32-12a, 32-13, 32-14a–c, 32-15a–b, 32-16a–b, 32-17a–d, 32-18, 32-19, 33-1a–b, 33-2, 35-5a–d, 35-5e, 36-7, 37-7a–b, 37-8, 38-7a, 38-10, 40-2, 40-3b, 45-3b, 45-12b, 55-4d
Bellini, Vincenzo	33-10a–c
Berg, Alban	50-2, 50-3a–b, 52-4, 55-5, 55-6, 55-7, 55-8, 55-9, 55-10, 55-11, 55-12, 55-13a, 55-13b, 58-17a, 58-18, 58-19, 58-20a–b, 58-20d–g, 58-21a, 58-21b, 58-22, 58-27b

Composer	Example nos. (chapter number followed by example number)
Berio, Luciano	66-8
Berlin, Irving	56-1b
Berlioz, Hector	38-6, 38-7b, 38-8, 38-9, 38-11, 38-12, 38-13
Bernhard, Christoph	21-11b
Binchois, Gilles	11-23, 11-27
Bizet, Georges	39-20, 44-10
Borodin, Alexander	39-21, 39-22a–c, 39-23, 46-16, 46-17, 46-18
Boulanger, Lili	48-33a–b, 48-33c
Boulez, Pierre	60-7a–b, 60-8, 60-9, 60-10
Bowman, Euday	57-3
Brahms, Johannes	17-5, 45-1, 45-3a, 45-4a–d, 45-5a–b, 45-6, 45-7a–b, 45-8b, 45-9, 45-10a–b, 45-11a–b, 45-12a, 45-13b–c, 45-14, 45-15, 45-16a–b, 45-17a–d, 45-18, 45-19a–c, 45-20, 45-21, 52-27, 52-28, 52-29, 53-1d
Britten, Benjamin	11-2, 64-1, 64-2, 64-3a–b, 64-4, 64-5, 64-6, 64-7, 64-8a–b, 64-9, 64-10a–h, 64-11a, 64-11b–c, 64-12
Broschi, Riccardo	23-7
Bruckner, Anton	46-1, 46-2, 46-3a–b
Busnoys, Antoine	12-1a–b, 12-11, 12-12, 12-13, 12-14, 12-15a
Buus, Jacques	15-7a–b, 15-9a–b
Buxtehude, Dietrich	25-6a
Byrd, William	16-17, 16-18, 16-19b, 16-20, 16-21
Caccini, Giulio	19-1c, 19-2, 19-6
Cage, John	61-1, 61-2, 61-3
Calvisius, Sethus	18-7
Campra, André	22-5
Cara, Marco	17-1
Carmen, Johannes	10-9
Carrillo, Julián	51-19
Carter, Elliott	65-1, 65-2, 65-3a–b, 65-4, 65-5, 65-6, 65-7, 65-8a–b, 65-9, 65-11, 65-12a–d, 65-13, 65-14a–b
Caserta, Philippus de	9-21, 9-22
Cavalieri, Emilio de'	19-1a–b, 19-10b
Chabrier, Emmanuel	48-1a–c, 48-4
Chaikovsky, Pyotr Ilyich	39-24a–c, 44-7a–b, 44-8a–d, 44-9, 46-19, 46-20, 46-21b, 46-22, 49-4a–b, 49-5, 49-7a–c, 54-4, 68-10b
Chant/Liturgical	1-1, 1-2, 1-3, 1-4, 1-5, 1-6, 1-7a–b, 1-8, 1-11a–b, 1-12, 2-1, 2-2a–b, 2-3, 2-5, 2-6, 2-7a–c, 2-8a–b, 2-9, 2-10, 2-11, 2-12a–b, 2-13, 2-14a–b, 2-15, 3-5, 3-6, 3-7a–b, 3-8, 3-9, 3-11a–b, 6-3a–d, 12a–b, 12-9b, 16-1, 18-2, 26-7a

Composer	Example nos. (chapter number followed by example number)
Chopin, Frédéric	39-1, 39-2, 39-3, 39-5, 39-6, 39-7a–b, 39-11, 39-12a–g, 46-21a, 50-5
Ciconia, Johannes	8-7a–c
Clemens non Papa	17-8b
Clemens, Jacobus	15-3a–b, 15-4
Coeur-de-Lion, Richard	4-3
Compère, Loyset	13-9
Copland, Aaron	57-6, 57-7a–d, 57-8, 57-17, 57-18, 57-20, 57-21d, 57-22, 57-23, 57-24, 57-25, 60-1, 62-3a–f, 62-4a–b, 62-5, 62-6a–b
Corelli, Arcangelo	24-1a–b, 24-3, 24-6a, 24-7a–b, 24-8a, 24-8b, 25-13
Cornysh, William	13-6a–b
Couperin, François	25-12a–b
Couperin, Louis	25-4
Cowell, Henry	51-23
Crawford, Ruth	51-20
Dargomïzhsky, Alexander	43-14
David, Félicien	39-17a–b
Davidovsky, Mario	63-5
Davies, Peter Maxwell	68-2
Debussy, Claude	48-6, 48-7a–c, 48-8a–c, 48-10a–d, 48-11, 48-12, 48-13, 48-14, 48-15, 48-16, 48-17, 48-18a–b, 57-1a–b
Del Tredici, David	68-4a–b, 68-5a–b
Delibes, Leo	49-3
D'India, Sigismondo	19-4a–b
Donizetti, Gaetano	33-11a–b, 33-12a–f, 33-13a–b
Dowland, John	17-21, 17-22, 17-23a, 17-23b
Du Fay, Guillaume	8-8, 8-9, 11-20a–c, 11-24a–b, 11-25, 12-16, 13-3a–b, 13-4, 13-5, 65-10
Ducis, Benedictus	18-8
Dukas, Paul	48-21
Dunstable, John	11-18, 11-19
Dussek, Jan Ladislav	34-1b
Dvořák, Antonín	46-4, 46-5a–b, 46-6, 46-7, 46-9a–b, 46-10, 46-11b
Eisler, Hanns	55-19
Erkel, Franz	53-2
Falla, Manuel de	55-4c
Farnaby, Giles	21-7
Fauré, Gabriel	48-19, 48-20a–b
Feldman, Morton	61-4b

Composer	Example nos. (chapter number followed by example number)
Ferrabosco, Alfonso, II	22-8
Fétis, François-Joseph	30-9
Févin, Antoine de	14-8
Field, John	34-4a – b
Fischer, Johan Caspar Ferdinand	25-2a
Fogelweide, Walther von der	See Walther von der Fogelweide
Folk Music	11-4b, 34-16b, 36-14c, 39-4, 39-16b, 41-2, 41-4b – c, 41-8a, 41-9, 41-11, 41-12, 44-2, 46-8, 49-22b, 49-23, 49-27a, 49-29c, 53-6b, 57-21a – d
Fomin, Yevstigney	36-12
Foster, Stephen	39-15b
Franck, César	46-12, 46-14
Frescobaldi, Girolamo	19-6, 19-7a – d, 21-2, 21-3, 21-5
Froberger, Johann Jakob	25-7b, 34-1a
Fux, Johann Joseph	24-2
Gabrieli, Andrea	18-14a, 18-15
Gabrieli, Giovanni	18-13, 18-17, 18-18
Gagliano, Marco da	19-3a – c
Gallus, Jacobus	18-11, 18-12, 18-9a – c
Galuppi, Baldassare	27-9b
Gershwin, George	57-9, 57-10a – e, 57-11, 57-12
Gesualdo, Carlo	17-20
Gherardello da Firenze	10-3, 10-6
Ghiselin, Johannes	13-19a
Giovanni de Cascia	10-1
Glass, Philip	67-9a – b
Glinka, Mikhail Ivanovich	36-14a – b, 36-14c, 36-14d, 36-15, 36-16, 36-17a – c, 36-18a – b, 39-19a, 40-5, 41-9, 41-10a, 41-10b – c
Gluck, Christoph Willibald	28-3, 28-4, 28-5a
Gombert, Nicolas	15-2
Gottschalk, Louis Moreau	39-13, 39-14, 39-15a, 39-16a
Gounod, Charles	44-14b
Guido d'Arezzo	3-14 (attrib.), 5-3, 5-4
Guillaume de Machaut	See Machaut, Guillaume de
Guiraut de Bornelh	4-1
Guymont	9-11
Guyot de Provins	4-12
Handel, George Frideric	24-13, 24-14, 26-1a – b, 26-2a – g, 26-4b, 26-5a – b, 26-6a – b

Composer	Example nos. (chapter number followed by example number)
Handy, W. C.	57-4
Hanson, Howard	57-16
Harris, Roy	57-13a–c, 57-14, 57-15
Hasse, Johann Adolf	23-6a–c
Hauer, Josef Matthias	58-1
Haydn, Franz Joseph	29-4a–d, 29-5a–d, 29-6a–h, 29-7a–g, 29-8a–b, 29-9a–b, 29-10a–g, 30-10a–c, 30-11, 35-4, 45-3c, 53-1b
Heller, Stephen	39-9
Henry, Roy	11-14
Henze, Hans Werner	66-7
Hildegard of Bingen	3-10
Hindemith, Paul	55-14, 55-16, 59-3, 59-4, 59-5a–b, 61-5, 62-1a–e
Hucbald of St. Amand	3-4
Humperdinck, Engelbert	54-5
Isaac, Henricus	13-16a, 13-18, 15-10, 18-3
Ives, Charles	51-1, 51-3a, 51-5a–b, 51-6, 51-7a–b, 51-8, 51-9, 51-10, 51-12, 51-13a–b, 51-14, 51-15, 51-16, 51-17a–c, 51-18, 65-8c
Jacopo da Bologna	10-2a–b
Jacquet of Mantua	16-3a
Janáček, Leoš	53-28, 53-29, 53-30, 53-31, 53-32a–e, 53-33a–b, 53-34a–b, 53-35, 53-36a–b
Janequin, Clément	17-9
Jean de Noyers	11-17
Josquin Dascanio	17-3
Josquin des Prez	12-17, 13-11, 13-12, 13-13a–b, 13-19b, 14-1, 14-2, 14-3, 14-4, 14-5, 14-6a–e, 14-9
Kodály, Zoltán	53-5
Korngold, Erich	55-21
Krenek, Ernst	55-15, 60-11, 62-9, 62-10
Landini, Francesco	10-5, 10-8
Lasso, Orlando di	17-10, 17-11, 17-12, 17-13a–b
Lawes, William	22-9, 22-10a–d
Le Jeune, Claude	54-1
Lennon, John	66-1a, 66-2, 66-3
Leoncavallo, Ruggero	44-17
Leonin	6-2 (attrib.)
Lerdahl, Fred	68-6, 68-7a–c, 68-8
Lewandowski, Louis	35-19

Composer	Example nos. (chapter number followed by example number)
Lewis, John	66-6
Liszt, Franz	37-3, 37-4, 37-5a–e, 37-6a–c, 37-9a–d, 37-10a–c, 39-10, 40-1, 40-4, 40-6, 40-7a, 40-7b, 40-8a–c, 42-18a, 42-19, 44-4, 53-3
Loewe, Carl	35-15a–b
Longueval	18-10 (*attrib.*)
Lully, Jean-Baptiste	22-1a–b, 22-3, 22-4a–f, 22-4h
McCartney, Paul	66-1a, 66-2, 66-3
Machaut, Guillaume de	*8-5, 8-6, 9-1, 9-2*, 9-3, 9-4, 9-5, 9-6, 9-7, 9-8, 9-10, 9-15, 9-16a–b, 9-17, 9-18, 9-20
Mahler, Gustav	47-1, 47-2, 47-3, 47-4a–b, 47-5a–b, 47-6a, *47-6b*, 47-7, 66-1b
Mahu, Stephan	18-5b
Marcello, Alessandro	24-9a–b
Marco da Gagliano	*See* Gagliano, Marco da
Marenzio, Luca	17-16
Marsh, Simeon B.	51-11a
Martini, Johannes	13-16b
Mascagni, Pietro	44-16
Masini, Lorenzo	10-4
Medtner, Nikolai	55-23a–b
Mendelssohn, Felix	35-16, 35-17, 35-18, 35-20a–c, 35-21
Mercury, Freddy	66-4
Merulo, Claudio	18-14b
Messiaen, Olivier	50-24, 50-25, 50-26, *50-27*, 60-3, 60-4, *60-5, 60-6*
Meyerbeer, Giacomo	36-8, 36-9, 36-10, 36-11a–c
Milhaud, Darius	56-8a–b, 56-9, 56-10a–b, 57-2, 57-3
Mondonville, Jean-Joseph Cassanéa de	27-7
Moniot d'Arras	4-5
Monk, Meredith	69-3
Monteverdi, Claudio	17-18a–b, 17-19, 18-1a–b, 20-1, 20-2, 20-3, 20-4, 20-5, 20-6, 20-7, 20-8, 20-9, 20-10, 20-11, 20-12, 20-13, 20-14, 20-15, 21-1, 22-4 g
Morlacchi, Francesco	38-3
Morley, Thomas	17-24a
Mozart, Wolfgang Amadeus	28-5b, 28-6a–b, 28-7a–b, 30-1a–g, 30-2a–c, 30-3, 30-4a–b, 30-5a–c, 30-6, 30-7a–b, 30-8a, *30-8b*, *30-8c*, 31-1a–b, 32-1b, 36-1a–b, 54-2
Muffat, Gottlieb	26-4a

Composer	Example nos. (chapter number followed by example number)
Musorgsky, Modest	42-20, 44-1, 44-3, 44-5
Nanino, Giovanni Maria	34-12
Neidhardt, Pseudo-	*See* Pseudo-Neidhardt
Nicolaus de Radom	9-25
Notker Balbulus	2-4a–b
Obouhov, Nikolai	50-22
Obrecht, Jacobus	12-9a, 12-9c–d, 58-23
Ockeghem, Johannes	12-1c, 12-6, 12-7a–b, 12-8a–d, 13-2, 13-10
Offenbach, Jacques	44-11
Orff, Carl	59-1a–c, 59-2
Orlandini, Giuseppe Maria	27-10
Ornstein, Leo	51-22a–b
Ortiz, Diego	15-11, 15-13
Osiander, Lucas	18-6a
Paganini, Niccolò	37-1a–e, 37-2a–d
Paisiello, Giovanni	33-3, 33-4a–b, 33-5
Palestrina, Giovanni Pierluigi da	16-2a–b, 16-3b–d, 16-4, 16-5a–e, 16-7, 16-8, 16-9, 16-10, 16-11, 16-12a–b, 16-13, 16-19a
Parker, Horatio	51-2, 51-3b, 51-4
Pärt, Arvo	67-11, *67-12a–f*, 67-13, 67-14a–b
Partch, Henry	69-1, 69-2a–b
Penderecki, Krzysztof	63-6
Pergolesi, Giovanni	27-11a–b
Peri, Jacopo	19-1d, 19-8, 19-9a–b
Perotin	6-4 (*attrib.*), 6-5a (*attrib.*), 6-5b–c, 6-6a–b (*attrib.*)
Petrucci, Ottavinao	17-2
Piccinni, Niccolò	28-1a–b, 28-2
Poulenc, Francis	56-2, 56-6, 56-7
Power, Leonel	11-13, 12-2b, 12-3a–b
Praetorius, Michael	18-6b, 21-10
Prokofieff, Serge	55-1, 55-2a–c, 55-3, 55-4a
Pseudo-Neidhardt	4-14
Puccini, Giacomo	44-18a–d
Purcell, Henry	22-12a–b, 22-13, 22-14, 22-15, 24-10, 24-11, 24-12
Pycard	11-12
Rachmaninoff, Sergei	39-19c–d, 55-22
Raimon de Miraval	3-13
Rameau, Jean-Philippe	22-2, 22-6
Ravel, Maurice	48-22a, 48-23, 48-24a–b, 48-25a–b, 48-26, 48-32a–b, 57-5a–c

Composer	Example nos. (chapter number followed by example number)
Reich, Steve	67-4, 67-5, 67-6, 67-7, 67-8
Reichardt, Johann Friedrich	35-2, 35-3
Reincken, Johann Adam	25-1a
Riley, Terry	67-3
Rimsky-Korsakov, Nikolai	48-28, 48-29a, 48-29b, 48-30, 48-31, 49-8, 49-29e, 49-31
Rochberg, George	68-1a–b, 68-3a–b
Rore, Cipriano de	17-15
Rossi, Michelangelo	21-4
Rossini, Gioacchino	33-6, 33-7, 33-9a–d
Rousseau, Jean-Jacques	27-12
Ruffo, Vincenzo	16-6
Ruggles, Carl	51-21
Ruzitska, Ignác	53-1a
Rzewski, Frederic	61-4a
Sachs, Hans	4-15
Saint-Saëns, Camille	38-14, 39-18, 46-15, 48-3
Sammartini, Giovanni Battista	29-1a–b
Saracini, Claudio	19-5a–b
Sartori, Balthasar	16-14
Satie, Erik	48-2a–b, 48-5a–c, 55-4d, 56-1a, 56-3, 56-4, 56-5
Scarlatti, Alessandro	23-1a–b, 23-2a–c, 23-3, 23-4a–c, 24-5
Scarlatti, Domenico	26-19, 26-20, 26-21a–b, 26-22a–b
Scheidt, Samuel	21-8a–e
Schein, Johann Hermann	21-9, 45-8a
Schillinger, Joseph	52-23
Schnittke, Alfred	68-10a, 68-11
Schoenberg, Arnold	47-9, 52-1, 52-2, 52-3, 52-5, 52-6, 52-7, 52-8, 52-9, 52-10, 52-11a–b, 52-12, 52-13, 52-14, 52-15b, 52-16a, 52-17, 52-18a–c, 52-19a–c, 52-20a–c, 52-21a–c, 52-24, 52-25a, 52-26a, 52-28, 52-29, 54-6, 54-7, 58-2, 58-3, 58-4, 58-5, 58-6, 58-7, 58-8, 58-9, 58-10, 58-11, 58-12, 58-13, 58-14a, 58-14b–c, 58-14d, 58-14e, 58-15, 58-16
Schönfelder, Jörg	17-4
Schubert, Franz	34-5a–b, 34-6, 34-7, 34-8, 34-10, 34-11, 34-13, 34-14a, 34-14b, 34-15, 34-16a, 34-16b, 34-16c, 34-17, 35-6, 35-7a–b, 35-8a–c, 35-9, 35-10a–c, 35-11, 35-12, 35-13a–b, 35-14, 40-3c, 53-1c
Schuller, Gunther	66-5
Schumann, Robert	38-1a–e, 38-2, 38-4a–c, 38-5, 39-8, 39-25, 45-2a–b

Composer	Example nos. (chapter number followed by example number)
Schütz, Heinrich	21-11a, 21-12a–d, 21-13, 21-14
Scriabin, Alexander	50-4, 50-6a–b, 50-7, 50-8, 50-9, 50-11, 50-12a, *50-12b*, *50-13*, 50-15, 50-16, *50-17*, *50-18*, *50-19*, 50-20a–e, *50-21a–b*
Senfl, Ludwig	14-7, 17-6
Sermisy, Claudin de	17-7, *17-8a*
Shostakovich, Dmitriy	42-5, 59-6, 59-7, 59-8, 59-9, 62-2
Smetana, Bedřich	41-1, 41-3, 41-4a, 41-5, 41-6, 41-7, 41-8b, 53-28
Solage	9-23
Stamitz, Carl	32-12b
Stockhausen, Karlheinz	60-12, 60-13a–b
Stradella, Alessandro	26-3
Strauss, Johann	44-12, 44-13a–c
Strauss, Richard	47-8, 47-10a–b, 47-11a–b, 47-12a, 47-13a–c, 47-14a–b, 47-15a–b, 47-16, 47-17a–b, *47-18a*, *47-18b*, 47-19, 47-20, *52-15a*
Stravinsky, Igor	*49-9*, *49-10*, *49-11*, *49-12a–f*, *49-13*, *49-14*, *49-15*, *49-16*, *49-17*, *49-18*, *49-19*, *49-20*, *49-21*, *49-22a–b*, *49-23*, *49-24*, *49-25*, *49-27a*, *49-27b*, *49-28a–f*, *49-29a–d*, *49-30*, *49-32*, *49-33*, *50-1*, *54-8*, *54-9*, *54-10*, *54-11a–d*, *54-12*, *54-13*, *54-14*, *54-15*, *54-16*, *54-17*, *55-4b*, *62-7a–b*, *62-7c*, *62-8*, *62-11*, *62-12*, *62-13*, *62-14*, *62-15*, *62-16*, *62-17*
Strozzi, Barbara	21-15a–c
Sullivan, Arthur	44-14a, 44-15
Sweelinck, Jan Pieterszoon	21-6
Tallis, Thomas	16-15
Tavener, John	*67-15*
Taverner, John	15-8a–b
Thibaut IV de Champagne	4-4
Thomas, Abroise	54-3
Thomson, Virgil	56-11, 56-12a–b, 56-13, 57-19
Tomášek, Václav Jan	34-2, 34-3
Tomkins, Thomas	22-11
Tye, Christopher	22-7a–c
Van Wilder, Philip	16-16
Varèse, Edgard	63-4
Varlamov, Alexander	44-6a–b
Vecchi, Orazio	17-24b

Composer	Example nos. (chapter number followed by example number)
Verdi, Giuseppe	43-1, 43-2a–b, 43-3, 43-4a–d, 43-5, 43-6, 43-7, 43-8, 43-9a–b, 43-10, 43-11, 43-12a–b, 43-13a–b, 43-15, 44-14a
Verstovsky, Alexey Nikolayevich	36-13
Victoria, Tomás Luis de	18-16
Vinci, Leonardo	23-5a–c
Vitry, Philippe de	8-1, 8-3
Vivaldi, Antonio	24-16, 24-17a–e, 24-18a–b, 24-19a–e
Volkonsky, Andrey	68-9
Wagner, Richard	33-8, 42-1, 42-2a–w, 42-3a–b, 42-4, 42-6, 42-7, 42-8a–b, 42-9, 42-10, 42-11, 42-12, 42-13, 42-14, 42-15, 42-16, 42-17, 42-19, 42-21a–b, 42-22, 42-23, 42-24, 52-16b
Walther von der Fogelweide	4-13
Walther, Johann	18-4
Ward, John	17-25
Weber, Carl Maria von	36-2, 36-3, 36-4a–b, 36-5, 42-18b
Webern, Anton	52-26b–c, 52-30, 58-24a–e, 58-25, 58-26, 58-27, 58-28, 58-29, 58-30, 58-31, 58-32
Weerbeke, Gaspar van	13-7, 13-8
Weill, Kurt	55-17, 55-18, 55-20a–b
Wert, Giaches de	17-17
Willaert, Adrian	15-5a–c
Wolpe, Stefan	60-2
Young, La Monte	67-1, 67-2
Zarlino, Gioseffe	15-1, 15-6
Zeuner, Charles	51-11b
Zhitomirsky, Alexander	48-22b

Master Index

Page numbers in *italics* indicate illustrations.

A

Aachen (Aix-la-Chapelle), 3:165

Aaron, Pietro, 1:576–78, *579*, 630

ABA. *See* da capo aria

Abbate, Carolyn, 1:827; 3:485, 493, 496; 4:90, 92

abbreviavit, translations of, 1:186

Abduction from the Seraglio (Mozart), 2:470–76, 479, 602, 678; 3:193, 386, 638

Abel, Carl Friedrich, 2:419, *420*, 508

Bach (J. C.) partnership with, 2:419

Sonata in B flat major, op. 2, no. 4, 2:429–32

Abélard, Pierre, 1:112, 172

Abe Lincoln (Robinson), 4:658, 669, 670

"Abraham Lincoln Brigade," 4:659

absolute music, 1:541–42, 610–11, 796; 3:306; 4:9, 150, 307; 5:177

autonomous art concept and, 2:599

Bach sons as harbingers of, 2:388, 418

baton conducting and, 3:222

Brahms and, 3:695, 698, 703, 712, 714–16, 729, 730

concept of, 2:648, 714

darkened theaters and, 3:564

exigesis and, 2:650

Franck and, 3:775, 776, 781, 782

listener involvement and, 3:341

music appreciation and, 3:783

New German School and, 3:698

Schubert and, 3:100, 139

values of, 3:22, 46

Wagner and, 2:714; 3:502

absolute truth, 1:629

absolutism

artistic expressions of, 2:14–15, 34, 111

British political end to, 2:114–15, 124, 126

contemporary modern examples of, 2:111–12

covert argumentation against, 2:110–12, 441–42, 443

Enlightenment thought vs., 2:110, 175, 443, 462

of French court, 2:88, 111, 647

Italian city-states and, 1:277

in musical performance tradition, 2:14, 110, 111–12, 174

music glorifying, 2:91–92, 111–12

abstract duration ratios. *See* rhythm

abstract number, 1:37

abstract pitch ratios. *See* intervals

Abstraktion und Einfühlung (Worringer), 4:474

Abu Hassan (Weber), 3:193, 386; 5:176

academia, 2:499–500

Academic Festival Overture (Brahms), 3:752

academic musicology. *See* musicology

academic style, 1:607–11

Palestrina and, 1:666

Académie de Poésie et Musique, 4:449

Académie des Beaux-Arts, 4:63–64, 70, 78

Académie Française, 2:90

Académie Royale de Musique (Paris), 2:89; 3:205–9, 211, 215, 217

Freischütz performance at, 3:335

Liszt and, 3:262

Rossini and, 3:11

academies, Florentine, 1:798–801, 818

académies de musique, 2:504

Academy (ancient Greece), 1:798

Academy of Antient (Ancient) Musick (London), 2:639

a cappella, 1:666–67

Good Friday settings and, 2:73

Monteverdi and, 2:6

Russian choral music and, 3:234

St. Mark's choir and, 1:780

Accademia degli Elevati (Florence), 1:818

Accademia degli Incogniti (Venice), 2:26–27

Accademia degli Invaghiti (Mantua), 2:18

Accademia dei Umidi (later Accademia Florentino), 1:798–99

Accademia Platonica (Florence), 1:798

accentus, 1:22

acciaccatura, 2.393. *See also* mordant

accidentals, 1:35, 274, 275, 596, 721; 2:212, 247

accompanied sonata, 2:427–32

"Account of a Very Remarkable Musician" (Barrington), 2:464

"Ächzen und erbärmlich Weinen" (J. S. Bach), 2:364–65

Acis and Galatea (Handel), 2:313–14

Ack, Värmaland, du sköna (Swedish folk song), 3:455–56

Acquila, Serafino dall', 1:552

acrostic, musical, 1:446, 704

Acte préalable (Scriabin), 4:224, 225, 226, 345

acting

by castrati, 2:86, 459

French court opera declamatory style, 2:99, 106

of liturgy, 1:52

monody and, 1:822

"natural," 2:459

See also drama; theater

Act of Supremacy (1534; England), 1:671, 675

Act of Uniformity (1549; England), 1:672–73, 675

Acts of the Apostles, Schütz setting of, 2:68–72

acute accent, 1:14

Adam, Adolphe, 4:134, 136

Giselle, 4:134, 135–36 141, 142

romantic ballet and, 4:134

Adam and Holstein (lithographers), 3:202

Adam de la Halle (Adam le Bossu), 1:120, 121–26

first opera and, 1:127

motet and, 1:122, 220–21, 233

Oswald von Volkenstein compared with, 1:142–43

polyphonic songs of, 1:122, 123, 142, 291

works of

Bone amourette, 1:123, 220

Dieus soit en cheste maison, 1:123–24

Fines amouretes ai, 1:124–25

Jeu de Robin et Marion, Le, 1:127, 233, 349

Robins m'aime, 1:127, 233

Adam of St. Victor (Adam Precentor), 1:89–90

Adams, John, 4:68; 5: 369, 379, 517, *517*

Death of Klinghoffer, The and, 5:517, 522–23

in conversation with David Gates, 5:473

neotonality and, 5:454, 455

works of

El Nino, 5:523–27

Nixon in China, 5:517–23, *518*, 522

added sixth, 3:649

Addinsell, Richard, *Warsaw Concerto*, 4:559

Addio alla Mamma" (Mascagni), 3:660

"Addio del passato" (Verdi), 3:582

Addison, Joseph, 2:313; 3:289–90

Ades, Thomas

Grawemeyer Award and, 5:454, 474

works of

Sur incises, 5:474

Adhémar, Bishop of Le Puy, 1:96, 98

"ad hoc" chord, Scriabin and, 4:210

Adler, Guido, 4:4, 15, 16, 23

Adlerian musicology, 4:4

Admonitio generalis (Charlemagne), **1:**5
Adonis (Marino), **2:**37
Adonis (mythology), **2:**97
Adoration of the Magi, The, **1:**177, *343*
Adorno, Theodor Wiesengrund, **4:**28, 189,
    335, 361, 421, 422, 444, 711; **5:**17, 89,
    108, 147, 395
    "autonomy," **5:**17
    "gemassigte Moderne," **5:**20
    utilitarian music and, **4:**559
    works of
        "Philosophy of New Music, The,"
        4:189, 335; **5:**17
Ad organum faciendum (anon.), **1:**162, 163
Adrian I, Pope, **1:**3
Adrian VI, Pope, **1:**630
Advent, **1:**12, 28, 42, 177, 758
    Bach (J. S.) cantata for, **2:**342, 348
Adventures in Harmony (Cowell), **4:**298
Adventures Underground (Del Tredici),
    5:442
AEG. *See* Allgemeine Elektrizitäts
    Gesellschaft, **5:**175
Aegidius of Murino, **1:**259
Aegisthus (mythology), **4:**49
Aeneid (Virgil), **2:**90, 132
Aeolian Hall, **4:**626
Aeolian mode, **1:**553, 596
Aeschylus, **3:**576; **4:**49
Aesopian discourse, **2:**442; **3:**622, 623
Aesthetica (Baumgarten), **2:**641
aesthetics *See* esthetics
"Aesthetics of Rock, The" (Meltzer), **5:**332
affections, doctrine of, **2:**643
affective style, **1:**737–38
Affektenlehre, **2:**680
Africaine, L' (Meyerbeer), **3:**219, 389–90
African Americans, **3:**766, 767, 768
African-American music, **4:**599, 602, 605,
    625, 626
Afro-Cuban rumba, **4:**486
"Afternoon of a Faun, The." *See* Prélude
    a L'apres-midi d'un faune ,
Against Interpretation (Sontag), **5:**325
"Against nature." *See* À rebours ,
"Against the grain." *See* À rebours agape
Agamemnon (mythology), **4:**48, 53
"Agamemnon" leitmotif, *Elektra* and, **4:**50,
    53
Agazzari, Agostino, **1:**650, 651
"aggregate compositions," Schoenberg and,
    4:681
aggregate harmony, **4:**192, 193–94, 195, 197
    Berg and, **4:**305
    Scriabin and, **4:**225–26
aggression, Risorgimento art as stimulus to,
    3:570, 660
Agincourt, battle of (1415), **1:**421, 447
"Agincourt Carol" ("Roy Henry"),
    1:418–21
Agnelli, Scipione, **2:**6
Agnus Dei, **1:**54, 58, 310

Bach (J. S.) Mass in B minor and, **2:**375
Byrd settings of, **1:**680, 681–83
Cambrai, **1:**314, 315
Caput Mass, **1:**470, 482
Du Fay *Missa Ave Regina coelorum* and,
    1:511–12
Gaspar Mass-substitution cycle and,
    1:520, 521
Isaac *Missa super La Spagna* and,
    1:622–25
Josquin *Missa L'Homme Armé super voces
    musicales* and, **1:**520, 499, 529,
    531–34
Kyrie pairing with, **1:**311, 314
Lutheran chorale replacement for,
    1:758, 769
in Mass ordo, **1:**61(table)
Missa L'Homme Armé and, **1:**487,
    488–89, 492, 493, 494, 495, 531
Ockeghem mensurated canon and,
    1:477–78, 531
Palestrina and, **1:**633, 635–37, 648, 653,
    659–63, 680
Sanctus pairing with, **1:**461
text and settings of, **1:**54, 56–57
votive Mass and, **1:**316, 317, 318
Agnus Dei II (Josquin), **1:**520, 529, 531–34
Agobard of Lyons, **1:**69
Agon (Stravinsky), **5:**122
Agoult, Countess Marie d', **3:**77, 78, 290
agrémens (embellishments), **2:**106, 278, 279
Agricola, Alexander, **1:**544
Agricola, Martin (Martin Sohr), **1:**762, 765
    Ein' feste Burg ist unser Gott, **1:**762, 763
"Ahavoh rabboh" mode, **4:**109, 110, 111
"Ah! bello a me ritorna" (Bellini), **3:**43
"Ahi caso acerbo" (Monteverdi), **2:**26
"Ah, quell'amor" (Verdi), **3:**581
Ai no polye lipin'ka, Rite of Spring, The, and,
    4:171
Aida (Verdi), **3:**565, 595, 643; **5:**20
air (ayre), **1:**813; **2:**120–22; **3:**119
"Air" (Berg), **4:**509–10
Air à trois (Lully), **2:**99–100
air chinois, **3:**192, 193
Air-Conditioned Nightmare, The (Miller),
    5:186
air de cour, **2:**98
"Air on the G String" (J. S. Bach), **4:**510
Aissi cum en genser pascors (Raimon),
    1:98–99
Aistulf, King of the Lombards, **1:**2
Aix-la-Chapelle (Aachen), **3:**165
Aix-la-Chapelle, Peace of (1749), **2:**306
Akademie, **2:**499–500
Akhmatova, Anna, **4:**795
"ala turca." *See* Turkish mode
alba (dawn-song), **1:**110–11
    Tagelied as equivalent of, **3:**549
Alba Madonna (Raphael), **1:**585
Albéniz, Isaac, *Cantos de Espana*, **4:**632

Albert, Prince Consort of Great Britain,
    3:173
Albert, Steven, neotonality and, **5:**454
Alberti, Domenico, **2:**425, 432
    Sonata in C major, op. 1, no. 3, **2:**432–33
Alberti bass, **2:**425, 428, 429, 432
Albertus Parisiensis, **1:**165–67, 172
Albigensian Crusade, **1:**116, 351
Albion and Albanius (Grabu), **2:**132–33
Alboni, Marietta, **3:**30
Albrechtsberger, Johann Georg, **2:**499,
    509, 652
Albright, Daniel, **4:**562, 576, 590
Alceste (Gluck), **2:**90, 453, 466–70
    Mozart's *Idomeneo* compared with,
        2:466–70
Alceste (Lully), **2:**90, 90
Alcestis (Euripides), **2:**90
Alcestis (mythology), **2:**90
"Alcotts, The" (Ives), **4:**267, 269, 270
Alcuin of York, **1:**4–5, 7, 37, 39; **2:**724
Alcyone (Marais), **2:**321
Aldimoro, L' (A. Scarlatti), **2:**186–87
Aldrich, Richard, **4:**752
"Alëa" (Boulez), **5:**65
Alembert, Jean d', **2:**461, 462
A l'entrada del tens clar (troubadour balada),
    1:113–14, 397
Alessandro, Lorenzo d', **1:**267
Alexander I, Emperor of Russia, **3:**347
Alexander II, Emperor of Russia, **3:**476
Alexander III, Emperor of Russia, **3:**800;
    4:142, 148
    assassination of, **4:**117
Alexander III (the Great), King of
    Macedonia, **1:**38
Alexander VI, Pope, **1:**458
Alexander VIII, Pope, **2:**151
Alfano, Franco, **3:**674
Alfieri, Vittorio, Count, **3:**569
Alfonsina, La (Ghiselin), **1:**544, 545
Alfonso I d'Este, Duke of Ferrara, **1:**544
Alfonso X (the Wise), King of Castile,
    1:128–29, 130
Alfonso and Estrella (Schubert), **3:**84
Alford, Henry, **4:**247
Alfred (Dvořák), **3:**753
Algorismus proportionum (Nicole d'Oresme),
    1:248
Alia musica (anon.), **1:**75, 79
Alice in Wonderland, Del Tredici and, **5:**442
Alice's Adventures in Wonderland, *Final
    Alice* (Del Tredici), and, **5:**443
Alice Symphony (Del Tredici), **5:**442
alienation, **2:**600, 737
*All American Music: Composition in the Late
    Twentieth Century* (Rockwell), **5:**333
All-American Symphony, **4:**649
Allanbrook, Wye J., **2:**435, 437, 620–21;
    3:35, 798; **4:**569
allegory
    court musical theater and, **2:**15

English masque and, 2:113, 132
Mendelssohn's *Paulus* oratorio as, 3:167
musical works as, 3:426–27
tragédie lyrique and, 2:89–94, 95, 96
Alleluia, 1:13, 24, 25, 26, 28, 41, 42–43, 79, 417
  Byrd setting of, 1:686–87
  jubilated singing and, 1:39, 98
  Marian text for, 1:209–11, 211, 212
  motet and, 1:233, 267, 269–71, 291
  polyphonic setting of, 1:155, 162, 178, 191–96
  prosulated, 1:41, 42
  as ritornello, 1:784–85
Alleluia Nativitas (Perotin, attrib.), 1:191–96, 191, 209
allemande, 2:37, 53, 120
  in *Don Giovanni*, 2:491
  gavotte contrasted with, 2:274
  history of, 2:260
  in suite format, 2:260, 262, 263–65, 266, 267
  See also balletto
Alle psallite cum luya (motet), 1:403
Allererst lebe ich mir werde (Walther), 1:135
Allgemeine Elektrizitäts Gesellschaft, 5:175
Allgemeine musikalische Zeitung (journal), 2:673; 3:174, 291, 343
Allgemeiner Deutscher Musikverein (All-German Musical Society), 3:417, 446
All in the Golden Afternoon (Del Tredici), 5:444
alliteration, Wagner and, 3:501, 504, 509
Allmacht, Die (Schubert), 3:138, 140
"All of Flesh Is Like the Grass" (Brahms), 3:704
allusive art, 1:327
  Brahms and, 3:688, 694, 707–8, 721–23, 726
"All we like sheep have gone astray" (Handel), 2:332, 335
alman. *See* allemande
Alma Redemptoris Mater (Marian antiphon), 1:99, 461, 462
Alma Redemptoris Mater (Power Mass), 1:462–65
Alouette, L' (Janequin), 1:711
alphabetic notation, 1:17, 17, 33, 45
  Greek system, 1:17, 77
  medieval modes, 1:76, 77, 99–102
Alpha Centauri, 1:476
Alpha Draconis. See Caput Draconis
"Alphorn theme" (Brahms), 3:720, 725–28
Also sprach Zarathustra (Nietzsche), 4:53, 580
alta capella, 1:621–22
Altamont Festival, 5:311
Altenberg, Peter, 4:193
  Altes Neues, 4:193
"Altenberg Lieder" (Berg), 4:195, 196, 197, 225

Alten, bösen Lieder, Die (Schumann), 3:304–5
alto, 1:468
Amadeus (Shaffer), 2:464
Amalar (Amalarius) of Metz, 1:37–39, 41, 42, 51, 56, 59, 66
Amalia Catharine, Countess of Erbach, 2:70
Amarilli mia bella (Caccini), 1:813–17, 814, 819
amateur musicians. *See* domestic entertainment
Amati, Niccolò, 2:2
Amati family, 2:2
Amati violins, 3:255
ambitus (range), 1:74
Ambrose, Bishop of Milan, 1:.48, 47, 63
Ambrosian rite (Milanese), 1:47, 63, 518
Ambrosian stanza, 1:49
Amen
  Byrd Mass, 1:686
  Machaut Gloria, 1:322–23, 326
  melismatic, 1:316, 317
  triple, 1:777
  Willaert cadence, 1:602, 603
"America" (song), 1:18; 4:291, 597
American academic serialism, 5:210
American Articles of Confederation, 3:764
American Ballads and Folksongs (Lomax-Lomax), 4:659, 660
American Civil Liberties Union, 5:107
American civil rights movement, Josephine Baker and, 4:602
American colonies, 2:111
American Communist Party, 4:651, 658
American Constitution, 2:111, 461–62
"American hustle," myth of, 4:622, 637
American in Paris, An (Gershwin), 4:628
American literary realism, 4:273
American Legion, 5:109
American neoromantic style, 4:647
"American Preludes" (Ginastera), 3:351
American Revolution, 3:764
"American school," 4:599, 610
American Society of University Composers (ASUC), 5:164
American Songbag, The (Sandburg), 4:659
American West, mythology of, 4:637–47
Americanism
  European backlash against, 3:384–85
  France and, 3:214
  musical, 4:588, 599
"Americanist" symphonies, 4:648–49
Amériques (Varese), 5:184
Amiel, Henri, 3:69
Amiens, 1:411
Amigoni, Jacopo, 2:172
A minor, as Mozart's "Turkish" key, 2:602
Amint (C. P. E. Bach), 3:120–21
Am leuchtenden sommermorgen (Schumann), 3:303–4
Am Meer (Schubert), 3:138, 139

Amor coniugale, L' (Mayr), 3:3
"Amour sacré de la patrie" (Auber), 3:212, 213
Ampex Company, tape recorders and, 5:176
Amsterdam, 2:44, 48, 177
Am Wegrand (Schoenberg), 4:335, 336, 337, 344, 353
Anabaptists, 3:218–19
anachronism, 1:127, 141–44, 792
  meaning of, 1:142–44
Anacreon, 3:120
Anacreontic verses, 2:3; 3:120, 125
Anaklasis (Penderecki), 5:217
anapestic meter, 1:197, 198
Ancient Voices of Children, Crumb and, 5:422, 423, 426
  Bach's "Notebook for Anna Magdalen" and, 5:423
  Lorca and, 5:422
  Mahler's "Farewell" motif from *Song of the Earth* and, 5:423
Ancient Voices of Children: no. 3, "Dance of the Sacred Life-Cycle," 5:424–25
ancient world, 1:29–35, 31, 32, 38, 47; 2:453, 724
  British music and, 1:387–88, 388
  Plato's Academy and, 1:798
  polyphony and, 1:147
  Renaissance interest in, 1:382–83, 384
  Wagner on, 3:488, 489–90
  See also classicism; Greek (Hellenistic) music theory
Andante de la Symphonie en La (Lami), 3:86, 87, 331
Andante pour le clavecin (Mozart), 2:463
Andate, oh miei sospiri (A. Scarlatti), 2:142, 143–47
An der schönen, blauen Donau, op. 314 (J. Strauss), 3:648, 649
An die ferne Geliebte, op. 98 (Beethoven), 2:673; 3:131–36, 154
  Schumann's (Robert) *Phantasie* and, 3:312–15, 324
An die Freude (Schiller), 2:675, 678, 680, 731
Andersen, Hans Christian, 4:240, 675
  "The Emperor's New Clothes," 4:360
Anderson, Laurie, 5:492–95, 492
  androgynous persona and, 5:492
  "punk"/unisex style and, 5:492
  self-parody and, 5:493
  technology and, 5:493
  vocoder and, 5:493
  "Voice of Authority" and, 5:493
  works of
    "O Superman," 5:493–94
    Walking the Dog, 5:494
Anderson, Marian, 3:771
Andriessen, Louis, 5:397–400, 407
  De Staat, 5:397, 398, 399–400
  De Stijl, 398, 5:399

Andriessen, Louis (*continued*)
  De Volharding (Perseverance) and,
    5:397
  Hague Conservatory and, **5:**398
  Hoketus and, **5:**397
Andromaque (Racine), **3:**333
Andromède (Corneille), **2:**87
Angelorum ordo (Notker sequence), **1:**42–43
Angelus Domini (Chartres fragment),
    1:155, 158
Angiolini, Gasparo, **4:**133
Anglican Church, **1:**402, 671, 672–75, 751;
    2:116, 125, 204
  Handel's *Messiah* and, **2:**325
Anglican liturgy, **1:**672–73, 675, 676,
    677–78
Anglo-American folklore, **4:**661, 671
Anglo-American school of symphony, **4:**6
Anglo-folklorism, **4:**662
Angsttraum (Schoenberg), **4:**326
anhemitonic pitch collections, Debussy
    and, **4:**83
anhemitonic scales, **4:**75, 101
Aniello, Tommaso (Masaniello), **3:**208
Anima 7 (Kosugi), **5:**91
animal magnetism, **3:**71
animal sounds, **1:**717
Anima mia che pensi (Cavalieri), **1:**833, 834
Anima mia che pensi (lauda), **1:**833, 834
Anjou, Count of, **1:**127
ANNA (madrigalist patron), **1:**353, 356
Anna Magdalena music book (J. S. Bach),
    2:262, 262
"Anna O.," **4:**327. *See also* "The Case of
    Anna O."
Anne (Anna Ioannovna), Empress of
    Russia, **3:**233–35
Anne, Queen of Great Britain, **2:**237
Années de pèlerinage (Liszt), **3:**432; **4:**112
Annette et Lubin, **3:**235
Annunciation, **1:**420, 565, 566
annus horribilis, **5:**310
Annuzio. *See* D'Annuzio, Gabriele
Anonymus IV, **1:**173–75, 177, 183, 184, 186,
    187, 192, 196, 198, 209, 233
  on English thirds, **1:**394
  on faburden, **1:**437
Another Dawn (Korngold), **4:**551
Ansermet, Ernest, **4:**563, 601, 602, 603, 607,
    612–13, 616–17
  Diaghilev's Ballets Russes and, **4:**601
  Stravinsky and, **4:**601
Anschütz, Heinrich, **2:**689
Antar (Rimsky-Korsakov), **3:**397
anthem, origin of, **1:**11, 94
anthem oratorio, Handel's *Israel in Egypt* as
    prototype of, **2:**316–21
Anthoni usque limina (Busnoys), **1:**456
Anthony, Susan B., Thomson's *The Mother
    of Us All* and, **5:**225–26
Anthony Adverse (Korngold), **4:**551
Anthony the Abbot, Saint, **1:**9, 456

Antiche arie e danze per liuto (Respighi), **4:**750
Antico, Andrea, **1:**691
antiphonal Mass, **1:**780
antiphonal psalmody, **1:**8, 11, 23, 611
  original meaning of, **1:**8
antiphoner, **1:**6, 7, 14, 17, 20, 41, 53, 62
  chant modal classification, **1:**78
  staffed neumes proposal, **1:**99
antiphons, **1:**8, 12, 20–29, 79, 80
  chant interval exemplars, **1:**100
  Communion, **1:**433–35
  cyclic Mass Ordinaries and, **1:**465, 693
  definition of, **1:**111
  English, **1:**612–14, 686–88
  Frankish mode theory and, **1:**76–86
  Gregorian, **1:**12–13, 34, 78
  grouping of, **1:**72–76
  neumated, **1:**13–17, 24
  psalm tone pairing with, **1:**20–21, 78, 83
  Song of Songs, **1:**429–33
  tonaries and, **1:**72–76
  troping of, **1:**50–53, 55
  See also Marian antiphons
antiphony, **2:**46, 59, 315, 378, 381
Antiphony I (Brant), **5:**421
Antique Theater (St. Petersburg), **1:**127,
    128
antiquity. *See* ancient world; classicism
anti-Semitism, **1:**88; **3:**772
  Dreyfus and, **4:**106
  in Germany, **3:**177
  Mahler and, **4:**7
  St. John Passion and, **2:**389–90
  Wagner and, **3:**177–79, 227–29, 480,
    559, 560
anti-Teutonic modernism, **4:**59–69
antithesis, **1:**723, 724, 733–34, 747, 749;
    3:424, 567
  Brahms and, **3:**704
  Bruckner and, **3:**746
  Hegelian dialectic and, **3:**412
Antokoletz, Elliott, **4:**119, 410
Antonio da Tempo, **1:**723
Antwerp, **1:**454, 459, 597, 676, 714
  English composers in, **2:**45
"Anvil Chorus" (Gilbert and Sullivan),
    3:653
"anxiety of influence" theory, **3:**695
Any Resemblance Is Purely Coincidental
    (Dodge), **5:**499
Anyuta (Russian opera), **3:**235, 236
Apel, Johann August, **3:**191
Apocrypha, *El Nino* and, **5:**526
Apocryphal themes, oratorio and, **3:**164
Apollinaire, Guillaume, **4:**564–67, 578, 579
  Les mamelles de Tirésias and, **4:**578, 578f,
    580–81
  "sur-réalisme" and, **4:**566–67, 578
Apollo (mythology), **1:**32, 802, 803, 804,
    824, 826; **2:**21, 47, 58, 88, 151;
    4:676, 677

Apollo 11 moon landing, *Night of the Four
    Moons* and, **5:**422
A poste messe (Lorenzo), **1:**366
apostles, **1:**719
Appalachian Spring (Copland), **4:**666
"Appassionata" Sonata in F minor, op. 57
    (Beethoven), **2:**670; **3:**11, 376
appoggiatura, **2:**254, 364, 413, 414;
    3:99–100; **4:**8, 28, 211, 276, 311, 319,
    320, 663
Apprenti sorcier, L' (Dukas), **4:**104
Appress' un fiume (Giovanni), **1:**356–59, 363,
    364
"Approaching a History of 18th-Century
    Music" (Heartz), **2:**400
Apt Codex, **1:**310, 311, 316
Aquitaine, **1:**50, 51
  ars subtilior composition and, **1:**342–45
  monastic polyphonic manuscripts and,
    1:156–62, 166, 307
  troubadours and, **1:**106–17, 351, 353
  See also Avignon papacy
"arabesques," Schoenberg's Quartet no. 2
    and, **4:**315–16, 317
"Arabian Dance" (Chaikovsky), **3:**406
Arabian Nights, **3:**193, 386, 397
  Sheherazade and, **4:**121
Arabic mathematics, **1:**252
Arabic music
  instruments, **1:**129, 130
  sung poetry, **1:**108
Arab-Israeli conflict, *The Death of
    Klinghoffer* and **5:**522
Arabskaya melodiya (Borodin), **3:**400–401
Aragon. *See* Spain
Araja (Araia), Francesco, **2:**158; **3:**234–35
  *Finto Nino, Il, overo La Semiramide
    riconosciuta*, **3:**234–35
  Tsefal i Prokris, **3:**235
Arcadelt, Jacques, **1:**723, 724, 725
  Bianco e dolce cigno, Il, **1:**724–25, 726
Arcadian Academy (Rome), **2:**150–52, 153,
    177, 192, 435
archaeology, **2:**453
Arditti Quartet, **5:**359
"Archduke" Trio in B-flat major, op. 97
    (Beethoven), **2:**655, 671
Archilei, Vittoria, **1:**804, 806–7
architecture, **1:**169, 797; **2:**35
  modern, **5:**412–13
  postmodern, **5:**412
arcigravicembalo (enharmonic keyboard),
    1:730, 732, 732; **4:**285
a realibus ad realiora and, **4:**217
À rebours (Huysmans), **4:**29, 57, 84
À rebours agape, **1:**13
Arel, Bülent, **5:**208
Arendt, Hannah, **4:**743
aria, **1:**803
  Bach (J. S.) and, **2:**370–74, 376–77
  Bellini and, **3:**40, 43, 71
  cantata, **2:**75, 348, 351, 352

cantata vs. operatic, 2:146
as concerto for voice and orchestra, 2:308
Farinelli's signature, 2:167–69
fermata in, 2:171
in *grand opéra*, 3:219–20
Handel and, 2:311–12, 317
improvisation and, 2:650
Metastasian librettos and, 2:153–54, 161–64, 166–67
monody and, 1:806–12
opera seria, 2:143–44, 145, 154, 311–12, 341
original meaning of, 2:144
origins of word, 1:627
Passion, 2:378–81
rage, 2:155, 308–11, 437, 481, 602, 678
recitative with, 2:25, 78, 142, 143–44, 154, 192, 342, 348, 349, 351–52, 378
Rossini new style of, 3:15, 27–35
siciliana, 2:144–46
simile, 2:161, 168–69, 231, 308
strophic, 2:33, 144
Verdi and, 3:570–72
See also da capo aria
aria cantabile, 2:154
aria d'affetto, 2:154
Aria della battaglia (A. Gabrieli), 1:787–89
aria di bravura
Handel and, 2:336–40
in Metastasian librettos, 2:154, 161
Aria di Fiorenza (Archilei), 1:804, 806–7
Aria di romanesca (Caccini), 1:823
Aria di romanesca (Frescobaldi), 1:823, 824, 825
aria di sorbetto, 2:154, 174
Ariadne (mythology), 2:104
Ariadne auf Naxos (Benda), 4:458
Ariadne auf Naxos (Hofmannsthal), 4:453
Ariadne auf Naxos (Strauss), 4:453
Ariane (Cambert), 2:89
Ariane et Barbe-bleue (Dukas), 4:104, 106
Arianna (Monteverdi), 2:104
"aria time," 3:69, 329
Augenblick and, 3:91
in Meyerbeer's *Les Huguenots*, 3:225
Rossini new style and, 3:28
Schubert and, 3:91, 94
Arie musicale (Frescobaldi), 1:821, 824–25
ariette
in cantata, 2:75
Rameau and, 2:107, 108
Arion (mythology), 1:804, 805, 809
arioso, 2:24, 133
aristocracy
Beaumarchais's Figaro plays and, 2:478
Beethoven and, 2:671
castrato singing and, 2:174
chamber music and, 3:730–31, 732
classicism and, 2:647
comédie larmoyante as lampoon of, 2:450
commercial (later comic) opera oppositional politics and, 2:17
darkened theater concerns of, 3:564

democratization of taste and, 3:251
English Civil War and, 2:124
English masques and, 2:113
entrepreneurial class challenges to, 2:115
in France, 2:85, 97; 3:214
Gluck's reforms and, 2:459
Grocheio's musical social theory and, 1:208
Haydn's relationship with, 2:527–28, 553–55, 577–78, 607
high art and, 1:115–16, 120, 226, 326–27, 336
Hungarian, 4:365
Italian court musical presentations and, 2:15–16
Italian musical preferences and, 1:351–52, 367
lied genre and, 3:130
madrigal and, 1:354–56, 368
meritocracy and, 1:121
Mozart subscription concerts and, 2:608
musical supply and demand and, 2:527–28, 553, 555
Nuove musiche song and, 1:812–13
opera seria and, 2:174–75, 447, 455
pastorelas and, 2:446
plot devices and, 2:446, 447, 448
rococo expression and, 2:279, 459
in Russia, 3:467
salons and, 3:74, 78
sexual behavior among, 3:36
troubadour art and, 1:109, 110, 111, 116, 208
vernacular song and, 1:695
virtuosity ban by, 2:15
women composers and, 2:79, 80–81
See also court music; court opera; cultural elite; patronage
aristocracy of talent, 1:552, 554, 608
Aristotle, 1:196, 248, 551, 587, 727; 2:15, 17, 151, 435, 706; 3:671
ars perfecta and, 1:615
"art imitates nature" doctrine of, 2:642–43
Mei treatise on, 1:799
Aristoxenus, 1:799
"chromatic tetrachord" and, 4:449
Armida (mythology), 2:94, 95
Armide (Lully), 2:94–96, 95, 155
armonica, 3:53, 73
Arnalta's gloating aria (Mozart), 2:27, 28–29
Arnaut Daniel, 1:110, 116, 352, 352
Arndt, Ernst Moritz, 3:158, 165, 168
Arne, Thomas, 2:158
Arnim, Achim von, 3:123; 4:20
Arnold, Matthew, 3:773, 774, 782, 783; 4:270, 272
Arnold Schoenberg's Society for Private Musical Performances, 5:158
Arnstadt, 2:239, 241
Arnt von Aich (Arnt of Aachen), 1:691–92

arpeggione, 3:85
Arras, 1:120
Arras Puy, 1:121
Arreglito, El (Yradier), 3:641
Ars Antiqua. *See* classicism
Ars cantus mensurabilis (Franco of Cologne), 1:215
ars combinatoria, motet as, 1:226
ars erotica (erotic art), 3:36
Ars Gallica, 4:59, 61
Ars musicae (Grocheio), 1:207
Ars Nova, 1:247–87
bottom-up techniques of, 1:291
conservative backlash to, 1:254–55
discordia concors belief and, 1:255, 261
distinguishing notational principles of, 1:258, 260–61
final phase of, 1:337
Italian music and, 277–281, 374. *See also* trecento
Machaut and, 1:270–73, 291, 295, 325, 326
notational representation and, 1:252–55, 260, 355
notational theory of, 1:248–50
patterning and, 1:261–66, 262
practice implications of, 1:250–52
spread of, 1:346, 348–50
trobar clus and, 1:326
Ars novae musicae (Jehan des Murs), 1:247–48
Ars nova (Vitry), 1:248, 258, 273, 337
ars perfecta, 1:585–628; 2:13
art of transition and, 1:600
Byrd and, 1:630, 678, 684, 686–87
challenges to, 1:687, 689, 721, 722, 725, 775, 780, 782, 783–84, 786, 797, 800, 831
concerto vs., 1:783–84
Counter Reformation musical departure from, 1:771, 775, 780, 782, 783–84, 786
distortion vs., 1:629–30
as ecumenical, 1:629, 630, 631, 642, 644–45, 646, 667, 684, 713, 722, 724, 771
English liturgical music contrasted with, 1:612–14
Galilei's view of, 1:800
Gregorian chant and, 1:631
harmony and, 1:588, 816
instrumental music and, 1:606, 617–28
Italy and, 1:699
Josquin and, 1:550, 755
Lasso and, 1:721, 722
Lutheran church music and, 1:755, 756, 769
madrigalism vs., 1:724, 725, 727, 733, 735
metrical psalms contrasted with, 1:599
motet and, 1:607, 641
Palestrina and, 1:630, 632–33, 652, 655, 663, 667, 713

ars perfecta (*continued*)
  Reformation hostility to, **1**:754
  as *stile antico*, **1**:831
  as utopian, **1**:629
  Willaert and, **1**:601–11
  written historical record of, **1**:617
ars poetica, **1**:290
ars subtilior, **1**:338–48, *341*
  centers of, **1**:342–46
  English composers and, **1**:409, 410, 424
  notational signs and, **1**:338, 339–42, 345, 355–56
art. *See* artistic creation
art, sacralization of, **4**:20
Art and Revolution (Wagner), **3**:488–91, 496
Artaria (Vienna publisher), **2**:541
"art-deco," **4**:776
Artaserse (Araja), **2**:158
Artaserse (Arne), **2**:158
Artaserse (J. C. Bach), **2**:158, 419
Artaserse (Cimarosa), **2**:158
Artaserse (Galuppi), **2**:158
Artaserse (Gluck), **2**:158
Artaserse (Hasse), **2**:158, 166
Artaserse (Isouard), **2**:158
Artaserse (Jommelli), **2**:158
Artaserse (London pastiche), **2**:311
Artaserse (Metastasio libretto), **2**:153, 158–68
  "geometry" of dramatis personae of, **2**:159, *160*
  myriad musical settings and performance places of, **2**:158, 419
  story of, **2**:159–61
  thirty arias in, **2**:161–71
Artaserse (Mysliveček), **2**:158
Artaserse (Paisiello), **2**:158
Artaserse (Piccinni), **2**:158
Artaserse (Sarti), **2**:158
Artaserse (G. Scarlatti), **2**:158
Artaserse (Vinci), **2**:158, 161–65
Art décoratif d'aujourd'hui, L' (Le Corbusier), **5**:209
Art de Dictier et de Fere Chançons (Deschamps), **1**:337
Arte dei rumori, L' (Russolo), **5**:179
Arte del violino, L' (Locatelli), **2**:299; **3**:252
Art et instruction de bien dancer, L' (Michel de Toulouze), **1**:621
art for art's sake, **1**:541; **2**:111, 590, 600; **3**:75, 595–96, 599
  See also absolute music
art history, **1**:382–83, *382*, 429, 585, 641, 653
  Baroque and, **1**:797
  Hegelian dialectic and, **3**:413
  mannerism and, **1**:733
Arthurian legend, **1**:119
Articles of Confederation (U.S.), **3**:764
Artikulation (Ligeti), **5**:52–53, 191, 214
artisan class, **1**:368
  See also guilds
Artis canendi (Heyden), **1**:550

artistic creation
  absolute music and. *See* absolute music
  accessibility/social relevance of, **3**:251
  alienation and, **2**:600, 737
  alternative views of, **1**:66
  anachronism and, **1**:143–44
  Ars Nova and, **1**:267–70, 337
  ars perfecta and, **1**:585–628, 629–30
  artificial conceptual subdivisions and, **1**:380–85
  aspirational view of, **3**:774
  authenticity and, **3**:62, 122, 124
  as autonomous. *See* autonomous art
  avant-garde and, **1**:326–27
  beholder's role in, **3**:305, 315–16, 341
  biblical Creator linked with, **2**:81
  biography of author and, **2**:620
  classical view of, **2**:642–43
  collective, **3**:306
  commodification of, **1**:542, 549; **2**:736; **3**:664, 682
  consciousness of style in, **1**:267, 270
  convention and, **1**:359, 363–64
  cultural bias and, **3**:298
  democracy and, **3**:383–86
  difficult vs. accessible works and, **1**:115–16, 120, 226, 228, 326–27, 459–60
  emancipation of, **2**:737
  emulation vs. imitation in, **1**:474–75
  Enlightenment thought and, **2**:495–96
  estheticism and, **3**:562
  free market and, **2**:600
  gender and, **2**:78–81
  genius and, **1**:551, 552, 570, 608; **3**:439, 451, 456
  German hegemonic claims to, **2**:389, 738
  German national identity and, **1**:141; **2**:388, 389
  group identity and, **2**:82, 83
  as higher truth, **3**:59
  in historical/political context, **2**:389–90, 397
  historiographic approach to, **1**:144–45
  home entertainment and, 3.63. *See also* domestic entertainment
  humanity represented in, **2**:464, 474, 475, 486, 495, 590–91, 643
  as imitation of nature, **2**:643; **3**:277, 324, 333, 618
  immanence of author's intentions in, **2**:620
  improvisation and, **1**:117
  innovation and, **2**:397
  interpretation of, **2**:680
  introspectivity subjectivity and, **2**:590–600, 643
  legendary status and, **1**:547–48
  linear historical view of, **1**:245, 247–48, 252, 580, 738–39
  lonely, suffering hero concept and, **2**:649

  masterwork concept and, **2**:639, 650; **3**:681
  medieval sense of, **1**:267, 270
  mimesis and, **1**:363
  of Mozart, **2**:495, 590–91, 599–600
  Mozart's "pleasing the ear" statement and, **2**:471–72, 494
  Musica and, **1**:69–76, 148, 248, 552
  musical historiography and, **2**:12–18
  music's purpose and, **2**:363–64, 486, 494
  myth of perfection and, **2**:235
  naturalism and, **2**:432–34
  neoclassic view of, **2**:453
  New German School view of, **3**:438–41
  nonpolitical appreciation of, **2**:111, 485
  objectivity and, **3**:315–16
  "original genius" concept and, **2**:329, 416, 641, 643
  Palestrina legend and, **1**:653
  performance separated from, **2**:639, 642, 655
  for personal satisfaction. *See* autonomous art
  personal taste and, **2**:87, 173
  poietic fallacy and, **2**:13
  political context of, **1**:653, 673; **2**:12–16, 111–12, 175–76
  politics separated from, **3**:62
  professional reviewers and. *See* criticism
  Romantic concept of, **1**:337; **2**:81, 590, 591, 600, 641–46. *See also* Romanticism
  Russian perspective of, **3**:622
  sacralization of, **2**:649–50
  as seeking and finding, **1**:606
  sense of style and, **1**:267
  sensibility and, **2**:409–18, 737
  social consequences of, **2**:14–15
  social import of, **2**:496
  social purpose of, **1**:144
  solitude and, **3**:64
  Sturm und Drang and, **2**:416, 417; **3**:121
  style-based judgments of, **1**:145
  stylistic evolution and, **1**:245, 247–48, 267–70
  sublimity vs. beauty in, **2**:643–46, 649
  subtle cleverness and, **1**:327–42
  synthesis of words and music in, **1**:337
  timelessness and, **1**:65
  transcendence and, **2**:706, 714, 720, 721
  truth and, **3**:64, 77, 229–30, 397
  universalizing resistance by, **2**:600
  utopian message drawn from, **3**:59
  verisimilitude and, **3**:229–30, 397
  virtuosity and, **1**:330. *See also* virtuosity
  Wagner on, **3**:488–90
  women's underrepresentation in, **2**:78–83
  See also composers
artistic truth, **3**:64, 77, 229–30, 397
artist managements, **3**:272
artist-prophet myth, **3**:59, 438, 439

art music
Art of Fugue, The (J. S. Bach), **2:**385–88;
    4:465, 703
Artôt, Désirée, **3:**409, 410
"Art poétique" (Verlaine), **4:**100
art-prose, **1:**39, 50
arts criticism. *See* criticism; musical analysis
art song, **3:**132
    Schumann (Robert) and, **3:**295
arts patronage. *See* patronage
Artusi, Giovanni Maria, **1:**735–36; **2:**2, 5
*Artusi, overo Delle imperfettioni della moderna
    musica, L'* (treatise), **1:**735–36
art vs. commerce controversy and, **3:**664,
    682
    lied and, **3:**132, 135
    nineteenth-century symphonic music
      and, **3:**682, 755
    sixteenth-century, **1:**724
    United States and, **3:**766–67, 768
Artwork of the Future, The (Wagner), **3:**675
Asafyev, Boris, **3:**633; **4:**526–27, 528, 550,
    780
"Ascendit in celum" (Nanino), **3:**102–4
asceticism, musical, **2:**68
Aschberg set. *See* A. Schbeg set
A. Schbeg set, **4:**324–25
"Λ Serpina penserete" (Pergolesi), **2:**439,
    440
Ashe, Andrew, **2:**568
Asian culture, **2:**721
Asian themes, **3:**192, 787
    See also orientalism
Askold's Grave (Verstovsky), **3:**236, 238
Association of Contemporary Music
    (ASM), **4:**657, 777
assonance, **1:**44
Assumption, **1:**523, 566
asterism, **3:**311
Astra tenenti (Play of Daniel conducti), **1:**95
astrology, **1:**615, 6116
Athens, **1:**798
Atlas (Monk), 490–91, 490
Atlas eclipticalis (Cage), **5:**75, 76, 88, 96
atomus, **1:**253
atonality, **1:**472, 729–30; **4:**218, 312–13
    Scriabin and, **4:**218–24
atonal triads, **4:**331–34
Attaingnant, Pierre, **1:**692–93, 692, 694,
    706, 710, 786
Attali, Jacques, **5:**346
    Brutis, **5:**346
Attic Greek amphora, **1:**32
Attilio Regolo (Metastasio libretto),
    2:155–58
    musical settings of, **2:**157–58
Attis (mythology), **2:**97
Atys (Lully), **2:**91–92, 97–106, 110
    contemporary subtext of, **2:**97
    overture to, **2:**91–92
    sommeil (sleep scene), **2:**100–102, 100

as "the king's opera," **2:**97
    third act of, **2:**97–106
Auber, Daniel François Espirit, **3:**798
    grand opéra and, **3:**207–8
    Muette de Portici, La, **3:**207, 208–14, 216,
      219
Aubigné, Françoise d'. *See* Maintenon,
    Mme de
auctoritas (authority), **1:**475
Aucun/Lonc tans (Petrus), **1:**238–41, 241
Audefroi le Bastart, **1:**119–20, 120
au-dela, **4:**85, 144
Auden, W. H., **3:**143; **5:**117, 228, 246, 343
    Paul Bunyan and, **5:**226
audible music. *See* musical sound
audience
    as arbiter of musical taste, **2:**173
    artist's representation to, **3:**64
    art vs. commerce controversy and, **3:**664
    Beethoven's consistent popularity with,
      2:655, 671, 691, 692
    buffi popularity with, **2:**434
    for chamber music, **3:**731
    commercial opera and, **2:**34
    democratization of taste and, **3:**251, 292
    disrupted musical expectations of,
      2:207–8, 223
    early music conventions and, **2:**233
    eighteenth-century aggressive responses
      by, **2:**223–24, 651
    empathy and, **3:**287
    expectations of, **2:**213, 305, 434
    as free market, **2:**571
    German music festival and, **2:**385
    grand opéra courting of, **3:**210–11
    interaction with music by, **2:**223, 611–13
    late-eighteenth-century spontaneity of,
      2:613, 651
    music criticism and, **3:**289, 290
    nineteenth- and
      post-nineteenth-century decorum
      of, **2:**223–24, 613, 651
    nineteenth-century mass musical
      appreciation by, **2:**736
    opera seria behavior of, **2:**153–54, 173–75,
      223
    opera's "two musics" and, **1:**827
    as oratorio participants, **3:**169
    Orfeo's appeal to, **2:**21
    response to musical representations of
      nature by, **2:**321
    for symphonic music, **2:**498; **3:**676–79,
      681
    twentieth-century etiquette instructions
      for, **2:**651
    "understandable" music and, **2:**234
    virtuoso performance effects on,
      1:616–17; **2:**16
Audience Pieces (Vautier), **5:**92
Audite nova (Lasso), **1:**717–18
Auferstehung (Mahler), **4:**9

Augenblick, in Schubert's works, **3:**91–92,
    110
Augenmusik (eye-music), **1:**778–79, 801;
    4:462; **5:**168, 425
augmented fourth, **1:**40, 152
augmented second, **1:**275
augmented sixth, **2:**364
    in Brahms's First Symphony, **3:**698
    nineteenth-century harmony and, **3:**73
    normal resolutions of, **3:**428
    Romantic introspection and, **3:**96
    Schubert's use of, **3:**92, 95, 98, 112
augmented triad, Liszt and, **3:**428, 435–36
Augsburg Confession, **2:**353–54, 402; **3:**167
Auguries of Innocence (Blake), **3:**277
Augustine, Saint, **1:**11, 25, 39, 47, 66, 70, 90,
    172, 433, 613, 646, 755
    definition of music by, **1:**69–70
    music treatise of, **1:**69–70, 175, 337
Augustinians, **1:**179, 539
Auner, Joseph, **4:**680
A un giro sol (Monteverdi), **1:**733–34, 735,
    736, 747; **2:**229
    Luther setting of, **1:**756, 758
    Sennfl setting of, **1:**757
aural conditioning, **1:**471–72, 739
aural learning. *See* oral tradition
Aurelian of Réôme, **1:**76, 77
Aureliano in Palmira (Rossini), **3:**20
Auric, George
    Les Six group and, **4:**588
Ausgleich, **4:**366, **4:**569, 570
Aus meinen thranen (Schumann), **3:**299–300
Austen, Jane, **2:**409
Austin, Larry, **4:**283
Austria, **2:**647
    Belgium and, **3:**212–14
    claim to Beethoven by, **2:**675–76
    Enlightenment thought and, **2:**462, 482
    folkishness connotation in, **2:**550
    Fux and, **1:**667, 669
    Haydn's nationalistic oratorio for, **2:**633
    Italy and, **3:**569, 570, 573, 573
    Napoleonic Wars and, **2:**577
    national anthem of, **3:**130
    nineteenth-century symphonic music in,
      3:677, 680, 745–51
    operetta in, **3:**644, 647–51
    "oratorio-style" Mass genre in, **2:**375
    Poland and, **3:**344, 357
    Slavic language speakers in, **3:**345
    symphony and, **2:**504
    Thirty Years War and, **2:**55–56
    waltz and, **2:**573
    See also Holy Roman Empire; Vienna
Austrian suzerainty, **4:**365
Austro-German *Anschluss* (annexation),
    4:551
Austro-German symphonic composition,
    conclusion of, **4:**6
Austro-Prussian War (1866), **3:**569
authenticity, **3:**62, 122, 124

authentic modal form, **1:**74, 76
authentic performance, **1:**782
"Authority" leitmotif (Wagner's
    Götterdämmerung), **3:**507, 516
autogenetic principle, **4:**638–39, 641–42
autonomous art, **2:**111, 208, 589–90, 599,
    642, 643, 670, 737
    criterion for, **1:**65–66
    earliest instrumental music and, **1:**541
    "loner" artist concept and, **1:**144
    as written, **1:**104
Autran, Joseph, **3:**425
Autre jour, L' (French double motet),
    1:222–24, *222*, 229
Autrier jost' una serbissa, L' (Marcabru), **1:**113
Available Forms I (Brown), **5:**96
avante-garde, **1:**326–27; **3:**483
    conservatism vs., **3:**285–86
    critique of Beethoven by, **2:**693
    historicist theory and, **3:**411, 416
    Italian Risorgimento period and, **3:**570
    Liszt and, **3:**418, 420
"Avant-Garde and Kitsch" (Greenberg),
    5:221–22
Ave Maria (antiphon), **2:**66
Ave Maria (Compère pastiche), **1:**523–26,
    583
Ave Maria (Gounod), **2:**251
Ave Maria (Josquin), **1:**606, 686
Ave Maria . . . Virgo serena (Josquin),
    1:565–73, 577–84
    dating of, **1:**578–80, 583–84
    emblematic status of, **1:**565, 577–78,
        588, 602–3
    text of, **1:**565–66
Ave Maria . . . Virgo serena (Sennfl),
    1:572–73, 588, 704
Ave maris stella (Frankish hymn), **1:**48, 49,
    83
    Du Fay fauxbourdon setting of, **1:**441,
        442–43, 446
Ave Regina coelorum (Du Fay), **1:**507–12,
    574
Ave verum corpus (Byrd), **1:**686, 687
Avignon papacy, **1:**249, 307–21, *310*, 331,
    337, 342, 348, 378, 424
awe, **1:**287
ayre (air), **1:**813; **2:**120–22; **3:**119

B
Ba. *See* Bamberg Codex
Babinski, Hubert, **3:**241
Babbitt, Milton, **4:**191, 195, 705, 732; **5:**94,
    135, 136–73, 177–205, 210, 277, 331,
    367, 374, 448, 453, 473
    Carl Hempel and, **5:**155
    "combinatoriality" and, **5:**424
    complementation, principle of, **5:**141
    "Composer as Specialist, The," **5:**157
    "Darmstadt method," **5:**140
    Grundgestalten, **5:**156

Joshua Rifkin and, **5:**330
"New Romanticism" festival and, **5:**474
"Past and Present Concepts of the
    Nature and Limits of Music"
    (lecture), **5:**155
Philomel, **5:**211
"pitch class," **5:**136
"Pointwise Periodic Homeomorphisms"
    (lecture), **5:**172
Princetonian serialism and, **5:**136
Princeton University, **5:**157
RCA Mark II music synthesizer and,
    5:198, 478, 497
"rhythmic series," **5:**140
Richard Maxfield and, **5:**94
Score, The, **5:**15
serialism and, **5:**474
"Some Aspects of Twelve-Tone
    Composition" (article), **5:**153–54
"The More Than Sounds of Music,"
    5:475
Vision and Prayer, **5:**210–11
"Who Cares If You Listen?," **5:**157–58,
    170, 331, 449, 454
works of
    Composition for Four Instruments,
        5:143–48, 153
    Composition for Twelve Instruments,
        5:148–53, 168
    "Function of Set Structure in the
        Twelve-Tone System, The"
        (essay), **5:**136
    Three Compositions for Piano, **5:**137–39,
        141, 153
    Perle's analysis of, **5:**137
    "Twelve-tone Rhythmic Structure
        and the Electronic Medium,"
        5:167, 172
Babylonian Captivity (papal), **1:**310
Babylonian musical notation, **1:**31–32
Bacchae (Euripides), **5:**343
Bacchanale (Cage), **5:**60–61, 74
Bacchanale (Fort), **5:**59, 73, 74
Bacchanale (Saint-Saëns), **3:**390–91, 397
Bach, Alexander, **3:**445
Bach, Anna Magdalena (J. S. Bach wife),
    2:262
Bach, Carl Philipp Emanuel (J. S. Bach
    son), **2:**240, 259, 400, 410–18, *411*,
    503, 527; **3:**363
    brother Bach (J. C.) compared with,
        2:402, 426–27, 428
    clavichord and, **2:**413
    concerto and, **2:**606, 622
    empfindsamer Stil and, **2:**410, 413, 414, 416,
        418, 426–27, 428–29, 508, 529,
        610, 624
    fantasias of, **3:**65, 312
    father Bach (J. S.) and, **2:**243, 346, 385,
        504
    Frederick II patronage of, **2:**410, *411*, 413,
        462

harmonics and, **3:**428
    as Haydn influence, **2:**518, 529
    inner-directed music of, **2:**410, 418
    Klopstock friendship with, **2:**410
    lied genre and, **3:**119–20
    Mozart as musical heir to, **2:**399, 410,
        601, 606, 622, 624
    "Prussian" sonatas of, **2:**413
    symphonic style of, **2:**508–16
    works of
        Amint, **3:**120–21
        Fantasia in C minor, **2:**414–16, 417,
            624
        Orchestral Symphony, first, **2:**510–16
        Sonata in F major, no. 1 ("Prussian"),
            2:411–13, 518
        Symphony in B minor, **3:**108
Bach, Johann Bernhard (J. S. Bach cousin),
    2:240
Bach, Johann Christian (J. S. Bach son),
    2:240, 418–26, *419*, 488, 503, 504
    Abel partnership with, **2:**419
    accompanied keyboard sonatas of,
        2:428–29
    Bach (C. P. E.) compared with, **2:**402,
        426–32, 428
    career of, **2:**53, 240, 418–19
    contrast and balance used by, **2:**420
    double exposition and, **2:**606
    fame of, **2:**418
    influence of, **2:**424
    Italian instrumental style and, **2:**208–16
    Marcello *Concerto a cinque* and, **2:**192
    modulatory maneuvering of, **2:**488
    as Mozart model, **2:**399, 464, 601–2,
        606, 622
    opera seria and, **2:**158, 240, 507
    status in own day of, **2:**234, 240
    symphonic development and, **2:**507–9
    versatility of, **2:**419
    works of
        Lucio Silla, **2:**507
        Sinfonia in B flat major, op. 18, no 2,
            2:507–11
        Sonata in D major, op. 5, no. 2,
            2:420–26
Bach, Johann Christoph (J. S. Bach uncle),
    2:240
Bach, Johann Ludwig (J. S. Bach cousin),
    2:240
Bach, Johann Michael (J. S. Bach uncle),
    2:240
Bach, Johann Nicolaus (J. S. Bach cousin),
    2:240
Bach, Johann Philipp (J. S. Bach relative),
    2:240
    Handel's musical differences with, **2:**345
Bach, Johann Sebastian, **2:**208–16,
    233–303, 238, 340–90, 433, 503,
    689; **3:**541, 566, 727; **4:**132, 266,
    281, 359, 361, 391, 449, 451, 452,

453–54, 480, 481, 527, 581, 735, 765, 767–68; 5:332, 347
anti-Enlightenment sentiments of, 2:364, 368–69, 390
Bach's (C. P. E.) musical outlook vs., 2:411, 413
Bach's (W. F.) style vs., 2:402, 406, 409
biographies of, 2:388, 3:716
Brahms and, 3:703, 716, 721
Brandenburg Concerto no. 4:3, 481
Brendel's view of, 3:414
BWV listing system for, 2:342
canonization of, 2:233, 235, 381, 388, 401; 3:680
cantata dating and, 2:342, 392
career and lifestyle of, 2:239–41, 261
career trajectory of (map), 2:236
Chopin and, 3:346–47, 366
chorale settings of, 2:50, 241, 255–57, 341; 3:168
death of, 2:385
family of, 2:240, 262. See also Bach sons
Frobinger's suite compared with, 2:266
George Crumb and, 5:423
German nationalism and, 2:235, 259, 385, 388; 3:712
Handel's approach to music contrasted with, 2:321, 345, 362, 364, 368, 374
Handel's career compared with, 2:236, 240, 305–6
improvisational mastery of, 2:241, 243, 384–85, 414
Italian style and, 2:280–85
Leipzig monument to, 3:177
Mendelssohn and, 2:381; 3:172, 178, 179, 180, 347
musically unmeetable performance demands of, 2:370–75
musical role models for, 2:241–42, 247, 248, 255
myth of perfection and, 2:235
"Notebook for Anna Magdalen," *Ancient Voices of Children* (Crumb) and, 5:423
numerological skill of, 2:384–4, 385
oratorios of, 3:163
as religious composer, 2:303, 305, 340, 363–83, 389
revival in nineteenth century of, 1:584; 2:234, 235, 364, 368, 375, 381, 383–85, 388, 389, 390, 399, 464; 3:129, 163
St. Thomas (Leipzig) cantorship of, 1:763; 2:.238, 53, 239, 239
Scarlatti (Domenico) compared with, 2:396
Schumann (Robert) and, 3:294
secular music and, 2:261–77, 305, 374–75
significant birth year of, 2:233, 235

social/political interpretations of musical transgressions of, 2:301–3, 368
sons of. *See* Bach sons
standard repertory and, 2:234
stylistic complexity of, 2:235, 241, 242–43, 248–50, 285–89
as teacher, 3:481
"testaments" of, 2:375–90
transformation of traditional techniques by, 2:254–55, 258–59
tuning practice of, 2:248
unique genius of, 2:254, 258, 287, 289, 364, 378, 383–84
Vivaldi arrangement by, 2:224–25
works of
    "Air on the G String," 4:510
    Anna Magdalena music book, 2:262
    Art of Fugue, The, 2:385–88; 4:465, 703
    Ave Maria (Gounod arrangement), 2:251
    B-A-C-H cipher, 2:385, 386–87, 388
    Brandenburg Concerto no. 5 in D major, 2:290, 291–300, 406; 5:368
    Brandenburg Concertos, 2:289–301, 305, 306, 619
    cantatas of, 2:340–75, 376, 378, 682; 3:168, 729
    Capriccio on the Departure of His Beloved Brother, 3:65
    Christ lag in Todesbanden, 2:50, 343–47
    Chromatic Fantasia and Fugue in D minor, 2:414
    Clavier-Übung (Well-Tempered Clavier), 2:262, 263, 281, 383
    "Coffee cantata," 2:374
    Concerto in C major for 2 Harpsichords, BWV 1061, 2:266–67
    Concerto nach italiänischem Gusto ("Italian Concerto"), 2:281–82, 285, 287
    C-sharp minor fugue, 3:155
    Du Hirte Israel, höre, BWV 104, 2:372–75
    Durch Adams Fall, 2:255, 257–58
    Ein' feste Burg, BWV 80, 2:353–63, 364, 402
    English Suites, 2:262
    Es ist genug, 4:715
    F-major keyboard invention, 4:340, 341
    Fifth Suite, 5:144
    French suites of, 2:262–67
    French Suite no. 5 in G major, 2:263–70, 271–74
    Fuga a 3 soggetii, 2:385
    Fugue in B minor, no. 24, 2:249, 251, 253–54, 279, 291
    Fugue in E major, subject, 2:248–49
    "Goldberg Variations," 2:383

    Jauchzet Gott in allen Landen, BWV 51, 2:374–75
    Kunst der Fuge, Die (*The Art of Fugue*), 2:385–88
    Magnificat, 3:711
    Mass in B Minor, 1:54; 2:110, 289, 373, 77, 383
    Meine Seufzer, meine Tränen, BWV 13, 2:364–65
    Musical Offering, 4:361, 465
    Musikalisches Opfer (*The Musical Offering*), 2:376, 384–85
    Nach dich, Herr, verlanget mich, 3:729
    Nimm von uns, Herr, Du treuer Gott, BWV 101, 2:365–68
    Nun komm, der Heiden Heiland, BWV 61, 2:342–43, 348–53, 354, 356
    Orchestral Suite no. 3, overture, 2:286–87, 288
    Orgelbüchlein, 2:255–56, 258
    Passacaglia in C minor, 2:247; 3:716
    Prelude in C major, no. 1, 2:249–50, 253
    Reincken Sonata no. 1 arrangement, 2:245–47, 249, 274
    St. John Passion, 2:377–81, 389–90
    St. Matthew Passion, 2:377–78, 381, 382, 389–90; 3:163–64
    Siehe zu, dass Deine Gottesfurcht, BWV 179, 2:370–72
    Suite in D major, 3:711, 714
    suites of, 2:260, 261–77, 286–89
    Toccata (organ) in F major, BWV 540, 2:208–16, 247, 295
    trio sonatas of, 2:428
    Wachet auf, ruft uns die Stimme, BWV 104, 2:375
    Well-Tempered Clavier, 4:486, 768
    Wo Gott der Herr nicht bei uns hält, BWV 178, 2:369–9
    Wohltemperirte Clavier, Das (*The Well-Tempered Clavier*), 2:247–51, 253, 291
Bach, Veit (J. S. Bach ancestor), 2:240
Bach, Wilhelm Friedemann (J. S. Bach son), 2:240, 401–9, 401, 424, 503, 504
    Ein' feste Burg arrangement, 2:353, 357, 402
    Harpsichord Sonata in F, 2:402–9, 413, 414
Bach, Wilhelm Friedrich Ernst (J. S. Bach grandson), 2:240
Bach-Abel Concerts (London), 2:419, 555
"Bach chorale" harmonization, 2:346
B-A-C-H cipher, 2:385, 386–87, 388; 4:313, 702, 704, 734–35, 739
Bach-Gesellschaft (Bach Society), 2:342, 392; 3:711; 4:453
Bach keyboard, 4:453
"Bach's Greatest Hits" (Swingle Singers), 5:347

Bach's motets, **4**:311

Bach sons, **2**:240, 399, 401–29, 432

  concerto style and, **2**:606

    Mozart as heir to, **2**:622, 624

    new musical style of, **2**:399, 418, 420,
      429, 433, 437

    Sammartini's music and, **2**:503, 504

  as symphonists, **2**:507–16

  See also Bach, Carl Philipp Emanuel;
    Bach, Johann Christian; Bach,
    Wilhelm Friedemann

Bach-Werke-Verzeichnis (BWV listing),
  2:342

Baciocchi, Princess Elisa, **3**:252

background music, **1**:611

Back to Methuselah (Shaw), **5**:198

Backus, John, **5**:165, 166

Baden-Baden Festival (Germany), **5**:198

Badener Lehrstück vom Einverständnis, Das
  (Brecht), **4**:541

Baez, Joan, **4**:659; **5**:315

Bagatelle ohne Tonart (Liszt), **3**:362, 363, 438,
  447

Bagatelle, op. 6, no. 2 (Bartók), **4**:388,
  389–90, 391, 398, 400

Bagatelle, op. 6, no. 4 (Bartók), **4**:381, 382,
  384

Bagatelle, op. 6, no. 7 (Bartók), **4**:386

Bagatalle, op. 6, no. 8 (Bartók), **4**:387, 388

Bagatelle, op. 6, no. 11 (Bartók), **4**:387, 388

Bagatelle, op. 6, no. 12 (Bartók), **4**:396

Bagatelles (Beethoven), **2**:686; **3**:65; **4**:347

  Liszt and, **3**:362, 363

Baini, Giuseppe, **1**:652

Bajocco e Serpilla (Orlandini). See *Marito
  giocatore e la maglie bacchettona, Il*

Bajocco's aria (Orlandini), **2**:436

Baker, James M., **4**:203

Baker, Josephine, **4**:602, 611

  American civil rights movement and,
    4:602

  Folies Bergere and, **4**:602

  La revue negre and, **4**:602

  Stork Club (New York) and, **4**:611–12

Baker's Biographical Dictionary of Musicians

  Richard Maxfield's entry in, **5**:94

Bakhtin, Mikhail, **2**:17; **3**:513

Bakunin, Mikhail, **3**:488, 489–90, 491

Balaam motet, **1**:399–402, 403

balada, **3**:126

  as troubadour genre, **1**:113–14, 131, 397

baladelle, **1**:290

Balakirev, Miliy Alexeyevich, **3**:468–78;
  4:9, 67, 620

  Borodin and, **3**:788

  Chaikovsky and, **3**:409–10

  folk songs and, **3**:469–77

  nervous breakdown of, **3**:477

  New Russian School and, **3**:395, 397,
    468, 474, 617, 625, 786, 788

  orientalism and, **3**:395–97, 409

  Smetana and, **3**:457–58

works of

  Ne poy, krasavitsa, **3**:394–97, 398, 474

  Overture on Russian Themes (1857–58),
    3:468–71

  Overture on Russian Themes (1864),
    3:470–78

  Rus', **3**:477–78

  Tamara, **3**:397

balalaika, **3**:236, 465

balance. *See* contrast-and-balance technique

Balanchine, George, **4**:144; **5**:122

  Imperial Theaters School and, **4**:144

ballad

  Loewe and, **3**:155, 158

  Schubert and, **3**:148–49

  volkstümlich Romantic poetry and,
    3:126–29, 367

ballade (piano work)

  Chopin and, **3**:367–76, 427

  Gottschalk and, **3**:378

ballade (song), **1**:124–25, 255, 290, 298–99,
  501

  ars subtilior and, **1**:342, 349

  Binchois and, **1**:446–52

  Cypriot manuscript and, **1**:345

  Deschamps and, **1**:336–37

  loftiness of, **1**:349

  Machaut and, **1**:302–5, 327, 338, 371

  Philippus and, **1**:338–42, 341

  unaccompanied performance of, **1**:452

  See also ballata; cantilena

Ballade no. 1 in G minor (Chopin),
  3:369–76

Balladen ohne Worte, **3**:368

"Ballad for Americans" (Robinson), **4**:662

ballad-narratives, Wagner and, **3**:486, 492,
  515, 522

"Ballad of Ozie Powell" (Hughes) **4**:662

Ballady i romanse (Mickiewicz), **3**:367

ballata, **1**:134, 364–74, 694–95; **3**:126

  Boccaccio texts for, **1**:366, 367

  fixed form of, **1**:724

  frottola and, **1**:696

  Landini and, **1**:368–71, 383

Ball at the Court of King Yon of Gascony
  (Liedet), **1**:622

ballet, **4**:131–89

  Russian "Imperial Style" and, **4**:144

ballet a grand spectacle, **4**:144

Ballet Caravan, **4**:662

ballet d'action, **4**:132–38, 139, 144, 151

  Chaikovsky's ballets, **4**:140–50

  French ballet, **4**:131–32, 151

  French opera and, **2**:100; **3**:12, 208

  in Glinka's *Life for the Tsar*, **3**:239

  Petrushka, **4**:159–70

  Rite of Spring, The, **4**:170–90

  Rossini works and, **3**:12, 13

  Russian ballet, **4**:138–40

  Stravinsky, **4**:152–90

  See also court ballet

ballet-féerie, **4**:144

Ballet from "Robert le Diable," The (Degas),
  3:217

"ballet réalliste," **4**:561

Ballet Russe de Monte Carlo, **4**:663

ballets de cour, Catherine de Médicis and,
  4:131

Ballets Russes, **3**:786–87

  Cocteau and, **4**:561

  Diaghilev and, **4**:159, 502, 561

  Massine and, **4**:561

  maximalism and, **4**:159

  Picasso and, **4**:561

  Satie and, **4**:561

balletto, **1**:746; **2**:37, 120, 260

  See also allemande

ballo, **1**:804, 806–7

ballroom dances, **1**:621, 626, 742; **2**:96, 503,
  506

  as aria models, **3**:35

  in Berlioz's *Symphonie fantastique*, **3**:328

  Chopin's works and, **3**:350

  suite adaptation of, **2**:259–61

  See also minuet; waltz

bal tedesco *See* allemande

Balthazar, Scott, **3**:3

Balzac, Honoré de, **3**:349; **4**:340, 344

  Séraphita, **4**:338–39, 344

Bamberg Codex, **1**:214–17, 220–21, 229,
  541

Bambini, Eustachio, **2**:441, 442, 443

Bamboula, danse des nègres, op.2
  (Gottschalk), **3**:377–79, 382

Bananier, Le, chanson nègre, op. 4
  (Gottschalk), **3**:377

Banchetto musicale (Schein), **2**:53

Banchieri, Adriano, **1**:780, 781, 792

  Concerti ecclesiastici a otto voci, **1**:780

banda (brass ensemble), **3**:41, 43

band concerts, **2**:499

Bang on a Can, **5**:399–400

Banister, John, **2**:499

Banjo, The (Gottschalk), **3**:378, 381

Bánk bán (Erkel), **3**:447, 448; **4**:369, 370

"ban on pathos," **4**:467, 475, 490, 573

Banquet of the Oath of the Pheasant, **1**:484

bar. *See* measure

Baraka, Amiri, **5**:335

Barbedette, Hippolyte, **3**:355

Barberini, Antonio Cardinal, **2**:88

Barber of Seville, The. See Barbiere di Siviglia, Il

barbershop quartets, **3**:382, 384

Barbican Centre (London), *El Nino* and,
  5:523

Barbier, Jules, **3**:640

Barbier de Séville, Le (Beaumarchais), **2**:477

Barbiere di Siviglia, Il (Paisiello), **3**:235

  overture, **3**:16–20

  "Yawning and Sneezing" trio, **3**:22–23

Barbiere di Siviglia, Il (Rossini), **3**:9, 10,
  22–24, 34, 240

  costume designs for, **3**:20

  Gilbert and Sullivan parody of, **3**:652

overture, **3**:9, 16–20, 109, 110

Barbieri, Filippo, **1**:719

Barcarolle (Chopin), **3**:350

Barcelona Mass, **1**:315–16

Bardac, Emma, **4**:106

Bardac, Sigismond
    Debussy and, **4**:100
    Faué and, **4**:100

Bardare, Leone Emanuele, **3**:577

Bardi, Giovanni de', Count, **1**:799, 800, 803, 804, 826

bar form, **1**:118, 181

Bargagli, Girolamo, **1**:803

Bargiel, Woldemar, **3**:675–76, 684

Baron, Samuel, **5**:213

Baroque, **1**:699
    alternate labels for, **1**:797–98
    aspects of, **1**:786
    "festival" orchestra, **3**:711
    first musical composition termed, **1**:797
    ground bass and, **2**:35
    Handel and, **2**:204, 437
    Monteverdi and, **1**:735; **2**:18, 35
    movement from *ars perfecta* toward, **1**:630, 689, 727
    original meaning of term, **1**:629
    Rameau and, **2**:110
    sociology of music of, **2**:14–15
    twentieth-century interest "boom" in, **2**:217

Baroque Beatles Book, The (Rifkin), **5**:332

Barrère, Georges, **5**:186

Barrington, Daines, **2**:464

Barron, Bebe, **5**:196

Barron, Louis, **5**:196

Bartered Bride, The (Smetana), **3**:458–59, 458, 463, 464

Bartlet, M. Elizabeth C., **3**:218

Bartók, Béla, **4**:349, 373–421, 373f, 422, 444, 445, 523, 553, 690, 699, 755, 765; **5**:19, 49, 50, 51, 108, 141, 326, 456
    axial symmetry and, **4**:390
    fugue and, **4**:398, 400
    György Ligeti and, **5**:438
    "impressionist" style and, **4**:380–81, 397
    Liszt and, **4**:373
    "night music" and, **4**:394
    Sonata for solo cello (Crumb) and, **5**:423
    works of
        Bagatelle, op. 6, no. 2, **4**:388, 389–90, 391, 394, 398, 400
        Bagatelle, op. 6, no. 4, **4**:380, 381, 382, 384
        Bagatelle, op. 6, no. 5, **4**:382, 383, 384
        Bagatelle, op. 6, no. 7, **4**:386, 387
        Bagatelle, op. 6, no. 8, **4**:387, 388
        Bagatelle, op. 6, no. 11, **4**:387, 388
        Bagatelle, op. 6, no. 12, **4**:394396
        Cantata profana, **4**:394
        Concerto for Orchestra, **4**:402; **5**:19, 229

Four Dirges, op. 9a, **4**:384, 385, 386, 387, 396

Fourteen Bagatelles, **4**:380, 388

Kossuth, **4**:373–74

Miraculous Mandarin, The, **4**:749

Music for Strings, Percussion and Celesta, **4**:394, 398, 399, 401, 402, 421

Piano Concerto no. 2, **4**:402

Quartet no. 4, **4**:402, 403, 404–5, 406–8, 409, 410, 411, 412–13, 416–17, 418, 419, 420, 421, 445; **5**:19

Quartet no. 5, **4**:402

Bartók chord, **4**:387

Bartók-Kodály, *Magyar népdalok*, **4**:375, 377

Bartoli, Cosimo, **1**:384, 641

Bartos, Frantisek, **4**:414

baryton (*viola paradon*), **2**:527, 527, 601

barzelletta (song genre), **1**:695–96

Barzun, Jacques, **3**:332, 480, 488, 559

Basel Chamber Orchestra, **4**:394

Basevi, Abramo, **3**:568

Basil, Bishop of Caesarea, **1**:9, 10; **3**:163

Basiron, Philippe
    Missa L'Homme Armé, **1**:493, 494
    Salve Regina, **1**:501–4

bass (voice), **1**:467, 468–71
    Caput Mass and, **1**:474, 475, 477, 482
    as intermezzo character, **2**:434, 438
    Missa L'Homme Armé and, **1**:492–93

bassadanza (basse danse), **1**:621, 622–23, 626

Bassarids, The (Henze), **5**:343, 344

basse fondamentale, **2**:189

basso buffo. See *buffo*

basso continuo. See Alberti bass; continuo

basso generale, **1**:783

bassoon, Vivaldi concertos for, **2**:217–24

basso seguente, **1**:781, 782, 783, 795

bassus voice. See bass

bass viol, **1**:741

Bastien und Bastienne (Mozart), **2**:656–58

bathtub aria (Hindemith, *Neues vom Tage*), **4**:531, 532–33, 550

baton conducting, **3**:222

Batstone, Philip
    Multiple Order Functions in Twelve-Tone Music (essay), **5**:160

battaglia, **1**:834

battle pieces, **1**:711–12, 787–89

"Battle Symphony" (*Wellington's Victory*) (Beethoven), **2**:672–73; **5**:177

Baucarde, Carlo, **3**:579

Baudelaire, Charles, **3**:354–55, 561; **4**:59, 84, 86, 216, 711
    "Correspondances," **4**:84
    "decadence" and, **4**:84
    De profundis clamavi, **4**:711
    Les fleurs du mal, **4**:84
    Symbolist movement and, **4**:86

Bauernfeld, Eduard, **3**:252–53

Baumgarten, Alexander Gottlieb, **2**:641

Bavaria. See Munich

bawdy songs, **1**:138, 710–11

Bayadère, La (Minkus), **4**:139

Bayreuth festival, **4**:60, 61, 142, 751
    Festspielhaus, **3**:498, 499
    invisible orchestra, **3**:564
    stage magic at, **3**:500
    Wagner and, **3**:498, 502, 512, 719

Beach, Amy Marcy, 3:769–73, 769, 783; **4**:124–25
    "Dark Is the Night," **3**:770
    Gaelic Symphony, **3**:770–73

Beach, Henry Harris Aubrey, **3**:770

Beach Boys, *Good Vibrations*, **5**:183

Beardsley, Aubrey, **4**:38f, 467

"Beardsley cult," **4**:467

beat, Ars Nova notation of, **1**:251–52

Beata viscera (conductus/motet), **1**:406–7, 433

Beata viscera (Perotin), **1**:173–74

beat generation, 62, 309

Beatles, **1**:617; **5**:316–33
    "concept albums," **5**:319
    concert at Shea Stadium, **5**:318
    George Martin and, **5**:318
    Liverpool, **5**:324
    plunderphonics compact disc and, **5**:504
    Requiem for a Young Poet (Zimmermann) and, **5**:420
    tribute to by Ned Rorem, **5**:431
    works of
        "Day in the Life, A," **5**:321–25
        "Eleanor Rigby," **5**:321
        Revolver, **5**:319
        Sgt. Pepper's Lonely Hearts Club Band, **5**:319
        "Taxman," **5**:319
        "Tomorrow Never Knows," **5**:319–20

"Beatles Revive Hopes of Progress in Pop Music, The" (article, Mann), **5**:324

Béatrice et Bénédict (Berlioz), **3**:320

Beatrice of Burgundy, **1**:134

Beatriz di Dia, **1**:113; **2**:79

Beaujoyeulx (né Belgioioso), Balthasar de, **4**:131

Beaumarchais, Pierre-Augustin Caron de, **2**:477–78; **3**:16
    "revolutionary" myth about, **2**:478
    Figaro trilogy, **5**:515

beauty
    art and, **3**:62, 440, 441, 528
    Brendel's view of, **3**:414, 440
    esthetics and, **1**:541; **3**:561
    Hanslick's theory of, **3**:531
    as music's purpose, **2**:363–64, 486, 494, 590–91, 599–600, 644, 649
    of pagan art, **2**:649
    realism and, **3**:622
    sublime vs., **2**:643–46, 649
    truth and, **2**:363; **3**:62, 440
    Wagner on, **3**:490

"beauty is truth" (Keats), **3**:62, 440

Bechet, Sidney, **4**:602, 612, 613

Becker, Carl Ferdinand, **3**:174

Becker, Cornelius, 2:59
Becker, Heinz, 3:216
Becker, John J., 4:295
Beckerman, Michael, 3:451, 452, 454, 760,
    764, 765–66; 4:425
"Becker Psalter," 2:59
Becket, Thomas. See Thomas à Becket
Beckett, Samuel, 5:89, 296
    Unnamable, The, 5:347
BecVar, Bruce, 5:317
Bedford, Duke of. See John of Lancaster
Beer, Amalia, 3:215
Beer, Juda Herz, 3:215
Beethoven, Johann van (father), 2:652
Beethoven, Karl van (nephew), 2:672, 682
Beethoven, Kaspar van (brother), 2:672
Beethoven, Louis (Ludwig) van
    (grandfather), 2:652
Beethoven, Ludwig van, 2:647, 648–89,
    691–735; 3:95, 179, 291, 543, 677,
    710; 5:71, 72, 73, 74, 76, 261, 269,
    305, 306, 347; 4:8, 12, 13, 16, 22, 104,
    124, 262, 264, 272, 306, 309, 420,
    506, 765, 777
  alienation and, 2:655, 671, 672, 737
  archaism and, 2:686–88
  atonality and, 4:312
  authority and influence of, 2:648, 650,
    689, 691, 693, 696, 706, 735–36,
    738–39
  Bagatelles, 4:347
  baton conducting by, 3:222
  Berlioz and, 3:324, 326, 327, 333–35, 421,
    440
  biographical interest in, 2:654, 672
  Bonn monument to, 3:309–10
  Brahms and, 3:686, 688, 690, 691,
    694–95, 697, 715, 720–26
  Brendel's view of, 3:414
  Bruckner and, 3:747–51
  as businessman, 2:653, 672–73
  cadenza scoring by, 2:650
  canonization of, 2:689, 691, 738
  career of, 2:652–55, 671–72
  chamber music and, 3:731, 754
  characteristic rhythm of, 2:696–97, 709,
    711, 713
  Chopin and, 3:346, 368
  Classical period and, 2:739
  C-minor moods and, 2:691–735
  concerto and, 3:273–76
  concert tours by, 2:653
  conflicting images of, 2:671
  creative dry spell of, 2:672–73
  critical resistance to, 2:677, 691, 692–93,
    738, 739
  in Danhauser's painting, 3:77
  David and, 3:387
  deafness of, 2:653–55, 671, 672, 676, 677,
    737; 3:690, 731, 800
  death of, 2:682, 687, 689
  Deity symbol of, 2:732

  distinctive tone of, 2:694
  ear trumpets made for, 2:.654
  Elysium and, 4:19
  emotional drains on, 2:671–72
  financial support of, 2:671; 3:443
  Franck and, 3:778
  fugal writing by, 2:686, 721–27, 729
  funeral of, 2:687, 689, 689
  Goethe and, 2:671–72, 689, 720; 3:132
  harmonics of, 3:428, 429, 436, 529
  Haydn and, 2:652, 653, 660, 692,
    694–95, 696, 698, 701, 702; 3:14
  Heiligenstadt Testament of, 2:654, 672;
    3:690, 800
  heroic style of, 2:656, 668–69, 670–71,
    689, 701–2
  higher realm and, 2:731
  "Immortal Beloved" letter by, 2:672
  improvisations and, 2:652, 653, 655
  incidental music and, 3:1–2
  infinite and, 2:648–49, 670, 731–32, 734
  instrumental music and, 3:7
  interpretation of, 2:680, 694
  intuition and, 2:720
  inward-turning by, 2:683–87
  Josquin parallels with, 1:547–49, 552,
    579
  Kampf und Sieg rhetoric and, 3:1, 198,
    694–95
  last completed work of, 2:682
  last public appearance of, 2:655
  late period of, 2:682–89, 693, 721, 726,
    732–33
  legacy of, 2:652, 686, 689, 735–39
  lieder and, 3:131–35
  Liszt and, 3:262, 268, 285, 287, 420, 421,
    424, 437
  Mass composition by, 1:54; 2:721
  mass public audience for, 2:655, 671, 691,
    692
  metronome tempo settings by, 2:673
  Mozart's works and, 2:651, 653, 656–58,
    660, 692, 696, 698, 702
  museum culture and, 2:639
  mythology of. See Beethoven myth
  New German School and, 3:439, 440,
    464, 719–20
  "Ode to Joy" and, 2:677–78, 680, 681,
    731
  opera and, 3:1–7, 567
  organic form of works of, 2:301, 701, 706,
    714
  orientalism and, 3:1, 386
  overture and, 3:197
  performance skill of, 2:652
  plunderphonics compact disc and, 5:504
  politics and, 2:655–56, 659, 670, 673,
    686, 721–24
  popular-appeal works of, 2:672
  posthumous legendary status of, 1:547,
    548, 579; 2:12, 651, 693
  post–World War I critics of, 2:693

  preface themes, 3:109, 112
  as public figure, 2:687
  Rochberg and, 5:436
  Rochberg's Music for the Magic Theater,
    and, 5:415
  regained creativity of, 2:674–75
  religiosity and, 2:686, 721, 732
  as Romantic icon, 1:548; 2:648–51,
    654–55, 656, 659, 675, 686, 692,
    702, 714, 717, 731, 735; 3:71, 77, 273,
    288
  Rossini contrasted with, 3:7–8, 10,
    13–14, 25, 34
  Schubert and, 3:80, 84, 93, 98, 103,
    108–10
  Schumann and, 3:294, 309–15, 324, 346
  self-assertion by, 2:653
  semiotics of works of, 2:718, 720
  Slava folk melody and, 3:625
  social attitudes of, 2:671
  sonata and, 3:109, 368
  song cycle of, 3:131–36
  as "sound poet," 5:514
  Stamitz and, 2:718, 719
  standard repertoire and, 3:3, 131, 679,
    680
  string quartet and, 2:653, 682–88
  struggle-to-victory paradigm of,
    2:654–55, 658–59, 670, 694
  study of, 2:683
  stylistic transformation by, 2:655–56
  the sublime and, 2:648–89, 656, 692,
    724, 732, 734
  symphony and, 2:653, 692, 705–20
  Symphony no. 9, Requiem for a Young
    Poet (Zimmermann) and, 5:420
  syncretism of, 3:14–15
  theatrical pathos and, 2:696, 697
  tormented soul image of, 2:691, 696
  transcendence and, 2:655, 656, 706
  victory music and, 3:1, 2
  vocal music and, 2:686
  Wagner and, 3:7, 178, 480, 483, 485, 547,
    558, 675, 719, 729
  Weber and, 3:197–99
  works of
    An die ferne Geliebte, op. 98, 2:673;
      3:131–36, 154, 312–15, 324
    "Archduke" Trio, op. 97, 2:655
    Bagatelles, 2:686; 3:65
    B-flat major Quartet, op. 130, 3:69,
      778
    Cello Sonata in D major, op. 102, no.
      2, 2:673, 724, 725
    Choral Fantasy, 2:655
    Consecration of the House Overture, op.
      124, 2:726
    Coriolan overture, 2:702–5, 721, 729;
      3:1, 4, 197, 419
    Diabelli Variations, op. 120, 2:674, 686,
      726; 5:83
    Die Geschöpfe des Prometheus, 4:133

Egmont, 3:11, 4, 197, 198, 222, 419; 4:650

Eroica Symphony, 4:13, 14

Fidelio (*Leonore*), 2:670, 676; 3:11–7, 2, 203, 246, 334–35

"Für Elise," 2:686

Glorreiche Augenblick, Der, 2:673, 686, 722–24; 3:708

Grosse Fuge, op. 133, 2:682, 728

"Hammerklavier" Sonata, op. 106, 5:177

Heiliger Dankgesang eines Genesenen an die Gottheit, in der lydischen Tonart, 2:721, 1108–1688; 5:430

König Stephan, 3:11–2

Last Symphony, 4:12

Missa solemnis (Mass in D), 2:376, 671, 674–75, 682, 686, 721; 3:14; 4:371

"Ode to Joy," 5:3

Piano Concerto no. 2 in B-flat major, op. 19, 2:652

Piano Concerto no. 3 in C minor, op. 37, 3:273–74

Piano Concerto no. 4 in G major, op. 58, 2:655; 3:275, 276

Piano Concerto no. 5 in E-flat major, op. 73 ("Emperor"), 2:671; 3:275

Piano Sonata no. 8 in C minor, op. 13 ("Pathétique"), 2:727, 728; 3:429

Piano Sonata no. 14 in C-sharp minor, op. 27 ("Moonlight"), 3:273

Piano Sonata no. 21, op. 53 ("Waldstein"), 2:670

Piano Sonata no. 23 in F minor, op. 57 ("Appassionata"), 2:670; 3:11, 376

Piano Sonata no. 28 in A major, op. 101, 2:686, 724, 725

Piano Sonata no. 29 in B flat, op. 106 ("Hammerklavier"), 2:673, 674, 686, 724, 726, 727

Piano Sonata no. 31 in A flat, op. 110, 2:686, 726

Piano Sonata no. 32 in C minor, op. 111, 2:674, 721, 727–35; 3:268

Piano Trio in B-flat major, op. 97, 2:655

Piano Trio in C minor, op. 1, no. 3, 2:653, 694, 695–701, 706–7, 721, 730; 3:14, 108–9, 112

Ruinen von Athen, Die, 3:11, 386

Schwer gefasste Entschluss, Der, op. 135, 3:424, 776

Septet for Winds and Strings, op. 20, 2:653; 3:103

String Quartets nos. 1–6, op. 18, 2:653, 671

String Quartets nos. 7–9, op. 59 ("Razumowsky"), 2:670, 671, 683, 721; 3:233

String Quartet no. 11 in F minor, op. 95 ("Serioso"), 3:11

String Quartet no. 12 in E-flat major, op. 127, 2:682, 683; 3:778

String Quartet no. 13 in B flat, op. 130, 2:682, 683, 684–85, 686, 726, 731

String Quartet no. 14 in C-sharp minor, op. 131, 2:682, 726, 727

String Quartet no. 15 in A minor, op. 132, 2:686–88, 721, 731; 5:290

String Quartet no. 16 in F major, op. 135, 2:682, 683

Symphony no. 1 in C major, 2:653

Symphony no. 2 in D major, op. 36, 3:690, 691, 692, 800

Symphony no. 3 (*Eroica*), op. 55, 2:110, 655–70, 671, 680, 685, 702, 718; 3:22, 95, 98, 275, 327, 366, 531, 704, 726, 742, 756, 759, 772, 788; 4:13, 648

Symphony no. 4 in B-flat major, op. 60, 3:16, 80; 4:619

Symphony no. 5 in C minor, op. 67, 2:507, 655, 671, 705–20, 721; 3:11, 4, 18, 80, 108, 109, 279, 282, 285, 331, 694–95, 699, 720, 724, 726, 778, 793; 4:12, 13, 202, 209, 267, 269

Symphony no. 6 in F major, op. 68 ("Pastoral"), 2:655, 671, 680, 682; 3:204, 273, 322–23, 334, 368, 375

Symphony no. 7 in A major, op. 92, 2:672; 3:16, 87, 331

Symphony no. 8 in F major, op. 93, 2:672

Symphony no. 9 in D minor, op. 125, 2:675–82, 683, 718, 721, 729, 731, 732; 3:14, 108, 109, 110, 184, 387, 415, 482, 483, 485, 675, 688, 690, 715, 719–23, 726, 729, 747, 749–51, 778; 5:3, 71, 347; 4:12, 13, 14, 18, 19, 21, 208, 266, 283, 312, 344, 345, 347, 703

Wellington's Victory ("Battle Symphony"), 2:672–73; 5:177

Beethoven: His Spiritual Development (Sullivan), 2:671

Beethovenian tradition, Mahler and, 4:13

Beethoven myth, 2:12, 651, 653, 672, 693; 5:222

contrary facts and, 2:672–73

Grillparzer's eulogy and, 2:689

Hoffmann's propagation of, 2:648–49, 670, 673, 692, 714, 717, 731, 739

Josquin myth and, 1:579

undesirable side effects of, 2:670–71

Beethoven, ses critiques et ses glossateurs (Ulybyshev), 3:439

"Beethoven's Instrumental Music" (Hoffmann), 2:648

Beethoven: The Man Who Freed Music (Schauffler), 1:579; 2:671

Beggar's Opera, The (Gay-Pepusch), 2:312, 312, 313; 4:536

"Beglückte Heerde, Jesu Schafe" (J. S. Bach), 2:372–75

Behrend, Jeanne, 3:382

Behrman, David, 5:366, 369

Columbia Records, 5:369

New Sounds in Electronic Music, 5:369

Bekker, Paul, 3:202

Belasco, David, 3:665, 667, 668

bel canto, 3:36–46

Bellini and, 3:36–46, 570

Chopin and, 3:346

Donizetti and, 3:37, 48, 578

Field and, 3:71

grand opéra and, 3:219

tenors and, 3:578

"Bel dí, Un" (Puccini), 3:668–72

Bele Ydoine (Audefroi), 1:120

Belgium, 1:536; 3:212–14

English composers in, 2:45, 47

Flemish composers, 1:277, 316, 453, 454, 455–59

Gombert and, 1:589–90

musician emigrés from, 1:277, 518–22, 544, 589, 605–6, 676–77, 713, 723, 733

Bell, Clive, 2:693

Bell, Daniel, 5:155, 312

Bell, The (journal), 3:476–77

"Bella figlia dell'amore" (Verdi), 3:587–89

Belle au bois dormant, La (Chaikovsky), 4:144

Belle Hélène, La (Offenbach), 3:644, 645, 648

"Belle nuit, ô nuit d'amour" (Offenbach), 3:657

Bellini, Giovanni, 5:343

Bellini, Vincenzo, 3:37, 93, 565, 567

background and career of, 3:37

bel canto and, 3:36–46, 578

Chopin and, 3:349, 373

coloratura and, 3:222

ensemble finales of, 3:210

Glinka and, 3:240

librettist of, 3:37

Wagner and, 3:481

works of

Capuleti e i Montecchi, I, 3:37, 45

Norma, 3:37–44, 40, 41, 49, 71

Puritani, I, 3:37

Sonnambula, La, 3:37

Bellman, Jonathan, *style hongrois* and, 4:373, 374

Belloni, Gaetano, 3:272

"Bells Are Ringing in Yevlashev Village, The" (Rimsky-Korsakov), 4:183

Bell Telephone Laboratories, development of transducer and, 5:495

Belmonte's aria (Mozart), 2:472–75

Belshazzar (Handel), 2:315

Belshazzar, King, 1:94

Belyayev, Mitrofan, 4:620

Bembo, Pietro, 1:723

Benda, Franticek, 2:411

Benda, George, 4:458

Ariadne auf Naxos, 4:458

Benedicamus Domino (response), 1:160–61

Benedict VIII, Pope, **1:**34

Benedict XIII, Antipope, **1:**378

Benedicta es, coelorum regina (Josquin), **1:**580–83, 601–2, 633

Benedicta es, coelorum regina (Willaert), **1:**601–4

Benedictines, **1:**22, 23, 50, 71, 76, 90, 93, 100, 111, 138, 387, 402, 408
   Gregorian chant revision and, **1:**631, 632

Benedict of Nursia, Saint, **1:**10–11

Benedictus (Isaac), **1:**543–44, 545

Benedictus (Taverner), **1:**612–13, 614

Benedictus (Victoria), **1:**789–90

Benediktbeuren abbey, **1:**138

benefices, **1:**315, 316

Beneventan chant, **1:**64

Benjamin, Walter, **5:**101, 169

Bennett, Tony, **1:**817

Benois, Alexander, **4:**146, 148, 149–51, 160, 170, 203
   "Colloquy on Ballet" (article), **4:**150

Bent, Margaret, **1:**417

Benti, Maria Anna (La Romanina), **2:**155

Benvenuto Cellini (Berlioz), **3:**339, 418

Berain, Jean, **2:**95, 100

Berberian, Cathy, **5:**193, 196

Berceuse (Chopin), **3:**350

Berceuse d'un bienheureux (Obouhov), **4:**228

Berenice, regina d'Egitto, ovvero le gare da amore e di politica (D. Scarlatti), **2:**390

Berenstadt, Gaetano, **2:**.307

Berezovsky, Maxim, **3:**235

Berg, Alban, **4:**193, 309, 315, 341, 344, 380, 505–26, 543, 628, 690, 710, 710, 719, 732, 738, 741
   "aggregate harmony" and, **4:**305
   "Air," **4:**509–10
   BACH cipher and, **4:**313–14
   Lyric Suite, Variazioni per orchestra (Crumb) and, **5:**423
   twelve-tone row technique, **4:**710, 712; **5:**415
   "Why Is Schoenberg's Music So Difficult to Understand?", **4:**342, 359
   "Wir arme Leut" leitmotif, **4:**511
   works of
     Altenberg Lieder, **4:**194, 195, 196, 197, 225
     Der Wein, **4:**749
     Fünf Orchesterlieder nach Ansichtskartentexten von Peter Altenberg, op. 4, **4:**193
     Kammerkonzert ("Chamber Concerto"), **4:**313–14, 342, 523, 525, 710
     Lulu, **4:**714
     Lyric Suite, **4:**523, 710, 711, 712–13, 714, 719, 721
     Schliesse mir die Augenbeide, **4:**710, 711
     Violin Concerto, **4:**714–15, 716, 718–19, 720–21

Wozzeck, **4:**506–26, 507f, 508. 539, 545–46, 559, 710, 711, 714, 719, 749, 789; **5:**223, 241

Wozzeck (Air) ("Wir arme Leut"), **4:**509–10

Wozzeck, Entr'acte between scenes 4 and 5, **4:**520, 521

Wozzeck, "Quasi Gavotte," **4:**511, 512

Berg, Wesley, **1:**27

Berger, Anna Maria Busse, **1:**185

Berger, Arthur, **5:**13, 165
   Perspectives of New Music, **5:**165

Berger, Karol, **3:**375–76, 529–30

Berger, Ludwig, **3:**184

bergerette (song genre), **1:**526–34, 695

Bergsma, William, **5:**368
   Steve Reich and, **5:**368

Bergson, Henri, **5:**277

Berio, Luciano, **5:**37, 65, 193, 195, 211, 212, 319, 346, 347, 348, 368, 396
   "Commenti al Rock" (article), **5:**328–30
   Sinfonia, collage technique and, **5:**417–418
   twelve-tone technique and, **5:**415
   works of
     "O King," **5:**348, 350
     "Omaggio a Joyce," **5:**193, V197
     Ritratta di citta, **5:**193
     Sinfonia, **5:**348, 349
     Thema, **5:**193

Berkeley Barb, **5:**326–27

Berkshire Music Center, **5:**157

Berlin, **2:**289, 410, 419; **4:**563, 624
   lied origins and, **3:**119–20
   music conservatory, **3:**769
   national theater, **3:**194

Berlin, Irving
   Tin Pan Alley and, **4:**563
   works of
     That Mysterious Rag, **4:**563, 566

Berlin Academy of Arts, **3:**174

Berlin Cathedral Choir, **3:**173

Berlin Conservatory, **4:**539, 628

Berlin Court Opera, **3:**658

Berlin New Music Festival, **4:**543

Berlin Opera Orchestra, **3:**173

Berlin Philharmonic Orchestra, **4:**781; **5:**343

"Berlin School," **4:**21

Berlin Singakademie, **3:**129, 174, 184, 215–16

Berlin song school, **3:**126

Berlin Wall, fall of, **5:**437, 508

Berlioz, Hector, **3:**318–41, 319; **4:**11, 18, 79, 101, 431
   Beethoven and, **3:**324, 326, 327, 333–35, 421, 440
   Chopin and, **3:**349
   civic ceremonial music and, **3:**319–20
   conducting by, **3:**323
   courtship and marriage of, **3:**320–21
   in Danhauser's painting, **3:**76–77

on David's *Le Désert*, **3:**388

Glinka and, **3:**465

Gluck and, **3:**324, 329

on imitation, **3:**332–35

imitation of nature by, **3:**324

instrumental music and, **3:**775

instrumental skills of, **3:**323

Liszt and, **3:**336, 421, 424

medical studies by, **3:**324

mélodie and, **4:**97

on Meyerbeer's *Les Huguenots*, **3:**225

music criticism by, **2:**737; **3:**291, 332–35, 583

"Neuf mélodies," **4:**97

New German School and, **3:**421–22, 685

orchestration technique of, **3:**323–24, 339

Paganini and, **3:**253

Rossini and, **3:**77

Schumann (Robert) and, **3:**683

Shakespearean subjects of, **3:**320

Wagner and, **3:**482, 483, 485

Weber's *Der Freischütz* and, **3:**208, 335

works of
   Béatrice et Bénédict, **3:**320
   Benvenuto Cellini, **3:**339, 418
   Damnation of Faust, The, **3:**654
   Épisode de la vie d'un artiste (Symphonie fantastique en cinq parties), **3:**320
   Francs-juges, Les, **3:**319, 331
   Grande messe des morts, op. 5, **3:**319
   Grande symphonie funèbre et triomphale, **3:**319–20, 331
   Harold in Italy, **3:**253, 421
   Herminie, **3:**326
   Lélio, or Returning to Life, **3:**387
   Roi Lear, Le, **3:**320
   Roméo et Juliette, **3:**320, 329, 482, 483, 788
   Sardanapale, **3:**326
   Symphonie fantastique, **3:**320–32, 335–40, 368, 387, 419, 420–21, 425, 482, 502, 793; **4:**79, 191, 431

Bernard, Jonathan W., **5:**454, 455

Bernard de Got. See Clement V, Pope

Bernardina, La (Josquin), **1:**544, 546

Bernard of Cluny, **4:**246, 247

Bernart de Ventadorn, **1:**108, 109, 109, 110, 117, 353

Bernhard, Christoph, **2:**58, 73
   luxuriant style and, **2:**59, 60

Bernhardt, Sarah, **3:**667; **4:**170

Bernini, Gian Lorenzo, **1:**772, 772; **4:**594

Berno, Abbot of Cluny, **1:**50

Bernsdorf, Eduard, **3:**228

Bernstein, Leonard, **4:**240, 262; **5:**6, 75, 96, 113, 198, 348, 431, 431
   Aaron Copland and, **5:**116
   Chichester Psalms, **5:**431
   New York Philharmonic and, **5:**431
   Serge Koussevitsky and, **5:**3

Bernstorff, Johann-Heinrich von, 3:228
Berry, Chuck, 5:396
Berry, Duchy of, 1:342–45
Berry, Wallace, 5:170–72
Bertin, Émile, 3:642
Bertrand, René, "dynaphone" and, 5:184
Betterton, Thomas, 2:126, 127, 128
B-flat mode, 1:273, 274, 275, 394, 554
    cadence and, 1:599–600
Bianco e dolce cigno, Il (Arcadelt), 1:724–25, 726
Bianconi, Lorenzo, 1:739; 2:37
Biba, Otto, 3:81, 84
Bible of Pedro de Pamplona, Seville, 1:48
biblical cento, 1:594, 595
biblical exigesis, 1:285
    Protestant Reformation and, 1:553, 753
biblical operas. *See* oratorio
biblical orientalism, 3:391–92
biblical prophecy, 1:719
Biblical Sonata (Kuhnau), 3:65
bibliophiles, 1:693
Biblioteca Colombina (Seville), 1:693
Bibliothèque Nationale (Paris), 1:109; 5:43
Biches, Les (Poulenc), 4:568
bicinia, 1:550, 604
"Bicycle Built for Two, A,"
    voice-synthesized rendition of, 5:496
Biedermeier genres, 3:84
big band battle-pieces, 1:786–87
"big Five-Ones," Mahler's Second and, 4:319
"big symphony from the West" (Harris), 4:638, 639, 649. *See also Symphony 1933*
"Big Troika" (Denisov, Schnittke, and Gubaidulina), 5:464
Billroth, Theodor, 3:730–31, 732, 743
Billy Budd, Melville and, 5:225
Billy Budd (op. 50) (Britten), 5:225, 227
Billy the Kid (Copland), 4:662, 663, 671, 672; 5:268
binaria, 1:176, 177, 187, 215
binarisms, 1:105–6
binary form
    ayre and, 2:120–21
    concerto and, 2:222, 606–7
    dance movement and, 2:146–48, 261
    keyboard sonata and, 2:402
    sonata and, 2:420–21, 426, 433
    symphonic. *See* sonata form
    "there-and-back" and, 2:267, 606, 660
Binchois, Gilles, 1:423, 425, 435, 439–40, 439, 455, 536
    career of, 1:439
    chanson and, 1:446–52, 706
    Ockeghem and, 1:454
    works of
        Deuil angoisseux, 1:447–52
        Veni Creator Spiritus, 1:439–41
Bingen, Hildegarde von, *El Nino* and, 5:524

Bins, Gilles de. *See* Binchois
Birchfield, David, "interactive sound installations" and, 5:514
"Birch Tree, The," 3:236
Bird, Bonnie, 5:56
    John Cage and, 5:56, 73
    Syvilla Fort and, 5:58
birdsong, 1:349, 711
    violin imitations of, 2:227–28
Birmingham Festival, 3:173, 657
Birtwistle, Harrison, 5:426, 429
bishop, 1:169, 170
Bismarck, Otto von, 3:710, 711
Bispham, David, 3:497
bithematic ternary model, 2:584
Bitter Music (Partch), 5:481, 483, 487
Bizet, Georges, 3:640, 641, 798
    orientalism and, 3:390, 641
    symphony and, 3:657, 676
    works of
        Carmen, 3:398–99, 400, 405–6, 641–43, 642, 648; 4:71
        Djamileh, 3:390
        Pêcheurs de perles, Les, 3:390
        Symphony in C Major, 3:657
Blacher, Boris, 3:256
Black Angels (Crumb), 5:424
Blackburn, Bonnie J., 1:536
Blacking, John, 5:380–83
    fieldwork among the Venda, 5:381, 383
    How Musical Is Man?, 5:380–83
    Queen's University, Belfast, 5:380
Blackmur, R. P., 5:39
    "Recent Advances in Musical Thought and Sound," 5:39
black nationalism, 4:612
black notes, 1:265
Black Panthers, 5:348–49
Black Romanticism
    Liszt and, 3:264
    Paganini and, 3:255
    Weber and, 3:194
Blake, William, 2:64; 3:277, 604
Blancheroche, M., 3:65
Blancrochet (lutenist), 2:265
Bland, John, 2:555
Blaník (Smetana), 3:452, 459–62
Blavatsky, Helena Petrovna, 4:203
    The Secret Doctrine and, 4:216
Blessed Virgin. *See* Marian antiphons; Virgin Mary
blind musicians
    famous organists, 1:374
    improvisational virtuosity of, 1:536
Blitheman, John, 2:49
Blitzstein, Marc, 4:127, 537, 649, 656, 661
    Cradle Will Rock, The, 4:649–51, 650f
Bloch, Ernest, 4:108, 263, 626
    The Sacred Service, 4:749
Bloch, Gregory, 5:392
Block, Adrienne Fried, 3:769
Blondel de Nesle, 1:117

Blood of a Poet, The (Cocteau), 5:290
Blood, Sweat, and Tears, 5:328
Bloom, Claire, 5:172
Bloom, Harold, 3:695; 4:124; 5:82, 434–35
Bloomfield, Mike, 5:334
    Bob Dylan and, 5:334
Blow, John, 2:132
"Blowin' in the Wind" (Dylan), 5:315
Blown-away Leaf, A (Janáček), 4:429
Blue Danube, The (J. Strauss), 3:648, 649
"blue notes," 4:607, 632, 633
"Blues," as musical term, 4:505
"Blues" (Ravel), 4:606
Blume, Friedrich, 2:346
Blumen, 1:140
Blut und Boden (blood and soil), 3:178
"B-minor Mass" (J. S. Bach). *See* Mass in B minor
B-minor mode
    Bach (J. C.) and, 2:488
    Vivaldi and, 2:222–23
Bobo phenomenon, 5:526–27
Boccaccio, Giovanni, 1:365–66, 367
    as proto-Renaissance figure, 1:382–83
Boccherini, Luigi, 2:600
body portraiture
    in Berlioz's *Symphonie fantastique*, 3:324
    in Chaikovsky's *Eugene Onegin*, 3:638
    in Mozart's *Die Entführung aus dem Serail*, 3:324, 638
Boethius, Anicius Manlius Severinus, 1:17, 69, 70–72, 71, 74, 77, 94, 185, 187, 196, 281, 291, 495, 552, 553, 585, 799
Bohème, La (Puccini), 3:666–67; 4:751
Bohemia. *See* Czech lands
"Bohemian Rhapsody" (Queen), 5:328, 329
Böhm, Georg, 2:241
Boito, Arrigo, 3:596, 599, 600, 606, 611, 639, 669
Bokhara, Khan of, 3:392
Bolcom, William
    neotonality and, 5:454
    View from the Bridge, A (opera), 5:515
Boldoni, Giovanni, 3:564
Boléro (Ravel), 5:424
Bologna, 1:352, 435, 780, 781
    cantata and, 2:75
    solo concerto and, 2:193
    See also University of Bologna
Bolshevik (Communist) party, 4:743
Bolshoi Theater (Moscow), 4:140, 141
Bolt, P., 2:492
Bonaparte. *See* Napoleon I
Bone amourete (Adam), 1:123, 220
Boni, Margaret B., *The Fireside Book of Folk Songs*, 4:657, 659
Boniface, Saint, 1:7
Boniface IX, Pope, 1:348
Bonitatem fecisti servo tuo, Domine (Carpentras attrib.), 1:554–55, 557
Bonn, 2:507, 652, 718, 736
Bonne Chanson, La (Fauré), 4:100–101

Bonne d'enfant (Poulenc), **4:**575
Bonner, Andrew, **3:**425
Bonney, William H., **4:**662
Bononcini, Giovanni, **2:**312
Bontempelli, Massimo, Italian fascism and, **4:**744
Booke of Common Praier Noted, The (Merbecke), **1:**673
Book of Common Prayer (Anglican), **1:**672–73, 675
Book of Hymns (Notker), **1:**41, 42
Book of Procurors, **1:**170
"Book of St. James". *See* Codex Calixtinus
Book of the Courtier (Castiglione), **1:**626, 698; **2:**15–16
Boretz, Benjamin, **5:**164, 165, 303
   Elliott Carter and, **5:**303–4
   Meta-Variations: Studies in the Foundations of Musical Thought, **5:**160
Borgia, Lucrezia, **1:**458, 544
Borgia family, **1:**458
Boris Godunov (Musorgsky), **3:**623–32, 624, 638, 754;**4:**66, 89, 149, 151, 153, 181, 207, 428
   coronation bells, **3:**544–45, 627
   Coronation Scene, **3:**624–28
   St. Basil's scene, **3:**628–31
Boris Godunov (Pushkin), **3:**623, 624, 629, 631
Born, Georgina, "ethnography" of IRCAM and, **5:**480
Borodin, Alexander, **4:**183
   background of, **3:**399–400
   New Russian School and, **3:**397, 399, 468, 474, 786
   orientalism and, **3:**397, 400–405, 786, 789
   works of
      Arabskaya melodiya, **3:**400–401
      In Central Asia, **3:**397, 401–3
      Prince Igor, **3:**397, 400–405, 400, 407, 789
      Symphony no. 1, **3:**788–89
      Symphony no. 2, **3:**789–91
Borromeo, Carlo Cardinal, Archbishop of Milan, **1:**650, 652
borrowings (musical), **2:**327–40, 331–40
Bortnyansky, Dmitiri, **3:**235
Bosanquet, Macdowall, **4:**285
Bose, Hans Jürgen von, Sonata for Solo Violin, **5:**432
Bossinensis, Franciscus (Francis from Bosnia), **1:**698–99
Boston, **3:**679, 768–69
Boston School, **3:**768–69, 774; **4:**266
Boston Symphony Orchestra, **3:**679, 770, 774; **4:**240, 619, 610f, 622, 637, 639, 647; **5:**157, 276
bottom-up techniques, **1:**291, 326, 403
   See also cantus firmus
Boucon, Anne Jeanne, **2:**428
"Boucon, La" (Rameau sarabande), **2:**428

Bouffes-Parisiens (Paris), **3:**645
Bouilly, Jean-Nicolas, **3:**2, 3
Boulanger, Lili, **4:**125, 125, 126
   Faust et Hélène, **4:**126
   Pie Jesu, **4:**126, 127–28
   Pour les funérailles d'un soldat, **4:**126
   Vielle priere bouddhique, **4:**126
Boulanger, Nadia, **4:**102, 125, 126, 127, 588, 599, 614–15, 620, 638
   Andrey Volkonsky and, **5:**111, 268, 461
   Elliott Carter and, **5:**268, 295
"Boulangerie" group., **4:**599, 614, 628, 638, 647, 648, 649, 651, 660; **5:**268
boulevard theaters, **3:**207, 644
Boulez, Pierre, **5:**19–22, 26–40, 43–44, 45, 50, 63, 65, 69, 84, 154, 183, 188, 189, 207, 216, 223, 277, 345, 396, 453, 463, 476–80
   electronic music and, **5:**495
   Ensemble InterContemporain and, **5:**478
   4X computer and, **5:**478
   Grawemeyer Awards and, **5:**474
   IRCAM and, **5:**471, 478–80
   New York Philharmonic and, **5:**477
   Olivier Messiaen and, **5:**1, 19, 26, 27, 37, 269
   Perspectives of New Music, **5:**165
   precompositional strategy, **5:**28
   Rene Leibowitz and, **5:**19
   "Schoenberg est mort," **5:**19, 27, 37, 154
   "total serialism," **5:**36, 37, 38, 39, 41, 42, 48
   twelve-tone technique and, **5:**415
   works of
      "Alea," **5:**65
      Incises, **5:**478
      Le Marteau sans Maitre, **5:**451, 452, 463
      Répons, **5:**478, 479
      Second Piano Sonata, **5:**63
      Structures, **5:**27–36, 38, 39, 41, 45, 47, 49, 50, 64, 140, 153, 165, 166
      Third Piano Sonata, **5:**65
Bourbon dynasty, **3:**11, 206, 214
Bourbon Restoration, **3:**14, 211
Bourgeois gentilhomme, Le (Molière), **3:**386
bourgeoisie
   ballata and, **1:**368
   chamber music and, **3:**732
   comédie larmoyante and, **2:**450
   democratization of taste and, **3:**251
   femininity notion and, **3:**36
   fiction motifs of, **2:**446
   French emergence of, **1:**120, 121
   French opera and, **3:**214–19
   grand opéra and, **3:**210–11
   opera patronage by, **3:**207
   operetta and, **3:**644
   as Piccini's audience, **2:**450, 459
   Romantic age linked with, **2:**647, 670
   in Russia, **3:**679
   salon culture and, **3:**78–79

symphony concert patronage by, **2:**498
verismo opera and, **3:**660
   See also middle-class values
bourgeois music. *See* domestic entertainment
Bourges, **1:**342, 458
bourrée, in suite format, **2:**263, 272–73
Boutique fantasque (Respighi/Rossini), **3:**12
Bowie, David, *Low*, **5:**391
Bowman, Euday, "Twelfth Street Rag," **4:**605
Boyé, Pascal, **2:**458
boy soprano, **2:**352, 370–71, 381
"Brahmin" critics, **4:**341
"Brahmin," Des Eissentes and, **4:**30
"Brahminism," **4:**60, 341–43
"Brahmins" (Brahms enthusiasts), **3:**736, 743, 750
Brahms, Johannes, **3:**657, 683–743, 683, 697, 730, 748, 783; **4:**2, 12, 18, 23, 69, 142, 266, 341, 354–55, 359, 360, 363, 420, 553, 555; **5:**261, 347
   Bach (J. S.) and, **3:**703, 716, 721
   background of, **3:**683
   Beethoven and, **3:**686, 688, 690, 691, 694–95, 697, 715, 720–26
   birthplace of, **3:**683
   Bruckner and, **3:**746
   Chaikovsky on, **3:**792, 798
   chamber music and, **3:**730–42, 754; **4:**304
   choral music and, **3:**703–16
   Debussy on, **3:**22
   Dvořák and, **3:**752, 754, 755
   German vernacular songs and, **1:**702, 703–4
   György Ligeti and, **5:**438
   Haydn and, **3:**690, 691, 716–19
   Liszt and, **3:**685, 696, 699–700
   Mahler and, **4:**7
   music room of, **3:**711
   nationalism and, **3:**703–4, 710–12, 719
   as New German School detractor, **3:**418, 684, 685, 692, 719, 727
   overture and, **3:**752
   Paganini and, **3:**256
   Schubert and, **3:**697–99, 703
   Schumann (Clara) and, **3:**684–85, 692–93, 697, 698, 720
   Schumann (Robert) and, **3:**683–88, 691, 694, 703
   string quartet and, **3:**731–42
   variation technique and, **3:**734–42
   Wagner and, **3:**695–96, 699, 719, 729, 743
   Wunderhorn poems and, **4:**21
   works of
      Academic Festival Overture, **3:**752
      Cello Sonata no. 2, op. 99, **4:**354–355, 556
      Deutsches Requiem, Ein, **3:**704–10
      Four Serious Songs, op. 121, **4:**356

Hungarian Dances, 3:717, 753; 4:632
Hungarian Dance no. 5, 4:369
Liebeslieder-Walzer, 3:717, 753
O Tod, 4:356, 357–58, 360
Piano Concerto in D minor no. 1, op.
   15, 3:686–89, 691, 704. 3.692, 776
Rinaldo, 3:703
Schicksalslied, 3:714–16, 714, 719, 781
Serenade no. 1 in D major, op. 11,
   3:690–92
Sonata no. 3, op. 5 in F minor,
   3:685–86
String Quartet no. 1 in C minor, op.
   51, no. 1 3:731–42
String Quartet no. 2 in A minor, op.
   51, no. 2, 4:355, 356
Symphony no. 1 in C minor, op. 68,
   3:685–86, 692–702, 716, 719–29,
   730, 742; 4:145
Symphony no. 4 in E minor, op. 98,
   3:724, 729, 745, 791–92
"Tragic Overture," 3:752
Triumphlied, 3:708–14
Variations for Orchestra on a Theme
   by Joseph Haydn, 3:716–19, 720
Von edler Art, 1:703–4
"Brahms line," 4:5
"Brahms the Progressive," 4:355–56,
   357–58, 359, 360, 361
Braid, James, 3:71–72
Branberger, Jan, 3:451
Brandenburg, 2:68, 235
   See also Prussia
Brandenburg Concertos (Bach),
   2:289–301, 306, 369
   Bach's calligraphic dedication, 2:.289
   eccentricities of, 2:289–90
   political interpretation of, 2:301–3, 369
Brandenburg Concerto no. 1 in F major
   (J. S. Bach), 2:289–90
Brandenburg Concerto no. 2 in F major
   (J. S. Bach), 2:290
Brandenburg Concerto no. 3 in G major
   (J. S. Bach), 2:290
Brandenburg Concerto no. 4 in G major
   (J. S. Bach), 2:290
Brandenburg Concerto no. 5 in D major
   (J. S. Bach), 2:290, 291–300, 406
   cadenza and, 2:298–300
   obbligato writing and, 2:300–301
   political/social interpretations of,
      2:301–3, 619
   sketches for third movement, 2:.705
Brandenburg Concerto no. 6 in B-flat
   major (J. S. Bach), 2:290
Brandenburgers in Bohemia, The (Smetena),
   3:448–50, 463
Branibooi v Eechách (Smetana), 3:448–50,
   463
Brant, Henry, 5:421–22, 424, 426
   collage technique and, 5:421–22
   maximalism and, 5:421

works of
   Antiphony I, 5:421
   Kingdom Come, 5:421
   Meteor Farm, 5:422
brass band, 2:287
brass ensemble, 3:41, 43
brass instruments, 3:168
   Bach (J. S.) and, 2:287
   opera seria orchestration and, 2:166
Brazil, Gottschalk concert in, 3:382–83
Brazilian maxixe, 4:486
"breaking a base," 2:120
Brecht, Bertolt, 4:534–35, 541, 542, 559–60,
   765
   "epic theater" and, 4:534
   works of
      *Das Badener Lehrstück vom
         Einverständnis*, 4:541
      Der Jasager, 4:543
      Der Neinsager, 4:547
      Der Oceanflug, 4:541
      Verfremdung, 4:534
Brecht, George, 5:91
   Organ Piece, 5:91
   Piano Piece 1962, 5:91
   Three Telephone Events, 5:91
Brecht-Weill-Hindemith, *Der
   Lindberghflug*, 4:541
Brendel, Karl Franz, 3:411–17, 412, 419,
   421–22, 425, 426, 440, 449, 482
   Neue Zeitschrift für Musik and, 3:416–17,
      683, 685
   Schumann (Robert) and, 3:416, 482, 685
   Wagner and, 3:492
Brentano, Antonie, 2:672
Brentano, Bettina, 2:672
Brentano, Clemens, 3:123; 4:20
Brescia, 1:787
Breton, André, 4:595
   "Surrealist Manifesto," 4:590
Brett, Philip, 5:248, 246, 247, 256; 5:229
Breuer, Josef, 4:327
breve, 1:197, 217, 355
   Marchetto classification and, 1:355, 356
   See also semibreve
Brian, Havergal, Symphony no. 2 (the
   "Gothic"), 4:22
Bride of Lammermoor, The (Scott), 3:46–48
Bride of Messina, The (Schumann),
   3:409–10
Brillez, brillez astres nouveaux (Rameau),
   2:108–9
"Bringing in the Sheaves" (Ives), 4:289
Brinkmann, Reinhold, 3:726, 728
British Broadcasting Corporation, *El Nino*
   and, 5:523
"British Grenadiers, The" (March), 4:274,
   275
British Isles. *See* Great Britain
British Library, 1:403, 409
British Museum, 1:387

Britten, Benjamin, 1:389, 391, 392; 3:13;
   5:224–59, 228, 429, 434
   homosexuality and, 5:246–47; 261, 265,
      295, 350
   life peerage and, 5:224
   Pacifist March and, 5:228
   Peace of Britain and, 5:227
   works of
      Billy Budd (op. 50), 5:225, 227, 250
      Burning Fiery Furnace, The, op. 77,
         5:225
      Ceremony of Carols, A, 1:391
      Coal Face and, 5:227, 228
      Curlew River, op. 71, 5:225
      Death in Venice, op. 88, 5:225, 249,
         254, 255, 257
      Gloriana (op. 53), 5:225
      Midsummer Night;s Dream, A,(op. 64),
         5:225, 250, 252
      Noye's Fludde (op. 59), 5:225
      Owen Wingrave, op. 85, 5:225
      Paul Bunyan, 5:226, 228, 229
      Peter Grimes (op. 33), 5:304, 225,
         229–51
      Peter Grimes, Passacaglia, 5:241–42
      Prince of the Pagodas, The (op. 57),
         5:225, 256
      Prodigal Son, The, op. 81, 5:225
      Sinfonia da Requiem, 5:228, 229
      Stay Down Miner and, 5:228
      Turn of the Screw, The, op. 54, 5:225,
         226, 249, 250, 253, 254–55
      Violin Concerto, 5:228
      War Requiem, op. 66, 5:257, 422
Britten of Aldeburgh, Lord, 5:224
Brno Organ School, 4:423
Broadway composers, 4:624. *See also specific
   names*
Broadway musicals, 2:33
Brockes (poet), 2:313, 377
Brockes Passion (Handel), 2:313
Brodbeck, David, 3:721
broken style (*style brisé*), 2:249–50, 251, 260,
   265, 274
Brooklyn Academy of Music
   Death of Klinghoffer, The and, 5:522
   Nixon in China and, 5:518
Brooks, David, *Bobos in Paradise*, 5:526–27
Broschi, Carlo. *See* Farinelli
Broschi, Ricardo, 2:158, 168–72, 311; 4:453
Brosses, Charles de, 2:217
Browder, Earl, 4:658
Brown, Earle, 5:75, 76, 95–98, 196, 197
   John Cage and, 5:75, 95
   works of
      Available Forms I, 5:96–97
      December 1952, 5:95
      Synergy, 5:95
Brown, Howard Mayer, 1:708
Brown, James, 5:313
   plunderphonics compact disc and, 5:504
Brown, Maurice, 3:83

Browne, John, **1:**513

Browning, Robert, **4:**297
 "Paracelsus," **4:**259, 270

Browne, Tara, **5:**321
 death of, **5:**321

Brown v. Board of Education, **5:**336

Bruckner, Anton, **3:**87, 657, 745–51,
  746;**4:**4, 16, 19, 765; , **5:**347
 background of, **3:**746
 Beethoven and, **3:**747–51
 Brahms and, **3:**746
 Franck and, **3:**774
 Mahler and, **4:**6
 Wagner and, **3:**746, 747
 works of
  Symphony no. 3 in D minor, **3:**747,
   776; **4:**6
  Symphony no. 7 in E major,
   3:747–51, 755
  Symphony no. 8 in C minor, **3:**748

Bruckner rhythm, **3:**747

Bruges, **1:**455, 536

Brunelleschi, Filippo, **1:**282

"Brünnhilde" leitmotif (Wagner), **3:**527

Brunswick, Duchess of, **2:**79

Brunswick, Duke of, **2:**15, 52

Brussels, **2:**259
 English composers in, **2:**45, 47

Brutis (Attali), **5:**346

Bruyère, Jean de la, **2:**88

"Bruyeres" (Debussy), **4:**78

Buchanan, Herbert, **4:**335

Buch der hängenden Gärten, Das,op. 15
  (Schoenberg), **4:**354

Buch der Lieder (Heine), **3:**154

Büchner, Georg, **4:**506, 519, 520, 525
 Woyzeck, **4:**506

Buckingham, Duke of, **2:**87

Buckingham, Earl of, **2:**429

bucolic poetry. *See* pastorals

Budden, Julian, **3:**15, 25, 569, 593–94, 600,
  671, 673

Buddhism, **2:**721

buffo, **2:**439–40, 447, 451; **3:**23
 definition of, **2:**433
 Diderot on art of, **2:**437, 442, 443
 French debate over. *See* War of the
  Buffoons
 popularity of, **2:**434
 Rousseau and, **2:**442, 443
 stock types, **2:**478, 488
 See also opera buffa

buffo ensemble. *See* ensemble

buffoon-battle. *See* War of the Buffoons

Building of Banba, The (Cowell), **4:**298

Bukofzer, Manfred, **1:**429, 460, 496;
  2:14–15, 18, 235, 706

Bull, John, **2:**45, 47, 49

Bülow, Hans von
 Brahms's First Symphony and, **3:**729
 as conductor, **3:**222, 418, 729
 Liszt (Franz) and, **3:**418, 729

marriage to Cosima Liszt of, **3:**418, 558,
  729

Buona Figliuola, La (Piccinni), **2:**445–52,
  453, 486
 literary source of, **2:**445–46
 second-act finale of, **2:**451–52
 success of, **2:**445

Buontalenti, Bernardo, **1:**809

Burckhardt, Jakob, **1:**382

burden. *See* refrain

Burgess, Guy, **5:**7

Burgstaller, Alois, **3:**522

Burgtheater (Vienna), **2:.**471
 Mozart productions, **2:**470, 478

Burgundy, **1:**314, 316
 fifteenth-century court composers,
  1:424, 439, 447, 455, 458, 535, 536
 Homme Armé Masses, L' and, **1:**484–86,
  495
 Hundred Years War and, **1:**421, 422

Burke, Edmund, **2:**644, 645; **3:**354

Burkholder, J. Peter, **3:**680, 682, 686;
  4:269, 270

Burleigh, Harry T., **3:**765

Burleske Musik (Hartmann), **4:**770

Burlesque (Copland), **4:**617

Burmeister, Joachim, **4:**17

Burmeister, L. P. A. (Lyser), **2:**647; **3:**254,
  254

Burney, Charles (Dr. Burney), **1:**388–89,
  480, 481, 547; **2:**17, 158–59, 165,
  166, 312, 395, 420, 455
 on Mannheim orchestra, **2:**505
 on purpose of music, **2:**363, 368, 391
 use of term vamp by, **2:**564

Burnham, Scott, **2:**659

Burning Fiery Furnace, The, op. 77 (Britten),
  5:225

Burr, Jessica, **4:**662

Busbey, Fred, **5:**107

Busenello, Giovanni Francesco, **2:**26–27

Busnoys, Antoine, **1:**455–59, 485, 518, 520,
  535, 547, 667; **2:**184
 autograph manuscript of, **1:**456, *456*
 bergerette genre and, **1:**529
 influence of, **1:**493, 497–98, 499
 works of
  In hydraulis, **1:**456, 495, 500
  J'ay pris amours tout au rebours, **1:**539
  Missa L'Homme Armé, **1:**486–93, 494,
   495, 497–98, 499, 500, 501
  Quant j'ay au cuer, **1:**543
  "Tu solus altissimus," **1:**490–92

Busoni, Ferruccio, **2:**495, 496; **4:**286, **4:**539;
  5:177, 181, 192, 207
 Ästhetik der Tonkunst ("Sketch for a New
  Esthetic of Music") (pamphlet),
  4:286
 "free music" and, **5:**184, 193
 Sketch of a New Asthetic of Music, **5:**177,
  182, 184
 third tones and, **4:**286

Bussotti, Sylvano, **5:**95, 96

"But who may abide the day of His coming"
  (Handel), **2:**336–40, 445, 459

Buus, Jacques (Jachet orJakob), **1:**605–11,
  617, 618, 783
 Ricercare no. 1, **1:**618–19, *619*, *620*
 Ricercare no. 4, **1:**608–11, 617

Buxtehude, Dietrich (or Diderik), **2:**241,
  247, 255
 Durch Adams Fall, **2:**255–56, 258

BWV (Bach-Werke-Verzeichnis) listing.,
  2:342

Byrd, William, **1:**630, 670, 673, 675–89,
  694; **2:**47
 ars perfecta and, **1:**630, 678, 684, 686–87
 career of, **1:**675–79
 as Catholic recusant, **1:**670, 675, 677,
  678, 679, 686, 742
 hermeneutics and, **1:**683–84
 Mass settings by, **1:**679–89
 music printing monopoly of, **1:**678, 741
 Sweelinck compared with, **2:**45
 vernacular songs, **1:**741–42
 versatility of, **1:**670
 works of
  Ave verum corpus, **1:**686, 687
  Cantiones sacrae, **1:**678–79
  Circumspice, Jerusalem, **1:**679
  Gradualia, **1:**679–80
  Infelix ego, **1:**679
  In Nomines, **2:**118
  Mass in Five Parts, **1:**682–86
  Mass in Four Parts, **1:**681–82
  Non vos relinquam, **1:**686–87, 688
  O Domine, adjuva me, **1:**679
  Psalmes, sonets and Songs of sadness and
   pietie, **1:**741
  Songs of sundrie natures. . ., **1:**741
  Tristitia et anxietas, **1:**679

Byrds, The, 334
 "Mr. Tambourine Man", cover of, **5:**334

Byrne, David, Philip Glass and, 391

Byron, Lord, **3:**194, 253

Byzantine chant, **1:**33–35, 41, 64
 Roman synthesis of, **1:**84
 traditional performance practice of,
  1:149

Byzantine Church. *See* Eastern Orthodox
  Church

Byzantine Empire, **1:**33, 484

"Byzantium" (Yeats), **3:**311

C

cabaletta. *See* cantabile/cabaletta; stretta

Caby, Robert, **4:**570

Cabezón, Juan de, **2:**47

caccia (canon), **1:**331, 363–65, 366, 371, 378,
  380, 711
 motet in style of, **1:**378–80

Caccia, La (Vivaldi), **2:**230

Caccini, Francesca, **2:**80, 81, 82

Caccini, Giulio, 1:804, 806, 811–17, 818, 821, 823, 826; 2:11, 15–16
  monody and, 1:812–13, 822
  on vocal technique, 1:816–17, 821
  works of
    Amarilli mia bella, 1:813–17, 814, 819
    Aria di romanesca, 1:823
    Euridice, 1:811, 812; 2:21, 23, 24
    Io che dal ciel cader, 1:804, 808–9
    Nuovo musiche, Le, 1:812–13, 816–17, 816, 821, 823
    Rapimento de Cefalo, Il, 1:813, 831
cadence, 1:20, 44, 46
  Aaron theory and, 1:577
  accelerated harmonic rhythm and, 1:628
  avoidance of, 1:603–5
  ballata and, 1:366, 368, 369–71
  bass progression and, 1:467, 468–72
  as cadenza ancestor, 2:609
  Caput Mass and, 1:468–71, 483
  changed articulation of, 1:471–72
  closure and, 1:305, 408, 471, 493, 587, 628
  counterpoint, 1:155, 168, 297–98, 301, 302, 305, 430
  deceptive, 1:603–4; 2:213, 214, 216, 220, 628–29
  definition of, 1:468–69
  on the dominant, 2:488
  dominant-tonic, 1:409, 447, 469, 470–72
  Dorian, 1:274
  double leading-tone, 1:276–77, 368, 408–9
  Du Fay and, 1:446–47
  elided, 2:561, 563, 576, 584, 658
  V–I pattern and, 1:409, 447, 469, 470–71
  Fortspinnung technique and, 2:212–13
  galliard, 1:742
  Gaspar's *Mater, Patris Filia* and, 1:520, 521
  ground bass and, 1:626, 627
  interrupted, 2:559, 562
  Landini (under-third), 1:368, 369–71, 470
  Landini madrigal in motet style, 1:374, 375–77
  Machaut and, 1:325
  medial, 1:446
  monodic harmony and, 1:815
  Neapolitan-sixth and, 2:74, 213
  by *occursus,* 1:154, 155, 356
  Ockeghem motet and, 1:505–6
  octave leap, 1:447, 448
  open, 1:408
  "open and closed," 2:432
  pavan, 1:742
  rule of closeness and, 1:276–77
  Schubert's "Unfinished" Symphony and, 3:110
  sequence-and-cadence model, 212; 2:189–98

  superius/tenor motion and, 1:470
  three-voice, 1:298–99
  transition and, 1:599–600
  Willaert and, 1:602, 603–5
cadenza
  concerto instrumental solo and, 2:298–300, 609–10
  female vocal duets and, 3:36
  fermata as signal for, 2:171
  improvisation of, 2:171–72; 3:287–88
  improvised vs. written, 2:171, 609–10, 613, 614–15, 650
  Lucia coloratura interpolation of, 3:55
  Mendelssohn and, 3:275–76
  Mozart and, 2:609–10, 613, 614–15
  as vocal display vehicle, 2:171–72
cadenza fiorita, 2:171
Cadmus et Hermione (Lully), 2:86
Caduta de' decemviri, La (A. Scarlatti), 2:148–50
Caesar, Julius, 3:41
Caffarelli (Gaetano Majorano), 2:173
Cage, John, 4:570–71, 597; 5:4, 55–101, 161, 162, 176–77, 181, 182, 185, 187, 189, 191, 192, 195, 196, 201, 212, 269, 322, 372, 402, 423, 448, 496
  Adolph Weiss and, 5:73
  Amadeo Roldan and, 5:58
  Beethoven critique by, 2:693
  Black Mountain College, 5:89
  Bonnie Bird and, 5:56, 73
  Brussels World Fair, 5:65
  childhood, 5:55
  Christian Wolff and, 5:82
  Composition of Experimental Music, 5:91
  "dadaist," 5:55, 372
  Darmstadt, 5:65, 77
  David Tudor and, 5:65
  divorce from Xenia, 5:59
  Earle Brown and, 5:75, 95
  education in California, 5:55
  "Future of Music, The: Credo" (lecture), 5:56
  Gita Sarabhai and, 5:61
  Henry Cowell and, 5:55, 59, 73
  Henry David Thoreau, kinship with, 5:74
  homosexuality, 5:59
  "How the Piano Came to Be Prepared," 5:73–74
  I Ching, 5:63, 65, 70, 74, 82, 371, 643
  James Joyce, kinship with, 5:74
  "Lecture on Nothing," 5:69
  Lejaren Hiller and, 5:74
  Louis Andriessen and, 5:397
  Merce Cunningham and, 5:58, 59
  Milton Babbitt and, 5:154
  modernism, 5:66
  Morton Feldman and, 5:77
  New School and, 5:91
  Notations, 5:95

  "prepared piano," 5:59
  "prophet of purity," 5:73
  Robert Rauschenberg and, 5:77, 353
  Schoenberg pupil, 5:55, 73, 74
  tala, 5:61
  Virgil Thomson and, 5:70
  "well-tampered clavier," 5:59
  Zen Buddhism and, 5:62, 62–64, 68–70, 74
  works of
    4'33", 5:73, 95, 355
    Atlas eclipticalis, 5:75, 76, 88, 96
    Bacchanale, 5:59, 60–61
    Constructions in Metal, 5:57, 58
    Fontana Mix, 5:196, 197
    "Future of Music: Credo, The" 5:175, V181
    HPSCHD, 5:74
    Imaginary Landscape No. 1, 5:56–58
    Imaginary Landscape No. 3, 5:70
    Imaginary Landscape No. 4, 5:70
    Imaginary Landscapes, 5:185
    "Living Room Music," 5:55
    Music for Piano, 5:65
    Music of Changes, 5:64, 66
    Perilous Night, The, 5:59, 60
    Primitive, 5:59
    Sonatas and Interludes, 5:59, 64
    Totem Ancestor, 5:59
    Williams Mix, 5:196, 197
Cage, Xenia, 5:58
Cahill, Thaddeus, 5:177
Caïd, Le (Thomas), 3:390
cakewalks, 4:599
Caldara, Antonio, 2:481
Calder, Alexander, 5:96
Cale, John, 5:362
  La Monte Young and, 5:362
"Calf of Gold" song (Gounod), 3:640
call and response, 1:113
Callistus (Calixtus) II, Pope, 1:162
"Calunnia è un venticello, La" (Rossini), 3:23
Calvin, John, 1:754
Calvinism, 1:754–55
  church music restrictions of, 2:46, 125, 261
Calvisius, Sethus, 1:768
  Ein' feste Burg ist unser Gott, 1:768–69
Calzabigi, Ranieri de', 2:90, 455, 457, 478; 3:37
Cambert, Robert, 2:89
  Ariane, 2:89
Cambini, Giuseppe Maria, 3:277
Cambrai Agnus Dei, 1:314, 315
Cambrai Cathedral, 1:441, 453, 458, 507, 558
Cambridge University, 1:166, 513
Camerata, 3:498
Camerata (Bardi circle), 1:800, 803, 804, 812, 818, 822
Cammarano, Salvadore, 3:46, 577–78

Campanella, La, 3:255, 266
Campion, Thomas, 2:114
Campra, André, 2:110
   Idomenée, 2:90, 106–17
Camptown Races (Foster), 3:378, 382; 4:668
"Canaries" (Carter), 5:273, 274, 275, 279, 285
cancan, 3:645–46
cancrizans motion (proceeding backward), 1:328
Cannabich, Christian, 2:506
canon (body of works)
   free-market formation of, 2:639
   repertoire vs., 3:665–66, 682
   See also canonization; standard repertory
canon (cathedral community), 1:169
canon (celebrant's prayer), in Mass ordo, 1:61(table)
canon (musical form), 1:330–36, 349; 2:402, 687
   Bach (J. S.) and, 2:383–85
   ballata and, 1:366
   Busnoys motet and, 1:457
   caccia and, 1:331, 363–65, 366, 371, 378, 380, 711
   chace and, 1:331–36, 349, 364, 366, 374, 491, 711
   complexity of, 1:331
   earlier meaning of, 1:330–31
   hunting pieces as, 1:364, 365
   J'ay pris amours arrangements as, 1:538
   madrigal and, 1:363–65, 374
   mensurated, 1:477–78
   Missa L'Homme Armé and, 1:485–86, 489, 491–92, 493, 520, 529
   Ockeghem Mass and, 1:477–78, 480, 641
   Palestrina Mass and, 1:637–41, 662
   Pycard Gloria and, 1:410
   Sumer, 1:388, 389–91, 397, 399, 409, 457
canon (notational rule), 1:262, 265, 280
Canonic Sonata in G minor, I, 1–8 (Fux), 2:180–81
canonization (musical), 2:3, 233, 326, 691
   of Beethoven, 2:689, 691, 738
   of composers of 1685, 2:233, 235, 289, 305, 381, 388
   of Handel, 2:233, 235, 639
   of Haydn and Mozart, 2:399, 400, 401, 463, 464, 481, 577, 638, 638–39, 643–48, 646, 738
   See also standard repertory
canon law, 1:170, 277
"Canon on Music to be Used in the Mass" (Council of Trent)., 1:650
Can shee excuse my wrongs (Dowland), 1:745
canso, 1:117, 124, 125
   ballade as descendant of, 1:349
   to Blessed Virgin, 1:98, 99, 128, 501, 533
   cantiga as equivalent of, 1:128
   description of, 1:107–8
   French *chanson courtoise* as, 1:117

Raimon and, 1:98–99
   regularized, 1:113
   strophic, 1:325
cantabile/cabaletta
   bel canto and, 3:37, 40, 41, 48
   Bellini aria and, 3:40, 43
   dances and, 3:35, 49
   Donizetti and, 3:48, 49, 52–53, 55, 59
   Paganini's variations on, 3:258–59
   Rossini and, 3:21, 27–35
   Rossini's "Di tanti palpiti" as, 3:28, 30–35, 41, 258–59
   solita forma and, 3:594
   Verdi and, 3:571–72, 579
cantata, 2:75–78, 340–75
   aria characteristics and, 2:146
   Bach (J. S.) and, 2:340–75, 376, 378, 392, 682
   Bach (W. F.) and, 2:402
   Beethoven and, 2:652
   Carissimi and, 2:75, 331
   Concert Spirituel (Paris) and, 2:499
   definition of, 2:75
   in Italy, 2:75–78
   liturgical function of, 2:349
   as musical sermon, 2:342
   Neumeister format for, 2:341, 342, 348, 351
   new style, 2:348–53
   old style, 2:343–47
   operatic links with, 2:75–78, 146, 349, 351
   Scarlatti (A.) and, 2:141, 142–47, 331
   Stravinsky, 5:118–22
   Strozzi and, 2:75–78, 81–82, 142
Cantata profana (Bartók), 4:394
Canterbury, 1:461
Canterbury Cathdral, 1:408, 408
Canterbury Tales (Chaucer), 1:365
canticle, 1:112
"Canticle of Mary." See Magnificat
Canti C numero cento cinquanta (Petrucci publication), 1:563
Canticum Sacrum (Stravinsky), 5:122
cantiga, 1:128–33, 134
   manuscript miniatures, 1:129–30, 130, 131, 133
Cantigas de Santa Maria (collection), 1:128
cantilena, 1:298–301, 312–13, 317, 318, 325, 397, 413, 417–18, 435
   motet as, 1:429–33, 501–46
Cantionalsätze, 1:765–68; 2:53; 3:164
Cantiones ab fual argumento sacras vocantur (Byrd and Tallis), 1:673, 677–78
Cantiones sacrae (Byrd), 1:678–79
Cantiones sacrae (Schütz), 2:58
canto, 1:542–46
Cantor, Georg, 5:136
Cantos de Espana (Albéniz), 4:632
cantus coronatus, 1:208
   See also song competitions
cantus firmus, 1:291, 311, 316, 326

Berlioz and, 3:339
   in Busnoys's *Missa L'Homme Armé*, 1:488(table)
   cantata and, 2:361
   Caput Mass transposition of, 1:475, 476, 482
   characteristic fifteenth-century Mass form of, 1:486–90
   chorale partita and, 2:50, 51–52
   conductus and, 1:397
   contratenor vs., 1:271
   counterpoint and, 1:156–57, 159, 161, 297–98, 307, 399
   countersinging, 1:438–39
   Cunctipotens genitor and, 1:306, 322
   cyclic Mass Ordinaries and, 1:461–71, 473–76, 482, 483–97, 501
   in Du Fay's Masses, 1:498
   in English church music, 1:439–40, 612, 613
   English descant and, 1:406, 407
   fantasia and, 2:115
   French motet and, 1:221
   imitative polyphony vs., 1:580–82
   In Nomine and, 2:115, 116, 118, 120
   Josquin's innovations and, 1:499, 529–30, 579, 580–81, 584, 602
   in Josquin's *Missa Hercules Dux Ferrariae*, 1:560–61
   in Josquin's *Missa L'Homme Armé*, 1:529
   Kyrie and, 2:43
   Lutheran chorales and, 1:761–62, 768
   Machaut Gloria paraphrase of, 1:325, 326
   Machaut Kyrie and, 1:322, 324
   Mass secular song basis of, 1:483–97
   paraphrase motet and, 1:503, 506, 507–8
   recercadas and, 1:620–21
   stile antico and, 1:667
   Sweelinck Chromatic Fantasia and, 2:45
   Tenorlied and, 1:756
   tenor part and, 1:468
Can vei la lauzeta mover (Bernart), 1:108
canzona, 1:786–96; 2:44, 114, 198
   big band battle-pieces and, 1:786–87
   church sonata and, 2:178, 179
canzona per sonare. See sonata
Canzone post il Comune (Frescobaldi), 2:44
canzonets, 1:746
Canzonets, or Little Short Songs to Four Voices: Selected out of the best and approved Italian authors (Morley), 1:746
canzonetti, 1:746; 3:130
Canzoni alla francese per sonar sopra stromenti da tasti (A. Gabrieli), 1:786
canzoni da sonare. See canzona
Canzoni et sonate a 3.5.6.7.8.10.12.14.15.&22. voci, per sonar con ogni sorte de instrumenti, con il basso per l'organo (G. Gabrieli), 1:790–91
Canzoni nove (songbook), 1:691
Capeol, Karl, 4:424

Capital Capitals (Thomson), **4**:592
capitalism. *See* free market
Capitulation (Wagner), **3**:560
Cappella Giulia (Vatican), **1**:631
capricci ad libitum, **3**:252
capriccio, **2**:299–300, 610
    Mozart's improvisation on, **2**:611
Capriccio (Janáček), **4**:424
*Capriccio on the Departure of His Beloved
        Brother* (J. S. Bach), **3**:65
Capriccio espagnol (Rimsky-Korsakov), **4**:121
caprice, **3**:252, 253, 255–57, 266, 292, 340
Caprice, op. 1, no. 13 (Paganini), **3**:255, 256
Caprice, op. 1, no. 17 (Paganini), **3**:255–57
Caprice, op. 1, no. 24 (Paganini), **3**:256,
        257, 340
"Capture of Burgoyne, The, **4**:661
Capuleti e i Montecchi, I (Bellini), **3**:37, 45
Capuleti e Montecchi (Romani), **3**:45
Caput Draconia, **1**:476, *476*
Caput Mass (anon.), **1**:465–71, 472, 474,
        481, 489, 493
    author's identity and, **1**:475–77, *476*
    emulations of, **1**:472–83, 493
Cara, Marco (Marchetto), **1**:695–96, 697,
        698, 699
    Mal un muta per effecto, **1**:695–96, 697,
        699
Carafa, Michele, **3**:208
Cardew, Cornelius, **5**:84–88, 101
    "List of 1001 Activities," **5**:87
    Michael Nyman and, **5**:355
    Royal Academy of Music, **5**:84
    training at, **5**:84
    Stratch Music, **5**:85, 87, 355
    Scratch Orchestra, **5**:84, 85
    Stockhausen Serves Imperialism, **5**:88
Carestini, Giovanni, **2**:161
Carissimi, Giacomo, **1**:484; **2**:73–75, 237
    cantata and, **2**:75, 81, 331
    Jephte, **2**:73–74, 76–77, 90
Carl Theodor, Elector of Palatine, **2**:505
Carmagnole, La (Paganini variation set),
        3:257
carmen (textless instrumental piece), **1**:543,
        544–46
Carmen (Bizet), **3**:398–99, 400, 405–6, 641,
        641–43, 642, 648; **4**:71
    "Habanera," **3**:398–99, 641, 642
Carmen, Johannes (pseud.), **1**:422, 423
    Pontifici decora speculi, **1**:378–80
carmina, **1**:543, 544–46, 559, 560–61
Carmina burana (1847), **1**:138, *139*, 201, 203
Carmina Burana (Orff), **1**:138–39; **4**:756,
        757–62, 764
Carnap, Rudolf, **5**:155
    Der logische Aufbau der Welt (treatise),
        5:155
Carnegie, Andrew, **3**:679
Carnegie Hall (New York City), **3**:679,
        755; **4**:627
carnival, **2**:12, *12*, 14, 16, 17, 113, 390

Carnival (Dvořák), **3**:755
carnival season, **1**:823, 826
carol, English, **1**:418–20
carole (dance-song), **1**:114, 120, 123–24, 131,
        349
    canon and, **1**:332, 349
    English version of, **1**:418–20
    instrumental accompaniment for, **1**:133
    Machaut and, **1**:294
    Carolingian Empire, **1**:2–7, 106, 141
    See also Franks
Carolingian Renaissance, **1**:4–7, *7*
    liberal arts curriculum, **1**:69, *71*
Carosfeld, Julius Schnorr von, **3**:486
Carpani, Giuseppe, **3**:333
Carpenter, John Alden, **3**:769
Carpentras (Elzéar Genet), **1**:555, 557
Carré, Michel, **3**:640
Carrelage phonique (Satie), **4**:570
Carreras, José, **3**:579
Carrillo, Julián, **4**:285–86, 292, 297
    microtonality and, **4**:292
    Preludio a Colón, **4**:292–93, 294, 295
    quarter tones and, **4**:286
    "sonido trece" system and, **4**:286
Carroll, Lewis, Del Tredici and, **5**:442
Carte, Richard D'Oyly. *See* D'Oyly Carte,
        Richard
Carter, Elliott, **4**:263–64, 265, 266, 787;
        5:224–225, 261–306, 332, 426, 442,
        448, 453, 474
    Benjamin Boretz and, **5**:303–4
    Celebration of Some 100 × 150 Notes, A,
        5:474–75
    Charles Ives and, **5**:268, 269
    David Schiff and, **5**:268, 280, 303
    early training, **5**:268
    Guggenheim Foundation Fellowship,
        5:280
    Harvard Francophile music department
        and, **5**:268
    hermetic image, **5**:280
    lecture at University of Texas, **5**:277
    Louisville Orchestra, **5**:295
    "Music and the Time Screen" (essay),
        5:277
    musical background, **5**:268
    Nadia Boulanger and, **5**:268, 295
    New Music Edition, **5**:153
    "New Simplicity" and, **5**:474
    Princeton Seminar in Advanced Musical
        Studies, **5**:295
    Pulitzer Prizes, **5**:300
    review of *Concord Sonata* (Ives), **5**:269
    Richard Franko Goldman and, **5**:269
    Stanley Quartet of the University of
        Michigan's commission, **5**:295
    on Susanne Langer, **5**:277
    String Quartet no. 1, **5**:415
    tempo modulation, **5**:275
    Walden Quartet of the University of
        Illinois and, **5**:293

    years in Paris, **5**:268
    works of
        "Canaries," **5**:273, 274, 275, 279, 285
        Cello Sonata, **5**:278–79
        Double Concerto, **5**:261, 262,
            265–268, 275, 280, 302–4
        cosmological allegory, **5**:303
        first performance of, **5**:265
        Eight Etudes and a Fantasy,
            5:269–73
        Eight Pieces for Four Timpani,
            5:273–75
        First String Quartet, **5**:280–85,
            287–98
        Fourth String Quartet, **5**:304
        Holiday Overture, **5**:276
        Piano Sonata of 1946, **5**:269
        Pocahontas, **5**:268
        Second String Quartet, **5**:295–300,
            328
        Six Studies for Four Timpani, **5**:269
        Symphony for Three Orchestras, **5**:301
        Third Quartet, **5**:300–301
        Variations for Orchestra, **5**:295
Cartesian period, **1**:797–98
Carthage, **2**:132, 155, 156
Cartier-Bresson, Henri, **5**:14
Carul cu boi (Popovici), **3**:456
Caruso, Enrico, **3**:579, 659; **4**:751, 752
    Any Resemblance Is Purely Coincidental
        (Dodge), **5**:499
Casanova (painter), **3**:417
Casella, Alfredo, **4**:647, 747, 750
    "minute stylizations" and, **4**:609–10
"Case of Anna O., The," **4**:327
"Casey Jones" (Hill), **4**:656
Casino de Paris, Josephine Baker and, **4**:612
cassatione
    definition of, **2**:498
    Haydn and, **2**:518
Casse-noisette (Chaikovsky), **4**:144
"Casta diva" (Bellini), **3**:39–44, 49, 71
Castel, Etienne, **1**:447
Castellanos, Rosario
    El Nino and, **5**:524
    Memorial de Tlatelolco, **5**:525
Castelli, Leo, **5**:76–77
Castellini, Teresa, **2**:172
Castiglione, Baldassare, **1**:626, 698; **2**:15
Castile. *See* Spain
Castle Church (Wittenberg), **2**:353
Castle, Irene, **4**:606
Castle, Vernon, **4**:606
Castor et Pollux (Rameau), **2**:91, 92–93, 94
    ariette, **2**:107, 108–9
    Atys compared with, **2**:110
    costume design, **2**:109
    moral of, **2**:94
    Prologue, **2**:93–94
castration
    Atys and, **2**:97
    illegality of, **2**:17

castrato, 2:16–17, 291, 376; 3:28, 38
  audience response to, 2:174–76
  in *Crociato in Egitto, Il,* 3:216
  English mocking of, 2:313
  Farinelli's fame as, 2:166–69, 237; 4:453
  French court opera and, 2:88, 97, 98
  Gluck and, 2:454
  Handel and, 2:307, 308, 311, 336, 339–40, 459
  haute-contre vs., 2:98
  Metastasian librettos and, 2:153, 155, 156, 161, 166–67
  modern musical counterpart of, 2:174
  Monteverdi roles and, 2:21, 27
  opera seria and, 2:153–56, 173–76, 307
  ornamentation and, 2:281
  Raguenet's description of, 2:86–87
  signature pieces of, 2:167–68
  soprano pairing with, 3:578
  symbolism of, 2:174
Casulana, Maddalena, 2:80
Catalogue d'oiseaux (Messiaen), 4:239–40
Catalonia, 1:128
categorical imperative, 3:61
Cathari, 1:116
catharsis, 3:671
cathedral architecture, 1:169
"Cathédrale engloutie, La" (Debussy), 4:78
Cathédrale, La (Huré), 4:196
Cathedral of Notre Dame. *See* Notre Dame de Paris
cathedral organization, 1:169, 170
  Italian arts patronage and, 1:277–81
  urban clerical class and, 1:207–8, 219
cathedral polyphony, 1:162–63
cathedral schools, 1:148, 149, 169, 170
  Beauvais, 1:94
Catherine II (the Great), Empress of Russia, 2:462, 631; 3:16, 235
Catherine of Valois, 1:421, 461
Catholic Church. *See* Roman Catholic Church
Catton, Bruce, 5:107
Catulli carmina (Orff), 4:760, 764
Catullus, 3:120
cauda, 1:124, 200, 201, 202, 203, 204, 403
Cavaillé-Coll, 3:774
Cavalieri, Emilio de', 1:804, 809, 812, 823, 826, 827
  Anima mia che pensi, 1:833
  Dalle più alte sfere, 1:804, 805
  O che nuovo miracolo, 1:804
  Rappresentatione di Anima, et di Corpo, 1:809, 811, 812, 823, 831, 832–34
Cavalleria rusticana (Mascagni), 3:659–61, 663
  Turiddu's arioso, 3:660–61
Cavalli, Francesco, 2:33, 75; 4:18
"Cav and Pag." *See Cavalleria rusticana; Pagliacci, I*
cavatina
  Beethoven and, 2:684–85, 726, 731; 3:69

Bellini and, 3:41
  meaning of, 2:684
Cavatine du Page (Meyerbeer), 3:220–22, 221, 227
Cavazzoni, Girolamo, 1:607
Cavazzoni, Marco Antonio, 1:607, 786
Cavell, Stanley, 5:42–43
  "Music Discomposed," 5:42
  nihilism, 5:42–43
Cavos, Catterino, 3:242
C clef, 1:99–100
Cech, Svatopluk, 4:423
Ce fut en mai (Moniot), 1:120–21, 131
celesta, 3:73; 4:145, 550
Celenus (mythological), 2:98, 99
Celestial County, The (Ives), 4:246, 247–48, 249–50, 286
Celestine I, Pope, 1:113
Cellarius, Andrea, 1:476
Celle m'as s'amour douné Qui mon cuer et m'amour a (refrain), 1:227
Cellini, Benvenuto, 3:116
cello
  accompanied sonata and, 2:428
  Beethoven sonatas for, 2:673, 724, 725
  Boccherini concerto for, 2:600
  Borodin theme, 3:789
  Haydn concertos for, 2:600
  in piano trio, 2:695
  Vivaldi concertos for, 2:217
Cello Concerto in B-flat major (Boccherini), 2:600
Cello Concerto in D major (Haydn), 2:600
Cello Sonata (Carter), 5:278–279
Cello Sonata in D major, op. 102, no. 2 (Beethoven), fugal finale, 2:724, 725
Cello Sonata, op. 99 (Brahms), 4:354–55
Celts, 1:119; 3:771–72
Cendrars, Blaise
  La création du monde, 4:571
  Relache, 4:571
censorship, 2:18, 88, 461
  in France, 3:211, 227, 577
  of Meyerbeer's *Les Huguenots,* 3:227, 230
  of religious service representations, 3:337
  in Russia, 3:227, 249, 478, 622, 623; 4:117
  of Verdi's *La traviata,* 3:580
  Wagner on, 3:489
Center of the Creative and Performing Arts in the State University of New York at Buffalo, 5:363
Cento concerti ecclesiastici, a una, a due, a tre & a quattro voci (Viadana), 1:780, 812; 2:52
centonization, 1:28
Cento partite sopra passacagli (Frescobaldi), 2:37, 40
Central Committee of the Soviet Communist Party, 5:9
"Ce qu'a vu le vent d'ouest" (Debussy), 4:78

Ce qu'on entend sur la montagne (Liszt), 3:429–30, 546, 699
Ceremony of Carols, A (Britten), 1:391
Cerha, Friedrich, 4:714
Cervantes, Miguel de, 3:188
Cervini, Marcello. *See* Marcellus II, Pope
Césaris, Johannes, 1:422, 423
Cetra, La (Vivaldi), 2:225
Chabrier, Emmanuel, 4:61, 65, 66
  España, 4:61
  Souvenirs de Munich, 4:61–62, 63
chace (canon), 1:331–36, 349, 491, 711
caccia vs., 1:364
  Lorenzo and, 1:366, 374
chacona, 2:37
chaconne, 2:39, 94, 135, 193, 261
Chadabe, Joel, 5:195
Chadwick, George Whitefield, 3:769, 770, 771, 772
Chaikovsky, Modest, 3:799, 800
Chaikovsky, Pyotr Ilyich, 2:16; 3:439, 632–39, 640, 791; 4:149, 454, 496, 555, 691, 751; 5:223, 244
  ballet and, 4:140–50
  Brahms and, 3:792, 798
  Carnegie Hall opening and, 3:679
  on darkened theaters, 3:564
  death of, 3:799–800
  1812 Overture, Schnittke's Concerto for Piano and Strings and, 5:467–68
  on German music, 3:440–41
  Glinka and, 3:464
  homosexuality of, 3:409, 795, 799–800; 5:248–49
  "Imperial" ballets and, 4:145
  on Mascagni, 3:663–64
  Mozart and, 3:796, 798
  on Musorgsky, 3:441
  New German School and, 3:799
  orientalism and, 3:406–10
  symphonic music, 3:657, 786, 789–801
  works of
    Casse-noisette, 4:144
    Eugene Onegin, 3:632–39, 663, 796–97; 4:7
    Iolanta, 3:406
    La belle au bois dormant, 4:144. See *Sleeping Beauty, The*
    Nutcracker, The, 3:406; 4:139
    Romeo and Juliet concert overture, 3:406–9, 663
    Swan Lake, 3:108
    Symphony no. 4 in F minor, 3:791–99; 4:140
    Symphony no. 6 in B minor, op. 74 (Pathétique), 3:108, 799–801; 4:19; 5:75
Chaillou, Raoul, 1:255, 258
chain finales, 3:5
Chaliapin, Fyodor, 2:16
Chamber Concerto (Berg), 5:265
chamber duet, 2:331–36

chamber music
  Beethoven and, 3:731, 754
  Brahms and, 3:730–42, 754
  cantata as, 2:146
  domestic performance of, 2:114, 419, 427,
    432
  Dvořák and, 3:754
  earliest instrumental, 1:541, 542–46
  as embodiment of transcendence
  English self-made class and, 2:124, 414
  galanterie and, 2:427–28
  late-eighteenth and nineteenth-century
    nomenclature for, 2:695
  Liszt on, 3:731
  New German School and, 3:731
  orchestral genre vs., 2:519
  origins of, 2:114–18, 695
  Raff and, 3:731
  Schubert and, 3:83, 84, 86, 731, 754
  Schumann (Robert) and, 3:731
  Smetana and, 3:731
  sonata and, 1:796
  Vienna public concerts of, 2:683
  vocal partbooks for, 1:539–40, 542
  See also specific forms, e.g. string quartet
chamber sonata, 2:178, 191, 193, 204, 497
  Bach (J. S.) work based on, 2:241
  church sonata compared with, 2:178–81
  courante and, 2:260
  end of church sonata distinction with,
    2:204
Chambonnières, Jacques Champion de,
    2:260
Chaminade, Cécile, *Piece dans le style ancien,*
    4:65
"Champagne aria" (Liszt), 3:270–71
"Champagne aria" (Mozart), 2:490, 491
Champion des dames, Le (Le Franc), 1:422,
    439, 536
Champmeslé, La (Marie Desmares), 2:106
Chandos, Duke of, 2:314
Chandos Anthems (Handel), 2:314
change, Hegel's theory of, 3:412–13
changeability, 2:437
"Change the World!" (Gold), 4:656
chanson, 1:435, 544, 706–9; 2:44
  accompanied, 1:131–33, 296
  bergerette and, 1:526–29
  Binchois and, 1:446–52, 706
  as canzona model, 1:786–87
  Du Fay and, 1:498, 706
  faux-naïve, 1:349–50
  fifteenth- vs. sixteenth-century, 1:706
  instrumental reworkings of, 2:114
  Janequin and, 1:710–13
  J'ay pris amours popularity as, 1:532–33,
    534–41
  lament genre of, 1:448, 452, 454
  Lasso and, 1:714–18
  lewd genre of, 1:138, 710–11
  Machaut and, 1:292–97, 298, 299–310

motet and, 1:218–19, *218*, 219, 220, 221,
    224–26, 233, 236, 238, 262,
    292–98, 301, 378, 429, 532, 706
onomatopoetic, 1:711, 712
organ arrangements of, 1:786–87
Parisian, 1:706–9, 710, 714, 786
social theory and, 1:208
tablatures of, 1:606
unaccompanied, 1:452
urbanization of, 1:206, 219
  See also troubadours; trouvères
chanson avec des refrains, 1:120, 123
chanson balladé. See virelai
chanson courtoise, 1:117
"Chanson hébraïque" (Ravel), 4:107
chansonniers, 1:109–10, 122, 353
chanson royal, 1:290
chansons couronées, 1:121
chansons courtoises, 1:122
chansons de geste, 1:120, 208
Chansons de maistre Clement Janequin
    (Janequin), 1:710–13
chansons de toile, 1:119–20
Chansons nouvelles en musique (songbook),
    1:692
chant, 1:11–35
  Ambrosian, 1:63
  Anglican, 1:672
  antiphons and responds, 1:12–13
  Beneventan, 1:64
  in Berlioz's *Symphonie fantastique,* 3:337,
    339
  Byzantine, 1:33–35, 64, 84
  concert performance of, 1:66
  contrapuntal amplification of, 1:435–39
  Dorian, 1:89
  Du Fay vs. Binchois paraphrase of, 1:441
  English sight-harmonizing of, 1:436
  evolution of, 1:12
  fauxbourdon and, 1:435–39, 501
  Frankish, 1:298
  Frankish additions, 1:37–67, 234
  French-Cypriot, 1:345
  Gregorian. *See* Gregorian chant
  Grocheio's social theory and, 1:208
  lesson and, 1:13
  Mozarabic, 1:63–64
  notation and, 1:1–2, 214
  Notre Dame settings of, 1:171–72
  Old Roman, 1:62, 63
  Ordinary, 1:58, 60–63, 310, 322, 324
  organ settings based on, 2:49
  paraphrased, 1:325
  Passion narrative, 1:776
  polyphonic settings, 1:147, 149–50, 156,
    162–68, 171, 185
  responsoraries, 1:11
  Roman, 1:1–7
  Russian tradition, 3:234
  tropes, 1:50–53
  unison, 1:47

Chantar m'er de so gu'en no volria (Beatriz),
    1:113
chant books, 1:15, *15*, 23, 78, 184, 462, 473
  "Credo I," 1:34
  Kyriale, 1:58, 322
  Machaut Mass discovery in, 1:325
  on rhythmic interpretation, 1:115
  See also antiphoner; graduale
Chant des oyseaux, Le (Janequin), 1:711
Chantilly Codex, 1:342–43
Chants polulaires (Ravel), 4:107–8
"Chaos" (Haydn), 2:633–37, 645; 4:345
Chapel of the Foundling Hospital
    (Dublin), 2:326
Chapel Royal (England), 1:513, 671–72,
    673, 679, 692; 2:49, 122, 127
Chaplin, Charlie, 4:563
characteristic piece, 3:65, 119
Charakterstück, 3:65, 119, 444
Charlemagne (Charles the Great), King of
    the Franks, 1:3–4, 5, 13, 37, 41, 49,
    53, 106, 111, 286; 2:139, 724
Charles I, King of England, 2:122, 124, 125
Charles II, King of England, 2:125, 132–33
Charles I, King of the Franks. *See*
    Charlemagne
Charles V, King of France, 1:317
Charles VI, King of France, 1:421, 461
Charles VII, King of France, 1:421,
    454–55, 458
Charles VIII, King of France, 1:457, 523
Charles IX, King of France, 1:719
Charles V, Holy Roman Emperor, 1:590,
    670
Charles VI, Holy Roman (Austrian)
    Emperor, 2:156, 438
Charles X, King of France, 3:11, 211
Charles d'Anjou, 1:120, 122
Charles, Ray, 5:313
Charles Ives and His Music (Cowell), 4:281
Charles Ives, My Father's Song (Feder), 4:251
Charles the Bold, Duke of Burgundy,
    1:455, 484–85, *485*, 486, 498, 518
Charles the Great. *See* Charlemagne
Charlotte, Queen Consort of Great
    Britain, 2:419
Charlotte de Bourbon, 1:345
Charlton, David, 3:679–80
Charpentier, Marc-Antoine, 2:73, 89
Chartres Cathedral, 1:453
Chartres counterpoint fragment, 1:155, 158
Chase, Gilbert, 3:377
Chasse, La (Janequin), 1:711
Chateaubriand, Vicomte de, 3:387, 392
Chaucer, Geoffrey, 1:290, 365
Chausson, Ernest, 3:783; 4:61, 70, 89, 90
chauvinism. *See* ethnocentrism
"Che faro senza Euridice" (Gluck),
    2:457–58, 459
cheironomy, 1:14
Chenneviere, Daniel (Dane Rudhyar
    pseud.), 4:295

Chernïshevsky, Nikolai, 3:622, 624
Cherubini, Luigi, 2:736; 3:2–3
chess champion, 2:499
Chesterfield, Lord, 2:340
chest of viols, 2:118, *120*
Chevalier, Maurice, 4:576
"Chez Pétrouchka," 4:164, 166, 167, 168,
    172, 204, 219, 221, 226
Chiabrera, Gabriello, 2:3
Chiang Kai-shek, 5:14
Chicago Eight, 5:310
Chicago Lyric Opera, Harbison's *The Great
    Gatsby* and, 5:515
Chicago Symphony, *Final Alice* and, 5:443
Chichester Psalms (Bernstein), 5:431
Chickering (piano manufacturer), 3:382
Chigi, Agostino, 1:457–58
Chigi Codex, 1:457–58, *458,* 473
Child Alice (Del Tredici), 5:442–45
"Child Falling Asleep" (Schumann), 3:360
child prodigies. *See* prodigies
Childe Harold (Byron), 3:253
Children's Corner (Debussy), 4:78, 599
children's songs, 1:18, 331, 389, 391, 392
child-sacrifice tragedies. *See* sacrifice of child
Chilesotti, Oscar, *Antiche arie e danze per
    liuto* and, 4:750
chimes, in Berlioz's *Symphonie fantastique,*
    3:338
"Chi mi frena" (Donizetti), 3:49–51, 587
"Ch'io parta?" (Hasse), 2:166, 167, 168, 169
chitarrone, 1:804–5, 809, 829
Choeur des Songes Funestes (Lully), 2:102–3
choeurs universels, 3:162–63
choirbooks, 1:457–58, 474, 496, 498, 507,
    555
    English, 1:513
    Milanese, 1:519
"choirbook style," 1:214
choirboys, 2:140
choirs
    antiphonal psalmody and, 1:8
    congregational singing vs., 1:758
    English, 1:513, 515, 517, 613, 671–72
    faburden and, 1:438
    intermedii, 1:804
    Mass Ordinary and, 1:310
    split, 1:611, 776, 780, 782–83, 787, 792
    stichic "arias," 1:24
    See also choral music
Chomsky, Noam, tonal music and, 5:446,
    447, 449
Chopin, Frédéric, 3:343–76, 386, 398, 447,
    482; 4:73, 100, 197, 556
    allure of, 3:406
    Bach and, 3:346–47, 366
    background of, 3:343–44, 347
    Beethoven and, 3:346, 368
    concerto and, 3:348
    esthetic credo of, 3:368
    étude and, 3:350
    George Crumb and, 5:423

Gottschalk and, 3:377, 382
illness and death of, 3:343, 354–55, 376
Liszt and, 3:349
mazurka and, 3:350, 357–60, 363,
    364–65
Mickiewicz and, 4:9
nationalism and, 3:344–47, 357–58, 367,
    375–76, 753
nocturne and, 3:348, 367; 4:553
patrons of, 3:348
performance practice of, 3:363–65
polonaise and, 3:347, 348, 350, 357, 367,
    796
portraits and drawings of, 3:343, 344,
    348, 349
prelude and, 3:350, 351–56, 438
salons and, 3:75, 78, 348
Sand and, 3:76, 349, 355, 368, 375, 376,
    385–86, 420
Schubert and, 3:346
Schumann (Robert) and, 3:343–47, 354,
    365–67, 368, 683
sonata and, 3:350, 365–67, 374
as teacher, 3:75, 348
works of
    Ballade no. 1 in G minor, 3:369–76
    Ballades, 3:367–76, 427
    Barcarolle, 3:350
    Berceuse, 3:350
    Étude in C major, op. 10, no. 2, 3:347
    Fantaisie, 3:350
    Fantasia on Polish Airs, 3:348
    Grande polonaise, 3:348
    Krakowiak, 3:347
    Mazurka, op. 17, 3:357–60
    Mazurka in F minor, op. 68, no. 4,
        3:347
    Mazurka in F-sharp minor, op. 6, no.
        1, 3:363, *363*
    Military Polonaise, op. 40, no. 1,
        3:796
    Prelude in C minor, op. 28, no. 20,
        4:200
    Preludes, op. 28, 3:351–56
    Sonata in B-flat minor, op. 35,
        3:365–67
    Sonata in B minor, op. 58, 3:365
Chopin, Nicolas, 3:344
Chopin Evoking Memories of Poland (Styka),
    3:343
"Chopsticks" (piano piece), 1:392
chorale, 1:758–69; 2:49–55
    Bach (J. S.) harmonization, 2:346
    in Bach (J. S.) Passions, 2:378, 382
    Bach (J. S.) settings, 2:50, 241, 255–57,
        341, 365
    cantata vs., 2:342
    four-part, 1:765–66
    harmonizations, 1:765–66
    Lutheranism and, 1:758–69; 2:49–55
    Lutheran oratorio form and, 2:341–42
    in Mendelssohn's *Paulus,* 3:167–70

nationalism and, 3:165–66
oratorio rebirth and, 3:164–66
partita and, 2:49–52, 262
polyphony and, 2:353
Sweelinck and, 2:48
vocal counterpart, 2:52–55
See also Lutheran chorale
chorale concerto, 2:52–72
chorale prelude (*Choralvorspiel*), 1:762;
    2:255–58, 378, 382
Choral Fantasy (Beethoven), 2:655
choral festivals, 3:162–63, 703
    in England, 3:173–74, 657
    Lower Rhine Music Festival, 3:156, 165,
        173
    oratorio rebirth and, 3:164
choral fugue, 2:724
Choralis Constantinus (Isaac), 1:679
choral music
    Beethoven and, 2:722–24
    bel canto opera and, 3:43, 48
    Brahms and, 3:703–16
    Counter Reformation and, 1:772–79,
        783–84
    earliest polyphonic, 1:314
    English Reformation and, 1:94
    foundations for English training, 1:94
    Handel and, 2:75, 237–38, 305, 313–40,
        314
    Männerchor and, 3:83, 84, 162–63, 202
    for multiple choirs, 1:776, 780, 782–83,
        791
    notation of, 3:162
    oratorio rebirth and, 3:164–66
    orchestration and, 1:782–84
    Romantic nationalism and, 3:162–63
    Schubert and, 3:83, 84
    sight-singing and, 1:617
    as Verdi's operatic set-pieces, 3:570–75
    voice parts for, 1:468
    See also choirs; oratorio
choral recitative
    Glinka and, 3:242
    Meyerbeer and, 3:242
Choralsätze. See chorale
choral societies, 3:703
    Romantic nationalism and, 3:162–63
Choralvorspiel (chorale prelude), 1:762;
    2:255, 255–58, 378, 382
"Chord of Prometheus," 4:215
"chord of the pleroma," Scriabin and, 4:216
chord roots, 1:813
chordal harmony
    Aaron on, 1:577
    basso continuo and, 1:781, 798
    Byrd and, 1:686
    English, 1:392, 407, 672
Chorus of Polovtsian Maidens (Borodin),
    3:401, 402
Chou-En-lai, *Nixon in China* and, 5:517–18,
    519
Chrétien de Troyes, 1:119

Christ Church (Canterbury), 1:461
Christe
    Busnoy *Missa L'Homme Armé*, 1:492–93
    Machaut Mass, 1:325, 530–34
    Palestrina *Missa Repleatur os meum laude*,
        1:639–40, 641
Christe eleison, 1:58, 103
Christe fili Dei (Josquin), 1:531–34
Christgau, Robert, 5:333
    Esquire, 5:333
    Village Voice, 5:333
Christian art, 2:112
    Bach's St. John Passion as, 2:377–81,
        389–90
    Handel's *Messiah* as, 2:325–26
    Romantic esthetic linked with, 2:649
Christianity
    "Credo I," 1:34–35
    Darwinism and, 3:480
    earliest surviving service music artifact,
        1:32, 33, 34
    early worship eclecticism, 1:12
    Jewish converts to, 3:166–67, 174, 177
    map of early monastic centers, 1:9
    Marxism and, 3:480
    music/Musica differentiation and, 1:71
    as oratorio theme source, 3:164
    psalmody of, 1:8–10
    in Russia, 3:234
    sybilline prophecy and, 1:719
    Wagner on, 3:488
    Western-Eastern schism in, 1:141
    Western musical unification and,
        1:61–64
    See also Eastern Orthodox Church;
        liturgical music; Protestantism;
        Roman Catholic Church; *specific*
        denominations
Christian IV, King of Denmark, 2:66
Christian Ludwig, Margrave of
    Brandenburg, 2:289
Christina, Queen of Sweden, 2:75, 142, 150,
    177
Christine de Pisane, 1:446–47, 448, 452
Christine of Lorraine, 1:803, 803
Christ ist erstanden (Leise), 1:758, 759
Christ lag in Todesbanden (J. S. Bach), 2:50,
    343–47
Christ lag in Todesbanden (hymn), 1:758, 759,
    760
Christ lag in Todesbanden (Osiander),
    1:766–67
Christ lag in Todesbanden (Praetorius),
    1:767–68; 2:55
Christ lag in Todesbanden (Scheidt), 2:50–52
Christ lag in Todesbanden (Schein), 2:52–54
Christ lag in Todesbanden (Walther),
    1:761–62
Christmas, 1:94
    Alleluia, 1:267, 269–71
    conductus, 1:199–201
    English carol, 1:420

Gloria in excelsis, 1:54
Gradual, 1:27, 173, 177, 177–78, 177, 178
    Handel's *Messiah* and, 2:325
    liturgical cycle, 1:12
    motet, 1:772–75
    neumes triplex, 1:37
    Palestrina motet-plus-Mass sets for,
        1:642, 643–44
    Palestrina Offertory, 1:663–66
    Schütz oratorio, 2:73
    trope, 1:52
    verse plays, 1:93
Christmas carol, 1:420
"Christmas Concerto" (Corelli), 2:189–92,
    499
Christmas Eve suite (Rimsky-Korsakov),
    4:121
Christus resurgens (processional), 1:155
chromatic descent. *See passus duriusculus*
Chromatic Fantasia and Fugue in D minor
    (J. S. Bach), 2:414
chromatic genus, 1:32–33
"chromatic tetrachord," Aristoxenus and,
    4:449
chromaticism, 1:273–76; 4:164, 312, 313
    adjustments of, 1:273–75
    aural conditioning and, 1:739
    Bach (C. P. E.) and, 2:385, 414
    Bach (J. S.) and, 2:254, 266, 267, 364, 385
    Bach (W. F.) and, 2:407, 414
    as both expressive and musical force,
        1:751
    Chopin and, 3:355–56
    Clemens and, 1:596, 597
    Du Fay and, 1:512
    early Greek origin of, 1:32–33
    Frescobaldi and, 2:43, 44
    Handel and, 2:317–18, 364
    Lasso and, 1:720, 721, 773
    Liszt and, 3:270, 280, 283–84, 428–38
    liturgical text and, 1:773
    Machaut motet and, 1:273
    madrigalistic, 1:724–25, 729–30, 732,
        734, 738, 739, 751, 773, 785
    monodic madrigal and, 1:819, 821
    Mozart and, 2:591, 624–25, 627, 631, 633
    musical color and, 3:203
    Paganini and, 3:255–56
    Palestrina and, 1:686
    Purcell and, 2:128, 135
    semitones and, 1:729–30
    singer adjustment to, 1:274
    Solage *ars subtilior* and, 1:343–44
    Sweelinck and, 2:46
    Wagner and, 1:738, 739
chronaca, theory of, 1:253
Chronicles of My Life (Stravinsky)
    (autobiography), 4:469
Chronological Thematic Catalogue (Köchel),
    2:463
Chrysander, Friedrich, 3:703, 722, 726
Chrysothemis, *Elektra* and, 4:51–54

Chrysostom, John, Saint, 1:10
church and state, 1:517, 670–75
church calendar, 1:12, 37–39, 177, 314
    Marian antiphons and, 1:96
    Parisan-style music books and, 1:171, 172
Church Fathers, 1:24, 69, 106
church music. *See* liturgical music
Church of England. *See* Anglican Church
Church of the Blessed Virgin (Lorento),
    1:578
church plays. *See* liturgical drama
church sonata, 2:177–84, 187–92, 208
    chamber sonata compared with,
        2:178–81
    end of chamber distinction with, 2:204
Churchill, Winston, 4:747; 5:6
    Requiem for a Young Poet and, 5:420
Church Windows (Respighi), 4:750
Chute de la maison Usher, La (Debussy), 4:86
chuvstvennost', 3:239
ciaccona, 2:30, 37, 38, 39, 193
    See also chaconne
Cicéri, Pierre, 3:207, 215, 217
Cicero, Marcus Tullius, 1:70, 459, 462, 550,
    554
    Academy and, 1:798
Ciconia, Johannes, 1:277–81, 282, 284–85,
    348, 424
Cimarosa, Domenico, 2:158, 646
    Matrimonio segreto, Il, 3:34
    as Rossini antecedent, 3:16
    in Russia, 3:235
Cimento dell'armonia e dell'inventione, Il
    (Vivaldi), 2:225
Cincinnati Symphony Orchestra, 4:666,
    670
Cinq pieces dans le style ancien (Castillon),
    4:65
Cinq poèmes de Baudelaire (Debussy), 4:86
Cipriano de Rore, 2:5
Circé, ou le Balet comique de la Royne, 4:131
circles of fifths, 1:30, 505, 666, 732;
    2:184–89, 212, 213, 216, 220;
    3:99–101, 697; 4:319
    Corelli and, 2:184, 188, 202
    diagram of, 2:185
    Schubert's use of, 3:99–101, 697
circumflex, 1:14
Circumspice, Jerusalem (Byrd), 1:679
Cirillo Franco, Bernardino, 1:646–47, 649
Cirque Napoléon (Paris), 3:678
civic ceremonial music, Berlioz and,
    3:319–20
Civil Rights Act, 5:307
civil servants, composers as, 2:53
Civil War (American), 4:659, 671
Civil War, English. *See* English Civil War
Clair René, *Entr'acte*, 4:572
Claparède, Count, 3:209
Clapping Music (Reich), 5:374–75, 385, 386
claque, Liszt and, 3:272
Clarence, Duke of, 1:409, 461

clarinet, **2:**505

Clarino Concerto in E-flat major (Haydn), **2:**600

class. *See* social class; *specific classes*

classical literature, **1:**356, 717, 719–22

See also permanent canon, and standard repertory

"classical" minimalism, **5:**368–72

classical music

Baroque label and, **1:**797

Beethoven as standard-bearer of, **2:**650, 692, 693, 738

birth of concept of, **2:**639

conservatories and, **3:**286, 287

German hegemony in, **3:**348

German universalizing and, **2:**738–39

Handel's *Messiah* as first work of, **2:**326

Hanslick and, **3:**442

improvisation skills excluded from, **2:**650–51

Italian terminology and, **2:**158

lonely artist-hero image and, **2:**649

modern listening to, **1:**610

Mozart as foundation of, **2:**464

music appreciation and, **2:**540, 738; **3:**442, 782–83, 785, 786

nineteenth-century symphonic music and, **3:**679–83, 686, 728

permanent canon and, **2:**34

political factionalism and, **3:**416

political freight of, **2:**111–12

"Preclassic" period and, **2:**401–2

as primarily literate, **1:**779

as Romantic creation, **2:**649–50

sacralization of, **2:**649–50, 651

trascendence and, **2:**706, 714, 720, 721

Classical period, **3:**286, 287

Beethoven and, **2:**739

delineation with Romantic period, **2:**646

as misnomer, **2:**647

Mozart and, **2:**16, 646–47, 739

classical repertory. *See* standard repertory

"Classical Symphony" (Prokofieff), **4:**496.

See also symphony

classicism

aim of, **1:**632

Der Rosenkavalier and, **4:**49

Enlightenment thought and, **2:**363

first writer of, **2:**739

Florentine academies and, **1:**799

genius concept and, **1:**552

German claims to, **2:**738, 739

Glareanus's modal theory and, **1:**554

Gluck and, **2:**453–54

Greek drama and, **1:**780, 799, 822–23

Haydn and, **2:**542, 646

hedonistic virtues of, **2:**649

high art definition and, **1:**459, 462

humanism and, **1:**615, 717, 730, 753, 780

Lasso text settings and, **1:**717, 719–22

Mozart and, **2:**646

musical expression and, **2:**642–43

musical historiography and, **1:**383–84

musical rhetoric and, **1:**550

music appreciation textbook on, **2:**738, 739

neoclassical revival and, **1:**797–834

neoclassicism vs., **2:**151–52

Plato's Academy and, **1:**798

post-Napoleonic nostalgia for, **2:**647

Renaissance and, **1:**382–83, 384, 586, 797

Romantic art vs. art of, **2:**649

romantic canonizations and, **3:**45

Romantic dichotomy with, **2:**642–43, 646–48, 649, 739

Schumann (Robert) and, **3:**316, 318

Viennese, **2:**542

Willaert and, **1:**604–7

See also ancient world; *ars perfecta*; Greek (Hellenistic) music theory; Greek drama; Greek mythology

"Classisch und Romantisch" (Gelbcke), **2:**646–47

Claudel, Paul, **4:**582

Claudin de Sermisy, **1:**692, 706–7, 714

Tant que vivray, **1:**706–7, 708, 709, 711, 712

clausula, **1:**180, 181–84, 296

Ex semine, **1:**.210, .211, .220, 196, 209–11, 212, 217

motet in relationship with, **1:**210, 214, 217, 219, 221, 228, 236, 259

prosulated, **1:**209

"substitute"/"ersatz," **1:**183–84

clavecinistes, **3:**119

claves, **1:**99–100, 101

clavichord, **2:**413

Clavier-Übung (J. S. Bach), **2:**262, 263, 281, 383

clefs, **1:**99–100, 312–13

Ockeghem Mass notation without, **1:**479–80

Clemens, Jacobus (Jacob Clement), **1:**593–99, 601, 602, 678, 754–55

In te, Domine, speravi, **1:**598–99

Qui consolabatur me recessit a me, **1:**594–97, 599

Souterliedekens, **1:**597–99, 754

Clemens non Papa, **1:**709; **2:**5

Musica dei donum, **1:**710

Clement V, Pope, **1:**310

Clement VII, Pope, **1:**630

Clement VIII, Pope, **1:**631, 670, 826

Clementi, Muzio, **3:**73–74, 351; **5:**326

Clemenza di Tito, La (Caldara), **2:**481

Clemenza di Tito, La (Mozart), **2:**481–82

clergy

cathedral, **1:**169, 207–8

papal schism and, **1:**277

Protestant Reformation and, **1:**753

Clocks and Clouds (Ligeti), **5:**438

closeness, rule of, **1:**276–77

closure, **3:**152, 528

Cluniac reform, **1:**50

Cluny monastery, **1:**50

Clytemnestra (mythology), **4:**48–49

C major

Ars Nova and, **1:**261, 262

Beethoven's Piano Sonata, no. 32, op. III first movement in, **2:**721, 732, 734

chord of six based on, **1:**588

C-minor trajectory to, **2:**694, 701, 702, 705, 717, 721

"grand military" affect and, **2:**718

as "purest" of keys, **2:**241

Schubert and, **3:**94–96

C-minor Fantasy, K. 475 (Mozart), **3:**314, 356

C-minor moods, **2:**691–735

Bach (C. P. E.) and, **2:**414–16, 417, 624

Beethoven's association with, **2:**653, 685, 691–735

Donizetti's *Lucia di Lammermoor* and, **3:**54

Haydn and, **2:**634–37, 638, 653, 692, 695, 696, 701, 721

Lawes and, **2:**120–21

Mozart and, **2:**625–31, 634, 637, 692; **3:**273–74

sign clusters associated with, **2:**727

Stamitz and, **2:**718

symbolic trajectory to C major, **2:**634–37, 693, 701, 702, 705, 717, 721

as tragic key, **2:**121, 696, 697, 701, 702, 705

Cocardes (Poulenc), **4:**575, 576, 577

Cock, Simon, **1:**597, 598

Coclico, Adrian Petit, **1:**552–53

Cocteau, Jean, **3:**504; **4:**562, 563, 566, 569, 587, 588, 589, 676

Ballets Russes and, **4:**561

Le train bleu and, **4:**569

Les mariés de la Tour Eiffel, **4:**589

coda, **1:**200; **2:**202

signification of, **2:**279

See also stretta

code-name, **1:**353

Code Napoléon, **3:**15

Code Rossini, **3:**14–22, 27, 239, 568

codetta

function of, **3:**95

Rossini overture and, **3:**18

Schubert "Great" C-major Symphony and, **3:**94–96

codex, definition of

Codex Calixtinus, **1:**162–68, *165*

Codex Rupertsberg (Hildegard), **1:**91

Coe, Richard, Philip Glass Ensemble and, **5:**392

"Coffee cantata" (J. S. Bach), **2:**374

"Cognitive Constraints on Compositional Systems" (Lerdahl) **5:**451–52

cognitive processes, **2:**208

cognitive symbolism, **3:**528, 531, 540

Cohan, George M., 4:257
Cohen, Samuel, 3:456
cold war, 2:739; 4:651, 5:6–18, 103–73, 460
  Central Committee of the Soviet
    Communist Party, 5:9
  "containment," 5:7
  "Cuban missile crisis," 5:8
  Cultural and Scientific Conference for
    World Peace, 5:106
  fall of Berlin Wall and, 5:437
  "formalism," 5:9
  "fraternal republics," 5:11
  "Great Patriotic War of 1941–1945," 5:8
  "mutual assured destruction" (MAD),
    5:8
  North Atlantic Treaty Organization
    (NATO), 5:7, 8
  Red Channels: The Reports of Communist
    Influence in Radio and Television,
    5:106
  Soviet atomic bomb explosion, 5:7
  "Soviet bloc," 5:7
  Stunde Null, 5:18
  Zhdanovshchina, 5:11
Colebault, Jacques. See Jacquet of Mantua
Coleridge, Samuel Taylor, 4:244, 495
Colette, L'enfant et les sortileges, 4:605
Colista, Lelio, 2:198
collage techniques, 5:415, 417–22
  Rochberg and, 5:415
  secret structure and, 5:415
  Zimmermann and, 5:418–21
Collect, in Mass ordo, 1:61(table)
collection. See Offertory
collective consciousness, 3:62
collective spirit, 3:122
collective works of art, 3:306
College of St. Edmund (Old Hall), 1:409
collegiate church, 1:170
Collegio Germanico (Rome), 2:73
Collegium Musicum (Leipzig), 2:286, 300,
    301, 340, 374
Collet, Henri, 4:588
Collin, Heinrich Josef von, 2:702
"Collines D'Anacapri, Les" (Debussy), 4:78
Collins, Judy, 5:315
Collins, Michael, 3:45
"Colloquy on Ballet" (Benois) (article),
    4:150
Cologne, 3:165
Colonne, Edouard, 3:678
color, coloration, 1:232, 262, 265–66, 269,
    337, 340; 3:203
  Berlioz's sense of, 3:323
  contratenor and, 1:270–71
    Dunstable motet and, 1:424–25, 427
    Machaut DAVID melisma and,
      1:291–92
    Power Mass and, 1:463
    Verdi's tinta and, 3:568–71, 573, 581, 592,
      604
"color chords," 4:33

Erwartung and, 4:303, 304
  harmonic porogression and, 4:310
coloratura
  bel canto tenors and, 3:578
  in Donizetti's Lucia di Lammermoor, 3:55
  lied lack of, 3:142
  Meyerbeer's use of, 3:222
  parody of, 3:655
  rage aria and, 2:311, 481
colorito. See tinta
Columba aspexit (Hildegard), 1:91–92
Columbia-Princeton Electronic Music
    Center, 5:208, 211, 478
Columbia University, 2:478; 3:768; 5:164,
    310
  computer music-synthesis program,
    5:497
Columbo, Russ, 1:817
Columbus, Ferdinand, 1:693
Combattimento di Tancredi e Clorinda
    (Monteverdi), 2:7–9, 110
combinatoria, 1:148
"combinatorial row forms," 4:705
"combinatoriality," Babbitt and, 5:424
Come Out (Reich), 5:369–70, 374
comédie larmoyante, 2:447, 450, 452
comedies-ballets, 2:127
comédies mêlées d'ariettes, 3:187, 188, 235
comedy
  naturalness and, 2:437
  opera and, 3:611–15, 617, 640, 658
  realism and, 3:631
Comedy Overture on Negro Themes (Gilbert),
    4:613
"Come, friends who plow the sea" (Gilbert
    and Sullivan), 3:653
"Come, Redeemer of the Heathen"
    (J. S. Bach), 2:342–43
comic baritone, operetta and, 3:655
comic opera, 3:611–15, 617, 640, 658
  Adam de la Halle and, 1:127
  class aspirations and, 2:17, 446–52
  complex ensemble finales in, 2:451; 3:12,
    23
  conventions of, 3:216
  dance and, 3:35
  earliest form of. See opera buffa
  earliest in standard repertory, 2:438
  eighteenth-century subtexts of,
    2:442–43, 445–52
  ensemble finales in, 3:22–27, 35, 48, 49,
    210
  folk songs and, 3:187, 448
  imbroglio element of, 2:451, 486, 490,
    492, 620
  intermezzos and, 2:434–37
  ironic contrast and, 2:439
  musical significance of, 2:434
  origins of, 3:187, 643–44
  Rossini first-act prototype of, 3:15
  in Russia, 3:235
  Smetana and, 3:462–63

spoken dialogue and, 1:827; 3:341
  Verdi and, 3:611
  See also opera buffa; singspiel
Comintern, 4:651, 657
commedia dell'arte, 2:439; 4:160, 457, 498
"Commenti al Rock" (Berio), 5:328
commercialism. See free market; mercantile
    economy
commercial music. See concerts; music
    publishing
commercial opera
  birth in Venice, 2:12, 16–33
  continual revisions of, 2:33, 33–34
  court opera and, 2:33–34, 87–88
  crowd-pleasing devices of, 2:17–18
  first Italian performance in Paris, 2:110
  intermezzo and, 2:436–39
  ongoing conventions of, 2:16
  political subtexts of, 2:110
  recitative/aria relationship and, 2:25
  Rossini's career and, 3:8–12
  women singers and, 2:80
  See also opera
Committee for a Sane Nuclear Policy,
    5:309
commixed mode (commixtus), definition of,
    1:83
common law, English, 2:124
commonplace book, 1:553
"Common Sense" (Paine), 2:460, 461
Common Sense Composers Collective,
    5:400
Commonwealth period (Britain), 2:124, 125
"Communication to My Friends"
    (Wagner), 3:493, 496, 498–501,
    504
Communion, 1:686
  antiphon, 1:433–35
  in Mass ordo, 1:61(table)
  See also Eucharist
Communist esthetic theory, 4:656
Communist Manifesto, The (Marx-Engels),
    4:745; 5:89, 93
Communist parties, 4:657–58
Communist Party, 4:671
Communist regimes, fall of, 5:508
community
  chorales and fostering of, 3:165, 169
  Herder's view of, 3:190–91
  Wagner and, 3:488, 490, 504–5
Como, Perry, 1:817
compact discs, 2:9
Comparaison de la musique italienne et de l
    musique française (Lecerf), 2:85–86
Compendium musices (Coclico), 1:552–53
Compère, Loyset, 1:459, 523–26, 535
  Ave Maria, 1:523–26, 583
competitions. See song competitions
"complexe sonore," 4:221, 224
Compline, 1:12, 94, 407, 677
Componimenti musicali (Muffat), 2:327, 329
  preeminence of, 2:737

"Composer as Specialist, The" (Babbitt), 5:157
"Composer in the Machine Age, The" (Gershwin) (essay), 4:628
composers, 1:64–67
  academic style and, 1:608–11
  ars subtilior and, 1:342–49
  Beethoven as ethical yardstick for, 3:10
  "borrowings" by, 2:327–31
  "borrowings" from self by, 2:331–40
  canonization (musical) of, 2:3, 399, 400, 401, 691, 738
  career periodization of, 1:381
  centonized chants and, 1:28
  as civil servants, 2:53
  concept of music's permanent value and, 2:639
  conservatories and education of, 3:286, 617
  as conservatory professors, 2:736
  creator ideal of, 2:655
  cyclic Masses and, 1:472–500
  earliest with unbroken performance record, 1:667
  elevation of, 2:655
  employer's needs and, 2:527–28
  emulation by, 1:474–75, 484, 486, 493, 497–98, 499
  as entrepreneurs, 2:283, 465
  first biographical work on, 2:388
  first concerted specifications by, 1:782
  first orchestration by, 1:782
  fourteenth-century technical competition for, 1:337–42
  freelance status of, 3:81
  free market and, 2:571
  Hegelian view of, 3:414
  imitation vs. emulation and, 1:474–75
  improvisation and, 2:610–11, 650
  intuition and, 2:720
  mode as guide to, 1:80–86
  music criticism by, 2:737; 3:290–94, 332–35, 336, 340–41, 343, 346, 583
  New German School view of, 3:421
  New Russian School view of, 3:393, 395–97, 468, 474, 617
  as nineteenth-century culture heroes, 2:655, 736
  nineteenth-century introspection of, 2:737
  "norms" and breaching of by, 2:532–33
  opera production process and, 3:9–10
  patrons of. *See* patronage
  performance separated from, 1:65, 299; 2:639, 642, 655
  as performers, 2:519, 600, 607, 610–14, 653
  polyphony and, 1:148–68, 301
  Romantic elevation of, 2:173, 655, 689
  royalist loyalties of, 2:124
  sensibility and, 2:409–18, 737

  seventeenth- and eighteenth-century status of, 2:173
  specialization by, 3:315, 656–57
  stylistic changes and, 1:245, 247–48
  subtilitas (subtlety) and, 1:327–42
  symbiosis with discerning patrons of, 2:527–28, 553, 555
  of troubadour songs, 1:110
  women's underrepresentation as, 2:78–81
  writing on "spec" by, 2:590, 601
  written music and, 1:104, 456
  See also artistic creation; *specific names*
Composers Collective of New York, 4:651–52, 656, 658, 659
  Workers, Songbook and, 4:651, 655
"Composers Forum" concerts (Columbia University), 5:192, 198
composite, 1:151
Composition for Four Instruments (Babbitt), 5:143–48, 153
Composition for Twelve Instruments (Babbitt), 5:148–53, 168
Composition with Arrays (essay, Winham), 5:159–60
Compositions 1960 (Young), 5:92, 355, 359
compositore scritturato, 3:568
Compostela manuscript, 1:162, 171
computer-assisted music, 5:495–96
"computer music," 5:495
Comte, Auguste, 3:287
"concatenationism," 5:511, 512
concert. *See* concerts
concertato. See concerto
concert booking agencies, 3:272
Concert de bruits (Schaeffer), 5:188
Concert de la Loge Olympique, Le (Paris), 2:557
concerted music, 1:780–96
  intermedii, 1:803, 804
  liturgical, 1:788–90, 794–95
  madrigal, 1:817
Concerted Piece for Tape Recorder and Orchestra (Ussachevsky), 5:198
"Concert Suite from *Dromenon*" (Maxfield), 5:92
concert halls
  audience etiquette instructions in, 2:651
  as museums, 2:639, 650, 651
  nineteenth-century construction of, 2:736
  nineteenth-century growth of, 3:677–79
  oratorio performances in, 2:325, 385
  See also concerts; opera houses; *specific names*
Concerti ecclesiastici a otto voci (Banchieri), 1:780
concerti futuristici, Russolo and, 5:179
Concerti Grossi, op. 6 (Handel), 2:204–8
concertmaster, 2:291; 3:173
concerto
  Bach (C. P. E.) and, 2:606, 622

Bach (J. C.) keyboard works, 2:606
Bach (J. S.) Brandenburg, 2:289–301
Bach (J. S.) keyboard arrangements, 2:282, 285
as Bach (J. S.) term for cantata, 2:341
Beethoven and, 2:652, 655
cadenza and, 2:298–300
Chopin and, 3:348
chorale and, 2:49–55
composer-performers of, 2:607, 609
double exposition technique and, 2:606–7
earliest solo keyboard work, 2:290
Gabrielis and, 1:780–86
genre transformation, 3:273–85
Haydn's limited output of, 2:600–601
improvisations and, 2:650
in Italian style, 2:177–231
Liszt and, 3:277–85, 287
Marcello and, 2:192
melodic elaboration and, 2:212
Mozart's transformation of, 2:606–25
opera seria kinship with, 2:222, 231, 308
original meaning of, 1:780–81; 2:497, 498
Paganini and, 3:252, 255, 256–57
as social paradigm, 2:221, 619–22
solos and, 2:193, 216, 220, 301–2
symphonic, 2:498
three-movement, 2:193, 216, 609
Vivaldi and, 2:193, 216–31, 609
See also piano concerto; violin concerto
Concerto (Monteverdi). *See* Seventh Book of Madrigals
Concerto a cinque in D minor, (A. Marcello), 2:192
concerto da camera. See chamber sonata
concerto delle donne (consort of women singers), 2:5, 80
Concert of Antient Music (London), 3:680
Concerto, op. 24 (Webern), 5:143, 153
Concerto for Bassoon in C major, F VIII/13 (Vivaldi), 2:217–24
Concerto for Four Violins in B minor, op. 3, no. 10 (Vivaldi), 2:222–26
  Bach (J. S.) keyboard arrangement of, 2:282, 287
Concerto for Orchestra (Bartók), 5:19, 229
Concerto for Piano and Strings (Schnittke), 5:467–70
Concerto for Piano and Winds (Copland), 4:621, 622–23
Concerto for Piano and Winds (Stravinsky), 4:491, 555
Concerto for Two Harpsichords in C major, BWV 1061 (Bach), 2:266–67
Concerto gregoriano (Respighi), 4:750
concerto grosso, 2:177–78; 3:277
  Corelli and, 2:177–84, 187–92, 193
  Handel and, 2:192, 204–8, 305, 327, 392

Concerto Grosso No. 1 (Schnittke),
  5:465–66
Concerto Grosso, op. 6, no. 7 (Handel),
  2:204–8, 392
Concerto Grosso, op. 6, no. 8 (Corelli),
  2:189–92, 499
Concerto in modo misolidio (Respighi), 4:750
Concerto nach italiänischem Gusto (J. S. Bach),
  2:281–82, 285, 287
concert oratorio movement,
  nineteenth-century, 2:385
concerto symphonique, 3:277
concert overtures
  Chaikovsky and, 3:406–9, 663
  Mendelssohn and, 3:183, 419
concerts
  Bach-Abel London series, 2:419
  Beethoven's successful tours of, 2:653
  behavior at, 2:651
  composer's "ex tempore" improvisations
    at, 2:611
  cyclic Mass Ordinary performances in,
    1:496
  early music and, 2:233
  as free market, 2:571, 639
  Gregorian chant revivals at, 1:66
  Handel oratorio performances at, 2:385
  London subscription, 2:419, 555, 556,
    571, 577, 639
  modern repertory foundation for, 2:738
  Mozart's subscription, 2:607
  nineteenth-century development of,
    2:385
  original meaning of, 2:498
  origin and development of, 2:498–507
  professional reviewers and, 2:571
  subscription symphony genre and,
    2:556, 557, 558
  symphonic development and, 2:498, 573
  typical eighteenth-century Viennese
    program, 2:499–500, 509
  Venetian cathedral services as earliest,
    1:789
  Vienna chamber music, 2:683
  See also audience; concert halls; standard
    repertory
Concert sans orchestre (Schumann), 3:309
Concerts Colonne, 3:678
Concerts Lamoureux, 3:678
Concert Spirituel (Paris), 2:226, 227,
    498–99, 505, 556; 3:277
  Mozart attendance at, 2:603
Concerts Populaires de Musique Classique
    (Concerts Pasdeloup), 3:678
concert symphony. See symphony
concitato style, 2:291
Concord, Massachusetts,
    Transcendentalism and, 4:244
Concord, Mass., 1840–60 (Ives piano
    sonata), 4:262, 265, 266, 270, 351;
    5:268, 269
conductor

absolutism of, 2:111–12, 291
baton use by, 3:222
Beethoven as, 3:222
Berlioz as, 3:323
first virtuoso baton, 2:677
interpretations of music by, 2:705
Mendelssohn as, 3:166, 172, 173, 317
Nikisch as, 3:747
oral transmission by, 1:18
Toscanini as, 3:572
von Bülow as, 3:222, 418, 729
Wagner as, 3:481, 483
conductus, 1:131, 162, 165, 166–67, 233, 296
  British, 1:387, 397–99, 403, 404–5, 406
  characteristics of, 1:198–99, 311, 314
  end of, 1:214
  motet and, 1:209–11, 219
  Notre Dame school and, 1:173–74,
    198–205
  versus and, 1:94, 95, 111
Condulmer, Gabriele Cardinal. See Eugene
    IV, Pope
Cone, Edward T., 3:323; 5:161–63
  "One Hundred Metronomes" (essay),
    5:162
Confession d'un enfant du siècle, La (Musset),
    3:76
Confessions (Augustine), 1:66
Confessions (Rousseau), 2:443, 641; 3:62
Confessions of an English Opium-Eater (De
    Quincey), 3:322
Confidence Man, The (Rochberg), 5:436
Confrérie des Jongleurs et des Bourgeois
    d'Arras, 1:120, 139, 142
Congaudeant catholici (Albertus), 1:165–67,
    166, 172
Congregational Church, 1:27, 28
congregational singing, 1:27–28, 47, 58,
    758, 765
Congress for Cultural Freedom, 5:21, 293,
    295, 304
  Nicolas Nabokov and, 5:21
Congress of Vienna (1815), 2:673, 673–74,
    722, 724; 3:212, 569
  masked ball celebration, 2:722
conjunct tetrachords, 1:151–52
Connotations (Copland), 5:115
Conon de Béthune, 1:120
Conrad, Tony, 5:362
  Theatre of Eternal Music, 5:362
Conradi, August, 3:419
Conrad II, Holy Roman Emperor, 1:86
Consecration of the House Overture, op. 124
    (Beethoven), 2:726
conservatism, 2:115, 235, 302, 724
  avant-garde vs., 3:285–86
  progressivism vs., 3:179
  conservatories, 2:650, 736
  in Naples, 2:140
  in Russia, 3:468, 617, 786
  spread of, 3:286–88
consonance, 1:153, 297–98, 397, 587; 2:497

cadence and, 1:468–69, 470, 587
culture-bound criteria of, 1:153
English harmony and, 1:407, 417, 423
Garlandia's tripartite division of, 1:196,
    394
harmonic balancing of, 1:153, 407
imperfect. See dissonance
normative polyphonic, 1:187–89
parallel-imperfect, 1:406–9
Pythagorean classification of, 1:29–31,
    70, 456, 495, 587
triads and, 1:168, 587
consonance and dissonance, 4:309–10, 312,
    340, 358
  Harmonielehre and, 4:309
consort music, 2:114–25
  ayres and suites, 2:120–22
  fantasy, 2:115–18, 120, 196–98
consort of viols, 1:741, 742
Constantine XI, Byzantine Emperor, 1:484
Constantinople, 1:484
Constitution (U.S.), 2:111, 461–62
Constitution Hall (Washington, D.C.),
    3:771
Constructions in Metal (Cage), 5:57, 58
"Constructions of Subjectivity in
    Schubert's Music" (McClary),
    3:117
contenance angloise, 1:422–52
  continental assimilation of, 1:441–52
  features and impact of, 1:423, 433, 452
  harmonizing and, 1:34–35
  significance of, 1:429, 461
  Tinctoris on, 1:514
  translation of term, 1:422
"content-determined form," 4:639
Contes d'Hoffmann, Les (Offenbach), 3:657
contests. See song competitions
Continental Congress (U.S.), 3:764
continental music. See international style
continuo, 1:780–82, 783, 784, 795, 798
  cantata and, 2:146
  earliest printed, 1:809, 811
  early keyboard sonatas and, 2:427–28
  early symphony and, 2:510
  end of popularity of, 2:428
  Gluck's elimination of, 2:457
  improvisation of, 2:291
  monodic madrigal and, 1:813–18, 821
  Monteverdi and, 2:3, 9
  opera's development and, 2:457
  original composition pf, 1:804, 808–9
  Peri's Euridice and, 1:829–31
  Schein and, 2:53
  tragédie lyrique and, 2:106
  See also Alberti bass
continuo songs (musiche), 1:813–18, 823–26
continuous finale, 3:210, 599
contrafactum, 1:48, 90
  definition of, 1:598
  Easter dialogue trope and, 1:52
  English round and, 1:392

contrafactum (continued)
   laude and, 1:133
   Lutheran chorales and, 1:759, 760
   Minnelieder and, 1:134, 143
   motet and, 1:217–21, 227–28
   vernacular psalm settings and, 1:598
contralto, 1:468; 3:36
contrapuntal style. See counterpoint
contrast-and-balance technique
   Bach sons and, 2:420, 429, 433, 437
   opera buffa and, 2:439
Contrastes (Davidovsky), 5:211
contratenor (fourth voice), 1:270–73,
     298–99, 301, 349, 374
   Binchois use of, 1:448
   caccia with, 1:378, 380
   Caput Mass and, 1:466, 468, 477
   defining characteristic of, 1:301
   Du Fay use of, 1:441–43, 446–47
   Josquin and, 1:529–31
   Machaut composition and, 1:325, 328,
     328
   Ockeghem's Ma bouche rit and, 1:529–30
contratenor bassus. See alto; bass
contredanse, 2:490; 3:35, 48
contretenor altus. See contralto
conventions, 1:359, 363–64
   opera, 3:4, 35–36, 45, 55, 216
   rejection of in music, 4:306
   Schubert's use of, 3:109
   stereotypes vs., 3:49
"conversation galante et amusante," 2:428
Converse, Frederick Shepherd, 3:769
Cooke, Deryck, 3:747
Coomaraswamy, Ananda, 5:68
Cooper, John (Coprario), 2:113
Cooper, Martin, 3:676
Copernican revolution, 1:577, 578
Copland, Aaron, 1:236; 4:102, 447, 448,
     449, 451, 456, 478, 614, 627, 629,
     632, 636, 638, 648, 651, 658,
     660–73; 5:3–6, 12, 16, 21, 104–16,
     120, 124, 172, 228, 268, 276, 431
   abandonment of jazz, 4:622–23
   American Legion target, 5:109
   Clifford Odets and, 5:10
   death of, 4:666
   "Effect of the Cold War on the Artist in
     the U.S., The" (speech), 5:108
   ethnic/racial origins, 4:621
   Harvard University, 5:116
   "Tradition and Innovation in Recent
     European Music" (lecture), 5:116
   homosexuality and, 5:248–49
   Leonard Bernstein and, 5:116
   Library of Congress archive, 4:662
   musical Americanism and, 4:662
   National Council of American-Soviet
     Friendship, 5:106
   Permanent Subcommittee on
     Investigations, 5:107–8
   "prairie" idiom and, 4:663, 668

rivalry with Roy Harris, 5:3
serialism and, 5:414
on women's lack of musical creativity,
     2:78, 79, 81
works of
   Appalachian Spring, 4:666
   Billy the Kid, 4:662, 663, 671, 672;
     5:268
   Burlesque, 4:617, 619
   Concerto for Piano and Winds,
     4:621, 622–3
   Connotations, 5:115
   "Dogmatic," 4:654
   Fanfare for the Common Man, 4:666,
     667; 5:3, 328
   "Git Along, Little Dogies," 4:662, 666
   Hear Ye! Hear Ye!, 4:653
   "Into the Streets, May First,"
     4:654–55, 656, 658
   "Jazzy," 4:614–15, 652
   "Jingo," 4:654
   Lincoln Portrait, A, 4:668, 669–70,
     671; 5:107, 109
   "Militant," 4:654
   Music for Radio, 4:661
   Music for the Theatre, 4:615–16,
     617–19, 620, 621, 627, 629; 5:3
   "Nocturne," 4:652
   Piano Fantasy, 5:112, 114
   Piano Quartet, 5:109–13
   Piano Variations, 4:652–53, 654
   Prairie Journal, 4:661
   Radio Serenade, 4:661
   Rodeo, 4:663
   Rodeo, "Corral nocturne," 4:663,
     4:665, 666
   Saga of the Prairie, 4:661, 672
   Second Hurricane, The, 4:661
   "Song of the Prairies," 4:672
   Statements for Orchestra, 4:654
   "Street in a Frontier Town," 4:662
   Symphony for Organ and Orchestra, 4:615
   Third Symphony, 5:3–5, 8, 105, 112
   "Ukelele Serenade," 4:652
"Coplandesque" moods, 4:668
Coppélia (Delibes), 4:136, 137–38
copperplate engraving, 1:693
copula, 1:179
copyright, 1:691
Corelli, Arcangelo, 2:150, 151, 177–81, 178,
     187–92, 193, 204, 228, 237, 260,
     281, 497
   career of, 2:177
   circles of fifths and, 2:184, 188, 202
   comparison of church and chamber
     sonatas by, 2:178–81, 208
   Fux comparison with, 2:180–81
   Handel and, 2:204
   legacy of, 2:177, 181, 184
   ornamentation models of, 2:281
   Purcell compared with, 2:196, 198
   tonality and, 2:184, 188–92

works of
   Concerto Grosso, op. 6, no. 8
     ("Christmas Concerto"),
     2:189–92, 499
   "Folia, La," 2:193
   Sonata da camera in G minor, op. 4,
     no. 2, 2:179–81, 189
   Sonata da chiesa in G minor, op. 3,
     no. 11, 2:179–81, 187–89
   Sonata in D major, Op. 5, no. 1,
     2:282–85
Corelli clash, 2:69
Corelli's graces, 2:281
Coren, Daniel, 3:86
Corigliano, John
   Ghosts of Versailles, The, 5:515
   neotonality and, 5:454
   Symphony no. 1, 5:516–17
Coriolan, a Trauerspiel (Collin), 2:702
Coriolan Overture (Beethoven), 2:702–5,
     721, 729; 3:1, 4, 197, 419
Coriolanus (Shakespeare), 2:702
Coriolanus, Gnaeus Marcius, 2:702
Corneille, Pierre, 2:87, 127, 307
Cornelius, Peter, 3:418, 419
Corner, Philip, 5:93
cornetto, 1:780, 783, 786, 791
Cornish Theatre, The, 5:73
Cornysh, William, 1:612, 672, 692
   Salve Regina, 1:513–18
"Coronation" Concerto in D major, no. 26,
     K. 537 (Mozart), 2:610–11, 612
Coronation of Poppea, The (Monteverdi). See
     Incoronazione di Poppea, L'
Corps glorieux, Les (Messiaen), 4:232
Correggio, 3:264
corrente (courante), 2:37, 261
"Correspondances" (Beaudelaire), 4:84
Corrette, Michel, 2:227
Corsi, Jacopo, 1:826, 829, 833
Corsica, 2:139
Corteccia, Francesco, 1:803
Coryat, Thomas, 1:789–90, 791, 795
Cosa rara, Una (Martín y Soler), 2:493
Così fan tutte, ossia La scuola degli amanti
     (Mozart), 2:478–79; 4:569
   as emblematic of Enlightenment, 2:479
cosmic harmony, 1:70, 71, 148
   discordia concors belief and, 1:148, 226,
     229, 236, 255, 261, 286
   Du Fay motet and, 1:284
   Machaut motet and, 1:271–73
   motet as Dante's metaphor for, 1:286
   music as metaphor for, 1:255
cosmological theory, 1:577; 2:634
cosmopolitanism, 3:228, 745
Cossacks, 3:478
Cöthen, 2:239, 240, 255, 261, 281, 286, 289,
     291
Council of Constance, 1:278, 281, 310
   English musical influence and,
     1:423–24, 433

Council of Trent
    anti-Semitic excises from liturgy by, 1:88
    liturgical music reform by, 1:649–50,
        653, 655, 656, 672, 789
    Pfitzner operatic portrayal of, 1:652
counter note, 1:436, 437
counterpoint, 1:147–68; 2:165–66; 3:413
    Bach (J. S.) and, 2:235, 242, 249, 364–65,
        383, 385–88
    Beethoven and, 2:687
    Brahms and, 3:692, 693–94, 726
    chant amplification and, 1:435–39
    Chartres fragment style of, 1:155
    compositional virtuosity and, 1:339
    definition of, 1:153
    distinguishing stylistic characteristics of,
        1:153
    Dunstable techniques and, 1:427, 429,
        430
    by ear, 1:392, 406
    English madrigal, 1:747
    example variants, 1:154
    Frankish vox organalis and, 1:44
    fugal, 2:198, 201–2
    Fux analysis of, 1:669; 2:180
    Guido of Arezzo and, 1:153–54, 156
    holding part in, 1:156, 157, 159–60
    homorhythmic. See homorhythmic
        counterpoint
    invertible, 2:201–2
    Jeppesen treatise on, 1:670
    "laws of," 1:168
    melismatic voice, 1:156, 156
    Monteverdi madrigal and, 1:736
    note-against-note, 1:155, 159, 168, 171,
        199, 667. See also discant
    organum, 1:156–57, 167, 171
    parsimony principle and, 1:154
    perfect parallel, 1:151–52, 153
    stile antico and, 1:667, 669; 2:165, 180, 518
    successive composition and, 1:301
    suspension chain and, 2:188–89
    Sweelinck and, 2:45–46, 48
    syncopation and, 1:368
    texts on, 1:669, 670
    top/bottom reversal in, 1:156–62, 161
    top-down composition and, 1:297–98
    two-part discant with occursus and, 1:356
    unwritten harmonizations and, 1:434, 436
    vernacular songs and, 1:697
    virtuosos improvisation of, 1:536, 538
    See also polyphony; tonality
Counterpoint (Jeppersen), 1:670
Counter Reformation, 1:771–96; 3:528,
    529
    Baroque and, 2:35
    favola in musica and, 1:832
    Kyrie changes, 1:59
    liturgical music and, 2:2, 10, 18, 35, 43,
        69, 112
    musical sensuality and, 1:772–77, 785,
        800

Passion settings and, 1:775–79
polychoral style and, 1:776–81
Reformation outlook vs., 1:771–72
Schütz's adoption of musical techniques
    of, 2:69
toccata as epitomizing idea of, 2:44
Tridentine reforms of. See Council of
    Trent
countersinging, 1:438–39
countersubject (CS) of fugue, 2:201
countertenor, 2:130
"Country Band March" (Ives), 4:275, 276
Country Dance (Hogarth), 2:574
Couperin, François, 2:277, 391, 392; 3:703
    Bach (J. S.) gigue comparison, 2:275–81
    harpsichord pièces, 3:119
    Pièces de clavecin, 2:269, 269
    Rossignol en amour, Le, 2:277–81, 282, 428
Couperin, Louis, 2:250–52
    couples dance, 1:626
    couplet, 1:39, 43, 44
    canso repeated, 1:113, 325
    chace (canon) and, 1:332, 333
    courante (corrente), 2:37, 53
    loure contrasted with, 2:274
    in suite format, 2:260–61, 262, 263,
        267–70
court ballet, 2:11, 349
    French court opera and, 2:99, 455
    Schütz and, 2:58
courtesans, 2:17, 80
"Courtesans, Muses or Musicians?"
    (Newcomb), 2:80
courtly love poetry and song, 1:98, 106–45,
    172, 351, 439
    Bembo publication and, 1:723
    canon and, 1:331, 333
    conventions of, 1:108–9, 111
    Germany and, 1:701
    Machaut redefinement of, 1:291–307,
        333–34
    Song of Songs antiphons and, 1:429–33,
        632
    See also ballade; canso; chanson; love
        songs
court music
    ars subtilior and, 1:342–45
    in Burgundy, 1:439–40, 484–85, 535,
        536
    in Cinchois, 1:448–49
    in Cöthen, 2:261–62
    in England, 1:671, 677
    fifteenth-century, 1:424, 439, 447, 455,
        458
    in France, 2:259–60
    in Italian city-states, 1:277–81
    late-eighteenth-century diminishment
        of, 2:607
    in Mannheim, 2:505–7
    monodies and ayres as, 3:119
    public concert replacement of, 2:639
    women performers and, 1:5; 2:80

court opera
    commercial opera and, 2:17, 33–34
    financing of, 2:15
    in France, 3:206
    French centralization of, 2:88
    French conventions of, 2:96–97
    French stage machinery for, 2:88, 106,
        127
    high-style theatrical declamation and,
        2:99, 106
    Italian challenge to, 2:110
    Lully and, 2:86, 89–106, 454, 455
    Monteverdi and, 2:2, 16
    neoclassical drama and, 2:151–52, 434
    orchestral storm scenes in, 2:321
    political function of, 2:14–15, 96
    prologue to, 2:93–94, 113
    spectacles and, 2:88, 94, 106, 127
    texts of, 2:33
    third act of Atys as perfect model of,
        2:97–99
    tragèdie lyrique and, 2:88–110
Coussemaker, Charles-Edmond-Henri de,
    1:127, 173
Cousser. See Kusser, Johann Sigismund
Covent Garden (London), 2:237, 326
    Peter Grimes and, 5:225
Cowboy Songs and Other Frontier Ballads
    (Lomax), 4:659
Cowell, Henry, 4:262, 281, 297–302, 298f,
    628, 637, 656, 666, 707; 5:192
    Celtic pieces and, 4:298, 302; 5:153, 268,
        269, 276
    John Cage and, 5:55, 59, 73
    "Music of the World's People" (course
        at New School), 5:74
    futurism and, 4:299
    New Music Edition, 5:153
    New Musical Resources, 5:268
    New Music Quarterly, 4:292, 295, 656
    "tone clusters" and, 4:298
    works of
        Adventures in Harmony, 4:298
        Building of Banba, The, 4:298
        Dynamic Motion, 4:299, 4:301–2
        The Tides of Manaunaun, 4:298, 302
        Voice of Lir, 4:299
Crabbe, George, 5:228, 229, 230, 232, 240,
    243, 242, 247
    The Borough and, 5:228, 229, 231
Cradle Will Rock, The (Blitzstein),
    4:649–51, 650f
Craft of Musical Composition, The
    (Schoenberg), 5:103
Craft, Robert, 4:361; 5:117–18, 206, 246, 261
    Igor Stravinsky and, 5:117, 126, 128–29,
        134
crafts guilds. See guilds
Craindre vous vueil (Du Fay), 1:444–46, 510
Cramer, Carl Friedrich, 2:417–18
Cranmer, Thomas, Archbishop of
    Canterbury, 1:672, 675

Crawdaddy!, **5**:332
    "Aesthetics of Rock, The" (Meltzer),
        5:332
Crawford, Ruth, **4**:295
    Prelude no. 6, **4**:296–97
Creation, The (Haydn), **2**:385, 633–37, 638;
        3:3; **4**:283, 449; **5**:347
    Prologue, **2**:633–634–637, 645, 692,
        694, 701, 702
Création du monde, La (Milhaud), **4**:603,
        609–10, 630
creation myth, **1**:175
creativity. *See* artistic creation
Credo, **1**:54, 310, 311
    Bach (J. S.) Mass in B minor and, **2**:375
    Byrd setting, **1**:680, 684, 685–86
    Caput Mass and, **1**:470, 482
    French-Cypriot setting, **1**:345–49
    Gloria pairing with, **1**:311, 312, 313,
        345–49, 461
    Machaut Mass and, **1**:325
    in Mass ordo, **1**:61(table)
    Missa L'Homme Armé and, **1**:490, 495,
        497–98, 529, 530
    Nicolaus de Radom and, **1**:348
    Palestrina *Missa O magnum mysterium*
        and, **1**:646
    Palestrina *Missa Papae Marcelli* and,
        1:653, 655, 655–56, 658–60, 680,
        684–85
    votive Mass and, **1**:316, 317, 318
"Credo I," **1**:34–35
Cremona, **2**:2
Crequillon, **2**:5
crescendo
    Beethoven's *Eroica*, **2**:669–70
    Rossini, **2**:669–70; **3**:18, 20, 21, 22
Crete, **2**:139
Crétin, Guillaume, **1**:455, *455*
Crimean War, **3**:476, 622
Critica musica (journal), **3**:290
criticism
    Beethoven scholarship and, **2**:671,
        691–92
    by Berlioz, **3**:291, 332–35, 583
    of cantabile/cabaletta combination,
        3:45–46
    composer-critics, **2**:737; **3**:290–94,
        332–35, 336, 340–41, 343, 346, 583
    by Cui, **3**:290, 458–59, 625
    exigetical interpretation and, **2**:650, 696,
        714
    first important modern music magazine
        for, **2**:673
    free-market concert life and, **2**:571
    German "absolute music" concept in,
        2:714
    Haydn's English reviews and, **2**:571
    hidden political messages in, **2**:442
    historicist assumptions and, **3**:415
    nineteenth-century birth of modern,
        2:571, 736, 737

professional development of, **3**:289–91
    Romantic ideal and, **2**:641–43, 649
    by Schumann, **3**:291–94, 336, 340–41,
        343, 346
    by Shaw, **3**:271, 290, 658
    Stendhal's biography of Rossini as, **3**:32
    Wagner and, **3**:483
    See also music analysis
Critique of Judgement (Kant), **5**:68
Croatia, **3**:345, 447–48
Croce, Benedetto, **4**:753
Croce, Johann Nepomuk della, **2**:621
Crociato in Egitto, Il (Meyerbeer), **3**:216
Crocker, Richard, **1**:219; **5**:161, 451, 452
Cromwell (Hugo), **3**:76
Cromwell, Oliver, **2**:124, 125
crooning (singing style), **1**:817. 2.15
Crosby, Bing, **5**:312
    tape-recording and, **5**:176
"crossover projects," 515
cross relation (harmonic), **1**:686
Crouch, Stanley, **5**:335
    critique on Miles Davis, **5**:335
    New Republic, The, **5**:335
    Cruda Amarilli (Monteverdi), **1**:735–38
Crumb, George, **5**:422–26, 422, 431, 524
    eclecticism and, **5**:423
    García Lorca, Federico and, **5**:422, 423,
        442
    Sonata for solo cello, Bartók and, **5**:423
    works of
        Ancient Voices of Children, **5**:422, 423,
            424, 426
        Black Angels, **5**:424
        Night Music, **5**:422
        Night of Four Moons, **5**:422, 423
        Songs, Drones, and Refrains of Death,
            5:422, 423
        Variazioni per orchestra, **5**:423
Crunden, Robert, **4**:262, 265
Crusades, **1**:96, 107, 108, 117, 135, 141
    Constantinople and, **1**:484
    Cyprus and, **1**:345
    Homme Armé Masses and, **1**:484–85
Cruz, Sister Juana Inés de la, *El Nino* and,
        5:524
"Crye" tradition, **2**:579
    Tye *In Nomines*, **2**:116
CS. *See* countersubject of fugue
"Cuban missile crisis," **5**:8
Cui, César, **2**:737
    Dargomïzhsky's *Stone Guest* and, **3**:612
    on double choruses, **3**:654
    as music critic, **3**:290, 458–59, 625
    New Russian School and, **3**:397, 468,
        625, 786, 787–88
    nom de plume of, **3**:311
    orientalism and, **3**:397
    Prisoner in the Caucasus, A, **3**:397
    on Smetana, **3**:458–59, 463
"Cujus animam" (Rossini), **3**:13
cult of personality, Liszt and, **3**:268

Cult of the Supreme Being, **3**:162
Cultural and Scientific Conference for
        World Peace, **5**:106
cultural conditioning, response to music
    and, **3**:298
cultural conservatism. *See* conservatism
cultural elites. *See* elite culture
cultural miscegenation, **5**:314
culture
    German *Kultur* and, **3**:123–24, 130, 132,
        228
    language communities and, **3**:122
    redemptive, **3**:772–73, 783
culture wars, **3**:22, 743
Cumaean sibyl, **1**:719, *719*
Cum jubilo (Kyrie IX), **1**:84–86, 89, 234
Cumming, Julie, **1**:286
Cunctipotens genitor (Ad Organum faciendum),
    1:163
Cunctipotens genitor (Codex Calixtinus),
    1:164, *165*, 306–7
    Machaut Kyrie and, **1**:322, 324–25
Cunctipotens genitor (Faenza Codex), **1**:306,
    322, 371
Cunctipotens genitor Deus (Kyrie IV), **1**:59,
    111, 306, 325
Cunningham, Merce, **5**:58, 92
    John Cage and, **5**:58
Cupid (Eros), **2**:331, 447, 453
Curlew River, op. 71 (Britten), **5**:225
Current Musicology, **5**:161
"Curse" leitmotif (Wagner), **3**:508, 520, 526
cursive principle, **1**:12
curtain-raiser. *See* overture
Cusick, Suzanne, **2**:81, 82
Cuzzoni, Francesca, **2**:307
Cybele (mythology), **2**:97, 100, 102, 103
"Cybele's lament" (Lully), **2**:103–4, 105, 106
cyclic form, **3**:750–51, 784
    Dvořák and, **3**:754–55
    Franck and, **3**:777
cyclic Mass Ordinaries, **1**:459–500, 501
    composers of, **1**:472–500
    constituent sections of, **1**:496
    emulation and, **1**:474–75, 484, 633
    English composers and, **1**:460–71
    fifteenth-century inception of, **1**:450–60
    four-part harmony and, **1**:466–71
    high style of, **1**:461–62, 465, 480–81,
        486
    Missa L'Homme Armé and, **1**:484–500,
        529
    modern concert audiences and,
        1:496–97
    Palestrina and, **1**:633–63
    Petrucci printed publication of,
        1:499–500
    Phrygian polyphony and, **1**:529
    votive motet substitutes in, **1**:518–26,
        529
    See also Mass Ordinary
Cypriot Codex, **1**:345–46

Cyprus, *ars subtilior* composition and, 1:345–46

Czech lands, 1:772; 2:505; 3:345, 446
  Dvořák and, 3:753, 754
  folk songs and, 3:444, 765
  Gluck and, 2:454
  modern literature and, 3:949
  nationalism and, 3:67, 445, 451–56, 463
  Nazi Germany and, 3:462–63
  nineteenth-century symphonic music and, 3:745
  opera and, 3:447–51, 463
  polkas and, 3:455, 754
  Smetana and, 3:443–45, 447, 448, 451, 461, 754
  Thirty Years War and, 2:55
  See also Prague

Czech language, 3:444, 445, 448, 765

Czerny, Karl (Carl), 2:606, 675; 3:261–62

D

da capo aria, 1:32; 2:144, 152, 317; 3:48, 71, 668–69
  cadenza and, 2:171–72, 609
  cantata and, 2:342, 369
  concerto compared with, 2:222, 609
  definition of, 2:144, 432
  in exit opera, 3:48
  Field and, 3:71
  format changes in, 2:165
  Handel oratorio and, 2:317
  Haydn oratorio and, 2:633
  Monteverdi and, 2:33
  Puccini's "Un bel dí" as, 3:668–69
  Scarlatti (Alessandro) and, 2:144, 146
  standardization and, 2:152
  symphonic thematic development and, 2:525

dactylic meter, 1:83, 111, 191–92, 197, 215, 218, 325; 2:378
  Parisan chanson and, 1:708

Dada movement, 4:567, 599

Dafne (Peri), 2:58

Dafne (Schütz), 2:15, 58

Dafne, La (Peri), 1:824, 826, 827–29, 831
  as first opera, 1:826

Da gaudiorum premia (Dunstable, attrib.), 1:461

Daguerre, Louis, 3:208

Dahlhaus, Carl, 2:650; 3:14, 78, 179, 415, 459, 463, 482, 732, 734–35, 755, 775, 785

Daily Worker, 4:652, 656, 657, 658

Dali, Salvador, 4:567

Dallapiccola, Luigi, 5:94, 295
  Richard Maxfield and, 5:94

Dalle belle contrade d'oriente (Rore), 1:726–27, 728–29, 802

Dalle più alte sfere (Cavalieri), 1:804, 805

Dame aux camélias, La (Dumas), 3:580

Damnation of Faust, The (Berlioz), 3:654

Damon, S. Foster, *Series of Old American Songs*, 4:659, 661, 668

Damrosch, Walter, 4:615, 617, 626, 627, 628, 636

Dance for Burgess (Varèse), 5:196

Dance in Place Congo, The (Gilbert), 4:613

dance music, 1:601–02; 2:574
  Austrian forms, 2:573
  ayres and, 2:120–25
  Baroque keyboard genres, 2:37
  Chaikovsky and, 3:796–97
  Chopin and, 3:348, 350, 357–60
  English incidental music and, 2:126
  English masques and, 2:113, 134
  English national dance and, 2:204, 205
  fiddler repertory of, 1:1131
  Glinka and, 3:242, 245
  Grocheio's social theory and, 1:208
  Handel concerto grosso and, 2:204, 205
  Handel suites and, 2:306
  Mozart and, 3:35, 114, 796, 798
  in operettas, 3:645–46, 648
  Scarlatti (Alessandro) overture and, 2:146–47, 148, 149–50
  Schubert and, 3:83, 84
  suites based on, 2:53, 259–60, 262, 263, 265–81
  tragédie lyrique and, 2:94, 96, 99, 100
  See also ballet; ballroom dances; *specific forms*

dance musice, French harpsichord *pièces* and, 3:119

"Dance of the Earth" (Stravinsky) (*Rite of Spring*), 4:177, 179–81, 181, 182

"Dance of the Sacred Life-Cycle" (*Ancient Voices of Children*), 5:424–25

"Dance of the Seven Veils," 4:37, 44–45

dance-song
  English vernacular, 1:742–46, 746
  opera vs., 1:827
  See also balada; ballata; carole; galliard; pastorelle; pavan; roudeau; virelai

Danger Music (Higgins), 5:94

Dangerous Moonlight (film), 4:558

Danhauser, Josef, 3:75–77, 76

Daniel (biblical), 1:94

Daniel, Arnaut, 2:6

Daniélou, Jean, 4:676

Danielpour, Richard, neotonality and, 5:454

D'Annuzio, Gabriele, 3:663, 664

"dans le style ancien," 4:65

"Danse des almées" (David), 3:388

Danse macabre (Saint-Saëns), 3:203, 339

"Danse russe," 4:170, 171, 172
  Petrushka and, 4:171

Danse sauvage (Ornstein), 4:299, 300

"Danseuses de Delphes" (Debussy), 4:78

Dantan, Jean-Pierre, 3:252

Dante Alighieri, 1:116, 139, 286–87, 290, 367, 384, 641
  Galilei musical setting and, 1:803

motet description by, 1:286
  as proto-Renaissance figure, 1:382, 383
  vernacular literature and, 1:351, 352, 383, 459

Daphne (Farnaby), 2:47

Daphne (mythology), 1:824, 829; 2:23, 47, 58

Da Ponte, Lorenzo, 2:476–79, 477, 493, 622; 3:16, 23, 25, 37, 52, 599
  Don Giovanni libretto, 2:485–94
  on finale, 2:487

Dargomïzhsky, Alexander, 3:612–15, 618
  Musorgsky and, 3:618
  Stone Guest, The, 3:612–15, 618, 619, 623

Dario, Rubén, *El Nino* and, 5:524

Darius, King of Persia, 1:94

Dark Ages, 1:798; 3:124

dark and light metaphor, Beethoven and, 3:3, 4

"Dark Is the Night" (Beach), 3:770

Darmstadt, 5:21–22, 27, 37, 38, 44, 45, 50, 54, 63, 65, 67, 77, 111, 121, 193, 345, 432, 463, 464

Darmstadt school, 5:432, 454, 463, 460, 463

Darmstadt serialism, 5:135

Darwin, Charles, 2:396; 3:287, 412–13, 480, 559

Darwinian historiography, 2:396–97

Darwinism, 3:480

Darwin, Marx, Wagner (Barzun), 3:480

Dascanio, Josquin. *See* Josquin des Prez

Da te parto (Saracini), 1:821, 821, 822

Daughter of the Regiment, The (Donizetti), 3:46

Daughters of the American Revolution (D.A.R.), 3:771

Daumer, Georg Friedrich (Eusebius Emmeran), 3:717

Daverio, John, 2:702; 3:294, 314

David (biblical), 1:10, 51

DAVID (Machaut melisma), 1:291–92

David, Félicien
  Beethoven and, 3:387
  orientalism and, 3:387–89
  works of
    Désert, Le, 3:387–89, 387, 390, 397, 419, 482
    Lalla-Roukh, 3:389

David-Néel, Alexandra, *Atlas* and, 5:490

Davidenko, Alexander, 4:654

Davidovsky, Mario, 5:211–13
  Contrastes, 5:211
  Synchronisms No. 1, 5:211–13

Davidsbund (Schumann journalistic pseudonym), 2:737

Davidsbündler, 3:293, 294, 309, 316, 343

Davidsbündlertänze (Schumann), 3:309

Davis, Miles, 5:335
  Bitches Brew, 5:335
  In a Silent Way, 5:335
  "Stella by Starlight" and, 5:415

Davis, Natalie Zemon, **1**:447

Davy, Richard, **1**:513

dawn-song, **1**:110–11; **3**:549

"Day in the Life, A" (Beatles), **5**:321–25

day offices, **1**:11

"Day of Wrath." *See Dies irae*

Dead Man Walking (opera), **5**:516

dean (cathedral), **1**:169, 170

"Death" leitmotif (Wagner), **3**:506, 513, 515, 516

Death in Venice (Mann), **5**:225

Death in Venice, op. 88 (Britten), **5**:225

Death of Klinghoffer, The (Adams), **5**:517

    Arab-Israeli conflict and **5**:522

    Alice Goodman and, **5**:517

    Peter Sellars and, **5**:517

Death without Weeping, The Violence of Everyday Life in Brazil (Scheper-Hughes), **5**:450

de Bäif, Jean-Antoine, **4**:449

debate-song (tenso), **1**:115–16, 121, 226

De bone amour vient seance et bonté (Thibaut), **1**:118–19

Deborah (Handel), **2**:314

Deburau, Jean-Baptiste-Gaspard, **4**:457

Debussy, Claude, **1**:152, 349; **5**:347; **4**:21, 59, 70–96, 70f, 102, 104–5, 106, 107, 108, 111, 120, 126, 200, 217, 231, 261, 266, 349, 380, 381, 395, 422, 443, 457, 469, 508, 567, 621, 751, 754

    absence of people in works of, **4**:78

    anhemitonic pith collections and, **4**:83

    impressionism and, **4**:76–78

    les phrases tricolores and, **4**:106

    meaning of "voiles," **4**:74, 76, 79, 83–84

    prelude and, **3**:351

    progressions and, **4**:70, 71

    Stravinsky's memorial to, **4**:469

    on thematic development, **3**:22

    works of

        Cinq poèmes de Baudelaire, **4**:86

        Children' Corner, **4**:78, 599

        "Golliwog's Cakewalk," **4**:599, 600, 601

        Jeux and, **4**:567

        La chute de la maison Usher, **4**:86

        Le diable dans le beffroi, **4**:86

        Le Printemps, **4**:78

        Nocturnes, **4**:78, 79

        Nuages, **4**:79, 80, 81, 82, 83, 204

        Pelléas et Mélisande, **4**:79, 86, 89, 443

        Prélude a L'apres-midi d'un faune, **4**:86

        Préludes for piano, **4**:73, 78, 79

        Sarabande from *Pour le piano*, **4**:71–73

        Suite: Pour de piano 1894–1901, **4**:70

        Voiles, **4**:73–74, 75–76, 313

decadence, **4**:29–36, 776, 303, 304

    Parnassians and, **4**:97

    Strauss's *Reverie* and, **4**:33

decadent style. *See* mannered style

Decaisne, Henri, **3**:422

Decameron (Boccaccio), **1**:365–66

de Castillon, Alexis, **4**:64

December 1952 (Brown), **5**:95

deceptive cadence, **1**:603–4; **2**:213, 215, 216, 220, 628–29

decimal system, **1**:252, 253

declamation, **1**:612, 646, 680, 712, 720, 722

declamation motet, **1**:429, 430, 432, 433, 566, 567, 577, 603

declamatory style

    Monteverdi and, **2**:59

    Schütz and, **2**:59

Declaration of Independence (U.S.), **2**:111, 461

Decline and Fall of the Roman Empire, The (Gibbon), **3**:489

declining and ascending historical curves, concept of, **2**:235

decoration. *See* ornamentation

Degas, Edgar, **3**:217

Degeyter Club, **4**:651, 654

Degeyter, Pierre, **4**:651

De harmonica institutione (Hucbald), **1**:77

Dehmel, Richard, **4**:33, 36, 38, 304

    as "decadent," **4**:33, 304

Dehn, Siegfried, **3**:240, 288

dehumanization," **4**:261, 474, 476

"dehumanization of art," French modernism and, **4**:60, 474

"Dehumanization of Art, The" (Ortega), **4**:476

De institutione musica (Boethius), **1**:38–39, 37, 39

De inventione et usu musicae (Tinctoris), **1**:453–54, 536

Delacroix, Eugène, **3**:347, 349; **4**:105

De la démocratie en Amérique (de Tocqueville), **4**:302

De l'Allemagne (Heine), **4**:134

De l'Allemagne (Staël), **2**:645–46

Delavigne, Germain, **3**:208

"Del ciel clemente" (Donizetti), **3**:55–56

Delibes, Léo, **3**:798; **4**:136–38, 139, 142

    symphonic ballet and, **4**:136

    works of

        Coppélia, **4**:136, 137–38

        Lakmé, **3**:390

        Le roi s'amuse six airs de danse le style ancien, **4**:65

        Sylvia, **4**:136, 138, 141

"delicious" neoclassicism, Mozart and, **4**:451

"delicious" pastiche, **4**:451

"De l'Imitation musicale" (Berlioz), **3**:332–35

Delle cristiana moderzione del theatro (Ottonelli), **2**:17

Deller, Alfred, **2**:130

Delphic Hymns, **1**:32, 33, 799

Del Tredici, David, **5**:438–44, 438, 459, 460

    serialism and, **5**:442

    works of

Adventures Undergrund, **5**:442

Alice Symphony, **5**:442

All in the Golden Afternoon, **5**:444

Child Alice, **5**:442–45

Final Alice, **5**:442–45

March to Tonality, **5**:444

In Memory of a Summer Day, **5**:443

Pop-Pourri, **5**:442

Syzgy, **5**:438–42

Vintage Alice, **5**:442

de Médicis, Catherine, *ballets de cour* and, **4**:131

De mensurabili musica (Garlandia), **1**:196–98

De mensuris et discantu. See Anonymus IV

democracy, **2**:111, 724; **3**:383–86

democratization of taste, **3**:251, 292

de Mille, Agnes, **4**:663

De modis musicis antiquorum (Mei), **1**:799

Demofoonte (Berezovsky), **3**:235

De musica (Augustine), **1**:37–38, 175, 337

De musica (Grocheio), **1**:207

De musica (John of Afflighem), **1**:155

De natura sonoris (Penderecki), **5**:217

Denisov, Edison, **5**:463, 464, 465, 471

    Sun of the Incas, The, **5**:463

Denmark, **2**:66; **3**:127

Dennis, John, **2**:312–13

Denon, Baron Dominique, **3**:387

DeNora, Tia, **5**:306

Densité 21.5 (Varese), **5**:186

Dent, Edward J., **2**:692; **3**:13

De numeris harmonicis (Gersonides), **1**:249

Deo Gratias, **1**:310, 316

Deo gratias Anglia ("Agincourt Carol") ("Roy Henry"), **1**:418–21

De plan musica (Garlandia), **1**:196

De profundis clamavi (Baudelaire), **4**:711

De Quincey, Thomas, **3**:322

de Régnier, Henri, **4**:111, 112, 146

De Rerum Natura (Lucretius), **5**:302

Dernova, Varvara, **4**:208

    "tritone link" and, **4**:200

Des Antonius von Padua Fischpredigy (Mahler), **4**:21

Des bohemiens et de leur musique en Hongrie (Liszt), **4**:371

Des Esseintes, **4**:29, 30, 57, 58, 84

Des Knaben Wunderhorn, **4**:20, 21, 22

"Des pas sur le neige" (Debussy), **4**:78

descant, English, **1**:155, 406–9, 417

    Beata viscera example of, **1**:406–7, 433

    distinguishing features of, **1**:423, 425, 429

    See also discant

Descartes, René, **1**:797–98; **2**:75

descending fifths, **1**:733

descending minor tetrachord, **2**:95

descending seconds, **1**:356

Deschamps, Émile, **3**:225

Deschamps, Eustache, **1**:336–37, 343

deschaunte, **1**:436

descort, **1**:113, 119

Description of Egypt (Jomard), **3**:387

Description of the Empire of China, A (Du Halde), **3**:192

Désert, Le (David), **3**:387–89, 387, 390, 397, 419, 482

Déserts (Varèse), **5**:207, 208, 211, 214, 415

Deshayes, Celestin, **3**.11

De Sica, Vittorio, **3**:674

Desiderius, King of the Lombards, **1**:3

Désir (Scriabin), **4**:215

desire

    music's induction of, **3**:529–30

    Russian *nega* and, **3**:399, 401–4, 407

    Wagner's channeling of, **3**:528–39

Desmares, Marie (La Champmeslé), **2**:106

despotism. *See* absolutism

determinism, **1**:144

Detmold, Germany, **3**:690

de Tocqueville, Alexis de, *De la démocratie en Amérique*, **4**:302

De tous biens plaine (Hayne), **1**:535, 536, 539

    instrumental arrangements of, **1**:544

    Josquin canon on, **1**:538

De toutes flours (Machaut), **1**:303–7, 308–9, 371, 373

Deuil angoisseux (Christine de Pisane), **1**:446–47

    Binchois setting of, **1**:447–52

deus ex machina, **2**:151–52, 448; **3**:197

Deus in adiutorium meum intende (doxology), **2**:19–20

Deutsch, Otto Erich, **3**:83

Deutsche Mythologie (Grimm), **3**:492

Deutschen Vaterland, Des, **3**:158, 160–61, 162

Deutscher Liederschatz (Erk), **3**:160–61, 162

Deutsche Sagen (Grimm brothers), **3**:122

Deutsches Requiem, Ein (Brahms), **3**:704–10

Deutsche Staatsbibliothek (Berlin), **2**:49

Deutsche Tänze (Deutscher), **2**:491, 573

Deutsche Volkslieder (Brahms, ed.), **1**:703–4

"Deutschland, Deutschland über alles" (German national anthem), **3**:130

Deux aveugles, Les (Offenbach), **3**:654

Deux mélodies hébraïque (Ravel), **4**:107–8

Devan, William Carrolle, **5**:43

"developing variation," **4**:695

development section

    of Beethoven's *Eroica* Symphony, **2**:658–64

    concerto, **2**:613

    Hayden's symphonic, **2**:520–25, 557, 572–73

Deveria, Achille, **3**:209

Devin du village, Le (Rousseau intermezzo), **2**:110, 442

De vita libri tres (Ficino), **1**:615–16

devotional songs, **1**:133–34

DeVoto, Mark, **5**:160

De vulgari eloquentia (Dante), **1**:351

Diabelli, Anton, **2**:674, 675, 682

    "Patriotic Anthology," **3**:262

Diabelli Variation (Liszt), **3**:262, 263

Diabelli Variations, op. 120 (Beethoven), **2**:674, 686, 726; **5**:83

Diable dans le beffroi, Le (Debussy), **4**:86

diabolus in musica, **3**:203

diactonic thirds, **2**:248

Diaghilev, Sergei, **3**:786; **4**:149, 149f, 151, 152, 159, 160, 450, 502, 503, 505, 560, 569, 662, 675, 776

    Ballets Russes and, **4**:561

    Jeux, **4**:567

Diaghilev Ballet, **4**:663

Dial, The (magazine), **4**:621

dialectic, Hegelian, **3**:412–15

Dialogo della musica antica e della moderna (Galilei), **1**:800

dialogue tropes, **1**:51–53

Dialogues of the Carmelites (Poulenc), **5**:225

Dialogus de musica (medieval treatise), **1**:77

Diamorphoses (Xenakis), **5**:189

diapente, **1**:150, 151

diatessaron, **1**:150, 152

diatonic circle of fifths. *See* circles of fifths

diatonic melody, parallel doubling and, **1**:149–50

diatonic motion, **1**:721, 729

diatonic pitch set, **1**:29–31, 32, 33, 35, 41, 74

    deduction from Pythagorean consonances, **1**:31

    internalization of, **1**:30

diatonic scale, **1**:686, 729

diatonic system, **1**:274; **3**:94

"Dicant nunc judei" (Chartres fragment), **1**:155, 158

Dic, Christi veritas (Philip the Chancellor), **1**:201–5

Dichterliebe, op. 48 (Schumann), **3**:295–306

Dichter und Bauer overture (Suppé), **3**:647

Dictionnaire de musique (Mondo), **4**:68

Dictionnaire de musique (Rousseau), **3**:192, 193; **4**:68

Didelot, Charles Louis, **4**:133, 139

Diderot, Denis, **2**:458

    on *buffi* art, **2**:435, 437, 442, 443

    Enlightenment and, **2**:443, 461, 462, 470

    Lully and Rameau style comparison by, **2**:109

Dido and Aeneas (Purcell), **2**:132–38

    Dido's lament, **2**:135–37, 138

    "Englishness" of, **2**:134–35, 138

    girl's school performance of, **2**:132, 138

    recitative and dance song, **2**:133–34

    rediscovery of, **2**:137–38

Dido and Aeneas story, **3**:219

    Metastasio and, **2**:155

    Purcell and, **2**:132–38

Didone abbandonata (Metastasio libretto), **2**:154–55

Didone abbandonata (Vinci), **2**:330

"Dido's lament" (Purcell), **2**:135–37, 138

Dies, Albert Christoph, **2**:517, 556, 569, 571

Dies irae, **1**:88–90, 719; **4**:18, 101, 126, 43

in Berlioz's *Grande messe des morts*, op. 5, **3**:319

in Berlioz's *Symphonie fantastique*, **3**:337–40

    burlesque treatments of, **3**:337, 339–40

in Verdi's Requiem Mass, **3**:595

Dies sanctificatus (Christmas Alleluia), **1**:267, 269–71

Dieus soit en cheste maison (Adam), **1**:123–24

diferencias (divisions), **2**:47

Difficiles alios (notation problem), **1**:536

difficult art. *See* high art

"Difficult Decision, The" (Beethoven), **3**:424, 776

digital audiotapes, **1**:65

"digital revolution," **5**:479–80

Dijkstra, Bram, **4**:57, 58

Diletsky (or Dilezki), Nikolai, **2**:185, 185; **3**:234

diminished fifth, **1**:35, 151

diminished fourth, **1**:512; **2**:727, 729

diminished seventh

    Bach (J. S.) and, **2**:213, 258

    Bach (W. F.) and, **2**:406

    Beethoven's C-minor moods and, **2**:716, 727, 729

    cyclic resolutions of, **3**:99–100

    Handel and, **2**:317

    harmonic dissolution and, **3**:361, 362

    Haydn and, **2**:531–32

    Liszt and, **3**:428, 432–35, 543, 544

    Mozart and, **2**:493

    normal resolutions of, **3**:428

    Romantic introspection and, **3**:96

    Scarlatti (Alessandro) and, **2**:142

    Schubert and, **3**:96, 99–100, 105

    Smetana and, **3**:448

    Weber and, **3**:203, 543

diminished volume, **1**:817

Dimitrov, Georgi, **4**:657

d'Indy. *See* Indy, Vincent d',

dinner music. *See* Tafelmusik

Dion, Partch's *Revelation* and, **5**:485–86

Dionysus (mythology), **4**:677

Dionysus, Partch's *Revelation* and, **5**:485–87

Diporti di Euterpe (Strozzi), **2**:75–78

Di quella pira (Verdi), **3**:579–80, 581, 654

discant, **1**:155, 159, 163, 165, 169, 171, 311, 577, 628

    cadence and, **1**:276, 297–98, 356

    definition of, **1**:587

    dissonance and, **1**:168

    Garlandia's division of, **1**:196

    Jacopo treatise on, **1**:354

    modal rhythm and, **1**:179, 187, 245

    motet as texted, **1**:209, 210, 221, 229–32, 229, 259

    Notre Dame settings and, **1**:171, 179, 180

    prosulated. *See* motet

    Song of Songs antiphons and, **1**:429–33

    three-part, **1**:165–67, 168

discant (continued)
  trecento style, 1:356–59
  two-part, 1:256
discanter, 1:436
discantus. See discant
disciplinati. See flagellants
"disco," 5:392–93
"disco" music, 5:367, 392–96
discordia concors, 1:148
  definition of, 1:261
  motet and, 1:226, 229, 236, 255, 286, 424
Discotheque, 5:392–93
disjunct tetrachords, 1:151
dismissal, 1:54, 311, 318, 321, 323–24, 326
Disney, Walt, Fantasia, 4:104
dissociation theme, 3:154
dissolution, harmonic, 3:358–63
dissonance, 4:5, 14, 309–10, 312, 313
  Bach (J. S.) and, 2:254, 364, 365–68
  Beethoven's Ninth and, 2:677–78
  Bellini and, 3:42
  cadence and, 1:276, 305, 470
  culture-bound criteria of, 1:153
  discant harmony and, 1:168
  Dunstable refinements of, 1:427,
    429–32, 433
  as English descant feature, 1:406–9, 417,
    423
  in final chord, 1:470
  Garlandia's tripartite division of, 1:196
  Handel and, 2:317
  harmonic balancing of, 1:153
  invertible counterpoint and, 2:201–2
  luxuriant style and, 2:59, 67
  monody and, 1:818
  Monteverdi and, 1:734–35; 2:59
  Mozart and, 2:494, 631
  Peri and, 1:829, 830
  polyphonic closure and, 1:168
  Purcell and, 2:128, 137, 196
  sixteenth-century
    rationalization/codification of,
    1:588–89
  stile antico and, 1:669
  Strozzi and, 2:76–77
  Tapissier motet and, 1:429
  Willaert and, 1:603
"Dissonance" Quartet in C major, K. 465
    (Mozart), 2:631–33, 634
  autograph score of, 2:629
  Fétis rewrite of, 2:632
"Di tanti palpiti" (Rossini), 3:28, 30–35, 41,
    258–59
Dithyramb, op. 65, no. 2 (Tomášek), 3:69,
    70
dithyrambs, Tomášek and, 3:67, 69, 70, 71
Ditié de Jeanne d'Arc, Le (Christine de
    Pisane)
dits (lengthy allegorical poems), 1:290
divertimento
  definition of, 2:498

Haydn and, 2:518, 526, 527, 541–42, 547,
    549
  Mozart and, 2:549
  See also string quartet
Divertimento in F major, K. 523 ("A
    Musical Joke") (Mozart), 2:549
divertissement, 2:95, 107
Divine Comedy (Dante), 1:286–87, 383, 803
divine harmony. See cosmic harmony
divine inspiration
  Josquin's status and, 1:548, 552, 553
  Musica and, 1:69, 70
  representations of, 1:6, 6
Divine Poem, The (Scriabin), 4:208, 209, 211,
    213
divine presence, 1:772
divine right of kings, 2:88, 92, 124, 125
divine service. See liturgical music
divine tuning, 1:255
divisiones via naturae, 1:355
division points. See measure
divisions, 2:47. See also variations
division viol, 2:120
Division-violist, The, or the Art of Playing
    Extempore upon a Ground
    (Simpson), 2:120
Djamileh (Bizet), 3:390
Dmitrij (Dvořák), 3:754
Dmitry, Tsarevich, 3:623
do (scale-singing syllable), 1:101
"Do-" clausulae, 1:180–83, 186, 198, 228
Dobson, Austin, 1:122
Docta sanctorum (papal bull; 1323), 1:311
Doctorum principem super ethera/Melodia
    suavissima cantemus (Ciconia),
    1:278–80, 284–85, 424
Doctrinale (Villedieu), 1:197
"dodecaphony," 4:688
Dodekachordon (Glareanus), 1:553–54
Dodge, Charles
  computer music and, 5:496, 497
  serialism and, 5:497, 498
  speech synthesis and, 5:498
  works of
    Any Resemblance Is Purely Coincidental,
      5:499
    Changes, 5:497
    Earth's Magnetic Field, The, 5:497–98,
      497, 498
    Speech Songs, 5:498–99
"Dogmatic" (Copland), 4:654
Doktor Faustus (Mann), 4:774
Dolan, Robert Emmet, Lady in the Dark,
    5:183
Dolmatovsky, Yevgeniy, 5:12
Dolmen Music (Monk), 5:489
Dombrowski, Jan, 3:357
Dôme des Invalides (France), 3:319
domestic entertainment, 2:426–32, 736;
    3:63
  Brahms's works for, 3:717
  canzona and, 1:787

chamber music and, 2:114, 419, 427, 432
empfindsamer Stil and, 2:410, 695
English consort music and, 2:118
lieder and, 3:119, 120
music book use for, 1:694–96, 698, 699,
    709, 787
printed music for, 2:419
rare use of minor key for, 2:695
Romantic art and, 3:63–64
salons and, 3:73–79
Schubert's music and, 3:110
two complementary sides of, 2:426–27
Domestic Romanticism, 3:68, 71
  salons and, 3:75
dominant seventh, 1:470
  Musorgsky and, 3:545
  Romantic introspection and, 3:96
  Schubert and, 3:96, 112–13, 143, 698
  Schumann and, 3:303
  in third inversion, 2:215
  Wagner and, 3:542, 543, 546, 558
dominant-tonic progression, 1:409, 447,
    469, 470–71; 2:539, 627–28. See
    also passus duriusculus
Domingo, Placido, 3:579
Dom pesni (House of Song), 4:108
"Dona nobis pacem," 1:661, 662–63
Donaueschingen Festival (Germany), 5:65,
    217, 463, 464
Don Carlos (Verdi), 3:594, 595, 596, 643
Don Giovanni (Mozart), 2:478, 485–96,
    492, 515, 590, 637; 3:23, 25, 34, 235,
    612; 4:7; 5:117, 280
  achievement of, 2:484–85, 495
  act finales pf, 2:490, 492–94, 645
  ballroom scene of, 2:490, 491, 573
  closure ensemble of, 2:494, 495
  Kierkegaard on, 3:271–72
  Liszt's "Don Juan Fantasy" and,
    3:268–72, 347
  overture to, 2:487–88, 504, 515; 3:16, 197
  "painful" music in, 2:493–94, 645
  poster for, 2:485
  stage music in, 2:490–91, 492–93, 631
Donizetti, Gaetano, 2:16; 3:47, 567; 5:343
  bel canto and, 3:37, 48, 578
  Chopin and, 3:373
  coloratura use by, 3:222
  ensemble finales of, 3:48, 49, 210
  "entrance opera" technique of, 3:48, 209
  Glinka and, 3:240
  librettist of, 3:46, 577
  operatic output of, 3:46
  works of
    Don Pasquale, 3:46
    Elisir d'amore, L', 3:46
    Fille du régiment, La, 3:46
    Lucia di Lammermoor, 3:46–59, 46, 73,
      144, 273
    Lucrezia Borgia, 3:45
Don Juan (Gluck), 4:133

Don Juan Fantasy (Liszt), **3:**268–72, 273, 347

Don Juan legends, **2:**478

"Donna è mobile, La" (Verdi), **3:**585–87, 591, 593, 606

Donna l'altrui mirar (Gherardello), **1:**371, 372–73

Don Pasquale (Donizetti), **3:**46

Don Quixote (Minkus), **4:**139

Don Sanche, ou Le château d'amour (Liszt), **3:**262

Donizetti, Gaetano, *Lucia di Lammermoor*, **4:**45, 437

Doppelgänger, **3:**100

Doppelgänger, Der (Schubert), **3:**153–57

Doré, Gustave, **3:**319

Dorian chant, **1:**89

Dorian melody, **1:**99, 136, 137
   Ave maris stella, **1:**83
   Salve, Regina, **1:**270–71

Dorian mode, **1:**79, 86, 312, 479, 509, 597, 681, 802; **4:**382, **4:**384
   chromaticism and, **1:**274, 275
   minor and, **1:**554

Dorian pentachord, **1:**276–77

Dorian scale, **1:**75–76, 274

Dorian signature, **2:**120

D'Orlando di Lassus il primo libro dovesi contengono madrigali, vilanesche, canzoni francesi e motetti a quattro voci (collection), **1:**714

Dorn, Heinrich, **3:**503

Dorset Garden (London), **2:**126, 127

Dostoyevsky, Fyodor, **4:**149, 170, 424
   Epokha and, **4:**140

double-action harp, **3:**328

double chorus, in operetta, **3:**654

Double Concerto (Carter), **5:**261, 262, 265–68, 275, 280, 302–4
   cosmological allegory, **5:**303
   first performance of, **5:**265

double cursus, **1:**44, 325, 424, 427

"Double Diaspason," **1:**150

double entendre, **1:**750–51

double-exposition, concerto modernization and, **2:**606–7

double fugue, **2:**201–2

double leading-tone cadence, **1:**276–77, 368, 408–9

double motet, **1:**210–13, 212, 214, 215, 222–24, 222, 229, 317

double notation, **1:**60, 210

double point, **1:**687

double return
   Bach (C. P. E.) and, **2:**413, 514
   Bach (J. C.) and, **2:**425–26, 488, 504
   Bach (W. F.) and, **2:**407–8, 504
   Beethoven's Piano Trio in C minor and, **2:**698
   eighteenth-century composition and, **2:**407–8

Haydn's symphonic form and, **2:**520, 557, 588
   Mozart and, **2:**488, 594, 618
   Sammartini and, **2:**504
   Scarlatti (Domenico) and, **2:**394–95, 407, 504

doubles (fancy ornaments), **2:**281

doubling-voice (*vox organalis*), **1:**150, 577
   fauxbordon and, **1:**435–39

Douce dame jolie (Machaut), **1:**295, 298

dove of the Holy Spirit, **1:**175

Dover priory, **1:**408

Dowland, John, **1:**742–45; **2:**120
   Can shee excuse my wrongs, **1:**745
   Flow My Tears, **1:**742, 743
   "Lachrymae Pavan, The," **1:**742, 744–45

Downes, Olin, **3:**290; **4:**292, **4:**620, 627, 633–34, 659; **5:**182
   Treasury of American Song (ed.), **4:**659

"Downstream on Mother Volga," **3:**242, 244

Downtown Music School (New York), **4:**651

doxology, **1:**11, 12, 21, 22, 23, 50, 54

D'Oyly Carte, Richard, **3:**651, 652, 658

Draco (constellation), **1:**476, 476

dragmas, **1:**341, 355

Dragon's Head, **1:**476, 476

drama
   Beethoven incidental music for, **3:**1–2
   classic. See Greek drama
   grand opéra tableaux and, **3:**223
   humorous. See *opera buffa*
   liturgical, **1:**52, 93–94, 131, 138, 495–96, 834
   neoclassical, **2:**151–52, 154, 706
   opera's musical values and, **3:**35
   symphony as, **2:**599
   Verdi's *Rigoletto* as, **3:**583–94
   See also music drama; theater; tragedy

"dramatick opera." See semi-opera

drame surréaliste, **4:**578

dramma giocoso. See *opera buffa*

dramma per musica ("drama through music"), **2:**87, 152, 378; **3:**487. See also *opera seria*

"Dream of the Witches' Sabbath" (Berlioz), **3:**203, 322, 335–39

"dream symphony" ("sleep scene"), **2:**100–102

Dreigroschenoper, Die (Brecht-Weill), **4:**535–41, 543, 544
   compared with *Wozzeck*, **4:**536–37

Drei Pintos, Die (Mahler), **4:**10

Drei Pintos, Die (Weber), **3:**193, 216; **4:**8

Dresden, **2:**157, 240, 341; **3:**482, 483, 677
   Bach (J. S.) Mass and, **2:**375
   court chapel choir, **2:**58
   Praetorius and, **2:**55, 57
   Schütz and, **2:**57–59, 73
   Thirty Years War and, **2:**66
   Vivaldi concerto for orchestra of, **2:**222

"Dresden Amen," **3:**167

Dreyfus affair, **4:**106

Dreyfus, Alfred, **4:**106

Dreyfus, Max, **4:**624

drinking songs, **1:**138

Druckman, H. Jacob, New York Philharmonic and, **5:**435

Druids, **3:**41

Drumming (Reich), **5:**379–80, 383, 384, 386

Drury Lane (London theater), **2:**89

Drury Lane Oratorio Concerts, **2:**633

Druschetzky, Georg, **2:**499

Dryden, John, **2:**127, 132
   Handel's alleged "borrowings from, **2:**327

Dubinsky, Gregory, **4:**707
   Nomos technique and, **4:**681

"Dubinushka" ("The cudgel"), **4:**670

Dublin, Handel's *Messiah* commission, **2:**326, 326

DuBois, Luke, "interactive sound installations" and, **5:**514

ducal motets, **1:**519–26

Duchamp, Marcel, **5:**72, 354
   Dadaist, **5:**354
   Fountain, **5:**72
   John Cage and, **5:**72

Ducis, Benedictus, **1:**769
   Lämmlein geht und trägt die Schuld, **1:**769, 770–71

duda (Polish bagpipe), **3:**358

Dudevant, Maurice, **3:**349, 355

Duèse, Jacques. See John XXII, Pope

duetto per camera, **2:**331
   Handel self-borrowing and, **2:**331–36

Du Fay, Guillaume, **1:**148, 281–85, 423, 439, 439, 441–46, 453, 473, 529, 536, 563, 667; **5:**43
   antiphon motet and, **1:**507–12
   career of, **1:**281–82, 445, 458, 558
   chanson and, **1:**498, 706
   Constantinopolitan laments of, **1:**484
   fauxbourdon and, **1:**436, 437, 441, 442–43, 446
   musical significance of, **1:**281, 429, 441–43, 495, 498–99
   works of
      Ave maris stella, **1:**441, 442–43, 446
      Ave Regina coelorum, **1:**507–12, 574
      Craindre vous vueil, **1:**444–46, 510
      Hélas mon deuil, a ce coup sui je mort, **1:**512
      Missa Ave Regina Coelorum, **1:**574
      Missa L'Homme Armé, **1:**497–99
      Missa Sancti Jacobi, **1:**434–35, 436, 437
      Missa Se la face ay pale, **1:**532
      Nuper rosarum flores, **1:**282–85, 429, 441
      Se la face ay pale, **1:**498
      Supremum est mortalibus bonum, **1:**282
      Vos qui secuti estis me, **1:**434–35

Du Hirte Israel, höre (J. S. Bach), **2:**372–75

"Duino Elegies" (Rilke), **5**:314

Dukas, Paul, **4**:104–6, 107, 108
  Messiaen and, **4**:231
  works of
    Ariane et Barbe-bleue, **4**:104, 106
    L'apprenti sorcier, **4**:104

Duke of Monmouth's Rebellion (1685),
  2:133

Duke's Theatre (Lincoln's Inn). *See* Dorset
  Garden

dukh, **3**:239

Dumas, Alexandre, **3**:580

Dun, Tan. *See* Tan Dun.,

Dunque dovro (Frescobaldi), **1**:824, 825

Dunque fra torbid' onde (Peri), **1**:810

Dunstable, John, **1**:421–22, 424–25,
  427–33, 461, 499, 513; **2**:59
  Caput Mass linked with, **1**:476–77
  musical significance of, **1**:422, 424, 427,
    429, 433, 454
  Quam pulchra es, **1**:429–33, 462
  Salve scema/Salve salus, **1**:424–25,
    427–29

Duo concertante (Rochberg), **5**:414

Duo for Pianists II (Wolff), **5**:82

duodecimal system, **1**:252–53

duodenaria, **1**:356, 363

Dupin, Amandine Aurore Lucie (Baroness
  Dudevant). *See* Sand, George

duple meter, **1**:248–52, 251
  Elizabethan dance-songs and, **1**:742–46
  ground bass *passamezzo* and, **1**:626
  Machaut and, **1**:295

duplum. *See* organum duplum

Duponchel, Charles, **3**:207, 215

Duprez, Gilbert, **3**:578

Duranowski, August, **3**:252

durational ratios. *See* rhythm

Durazzo, Giacomo, Count, **2**:217

Durch Adams Fall, Buxtehude's vs. Bach's
  (J. S.) versions, **2**:255–58

durchkomponiert. See through-composed
  settings

Durey, Louis
  Ho Chi Minh and, **4**:589
  Les Six group and, **4**:588
  Mao Tse-tung and, **4**:589

durus (ut mode), **1**:102

Dussek, Jan Ladislav, **2**:556; **3**:65, 67–68

Düsseldorf
  musical directors, **3**:172, 294
  music festivals, **3**:165, 166
  Schumann concert in, **3**:302
  as Schumann suicide attempt site, **3**:318,
    318

Dutch language, **1**:597

Dutch Reformed Church, **2**:46

Dutschke, Rudi, **5**:344
  German Student Socialist League,
    5:344

Duvernoy, Victor Alphonse, **4**:134

Dvořák, Antonín, **2**:94; **3**:752–67, *752*;
  4:246, 263, 271, 427, 610–11, 613,
  614, 632, 633, 638, 640, 641, 649
  background of, **3**:753
  Beach and, **3**:770, 771
  Brahms and, **3**:752, 754, 755
  chamber works of, **3**:754
  early publications of, **3**:752–53
  nationalism and, **3**:753
  in New York City, **3**:753, 755, 760, 765,
    768
  Schubert and, **3**:87, 754, 755
  symphonic music of, **3**:754
  versatility of, **3**:754
  Wagner and, **3**:753, 754
  works of
    Alfred, **3**:753
    Carnival, **3**:755
    Cello Concerto, op. 104, **3**:754
    Dmitrij, **3**:754
    Hiawatha, **3**:760, 764–66
    King and the Charcoal Burner, The,
      3:753–54
    My Home, **3**:755
    Othello, **3**:755
    Rusalka, **3**:754
    Slavonic Rhapsodies, **3**:755
    Symphonic Variations, **3**:755
    Symphony no. 8 in G major, **3**:765,
      766
    Symphony no. 9 in E minor, op. 95
      (*New World*), **3**:754, 755–66, 770,
      772, 773, 774

Dwight, John Sullivan, **3**:385

Dying Poet, The (Gottschalk), **3**:380

Dylan, Bob, **5**:315, 324, 332, 334
  "Blowin' in the Wind," **5**:315
  Mike Bloomfield and, **5**:334
  "Mr. Tambourine Man," **5**:334
  Newport Folk Festival, **5**:334

Dynamic Motion (Cowell), **4**:299, 301–2

dynamics
  as emotional change delineators,
    2:414
  first indications of, **1**:792

Dynamophone, **5**:177

"dynaphone," **5**:184

Dzerzhinsky, Ivan, *Quiet Flows the Don*,
  4:790

Dziady I, "Gustav poem" and, **4**:10

Dziady (Mickiewicz), **4**:9, 10

E

Eames, Emma, **3**:565

Early Modern period, **1**:797; **4**:1

early music revival, **2**:138, 233
  Adam's *Jeu de Robin et Marion* and, **1**:127
  authentic performance movement and,
    1:782; **2**:233, 362–63
  cantigas and, **1**:130
  countertenor voice and, **2**:130
  definition of "early music" and, **2**:233
  Gesualdo and, **1**:739–40

Gregorian chants and, **1**:66
  Josquin's *Ave Maria . . . Virgo serena* and,
    1:565
  Josquin's *El Grillo* and, **1**:699
  Machaut's works and, **1**:290, 295
  modern esthetic response to, **1**:495–96
  Muffat treatise and, **2**:259
  Play of Daniel, **1**:93, 94
  speculative performance practice,
    1:158–59, 452
  standard repertory vs., **2**:233
  Vivaldi popularity and, **2**:217, 226

Earth's Magnetic Field, The (Dodge),
  5:497–98, *497, 498*

ear training, **1**:76, 99–104
  harmony and, **1**:46, 168, 392, 394, 406,
    434

ear trumpet, **2**:654

East Franks. *See* Germany

East, Thomas, **1**:741

East Village Other, The, **5**:327

Easter
  dating of, **1**:12
  dialogue trope, **1**:51–52, 53
  Frankish sequence, **1**:86–88
  Gloria, **1**:54
  Gradual, **1**:26, 27, 221
  Handel's *Messiah* and, **2**:325
  Introit, **1**:*15*, 24, 51–52, 82–83
  liturgical cycle, **1**:12
  Lutheran chorale, **1**:758
  Marian antiphon, **1**:389
  Mass counterpoint, **1**:155
  matins responsory, **1**:631–32
  oratorios, **2**:73, 313, 341
  Passion settings, **1**:775–77

Eastern Orthodox Church, **1**:484; **3**:234
  Byzantine chant of, **1**:33–35, 64, 84
  "Credo I" and, **1**:34–35
  earliest surviving music text of, **1**:33
  eight-mode system of, **1**:28, 73
  Frankish mode theory and, **1**:73, 76
  hymnody of, **1**:33–34, 47, 48
  instrument ban by, **1**:8
  Kyrie and, **1**:58
  music theory imports from, **1**:72–73, 84
  Western Roman schism with, **1**:141–1

Eastern Roman Empire. *See* Byzantine
  Empire

Eastman, George, **4**:647

Eastman School of Music (Rochester,
  NY), **4**:647, 649

Eaux de la grace, Les (Messiaen), **4**:232, 233

Eberlin, Johann Ernst, **4**:458

Ebbo, Book of, **1**:6

Ecce sacerdos magnus (Gregorian antiphon),
  1:633

Ecclesie militantis Roma sedes (Du Fay), **1**:282

échappée figure, **3**:424, 776

echo-fantasia, **2**:46

echo pieces, **1**:792

echoplex, **5**:362, 370

Eck, Johann von, **1:**763

Eckermann, Johann Peter, **3:**151, 343

Eco, Umberto, *Name of the Rose, The,*
    5:434–35

eclogue, **1:**356, 811–12; **3:**67–69, 71, 92

Eclogue, op. 35 (Tomasek), **3:**68–69

economic libertarianism. *See* free market

economy. *See* mercantile economy

écossaise, **3:**35

ecphonetic neumes, **1:**16

écriture feminine, **2:**82

ecstasy, **1:**772

Ecstasy of Saint Teresa of Avila, **1:**772, 772

Ecuatorial (Varese), **5:**186, **5:**209

Eddas (Icelandic epics), **3:**492

Edi beo thu, hevene Quene (English
    twinsong), **1:**394–95

Editio Medicaea, **1:**631

Éditions Russes de Musique, **5:**229

Ed Sullivan Show, **5:**314

education. *See* academies; cathedral schools;
    liberal arts curriculum; music
    education; university

Edward II, King of England, **1:**122

Edward III, King of England, **1:**410

Edward IV, King of England, **1:**455

Edward VI, King of England, **1:**672, 673,
    675

Edwards, Allen, **5:**276, 280, 284
    Elliott Carter and, **5:**280, 284
    Flawed Words and Stubborn Sounds, **5:**276

"Effect of the Cold War on the Artist in
    the U.S., The" (Copland, speech),
    5:108

effeminacy, **3:**77–78, 406

E-flat clarinet, Berlioz's use of, **3:**337

E-flat modulation, **2:**507, 718

egalitarianism. *See* equality

Egbert, Bishop of York, **1:**7

Egeria (Spanish nun), **1:**8

Église de la Saine-Trinité (Paris), Messiaen
    and, **4:**230

Egmont (Goethe), **3:**11

Egmont Overture (Beethoven), **3:**11, 4, 197,
    198, 222, 419; **4:**650

Egypt, **3:**565

"1848: The Revolution of the Intellectuals"
    (Namier), **3:**375

Ehenburg, Ilya, "Thaw" and, **5:**460

Eight Etudes and a Fantasy (Carter),
    5:269–73

*Eight Hitchhiker Inscriptions from a Highway
    Railing at Barstow, California*
    (Partch), **5:**482, 483–85, 486

Eight Pieces for Four Timpani (Carter),
    5:273–75

Eight Songs for a Mad King (Davies)
    King George III and, **5:**427
    Pierrot Players and, **5:**426–27
    Randolph Stow and, **5:**427

eighteenth century
    classicism of, **2:**454

comic style and, **2:**437, 443–44

compositional "borrowings" in, **2:**327

concert programs in, **2:**499–500

domestic music, **2:**426–32

Enlightenment and, **2:**443–44, 460–96

as esthetic battleground, **2:**274–75

High Baroque and, **2:**1201

intermezzo's importance in, **2:**434–35

intermission plays, **2:**434–37

Italian musical hegemony in, **2:**158

late-century Classical period, **2:**646

late-century *Kapellen* disbandments in,
    2:607

mannerisms, **4:**448, 449

mid-century black hole, **2:**400, 432,
    434–35

mid-century social changes, **2:**419

mid-century sonatas, **2:**427–32

Mozartean concerto transformation
    and, **2:**606–25

opera buffa/opera seria division and, **2:**17,
    433–34, 445–60, 464, 485

opera seria's end in, **2:**485

semiotic codes of, **2:**538, 539–40, 680,
    682

symphony development and, **2:**497–588

Vivaldi concertos and, **2:**216–31

Eighth Book of Madrigals (Monteverdi),
    2:6–12, 10, 11

eighth century, **1:**11–35
    Gregorian chant, **1:**5–35
    map of Europe, **1:**3

Eighth Congress of the International
    Society for Musicology, **5:**265

eighth mode, **1:**83–84, 466

eighth notes, **1:**261, 355, 363

Eighth Sonata for piano (Prokofieff), **5:**9

Eighth Symphony (Shostakovich), **5:**8

Eighth Symphony in G major (Dvořák),
    3:765
    flute solo, **3:**766
    woodwinds, **3:**766

eight-mode system, **1:**22, 28, 553
    Aurelian and, **1:**76
    medieval, **1:**73–76

Eile mich, Gott, zu erretten (Schütz), **2:**66–68

Eimert, Herbert, twelve-tone music and,
    5:19, 37, 44, 51, 189
    György Ligeti and, **5:**49

Ein' feste Burg ist unser Gott. See Feste Burg . .
    ., Ein',

Ein Gespenst geht um in der Welt (Nono),
    5:89, 90

Ein Heldenleben (Strauss), **4:**374

"Einigkeit und Recht und Freiheit" (West
    German national anthem), **3:**130

Einstein, Albert, **4:**765; **5:**2–3, 321

Einstein, Alfred, **2:**457

Einstein on the Beach (Glass), **5:**388–89

"Einverständnis," **4:**544

Eisenhower, Dwight David, 107, 109

Eisenach, **2:**235, 239

Eisenstadt (Burgenland), **2:**526, 527, 538

Eisler, Hanns, **4:**541–43, 559–60, 649, 654,
    656, 658, 661, 765; **5:**11, 13, 83, 106
    kampflied and, **4:**658
    works of
      "Ändere die Welt, sie brauchtes,"
        4:542
      Die Massnahme, **4:**541, 543
      Massenlieder, **4:**542, 544

Either/Or (Kierkegaard), **3:**271–72

Eleanor of Aquitaine, **1:**106, 109, 110, 117,
    117, 118

"Eleanor Rigby" (Beatles), 321, 324

"Election, An" (Ives), **4:**257

Elector Palatine, **2:**505–7, 505, 525

Electra (mythology), **4:**48–49, 57

"electronic glove," **5:**509, 509

electronic music, **5:**189, 495

Elegie (Poulenc), **5:**103

Elegy (Massenet), **5:**181

Elektra, Hofmannsthal and, **4:**49, 57

Elektra (Strauss), **4:**48–58, 164
    Strauss's maximalist extreme and, **4:**49

Elektrax, John Oswald and, **5:**504

elektronische Musik, **5:**189

Elektronische Studie II (Stockhausen), **5:**190,
    190

Elementi teorico-pratici di musica (Galeazzi),
    2:702

Elements (Euclid), **1:**253

Elevation toccata, **2:**44

eleventh century, Winchester Tropers,
    1:93, 155, 402

"elfin" style, Mendelssohn (Felix) and,
    3:179–81

Elgar, Edward, **4:**266

Elias, Norbert, **3:**124

elided cadence, **2:**561, 563, 576, 584, 658

Elijah (Mendelssohn), **3:**173–74

Eliot, George, **3:**417

Eliot, T. S., **4:**525–26
    The Waste Land, **4:**473

Elisabeth Christina, Empress Consort of
    Holy Roman (Austrian) Empire,
    2:438

Elisabeth von England (Klenau), **4:**774

Elisir d'amore, L' (Donizetti), **3:**46

elite culture
    artistic cleverness/subtlety and,
      1:327–37
    court opera and, **2:**14
    in democratic age, **3:**742–43
    fifteenth-century, **1:**453
    high art and, **1:**116, 226, 326–27;
      2:112–13
    modern music and, **3:**416
    motet and, **1:**226–28, 236, 237–38, 239
    political climate and, **2:**125
    Romanticism and, **2:**645, 649
    salon culture and, **3:**75, 78, 79
    social, **3:**673
    Tinctoris generation of, **1:**454–59

elite culture (*continued*)
  See also high art
Elizabeth, Empress of Russia 3:235
Elizabeth I, Queen of England, 1:649, 671,
    673, 675, 676, 677, 678, 742
  Triumphs of Oriana madrigal collection
    to, 1:746
Elizabethan music, 2:115, 116
  keyboard, 2:45
Elizabethan Settlement, 1:675
Ellis, William Ashton, 3:493
Elman, Mischa, 4:256
El mois de mai/De se debent bigami (motet),
    1:234–515, 236, 239
Elsner, Józef, 3:447
Elysium, Beethoven and, 4:19
emancipation, nineteenth-century, 1:143;
    2:737–38
Emancipation Act (1861; Russia), 1:143
"emancipation of dissonance," 4:308–10,
    326, 332, 337, 340, 341, 342, 353, 358,
    465, 510, 522, 692
embellishment. *See* ornamentation
Emerson, Keith, 5:328
Emerson, Lake, and Palmer, 5:328
Emerson, Ralph Waldo, 4:267, 287, 354
  over-soul and, 4:244, 273
  works of
    "Over-Soul, The" 4:243
    "Self-Reliance," 4:143
Emmeran, Eusebius. *See* Daumer, Georg
    Friedrich
emotional expression. *See* musical
    expression; subjectivity
empathy, audiences and, 3:287
"Emperor" Concerto no. 5 in E-flat major,
    op. 73 (Beethoven), 2:671; 3:275
Emperor Quartet in C major (Haydn),
    3:130
empfindsamer Stil, Bach (C. P. E.) and,
    2:410, 413, 414, 416, 418, 426,
    437–29, 508, 529, 610, 624
Empfindsamkeit
  Beethoven's *Heileger Dankgesang* and,
    2:687
  definition of, 2:409–10
  fantasy style and, 3:65
  galanterie vs., 2:426–27, 428–29
  improvisation and, 2:414
  instrumental recitative and, 2:413
  lieder and, 3:120
  musical examples of, 2:411–13
  Sturm und Drang and, 2:416, 417, 529
  symphonies and, 3:108
Empfindung, definition of, 2:409–10
empiricism, 1:196, 798
Empress of Morocco, The (Settle), 2:126
emulation
  fifteenth-century, 1:474–75, 484, 486,
    493, 497–98, 499
  by Palestrina, 1:633–41

Encyclopédie (Diderot and Alembert, eds.),
    2:435, 435, 461, 462
endless melody (*unendliche Melodie*), 3:486,
    521, 547, 751
Enfant de troupe (Poulenc), 4:575
Enfant et les sortileges, L' (Ravel), 4:605
Engel, Joel, 4:108
Engel, Carl, 4:627
Engels, Friedrich, 4:745; 5:89
  Communist Manifesto, 4:745; 5:89
"Énigme éternelle, L'" octatonic-diatonic
    interaction and, 4:110, 111
"Énigme éternelle, L'" (Ravel), 4:108, 110, 111
England. *See* Great Britain; London
Engländer, Richard (Peter Altenberg
    pseud.), 4:193
English Channel, 1:421
English Civil War (1642–48), 2:124–27
English language
  Anglican chant setting in, 1:672
  musical setting of, 2:133, 134, 138
  Sumer is icumen in/Lhude sing cuccu!,
    1:387–88
English Opera Group, Britten and, 5:225
English style. *See* *contenance angloise*
English Suites (J. S. Bach), 2:262
Enguerrand de Marigny, 1:258
enharmonic genus, 1:32–33
"enlightened despotism," 2:462, 538
Enlightenment, 2:460–96; 3:25, 124, 166,
    287; 4:2
  Bach's (J. S.) church music as contrary
    to, 2:363–64, 368, 369, 390
  Burney's definition of music and, 2:363
  concert music and, 2:498
  Freemasons and, 2:479–80
  Haydn and, 2:577, 643
  ideas of, 2:368, 460–62, 475, 479, 481,
    495, 496, 600, 620, 621
  Leopold II's reactionism and, 2:460–61,
    621
  Mozart and, 2:463, 470, 472, 475,
    479–80, 481, 482, 494, 495
  Mozart's *Cosi fan tutte* as emblematic art
    work of, 2:479
  music as enjoyment view of, 3:294
  nineteenth-century historicism and,
    3:411
  opera buffa and, 2:443–44, 477
  opera seria as counter to, 2:175
  perversion of message of, 3:61
  political absolutism vs., 2:110, 435, 443,
    538
  political reactions against, 2:645
  "public sphere" concept and, 3:289
  Romanticism contrasted with, 2:390,
    460, 600, 645, 706, 724
  Scarlatti (Domenico) and, 2:390
  truth concept of, 3:61, 122
  universality as basis of, 2:302, 600, 645,
    738; 3:61, 121, 188
  War of the Buffoons and, 2:110, 443

En mon cuer (Machaut), 1:296–97, 298, 299
Eno, Brian, 5:328, 351, 352, 387–88
  education, 5:352
  Low, 5:391
  Theatre of Eternal Music, 5:362
Enoch Arden (Strauss), 4:459
Enoch Arden (Tennyson), 4:459
En remirant (Philippus), 1:338–39, 341, 341
ensemble
  Bellini finales, 3:210
  Code Rossini and, 3:15, 22
  finales, 3:22–27, 35, 38, 48, 49, 210
  Romantic opera and, 3:35, 46, 48, 210
  in Rossini operas, 3:12, 23
Ensemble InterContemporain, Pierre
    Boulez and, 5:478
Ensemble of the 13th Tone in Havana,
    4:292
entarte Kunst ("degenerate art"), 3:440, 531;
    4:755
Entartete Musik, 4:755
entertainment music, nineteenth-century
    origins of, 3:682
Entführung aus dem Serail, Die (Mozart),
    2:470–76, 479, 602, 678; 3:193,
    386, 638
"entrance opera" technique, 3:48, 209
en travesti. *See* trousers role
entrepreneurial class, 2:115. *See also*
    self-made man
"Entrücking," 4:315, 316–17, 318–19, 339
enueg (troubadour genre), 1:107
Epic and Novel (Bakhtin), 3:513
epic chronotope, 3:513
epic romances, 1:119, 422
epics, 3:119
  America's *Hiawatha*, 3:123, 763, 764
  Finnish *Kalevala*, 3:123, 126, 763
  Icelandic *Eddas*, 3:492
  Russia's *Song of Igor's Campaign*, 3:400
epic songs, 1:120, 208
Epiphanium Domino (Balaam motet), 1:399,
    401
Epiphany, 1:12, 399
*Épisode de la vie d'un artiste, Symphonie
    fantastique en cinq parties* (Berlioz),
    3:320
Epistle reading, in Mass ordo, 1:61(table)
Epokha (journal), 4:140
Epstein, Paul, 5:374
  Temple University, 5:374
equality
  Enlightenment, 2:111
  War of the Buffoons and, 2:111
equal temperament tuning, 2:247–48
Eraclea, L' (A. Scarlatti), 2:146, 147
Era of Common Practice, 2:189, 192
Erard, Sebastian, 2:653; 3:328
Erasmus, Desiderius, 1:438, 553, 672
Erbach, Christian, 2:49
Erbach, Countess of, 2:79
Erbauliche Gedancken (Picander), 2:378

Erben, Karel Jaromir, 3:463, 755

Ercole (Hercules) d'Este, Duke of Ferrara, 1:459, 523, 559–63, 696

"Erda" leitmotif (Wagner), 3:505, 513

Erk, Ludwig, 3:162

Erkel, Ferenc, 3:447–48; 4:369

　Bánk bán, 3:447, 448; 4:369, 370

　Hunyádi László, 3:447

Erlebnisse, 3:294, 296

Erlkönig (Goethe), 3:80, 126–29, 144, 158, 367, 369, 372

Erlkönig (Loewe), 3:155, 158–59, 367

Erlkönig (Reichardt), 3:126–28, 132, 149, 158, 367

Erlkönig (Schubert), 3:80, 81, 145–46, 148–52, 155, 158, 367, 371, 372

Erlkönig (Schwind), 3:129

Ernani (Verdi), 3:569, 574–75, 583

Ernoul Caupain, 1:120

Ernste Musik ("E-Musik"), 5:15, 189

Eroica Symphony (Third Symphony, op. 55; Beethoven), 2:110, 655–70, 671, 718; 3:275; 4:13, 14, 16, 648

　Beach's Gaelic Symphony and, 3:772

　Berlioz and, 3:327

　Borodin's First Symphony and, 3:788

　Brahms and, 3:704, 726, 742

　Chopin and, 3:366

　crescendo in, 2:669–70

　Dvořák's "New World" Symphony and, 3:756, 759

　first movement, 2:656–70

　four-bar opening of, 2:656–58

　"Marcia funebre," 2:685, 702

　rescinded dedication of, 2:656

　Rossini and, 3:22

　Schubert and, 3:95, 98

　second movement "Funeral March" in C minor, 2:702

　as sinfonia caratteristica, 2:680

　Wagner and, 3:531

Eros (Cupid), 2:331, 447, 453

erotic art (ars erotica), 3:36

eroticism

　alba (dawn-song) and, 1:110–11

　Arabic sung poetry and, 1:108

　duetto per camera and, 2:331–32, 340

　Gesualdo madrigal and, 1:738

　spiritual ecstasy and, 1:772

Erwartung ("Anticipation") (Schoenberg, op. 2, no., 1), 4: 33, 34–35, 303, 304, 310, 323, 326, 327, 330, 331, 341, 344, 345, 414, 516–17, 678, 679, 691

　harmonic progression and, 4:310

　"intuitive aesthetic" and, 4:680

　Mahler symphonies and, 4:303

　melodic motif in, 4:334–35

　Strauss operas and, 4:303

Erwin und Elmire (Goethe), 3:130

"Escape from Freedom" (Fromm), 5:2

"escape tone" (counterpoint), 1:368, 439

Escenas campestres (Gottschalk), 3:380

Eschberg set, 4:314, 315, 316, 317

　transposition of, Schoenberg and, 4:316

Eschenbach. See Wolfram von Eschenbach

esclamazione (vocal technique), 1:817, 821

Escudier (Paris publisher), 3:378

Es fuegt sich (Oswald), 1:142

España (Chabrier), 4:61

Essay in Composition Instruction, An (Koch), 2:622

Essay on the True Art of Playing Keyboard Instruments (C. P. E. Bach), 2:410–11, 414, 418

Essay upon Publick Spirit (Dennis), 2:312–13

Essays before a Sonata (Ives), 4:265, 267, 270, 273, 281

essence, 5:2

essences, Platonic, 1:37, 827; 2:720

essentialism, 1:381, 382, 385; 3:483

　women's creativity and, 2:82

Essercizi per gravicembalo (D. Scarlatti), 2:396

"Established Rules of Harmony, The" (Zarlino), 1:586–87

estampie, 1:294

"Est-ce Mars?" (song), variations on, 2:47–48

Este, Ercole d'. See Ercole (Hercules) d'Este, Duke of Ferrara

Este, Isabella d', 1:696

Esterháza palace (Eisenstadt), 2:526, 527, 538, 539

　main gate, 2:526

Esterházy, Anton, Prince, 2:555

Esterházy, Johann (János Nepomuk), Count, 2:608

Esterházy, Nikolaus Joseph, Prince, 2:526–27, 538, 539–40, 541, 553, 555, 571, 600, 601, 682; 3:261, 716

　baryton compositions for, 2:527, 527, 601

Esterházy, Paul Anton, Prince, 2:525–26

Esterházy family, 2:525–30, 555, 607; 3:79; 4:365

Esther (pastiche of Handel work), 3:314, 315

esthesic, meaning of, 2:13, 14

esthetic ecstasy, 3:528

estheticism, 3:62, 561–62; 4:145

esthetics, 1:541; 3:45, 115–16, 305

　ancient and medieval service music and, 1:65, 66

　Arcadians' neoclassicism and, 2:151

　Brendel's view of, 3:414

　earliest art-for-art's sake example and, 1:541

　Empfindung and Empfindsamkeit and, 2:409–10

　of Enlightenment, 2:390, 494

　of fourteenth-century, 1:359, 363–64

　Hegel's treatise on, 3:415

　of Lutheran church music, 1:769; 2:68

　of musical sounds, 2:363–64, 471–72, 494

　music historiography and, 1:472

paradox of, 1:496–97

　radical humanism and, 1:803–5

　Romantic, 1:142, 144, 359; 2:641, 701, 714

　of standard repertory, 2:289

　Winckelmann neoclassic, 2:453

　See also artistic creation; musical taste

Estro armonico, L' (Vivaldi), 2:224–25

Ethelwold, 1:93

"etherphone," Terman and, 5:181

ethnicity, 2:139, 550; 3:491, 767, 786

　nationalism and, 3:62–63, 178, 480

　otherness and, 3:405–6

ethnocentrism, 1:143–44, 185; 3:63, 345

　Beethovenian Romanticized ideal and, 2:670

　universality claims vs., 2:739

ethnomusicology, 5:382

ethos, 1:38, 131, 732, 815

etiquette books, 1:694, 709

Eton Choirbook, 1:513–18, 612

Eton College choir, 1:513, 515, 517

Étude aux casseroles (Schaeffer), 5:188

Étude aux chemins de fer (Schaeffer), 5:188

Étude en douze exercices (Liszt), 3:262

Étude noire (Schaeffer), 5:188

Étude pour Espace (Varese), 5:186

Études d'exécution transcendante d'après Paganini (Liszt), 3:266–68

Étude violette (Schaeffer), 5:188

Etymologiae (Isidore), 1:6

Eucharist, 1:8, 13, 24, 34, 53, 54, 313

　Lutheran chorale and, 1:758

　in Mass ordo, 1:61(table)

　tropes and, 1:50

　See also Mass

Euclid, 1:253

Eudes (or Odo) de Sully, Bishop of Paris, 1:174, 187

Eugene IV, Pope, 1:282

Eugene Onegin (Chaikovsky), 3:632–39, 663; 4:7

　Act III, polonaise, 3:796–97

　"Slïkhal li vï," 3:634–36

　Tatyana's leitmotif, 3:633, 636, 637

　Tatyana's letter scene, 3:636–39

Euphrosine, ou Le Tyran corrigé (Méhul), 3:2

Euridice (Caccini), 1:811, 812

Euridice (Peri), 1:811, 812, 813, 823, 824, 826; 2:21, 23, 24, 454

　musical significance of, 1:829–32

Euridice (Rinuccini), 1:811–12, 826

Euripides, 4:49

　Bacchae, Harry Partch and, 5:485–86

　Gluck operas and, 2:453, 459, 460

　Lully opera and, 2:90

Europe

　seventeenth-century status of, 2:139, 140(map)

　See also specific countries, cities, and city-states

European jazz, 4:599–13

Euryanthe (Weber), 3:193, 544

Eurydice (mythology), 1:811–12, 829, 832; 2:21–25, 88, 126, 454

Eusebius (Davidsbund character), 3:293, 294, 309, 317, 343

Evangeline (Longfellow), 3:158

Evangelisches Andachts-Opffer (Franck), 2:353

Evangelist, 1:776, 777; 2:73, 378

Evensong
    Anglican, 1:677
    See also Vespers

Evesham abbey, 1:402

evolution theory, 2:396; 3:412–13

Excita Domine (Alleluia), 1:42

existentialism, 3:272

existential loneliness, 2:600

exit opera, 3:48

Exodus, Book of, 2:316, 321

Exos Dexterous Hand Master ("Electronic glove), 5:509, *509*

exoticism
    Beethoven and, 3:11
    Dvořák and, 3:752–53, 767
    Gottschalk and, 3:377–78, 380
    nationalism and, 3:192–93, 347–48, 386, 393
    opera locales and, 3:667
    Russian music and, 3:786–87
    See also orientalism

Expert, Henry, *Les maitres musiciens de la Renaissance*, 4:67

"Explication des agrémens et des signes" (Couperin), 2:279

exponential powers, theory of, 1:248

exposition
    piano concerto, 2:609
    symphonic, 2:525

Exposition du système du monde (Laplace), 2:634

Exposition Internationale des Arts Décoratifs et Industriels Modernes, 4:776

exposition of fugue, 2:198, 201–2
    Bach (J. S.) shaping of, 2:242
    episodes between, 2:202, 220
    gigue and, 2:274

expression. *See* musical expression; self-expression

Expression musicale mise au rang des chimères, L' (Boyé), 2:458

expressionism, 4:28, 197, 307

"expressionist" school, formation of, 4:309

Ex semine clausula, 1:196, 209–11, *210, 211, 217, 218,* 222
    different texts for, 1:217–21, *218,* 222
    double motet on, 1:212, 215, 217

Extase-chord, 4:215
    manipulation of, 4:215, *216*

extempore fantasias, 3:262, 288

extemporization. *See* improvisation

extended exit, 3:654

Extensions (Feldman), 5:98

"Extents and Limits of Serial Technique" (Krenek), 5:40

extroversive semiotics, 1:652–54, 658; 2:539–40, 550, 571, 661, 680, 682, 718; 3:528, 756, 759

Eya dulcis/Vale placens (Tapissier), 1:423–24, *425–26,* 429

"eye-music" (Augenmusik), 1:778–79, 801

F

Fabula di Orfeo (musical drama), 1:823

faburden, 1:436, 437

Factue tue, 1:1

Fadeyev, Alexander, 4:793

Faenza Codex, 1:306–7, 322, 324, 371

Faeroe Islands, 1:393

"Fairies Song" (Shakespeare), 2:130

Fair Phyllis (Farmer), 1:750–51

Fairy Queen, The (Purcell), 2:127, 128, 130–31

"Faites lui mes aveux" (Gounod), 3:653

faith, 1:765
    Reformation vs. Counter Reformation source of, 1:771–72

fake-book, 1:130–31, *132*

fakesongs, 3:236

falala (nonsense refrain), 1:746

Falcon, Cornélie, 3:225

Falla, Manuela de, 4:506
    El sombrero de tres picos, 4:502, *504–5*

fallacies, 1:221
    essentialism as, 1:381
    genetic, 1:42, 221, 472
    poietic, 2:13, 14

false relation. *See* cross relation

falsetto, 2:98, 130; 3:578

falsobordone, 1:776; 2:18

Falstaff (Verdi), 3:599, 611, *611*
    opera comedization and, 3:615
    "Quand'ero paggio," 3:614, 615, 660

Fanciulla del west, La (Puccini), 4:751

Fanfare for Russia (Taylor), 4:670

Fanfare for the Common Man (Copland), 4:666, *667*; 5:13

fanfares, 1:424, 563

Fantaisie (Chopin), 3:350

Fantaisie in A minor for Piano and Orchestra (Schumann), 3:316–17, 336, 419

Fantaisies pittoresques, 3:471
    Glinka and, 3:464–65

fantasia (fantasy)
    Bach (C. P. E.) and, 2:414–16, 607, 624; 3:65, 312
    Bach (J. S.) and, 2:414
    cadenza and, 2:609–10
    Characterstück origins and, 3:119
    consort music and, 2:115–18, 120
    extempore, 3:262, 288
    fugue paired with, 2:247
    as Haydn's *Creation* Introduction precedent, 2:633–34

In Nomine, 2:115–20
    Josquin and, 1:546
    Lawes and, 2:122
    as metaphor, 2:634–35
    Mozart and, 2:611, 613, 624–34; 3:312, 314, 542
    musical meanings of, 1:546, 616
    Purcell and, 2:196–98, 202
    Sweelinck and, 2:44–46

Fantasia chromatica (Sweelinck), 2:44, 46

Fantasia in C minor (C. P. E. Bach), 2:414–17, 624
    Shakespearean text of, 2:416, 417

Fantasia in C minor, K. 475 (Mozart), 2:625–31, 634, 637, 692

Fantasia in D minor, K. 397 (Mozart), 2:624–26

Fantasia on Polish Airs (Chopin), 3:348

Fantastic Romanticism, 3:179–80

fantasy. *See* fantasia

fantazia. See fantasia

"Fantazia 7" (Purcell), 2:205–197

"Farben" (Schoenberg), 4:339

farce, 1:746; 2:447
    "fourth wall" and, 4:495

"Farewell" Symphony in F-sharp minor, no. 45 (Haydn), 2:534–40, 553
    dropping out of instruments from, 2:537–38, *539,* 540
    enigmas of, 2:537–38
    finale of, 2:534–38
    first movement of, 2:530–31, 540
    introversive/extroversive signs in, 2:539–40, 682
    movement linkage of, 2:533, 540
    story behind, 2:538
    Sturm und Drang and, 2:528–29, 530
    as unique tour de force

Farewell to Arms, A (Hemingway), 4:473

Farewell to Pioneers: Symphonic Elegy, A (Harris), 4:640–42

Farinelli (Carlo Broschi), 2:166–71, *172, 173, 174,* 237; 3:25
    cadenza and, 2:298, 299
    Handel snubbed by, 2:311, 340
    Metastasio friendship with, 2:172
    signature aria, 2:167–72

Farmer, John, 1:750
    Fair Phyllis, 1:750–51

Farnaby, Giles, 2:47, 48

Farrenc, Aristide, 3:364

Farwell, Arthur, 4:638

Fate motif
    Chaikovsky and, 3:796, 797
    Shostakovich and, 3:514–15
    Wagner and, 3:505, 513–17, 520, 528, 776
    Wolzogen and, 3:514, 515

Fathers of the Church, 1:24, 69, 106

Faugues, Guillaume, 1:458, 574
    Missa L'Homme Armé, 1:493

Fauré, Gabriel, 4:62, 97–107, *97*
    death of, 4:102

"decadent" poetry and, **4:**97
mélodies and, **4:**97, 100
neomedievalism and, **4:**101
Ravel and, **4:**111
Symbolist poetry and, **4:**97
works of
 Fantaisie for harp, **4:**101
 In paradisum deducant te Angeli, **4:**101–2
 La Bonne Chanson, **4:**100–101
 Le parfum impérissable, **4:**97, 98–99
 Requiem, In paradisum, **4:**102–3
 Une sainte en son auréole (poem), **4:**100, 101
Fauser, Annegret, **4:**125
Faust (Goethe), **3:**69, 71, 80, 151, 337, 596, 639; **4:**23, 126
Faust (Gounod), **3:**639–40, 640, 653
Faust et Hélene (L. Boulanger), **4:**126
Faust-Symphonie (Liszt), **3:**435–37, 546
fauxbourdon, **1:**435–39, 441, 442–43, 446, 501, 776
 meaning of, **1:**435–36
faux-naïveté, **1:**349–50; **3:**158
 Jeu de Robin et de Marion, Le (Adam), **1:**127, 128, 233, 349
Favola del figlio cambiato, La (Malipiero), **4:**749
favole in musica (musical tales), **1:**826–27, 832–34; **2:**11, 13–14, 15, 21, 23, 27; **3:**645
favole pastorale. See pastorals
"Favourite Songs in the Opera call'd Artaxerxes by Sig. Hasse," **2:**169
F-based hexachord, **1:**273
F clef, **1:**99–100
Feast of Corpus Christi, **1:**48, 89, 686
Feast of St. Mary's Nativity, **1:**191–92, 291
Feast of St. Maximinus, **1:**91
Feast of St. Stephen the Martyr, **1:**173, 174
Feast of the Annunciation, **1:**565, 566
Feast of the Assumption, **1:**523, 566
Feast of the Circumcision, **1:**94, 173, 177
Feast of the Holy Innocents, **1:**37
Feast of the Immaculate Conception, **1:**566
Feast of the Nativity, **1:**566
Feast of the Pentecost, **1:**686
Feast of the Reformation, **2:**353
feasts, Roman Catholic cycle of, **1:**12, 171, 173, 314, 632, 642
 Marian, **1:**566
February Revolution (Russia), **4:**743, 744f
Fébus, Gaston. *See* Gaston III of Languedoc
Feder, Stuart, **4:**251, 253, 283, 284–85
 Charles Ives, My Father's Song, **4:**251
Federal Theatre Project, **4:**650
Feeling and Form (Langer), **5:**277, 332
Feen, Die (Wagner), **3:**481
feierlich, oratorios and, **3:**164
feint, Wagner's use of, **3:**542, 552
Feldman, Martha, **2:**159–60, 174, 175

Feldman, Morton, **5:**77, 98, 351, 359
 "free-rhythm notation," **5:**100
 John Cage and, **5:**77
 Stefan Wolpe and, **5:**98
 works of
  Extensions, **5:**98
  For Philip Guston, **5:**101
  Intersections, **5:**98
  Piece for Four Pianos, **5:**99–100
  Projection I, **5:**98–99
  Projection II, **5:**99
  Projections, **5:**98
  Second String Quartet, **5:**101
Felicianus of Musti, **1:**70
Felix Kon School of Higher Musical Education, **4:**777
Felix virgo/Inviolata/AD TE SUSPIRAMUS (Machaut), **1:**270–73, 291, 301, 302
Fellini, Federico, **3:**674
"feminine endings," **2:**413
femininity
 bourgeois notions of, **3:**36
 as salon music characterization, **3:**77–78
feminist movement, performance art and, **5:**492
feminist musicology, **2:**78, 82, 619–20
Ferdinand, Emperor of Austria, **3:**445
Ferdinand I, Archduke of Austria, **1:**762
Ferdinand I, King of Naples, **1:**453
Ferdinand II, King of Aragon (Spain), **1:**724
Ferdinand IV, King of Naples, **2:**601
Ferdinandus, M., **3:**496
fermata, **1:**433, 611; **2:**171
 Beethoven and, **3:**109, 110
 C-minor moods and, **2:**697, 698, 699–700, 706, 718, 727
 Schubert and, **3:**110
Ferne, op. 9, no. 9 (Mendelssohn), **3:**185
Ferneyhough, Brian
 Darmstadt Summer Courses and, **5:**475
 "nested rhythms" and, **5:**476
 String Quartet no. 2, **5:**476
Ferrabosco, Alfonso, **1:**677–78; **2:**114
 In Nomines, **2:**118–19
Ferrante Gonzaga of Mantua, **1:**715
Ferrara, **1:**523, 544, 545, 559–63
 virtuoso women singers in, **2:**80
Ferrari, Benedetto, **2:**33
Fervaal (D'Indy), **4:**61
Feste Burg ist unser Gott, Ein' (Agricola), **1:**762, 763
Feste Burg ist unser Gott, Ein', BWV 80 (J. S. Bach), **2:**353–63, 364, 402
Feste Burg ist unser Gott, Ein' (Calvisius), **1:**768–69
Feste Burg ist unser Gott, Ein', (Luther), **1:**760, 761; **3:**167–68, 229–32
 Les Huguenots and, **3:**229–32
Feste Burg ist unser Gott, Ein' (Mahu), **1:**762, 764

Feste romane (Respighi), **4:**750
"festival" orchestra, **3:**711
festival song, English, **1:**420
Festspielhaus (Bayreuth), **3:**498, 499
Fete d'eau (Ravel), **4:**111
Fêtes de la Révolution (France), **3:**319
Fétis, François-Joseph, **2:**637; **3:**333, 340, 341
feudalism, **1:**107–43, 406
 basis of, **1:**107, 141
 cathedral clerical hierarchy and, **1:**169, 207–8
 eastward progression of, **1:**143
 hierarchy in, **1:**107
 Protestant Reformation as anti-, **1:**753
 Roman Catholic hierarchy and, **1:**772
 urbanization's inroads on, **1:**120, 143
Feuermann, Emanuel, **4:**765
"Feuilles mortes" (Debussy), **4:**78
Févin, Antoine de, **1:**555, 573–76
 Missa super Ave Maria, **1:**574–76
"Few Drops of Phenomenology, A" (Ortega), **4:**519
Fibonacci series, **5:**51
Ficino, Marsilio, **1:**615–16, 798
fiddlers
 "In seculum," **1:**232, 233
 madrigal accompaniment, **1:**352
 medieval, **1:**131, 132, 141
 virtuosos improvisation by, **1:**536, 538
Fidelio (Beethoven), **2:**670, 676; **3:**1–7, 2; **4:**458
 Berlioz on, **3:**334–35
 Dungeon Scene, **3:**203, 246
 earlier versions of, **3:**2–3
 Finale, **3:**4, 5–7
fiefs, **1:**107
Field, John, **4:**352
 Chopin and, **3:**346, 348
 Liszt on, **3:**64–65, 71, 292
 Nocturne no. 4 in A major, **3:**71–74
 nocturnes, **3:**64–65, 68, 71–74, 348
 in Russia, **3:**73–75
 salon music, **3:**74, 75, 78
 Schubert and, **3:**87, 88
 as teacher, **3:**75
Fierabras (Schubert), **3:**140
fifteenth century
 cyclic Mass Ordinaries, **1:**459–500
 emulative composition and, **1:**474–75, 484, 486, 493, 497–98
 English style and, **1:**422–52, 461
 V-I bass introduction and, **1:**471
 gymel, **1:**395
 harmonic changes and, **1:**471–72
 instrumental music and, **1:**536–46
 international style of, **1:**378, 380, 384, 422, 453–59
 Italian arts patronage and, **1:**277–81
 motet and, **1:**280–87, 399–433, 461, 501–26
 musical coloration and, **1:**266
 musical Mariolatry and, **1:**501

fifteenth century (continued)
  syncopated counterpoint and, 1:368
  vernacular genres and, 1:526–34
  virtuoso improvisation and, 1:536–41
  See also Renaissance
Fifth Book of Madrigals (Monteverdi) 2:2, 4–5
Fifth Brandenburg Concerto (J. S. Bach). See Brandenburg Concerto no. 5 in D major
fifth equivalence, 1:151, 495
fifth mode. See spondaic meter
fifths. See circle of fifths; pentachord; V–I cadence
Fifth Brandenburg Concerto (Bach), 5:368
Fifth Suite (Bach), 5:144
Fifth Symphony in B-flat major (Schubert), 3:80
Fifth Symphony in C minor, op. 67 (Beethoven), 2:692, 705–20; 3:1, 4, 108, 109, 331, 778
  Borodin's Second Symphony and, 3:789
  Brahms and, 3:694–95, 699, 720, 724, 726
  Chaikovsky and, 3:793
  coded elements in, 2:718
  critiques of, 2:692
  finale's fifty-four bar coda, 2:721
  first performance of, 2:655
  four-note opening as germinal seed of, 2:706–12, 713, 717
  Hoffmann's exigesis of, 2:705–6, 709
  Liszt's Piano Concerto no. 1 and, 3:279, 282, 285
  "new theme" in coda of, 2:713–14
  organic sound structure and, 2:714
  Paisiello and, 3:18
  Piano Trio, op. 1, no. 3 compared with, 2:706–7
  scherzo, 2:718
  scherzo-finale interrelationship, 2:718, 720
  Schubert and, 3:80
  second movement, 2:714–17
  Stamitz's Orchestra Trio in C minor and, 2:507, 718, 719
  struggle-to-victory narrative of, 2:694
Fifth Violin Concerto in A major, no. 5, K. 219 (Mozart), 2:602–7
fifth voice, 1:597
50 Präludien (Moscheles), 3:351
Figaro plays (Beaumarchais), 3:16
figurae, 2:59
figural music. See polyphony
figured (figuralis) song, 1:439
figured bass. See continuo
Figurenlehre (Bernhard theory), 2:59
Fille du régiment, La (Donizetti), 3:46
Final Alice (Del Tredici), 5:442–45
finales, 3:210
  Beethoven's Fifth Symphony, 2:721

Beethoven's fugal preoccupation and, 2:727
  chain, 3:5
  continuous, 3:210, 599
  Da Ponte on, 2:487
  Haydn's "Farewell" Symphony, 2:534–38
  Haydn's "Surprise" Symphony, 2:573–77
  late Haydn characteristics of, 2:577
  Mannheim symphonies, 2:506
  of Mozart, 2:622
  Mozart's Don Giovanni, 2:490, 491
  operatic ensembles and, 3:22–27, 35, 38, 48, 49, 210
  Piccinni's Buona Figliuola, 2:451–52
  Rossini first-act, 3:25–27
finals, 1:73–76, 77–79
  C and A as, 1:553–54, 572, 587, 592
  four, 1:73–74, 76, 77–78, 99, 587
  parallel doubling and, 1:152
  three, 1:99
fin' amors
  conventions of, 1:108–9, 111
  French variant, 1:118
  Machaut refinement of, 1:291–98
finary form, Scarlatti (Domenico) keyboard pieces and, 2:391
Finck, Henry Theophilus, 4:255
Finck, Hermann, 1:589
Fine, Irving, 4:614f
fine amours. See fin' amors
Fines amouretes ai (Adam), 1:124–25
"Fingal's Cave" (Mendelssohn), 3:183
Fink, Robert, 3:695
  "Madison Avenue" and minimalism, 5:396
Finland, Kalevala epic, 3:123, 126, 763
Finley, Karen, aggressive feminism and, 5:492
Finnissy, Michael
  Darmstadt Summer Courses and, 5:475
  History of Photography in Sound, 5:476
Finta semplice, La (Mozart), 2:464–65
Finto Nino, Il, overo La Semiramide riconosciuta (Araja), 3:234–35
Fiori musicali (Frescobaldi), 2:43, 49
fioritura (florid singing), 1:356
Firebird (Stravinsky), 4:152, 154–59, 160, 170, 240, 447; 5:127, 134
  Petrushka-chord and, 4:164
Fireside Book of Folk Songs, The (Boni), 4:657, 659
Fireside Tales (MacDowell), 3:768
First Berlin School, 3:126, 130
First book of ballets to five voyces, The (Morley), 1:746
First Crusade, 1:96
First Delphic Hymn, 1:33
first-inversion triads, 1:406
first mode. See trochaic meter
first-movement form. See sonata form

first practice. See stile antico
First String Quartet (Carter), 5:280–85, 287–98
First Symphony (Mahler), 5:343
First Violin Sonata (Ives), 5:284
First World War. See World War I
First Zionist Congress, 3:456
Fischer, C., 3:417
Fischer, Johann Caspar Ferdinand, 2:248–49, 259–60
  Journal de printemps, Le, 2:259–60
  Musicalisches Blumen-Büschlein, op. 2, 2:260
Fischer, Kurt von, 1:352
Fischer, Wilhelm, 2:212, 400
Fischer-Dieskau, Dietrich, 5:258
Fischerin, Die, 3:126
Fitzgerald, F. Scott, 4:589
  The Great Gatsby, 5:515
Fitzwilliam Museum (Cambridge), 2:45
Fitzwilliam Virginal Book, 2:45, 47
five-note scale. See pentatonic scale
  V–I cadence, 1:409, 447, 469, 470–71
Five Orchestral Pieces, op. 16 (Schoenberg), 4:307, 339, 342
Five Pieces for Orchestra, op. 10 (Webern), 4:347, 351, 692
fixed tune. See cantus firmus
flagellants (flagellanti), 1:133–34
flageolet, Vivaldi concerto for, 2:217
Flaminio, Il (Pergolesi), 2:440
Flanders. See Belgium
Flanders and Swann (comedy team), 3:801
Flaques sonores ("sound puddles"), 4:563
flat keys, as pathos connotation, 2:121, 686
flat submediant, 3:66
  Beethoven and, 3:69
  Schubert and, 3:87, 88, 92, 94–101, 111–12
  Tomášek and, 3:69, 70
Flatterzunge, 4:615
flatward modulation, 2:370
Flaubert, Gustave, 3:397, 631
Flavio (Handel), 2:307
Flawed Words and Stubborn Sounds (Edwards), 5:276
Fledermaus, Die (J. Strauss), 3:648–51
"Fledermaus Waltz" (J. Strauss), 3:648, 649–51
Fleet Prison (London), 2:46
Flegeljahre, Die (Jean Paul), 3:294
Flemish composers. See Belgium
Fleurs du mal, Les (Baudelaire), 4:84
Fleury, Hélene, 4:125
Fleury Play-book, 1:93
Fliegende Holländer, Der (Wagner), 3:483–85, 484, 487, 501, 504
Flight into Egypt, 1:177
Flo. See Florence Codex
Florence, 2:80, 81, 139
  academies, 1:798–801, 818
  Boccaccio and, 1:365–66

cathedral dedication, 1:282, 285
Dante and, 1:351, 367
Euridice performance, 1:832–33
Handel in, 2:237
intermedii and, 1:803–5, 831, 832
literary music and, 1:722
madrigalists, 1:353, 723, 818
monodic revolution and, 1:823, 826
musical drama and, 2:14, 16
musical tales and, 1:826–27
Renaissance art, 1:382
trecento, 1:351–74, 382
urban elite of, 1:367, 368, 383
See also Medici family
Florence Codex (Flo), 1:177, 179, 180,
    181–83, 186, 187, 198, 199, 202, 203,
    402
    earliest surviving Latin-texted motets in,
    1:219
    measurement dimensions of, 1:184
    Veris ad imperia conductus, 1:397–99
Florestan (Davidsbund character), 3:293,
    294, 295, 309, 317, 340
florid style, 1:356, 363, 373, 667
Flos regalis (conductus), 1:403, 404–5, 406
Flow My Tears (Dowland), 1:742, 743
Fluorescences (Penderecki), 5:217
flute
    Atys "sleep scene" and, 2:100
    Bach's (J. S.) music for, 2:291, 293, 295,
    300
    Couperin and, 2:279
    in Dvořák's Eighth Symphony, 3:766
    keyboard sonata obbligato of, 2:428
    Lucia duet with, 3:53–54, 59
    Vivaldi concertos for, 2:217
    Vivaldi's *Primavera* arranged for, 2:227
Fluxus, 5:91–95
Flying Dutchmen, The (Wagner), 3:483–85,
    484, 487, 501, 504
Flynn, Errol, 4:551
F-major mode, 1:274, 394, 425, 447, 448
Foà, Roberto, 2:217
Foix, county of, 1:342–45
Fokine, Mikhail, 4:152
folia (ground bass), 1:626
"Folia, La" (Corelli), 2:193
Folies Bergère, Josephine Baker and, 4:602
folk dances
    Chopin and, 3:348, 357
    Dvořák and, 3:754
folkishness, eighteenth-century connotation
    of, 2:550
folklore
    German, 3:122–29, 166, 422
    German Romanticism and, 1:138
    Glinka's *A Life for the Tsar* and, 3:233,
    241–46
    Irish, 3:771
    nationalism and, 3:122
    Russia and, 3:233, 464
    Verdi's *Va, pensiero* and, 3:572–73

Wagner and, 3:485, 501, 504
Weber's *Der Freischütz* and, 3:197
folk music, 1:65; 2:432; 5:314–16
    Balakirev and, 3:469–77
    ballads and, 3:126–29, 367
    ballata inception as, 1:364
    British round and, 1:387–92
    chorales and, 3:166
    Czech, 3:444, 765
    Glinka and, 3:237–38, 242, 465–67
    Haydn arrangements of, 3:130
    Haydn's musical spoofs on, 2:549, 550
    Herder's anthology of, 3:123, 126
    lieder and, 3:120, 123, 132, 155
    as metrical psalm settings, 1:597
    Minnesingers and, 1:136–37
    Mozart and, 2:480, 549
    opera and, 3:187, 194, 448–51
    in Puccini's *Madama Butterfly*, 3:667
    revival, 4:649, 659
    Romanticism and, 1:703
    Russian, 3:233, 236, 242, 397, 469–76,
    624–25
    Schumann on, 3:345
    Tenorlied and, 1:701
    troubadour genres and, 1:113, 397
    Weber and, 3:194
"Folksong — American Big Business"
    (Harris) (article), 4:672
"Folksong Jamboree" (Harris), 4:671
"Folksong Symphony" (Harris), 4:671
Folle journée, ou le mariage de Figaro, La
    (Beaumarchais), 2:477–78
Fomin, Yevstigney, *Yamshchiki na podstave*,
    3:236, 237
Fons bonitatis (Kyrie verse), 1:111
Fontainebleau, 2:442; 4:614, 623, 649; 5:389
Fontana Mix (Cage), 5:196, 197
Fontane di Roma (Respighi), 4:750
Fontegara (Ganassi dal Fontego), 1:620
Fontenelle, Bernard Le Bovier de, 2:208,
    229, 392, 642
foot, musical. *See* metric foot; *pes*
Foote, Arthur William, 3:769
For Philip Guston (Feldman), 5:101
forest horns. See *Waldhörner*
Forkel, Johann Nikolaus, 2:388; 3:712
formalism, 3:783; 5:9
Formenlehre, 3:315, 421
formes fixes (lyric poetry), 1:125–26, 143
forms (Platonic), 1:69, 71
Forster, E. M., 5:228, 229, 230
Fort, Syvilla, 5:58, 73
    Bacchanale, 5:59, 73
    Bonnie Bird and, 5:58
Forte, Allen, 4:314, 316, 360
Fortner, Wolfgang, 5:20–21, 94
Fortspinnung (melodic elaboration),
    2:212–13, 242
Fortuna desperata (Busnoys attrib.), 2:184,
    184
Fortuna desperata (Greiter), 1:732

Fortunatus, Venantius, Bishop of Poitiers,
    1:47, 48
"For unto us a Child is born" (Handel),
    2:332, 334–35, 336
Forza del destino, La (Verdi), 3:594, 595
Foster, Stephen, 1:18; 3:378, 380
    "Camptown Races," 3:378, 382; 4:668
    "Massa's in de Cold, Cold Ground,"
    4:275
Foucault, Michel, 3:36, 61; 4:85
Foundling Hospital chapel (London),
    2:326
Fountain (Duchamp), 5:72
Fountain of Youth, 1:257, 258
Fouquet, Jean, 1:455
Four Dirges, op. 9a (Bartok), 4:384, 385, 386,
    396
Four Dreams of China, The (Yooung), 5:359
four elements, 1:71
four finals, 1:73–74, 76, 77–78, 99, 587
Four Organs (Reich), 5:375–79, 384, 386
four-part polyphony, 1:174, 187, 198,
    298–305, 318
    canzona books and, 1:787
    conductus, 1:199–201, 199
    contratenor, 1:270–73, 298–99, 301, 302
    Du Fay Credo and, 1:498
    Lutheran chorale and, 1:765–66
    Masses and, 1:782
    Miss Caput and, 1:466–71, 482
    Morley madrigal and, 1:746
    as Passion text setting, 1:776–77
    vernacular songs and, 1:697
four-part texture, 1:301–5, 318
Four Passions cycle, 5:524
Four Saints in Three Acts (Thomson-Stein),
    4:589, 660; 5:394
Four Seasons, The (Vivaldi), 2:225–31, 317;
    5:75
    popularity of, 2:226
    Spring, 2:225–31
    in standard repertory, 2:234
Four Serious Songs, op. 121 (Brahms), 4:356
four species of fifths, 1:73–74
4'33" (Cage), 5:73, 95, 355
fourteenth century
    Ars Nova, 1:248–87
    Avignon Ordinary styles, 1:310–21
    English musical nationalism and, 1:409
    esthetics, 1:359, 363–64
    Italian vernacular song and, 1:350,
    351–85
    madrigalists and, 1:352–85
    mathematics and, 1:248–55
    motet and, 1:232, 236, 248–87, 311, 461
    musical coloration and, 1:266
    musical technical competition and,
    1:337–42
    standard cadence in, 1:276
fourth (Hypophyrgian), 1:82
fourth equivalence, 1.495 See also tetrachord
Fourth Quartet (Bartók), 5:19

Fourth Quartet (Schoenberg), **5:**153
Fourth String Quartet (Carter), **5:**304
Fourth Symphony (Ives), **5:**268
"fourth wall," theater and, **4:**495–96, 537
Foweles in the frith (English twinsong), **1:**395
Fox, Christopher, **5:**476
Fox, Oscar J., **4:**662, 663
   "Git Along, Little Dogies," **4:**664
foxtrot, **4:**606
fractio modi, **1:**181
fragments, musical, **3:**315
   Chopin and, **3:**350–51
Fra i due litiganti il terzo gode (Sarti), **2:**493, 631
France
   Albigensian Crusade and, **1:**116
   ARS GALLICA and, **3:**775
   Ars Nova and, **1:**248–87
   ars subtilior composition and, **1:**342–46
   Avignon papacy amd, **1:**249, 307–14, *310*
   Berlioz and, **3:**318–41
   Bourbon dynasty and, **3:**11, 14, 206, 211, 214
   censorship in, **3:**211, 227, 577
   centralized power of, **2:**68
   choeurs universels and, **3:**162–63
   civic ceremonial music and, **3:**319–20
   Code Napoléon and, **3:**15
   comédie larmoyante and, **2:**447, 450
   comic opera origins and, **2:**447; **3:**187
   concert music's birth in, **2:**498–99
   conservatories in, **2:**736
   consistent national borders of, **2:**139
   court opera and, **2:**88, 96–97, 106, 127; **3:**206
   as Cypriot cultural influence, **1:**345
   English cultural interchange with, **1:**397–407, 409, 410–11, 413, 421–22
   English invasion of, **1:**421, 422, 433, 461
   English musical influence on, **1:**422, 423, 433–52
   Enlightenment in, **2:**443, 460–61, 462, 706
   feudalism in, **1:**107, 143
   as German musical influence, **2:**259–61
   German nationalism and, **1:**142
   Germany and, **3:**121, 124, 158, 560, 712, 776, 786
   Gluck and, **2:**459–60
   grand opéra and, **3:**11, 207–14
   grand siècle and, **2:**111, 454
   Hundred Years War and, **1:**408, 421, 422, 447
   Italian musical style vs., **2:**86
   as Italian trecento influence, **1:**366–67, 368, 371, 374–78
   Italy and, **3:**569
   July Monarchy of, **3:**205–6, 214, 218, 266, 319, 348
   July Revolution of, **3:**206, 212, 214, 319
   Lully and, **2:**85–104

   Machaut and, **1:**270–73, 289–307, *289*, 317–36
   Machaut's artistic heirs and, **1:**336–42
   motet and, **1:**219–21, 229–36, *229*, *233*, 255–77, 286, 378
   music journalism in, **2:**737
   music publishing in, **1:**692, 694, 706, 708, 710
   national anthem of, **3:**130, 223
   nationalism and, **3:**205–6, 567, 775–76
   nineteenth-century symphonic music in, **3:**677–78, 679–80, 745, 774–81, 783–86
   opera in. *See* French opera
   opéra lyrique and, **3:**639–43, 653
   operetta and, **3:**644–47
   orientalism and, **3:**387–91, 393
   ornamentation and, **2:**281, 282
   piano trio genre and, **2:**695
   polyphonic style and, **1:**429
   Reign of Terror in, **3:**61, 211, 214
   Revolution of 1789 of, **1:**253, 579; **2:**302, 443, 462, 577, 645, 736; **3:**61, 162
   Romanticism in, **3:**318
   Romantic opera in, **3:**205–30
   Second Empire, **3:**646
   style brisé (broken style) and, **2:**249–50
   Thirty Years War and, **2:**56
   trouvères in, **1:**116–27, 142, 219
   urbanization in, **1:**120, 207
   vernacular song in, **1:**106–7, 351, 706–13
   Vitry and, **1:**248, 249, 256–58, 259, 261, 267, 281, 286
   Vivaldi's *Primavera* popularity in, **2:**226, 227
   Wagner's hostility toward, **3:**559, 560–61
   See also Aquitaine; Burgundy; Franks; Paris; Provençal
Francesco I, Grand Duke of Tuscany, **1:**799, 803, 804
Francesco da Milano, **1:**616, 617, 620
Franchomme, Auguste, **3:**350
Francis, Kay, **4:**551
Francis (François) I, King of France, **1:**558, 581, 706, 708, 711
Francis II, Emperor of Austria, **2:**462
Franciscans, **1:**133
Francis from Bosnia, **1:**698–99
Francis of Assissi, Saint
Franck, César, **3:**774–81, *774*, *783*; **4:**61, 230, 266, 636; **5:**430
   harp use controversy and, **3:**328
   Liszt and, **3:**777
   works of
      Piano Quintet in F minor, **3:**776
      Piano Trio in F-sharp Minor, op. 1, no. 1, **3:**777
      Psyche, **3:**776
      "Symphonic Variations," **3:**776
      Symphony in D minor, **3:**774, 776–81, 784; **4:**210, 266, 269

Franck, Salomo, **2:**353, 354, 355
Franconian notation, **1:**212–17, 234–35, 238, 248, 249, 250
   Ars Nova notation and, **1:**355
   examples of principles of, **1:**216
Franco-American Musical Society, **4:**286, 291, 379
Franco of Cologne, **1:**250, 254
   on conductus, **1:**198–99, 403
   mensural notation treatise by, **1:**215, 248
   See also Franconian notation
Franco-Prussian War (1870–71), **3:**560, 566, 569, 710, 719, 775, 776; **4:**106
Franco-Roman chant. *See* Gregorian chant
Francs-juges, Les (Berlioz), **3:**319, 331
Frank, Joseph, **4:**595, 598
Frankenstein, Alfred, **5:**365
Frankenstein (Shelley), **3:**194
Frankish mode theory, **1:**28–29, 48, 72–104, 553, 587
   classification and, **1:**74–75, 378–80
   composition and, **1:**80–86
   Hermann Contractus and, **1:**99–100
   versus and, **1:**86–95
Frankist chant, **4:**101
Franklin, Benjamin, **3:**53
Franks, **1:**2–5
   Carolingian Empire, **1:**2–7, 106, 141
   chant and, **1:**5–7, 13, 21, 40, 234
   chant and liturgical reform of, **1:**37–67, 111, 298
   "Credo I" and, **1:**34
   harmony and, **1:**147
   high art doctrine and, **1:**459
   hymns and, **1:**41–43, 47–49
   Mass ordinary standardization by, **1:**53–62
   monastic music theory and, **1:**71–76
   music treatise of, **1:**17, 44, 45
   neumes and, **1:**14–18, 62
   notation and, **1:**28, 47
   polyphony and, **1:**44–47, 45
   tonaries and, **1:**72–76
   tropes and, **1:**50–53
   See also Frankish modal theory
Franz Joseph, Emperor of Austria, **3:**445, 710; **4:**366
Franz Liszt als Symphoniker (Brendel), **3:**421
"Franz Liszt Exerts His Spell on the Ladies in the Audience" (caricature), **3:**267, 268, 269, 292
Frappolone e Florinetta (intermezzo), **2:**434–35
"Fraternal republics," **5:**11
Frauenlob (Heinrich von Meissen), **1:**140, *141*
Frazer, Sir James, **4:**188
Frederick I (Barbarossa), Holy Roman Emperor, **1:**134
Frederick II (the Great), King of Prussia, **2:**385, 410, *411*, 413, 462, 509; **4:**361
Frederick II, Holy Roman Emperor, **1:**135

Frederick August II, Elector of Saxony, **2:**157, 222, 375, 376

Frederick William, King of Prussia, **2:**509

"free association," **4:**326, 327

free intellect, **2:**460–61

free market, **2:**114, 115

  canon formation in wake of, **2:**620

  Handel as composer of, **2:**239, 340

  Haydn as composer of, **2:**541, 555, 571, 607, 639

  Mozart as composer of, **2:**600, 607–8, 620, 649

  music composition and, **2:**737

  public concert series as, **2:**571

  See also mercantile economy

Free Music for string quartet (Grainger), **5:**182

Free Music No. 2 (Grainger), **5:**182, 184

"Free Music Machine," Grainger and, **5:**183

Free Speech Movement, **5:**94

Freed, Alan, **5:**313

  coining term "rock 'n' roll," **5:**313

freedom, in Hegelian theory, **3:**413, 414

Freeman, Jason, "interactive sound installations" and, **5:**514

Freemasons, **2:**479, 557

free-standing note (*nota simplex*), **1:**187, 192, 197, 209, 217

Freigedank, K. (Richard Wagner), **3:**177–79

Freischütz, Der (Weber), **3:**191–205, 208, 217, 236, 447, 455, 763; **4:**135, 458

  criticism of, **3:**204–5

  Gilbert and Sullivan parody of, **3:**652

  Overture, **3:**197–202, 204, 419

  "Volkslied," **3:**194–96

  Wagner on, **3:**194–97, 208, 479

  Wolf's Glen scene, **3:**198, 202–5, 202, 217, 225, 335

French ballet, **4:**131–32, 151

French horn, Rossini and, **3:**21

French language, **1:**102; **2:**695; **3:**345

  accent signs, **1:**114

  as German court language, **2:**289

  Italian mercantile elite and, **1:**367

  motet text in, **1:**219, 220

French modernism, **4:**59–60

French opera

  background of, **2:**87–89

  ballet in, **2:**100; **3:**12, 200

  bourgeois interests and, **3:**214–19

  comédie larmoyante and, **2:**447, 450, 452

  first officially sponsored work, **2:**87–88

  Gluck and, **2:**459–60

  grand opéra and, **3:**11, 207–23

  grand siècle and, **2:**111, 454

  Italian opera contrasted with, **2:**88–89, 103

  Italian singers and, **2:**88

  Italizan hybridization with, **2:**459–60

  Lully and, **2:**86, 89–106

  political debates and, **2:**86

production process of, **3:**217–18

Purcell's importations from, **2:**135

Rameau and, **2:**109–10

rescue theme in, **3:**2–3, 239, 249

Romantic opera and, **3:**205–30

Rossini and, **3:**11, 775

Rousseau's commentary on, **2:**442, 443

stage machinery of, **2:**88, 106, 127

War of the Buffoons and, **2:**110, 443

See also tragédie lyrique

French Revolution, **1:**579; **2:**302, 443, 462, 577, 736; **3:**61, 162; **4:**471

  backlash against, **2:**645

  ballet and, **4:**133

  decimal system and, **1:**253

French sixth chord, **4:**54, 198, 199, 205, 206, 209, 211, 215, 217, 218, 221

French Suites (J. S. Bach), **2:**262–77

  no. 5 in G major, **2:**263–66, 267–74

French surrealism, **4:**660

"Frère Jacques" (round), **1:**331, 399

Frescobaldi, Girolamo, **1:**821, 823; **2:**35–44, 35, 53, 120, 259, 260

  improvisations of, **2:**37

  keyboard publications of, **2:**36, 37

  toccata use by, **2:**37, 40–44

  works of

    Aria di romanesca, **1:**823, 824, 825

    Arie musicale, **1:**824–25

    Cento partite sopra passacagli, **2:**37, 39, 40

    Dunque dovro, **1:**824, 825

    Fiori musicali, **2:**43, 49

    Primo libro d'intavolatura, **2:**41–42

    Toccata nona (Toccata IX), **2:**41–42

Freud, Sigmund, **2:**599; **3:**155, 293, 559; **4:**308, 327, 567; **5:**93, 415

  "ego" vs."id," **4:**330

  Oedipus complex and, **4:**124, 676

  psychoanalysis and, **4:**307

Freunde von Salamanka, Die (Schubert), **3:**84

Friedan, Betty, **5:**307

Feminine Mystique, The, **5:**307

Friedrich. *See* Frederick

Friedrich, Caspar Friedrich, **2:**644

Frigyesi, Judit, **4:**374, 375

Fripp, Robert, **5:**328

Frisch, Walter, **3:**741–42

Froberger, Johann Jacob, **2:**259, 260–61, 262; **3:**65–66

  suite components of, **2:**260–61, 263, 270

  works of

    Diverse curiose partite, di toccate, canzone, ricercate etc., **2:**259

    Dix suittes de clavessin, **2:**259

    Suite in E minor, Allemande, **2:**261, 265–66

Froissart, Jehan, **1:**342

Frölich, Josephine, **3:**85

"From Paracelsus" (Ives), **4:**262

From the House of the Dead (Janáček), **4:**440, 442, 443

Fromm, Erich, **5:**2

Fromm Music Foundation, **5:**261, 262

Fromm, Paul, **5:**164–65, 261

  Seminar on Advanced Musical Studies, **5:**164

Frondists, **2:**89

Frothingham, Octavius B., **4:**244

frottola, **1:**666, 694–701, 706, 708, 722, 834

  villanella and, **1:**716

Fuchs-Robettin, Hanna, **4:**711, 712

Fuga a 3 soggetii (J. S. Bach), **2:**385

fugato form, **2:**727

fugue, **2:**198–203

  Bach (J. S.) and, **2:**238, 242–43, 247, 248–49, 251, 253–54, 287, 384, 385–88

  Beethoven and, **2:**686, 721–27, 729

  counterpoint and, **2:**198–99, 201–2

  countersubject of (CS), **2:**201

  definition of, **2:**198

  double, **2:**201–2

  episodes in, **2:**202, 220

  exposition in, **2:**198, 201–2, 242, 274

  fantasia paired with, **2:**247

  Germanic traits in, **2:**241–42

  gigue and, **2:**274

  Handel and, **2:**204, 207, 208

  Mozart and, **2:**494, 646

  prelude and, **2:**247–51

  Purcell and, **2:**198–203, 204, 208

  sonata genre vs., **2:**726–27

  subject of, **2:**198, 201, 202, 241–42

  toccata paired with, **2:**247

Fugue in B-minor, no. 24 (Bach), **2:**249, 251, 253–54, 279, 291

Fugue in E major (Fischer), **2:**248

  Bach expansion of, **2:**248–49

Fulcher, Jane, **3:**211, 212

Fuleihan, Anis, **5:**182, 183

fumeux (literary group), **1:**343

Fumeux fume (Solage), **1:**342–45

"Function of Set Structure in the Twelve-Tone System, The" (essay, Babbitt), **5:**136

fundamento, **2:**18, 22

"Funeral March" in C-minor (Beethoven), **2:**685, 702

Fünf Orchesterlieder nach Ansichtskartentexten von Peter Altenberg, op. 4 (Berg), **4:**193

Funfftzig geistliche Lieder und Psalmen mit vier Stimmen auff contrapunctsweise . . . (Osiander), **1:**765, 766

Für die Sünde der Welt gemartete und sterbende Jesus (Handel), **2:**313

"Für Elise" (Beethoven), **2:**686

furiant, **3:**754

"Furie di donna irata" (Piccini), **2:**449–50

furore, **2:**437

Fürstenberg, Prince Egon, **4:**444

Furtwängler, Wilhelm, **4:**756, 765

Fussell, Paul, **4:**473

"Future of Music: Credo, The" (Cage),
5:56, 175
"Future Tense: Music, Ideology, and
Culture" (Meyer), 5:411
Futurism, 5:188, 189, 209
futurismo, 5:178
Futurist Manifesto of 1909 (Marinetti),
5:178
futuristi, 4:299
Fux, Johann Joseph, 1:667, 669; 2:180–81
Canonic Sonata in G minor, I, 1–13,
2:180–81
Gradus ad Parnassum, 1:667, 669
textbook by, 2:180, 518

G

Gabriel (archangel), 1:420, 566, 572
Gabrieli, Andrea (uncle), 1:605, 779–80,
782, 783, 786, 787–89; 2:149, 208
Aria della battaglia, 1:787–89
Canzona incipit, 1:787
*Canzoni alla francese per sonar sopra
stromenti da tasti*, 1:786
Gabrieli, Giovanni (nephew), 1:782–86,
790–96; 2:5, 10, 15, 208, 497; 3:711
orchestration by, 1:782–83
scholarly biography of, 1:792
Schütz's studies with, 2:57, 59, 66, 68,
69, 341
works of
Canzoni et sonate. . ., 1:790–91
In ecclesiis benedicite Domino, 1:783–86
Sonata per tre violini, 1:795–96
Sonata pian'e forte, 1:791–94
Sonate per tres violini, 2:223
Symphoniae sacrae, 1:782–86, 790–92;
2:59, 60–66, 497
Gade, Niels, 3:675–76, 681, 684
Gaea (mythology), 1:824
Gaelic Symphony (Beach), 3:770–73
Gafori, Franchino (Gaffurius), 1:519
Gagliano, Marco da, 1:817–18, 826
Dafne, La, 1:826
Valli profonde, 1:818–19
gagliarda, 2:53
Gainsborough, Thomas, 2:419, 420
galant
Bach (J. C.) and, 2:420
Bach (J. S.) and, 2:376, 406
rococo and, 2:279
galanterie, 2:427–28
convivial spirit of, 2:427, 428
Empfindung contrasted with, 2:426–27,
428–29
meaning of, 2:263
suite and, 2:263, 270, 271–74
Galeazzi, Francesco, 2:702, 718
Galicia, 3:345
Galician-Portuguese vernacular, 1:128
Galilei, Vincenzo (father), 1:724, 799–803,
800, 804, 822

Galileo Galilei (son), 1:797, 799
Galitzin. *See* Golitsyn
galliard, 2:120, 126
Dowland's ayres and, 1:742
Gallican rite, 1:5, 47
Galli-Curci, Amelita, 4:626
Gallus, Jacobus (Jakob Handl), 1:772, 801
Mirabile mysterium, 1:772–75
Opus musicum, 1:772
St. John Passion, 1:775, 776, 777–79,
801
Galop chromatique (Liszt), 3:273
Galuppi, Baldassare, 2:158; 3:235; 4:453
keyboard sonatas of, 2:432–33
opera buffa and, 2:433
"Game of Abduction," 4:171, 172, 175
Gamesters, The (Orlandini intermezzo),
2:435
Gamma ut, 1:101–2
gamut, origin of word, 1:102
Ganassi dal Fontego, Sylvestro di, 1:620,
698
Gandhi, Mahatma, 5:321
Satyagraha and, 5:397
Gann, Kyle, 5:426, 480, 492, 502, 509–10,
511
computer music and, 5:496
gap (troubadour genre), 1:107
Garafola, Lynn, "lifestyle modernism"
genre and, 4:568, 569
Garbutt, J. W., 5:243–245, 247
García Gutiérrez, Antonio, 3:577
Gardane, Antonio, 1:600–601, 611–12, 781,
782, 790–91
Garibaldi, Giuseppe, 3:569
Garlandia, Johannes de, 1:196–98, 215,
249, 250, 325, 394
Garrick, David, 2:459; 4:133
Garroway, Dave "Today" show and, 5:198
Gasparini, Francesco, 2:142
Gaspar van Weerbeke, 1:518–23, 583
Mater, Patris Filia, 1:520–21, 528, 583
Quem terra pontus aethera, 1:521–22, 583
Gaston III (Fébus) of Languedoc, 1:342
Gatti-Casazza, Giulio, 3:665
Gaudeamus Introit (West Frankish/East
Frankish versions), 1:62
Gaul, 1:2
Gaultier, Denis, 2:249, 260
Gautier, Théophile, 3:219; 4:97, 134, 135
Gaveaux, Pierre, 3:3
gavotte, 2:96, 104, 190; 4:452
allemande contrasted with, 2:274
in suite format, 2:263, 271, 272, 274
Gay, John, 2:312, 312; 4:536, 537
The Beggar's Opera, 4:536
Gay, Peter, 3:75, 681
Gazzelloni, Severino, 5:212
Gazzetta ufficiale di Venezia, 3:593
Gebrauchsmusik, 4:527, 543, 559, 777
Gebrauchsmusiker
Hindemith and, 5:419–20

Stockhausen and, 5:419
Zimmermann and, 5:419
Gebüsche, Die (Schlegel), 3:310
"gefiltefish orchestration," 4:637
Geisslerlieder, 1:134
Geist (Spirit), 3:13, 22, 239
Geistererscheinungen, 3:202
Geisterschiff, Das (Tausig), 3:431
Geistliche Chor-Music (Schütz), 2:59, 68
Geistliche Lieder, 3:164; 4:21
Geistliche Lieder auffs new gebessert
(sacred-song book), 1:760
Geistreichen Gesangbuch (Bernhard), 2:58
Gelatt, Roland, 5:157
High Fidelity, 5:157
Gelbcke, Ferdinand, 2:646–47
gematriya device, 2:384
Gemeinschaft, 1:755
oratorios and, 3:165, 169
Wagner on, 3:488, 490
Gemini (constellation), 2:91
Geminiani, Francesco, 2:227–28, 392
Gemütlichkeit, choral music and, 3:162
gender
artistic greatness concept and, 2:81
Beethovenian ideal and, 2:670
bourgeois notions of, 3:36
castrati singing and, 2:86–87, 153
chanson de toile and, 1:119–20
fin' amors and, 1:108–9
mainstreaming and, 2:80
male and female operatic roles and, 3:36,
578
Mozart operas and, 2:478–79, 495–96
musical endowment and, 2:78–83
musical expression and, 2:82
opera seria and, 2:153, 175
Orfeo and, 2:21
salon culture concerns of, 3:77–78
sexual role conformity and, 3:78
See also patriarchy; women in music
General History of Music (Burney),
1:388–89; 2:363, 420, 564
*General History of the Science and Practice of
Music, A* (Hawkins), 1:388
Generative Theory of Tonal Music, A
(Lerdahl-Jackendoff), 5:446–48,
453
Genesis, Book of, 1:175; 2:637, 645
ecphonetic neumes, 1:16
"Genesis" leitmotif (Wagner), 3:506, 515
Genesis of a Music (Partch), 5:482
Genet, Elzéar. *See* Carpentras
genetic fallacy, 1:42, 221, 472
Geneva Psalter, 1:754
genius
as ancient concept, 1:552
Chopin described as, 3:343, 350, 354
Josquin's reputation as, 1:554, 570, 572
original meaning vs. familiar definition
of, 1:551, 552

Romantic notion of, **2**:329, 416, 641, 643, 648–49
Weltgenie concept and, **3**:439, 451, 456
Genoa, **2**:139; **3**:252
Genoveva (Schumann), **3**:418
genre rappresentativo, **2**:6–7
Gentili, Alberto, **2**:117
gentry (gentlemen)
    chamber music and, **2**:114
    English Civil War and, **2**:124
geometry, **1**:253
George I, King of Great Britain, **2**:237, 306, 313
George II, King of Great Britain, **2**:306
George III, King of Great Britain, **2**:315, 419, 464, 577–78
    Eight Songs for a Mad King and, **5**:427
George Louis, Elector of Hanover. *See* George I, King of Great Britain
George Gershwin: A Study in American Musi (Isaac) (biography), **4**:636
George, Stefan, **4**:315, 354, 711
    "Entrücking" and, **4**:315, 339
"Georgian Song". *See Ne poy, krasavitsa*
Gerald de Barri. *See* Giraldus Cambrensis
Gerasch, Franz, **3**:80
Gerber, Ernst Ludwig, **3**:165–66
Gericke, Wilhelm, **3**:770, 774
German art, expressionism and, **4**:307
German Bach Society, **2**:342
German language, **1**:102; **3**:345
    Herder theory and, **3**:122–24, 146
German music tradition, **4**:4
German National Library (Berlin), **2**:49
German opera, **3**:566, 567, 642
    Romantic, **3**:187–205
    See also Wagner, Richard; Weber, Carl Maria von
German philosophers, metaphysical issues and, **4**:6
German Romanticism, **2**:533, 659
    absolute music and, **3**:502
    Beethoven and, **2**:670, 705–6, 720, 731–32, 739
    Beethoven vs. Rossini and, **3**:7–8, 10, 13–14, 25, 34
    folklore and, **1**:138
    French esthetics and, **1**:142
    Herder's philosophy and, **3**:120–23, 345
    Hoffmann and, **2**:641–46, 647, 651, 655, 670
    "I" and "We" concept and, **3**:62–63, 120, 293
    Italian opera critiques and, **3**:45–46
    Kampf und Sieg theme and, **2**:654–55, 658–59, 694
    Kultur and, **3**:123–24, 132
    lieder and, **3**:124
    lyric poetry and, **3**:124–26
    Minnesinger art and, **1**:138, 139, 141
    narratives and, **3**:126–29
    oratorio rebirth and, **3**:163–66, 171

Russian view of, **3**:239
Schopenhauer and, **2**:720–21
Shakespeare and, **2**:706
Sturm und Drang and, **2**:416, 417, 529; **3**:121
sublime and, **2**:732
See also Romanticism
German sixth chord
    Schubert and, **3**:92, 96, 143, 155, 698
    Schumann and, **3**:303
German Student Socialist League, **5**:344
German vernacular comedy. *See* singspiel
Germany
    absolute music concept and, **2**:388, 418. 1.541; **3**:698
    anti-Semitism in, **3**:177
    "art and learning" emphasis of, **2**:388
    artistic hegemony of, **2**:533, 738, 739
    artistic purity and, **1**:141
    Bach (J. S.) revival in, **2**:234, 235, 364, 368, 375, 381, 383, 385, 388, 389, 399; **3**:129, 163
    Bach family and, **2**:235, 239–41, 401–26
    Baroque and, **1**:797
    Beethoven and, **2**:652–89; **3**:14
    Carmina burana and, **1**:138
    comic opera origins and, **3**:187
    concert oratorio movement in, **2**:385
    concert repertory dominance by, **2**:738
    conservatories in, **2**:736
    eighteenth-century music historiography and, **2**:400–401
    Empfindsamkeit and Empfindung and, **2**:409–10, 413, 414, 416
    Enlightenment backlash in, **2**:645
    Enlightenment in, **2**:461, 470
    exigetical music interpretation in, **2**:706, 714
    feudalism's duration in, **1**:143
    first musical play and, **2**:15
    flagellants and, **1**:134
    folklore and, **1**:138; **3**:122–29, 166, 422
    France and, **3**:121, 124, 158, 560, 712, 776, 786
    French style influences in, **1**:142; **2**:259–61, 285
    "Goethezeit" era in, **2**:659
    guild poets and, **1**:118
    Handel and, **2**:235–39, 385
    humanism and, **1**:549, 550, 581
    instrumental music and, **2**:533; **3**:414, 566–67
    Italianate influence in, **2**:68, 69, 259, 285
    Jews in, **3**:174, 177–79
    language communities of, **3**:123–24
    lied and, **3**:119–20, 123–26, 158, 160–63
    Liederkranz movement and, **3**:163
    liturgical organ music and, **2**:48–49
    Lutheran music and, **1**:758–69; **2**:68
    Luther's 95 theses and, **1**:753
    Meistersingers and, **1**:118, 139–44
    municipal music in, **2**:287

musical universality and, **2**:235, 258–59, 389, 738–39
music criticism in, **3**:32–33, 291
music festivals in, **2**:385
music journalism and, **2**:737
music publishing in, **1**:550–51, 691–92, 701, 760, 762, 765
nascent Romanticism in, **2**:533
national anthem of, **3**:130
national character concept and, **2**:670
nationalism and, **1**:138, 141; **2**:235, 259, 385, 388, 389, 670, 689, 739; **3**:8, 14, 62, 121, 123–24, 129, 158, 160–68, 171, 177, 194–97, 205, 345, 417, 422, 704, 710–12, 719
Nazis and, **1**:138; **2**:111, 369; **3**:177, 462–63
New German School and, **3**:416–22, 426, 427
Nibelungenlied epic and, **3**:492
nineteenth-century historicism and, **3**:411
nineteenth-century musical hegemony of, **2**:736–39; **3**:348, 411, 422, 464, 467, 786
nineteenth-century symphonic music and, **3**:376, 566, 677, 679
opera in. *See* German opera
oral music tradition of, **2**:49
oratorio and, **2**:313, 385
oratorio rebirth and, **3**:163–66
Paganini concerts in, **3**:253
poetry and, **3**:124–29
political subdivisions in, **1**:141; **2**:68, 139, 388
Protestantism and, **1**:549, 753–69; **3**:167
Roman Catholicism and, **3**:165
Romantic opera in, **3**:187–205
Schütz and, **2**:56–73
sonata in concerto style and, **2**:301
Sturm und Drang and, **2**:416, 417, 528–29
suite format and, **2**:260–61
Sweelinck pupils in, **2**:48, 49
symphonic development and, **2**:504–7
Tenorlied, **1**:701–6, 717, 756, 758, 760
Thirty Years War and, **2**:55–56, 66, 67
trouvère influence in, **1**:142
unification movement in, **1**:138, 141; **3**:165, 177, 416–17, 492, 710
vernacular song and, **1**:134–42, 351, 701–6, 717
Vormärz period, **3**:177
See also Berlin; Brandenburg; Dresden; Mannheim; Palatinate; Prussia; Saxony
Germi, L. G., **3**:257, 261
Gershkovich, Filip, twelve-tone score and, **5**:461, 463
Gersho, Levi ben. *See* Gersonides
Gershwin, George, **4**:623–37, 623f, 638, 662; **5**:327
    Broadway scores and, **4**:624

Gershwin, George (*continued*)
  conquest of Europe, 4:628
  ethnic/family background, 4:623
  financial success, 4:627–28
  Gersonides, 1:249
  prelude and, 3:351
  works of
    An American in Paris, 4:628
    Concerto in F (*New York Concerto*),
      4:627, 629
    Lady, Be Good!, 4:625
    Porgy and Bess, 4:628, 636
    Rhapsody in Blue, 4:626–36
    Swanee, 4:624
    "You Don't Know the Half of It,
      Dearie," 4:625
Gershwin, Ira, 4:628
Gerstenberg, Heinrich Wilhelm von,
  2:416–18
Gerstl, Richard, 4:309
Gerusalemme liberata (Tasso), 2:7–9, 94;
  3:164, 326, 703
Gervais du Bus, 1:255, 258
Gesamtkunstwerk, 3:306, 488, 719; 4:150,
  224, 469
  Partch and, 5:482, 485
Gesang, 4:19, 20
Gesang der Jünglinge (Stockhausen), 5:191
*Geschichte der Musik in Italien, Deutschland
  und Frankreich von den ersten
  christlichen Zeiten bis auf die
  Gegenwart* (Brendel), 3:411–12, 414,
  415, 417, 419
Geschichten aus dem Wienerwald, op. 325
  (J. Strauss), 3:648
Geschöpfe des Prometheus, Die (Beethoven),
  4:133
Gesualdo, Carlo, 1:738–41, 751, 773, 818,
  819
  madrigals and, 4:197
  modern reputation of, 1:738–40
  Moro, lasso, 1:739, 740
Gettysburg Address, 4:668
Gevaert, François-Auguste, 2:600
Gewerbehaussal (Dresden), 3:677
Geystliches gesangk Buchelyn (Walther),
  1:760–61
ghazals, 3:116
Gherardello da Firenze, 1:365
  Donna l'altrui mirar, 1:371, 372–73
  Tosto che l'alba, 1:365, 371
Ghezzi, Pier Leone, 2:193, 438
Ghiselin, Johannes (Verbonnet)
  Alfonsina, La, 1:544, 545
Giacobbi, Girolamo, 1:781
Giacosa, Giuseppe, 3:666
"Giant Awakens, The!" (Herzen editorial),
  3:476–77
Gibbon, Edward, 3:489
Gibbs, Sir Philip, 4:472
  Now It Can Be Told, 4:472–73
gigue

Bach (J. S.)-Couperin comparison,
  2:275–81
  in suite format, 2:261, 262, 263, 274,
  275–76
  in symphony movement., 2:506–7
Gigue for piano, K.574 (Mozart), 4:451
Gilbert, Henry F., 4:613
  "Indianist" compositions and, 4:613
  works of
    Comedy Overture on Negro Themes,
      4:613
    Dance in Place Congo, The, 4:613
    Intimate Story of Indian Tribal Life, The;
      or, The Story of a Vanishing Race,
      4:613
    Negro Episode, 4:613
    Uncle Remus, 4:613
Gilbert (William S.) and Sullivan
  (Arthur), 3:651–56
  mistaken identity device of, 2:448
  works of
    *HMS Pinafore; or, The Lass That Loved
      a Sailor*, 3:652
    Iolanthe, 3:655
    Mikado, The, 3:40
    Pirates of Penzance, The, 3:652, 653–54,
      655
    Ruddigore, 3:655–56
    Sorcerer, The, 3:652
    Thespis; or, the Gods Grown Old, 3:651
    Trial by Jury, 3:651–52
"Gilded Age, The," 4:253', 5:523
Gilles de Bins. *See* Binchois
Gillmor, Alan M., 4:67, 102
Gilman, Lawrence, 4:262–63, 264, 265, 351
Ginastera, Alberto, "American Preludes,"
  3:351
Giocatore, Il (Orlandini), 2:435, 436, 441
Gioconda, La (Ponchielli), 3:669
Giordano, Filippo, 2:217
Giotto di Bondone, 1:382–83, 382
Giovanni de' Bardi. *See* Bardi, Giovanni de',
Giovanni de Cascia, 1:352, 352, 353, 353
  Appress' un fiume, 1:356–59, 363, 364
Giraldus Cambrensis (Gerald de Barri),
  1:147, 262, 392, 402, 403, 410, 425,
  427, 438
Giraud, Albert, 4:457–58
  rondels, 4:461
Giselle (Adam), 4:134, 135–36, 135f, 141, 142
"Git Along, Little Dogies" (Copland),
  4:662, 664, 666
"Git Along Little Dogies" (Thomson),
  4:660, 662
Gitlin, Todd, 5:312
  "cultural miscegenation," 5:314
Giugno, Giuseppe di, 4X computer and,
  5:478
Giustiniani, Leonardo (Giustinian), 1:697
Glagolská mse (Janáček), 4:424
Glanville-Hicks, Peggy, 4:68

Glareanus, Henricus (Heinrich Loris),
  1:481, 549, 553–56, 554, 558, 559,
  563, 572, 574, 600; 2:538
  on Mouton, 1:589
  music theory and, 1:553–56, 581, 587,
  592, 799
Glasperlenspiel, Das (Hesse), 5:44
Glass, Philip, 5:388–96, 402, 411–12, 413,
  519
  "additive Structure" and, 5:390
  background, 5:389–90
  "crossover" and, 5:391–92
  David Byrne (Talking Heads) and, 5:391
  Einstein on the Beach, "Spaceship" finale,
    5:395
  minimalism and, 5:388–96
  "module" procedure, 5:392–93
  "packages language" and, 5:392
  Paul Simon and, 5:391
  rock appeal and, 5:393
  rock influence and, 5:391
  Tibetan Buddhism and, 407
  works of
    Einstein on the Beach, 5:388–89, 391,
      393–95, 397
    Fifth Symphony, 5:523, 527
    Low Symphony, 5:391
    "Night Train, 5:394, 395
    Satyagraha, 5:397
    Strung Out, 5:390–91
    Two Pages for Steve Reich, 5:391
    Voyage, The,389, 5:515–16, 516, 518
Glazunov, Alexander, 4:145, 151, 628, 636,
  755
glee clubs, 1:746, 750
Gliere, Reinhold, 4:778
Glinka, Mikhail Ivanovich, 3:240, 398, 448,
  464–67, 618; 4:71, 212, 253
  background and career of, 3:239–40
  Bellini and, 3:240
  Berlioz and, 3:465
  Donizetti and, 3:240
  Field and, 3:74
  folk style and, 3:238, 464–67
  on Liszt, 3:288
  nationalism and, 3:237–39, 449
  New Russian School veneration of,
    3:788
  whole-tone scale and, 3:430–31, 447
  works of
    Fantaisies pittoresques, 3:464–65
    Kamarinskaya, 3:465–71, 474, 475,
      478; 4:177
    Life for the Tsar, A, 3:233, 236–50, 245,
      286, 447, 710, 763, 788; 4:369
    Ne poy, krasavitsa ("Georgian Song"),
      3:393–95
    Ruslan and Lyudmila, 3:73, 399, 400,
      430–31, 430, 457; 4:443
Glinka, Sergey Nikolayevich, 3:242
Glinsky, Albert, 5:183
Glock, William, 5:293, 296

Glockenklavier, 550

glockenspiel, 3:73

Glogauer Liederbuch, 1:539, 540, 541, 542–43, 544

Gloria, 1:53, 58, 310

Bach (J. S.) Mass in B minor and, 2:375, 376–77

Caput Mass and, 1:470, 475, 481–83, 493

Credo pairing with, 1:311, 312, 313, 345–49, 461

French-Cypriot setting of, 1:345–49

Great Schism and, 1:348

by Hucbald in mode six, 1:80–82

Machaut La messe de Notre Dame and, 1:320–21, 325–26

in Mass ordo, 1:61(table)

Missa L'Homme Armé and, 1:487, 490–92

Monteverdi "Gloria concertata" and, 2:10, 376

Nicolaus de Radom setting of, 1:348

organ setting of, 2:49

Palestrina Missa O magnum mysterium and, 1:645

Palestrina Missa Papae Marcelli and, 1:655

Power setting of, 1:413, 416, 463, 464

Pycard setting of, 1:409–11, 413–15, 433

"Roy Henry" setting of, 1:417–18

text and settings of, 1:54, 55, 311

tropes, 1:55–56

votive Mass and, 1:316, 317, 318

Gloriana (op. 53) (Britten), 5:225

Glorious Revolution of 1688 (Britain), 2:114–15, 124, 126

Glorreiche Augenblick, Der (Beethoven), 2:673, 686, 722–24; 3:708

"Glory to thee, O Trinity" (Vespers antiphon), 2:116

Gloucester, Duke of, 1:421

Gluck, Alma, 4:133, 626

Don Juan, 4:133

Gluck, Christoph Willibald, 2:452–59, 453; 3:485, 488, 498

Berlioz and, 3:324, 329

Brendel's view of, 3:414

cosmopolitan background of, 2:454–55

librettists of, 2:90, 453, 455, 460, 478; 3:37

as Mozart's Idomeneo model, 2:465–66

opera and, 3:611, 703

operatic debut of, 2:158

operatic reform principles of, 2:452–59, 465–66

Orpheus myth and, 3:645, 646

Piccinni rivalry with, 2:441, 445, 455, 460

Salieri as pupil of, 2:454, 464

tragédie lyrique and, 2:459–60

works of

Alceste, 2:90, 453, 466–68

Iphigenia in Tauris, 2:460, 465

Ipigénie en Aulide, 2:459, 465

Orfeo ed Euridice, 2:452–59, 464

Parnasso confuso, Il, 2:454

Roland, 2:460

Glückliche Hand, Die, op. 18 (Schoenberg), 4:679–80

Glyndebourne Festival (Scotland), The Death of Klinghoffer and, 5:522

G-major dominant chord, 1:627

Gnesin, Mikhail, 4:778

"God Save the King" (British national anthem), 2:672; 3:130

God Save the King (Paganini variation set), 3:257–58

"Goddess of Liberty" (Ives), 4:277

Godowsky, Leopold, 4:626

Godunov, Boris, 3:623

Goebbels, Joseph, 5:18

Requiem for a Young Poet and, 5:420

Goehr, Lydia, 5:71

Goethe, Johann Wolfgang von, 1:141; 2:479, 528, 659, 659, 660; 3:343, 374, 703; 4:21, 104

ballads adapted from, 3:126–29

Beethoven and, 2:671–72, 689, 720; 3:132

folk style and, 3:124, 145

lieder and, 3:129–30

Massenet opera adapted from, 3:640

Mendelssohn (Fanny) and, 3:185

Mozart admiration of, 3:130

nature imitation concept, 3:277

on Paganini, 3:253

as Romanticism foe, 3:69, 71

Schubert and, 3:129, 151

strophic setting preference, 3:146

works of

Egmont, 3:11

Erlkönig, 3:80, 126–29, 144, 158, 367, 369, 372

Faust, 3:69, 71, 80, 151, 337, 435, 596, 639, 640; 4:23, 126

Wilhelm Meisters Lehrjahre, 4:452

Goethe in the Roman Campagna (Tischbein), 2:659

"Goethezeit," 2:659

Goetz, Hermann, 5:261

Gogol, Nikolai, 3:236, 619; 4:782, 785

"Goin' Home" (spiritual), 3:765–66

Gold, Michael, 4:658

"Change the World!," 4:656

Goldberg, Isaac, George Gershwin: A Study in American Music, 4:636

Goldberg, Johann Gottlieb, 2:383

Goldberg bass (J. S. Bach), 2:383–84

"Goldberg Variations" (J. S. Bach), 2:383

Golden Bough, The (Frazer), 4:188

Golden Fleece. See Order of the Golden Fleece

Golden Legend, The (Sullivan), 3:657

Goldener Saal. See Grosser Saal

Golden Section, 5:50

"Golden Touch, The." See Die glückliche Hand

Goldman, Richard Franko, 5:269, 275

Elliott Carter and, 5:269

Goldmark, Karl, 4:614

Goldmark, Rubin, 4:614, 628

George Gershwin and, 4:623

Hiawatha overture and, 4:614

Negro Rhapsody and, 4:614

Goldoni, Carlo, 2:226, 493

Mozart libretto by, 2:465

opera buffa and, 2:433, 446

opera seria parody by, 2:155

Pamela adaptation by, 2:446–47

"Gold's Dominion" leitmotif (Wagner), 3:507, 520

goliards, 1:138, 139

Golijov, Oswaldo, Four Passions cycle and, 5:524

Golitsyn, Dmitriy Mikhailovich, 2:608

Golitsyn, Nikolai Borisovich, Prince, 2:675

Beethoven late quartets and, 2:682, 683

"Golliwog's Cakewalk" (Debussy), 4:599, 600, 601

double parody in, 4:599, 600

Golyscheff, Yefim, 4:681

Gombert, Nicolas, 1:589–97, 601, 602, 678; 2:5

In illo tempore loquente Jesu ad turbas, 1:590–93

Musae Jovis, 1:589

Gomulka, Wladsyslaw, Communist Part and, 5:216–17

Gonzaga, Francesco, Duke of Mantua, 2:2, 5, 14, 14, 21

Gonzaga, Vencenzo, Duke of Mantua, 2:2, 5

Good Friday, 1:832

Bach (J. S.) Passions for, 2:377–81

Schütz settings for, 2:73

Goodman, Alice, The Death of Klinghoffer and, 5:517

Goodman, Benny, 4:628

"Good Vibrations" (Beach Boys), 5:183

Goossens, Eugene, 4:666, 670

Gorbachev, Mikhail, glasnost' and, 5:465

Gorecki, Henryk, 5:407, 526

"Holy minimalism" and, 5:408

Third Symphony, 5:407–8

gorgia (throat-music), 1:816–17, 816, 821; 2:15

Gorky, Maxim, 4:775, 779

Gorman, Ross, 4:629

gospel motet, 1:595

Gospels, 1:6, 13, 25, 42, 758, 775

Bach (J. S.) Passions based on, 2:375, 377, 389–90

oratorios based on, 2:73, 325–26

Gossett, Philip, 3:8, 9

Göteborg, 3:445–46, 447, 455

Gothic romance, 3:47

Gothic style, 1:169, 631

Götterdämmerung (Wagner), **3:**495, 497, 503, 504, 539–40, 543, 610, 643; **4:**13, 20
  Act I, scene I, **3:**523
  leitmotif, **3:**506, 515, 516, 520, 523, 524, 538
  Prologue leitmotives, **3:**505–8, 511–28, 530–38, 759
  Siegfrieds Rheinfahrt, **3:**522
  Valkyries' Song, **3:**532, 537
"Gott, erhalte Franz den Kaiser!" (Haydn), **3:**130–31; **4:**374
"Gottes Zeit ist die allerbeste Zeit" (J. S. Bach), **3:**721–22
Gottschalk, Louis Moreau, **3:**377–86, 377, 618, 768
  Chopin and, **3:**377, 382
  collapse and death of, **3:**383
  criticism of, **3:**385
  hocketing hands-exchange technique of, **3:**378
  Latin American rhythm use by, **3:**378, 380
  musical training of, **3:**377, 385
  nervous breakdown of, **3:**379–80
  ragtime foundations and, **3:**378, 382
  works of
    Bamboula, danse des nègres, op. 2, **3:**377–79, 382
    Bananier, Le, chanson nègre, op. 4, **3:**377
    Banjo, The, **3:**378, 381
    Dying Poet, The, **3:**380
    Escenas campestres, **3:**380
    Last Hope, The, **3:**380
    Maiden's Blush, The, **3:**380
    Marcha solenne brasileira, **3:**383
    Morte!, **3:**380, 383
    Nuit des tropiques, La, **3:**380
    Savane, La, ballade créole, op. 3, **3:**377, 378
    Souvenir de Porto Rico, Marche des Gibaros, **3:**378, 380–81, 382
    "Tropical Night" Symphony, **3:**383
    Union, **3:**381–83
Goudimel, Claude, **1:**754
Gould, Glenn, Soviet tour and, **5:**460
Gounod, Charles-François, **3:**565, 798; **4:**63
  Mendelssohn (Fanny) and, **3:**185–86, 676
  symphony and, **3:**676, 679–80
  works of
    Ave Maria arrangement, **2:**251
    Faust, **3:**639–40, 640, 653
    Roméo et Juliette, **3:**639, 640
Gozzi, Carlo, **3:**192, 193, 481, 673; **4:**498, 499, 502
Grabu, Luis, **2:**132–33
grace (religious), **1:**552
graces (embellishments), **2:**278, 281
Grädener, Carl, **3:**676
Gradual, **1:**25, 26–27, 28, 40, 79–80, 171
  chorale replacement of, **1:**758
  church sonata and, **2:**178, 180

Isaac's *Choralis Constantinus* and, **1:**679
  in Mass ordo, **1:**61table
  motet and, **1:**221, 229, 328
  polyphonic setting of, **1:**162, 177, 178, 679
graduale, **1:**15, 40, 53, 58, 60, 62
  chant modal classification in, **1:**78
Gradualia (Byrd), **1:**679–80, 686, 688
Gradus ad Parnassum (Fux), **1:**667, 669; **2:**180, 518
Graham, Martha, **4:**666; **5:**325
Grainger, Percy, **5:**182, 184
  Free Music for string quartet, **5:**182
  Free Music No. 2, **5:**182, 184
  "Free Music Machine" and, **5:**183
Grammatika musikiyskaya (Diletsky), **3:**234
Granados, Enrique, **2:**391–92
grand concerto. *See* concerto grosso
Grand Duchess of Gérolstein, The (Offenbach), **3:**644
Grand macabre, Le (Ligeti), **5:**438
grande bourgeoisie, middle class imitation of, **3:**78
Grande fantaisie de bravoure sur La Clochette de Paganini (Liszt), **3:**264
  "Variation à la Paganini," **3:**264, 265
Grande messe des morts, op. 5 (Berlioz), **3:**319
Grande polonaise (Chopin), **3:**348
Grande Salle (Paris), **3:**677
Grandes Chroniques, Les" (manuscript), **1:**207
Grande symphonie funèbre et triomphale (Berlioz), **3:**319–20, 331
Grandi, Alessandro, **2:**75
Grandma Moses, **5:**330
grand opéra, **3:**207–23, 323, 639, 643
  arias in, **3:**219–20
  Auber and, **3:**207, 208–14, 216, 219
  Glinka and, **3:**239
  historical dramas and, **3:**218–19, 622
  leading proponents of, **3:**207–8
  Meyerbeer and, **3:**207, 215, 216–19
  Neyerbeer and, **3:**215, 218–32
  Rossini and, **3:**11
  values of, **3:**214–15, 220
Grand Overture style (concert symphonies), **2:**556, 558
grand siècle (France), **2:**111, 454
Grands vents venus d'outremer, Les (Ravel), **4:**111
Grassi, Cecilia, **2:**419
Graudal of St. Yrieux, **1:**39–41
Graupner, Christoph, **2:**240
Grawemeyer Awards, **5:**454
  Incises (Boulez) and, **5:**478
  Pierre Boulez and, **5:**474
"Great American Novel," **4:**637
Great Britain, **1:**387–452
  American Revolutionary and, **3:**764
  arts criticism's inception in, **2:**571
  Bach's (J. C.) career in, **2:**419
  ballads and, **3:**126, 367

Birmingham Festival and, **3:**173, 657
Byrd and, **1:**670–89, 741–42
Caput Mass and, **1:**465–71, 472, 474, 475, 476–77, 481
chamber music and, **2:**114
choral foundations in, **1:**94, 614
comic opera origins in, **3:**187
composers in Belgium from, **2:**45, 47
concerts and repertory in, **2:**738
consistent national borders of, **2:**139
consort music and, **2:**114–18
contenance angloise and, **1:**422–52
continental cultural interchange with, **1:**397–407, 409, 421–22, 676, 678
countertenor voice and, **2:**130
cyclic Mass Ordinary and, **1:**460–71, 473, 474
descant and, **1:**406–9, 411, 423, 425, 429
destruction of pre-Reformation liturgical manuscripts in, **1:**402–3, 513, 672
Dowland and, **1:**742–43
Dunstable and, **1:**421–22, 424–25, 427–33, 461
early music manuscript of, **1:**387–88, 388
early sixteenth-century church music of, **1:**612–14
eighteenth-century novel in, **2:**445–46
Enlightenment backlash in, **2:**645
Enlightenment in, **2:**461
fifteenth-century musical prestige of, **1:**422–52, 461
Glorious Revolution of 1688 in, **2:**114–15, 126
Handel's career in, **2:**204–8, 237–39, 306, 307–40, 401
Handel's oratorios and, **2:**237–38, 314–40, 385, 578, 633
Haydn in, **2:**555–88, 633, 695
identification with Old Testament Israelites by, **2:**315
imperialism of, **3:**392
insular musical idiom and, **1:**396–97, 399, 405, 406, 409, 613–14
interregnum in, **2:**124–25
Italian musical craze in, **1:**743–44
Italian opera as suspect in, **2:**312–13, 340
Italian style adopted in, **2:**196–204
jig and, **2:**261
keyboard music and, **2:**45, 46–47, 49
liturgical drama in, **1:**93
liturgical music and, **1:**612–14, 672
madrigal and, **1:**742, 744, 746–51
magic plays and, **3:**188
masques and, **2:**113–14, 126, 127, 130–31, 132, 134, 137
Mass ordo standardization and, **1:**60, 61(table)
medieval monasticism and, **1:**4–5, 7, 387
Mendelssohn (Felix) and, **3:**173
metric system and, **1:**253

motet and, **1:**399–403, 405, 406–7, 408–11, 423–33, 460, 462, 512–18
musical importance of, **1:**422–52
musical nationalism and, **2:**133, 138, 321
musical reticence and, **1:**751
music criticism in, **3:**289–90
music publishing in, **1:**678, 679, 692, 694
national anthem of, **3:**130
nationalism and, **1:**389, 399, 405–6, 409, 670, 746; **2:**238, 315, 321, 385, 388, 633
nineteenth-century symphonic music in, **3:**678, 680
Norman Conquest of, **1:**397, 397
Notre Dame/University of Paris students from, **1:**172–73
novel and, **2:**445–46, 450; **3:**131
Old Hall manuscript and, **1:**409–18, 429, 461, 513
opera and, **2:**131, 132–38, 237, 311–12
operetta and, **3:**644, 651–56
oratorio and, **2:**75, 237–38, 305, 313–40, 314, 385, 464, 578, 633; **3:**163
pan-European musical style and, **1:**422
parish church musical oral tradition and, **1:**27
political institutions in, **2:**388
political upheaval in, **2:**122–25
polyphony and, **1:**155, 387–99, 402–3, 612–14
public sphere concept in, **3:**289
Purcell and, **2:**127–38, 196–204
Reformation in, **1:**387, 402, 518, 670–73, 686, 753
Restoration in, **2:**124, 125–27
Roman Catholic recusants in, **1:**670, 675, 675, 677, 678, 679, 686, 742
Romantic literature and, **3:**64
self-made class and, **2:**114, 237, 450
semi-opera of, **2:**126–27, 128, 130–31
seventeenth-century music in, **2:**113–38
social class and, **2:**114, 125
song cycle origins in, **3:**131
Sumer Canon and, **1:**387–92, 394, 397, 399, 408, 419, 457
Sweelinck's works and, **2:**45
Tallis and, **1:**673–75
theatrical tradition in, **2:**87, 113, 125–27
twinsong and, **1:**392, 394–96, 408
vernacular song and, **1:**387–95, 419–20, 741–51
Vikings and, **1:**392–93, 399
votive antiphons and, **1:**94
See also London
Great Depression, **4:**548, 637
Greater Doxology. See Gloria
Greater Perfect System, **1:**70, 77
greatness, **2:**649–50
"great persuader," music as, **3:**557
"Great Sacrifice, The" (Stravinsky), **4:**170, 171, 172

Great Schism (papacy), **1:**278, 281, 310–14, 348, 423–24
Great War. See World War I
Greco, El, **2:**122
Greek art, eighteenth-century classicism vs., **2:**453–54
Greek chorus, **3:**341
Greek drama, **1:**780, 799; **2:**15; **3:**619
Aristotle and, **2:**151, 435
Gluck operas and, **2:**453, 459
Metastasio librettos and, **2:**152–53, 154
monodist re-creations and, **1:**822–23, 832
Greek (Hellenistic) music theory, **1:**29–35, 32–33, 32, 69–70
alphabetic notation, **1:**17, 77
ethos concept and, **1:**38, 131, 732, 815
Greater Perfect System, **1:**70, 77
Mei treatises on, **1:**799, 800
mimesis and, **1:**363
monophony and, **1:**799
nomenclature, **1:**74–75, 77
nondiatonic modes, **1:**730, 732
prosodia daseia, **1:**47
tone system, **1:**29, 74–75, 799
Greek mythology, **1:**29, 32, 374, 384; **2:**15, 21–25, 91–92
first "true" opera and, **1:**824–26
intermedii texts and, **1:**804, 811–12
See also Orpheus legend
Greek odes, **3:**120
Greek Orthodox (Byzantine) Church. See Eastern Orthodox Church
Greek siren songs, **3:**127
Green, Douglass, **4:**711
"Green" movements, postmodernism and, **5:**414, 513
Greenberg, Clement, **5:**264, 303, 304
"Avant-Garde and Kitsch," **5:**221
Greenberg, Noah, **1:**93, 94
Greenland, **1:**393
Gregorian chant, **1:**6–35; **2:**326; **3:**13, 619; **4:**29, 67, 101, 284, 312, 642; **5:**510
accentus and, **1:**22
antiphon classification, **1:**72–76
antiphons, **1:**12–13, 34, 83, 633
background of, **1:**5–12
binariae, **1:**215
centonized, **1:**28
chorale replacement of, **1:**758
compact disc of, **1:**66
concert hall performance of, **1:**66
Counter Reformation changes in, **1:**59
"Credo I" and, **1:**35
dialects and, **1:**304–64
diatonic pitch set and, **1:**30, 32
discant and, **1:**297–98
Franco-Roman, **1:**60–62
Frankish manuscript uniformity and, **1:**62
Frankish modal theory and, **1:**41–67, 553

Frankish reorganization of, **1:**37–64, 40, 234, 298
Greek modal system and, **1:**29–35
Kyrie IX, **2:**43
Liber usualis edition of, **1:**23, 87
Mass psalmody and, **1:**23–25
melismatic embellishment and, **1:**28, 228–29
modal classification of, **1:**72–76, 78
as monophonic, **1:**47, 120, 148
motet and, **1:**228, 234, 267, 269–71, 282, 507–8, 566, 601–2, 604, 641
neumes and, **1:**13–16
nineteenth-century reediting of, **1:**22
notation following practice in, **1:**1–2, 184
Notre Dame settings for, **1:**171–72
"Old Roman" variant of, **1:**62, 64
oral tradition of, **1:**6–12, 13, 17–20, 26–29
origin of, **1:**6, 7–9, 10, 368
Palestrina revision of, **1:**631
polyphony and, **1:**147, 148, 149–50, 156, 162–68, 171
as psalmodic, **1:**13, 23–25, 47
repertory of, **1:**21
repetition function in, **1:**26–27
resistance elements to, **1:**63–64
Respighi and, **4:**750
restoration of, **3:**13
rhythmic indeterminacy and, **1:**114, 157
scale mapping, **1:**101
Second Vatican Council decanonization of, **1:**278
shared material, **1:**28
tonal range of, **1:**99
tropes and, **1:**50–53
troubadour melodies and, **1:**111, 114, 131, 136
unaccompanied unison style of, **1:**47, 130
See also psalms and psalmody
Gregorian hymn, **2:**342
Gregorius Praesul, **1:**7
Gregory I (the Great), Pope, **1:**5–7, 6, 47, 58, 63, 79, 175, 368, 452, 548, 631
Gregory II, Pope, **1:**7
Gregory XI, Pope, **1:**310
Gregory XIII, Pope, **1:**631, 675
Greiter, Matthias, **1:**722; **2:**184
Gretchen am Spinnrade (Schubert), **3:**80, 81, 151–54
Grétry, André, **1:**117–18
Richard Coeur-de-Lion, **3:**2
Griboyedov, Alexander, **3:**395
Griechen und Römer, Die (Schlegel), **3:**310
"Grief" leitmotif (Wagner), **3:**507, 517, 519
Grieg, Edvard, Norwegian Dances, **4:**632
Griesinger, Georg August, **2:**527, 538
Griffiths, Paul, **5:**25, 305
Grillo, El (Josquin), **1:**699–701
Grimaldi, Nicolo. See Nicolini
Grimm brothers, **4:**459
Grimm, Jacob, **3:**122, 123, 492

Grimm, Melchior von, 2:470

Grimm, Wilhelm, 3:122, 123

Grisey, Gérard, 5:499–501

    Les espaces acoustiques, 5:500

    musique spectrale and, 5:499–500

Grisi, Carlotta, 4:134

Grisi, Giulia, 3:30

Gritti, Andrea, 1:600

Grocheio, Johannes de, 1:207–8, 211, 219, 221, 226, 229, 233, 236, 262

Grofé, Ferde, 4:626, 627, 630

Gropius, Manon, 4:714

Gropius, Walter, 4:714

Group for Contemporary Music at Columbia University, 5:164

Groupe des Six. *See* Les Six group

Grosse Fuge, op. 133 (Beethoven), 2:682, 726

Grosse Heidelberger Liederhandschrift, 1:141

grosse romantische Oper, 3:194

Grosser Saal (Vienna), 3:677, 678

Grosse Sonate f. d.Pianoforte für Beethovens Denkmal (Schumann), 3:309–10

Grosse Sonate für das Pianoforte (Schumann), 3:309

Gross senen (J'ay pris amours), 1:540–41

grotesque

    Chopin prelude and, 3:353, 354

    Paganini use of, 3:255

Grouchy, Jean de. *See* Grocheio, Johannes de

ground bass, 1:625–28, 658, 666, 803, 804

    from Bach's "Gottes Zeit ist die allerbeste Zeit," 3:721–22

    Baroque compositions and, 2:35, 36

    Brahms and, 3:721

    "breaking a base" (variations), 2:120

    chaconne (ciaccona(or passacaille (passagli) over, 2:38, 94

    Italian string repertory and, 2:193

    monodic songs and, 1:821, 823–28, 823

    Monteverdi and, 2:10, 35

    Purcell's gift for, 2:135, 137, 138

    sacra rappresentazione and, 1:834

    Scarlatti (Alessandro) and, 2:186–87, 189

    Schubert and, 3:154–55

    significance of, 1:627

    traditional tenors and, 1:626

Group des Six, Le 4:588f, 628

    Honegger and, 5:183

group identity, artistic creativity and, 2:82, 83

Grout, Donald Jay, 2:142, 151, 173, 329

Grove Dictionary of Music, 1:389

Groven, Eivind, 4:285

Grundgestalt (Schoenberg term), 2:701; 4:325, 336, 343, 353, 354, 355, 363, 461, 687, 688, 689, 690, 692, 704, 714, 734, 738

    spectral music and, 5:500

Grünewald, Matthias, 4:767

gruppo ("note-group"), 1:816, 817. *See also* trill

Guadagni, Gaetano, 2:336, 339–40, 459

Guárdame las vacas (folk tune), variations on, 2:47

Guarini, Giovanni Battista, 1:736–37, 813

    Pastor Fido, Il, 1:736–37, 813

Guarneri del Gesù violins, 3:255

Gubaidulina, Sofia, 5:464, 471

    Four Passions cycle and, 5:524

    Offertorium, Concerto for Violin, 5:464

Guelphs and Ghibellines, 1:286, 354

Guelphs and the Ghibellines, The (opera), 3:227, 230

Guerre, La (Janequin), 1:711–12, 787

    parody Mass on, 1:788, 789

Guerre des Bouffons. See War of the Buffoons

Guhr, Karl, 3:261

Guidiccioni, Laura (née Lucchesini), 1:823

Guido d'Arezzo. *See* Guido of Arezzo

Guidonian hand, 1:101–3, 103, 104, 275, 368, 499

Guidonian hexachord, 2:45

Guido of Arezzo, 1:273, 276, 281, 617, 682

    counterpoint innovation and, 1:153–54, 155, 156, 161

    rhyming rules of, 1:185, 368

    sight-singing rules and, 1:99–104, 153

    staff invention by, 1:16, 102, 153

guild musicians, 1:131, 139, 143, 608, 622, 760

guild poets, 1:118

guilds, 1:120, 291; 2:287

Guillaume I. *See* William I

Guillaume IX. *See* William IX

Guillaume de Amiens. *See* William of Amiens

Guillaume de Machaut. *See* Machaut, Guillaume de

Guillaume Tell (Rossini), 3:11–12, *11*, 18, 273, 578, 579

Guillaume Tell (Schiller), 3:11

Guillaume the Pious. *See* William I (Guillaume) the Pious

Guillemain, Louis-Gabriel, 2:427–28

Guiraud, Ernest, 3:657; 4:71

Guiraut de Bornelh, 1:110–11, 115–16

Guiraut Riquiet, 1:116

guitarists

    passacagli and, 2:38

    tabulature for, 1:606

    vamping by, 2:38

Günther, Ursula, 1:338

Gurrelieder (Schoenberg), 4:305, 306, 344, 347, 460

    "decadent" erotic manner of, 4:305

"Gustav poem," *Dziady I* and, 4:10

Gutenberg (Loewe), 3:164

Guthrie, Woody, 5:334

Guymont, Kyrie, 1:312

Guy of Lusignan, 1:345

Guyot de Provins, 1:134, 135

Gwynn, Nell, 2:125–26, *126*

gymel (twinsong), 1:395, 517

gymnopédies, 4:67–68

    Debussy and, 4:70

Gypsy music, Liszt and, 3:261, 433

Gypsy style, 4:367. *See also style hongrois*

Gyrowetz, Adalbert, 3:347

H

Haar, James, 1:697, 699, 723

Hába, Alois, 4:286

"Habanera" (Bizet), 3:398–99, 641, 642

Habeneck, François-Antoine, 3:323, 327, 331, 677

Habermas, Jürgen, 5:508

    "Modernity — An Incomplete Project," 5:221

Habilitationsschrift, 5:50

Haec dies (Easter Gradual), 1:27, 221, 228

    West Frankish/East Frankish versions, 1:62

"Haffner" Symphony in D major, K. 385 (Mozart), 2:589

Haggh, Barbara, 1:148

Haight-Ashbury, 5:309

"Hail, Hail, the Gang's All Here" (Gilbert and Sullivan), 3:653

"Hail, Mary" (prayer), 1:523–26, 565–66, 572, 606

Hail Columbia (song), 3:381, 382

Haimo, Ethan, 4:703

Haionhwat'ha, 3:764

Hakobian, Levin, Schnittke and, 5:467

Hakon Jarl (Smetana), 3:446, 452

Halaphone, 4X computer and, 5:478

Halde, Jean-Baptiste Du, 3:192

Halévy, Jacques Fromental, 3:207, 215

    Juive, La, 3:215, 218

Halévy, Ludovic, 3:648

half-aria (*mezz'aria*), 2:349, 351

half-cadence, 2:488

half-step adjustments, 2:594

half-steplessness, 4:69–76, 129

Halka (Moniuszko), 3:447

Halle, 2:48, 402

    as Handel's birthplace, 2:235, 236, 239

Halle, Adam de la. *See* Adam de la Halle

Hallé, Charles, 3:364–65, 385

Hallelujah Chorus (Handel), 3:180

Halm, August, 2:726

Haman and Mordecai (Handel), 2:313–14

Hamburg, 3:290

Handel in, 2:236–37

    Klopstock-C. P. E. Bach connection, 2:410

    organ posts, 2:48

Hamlet (Liszt), 3:446

Hamlet (Shakespeare), 2:416, 417, 645; 3:320, 558; 4:498

Hamlet (Thomas), **3**:640

Hamm, Daniel, **5**:370

"Hammerklavier" Sonata in B flat, op. 106 (Beethoven), **2**:673, 674, 724, 726, 727; **5**:177

hand, as mnemonic device, **1**:102–3

Handel, George Frideric, **2**:204–0, 241, 303, 305–40, 305, 306, 402, 409, 411, 455, 689; **3**:163, 172, 592; **4**:449, 453

  adaptability of, **2**:340

  Bach's (J. S.) approach to music contrasted with, **2**:321, 345, 362, 364, 368, 374

  Bach's (J. S.) career compared with, **2**:236, 240, 305–6, 418, 419

  Beethoven's tribute to, **2**:724

  "borrowings" by, **2**:327–31, 392

  Brendel's view of, **3**:414

  business bankruptcy of, **2**:313, 314

  business sense of, **2**:237, 239, 240, 313, 340

  canonization of, **2**:233, 235, 639

  career and lifestyle of, **2**:235–39, 400–401

  career trajectory of (map), **2**:236

  closeted sexual orientation of, **2**:340

  concerto grosso and, **2**:192, 204–8, 305, 327

  conservativism of, **2**:235

  contemporary musical taste and, **2**:363

  death date of, **2**:326

  duetto per camera and, **2**:331–32

  English nationalism and, **2**:238, 315, 321, 385, 633

  Englishness vs. Germanness of, **2**:385, 739

  English royal patronage of, **2**:237, 306

  financial success of, **2**:237, 239, 419, 517

  as first modern composer, **2**:340

  fugue and, **2**:204, 207, 208

  German reclamation of, **2**:385

  Gilbert and Sullivan's parody of, **3**:652

  as Haydn inspiration, **2**:633

  Haydn's career compared with, **2**:578

  High Baroque style and, **2**:194

  internationalism of, **2**:239

  librettists of, **2**:307, 316, 325

  London music scene and, **2**:237–39, 306, 307–40, 401, 419

  masques of, **2**:313–14

  Mendelssohn and, **3**:180

  Mozart modernized scores of, **2**:399

  music historiography and, **2**:400–401

  nationalism and, **2**:385

  opera and, **3**:703

  opera seria of, **2**:109, 236–37, 238–39, 306–12, 313, 351

  oratorio and, **2**:75, 237–38, 305, 313–40, *314*, 385, 464, 578, 633; **3**:163, 164, 657; **5**:525–26

  orchestral suites of, **2**:234

  Orlandini's style compared with, **2**:437

  rage arias of, **2**:308–9, 437

  rediscovery/public revival of, **2**:385

  Scarlatti (Domenico) compared with, **2**:396

  as self-made man, **2**:237, 240, 313, 340, 419, 517

  significant birth year of, **2**:233, 235

  speed of composing by, **2**:326, 327

  standard repertory inclusions of, **2**:234, 235; **3**:680

  stroke suffered by (1737), **2**:328

  unique genius of, **2**:313

  works of

    Acis and Galatea, **2**:313–14

    Belshazzar, **2**:315

    Brockes Passion, **2**:313, 377

    Chandos Anthems, **2**:314

    Concerto Grosso in B-flat Major, Op. 6, no. 7, **2**:204–8, 327, 392

    Deborah, **2**:314

    Für die Sünde der Welt gemartete und sterbende Jesus, **2**:313

    Haman and Mordecai, **2**:313–14

    Israel in Egypt, **2**:315–25, 327, 331, 345, 364, 368; **3**:331, 333–34, 335

    Jephtha, **2**:75

    Joshua, **2**:315

    Judas Maccabeus, **2**:315; **3**:164

    Messiah, **2**:316, 325–27, 331–40, 377, 399, 459; **3**:174, 180

    Ode for St. Cecilia's Day, **2**:330

    Rodelinda, **2**:306–11

    "Royal Fireworks," **2**:306, 362

    Samson, **2**:75, 315, 339

    Saul, **2**:314–15, 316

    Solomon, **2**:315

    Vivi, tiranno!, **2**:308–11, 340, 437

    "Water Music," **2**:306

Handl, Jakob (Jacobus Gallus), **1**:679, 772

Handy, W. C., **4**:609, 625, 629

  St. Louis Blues, **4**:606–7

Hangmen Also Die (Lang), **4**:560

Hanover dynasty, **2**:237, 306

Hanover Square (London), **2**:555

Hanover Square Rooms (London), **3**:678

Hänsel und Gretel (Humperdinck), **4**:459

Hansell, Kathleen, **2**:174

Hansen, Al, **5**:92

Hansen, Theophil, **3**:678

Hanslick, Eduard, **2**:336, 458; **3**:443, 715, 752; **4**:4

  Bruckner and, **3**:746

  as music critic, **3**:290, 745

  as music professor, **3**:769

  as New German School opponent, **3**:441–42, 531

Hanson, Howard, **4**:647–48, 649, 666

  Symphony no. 3, **4**:647, 648

Hanswurst ("Johnny Sausage") shows, **2**:518; **3**:188

"Happy Birthday to You" (song), **1**:18; **5**:481

happy ending, operatic, **2**:151, 446–47

Hapsburg dynasty, **2**:504, 525, 550, 607; **3**:130, 206, 212, 392, 445; **4**:365

  See also Austria; Holy Roman Empire

Haraszti, Emil, **3**:425, 426

Harbison, John, **5**:516

  Great Gatsby, The (opera), **5**:515

  neotonality and, **454**

Harding, Warren G., **4**:257, 259, 562

Hardy, Thomas Bush, **2**:517, 555

Hare, John, **2**:177

"Hark! the ech'ing air" (Purcell), **2**:131

Harlem nightclubs, **4**:602

Harley, Robert, first Earl of Oxford, **1**:387

Harley manuscript, **1**:387, *388*

harmonia perfetta, **1**:587

harmonic consonances, **1**:29, 30

harmonic dissolution, **3**:358–63

Harmonice musices odhecaton (partbook), **1**:542

harmonic minor, **1**:277

harmonic numbers, theory of, **1**:248, 249

harmonic progression, color chords and, **4**:310

harmonic proportions, **1**:249, *250*

harmonic ratios, **1**:5, 29, 284–85

harmonic rhythm, **1**:628; **2**:188

harmonic tonality. *See* tonal harmony

Harmonie (wind ensemble), **2**:509

Harmonielehre (Schoenberg), **4**:309–10, 311, 331, 339, 386, 680

Harmonies poétiques et religieuses (Lamartine), **3**:264

harmonizing, **1**:168, 472

  extemporized by ear, **1**:392, 394, 406, 452

  fauburden and, **1**:436, 437

  Geneva Psalter and, **1**:754

  metrical psalms and, **1**:598

  sight-singing and, **1**:434–35

harmony

  Aaron's treatises on, **1**:576–77

  abstract musical forms and, **1**:37, 798

  added sixth and, **3**:649

  ars perfecta and, **1**:588, 816

  augmented sixth and, **3**:73, 92, 95, 96, 98, 112, 428, 698

  augmented triad and, **3**:428, 435–36

  Bach (C. P. E.) and, **2**:413, 414, 514–15

  Bach (J. S.) and, **2**:211–16, 242, 248, 249, 251, 253–54, 266, 285, 346, 361, 370, 372, 381

  Bach (W. F.) and, **2**:407

  Balakirev and, **3**:471–76

  Baroque, **1**:796

  basso continuo and, **1**:780–81, 796, 809

  Beethoven and, **2**:660–67, 677–78; **3**:428, 429, 436, 529

  Brahms and, **3**:695–99, 735, 737–39

  Caput Mass and, **1**:475

  Chaikovsky and, **3**:637–38

  Chopin and, **3**:352–56

  chromatic, **1**:32–33, 273–74; **3**:203

  closure and, **1**:471

harmony (*continued*)

consonances and, 1:29–31, *30, 32,* 153, 407

Corelli and, 2:181–84

Counter Reformation liturgical music and, 1:773–77, 785

definition of, 1:153

diatonic circles of fifths and. *See* circles of fifths

diminished seventh and, 3:96, 99–100, 105, 203, 361, 362, 428, 432–35, 448, 543, 544

distinguishing stylistic characteristics of, 1:153

by ear, 1:46, 168, 435–39

English, 1:403, 405–6, 407, 408–9, 417, 423–29, 435–39, 447–48, 614, 686

flat submediant and, 3:66, 69, 70, 87, 88, 92, 94–101, 111–12

genetic fallacy and, 1:42, 221, 472

German sixth chord and, 3:92, 96, 143, 155, 303, 698

Gesualdo and, 1:738, 739

ground bass effects on, 1:625–28

higher levels of Musica and, 1:38

homologous chords and, 3:96

improvisation of, 1:392, 394

Lasso and, 1:720–21, 739

Liszt and, 3:428–38, 627–28

Lutheran chorale and, 1:765–66, 768

melodic sixths and, 3:633, 636–38

modulation and, 1:471

monody and, 1:802–3, 813, 815–16, 818–19

Monteverdi and, 2:2, 5, 23–24

motet and, 1:271–76, 286

Mozart and, 2:486, 488, 489, 490, 492, 493, 494, 495, 609, 618, 620–21, 624–25, 631, 632–33, 634

Musorgsky and, 3:621, 626–28

Neopolitan, 2:142, 144

Paganini and, 3:256–57, 264

pendular plan and, 2:267, 606, 660

pivots and, 3:299

printed bass line and, 1:781–82

Rameau treatise on, 2:192

Scarlatti (Alessandro) and, 2:142, 144, 146

Scarlatti (Domenico) and, 2:391, 392, 396, 620

Schubert and, 3:89, 92–94, 96, 99–107, 115, 117, 428–30, 436, 550, 697

Schumann and, 3:295, 298–305, 313, 314, 315

sixth degree, 3:649–51

standardization of, 2:181–82, 234

strategic delays and, 3:528

Strauss (Johann) and, 3:649

Sumer canon and, 1:392

tempered tuning and, 1:730

tonal, 1:471–72; 2:181–203, 234, 248

triadic, 1:168, 433, 447, 470, 587–88

triad in first inversion and, 1:813

Vivaldi and, 2:220

Wagner and, 3:521–28, 531–54, 547, 702

Willaert and, 1:603–4

Zarlino treatise on, 1:586–87

See also cadence; counterpoint; discant; polyphony

harmony of cosmos. *See* cosmic harmony

harmony of the spheres, 1:152, 804

Harold in Italy (Berlioz), 3:253, 421

Haromia Macrocosmica (Celarius), 1:476

harp

Babylonian, 1:31, *31*

in Berlioz's *Symphonie fantastique*, 3:328

double-action, 3:328

medieval, 1:132, 147, 392

harpsichord

accompanied sonata, 2:427–32, 695

Bach (J. S.) works for, 2:192, 224–25, 241

Bach's (J. S.) Fifth Brandenburg Concerto solo role of, 2:290, 291–300, 301

Couperin and, 2:279, 282

English virginal and, 2:45

Haydn concerto for, 2:600

obbligato provided by, 2:300–301, 428

pièces for, 3:119

Scarlatti (Domenico) and, 2:390–96

Sweelinck fantasias and, 2:46

Harpsichord Concerto in D major (Haydn), 2:600

Harpsichord Sonata in F (W. F. Bach), 2:402–9, 413, 414

Harris, Joel Chandler, 4:613

Harris, Roy, 4:637–49, *637,* 662, 666, 671, 672; 5:21, 268

background, 4:638

"Folksong—American Big Business" (article), 4:640

"The Growth of a Composer" (article), 4:640

rivalry with Aaron Copland, 5:3

works of

Farewell to Pioneers: Symphonic Elegy, A, 4:640–42

"Folksong Jamboree," 4:671

"Folksong Symphony," 4:671

"Negro Fantasy," 4:672

Symphony 1933, 4:639

Symphony no. 3, 4:641, 643–46, 647, 648; 5:3

Symphony no. 4, 4:671–72

Symphony no. 5, 4:671

"Western Cowboy," 4:672

"When Johnny Comes Marching Home Again," 4:671–72

Harrison, Frank Llewellyn, 1:389, 390–91, 513

Harrison, George, 5:317, 318

performance on Indian sitar, 5:317–18, 320

"Taxman," 5:319

Hartlaub, Gustav, 4:527

Hartleben, Otto Erich, 4:457

Hartmann, Karl Amadeus, 4:769–72, 773

Burleske Musik, 4:770

Jazz-Toccata und Fuge, 4:770

Musica Viva and, 4:772

Sinfonia dramatica: China kämpft, 4:772

Tanzsuite, 4:770

Harty, Sir Hamilton, 2:306

Harvard University, 3:769; 5:116, 268

Hasse, Johann Adolf, 2:157, *157,* 158–59, 161, 400

Artaserse settings, 2:158, 166

Hasser, Hans Leo, 2:49

Hatikvah (Zionist hymn), 3:456

Hatwig, Otto, 3:85

Hauer, Josef Matthias, 4:680, 684, 689, 692

Nomos, op. 19, 4:681, 682, 685, 686, 688, 692, 707

Nomos technique and, 4:681

Prioritätstreit and, 4:686–87

Zwölftontechnik and, 4:688

Hauptthemen, 3:502

Hausen, Friedrich von, 1:135

Hauser, Arnold, 2:736, 737

haute-contre (French high tenor), 2:98, 100, 130, 459

hauteur, musical meaning of, 1:448, 452

Hawkins, Sir John, 1:388, 389

Hawthorne, Nathaniel, 4:267, 270

Haydn, Franz Joseph, 2:479, 499, 515–88, 517, 557, 642; 3:287, 445, 678, 799; 4:18, 19, 104, 124, 309, 367, 368, 374, 435, 496, 630, 632; 5:368

absolute music and, 2:646

Bach (C. P. E.) as influence on, 2:518, 529

background and career of, 2:517–20, 525–28, 607

Beethoven as heir-apparent to, 2:653, 660; 3:114

Beethoven's studies with, 2:652, 653

Beethoven's use of C-minor and, 2:653, 692, 694–95, 696, 698, 701, 702

biography of, 3:333

Brahms and, 3:690, 691, 716–19

Brendel's view of, 3:414

canonization of, 2:399, 400, 401, 638–39, 646, 738

canzonetta and, 3:130

celebrity of, 2:517, 541, 557, 607

Classical period and, 2:739

C-minor mood and, 2:634–37, 692, 694–95, 701, 702, 721

concerto and, 2:600–601

concision of, 2:578–88, 591

Dussek and, 3:65

Enlightenment and, 2:577, 643

Esterházy patronage of, 2:525–28, 538–41, 553, 555, 607, 682; 4:365

financial success of, 2:517, 556, 607

folk song arrangements by, 3:130

freelance status of, **2:**541, 555, 577, 607, 639

fugal sonata movements and, **2:**726–27

Fux's text and, **1:**669

Handel oratorios and, **2:**385, 578, 633

Hoffmann's appraisal of, **2:**643, 645–46

innovations of, **2:**571

late symphonies of, **2:**557–88

lied and, **3:**130

London tours of, **2:**555–88, 589, 607, 633, 652, 695

Mass composition of, **2:**376, 633

Mozart's interrelationship with, **2:**589, 590, 591, 593, 601, 607, 631, 634, 637

musical predecessors of, **2:**400

musical wit of, **2:**540–41

nocturne and, **3:**64

operas of, **2:**464, 526

opus numbers and, **2:**541

oratorios of, **2:**385, 633–37; **3:**165

Oxford honorary degree of, **2:**556

Paris symphonies of, **2:**556–57

patrons of, **2:**519–20, 525–28, 538, 607, 655; **3:**79, 261

performance skill limitations of, **2:**590, 601

piano trios of, **2:**695

reasons for success of, **2:**516

Romantic esthetic and, **2:**643, 645–46, 647, 648

Salomon contract with, **2:**555–56

as self-made man, **2:**517, 525, 538

sonata form and, **2:**10–533, 520–25, 540, 549, 557, 584, 660

standard repertory and, **2:**399, 464, 578, 646; **3:**679, 680

string quartets of, **2:**518–19, 526, 541, 578, 600, 721

structural efficiency of, **2:**578–88

Sturm und Drang and, **2:**528–29

symphonies concertante and, **3:**277

symphony and, **1:**175, 632; **2:**515–40, 542, 549, 556–88, 600, 601, 717

technical virtuosity of, **2:**579

trios of, **2:**695–96

waltz dissemination by, **2:**573

Weber and, **3:**192

whimsical fugalism and, **2:**721

works of

Cello Concerto in D major, **2:**600

Clarino Concerto in E-flat major, **2:**600

Creation, The, **2:**385, 633–37, 638, 645, 692, 694, 701; **3:**3; **4:**283, 449

Harpsichord Concerto in D major, **2:**600

"In Distress" ("Lord Nelson Mass"), **2:**577, 633

"In Time of War," **2:**577, 633

Kaiserhymne ("Gott, erhalte Franz den Kaiser!"), **3:**130–31; **4:**374

London Symphony, **3:**16, 691, 692

Quartet in C major, op. 76, no. 3 (Emperor Quartet), **3:**130

Seasons, The, **2:**385, 388, 633; **4:**449

String Quartet, op. 103 (unfinished), **2:**542

String Quartet in E-flat major, op. 33, no. 2 ("The Joke"), **2:**542, 555, 558, 565, 591, 593

String Quartets, op. 33 ("Russian"), **2:**541–42, 589

String Quartets, op. 42, **2:**542

String Quartets, op. 50, **2:**542

String Quartets, op. 64, **2:**542, 556

String Quartets, op. 76, **2:**542

String Quartets, op. 77, **2:**542

String Quartets, opp. 54/55, **2:**542

String Quartets, opp. 71/74, **2:**542

Symphony "A," **2:**520–24

Symphony nos. 6–8 ("Morning", "Noon" and "Night"), **2:**528

Symphony no. 24 in D major ("London"), **2:**578–88

Symphony no. 31 ("Hornsignal"), **2:**527

Symphony no. 45 in F-sharp minor ("Farewell"), **2:**528–40, 553, 682

Symphony no. 46 in B major, **3:**108

Symphony no. 48 in C major, **2:**526

Symphony nos. 82–87 ("Paris"), **2:**557–58

Symphony no. 92 in G major ("Oxford"), **2:**556

Symphony no. 94 in G major ("Surprise"), **2:**557–77, 557, 584

Symphony no. 95 in C minor, **2:**695

Symphony no. 96 in D major ("Miracle"), **2:**556

Symphony no. 100 in G major ("Military"), **2:**558, 577

Symphony no. 104 in D major ("London"), **2:**578–88; **4:**19

Haydn, Michael (brother), **2:**517; **3:**191

Haydn, Mozart and the Viennese School: 1740–1780 (Heartz), **2:**400

Haydn Variations. *See* Variations for Orchestra on a Theme by Joseph Haydn

Hayes, Alfred, **4:**658

Haym, Nicola Francesco, **2:**307

Hayne van Ghizeghem, **1:**535, 536

Hazlitt, William, **3:**64

head voice. *See* falsetto

Hear Ye! Hear Ye! (Copland), **4:**653

hearing. *See* musical sound

"Heart and Soul" (piano piece), **1:**392

Heartz, Daniel, **1:**693; **2:**400, 409, 434, 437, 466, 470, 477, 488

Heaven and Earth (Rimsky-Korsakov), **4:**120

Hebrew language, **1:**16, 54

Hebrews (biblical). *See* Israelites

Hebriden, Die (Mendelssohn), **3:**183

Hefling, Stephen, **4:**9, 10

"He gave them hailstones (Handel), **2:**321, 322–23, 327

Hegel, Georg Wilhelm Friedrich, **2:**670; **3:**412–13, 412, 415, 416, 422, 423, 459, 735

Phenomenology of Spirit, **5:**332

Überseele and, **4:**44

"world-historical" figure and, **4:**308

Heggie, Jake, *Dead Man Walking* (opera), **5:**516

Heidenröslein (Goethe), **3:**124, 130, 146

Heidenröslein (Reichardt), **3:**124–26

Heidenröslein (Schubert), **3:**145–48, 189

Heifetz, Jascha, **4:**551, 626

Heilbroner, Robert, **5:**413

"Historic optimism," and, **5:**413–14

Heiligenstadt Testament (Beethoven), **2:**654, 672; **3:**690, 800

Heiliger Dankgesang eines Genesenen an die Gottheit, in der lydischen Tonart (Beethoven), **2:**686–88, 721, 731

Heine, Heinrich, **3:**295, 304, 308; **4:**19

Chopin and, **3:**349

De l'Allemagne, **4:**134

Liszt's *Die Lorelei* and, **3:**543

on Liszt's personal manager, **3:**272

mental state depiction by, **3:**154

Paganini concert memoir, **3:**253

Schubert's *Am Meer* and, **3:**138

Schumann's *Dichterliebe* and, **3:**295–96, 301, 303

Wagner's *Der fliegende Holländer* and, **3:**485

Heinichen, Johann David, **2:**261

Heinrich von Meissen (Frauenlob), **1:**140, 141

Heir beginnis countering (plainchant), **1:**438–39

Hélas mon deuil, a ce coup sui je mort (Du Fay), **1:**512

"heliotropic" melodies, **4:**639, 640, 641, 643, 666

"heliotropisms," **4:**647

Hellenism, **1:**70. *See also* Greek (Hellenistic) music theory

Heller, Stephen, **3:**365

Spaziergänge eines Einsamen, op. 78, **3:**361, 363

Helm, Everett, **5:**20

Helmholtz, Hermann Ludwig Ferdinand von, *On the Sensations of Tone,* **4:**287

Help, Help, the Globolinks! (Menotti), **5:**226

Hemingway, Ernest, **4:**474, 589

A Farewell to Arms, **4:**473

hemiola, **1:**341, 345, 368, 742, 745

pattern of beats, **2:**267

Hempel, Carl, **5:**155, 162

Milton Babbitt and, **5:**155

Henderson, Robert, **5:**342–43

Henderson, W. J., **4:**627

Hendricks, Barbara, *Final Alice* and, **5:**443

Henrici, Christian Friedrich (Picander),
    2:378
Henricus Glareanus. *See* Glareanus,
    Henricus
Henricus Leonellus, 1:175
Henry II, King of England, 1:106, 408
Henry III, King of England, 4:131
Henry IV, King of England, 1:409, 416
Henry IV, King of France, 1:812
Henry V, King of England, 1:409, 416,
    418–21, 461
Henry VI, King of England, 1:417, 421,
    461, 513
Henry VII, King of England, 1:513
Henry VIII, King of England, 1:513, 613,
    670–72, 671, 675, 676, 692
Henry IV (Shakespeare), 3:623
Henry V (Shakespeare), 1:420
Henry, Pierre, 5:188
    Groupe de Recherche de Musique
        Concrete and, 5:188
    Orphée, 5:188
    "Veil of Orpheus, The," 5:188
Henry Street Settlement, 4:661
Hensel, Fanny. *See* Mendelssohn, Fanny
Hensel, Sebastian, 3:185
Hensel, Wilhelm, 3:184, 185, 295
Hentoff, Nat, 5:318
Henze, Hans Werner, 5:18, 21–22,
    342–46, 474
    Darmstadt, 5:342
    emigration to Italy, 5:342
    Lehrstück vom Einverständnis, 5:21
    The Rolling Stones and, 5:343–44
    works of
        Bassarids, The, 5:343, 344
        Musen Siziliens, 5:344–45, 346
"Henze Turns the Clock Back"
    (Stuckenschmidt), 5:345
Herbert, Victor, 4:624
    Suite of Serenades, 4:626
Herculaneum, 2:453
Hercules. *See* Ercole
"Hercules, Dux Ferrari(a)e" (in musical
    notation), 1:560
Herder, Johann Gottfried von, 3:73,
    120–23, 183, 367, 386, 422; 4:2, 21,
    371, 379, 422, 42
    folk songs and, 3:123, 126, 127, 155
    human culture origin concept of,
        3:190–91
    human differences view of, 3:121, 231–32,
        345, 567
    language view of, 3:121–22, 146, 190–91,
        345
    Urwüchsigkeit concept, 3:146, 191
"Here Comes the Bride" (Elsa's bridal song;
    Wagner), 3:487
Hermann Contractus (Hermann the
    Lame), 1:99, 102
hermeneutics, 1:683–84
Herminie (Berlioz), 3:326

hermit songs, 1:818, 821
Hernani (Hugo), 3:76, 574, 576
Herod, 2:68, 73
heroic roles, voice range and, 3:36, 578
heroic style, 2:738
    Beethoven's *Eroica* Symphony's
        earmarks of, 2:655–56, 668–69
    Beethoven's works and, 2:670, 689
    C-minor mood and, 2:701, 702, 705
    undesirable side effects of, 2:670–71
heroism, Romantic, 3:273, 275
Herrmann, Bernard, 5:184
Hervé (Louis August Joseph Florimond
    Ronger), 3:644, 647
Herz, Djane Lavoie, 4:295, 296
Herzen, Alexander, 3:476–77, 478
"He sent a thick darkness" (Handel), 2:321,
    324
"He smote all the first-born of Egypt"
    (Handel), 2:321, 325
    Stradella's *Quel prodigio e ch'io miri* and,
        2:327, 328
"He spake the word" (Handel), 2:317,
    319–20, 327
Hess, Rudolf, 4:764
Hesse, Hermann
    Das Glasperlenspiel, 5:44
    Steppenwolf, 5:415–16
heterosexual, coining of term, 3:36
hexachord
    C-A module, 1:99, 100–101, 102
    hard, soft, and natural, 1:102, 103–4
    Palestrina Mass based on, 1:634, 635
    syllables of, 1:102, 499
*Hexachord and Its Relation to the Twelve-Tone
    Row, The* (Rochberg), 5:414
Heyden, Seybald, 1:550, 578
Hiawatha (Dvořák), 3:760, 764–66
Hiawatha overture (Goldmark), 4:614
Hiawatha's Departure (painting), 3:763
Hicks, Michael, 4:299, 302
Hicks, Thomas, 3:380
Hidden Persuaders, The (Packard), 5:396
Hiemer, F. K., 3:715
hiermos, 1:34
Higgins, Dick, 5:91, 93
    Danger Music, 5:94
high art
    academic style and, 1:607–11
    classical doctrine of, 1:459, 462
    emulation and, 1:474–75
    entertainment separated from, 2:655
    Josquin and, 1:500, 579
    Machaut and, 1:326–27
    popular art vs., 1:115–16, 120, 226, 228,
        326–27
    social/political elites and, 2:112–13
    See also classical music; high style
High Baroque, 2:298
    Bach (J. S.) and, 2:345
    Handel and, 2:194, 345

High Church style (England), 1:518, 526,
    612–14
high culture, 3:743
    Gottschalk and, 3:377, 379, 380, 384
higher truth, 3:59
High Fidelity, 5:157
High Renaissance music, 1:577–84,
    585–628
high style
    cyclic Mass Ordinary as, 1:461–62, 465,
        480–81, 497
    English antiphon motet and, 1:517–18
    Ockeghem's bergerette and, 1:529
    Tinctoris's genre ranking and,
        1:459–60, 486, 517
    of troubadour, 1:110–13, 114, 131
"Hi ho, nobody home" (round), 1:331
Hilburn, Robert, 5:333
    Los Angeles Times, 5:333
Hildegard of Bingen, 1:190–92, 91, 93
    Columba aspexit, 1:91–92
    Ordo virtutum, 1:93
    textual preservation of works of, 2:79
Hildesheim, 2:66
Hildesheimer, Wolfgang, 2:464
Hill, Edward Burlingame, 3:769, 774–75;
    4:266, 636, 705
Hill, Joe, 4:656
    "Casey Jones," 4:656
Hill, Junius W., 3:770
Hill, Peter, 5:27
Hill, Richard S., twelve-tone technique
    and, 4:704–5
Hiller, Ferdinand, 2:724; 3:294, 685
Hiller, Johann Adam, 2:445
Hiller, Lejaren, 5:74
    John Cage and, 5:74
Hillier, Paul, Arvo Pärt and, 5:402, 403
Hillstrom, Joseph. See Hill, Joe
Hindemith, Paul, 3:192, 193; 4:528, 540, 541,
    543, 548, 555, 765, 766–773; 5:21,
    103–4, 326, 449
    Das Marienleben, 4:769, 770–71
    Das Nusch-Nuschi, 4:528
    Fugue no. 5, 4:768, 769
    Kammermusik Nr. 1, 4:528
    Konzertstück, 5:184
    Ludus tonalis, 4:768
    Mathis der Maler, 4:767, 768
    "minute stylizations" and, 4:609–10
    Mörder, Hoffnung der Frauen, 4:528
    Neues vom Tage, 4:530, 532
    Neues vom Tage, bathtub aria, 4:531,
        532–33, 550
    Sancta Susanna, 4:528
    "Series I" from *Unterweisung in Tonsatz*,
        4:768
    Sonata for solo viola, op. 25, no. 1, 4:528
    Suite "1922," 4:528, 528
    Tuba Sonata, 5:104
Hindenburg, Paul von, 4:748
Hindus, Sanskrit and, 4:307

Hinton, Stephen, 4:545
Hiob (Fanny Mendelssohn), 3:184
Hippolyte et Aricie (Rameau), 1:797
Histoire du chevalier des Grieux et de Manon Lescaut, L' (Prévost d'Exiles), 3:641
Histoire du soldat (Stravinsky), 4:486, 600
Historia der freuden und gnadenreichen Geburth Gottes and Marien Sohnes, Jesu Christi, unsers einigen Mitlers, Erlösers und Seeligmachers (Schütz), 2:73
historical concerts, 3:680–81
historical opera
    France and, 3:205–6, 622
    Russia and, 3:621–31
historicism, 2:390; 3:411–16, 640, 719–30; 5:413
    anachronism and, 1:143–44
    art history and, 1:653
    binarisms and, 1:105–6
    Brahms and, 3:691–92
    Brendel and, 3:411–15, 440
    canon vs. repertoire and, 3:665–66, 682
    "classical" genre view and, 3:676
    conceptual subdivisions and, 1:380–85
    context in, 1:739, 741
    dating of Josquin's *Ave Maria. . .* and, 1:579–81, 584
    deterministic, 1:144
    economic forces and. *See* free market
    essentialism and, 1:381, 382, 385
    estheticism and, 3:561, 562
    Hegel's change theory and, 3:412–13
    Herder and, 3:121
    morality of great works and, 2:389–90, 495–96
    nineteenth-century symphonic music and, 3:680, 681–82
    operetta appraisal and, 3:649
    political implications of "classical" art and, 2:389–90
    Puccini's standing and, 3:665–66
    teleological, 1:144, 381, 383, 738–39
    Wagner's *Tristan und Isolde* and, 3:545–46
    on women's underrepresentation in music, 2:78–81
    See also music historiography
historien. *See* oratorio
historiography. *See* historicism; music historiography
History of Music (Burney). *See General History of Music*
History of Photography in Sound (Finnissy), 5:476
Hitchcock, Alfred
    Spellbound, 5:183
    To Catch a Thief, 5:198
Hitler, Adolf, 4:476, 559, 747
Hiugens, Christiaan, 4:285
HMS Pinafore; or, The Lass That Loved a Sailor (Gilbert and Sullivan), 3:652
Ho Chi Minh, Louis Durey and, 4:589

Hobrecht, Jacobus. *See* Obrecht, Jacobus
Hochschule für Musik (Berlin), 3:769
hocket, 1:191, 199, 613
    canon and, 1:331, 332
    English motet and, 1:410
    Gloria *pax* and, 1:348
    Mass Ordinary and, 1:311, 316, 317, 323, 326, 345
    motet and, 1:227–28, 233, 262, 265, 266, 269, 271, 311
hocketing hands-exchange technique, 3:378
Hoepffner (biographer), 1:343
Hoffman, Stanley, 2:739
Hoffmann, E. T. A., 2:600, 642, 647, 651, 739; 3:35, 178, 657; 4:136, 144, 306, 307
    art vs. entertainment distinction of, 2:655
    on Beethoven, 2:648–49, 670, 680, 692, 714, 717, 731, 739; 3:32–33, 291, 440
    on Beethoven's Fifth Symphony, 2:705–6, 709, 720
    on *Don Giovanni* as "opera of operas," 2:485, 487
    on Haydn's musical gifts, 2:643, 644–46, 668
    "Hoffmanesque" romantic concept, 4:307
    on Mozart's sublimity, 2:643–46, 648
    on music as most Romantic of all arts, 2:641–42, 735
    on Rossini, 3:13, 34
    on Weber, 3:205
Hoffman von Fallersleben, August Heinrich, 3:114, 130
Hofmannsthal, Hugo von, 4:57
    Ariadne auf Naxos, 4:453
    Der Rosenkavalier, 4:49, 453
    Elektra, 4:49, 4:57, 4:453
Hofstadter, Richard, 4:273
Hofweise (melody), 1:701, 704, 706, 758, 759, 760
Hogarth, William, 2:312, 574; 5:117
Hohenheim, Philippus Aureolus von, 4:259
Holbein, Hans, the Younger, 1:671
Hölderlin, Friedrich, 3:714, 715, 715
Holford, Robert, 4:285
holiday liturgical music. *See* church calendar; *specific holidays*
Holiday Overture (Carter), 5:276
Holland, Charles, 5:493
Hollander, John, 5:65
    Philomel and, 5:201
Hölle Rache, Der (Mozart), 2:481, 482–83
Hollywood, 4:551, 628
Holmes, William C., 2:447
Holoman, D. Kern, 3:324, 335
"Holy Minimalists," 5:526
Holy Roman Empire, 1:286, 289, 421, 704, 772; 3:62, 165, 206
    arts and, 2:15, 152, 504–7

Council of Trent and, 1:653
    diminished power of, 2:68, 139
    disbanded *Kapellen* in, 2:607
    Elector Palatine and, 2:505
    Esterházy Princes and, 2:525
    formation of, 1:4
    multinational makeup of, 1:11, 13; 2:550
    northern Italian musical developments and, 2:152
    Protestant Reformation and, 1:753, 756, 758, 762
    Thiry Years War and, 2:55–56, 68
    See also Austria
Holy Spirit, 1:773
Holy Trinity, 1:333, 334
Holy Week, 1:465, 775
home entertainment. *See* domestic entertainment
"Home on the Range" (song), 1:18
Home on the Range (Westley), 3:384
Homer, 2:26; 3:513; 4:525
Hommage . . . John Cage (Paik), 5:92, 94
Homme Armé, L' (Davies), 5:427
Homme Armé, L' (Masses), 1:484–500, 529, 655
    Busnoy's *Missa* as genre archetype, 1:495, 500, 501
    characteristic cantus firmus of, 1:486–90
    Morales and, 1:634
    origins of, 1:484–85
    Palestrina and, 1:634, 635–37
    printed texts of, 1:499
    See also Missa L'Homme Armé
Homme Armé, L' (secular song), 1:484, 485–86, 485, 486–87
Homme et son désir, L' (Milhaud), 4:582
homoerotic art, 1:108
homologous chords, 3:96
homorhythmic counterpoint, 1:122, 146, 199, 296, 403, 577
    Avignon-style Mass Ordinary and, 1:311, 314, 316, 317
    Byrd vs. Palestrina use of, 1:680
    Dunstable motet and, 1:429–30, 432
    Gaspar motet and, 1:521
    Old Hall Sanctus and, 1:417
homosexuality, 2:312, 313, 340
    Cellini and, 3:116
    Chaikovsky and, 3:409, 795, 799–800
    coining of term, 3:36
    Schubert and conjecture concerning, 3:116–18
Honegger, Arthur, 5:13
    Les Six group and, 4:588; 5:183
Honoloulou (Makoko), 4:573
honor, 1:107, 109, 117
Hook, Sidney, 5:293, 294
Hoole, John, 2:156
Hoquetus In seculum (anon.), 1:233
Hora novissima (Parker), 4:246, 247, 248–49, 251, 252

Horace, **1:**115, 477, 552, 554, 570, 691; **2:**410, 461; **3:**120

"Horizons' 83: Since 1968, A New Romanticism?," Jacob Druckman and, **5:**435–36

horn call, **1:**485, 711

hornpipe, **2:**204, 205

horns
  Beethoven's *Eroica* false entrance by, **2:**664, 667
  forest, **3:**158, 199–202
  Haydn's orchestration and, **2:**527
  muted valve, **3:**335
  nature evocation and, **3:**158, 200, 202
  opera seria orchestration and, **2:**166
  Rossini and, **3:**21
  Wagner and, **3:**512
  Weber and, **3:**199–202, 204
  See also French horn

"Hornsignal" Symphony (Haydn), **2:**527

horror, musical expression of, **2:**317–21, 364, 365–68, 369, 470, 494

horror stories, **3:**194

Horthy, Nicholas, **4:**746

Hortus Musicus, **5:**401

Hortus musicus, Sonata no. 1 (Reincken), **2:**242, 243–44, 402
  Bach (J. S.) arrangement of, **2:**245–47

Hosanna (Josquin), **1:**560–63

"Houlihan" (a.k.a. "I Ride an Old Paint") (Thomson), **4:**660

"House Party, The." See *Les biches* ,

household entertainment. *See* domestic entertainment

household romance songs, **3:**633

Houston Grand Opera, *Nixon in China* and, **5:**518

Hove, Pieter van den. *See* Petrus Alamire

Howard, Hugh, **2:**178

How Firm a Foundation (Scottish hymn), **4:**660

"Howld Fast" (Tye), **2:**116, 117

How Musical Is Man? (Blacking), **5:**380–83

"How Rock Communicates" (Williams), **5:**332

"How the Piano Came to be Prepared" (Cage), **5:**73–74

HPSCHD (Cage), **5:**74
  commission of, **5:**74

Hrabanus Maurus, Archbishop of Mainz, **1:**49

Hrabovsky, Leonid, **5:**463, 471

Hucbald, **1:**77–78, 80
  Gloria trope by, **1:**80–82

Hughes, Langston, "Ballad of Ozie Powell," **4:**662

Hugo, Victor, **3:**318, 323, 430, 431, 594
  in Danhauser's painting, **3:**76
  opera adaptations from works of, **3:**45, 569, 574, 577, 583
  orientalism and, **3:**387
  revolutionary politics and, **3:**265

Shakespeare invocation by, **3:**576

Hugo Sprechtshart von Reutlingen, **1:**134

Huguenots, **1:**754

Huguenots, Les (Meyerbeer), **3:**215, 218–32, 286
  Act IV, **3:**219, 223–27
  Cavatine du Page, **3:**220–22, 221, 227
  Feste Burg, Ein' and, **3:**229–32
  Schumann (Robert) critique of, **3:**229, 230, 292
  "Tu l'as dit!," **3:**225–27

Hull, Arthur Eaglefield, **4:**216

Hulme, Thomas Ernest (T.E.), **4:**474, 467, 476, 550
  French Revolution and, **4:**471
  "Modern Art and Its Philosophy," **4:**467–68, 474–75
  "Romanticism and Classicism," **4:**467

human difference, **3:**191
  Herder's view of, **3:**121, 231–32, 345, 567
  orientalism and, **3:**193

humanism, **1:**382, 383, 547–84, 615–16, 630, 687
  ancient music theory and, **1:**799–800
  Byrd and, **1:**679
  classicism and, **1:**615, 717, 720, 730, 780
  Clemens and, **1:**593–94
  English church music as untouched by, **1:**613
  extroversive semiotics and, **1:**643
  Josquin and, **1:**547, 551–54, 566, 570, 572, 578–79, 581, 584, 687
  Lasso and, **1:**720
  literary music and, **1:**723, 724, 725
  Monteverdi and, **2:**4, 9, 21
  occultism and, **1:**615–16
  opera's invention and, **3:**618–19
  Palestrina and, **1:**641, 642, 647
  Parisian chanson and, **1:**708
  printing industry and, **1:**754
  Protestant Reformation and, **1:**753
  radical. *See* radical humanism
  Verdi's musical approach and, **3:**610
  See also ars perfecta

humanity, representation of, **2:**464, 474, 475, 486, 495, 590–91, 643

human unconscious, exploration of, **4:**307

Hume, Paul, **5:**107

Hummel, Johann Nepomuk, **3:**262, 351

humor, musical. *See* joke, musical

humorous drama. *See* opera buffa

humors, theory of, **1:**71

Humperdinck, Engelbert, **4:**459, 460, 539
  Die Königskinder, **4:**459
  Hänsel und Gretel, **4:**459
  Sprechnoten and, **4:**459

Humphrey, Duke of Gloucester, **1:**421

Hundred Variations on Passacalles, A (Frescobaldi), **2:**37

Hundred Years War, **1:**408, 421, 422

Hungarian Coronation Mass (Liszt), **4:**371, 372

Hungarian Dances (Brahms), **3:**717, 753; **4:**632

Hungarian Fantasia (Liszt), **4:**371

Hungarian Historical Portraits (Liszt), **4:**371

Hungarian kingdom, reunification of, **4:**365

Hungarian musical nationalism, **4:**373

Hungarian nationalism, **4:**365

"Hungarian Rhapsodies" (Liszt), **3:**433, 449; **4:**626, 632

Hungarian style, **4:**365–78

Hungary, **3:**11–2, 445, 447
  Esterházy family and, **2:**525–26, 526
  Liszt and, **3:**261

Hunnenschlacht (Liszt), **3:**446

hunt
  as caccia subject, **1:**364, 365
  onomatopoetic sounds of, **1:**711

Hunyádi László (Erkel), **3:**447

hurdy-gurdy, **1:**805

Huré, Jean, **4:**196

Hurrian cult song, **1:**31, 32

"Hurrian" (or Sumerian) hymn, **5:**451

Hus, Jan, **1:**753; **3:**164, 452

Huysmans, Joris-Karl, **4:**29
  À rebours, **4:**29, 57, 84

hymnbooks, Lutheran, **3:**171

hymn-march, **3:**247, 248

Hymnen (Stockhausen), **5:**191, 420

hymns and hymnody
  Ambrosian stanza, **1:**49
  Augustine definition of, **1:**11
  Babylonian, **1:**31
  Byrd and, **1:**686
  Byzantine church and, **1:**33–34, 48
  choral, **2:**49–50, 53
  Christmas carols as, **1:**420
  Delphic, **1:**32
  by Du Fay, **1:**444–46
  early Greek Christian, **1:**33
  English, **1:**439–40, 673–74
  Frankish, **1:**41–43, 47–49, 50–86
  Lutheran chorale translations of, **1:**758–69
  Nordic, **1:**392–94, 393
  oral tradition and, **1:**27, 39
  organ settings of, **2:**49–50
  polyphonic settings of, **1:**159
  psalmody vs., **1:**48
  revolutionary, **3:**162–63
  rhythmic performance speculation, **1:**114
  sequence-like, **1:**43–45
  trochaic meter, **1:**47
  Vesper, **1:**632

"Hymn to St. Magnus" (Nordic hymn), **1:**393–94, 393

Hymn to the Trinity, **1:**33, 34

"Hyperion's Song of Fate" (Hölderlin), **3:**714

Hyperprism (Varese), **5:**185

hypnotism, **3:**71–73

Hypodorian ambitus, **1:**89

Hypolydian mode (sixth), **1:**80, 85–86

Hypophyrygian mode (fourth), **1:**82
Hyppolite et Aricie (Rameau), **2:**110
Hystorie sacre gestas ab origine mundi (Leonius), **1:**175, 191

I

iambic meter, **1:**176–77, 197, 198
iambic pentameter, **1:**378, 742
"I Am the Very Model of a Modern Major-General" (Gilbert and Sullivan), **3:**655
"I" and "We" concept, **3:**293
    lieder and, **3:**120, 124, 135, 138, 142
    nationalism and, **3:**61–63, 124, 163
I Ching, **5:**63, 65, 70, 74, 82
"I" matrix, **5:**29
Iberian peninsula. *See* Spain
Iceland, **1:**393; **3:**492
Ich grolle nicht (Schumann), **3:**301–3
iconic represensentation, **1:**363
"Idaho Bill," **4:**672
idée fixe
    Berlioz and, **3:**321, 324, 326–31, 336, 419, 425, 502
    Smetana and, **3:**444
Idelsohn, Abraham Zvi, **4:**108–9
Idols of Perversity (Dijkstra), **4:**57
Idomenée, re di Creta (Campra), **2:**90, 465, 465–70, 474
    final mad scene, **2:**106–7
Idomeneo, di Creta (Mozart), **2:**90, 465–70, 466, 645
Idomeneus, King of Crete, **2:**90
idylls, **1:**356
Ier mains pensis chevauchai (Ernoul Caupain), **1:**120
Ignatius of Loyola, Saint, **1:**666, 771
Ile fantazies de Joskin (Josquin), **1:**545–46
Illica, Luigi, **3:**666
illuminated manuscripts, **1:**6–7, 6, 71, 71
Illumination of St. Petersburg at Night (Vasilyev), **3:**787
"illusionist" theater, **4:**495
Illustrated History of Music (Naumann), **3:**676
Illustrazione italiana (magazine), **3:**596, 611
imagery, **1:**91
    of courtly love, **1:**108
Imaginary Landscapes (Cage), **5:**185
    No. 1 (Cage), **5:**56–58
    No. 3 (Cage), **5:**70
    No. 4 (Cage), **5:**70
imagination, **3:**205
    of the beholder, **3:**305, 306, 315
    Schumann on, **3:**341
Imber, Naftali Herz, **3:**456
"imbricated arches," **4:**640
imbroglio (tangled plot), **2:**451, 486, 490, 492, 620; **3:**25, 47
imitation. *See* mimesis
imitatio technique, **1:**574

imitative polyphony, **1:**337, 493, 546, 574, 577, 579, 589, 596
    canon as, **1:**330–36
    cantus firmus and, **1:**580–82
    Gabrieli's (Giovanni) absence of, **1:**786
Immaculate Conception, **1:**566
"Immortal Beloved" letter (Beethoven), **2:**672
"I'm off to Constantinople" (round-dance tune), **3:**472
imperfect consonants. *See* dissonance
Imperial Chapel (Vienna), **3:**746
"Imperial" style, **4:**456
Imperial Theaters School, Balanchine and, **4:**144
imperialism
    British, **1:**406; **3:**392
    justification for, **3:**61
    orientalism and, **3:**387, 392
    Russian, **3:**392, 457, 459
implication/realization model, **2:**208
Impressario, The (Mozart), **2:**481
Impression: Sunrise (Monet), **4:**76, 77f
impressionism, **4:**145
    musical, **4:**76–83
Impressionism school of painting, **4:**76, 84
Impromptu in A-flat major, op. 142, no. 2 (Schubert), **3:**110–11
Impromptu in E-flat, op. 90, no. 2 (Schubert), **3:**87–89, 92, 100, 101
impromptus, **3:**87–88
improvisation
    arias and, **2:**650
    Bach (J. S.) and, **2:**241, 243, 384–85
    Baroque and, **2:**35, 37
    Beethoven and, **2:**652, 653, 655
    Bruckner and, **3:**746–47
    cadenza and, **2:**171, 609–10, 650
    Chopin and, **3:**350
    chorale and, **2:**255
    by composer, **2:**610–11
    concerto and, **2:**650
    continuo and, **2:**291
    definition of, **1:**17
    Empfindsamkeit vogue and, **2:**414
    as ground bass forerunner, **2:**186
    harmonic, **1:**392, 394, 406, 434–39, 452
    as instrumental vocal accompaniment, **1:**307
    jazz and, **1:**17, 307, 536; **2:**174, 223, 611, 650–51
    lute strumming as, **2:**249–51
    Lutheran cantus firmus and, **1:**762
    Mozart and, **2:**610–11, 624, 625–31, 650
    opera seria and, **2:**174
    oral tradition and, **1:**17–18, 666–67, 821
    organists and, **1:**437, 607, 617, 781; **2:**37, 43, 44
    ornamentation and, **1:**783, 821
    by performers, **3:**287–88
    polyphonic, **1:**758
    pop music and, **2:**174, 609, 611, 650–51

ricercari and, **1:**606–7
toccatas and, **2:**40–44
vernacular song and, **1:**697
virtuoso fifteenth-century, **1:**536–41
written examples as cream of, **2:**35, 44
Im wunderschönen Monat Mai (Schumann), **3:**296–99
In a Silent Way (Davis), **5:**335
In C (Riley), **5:**363–68, 369, 373
    algorithmic composition of, **5:**364
    premiere performance of, **5:**365
    reception of, **5:**365
Incantation (Luening-Ussachevsky), **5:**198
Incarnation, **1:**772–73
Incenerite spoglie (Monteverdi), **2:**6, 7
In Central Asia (Borodin), **3:**397, 401–3
In Contra mortem et tempus (Rochberg), **5:**415
"In Flanders Fields" (McCrae), **4:**291
In Memoriam Dylan Thomas (Stravinsky), **5:**122
In Memory of a Summer Day (DelTredici), **5:**443
In paradisum deducant te Angeli (Fauré), **4:**101–2
In Search of Lost Time (Proust), **4:**79, 97
incidental music
    Beethoven and, **3:**1–2
    English theater and, **2:**113, 126, 127
    Lully and, **3:**386
    Schubert and, **3:**81, 108
    Weber and, **3:**192, 193, 386
Incises (Boulez), **5:**478
"incomplete neighbor" (counterpoint), **1:**430
Incoronazione di Poppea, L' (Monteverdi), **2:**1–2, 13, 26–33, 87–88, 146, 148; **3:**611
    ground bass and, **2:**35
    Nerone and, **2:**140
    Pur ti miro and, **2:**30, 32–33, 77
    revived (1650s) version of, **2:**33, 37, 77
    Rossi's *Orfeo* and
Indebtedness of Handel to Works by Other Composers, The (Taylor), **2:**327
Indes galantes, Les (Rameau), **2:**321
India, Sigismondo d', **1:**818–19
    Piange, madonna, **1:**819–20
Indianists, **3:**767
"Indianist" compositions, Gilbert and, **4:**613
"Indian Suite" (MacDowell), **3:**768
In diesen heil'gen Hallen (Mozart), **2:**481, 484–85
"In Distress" ("Lord Nelson Mass") (Haydn), **2:**577
individual consciousness, **3:**62
individualism, **1:**548, 549; **2:**409, 643, 670, 737
    Protestant Reformation and, **1:**753, 765, 771
    Romanticism and, **3:**15, 62, 63, 273, 570
indulgences, **1:**315, 316, 753
Indy, Vincent d', **3:**777, 783; **4:**61, 266

Indy, Vincent d' (*continued*)
  Suite dans le style ancien, 4:65
In ecclesiis benedicite Domino
  (G. Gabrieli), 1:783–86
Infelix ego (Byrd), 1:679
Inferno (Dante), 1:803
infinite
  Beethoven and longing for, 2:648–49,
    670, 731–32, 734
  music's disclosure of, 2:641–42, 643–45,
    646
Ingarden, Roman, 5:69
Ingegneri, Marc'Antonio, 2:2, 5
in hexatono, 3:102
In hydraulis (Busnoys), 1:456–57, 495, 500
In illo tempore loquente Jesu ad turbas
  (Gombert), 1:590–93
inner life. *See* subjectivity
Innigkeit/Innerlichkeit, 3:63, 75, 113, 138;
  4:306
Inno alla vita (Pratella), 5:178
Innocent III, Pope, 1:112
In Nomine fancies, 2:115–20
Innsbruck, ich muss dich lassen (Isaac), 1:759,
  760
inordinato, 1:724
in partitura, 2:36
Inquisition, 1:653, 772
inscription. *See* written music
In seculum breve, 1:232
In seculum longum, 1:232
"In seculum" melisma, 1:222–24, 227–33,
  229
  textless pieces to, 1:229–33, 233, 424
In seculum viellatoris, 1:232, 541
inspiration, trance state and, 3:73
"instant classics," 3:682
Institut de Recherche et Coordination
  Acoustique/Musique (Paris). *See*
  IRCAM
instrumental drama
  Balakirev and, 3:471, 478
  Berlioz and, 3:321–31, 336–39
instrumental music, 1:534–46
  as absolute music, 2:418; 3:502, 775
  ars perfecta and, 1:606, 617–28
  Bach (J. S.) and, 2:261–301
  Beethoven's legacy to, 2:686
  Beethoven's Romanticism and,
    2:648–85, 702, 714, 724; 3:7
  Berlioz and, 3:323, 775
  big band battle-pieces, 1:787–89
  Brendel's view of, 3:414, 415
  Buus and, 1:606
  Byrd and, 1:670
  Calvinist ban on, 2:46
  canzona and, 1:787–96
  chorale prelude and, 1:762
  concerted style and, 1:780–81
  Corelli's legacy to, 2:177, 181–84
  cultural prestige of, 2:539
  domestic entertainment and, 3:63–64

earliest functionless form of, 1:541
empfindsamer Stil and, 2:413, 414, 416, 418
English "act tunes" and, 2:126
exigetical interpretation of, 2:650, 706,
  714
expressive potential of, 2:222, 539
fifteenth-century, 1:536–46
Franck and, 3:775
of French court, 2:259–60
Gabrielis' dramatization of, 1:786, 787
German, 2:533. 3.46
German emphasis on, 2:533. 3.46
Handel and, 2:305–6
Haydn and, 2:518, 600, 643, 646, 648
imitation of nature by, 2:227–31, 316,
  317–21
interactive, 2:223
intermedii as, 1:803, 804
interpretation of, 3:427
introversive and extroversive signs in,
  1:652–54, 658; 2:539–41, 542, 545,
  546, 550–53, 571, 588, 591, 599, 661,
  680, 682, 717, 718; 3:528, 756, 759
Italian development of, 2:177–231, 234,
  281
Jacobean consort and, 2:114–24
key system and, 1:44
Liszt recitals of, 3:272–73
method books, 1:620–21
mid-eighteenth-century newness of,
  2:399–434, 437
motet and, 1:222–24, 222, 227–28,
  229–33, 229, 233
Mozart and, 2:475, 589–639, 643, 646,
  648
as Musica metaphor, 1:38
New German School and, 3:440, 675
opera's stylistic impact on, 2:281, 433
orchestration origins and, 1:782–86
ornamentation and, 2:281
printing and, 1:542–46
Purcell and, 2:127–30
Romantic exaltation of, 2:591, 642; 3:69
Rossini's illustrative effects with, 3:24
as secularized, 2:204
seventeenth-century development of,
  1:798; 2:36–37
signification and, 2:539–55
sixteenth-century, 1:606, 617–28,
  780–81, 786–96
solo recitals of, 3:272–73
sonata and, 1:791, 792
standard forms of, 2:234
Tafelmusik as, 2:53
textual sanctity of, 2:650–51
tonality and, 2:188–98
Venetian cathedral performances of,
  1:790–96
virtuosos. *See* virtuosity
as vocal accompaniment, 1:131–33, 296,
  307, 352, 741–42, 780

See also chamber music; concerto;
  keyboard music; *specific instruments*;
  symphony
instrumental recitative, 2:413, 414
instruments
  design of, 2:736
  Janissary, 2:470–71, 602, 675, 678
  liturgical bans on, 1:8
  making of, 2:435
  miniatures of medieval, 1:129–30
  resurrection of "original," 2:233
  tuning of, 2:247–48
Intabolatura de lauto (Spinacino), 1:606
Intabolatura d'organo di recercari (Buus),
  1:619
intabulation (tablature), 1:307, 606
In te Domine speravi (lauda), 1:699
In te Domine speravi (Clemens), 1:598–99
Intégrales (Varese), 5:185
intellectual cleverness, 1:327–42
  fifteenth-century, 1:456
intellectual elites. *See* elite culture
intellectuals
  Busnoys's skills as, 1:456
  cathedral, 1:207–8
  high art and, 1:326–27
  See also elite culture
"intelligibility" (liturgical music) movement,
  1:647, 649–53, 671, 672, 769
In tempore belli (Haydn), 2:577, 633
"interactive sound installations," 5:513–14
intermedii. See intermezzo
intermezzo, 1:769; 2:12, 13, 434–37;
  3:643–44
  character conventions of, 2:434, 435,
    438–39
  English masque vs., 2:126
  farce and, 2:447
  first international hit, 2:435–37
  foreign reactions to, 2:435, 437
  monody and, 1:806–12, 823, 826
  as Mozart's first dramatic work, 2:464
  opera buffa and, 2:447; 3:187
  Pergolesi's *Serva padrona* as masterwork
    of, 2:438–52
  plot line of, 2:435, 438–39, 477
  Rousseau and, 2:442–43
  Schütz oratorio and, 2:73
  sixteenth-century Florentine *intermedii*,
    1:803–12, 831, 832
intermission play. *See* intermezzo
International Chopin Competition
  (Warsaw), 4:781
"Internationale" (Communist hymn),
  4:651–52
International Society of Contemporary
  Music, 2:693
international style, fifteenth-century, 1:378,
  380, 384, 422, 453–59
International Summer Courses for New
  Music, 5:20
internationalism

artistic content need for, 3:464
cultural conditioning and, 3:298
instrumental music and, 3:427
of Italian operas, 3:426
of musical works, 3:425–27
nineteenth-century national opera and, 3:250
poetic content and, 3:425–27
politics of, 3:476–78
in Puccini's operatic style, 3:667, 668
Wagner's view of, 3:559; 2:680, 682, 694
Intersections (Feldman), 5:98
intervals, 1:5, 73, 76, 284, 285
basso continuo, 1:809, *811*
counterpoint and, 1:154, 406
demonstration of, 1:73
diatonic pitch set and, 1:29–30, 35
ear training in, 1:76, 100–101, 406
parallel doubling and, 1:149–53
perfect, 1:274
as pitch ratio, 1:73
simultaneous. *See* consonance
staff, 1:29–30, 35, 73
as *symphoniae*, 1:149
"In Thee, O Lord, have I placed my hope" (Clemens), 1:598–99
Intimate Story of Indian Tribal Life, The; or, The Story of a Vanishing Race (Gilbert), 4:613
"In Time of War" (Haydn), 2:577, 633
intonarumori ("noise intoners"), 5:179, *180*
intonation, 3:633
Chaikovsky's use of, 3:633
"Into the Streets, May First" (Copland) 4:654–55, 656
intrasyllabic melodic expansion, 1:171–72
Introduction and Variations on "Dal tuo stellato soglio" (Paganini), 3:258
introduzione. See overture
Introit, 1:13, *15*, 23, 24, 79
in Mass ordo, 1:61(table)
troping of, 1:50, 51, 52, 64, 82
introspection
Enlightenment's universality standard vs., 2:600
humanism and, 1:383
late-eighteenth-century composers and, 2:588, 589
mid-eighteenth-century composers and, 2:409, 426–27
nineteenth-century composers and, 2:737
Romanticism and, 2:599; 3:86, 92–93, 96
introversive semiotics, 1:643; 3:528, 756, 759
Beethoven and, 2:680, 682, 717, 718
Haydn and, 2:539–41, 542, 545, 546, 551, 552, 553, 588, 591, 717
Mozart and, 2:591, 717
Romanticism and, 2:599
intuition, 2:720

"intuitive aesthetic," *Erwartung* and, 4:680
"inversion," homosexuality and, 5:248
inversions, 1:813
invisible orchestra, 3:563, 564
"Invitation to the Dance" (Weber), 3:208
inwardness
Romanticism and, 3:62, 63, 66, 69, 73, 86–87, 124
Schubert's representation of, 3:92–94, 96, 109, 152
Io che dal ciel cader (Caccini), 1:804, 808–9
Iolanta (Chaikovsky), 3:406
Iolanthe (Gilbert and Sullivan), 3:655
Io me son giovinetta (ballata), 1:366
Ionian mode, 1:553, 572, 592, 596
Ionisation (Varèse), 5:185, 186,2 09
Ionesco, Eugène, 5:89
Ipanema (Milhaud), 4:582
Iphigenia in Tauris (Euripides), 2:460
Iphigenia in Tauris (Gluck), 2:460, 465
Iphigenia in Tauris (Piccini), 2:460
Iphigénie en Aulide (Gluck), 2:459, 465
IRCAM, 471, 5:501
Irish jig, 2:261
Irish Melodies (Moore), 4:97
Iron Curtain, 5:6, 508
irony, 4:2, 479
artistic conventions and, 1:359, 363, 364
Chaikovsky's use of, 3:632
comic contrast and, 2:439
in Schubert's works, 3:142–47, 149
Verdi's use of, 3:577, 583–87
Iroquois League, 3:764
Isaac, Henricus, 1:536, 538–39, 544, 545, 547, 559, 572, 622, 679, 704, 759, 798, 823, 834; 3:703; 4:722
Choralis Constantinus, 1:679
Innsbruck, ich muss dich lassen, 1:759, 760
J'ay pris amours, 1:536, 538–39
Missa Quant j'ay au cuer, 1:543–44, 545
Missa super La Spagna, 1:623–25
SS. Giovanni e Paolo, 1:823, 827, 834
Isabella I, Queen of Spain, 1:724
Isabey, Jean Baptiste, 2:673
Isaiah, Book of, 1:52, 54
Isherwood, Christopher, 5:228, 234, 246
Isidore, Bishop of Seville, 1:6, 452
Isis (Lully), 2:102
Islam, 1:63–64, 106, 484; 3:392
themes from, 3:192, 397
Isolde's *Verklärung* (Wagner), 3:555–57
isorhythm, 1:266–67, 272, 278–85, 291, 311, 316, 325, 374, 495, 507
British motet and, 1:410, 424, 461
caccia motet and, 1:378, 380
chanson and, 1:708
cyclic Mass Ordinaries and, 1:461
isosyllabic scheme, 1:115, 159, 166
Isouard, Nicolas, 2:158
Israel, State of
national anthem, 3:456
Wagner composition ban in, 3:480

Israel in Egypt (Handel), 2:315–25, 331, 345; 3:331, 333–34, 335
Bach (J. S.) Cantata 101 contrasted with, 2:364, 368
"borrowings" in, 2:327
Israelis Brünlein (Schein), 3:704
Israelites (biblical), 3:163
British self-identification with, 2:314–15, 321
Istituzioni harmoniche, Le (Zarlino), 1:586–87, 600, 603, 604–5, 799–800
Italiana in Algeri, L' (Rossini), 3:10, 11, 20, 386
first-act finale, 3:25–27
"Italian Concerto" (J. S. Bach), 2:281–82, 285
Italian concerto style, 2:177–231, 234
Bach (J. S.) and, 2:281–85
in England, 2:196–204
fugal form and, 2:198–203
tonality and, 2:181–98
Vivaldi and, 2:216–31
Italian Girl in Algiers (Rossini), 3:10, 11, 20, 386
first-act finale, 3:25–27
Italian language, 1:200, 352, 383; 2:133
musical vocabulary and, 2:158–59, 203
Palestrina motet texts in, 1:632
poetry in, 1:722–23
Italian Madrigals Englished (Watson), 1:746
Italian opera, 3:376
Arcadian reforms and, 2:151–52, 153
Bellini and, 3:36–46
cantata and, 2:75–78, 146, 349, 351
Code Rossini and, 3:15, 568
English suspicion of, 2:312–13
ensemble finales, 3:22–27, 48, 49
French court opera contrasted with, 2:88–89, 103
Gluck reforms of, 2:452–60
Goldoni librettos for, 2:433, 446–47
Haydn's works and, 2:526
hegemony of, 2:158
intermezzos and, 2:434–37
interpretation of, 3:426
in London, 2:237, 307–12, 340
Mascagni and, 3:659–64
Metastasio librettos and, 2:152–65
mid-twentieth-century critiques of, 3:45–46
Monteverdi and, 2:12–34
Naples and, 2:140–52
nineteenth-century factory system in, 3:9, 568
oratorio and, 2:313
ornamentation and, 2:279, 281
preeminence of, 3:566–67
production process, 3:9, 217, 568
Puccini and, 3:664–74
Purcell's importations of, 2:135
Rome and, 2:150–51

Italian opera (*continued*)
  Rossini aria symbolizing, 3:28
  Russia and, 3:14, 233–35, 239, 240, 617
  Scarlatti (Alessandro.) and, 2:141–52, 186–87
  symphony as curtain-raiser for, 2:497, 498, 499, 500
  "unself-consciousness" of, 3:568
  Venice and, 2:12, 16, 126, 139
  Verdi and, 3:563, 565, 568–615
  verismo and, 3:641, 658–64
  vocal virtuosity and
  War of the Buffoons and, 2:110
  women composers and, 2:80, 81
  women singers and, 2:80
  See also opera buffa; opera seria
Italian style, Schubert and, 3:81
Italy
  academies in, 1:798–801, 818; 2:150–52
  ars perfecta and, 1:585–628
  Austria and, 3:569, 570, 573, 573
  ballata and, 1:364–74
  Baroque and, 1:630, 797
  castrati and, 2:16–17
  chamber music forerunners in, 2:114
  city-state political structure of, 1:277, 453
  concerted music in, 1:780–81
  concerts in, 2:500
  English musical influence of, 1:743–44
  fifteenth-century arts patronage and, 1:277–81
  fifteenth-century musical developments and, 1:453, 458–59
  film directors and, 3:674
  flagellants and, 1:133–34
  fourteenth-century vernacular music and, 1:351–85
  France and, 3:569
  French fourteenth-century musical stylistic influence, 1:366–67, 368, 371, 374–78
  French musical style vs., 2:86
  frottola and, 1:666, 694–99, 706, 722
  German musical imports from, 2:259
  Handel in, 2:237
  humanism and, 1:647, 720
  improvisatory tradition of, 1:666
  instrumental music amd, 2:177–231, 234, 281
  intermezzo and, 1:769, 803–5; 2:12, 13, 434–37; 3:643–44
  keyboard sonatas in, 2:432–34
  literary music development in, 1:722–51
  madrigals and, 1:352–64, 728–41, 750; 2:57
  Meyerbeer and, 3:216
  Monteverdi and, 2:1–34
  motet and, 1:277–87
  musical hegemony of, 1:666, 797; 2:158–59
  nationalism and, 1:666; 3:62, 567, 660

nineteenth-century symphonic music in, 3:745
northern city-states of, 2:139
notation and, 1:341
oltremontani musical idioms and, 1:723
opera censorship in, 3:580
oratorio in, 2:73–345, 73–75, 237, 313, 314
Palestrina and, 1:630–70
Papal States and, 1:2–3, 310
Risorgimento of, 3:569–70, 573, 580, 595, 660
Romanticism and, 3:570
Rossini and, 3:7–35
Scarlattis and, 2:141–50, 390–97
Schütz as German musical conduit from, 2:68, 69
sixteenth-century musical importance of, 1:605
songbooks and, 1:691
string music and, 2:177–231
string virtuosity tradition of, 3:251, 252
subethnic political divisions in, 2:139
Thirty Years' War and, 2:56
troubadour influence in, 1:116, 133–34, 351
unification of, 1:3; 3:566, 569, 572–73, 573
vernacular song and, 1:133–34, 350, 351–52, 694–701
vocal music and, 3:566–67
Willaert and, 1:600
See also Florence; Genoa; Lombardy; Milan; Naples; Rome; Venice
Ite/Deo gratias (Mass IX), 1:86
Ite, missa est (dismissal), 1:310, 311, 312, 316, 323–24
itinerant musicians, 3:251
Itinerary from Paris to Jerusalem (Chateaubriand), 3:387, 392
It's Gonna Rain (Reich), 5:369–70
"It was a lover and his lass . . ." (Morley setting)
Iudochus de Picardia, 1:558, 559, 584
Ivan IV (the Terrible), Emperor of Russia, 3:623
Ivanhoe (Sullivan), 3:658
Ivanov, Lev, 4:139, 152
  Nutcracker and, 4:144
Ivanov, Vyacheslav, 4:205–6, 213, 219
  a realibus ad realiora and, 4:217
  realiora and, 4:216, 224
Ivanovskaya, 4:171, 172
Ivashkin, Alexander, Alfred Schnittke and, 5:466–67
Ives, Charles, 4:192, 195, 197, 245–92, 245f, 253f, 339, 345, 387, 473, 681, 5:418; 5:21, 93, 268, 296, 326
  aggregate harmony and, 4:333
  as Americanist, 4:257–58
  background, 4:245–54
  death of father, 4:251

Elliott Carter and, 5:268, 269
"epiphany" form and, 4:261
fear of effeminacy, 4:254, 266
as founding father of American music, 4:262
George Rochberg and, 5:415
as internationalist, 4:257–58
manuscript dating dispute and, 4:264–65
maximalism and, 4:244, 250, 254, 257, 261, 266, 272, 281, 282, 292
modernism and, 4:263
quarter-tone music and, 4:379
ragtime "stylizations" and, 4:613
resistance to decadence, 4:266
"scherzoids" and, 4:272, 273, 282, 286
"tempo simultaneity" and, 5:415
Transcendentalism and, 4:244
twelve-tone technique and, 5:415
works of
  "An Election," 4:257
  "Bringing in the Sheaves," 4:289
  Celestial Country, The, 4:246, 247–48, 249–50, 286
  Concord Sonata, 4:262, 265, 266, 267, 270, 351; 5:268
  Concord Sonata ("Emerson"), 4:267–68
  Concord Sonata ("Hawthorne"), 4:267, 275
  Concord Sonata ("The Alcotts"), 4:267, 271
  Concord Sonata ("Thoreau"), 4:267, 269–70
  "Country Band March," 4:275, 276
  Essays before a Sonata, 4:265, 267, 270, 273, 281
  First Violin Sonata, 5:284
  "Fourth of July" rhetoric, 4:654
  Fourth Symphony, 5:268
  "From Paracelsus," 4:259, 260–61, 262
  "Goddess of Liberty," 4:277
  Memos, 4:253, 254, 255, 273, 279, 281, 283, 290
  "Nov. 2, 1920" (a.k.a. "An Election"), 4:257, 258–59
  Overture "1776," 4:276
  Piano Sonata no. 2, 4:262, 263
  "Putnam's Camp" (*Three Places in New England*), 4:273, 275, 276–77, 278–79, 280
  Quartet no. 2, 4:257; 5:296
  114 Songs, 4:262
  String Quartet no. 2, 4:254, 255–56
  Symphony no. 1, 4:246
  Symphony no. 2, 4:250, 262
  Symphony no. 4 ("Comedy"), 4:275
  Three Places in New England, 4:262, 265, 273; 5:268, 272
  Three Quarter-Tone Pieces, 4:286, 288–89, 290, 291

Unanswered Question, The, **5:**290, 300
"Universe in Tones," **4:**282, 284, 285
Universe Symphony, **4:**192, 282f,
   284–85, 297; **5:**359
Yale-Princeton Game, A, **4:**273
Ives, George, **4:**245, 251, 253, 284
ivory book cover, **1:**53
Ivrea Codex, **1:**310, 311, 312, 313, 314, 316,
   331–32, 333, 349, 402

J
Jackendoff, Ray, **5:**446–52
Jackson, Aunt Molly (Mary), **4:**656
Jackson, George Pullen, **4:**660
   White Spirituals in the Southern Uplands,
     4:659
Jackson, Michael, **1:**617
   plunderphonics compact disc and, **5:**504
Jacob, Max, **4:**570
Jacobean England, **2:**113–38
Jacobsen, Jens Peter, **4:**305, 306
Jacobus de Liège, **1:**254, 299
Jacopo da Bologna, **1:**352, 352, 353, 354, 364
   Oselleto salvagio, **1:**359–64
   university background of, **1:**354
Jacopone da Todi, **1:**134
Jacques de Liège. *See* Jacobus de Liège
Jacquet of Mantua (Jacques Colebault),
   1:536–38, 641
Jadassohn, Salomon, **3:**675–76, 681
Jahreszeiten, Die (Haydn)., **2:**385, 388, 633
J'ai les maus d'amours/que ferai
   (rondeau-motet), **1:**227–28, 233
"J'ai perdu mon Eurydice!" (Gluck), **2:**458
"J'ai perdu mon serviteur" (Rousseau),
   2:443
Jakobsleiter, Die (Schoebnerg), **4:**192, 344,
   345, 347; **5:**347
James, Saint, **1:**435, 436, 436
James I, King of England, **1:**742; **2:**113, 122,
   237
James II, King of England, **2:**114, 126, 132
James the Greater, Saint, **1:**162
James, Henry, **4:**472
   Turn of the Screw, The, **5:**225
James, William, **4:**590
Jameux, Dominique, **5:**479
Janáček, Leoš, **4:**421–45; **4:**426f
   maximalism and, **4:**422, 425, 429, 430
   works of
     Blown-away Leaf, A, **4:**429
     Capriccio, **4:**424
     From the House of the Dead, **4:**440, 442,
       443
     Glagolská mse, **4:**424
     Její pastorkyna, **4:**423
     Jenufa, **4:**423, 428, 430
     Kát'a Kabanová, **4:**430, 431, 432, 433,
       434–35, 435–36, 437, 438–40,
       441–42, 443, 444
     Listek odvanuty, **4:**429

Makropoulos Affair, The, **4:**425
Prihody Lisky Bystrousky, **4:**424
Šárka, **4:**427
Sinfonietta, **4:**424
Vec Makropoulos, **4:**424. See
   also *Makropoulos Affair, The*
Vylet pana Broucka do XV.stoleti, **4:**423
Z mrtvého domu, **4:**424
Zápisník zmizelého, **4:**424
Jander, Owen, **3:**275
Janequin, Clément, **1:**710–13, 786
   Alouette, L', **1:**711
   Chant des oyseux, Le, **1:**711
   Chasse, La, **1:**711
   Guerre, La, **1:**711–12, 787, 788, 789
Janissaries, **2:**470
Janissary instruments, **2:**470–71, 602, 675,
   678
Ja nun hons pris (Richard Lion-Heart),
   1:117–18
Janus, King of Cyprus, **1:**345
Japart, Jean, **1:**539
Jarocinski, Stefan, **4:**89
Jasager, Der (Weill-Brecht), **4:**543–47, 548,
   661
Jauchzet Gott in allen Landen (J. S. Bach),
   2:374–75
Jaufre Rudel, **1:**136
J'ay pris amours (anon.), **1:**532–33, 534–41
   instrumental duo on, **1:**536, 537
   partbook arrangements of, **1:**540–41,
     542
J'ay pris amours (Isaac), **1:**538–39
J'ay pris amours (Japart), **1:**539
J'ay pris amours (Martini), **1:**538, 539
J'ay pris amours (Obrecht), **1:**539
J'ay pris amours tout au rebours (Busnoys),
   1:539
jazz
   improvisation and, **1:**17, 307, 536; **2:**174,
     223, 611, 650–51
   unwritten conventions in, **1:**17, 261
"jazz age," **4:**628, 637
Jazz-Toccata und Fuge (Hartmann), **4:**770
"Jazzy" (Copland), **4:**614–15, 652
Jean, Duke of Berry, **1:**342
Jean de Grouchy. *See* Grocheio, Johannes
   de
Jean de Noyers. *See* Tapissier
Jeanneret, Charles (Le Corbusier), **5:**77
Jean Paul (Johann Paul Friedrich Richter),
   3:294
Jefferson, Thomas, **4:**658
Jehan Bretel, **1:**120, 121
Jehan des Murs, **1:**247–48, 249–50, 252,
   254
   harmonic proportions of, **1:**249, 250
Jehannot de l'Escurel, **1:**123
Jehan Robert (Trebor), **1:**342
Jeitteles, Alois, **3:**131
Její pastorkyna (Janáček), **4:**423
Je l'ayme bien (Lasso), **1:**714, 715

Jencks, Charles, **5:**412–13, 454
   "double coding" and, **5:**412, 437
   pluralism and, **5:**412
   postmodern architecture and, **5:**412–13
   What Is Post-Modernism?, **5:**411
Jennens, Charles, **2:**316, 325, 327, 330
Jenufa (Janáček), **4:**423, 428, 430
Jephte (Carissimi), **2:**73–74, 76–77, 90
Jephté (Montéclair), **2:**91, 93
Jephtha (Jephte) (biblical), **2:**73–74, 74,
   90, 91
Jephtha (Handel), **2:**75
Jeppesen, Knud, **1:**670
Jeritza, Maria, **4:**423
Jerome, Saint, **1:**20
Jérusalem (Verdi), **3:**568
Jerusalem, Latin Kingdom of, **1:**107, 345
Jerusalem Delivered (Tasso), **2:**7–9, 94;
   3:164, 326, 703
Jerusalem Temple, **1:**7, 8, 10
Jesu Cristes milde moder (twinsong), **1:**394,
   396
Jesuit German College (Rome), **2:**73
Jesuits, **1:**666, 667, 675, 679; **2:**461
Jeu de Robin et de Marion, Le (Adam), **1:**127,
   128, 233, 349
Jeux (ballet), **4:**567
   choreographed by Nijinsky, **4:**567
   produced by Diaghilev, **4:**567
   use of Debussy's music, **4:**567
Jeux d'eau (Ravel), **4:**111,112–16, 117, 119, 120,
   121, 164
"Jeux d'eaux a la Villa d'Este, Les" (Liszt),
   4:112
jeux-partis (mock-debates), **1:**121, 122
Jews and Judaism, **3:**163, 772
   assimilation of, **3:**177, 186
   Christian art and, **2:**112, 389–90
   Christian liturgy and, **1:**7–8, 10, 12, 13,
     21, 54
   Diaspora and, **3:**344
   emancipation of, **3:**166, 174, 186, 215, 228
   in Germany, **3:**174, 177–79
   as *grand opéra* proponents, **3:**215
   modernism and, **4:**3–4
   Reformed movement, **3:**174
   Wagner on, **3:**177–79
   See also anti-Semitism
Jherusalem, two counterpoints to, **1:**154
jig, **2:**261
   English theatrical incidental music and,
     2:126
   See also gigue
"Jingle Bells" (song), **1:**18
jingles, **1:**185
"Jingo" (Copland), **4:**654
"Jingo" statement, **4:**654
Joachim, Joseph, **3:**686
   Brahms and, **3:**684, 685
   Liszt and, **3:**418, 684
   Schumann (Clara) and, **3:**692–93, 698
Joan of Arc, **1:**421, 447; **4:**105

joc-partit. See tenso
Jockey Club, ballet and, 4:133
Joe, 5:310–11
Joe Hill (Robinson), 4:657f, 658
joglars. See minstrels
Johannes de Garlandia. *See* Garlandia, Johannes de
Johannes de Grocheio. *See* Grocheio, Johannes de
Johannes de Muris. *See* Jehan des Murs
Johannes Gabrieli und sein Zeitalter (Winterfeld), 1:792
Johanneum (Hamburg), 2:410
Johann Georg, Elector of Saxony, 2:68
Johann Hus (Loewe), 3:164
John, Gospel according to, 1:465; 2:73, 375, 377
   Passion settings and, 1:775–77
John, Saint, 1:6
John XXII, Pope (1245–1334), 1:311, 316, 433
John XXIII, AntiPope (1410–15, 1410–15), 1:278, 310
John XXIII, Pope (1881–1963), 1:278
John of Afflighem, 1:155, 161, 185
John of Cotton, 1:30
John of Gaunt, Duke of Lancaster and Aquitaine, 1:410–11, 417
John of Lancaster, Duke of Bedford, 1:421, 422, 433
John of Luxembourg (later King of Bohemia), 1:289
John of Salisbury, 1:172, 646
John Paul II, Pope, 1:310, 630
John the Baptist, Saint, 1:26, 37, 38, 42, 100
John the Deacon, 1:5, 6
Johnson, Lyndon (U.S. President), 5:309
Johnson, Robert, 2:114
Johnson, Robert Sherlaw, 5:25
Johnson, Samuel, 5:250
Johnston, Ben, 4:285; 5:485, 487
joke, musical, 1:359, 701, 801; 2:321
   Du Fay and, 1:511
   Haydn and, 2:540–41, 542, 545, 547, 548, 549, 551–54, 571
   Josquin and, 1:529–30
   Machaut and, 1:327
   Mozart and, 2:549
   Sennfl and, 1:705
   Ward and, 1:749
"Joke Quartet" in E-flat major, op. 33, no. 2 (Haydn), 2:542–55, 565, 591
   first movement, 2:542–47, 559
   fourth movement "joke" of, 2:551–54
   as mock-primitive piece, 2:549
   second movement, 2:547–49, 593
   third movement, 2:550–51
Jolson, Al, 4:624
Jomard, Edme François, 3:387
Jommelli, Niccolò, 2:158
Jones, Daniel, 5:348

Jones, Spike, 5:505, 506. *See also* Spike Jones and His City Slickers
jongleurs. See minstrels
Jonny spielt auf (Krenek), 4:529, 532, 536, 756; 5:38
Jonson, Ben, 2:113, 114
Jordan, Thomas, 2:124
Joseph II, Emperor of Austria, 2:647, 652; 4:365
   Beaumarchais and, 2:478
   Enlightenment reforms of, 2:462
   Mozart and, 2:462–63, 470, 476, 477, 478, 646
   operatic taste of, 2:470, 476, 478
   successor to, 2:462, 481–82, 652
Josephson, David, 1:517–18
Joshua (biblical), 1:286
Joshua (Handel), 2:315
Josquin Companion, The (Sherr, ed.), 1:558
Josquin des Prez, 1:499, 538, 539, 544, 547–84, 548, 612, 632, 667, 687, 706, 768, 786; 2:5, 12
   background and career of, 1:558–60, 563
   Beethoven parallel with, 1:547–49, 552, 579
   canon *in hexatono* and, 3:102
   as character in Pfitzner opera, 1:652
   death and will of, 1:563
   exemplary work by, 1:565–79
   frottola genre and, 1:699–701
   instrumental music and, 1:544, 545–46
   legacy of, 2:463, 464
   legendary status of, 1:547–49, 551–55, 558, 560, 572, 577, 579, 600
   Louis XII patronage of, 2:538–39
   Luther's admiration for, 1:755, 756
   misattributed works to, 1:549, 554–55, 563
   Mouton and, 1:589
   musical popularization of, 1:553–55
   myth and, 1:579
   Ockeghem and, 1:500, 529–30
   "paired imitation" style of, 1:555, 556, 589
   Palestrina's musical homage to, 1:633
   parody and, 1:572–76, 588, 641
   patrons of, 1:554–55, 559–63, 578, 578, 584, 696, 699
   Phyrgian polyphony and, 1:529–30
   posthumous period of, 1:552–53, 558, 581
   post-Josquin style and, 1:589–99
   printing revolution and, 1:499, 542, 549, 557–58, 559
   scholarship on, 1:558–60, 576–84
   stylistic chronology of, 1:564–65, 577–80
   voces musicales and, 1:499–500, 560
   Willaert's style and, 1:589, 601–3
   works of
      Agnus Dei II, 1:520, 529, 531–34
      Ave Maria, 1:606, 686

      Ave Maria . . . Virgo serena, 1:565–72, 577–84, 588, 602–3
      Benedicta es, coelorum regina, 1:580–83, 601–3, 633
      Bernardina, La, 1:544, 546
      Christe, Fili Dei, 1:530–34
      Grillo, El, 1:699–701
      Ile fantazies de Joskin, 1:545–46
      Memor esto verbi tui servo tuo, 1:554, 556, 557–58
      Missa Hercules Dux Ferrariae, 1:560–63, 696
      Missa L'Homme Armé super voces musicales, 1:499–500, 520, 529, 530–34
      Missa Pange lingua, 1:555–57, 566, 641
Journal de printemps, Le (Fischer), 2:259–60
Journal des débats (newspaper), 3:291, 583
Journal of Music Theory, 5:169
"Joy" leitmotif (Wagner), 3:507, 519
Joyce, James, 4:525–26, 595; 5:74, 193, 332
   Syzgy (del Tredici), and, 5:438, 442
   Ulysses, 4:525; 5:193
Juan del Encina, 1:724
Jubal, 1:175
jubilated singing, 1:11, 24, 26, 38–39, 98, 613
Jubilemus, exultemus (versus), 1:156, 157, 158, 162
Judah Maccabee (biblical), 1:286
Judaism. *See* Jews and Judaism
Judas Maccabeus (Handel), 2:315; 3:164
Judenthum in der Musik, Das (K. Freigedank [Wagner]), 3:177–79, 227–28
Judges, Book of, 2:73
Judith (Serov), 3:391–92
Judt, Tony, 4:472
Jugement de Paris, Le (Noverre), 4:133
Jugend (magazine), 4:34
Jugendstil ("youth style"), 4:34–35, 36f, 303
   Erwartung and, 4:303
Juilliard Quartet, 5:164, 296, 300
Juilliard School of Music (New York), 4:648, 649; 5:163, 300
Juive, La (Halévy), 3:215, 218
"Julio da Modena." *See* Segni, Julio
Julius III, Pope, 1:631, 634
July Monarchy (1830–48; France), 3:205–6, 214, 218, 266, 319, 348
July Revolution (1830; France), 3:206, 212, 214, 319
Jumièges abbey, 1:41
Junge Siegfried, Der (Wagner), 3:496, 497
Jupiter (mythology), 2:94, 107
"Jupiter" Symphony in C major, K. 551 (Mozart), 2:590, 646
justice, 1:286
Justin (Marcus Junianus Justinus), 2:159
Justinian, Emperor of Rome, 1:798
Justin Martyr, 1:8
Justus ut palma
   as Alleluia, 1:25, 41, 42–43
   as antiphon, 1:20, 21, 23

as Gradual, **1**:26, 79
as Introit, **1**:24, 79
as Offertory, **1**:24–25, 35, 79

K
Kaiser, Georg, **4**:540
Kaiserhymne (Haydn), **3**:130–31
Kalbeck, Max, **3**:686
Kalevala (Finnish epic), **3**:123, 126, 763
Kallberg, Jeffrey, **3**:77
Kallman, Chester, **3**:143; **5**:117, 343
Kamarinskaya (Glinka), **3**:465–71, 474, 475, 478; **4**:177
folk themes in, **3**:465–66
motivic derivations in, **3**:466
Kamarinskaya dance, **3**:465, *465*
Kammerkonzert ("Chamber Concerto") (Berg), **4**:313–14, 342, 523, 525, 710
Kammermusik Nr. 1 (Hindemith), **4**:528
Kampflied, **4**:658
Kampflieder (Wolpe), **5**:13
Kampf und Sieg, **2**:654–55, 658–59, 694
Beethoven and, **3**:1, 198, 694–95
Brahms and, **3**:694–95
Liszt and, **3**:423
Weber and, **3**:198
Kandinsky, Wassily, **4**:215, 306, 307, 310, 314, 330, 338, 344
Über das Geistige in der Kunst, **4**:338
Kangourou, Makoko, *Honoloulou*, **4**:573
kanon, **1**:34
kant, **3**:234, 247–48
Kant, Immanuel, **1**:541; **2**:461, 462, 634, 643, 644, 648, 720; **3**:61, 121, 294, 596; **4**:244; **5**:42, 68, 371
on instrumental music, **2**:642
on mathematical sublime, **2**:646, 732
Kapelle. See orchestra
Kapellen. See court music
Kapital, Das (Marx), **4**:745
Kaplan, Richard, **3**:427–28
Kaprow, Allan, **5**:91, 332
Fluxus, **5**:91
Karl I, Emperor of Austria, **3**:130
Karlowicz, Mieczyslaw, **5**:437
Kärntnerthor Theater (Vienna), **2**:518, *676*; **3**:3
Kashchey the Deathless (Rimsky-Korsakov), **4**:153, 154, 160
Kassel, Richard, **5**:483, 486
Kassler, Michael, **5**:160
Trinity of Essays, A (dissertation), **5**:160
"Toward a Theory That Is the Twelve-Note-Class System," **5**:160
Kát'a Kabanová (Janáček), **4**:423, 430, 431, 432, 433, 434–35, 435–436, 437, 438–40, 441–42, 443, 444
Kater, Michael, **4**:772
Katharine, Saint, **1**:424
Katharine of Aragon, **1**:670–71, 675
Kathrin, Die (Korngold), **4**:551

Katona, József, **4**:369
Kayenbergh, Albert, **4**:457
Kayserling, Count, **2**:383
Keats, John, **3**:62, 440
Keegan, John, **4**:472
Kellman, Herbert, **1**:563
Kemble, Charles, **3**:320
Kennan, George F., **5**:7
Kennedy Center for the Performing Arts, *Nixon in China* and, **5**:518
Kennedy, Jacqueline, **5**:113
Kennedy, John F. (U.S. President), **5**:310
assassination of, **5**:310
Kennedy, Robert F., **5**:310
assassination of, **5**:310
Kerman, Joseph, **1**:594, 678, 679, 680, 751; **2**:495, 677, 686; **3**:45–46, 138, 640, 664; **4**:526; **5**:160, 243
on Beethoven's C-minor mood, **2**:691
on lieder, **3**:132, 140
Kern, Jerome, **4**:624
Kernfeld, Barry, **5**:335
Kernis, Aaron Jay, neotonality and, **5**:454
Kernweise. See Tenorlied
Kerouac, Jack, **5**:62
Key, Francis Scott, **1**:409; **3**:120
keyboard miniatures, **3**:185
keyboard music
accompanied, **2**:427–32, 695
allemande and, **2**:260
Bach (C. P. E.) and, **2**:410
Bach (J. C.) and, **2**:420, 606
Bach (J. S.) and, **2**:192, 224–29, 234, 241, 247–51, 262–77, 306, 383, 402
Bach (J. S.) compared with Couperin, **2**:275–81
Bach (W. F.) and, **2**:402–9
Beethoven and, **2**:652, 653, 655, 686
Byrd and, **1**:670
domestic performance of, **2**:419, 427
earliest extant manuscript, **1**:305–7, 371
earliest solo concerto, **2**:290
English, **2**:45, 46–47, 49, 53
French *style brisé* and, **2**:249–50
Frescobaldi and, **2**:36–44
Haydn and, **2**:600
Italian composers of, **2**:432–34
Landini and, **1**:373, 374
Mozart and, **2**:601–34
ricercari and, **1**:607
Scarlatti (D.) and, **2**:234, 390–96
Schein variation technique, **2**:53
Sweelinck and, **2**:44–46, 53
tuning and, **2**:247–48
variation technique, **2**:53
See also organ music; *specific genres and instruments*
key signature, **1**:71, 72, 76; **2**:247–48
Clemens and, **1**:596–97
feelings associated with, **2**:686
Khachaturian, Aram Ilyich, **5**:9
"Sabre Dance," **5**:9

Simfoniya-Poema, **5**:12
khoroviye kontsertï, **3**:234
Khrushchev, Nikita, **5**:103
Khubov, Georgiy, **4**:795
khudozhestvennaya pravda ("artistic truth"), **3**:397
Kierkegaard, Søren, **2**:486, 487, 493; **3**:271–72, 530
Kiesewetter, Raphael Georg, **3**:7, 8
Kiev composers, twelve-tone compositions and, **5**:463
Kilmer, Anne Draffkorn, **1**:32
Kimbell, David, **3**:570
Kind im Einschlummern (Schumann), **3**:360
Kinder und Hausmärchen (Grimm brothers), **3**:122
Kinderman, William, **2**:732
Kinderscenen, op. 15 (Schumann), **3**:360–61
Kinderstück (Webern), **4**:720
King and the Charcoal Burner, The (Dvořák), **3**:753–54
King James Bible, **1**:20, 760
King Lear (Shakespeare), **3**:576–77, 591
King Lear, Orson Welles and, **5**:198
"King Lear Suite" (Luening-Ussachevsky), **5**:214
King, Martin Luther, Jr., **5**:309, 349, 350
assassination of, **5**:310
boycott of city buses in Montgomery, **5**:309
Kingdom Come (Brant), **5**:421
King Oedipus (Partch), **5**:481, 485
King's College (Cambridge University), **1**:513
"King's Grand Ball" (P. Rameau), **2**:92
Kings, Second Book of, **1**:285
King Stephen (Beethoven), **3**:1–2
King's Theatre (London), **2**:237, 307, 314, 419; **4**:133
Kingston Trio, **5**:315
King Theodore (Paisiello). *See Re Teodoro, Il*
Kinninger, Vincenz Georg, **2**:492
Kipling, Rudyard, **3**:233, 392
Kircher, Athanasius, **2**:74–75
Kirkpatrick, John, **4**:262–63
Kirkpatrick, Ralph, **2**:392, 395; **5**:302
Kirov ballet, **4**:139
Kirstein, Lincoln, **4**:662
Kismet (musical), **3**:401
"Kiss, A" (Dobson), **1**:122
Kiss of Judas, The (Giotto), **1**:382
Kisselgof, Zinoviy (Süssman), **4**:108
Kivy, Peter, **2**:329
Klangfarbenmelodien, **4**:339, 348, 351, 361
Klavierstück X (Stockhausen), **5**:83
Klavierstück XI (Stockhausen), **5**:54, 64, 82
Klein, Fritz Heinrich, **4**:710, 712
Kleine geistliche Concerte (Schütz), **2**:66–69
Kleine Klavierstücke, op. 19 (Schoenberg), **4**:347, 348, 363
Kleine Nachtmusik, Eine (Mozart), **3**:64
Klemperer, Otto, **4**:749, 765

Klenau, Paul von, **4:**774
  Elisabeth von England, **4:**774
  Michael Kohlhaas, **4:**774
  Rembrandt van Rijn, **4:**774
Klinger, F. M. von, **2:**528
Klopstock, Friedrich Gottfried, **2:**410, 416; **4:**22
  Aufersteh'n, **4:**21
Klug, Joseph, **1:**760, *761*
Knaben Wunderhorn, Des (Arnim and Brentano), **3:**123
Knapp, Raymond, **3:**719
Knecht, Joseph, **5:**44
Kneisel Quarter, **4:**254
Kneller, Gottfried, **2:**241
knightly poets. *See* troubadours
knowledge, Enlightenment, **2:**461
Knussen, Oliver, **5:**44
Koblyakov, Lev, **5:**451
Koch, Heinrich Christoph, **2:**606, 607, 609–10, 621, 622
Köchel, Ludwig von, **2:**463; **3:**83
Kodály, Zoltán, **4:**375, 376, 375f, 377, 379, 380
Koechlin, Charles, **4:**196, 490
  Traité de l'harmonie, **4:**195–96
Kolokol (journal), **3:**476–77
Komar, Arthur, **5:**160
Komm, Gott Schöpfer, Heiliger Geist (chorale), **1:**758
"Kommt, ihr Töchter, helft mir klagen" (J. S. Bach), **2:**378
Königskinder, Die (Humperdinck), **4:**459
König Stephan (Beethoven), **3:**1–2
kontakion, **1:**34
Kontakte (Stockhausen), **5:**191
Kontrapunkt (Jeppesen), **1:**670
Konyok-gorbunok (Pugni), **4:**139
Konzertstück in F minor for piano and orchestra (Weber), **3:**275
Konzertstück in *Petrushka,* "Danse Russe" (Stravinsky), **4:**161, 162–63, 166–67, 168
Korngold, Erich Wolfgang, **4:**549–52, 556, 557, 558
  leitmotifs and, **4:**550
  orchestral portramento and, **4:**550
  works of
    Another Dawn, **4:**551
    Anthony Adverse, **4:**551
    Die Kathrin, **4:**551
    Sinfonietta, op. 5, **4:**549
    Die tote Stadt, **4:**550
    Das Wunder der Heliane, **4:**550, 756
    Violin Concerto, **4:**551
Korot, Beryl, **5:**504
Kossmaly, Carl, **2:**388
Kossuth (Bartók), **4:**373–74
Kossuth, Lajos (Louis), **4:**365, 365f, 366, 371
Kosugi, Takehisa, **5:**91
  Anima 7, **5:**91
Kostelanetz, André, **4:**668, 670

Kostelanetz, Richard, **3:**416
Kotzebue, August von, **3:**1
Koussevitzky Music Foundation, **5:**229
Koussevitzky, Natalie, **5:**229
Koussevitzky, Serge, **4:**619, 620–21, 620f, 637, 638, 639, 641, 647; **5:**3, 229, 276
  Leonard Bernstein and, **5:**3
Kozinn, Allan, **5:**324
Krafft-Ebing, Richard von, **4:**30
Kraft, Anton, **2:**600
Krainev, Vladimir, Schnittke's Concerto for Piano and Strings and, **5:**467–68
Kraków, **1:**346, 347, 348
krakowiak, **3:**455
Krakowiak (Chopin), **3:**347
Kramer, Jonathan, **5:**471, 506, 511
  Time of Music, The, **5:**473
Kramer, Lawrence, **4:**257
Kramer, Richard, **3:**154
Krasner, Louis, **4:**714
Krasnïy sarafan (Varlamov), **3:**633
Krause, Christian Gottfried, **3:**120
Krehbiel, Henry, **3:**194, 202, 764, 765
Kreisler, Fritz, **4:**626
Krenek, Ernst, **4:**196, 540, 548; **5:**38–44, 123–26, 296, 448
  analysis of Webern's symmetrical row structures, **5:**123
  "Extents and Limits of Serial Technique," **5:**40
  "rotation" technique, **5:**123–24
  Studies in Counterpoint, publishing of, **5:**123
  Vassar College, **5:**123
  works of
    Jonny spielt auf, **4:**529, 532, 536, 755, 756; **5:**38
    Lamentations, **5:**123, 126
    "Leb' wohl, mein Schatz," **4:**530–31
    Sestina, **5:**39, 40, 140
Kreutzer, Rodolphe, **3:**2
Kreuzspiel (Stockhausen), **5:**44, 45–48, 153
Krik Petrushki ("Petrushka's shriek"), **4:**159
Kronos Quartet, **5:**503–4, 506
Kropotkin, Pyotr, Prince, **3:**647
Krosnick, Joel, **5:**164
Krügner, Johann Gottfried, **2:**239
Krukowski, Damon, **5:**487
Krumme Teufel, Der (Haydn), **2:**518
Ktož jsú Boži bojovníci (Hussite hymn), **3:**452, 459
Kubrick, Stanley, *2001: A Space Odyssey,* **5:**220, 496
Kuhnau, Johann, **2:**262, 265
  Biblical Sonatas, **3:**65
kujawiak, **3:**357
Kultur, **3:**130, 132
  anti-Semitism and, **3:**228
  German nationalism and, **3:**123–24
Kunst der Fuge, Die (J. S. Bach). *See* Art of Fugue

Kunst, Jaap, **5:**381
Kunstidee des Producenten, **3:**439, 441, 451, 452, 456
Künstlerverein orchestra, **3:**677
Kunst und die Revolution, Die (Wagner), **3:**488–91, 496
Kunstwerk der Zukunft, Das (Wagner), **3:**488
Kusser, Johann Sigismund, **2:**259–60
Kyriale (chant book), **1:**58, 322
Kyrie, **1:**53, 58–60, 89, 111, 234–36, 236, 461
  Agnus Dei pairing with, **1:**311
  Avignon-style, **1:**311–13, 316
  Bach (J. S.) Mass in B minor and, **2:**375
  Caput Mass and, **1:**458, 466, 467, 469, 473–74, 475
  Cum jubilo and, **1:**84–86, 89, 234
  Cunctipotens genitor and, **1:**59, 111, 163, 164, 165, 306–7, 325, 371
  English Old Hall manuscript and, **1:**409, 461
  Févin's *Missa super Ave Maria* and, **1:**574–76
  Frescobaldi and, **2:**43–44
  Josquin's *voces musicales* and, **1:**499, 500
  Machaut *La messe de Notre Dame* and, **1:**318–19, 322–25, 326
  in Mass ordo, **1:**61(table)
  melismatic and texted side-by-side, **1:**58–60
  Missa L'Homme Armé and, **1:**486–89, 495
  Ockeghem *Missa cuiusvis* and, **1:**479–80, 499
  organ settings of, **2:**49
  Palestrina *Missa O magnum mysterium* and, **1:**644
  Palestrina *Missa Papae Marcelli* and, **1:**654–55, 660
  Palestrina *Missa Repleatur os meum laude* and, **1:**637, 638–39, 640–41
  performance practice of, **1:**310, 614
  polyphonic setting of, **1:**162–63, 307, 310–13
  troubadour melody compared with, **1:**111
  votive Mass and, **1:**316, 317, 318
Kyrie I (Josquin), **1:**557
Kyrie II, **1:**111
"Kyrie IV, **1:**58–59, 325
Kyrie IX, *Cum jubilo,* **1:**84–86, 111; **2:**43; **5:**510
  structure of, **1:**85table
  voces for, **1:**103–4
"Kyrie Cuthbert," **1:**409
Kyrie eleison. See Kyrie

L

labor unions, **2:**112
"laceramento della poesia," **1:**742, 744–45
Lachen und Weinen (Schubert), **3:**135–36, 144

Lachner, Franz, **4**:454
"Lachrymae Pavan, The" (Dowland), **1**:742, 744–45
"Là ci darem la mano" (Chopin), **3**:347
"Là ci darem la mano" (Liszt), **3**:269, 270, 347
"La méchanisation de la musique" (Paris), **5**:185
Lady, Be Good! (Gershwin), **4**:625
Lady in the Dark (Dolan), **5**:183
Lady Macbeth of the Mtsensk District, The (Leskov), **4**:785–91, 787f,
Lady Macbeth of the Mtsensk District, The (Shostakovich), **5**:230–31, 241, 243
Lady Massess, **1**:314, 316, 317–26, 595
Lafayette, Marquis de, **3**:214
Lago, Giovanni del, **1**:551
Lagrime d'amante al sepolcro dell'amata (Monteverdi), **2**:6
Lagrime mie (Strozzi), **2**:75–78, 81
La Harpe, Jean-François de, **3**:33
lai (stanza sequence), **1**:119, 131, 332
Lai de confort (Machaut), **1**:332
Lai de la fonteinne (Machaut), **1**:332–36
laissez-faire. *See* free market
Lake, Greg, **5**:328
Lakmé (Delibes), **3**:390
Lalla-Roukh (David), **3**:389
Lamartine, Alphonse de, **3**:264, 422–26, 422
Lambe, Walter, **1**:513
Lambertus, Magister, **1**:214–15
Lambroso, Cesare, **4**:754
lament, **1**:448, 452, 454, 484, 500, 747
 Carissimi *Jephte*, **2**:74, 76
 Lully's *Atys*, **2**:103–4
 Monteverdi's *Lamento d'Arianna*, **2**:104
 Monteverdi's *Lamento della ninfa*, **2**:10, 11, 125
 Purcell's *Dido and Aeneas*, **2**:135–37, 138
Lamentations (Krenek), **5**:123, 126
Lamento d'Arianna (Monteverdi), **2**:104
Lamento della minfa (Monteverdi), **2**:10, 11
Lamento della ninfa (Rinuccini), **2**:10
Lami, Eugène, **3**:86, 87, 331
Lämmlein geht und trägt die Schuld, Ein (Ducis), **1**:769, 770–71
Lamoureux, Charles, **3**:678
Lampadius of Lüneburg, **1**:577–78
Lancaster dynasty, **1**:411, 417
Landini, Francesco, **1**:355, 366–78, 380, 383, 429
 background of, **1**:366, 368, 371, 374
 ballata cadences of, **1**:368, 383
 Non avrà ma' pietà, **1**:368–71, 373–74
 Sy dolce non sonò con lir' Orfeo, **1**:374–78, 380, 384
Landini cadence (sixth), **1**:368, 383, 441, 470
Ländler, **3**:113, 114
Landon, **2**:538, 539, 577
Lang, Fritz, *Hangmen Also Die* and, **4**:560
Lang, Paul Henry, **2**:738, 739; **3**:229; **4**:766

Lange, Joseph, **2**:474
Langer, Susanne, **5**:277, 332
 Feeling and Form, **5**:277
Langlais, Jean, **1**:374
language
 Herder theory of, **3**:121–22, 146, 190–91, 345
 medieval Europe polyglot, **1**:142
 Monteverdi and, **2**:10
 musical setting of, **2**:133, 134, 138
 musical vocabulary and, **2**:158–59
 nationalism and, **3**:62–64, 122
 operatic singing and, **2**:97
 Slavic, **3**:345
 verismo use of dialect, **3**:658–59, 660
 See also prosody; vernacular; word-music relationship; *specific languages*
language communities, **3**:122–24, 146
Languedoc region, **1**:107–16, 152
 ars subtilior composers and, **1**:342–45
 map of, **1**:111
 Mass of Toulouse and, **1**:315
 See also troubadours
Lanier, Nicholas, **2**:114
Lansky, Paul, **5**:501
 in conversation with Kyle Gann, **5**:473
Laplace, Pierre Simon de, Marquis de, **2**:634
"Largo al factotum" (Rossini), **3**:23, 24
largo concertato, caricatures of, **3**:652
Laroche, Hermann, **3**:391–92, 397, 612
Larsen, Libby, neotonality and, **5**:454
LaRue, Jan, **2**:497, 528
La Rue, Pierre de, **2**:5
La Scala (Teatro alla Scala; Milan), **3**:570, 571, 572, 573, 579; **4**:751, 752
 Peter Grimes and, **5**:225
Lasky, Melvin, **5**:293
Lasse/se j'aime/POURQUOY (Machaut), **1**:292, 293–94, 298
Lasso, Orlando di, **1**:678, 712–22, 713, 773, 786; **4**:18
 background and career of, **1**:713–14
 fame of, **1**:715
 Gabrieli (Giovanni) and, **1**:786
 madrigal and, **1**:724, 738, 739, 792
 Palestrina compared with, **1**:713
 voluminous published works of, **1**:713–14
 works of
  Audite nova, **1**:717–18
  Je l'ayme bien, **1**:714, 715
  Matona mia cara, **1**:714–17
  "O là o che bon eccho," **1**:792
  Prophetiae Sibyllarum, **1**:717, 719–22, 773
Lassus. *See* Lasso, Orlando di
Last Hope, The (Gottschalk), **3**:380
Last Judgment, **1**:719
Last Savage, The (Menotti), **5**:226
Last Supper, **1**:13
Lateran palace, **1**:6

Latin American dance genres, **4**:486
Latin American rhythms, **3**:378, 380
Latinate style, **1**:110–13, 298
Latin church plays. *See* liturgical drama
Latin Kingdom of Jerusalem, **1**:107, 345
Latin language
 Anglican Church and, **1**:672–73, 675, 676
 bawdy song collection in, **1**:138
 British liturgical manuscript destruction and, **1**:402
 British manuscript in, **1**:387
 British printed music in, **1**:678
 classical authors and, **1**:356
 Guido of Arezzo rhyme in, **1**:185
 liturgical decanonization of, **1**:278
 macaronic texts and, **1**:113, 233–34, 420
 motet text in, **1**:219, 311
 poetic meter and, **1**:191
 psalmody and, **1**:20–22
 sung verse play and, **1**:93
 vernacular vs., **1**:351, 459
La Tour, Maurice Quentin de, **2**:427, 442
Laubenstein, Paul Fritz, **4**:621
Lauda Sion Salvatorem/Lauda crucis attolamus (Adam sequence), **1**:89–90
lauda spirituale, **1**:133–34
Laudate Dominum (hymn), **2**:227
laude, **1**:133–34, 691, 834
Laudes crucis attollamus (Adam)
Lauds, **1**:11, 12
Laun, Friedrich, **3**:191
Lavignac's *Encyclopédie de la musique etdictionnaire du conservatoire*, **4**:237
"law of stylistic succession," **4**:559
Lawes, William, **2**:120–22, 124, 128, 134
 Ayre in six parts, **2**:120, 121
 fantasia themes, **2**:122
Lawrence, D. H., **5**:93
lay fraternities (*laudesi*), **1**:133–34, 691, 834
League of Composers, **5**:107
"League of David" (Schumann journalistic pseudonym), **2**:737
Lear, Edward
 "Owl and the Pussy-Cat, The," **5**:128
Leaves of Grass (Whitman), **4**:243
Lebedinoye ozero (Chaikovsky). *See Swan Lake*
Lecerf de la Viéville, Jean Laurent, **2**:85–86
Leclair, Jean-Marie, **2**:499
Leconte de Lisle, Charles-Marie-René, **4**:97
Le Corbusier (Charles Jeanneret), **4**:680; **5**:77
 definition of a house, **5**:412
lection tones, **1**:21
"Lecture on Nothing" (Cage), **5**:69
Lectures on the Philosophy of History (Hegel), **3**:413
Leeds Festival (England), **3**:657
Lefferts, Peter, **1**:277
Le Franc, Martin, **1**:422, 423, 424, 429, 435

Le Franc, Martin (*continued*)
   Champion des dames, Le, **1:**422, 439, 536
left-hand pizzicato, Paganini and, **3:**256
Legend of the Invisible City of Kitezh, The
   (Rimsky-Korsakov), **4:**179
Lehár, Franz, **3:**269
Lehre von der musikalischen Composition, Die
   (Marx), **3:**287
Lehr-Institut im Pianoforte-Spiele
   (Prague), **3:**444
Lehrstück, **4:**541, 543, 544, 547
Lehrstück vom Einverständnis (Henze), **5:**21
Leibowitz, Rene, **5:**15–20, 108
   Anton von Webern and, **5:**16
   Arnold Schoenberg and, **5:**16
   Schönberg et son École: L'État contemporaine
     du langage musical, **5:**15–16
Leichte Kavallerie (Suppé), **3:**648
Leipzig, **1:**763, 768; **2:**509, 739
   Bach (J. S.) and, **2:**53, 239–40, 262, 286,
     300, 341–42, 346, 353, 362–63, 364,
     365, 368, 370, 375, 377, 378, 381, 402
   birds-eye view of, **2:**238
   modern music criticism origins in, **3:**291
   municipal music in, **2:**287
   nineteenth-century symphonic music in,
     3:676, 677, 679, 680
   St. Thomas Square, **2:**239
   Schein and, **2:**53
Leipzig Conservatory, **3:**173
Leipzig Gewandhaus, **3:**172–73, *173,* 177,
   177, 317, 676, 677, 679
   Schnittke's Third Symphony and, **5:**467
Leipzig Thomasschule. *See* St. Thomas
   Church and School
Leise, **1:**758
"leitharmonie," *Elektra* and, **4:**51
leitmotif
   Chaikovsky and, **3:**633, 636, 637
   Puccini and, **3:**667
   Wagner and, **3:**503–28, 530–38, 540,
     541, 557, 560, 565, 734, 735, 759
Le Jeune, Claude, **4:**449
   Qu'est devenuece bel oeil, **4:**450
Lélio, or Returning to Life (Berlioz), **3:**387
Lemercier (lithographer), **3:**209
Lendvai, Erno, **5:**50–51
Lenin, Vladimir Ilich, **4:**542, 743, 776, 777,
     779, 780; **5:**86, 181
Lennon Companion, The, **5:**330
Lennon, John, **5:**317, 318, 332
   "Not a Second Time," **5:**318
   Tavener's *The Whale* and, **5:**408
Lenten season
   favole in musica and, **1:**834
   liturgical music, **1:**12, 28
   Mozart subscription concert
     performances, **2:**608
   opera house closure during, **2:**313, 470,
     499, 608
   oratorio and, **1:**834; **2:**73, 237, 313

symphony concert performances, **2:**499,
   500
Lenya, Lotte, **4:**533, 536
Lenz, Wilhelm von, **3:**364
Leo III, Pope, **1:**3, 4
Leo IX, Pope, **1:**141
Leo X, Pope, **1:**555
Leo XI, Pope, **3:**102
Leo Hebraeus. *See* Gersonides
Leoncavallo, Ruggero, **3:**659, 664
   Pagliacci, I, **3:**659–60, *659,* 662–63; **4:**751
Leonel Power. *See* Power, Leonel
Leonhardt, Ruth, **4:**661
Leonin (Leoninus magister), **1:**173, 174, 175,
   177, 179, 183, 184, 185, 186, 187, 249
Leonius (poet), **1:**175, 184, 185, 191
Leonora ossia L'amore conjugale (Paer), **3:**3
Leonore (Beethoven) *See Fidelio*
Leonore, oder Der Triumph der ehelichen Liebe
   (Sonnleithner), **3:**2, 3
Léonore, ou L'amour conjugal (Bouilly), **3:**3
"Leonore" story, **3:**2–3
Leopardi, Giacomo, **3:**570
Leopold, King of Belgium, **3:**213
Leopold II, Emperor of Austria, **2:**462,
   481–82, 499, 652
Leopold V, King of Austria, **1:**117
Leopold, Prince of Anhalt-Cöthen,
   2:261–62
Lepanto, battle of (1571), **1:**779, 787
Leporello's "Catalogue aria" (Mozart),
   2:489, 490
Leppert, Richard, **2:**340
Lerdahl, Fred, **5:**445–60, 463
   Generative Theory of Tonal Music, A (with
     Ray Jackenoff), **5:**446–48, 453
   "Cognitive Constraints on
     Compositional Systems," **5:**451–52
   "Composing and Listening: A Reply to
     Nattiez," **5:**411
   composing style of, **5:**455–60
   String Quartet no. 1, **5:**456–60
Lermontov, Mikhail, **3:**397
Les Six. *See* Group des Six, Le
Leskov, Nikolai, **4:**785
   The Lady Macbeth of the Mtsensk District,
     4:785–91, 787
lesson chants, **1:**13, 25, 171, 775
Le Sueur, Jean-François, **3:**318–19
Lettera amorosa (Monteverdi), **2:**6, 8
*Letter: A Depression Message from a Hobo
   Friend, The* (Partch), **5:**482
"Letter Concerning the Prison of Human
   Life" (Christine de Pisane), **1:**447
"Letter on French Music" (Rousseau),
   2:442
Letters on a Regicide Peace (Burke), **2:**645
"Letters to His Son" (Lord Chesterfield),
   2:340
Leuven, Adolphe de, **3:**641
Levant, Oscar, **4:**628
Levi ben Gershom. *See* Gersonides

Levi-Strauss, Claude, **5:**347
   Raw and the Cooked, The, **5:**347
Levine, Lawrence, **3:**385
Levinson, Jerrold, *Music in the Moment,*
   5:511–14
Levy, Beth, **4:**640, 672
Lewandowski, Louis, **3:**174
   Ma towu oholecho Jaakow, **3:**175–76
lewd songs. *See* bawdy songs
Lewin, David, **5:**496
Lewis, John, **5:**336–37, 339–42
   Manhattan School of Music, **5:**336
   Milt Jackson Quartet (MJQ) and, **5:**337
   Sketch, **5:**337, 341–42
Lewis, Wyndham, **4:**753
Lewontin, Richard, *Darwin's Revolution,*
   5:221
Leyer, Leonard, **5:**414
Liberal Arts, The: Music (Perréal), **1:**548
liberal arts curriculum, **1:**4, 69, 71, 248, 550
   madrigals and, **1:**354
liberalism
   backlash against, **3:**174
   tradition and, **3:**724, 728
Libera me (responsory verse), **1:**88–89
"Liberation of Sound, The" (Varèse),
   5:184, 187
Liberazione di Ruggiero dall'isola d'Alcina, La
   (Caccini), **2:**80
Liber de civitatis Florentiae famosis civibus
   (Villani), **1:**353
Liber hymnorum (Notker), **1:**41, 42
Liber primus missarum Josquini (Petrucci
   music book), **1:**559
Liber responsorialis (Benedictine), **1:**22
Liber sancti Jacobi. See Codex Calixtinus
"Liberty Bell" (Sousa), **4:**275
"Liberty Leading the People" (Delacroix),
   4:105
Liber usualis (chant book), **1:**23, 87, 177, *177,*
   178, 462
libretti (little books), **2:**159, 438
librettists
   Barbier, **3:**640
   Boito, **3:**596, 599, 600, 606, 611, 639, 669
   Bouilly, **3:**2, 3
   Busenello, **2:**26–27
   Calzabigi, **2:**453, 455, 478
   Cammarano, **3:**46, 577–78
   Carré, **3:**640
   Da Ponte, **2:**476–79, 485, 487
   Dryden, **2:**132
   of English oratorios, **3:**163
   Gagliano, **1:**818–19, 826
   Giacosa, **3:**666
   Gilbert, **3:**651
   Goldoni, **2:**433, 446–47, 467, 493
   Halévy (Ludovic), **3:**648
   Haym, **2:**307
   Illica, **3:**666
   Locle, **3:**595
   Meilhac, **3:**648

Metastasio, 2:152–72, 174, 175, 434, 438, 452, 453, 455, 481; 3:207, 235
Ottoboni, 2:151
Piave, 3:575–76, 577, 580, 583, 594
Quinault, 2:90, 94, 97, 155, 478
Rinuccini, 2:19, 15, 21, 23
Romani, 3:37, 44, 45
Sabina, 3:448
Schikaneder, 3:188
Scribe, 3:207–10, 215, 219, 220, 223, 225
seventeenth- and eighteenth-century power of, 2:173
Solera, 3:571, 573, 576
Sonnleither
Sonnleithner, 3:2, 3
Striggio, 2:14, 18, 21
Strozzi (Giulio), 2:75
Tate, 2:132, 155
Wagner as own, 1:337
Zeno, 2:152
librettos
for Beethoven
for Bellini, 3:37, 44
cantata conventions, 2:76
comic opera conventions, 2:450–51
Dargomïzhsky's dispensing with, 3:612, 618
darkened theaters and reading of, 3:564
for first intermezzos, 2:434–35
for Gluck, 2:453, 455, 478
for Handel, 2:307, 316, 325
for Haydn, 2:633
for Lully, 2:36, 310, 313, 478
Metastasian style, 2:153–54
most frequently reused, 2:158
for Mozart, 2:465, 466
musical relationship with, 2:486–87
Musorgsky's use of prose for, 3:618–21, 629, 631
neoclassic elements in, 2:151–52, 434
novels as plot sources for, 3:46, 47
opera seria and, 2:174
printed, 2:159, 438
Romanticism and, 3:44–45
Verdi's demands concerning, 3:575–76
Wagner's writing of, 3:487, 492, 576
Libro de villanelle, moresche, et altre canzoni (song collection), 1:715
libro d'intavolatura (Frescobaldi), 2:36, 38–39, 43
libro d'intavolatura (Rossi), 2:42
Libuše (Smetana), 3:461–63
Lichfield, Bishop of, 1:423
Lichnowsky, Karl von, Prince, 2:653, 675, 683, 694
Lieberson, Goddard, 5:366
Liebesbund, 3:537
Liebeslieder (Brahms), 3:717
Liebeslieder-Walzer (Brahms), 3:753
Liebesnot, 3:537
Liebestod (Wagner), 3:555
    Pelléas and Mélissande and, 4:44

Tristan und Isolde and, 4:240, 619
    Salomé and, 4:44
Liebesverbot, Das (Wagner), 3:481
"Liebe-Tragik" leitmotif (Wagner), 3:507, 519, 538
Liebfrauenkirche (Halle), 2:402
"Liebster Gott" (J. S. Bach), 2:370–72
lied, 3:119–20, 123–63
    Beethoven and, 3:131–35
    folk songs and, 3:120, 123
    German national identity and, 3:124, 158, 160–63
    Haydn and, 3:130
    maturing of form, 3:129–35
    Meisterlied (master-song) and, 1:139–40
    Mendelssohn (Fanny) and, 3:185
    Minnelied and, 1:134–39, 143
    Mozart and, 3:130–31
    origins of, 3:119–20
    Schubert and, 3:135–55, 189
    strophic settings and, 3:145–48, 152, 189
    volkstümlich poetry and, 3:125–26
Liedbearbeitung, 1:541
Liederbuch (Schöffer), 1:701
Lieder eines fahrenden Gesellen (Mahler), 4:13
Lieder für das Pianoforte, 3:184
Liederkranz movement, 3:163
Lieder ohne Wörte
    Mendelssohn (Fanny) as originator of, 3:184, 185
    Mendelssohn (Felix) and, 3:184, 368
Liedet, Lyset, 1:622
Liedsätz, 1:761–62, 765
    See also Lutheran chorale
Lied von der Erde, Das (Mahler), 4:6, 717; 5:318, 319
Liedweise, 1:701
lieto fine (happy ending), 2:151
Life and Times of Joseph Stalin, The, Robert Wilson and, 5:393
Life for the Tsar, A (Glinka), 3:233, 236–50, 245, 286, 447, 710, 763, 788; 4:369
Life of Rossini (Stendahl), 3:32–34
"lifestyle modernism" genre, 4:567–72, 588
ligatures, 1:176, 177, 179, 180, 199
    Franconian, 1:215–17
    isosyllabic scheme, 1:159
    melisma and, 1:199, 200
    pitch and, 1:176
Ligeti, György, 5:41, 42, 49–54, 162, 165, 220, 437, 463
    Darmstadt, 5:50
    "electronic music," 5:51
    Herbert Eimert and, 5:49
    Karlheinz Stockhausen and, 5:49
    Liszt Conservatory, 5:49
    works of
        Apparitions, 5:51
        Artikulation, 5:52–53, 191, 214
        Atmospheres, 5:214, 215, 217, 219–20, 363, 501

Clocks and Clouds, 5:438
Le grand macabre, 5:438
Mikropolyphonie and, 5:215
Poème symphonique, 5:162, 373
"Self-Portrait with Reich and Riley (and Chopin in the Background), 5:438
Three Pieces for Two Pianos, 5:438
Trio for Violin, Horn, and Piano, 5:438
light shows, 3:202–3
light verse, 1:122
lilt, prolation, 1:261, 262
Limoges, 1:111, 112, 157
Lincoln, Abraham, 4:668, 669
    First Inaugural Address, 4:658
    Gettysburg Address, 4:668
    as Great Emancipator, 4:658
Lincoln Center for the Performing Arts (New York), 5:113, 114, 116
    El Niño and, 5:523
Lincoln Portrait, A (Copland), 4:668, 669–70, 671; 5:107
"Lincoln Symphony" (Mason), 4:621
Lind, Jenny, 3:286
Lindbergh, Charles, 4:541
Lindberghflug, Der (Brecht-Weill-Hindemith), 4:541
Lindenberger, Herbert, 4:525
Linear Contrasts (Ussachevsky), 5:198
Linhaure (Raimbaut d'Aurenga), 1:115–16, 226
Linley, Thomas, 2:633
Lipatti, Dinu, 5:461
Lippman, Edward, 3:309
liquescent neumes, 1:24
lira da braccio, 1:697, 697
lira grande, 1:829
lira organizzata, Haydn compositions for, 2:601, 601
Lisbon Cathedral, 2:390
Lisinsky, Vatroslav
    Ljubav i zloba, 3:447–48
Lissitzky, Lazar (El), 4:776
"List of 1001 Activities, by Members of the Scratch Orchestra," 5:86
Listek odvanuty (Janáček), 4:429, See also Blown-away Leaf, A
listeners. See audience
Listenius, Nikolaus, 1:550–51, 553, 577–78
Liszt, Cosima. See Wagner, Cosima Liszt
Liszt, Eduard, 3:284
Liszt, Franz, 1:617; 3:261–73, 262, 287, 317, 482, 4:120, 197, 200, 205, 207, 210, 224, 231, 266, 304, 352, 360, 373, 397, 398, 410, 454, 553, 632, 699; 5:77
    d'Agoult and, 3:77
    background of, 3:261–62
    Beethoven and, 3:262, 268, 285, 287, 309, 420, 421, 424, 437
    Belloni as personal manager of, 3:272
    Berlioz and, 3:336, 421, 424

Liszt, Franz (*continued*)
    Berlioz's *Symphonie fantastique*
        transcription and, 3:324, 325–26,
        340
    Brahms and, 3:685, 696, 699–700
    Brendel and, 3:417, 419, 421–22, 425, 426
    caricature of, 3:267, 268, 269, 292
    on chamber music, 3:731
    Chopin and, 3:349
    concerto and, 3:277–85, 419
    Danhauser's painting of, 3:75–77
    on Field, 3:64–65, 71, 292
    Franck and, 3:777
    harmonics, 3:428–38, 627–28
    Hungarian persona of, 3:261
    improvisation by, 3:287–88
    as instrumental recital pioneer,
        3:272–73
    Joachim and, 3:418, 684
    MacDowell and, 3:768
    Mozart and, 3:287–88
    as music critic, 3:290
    New German School and, 3:417–22,
        426, 428–38, 676, 692; 4:371
    Paganini and, 3:253, 256, 261, 264,
        266–68, 292
    public support of, 3:292
    revolutionary politics and, 3:264–66
    Saint-Saëns and, 3:784
    salons and, 3:75–77, 273
    Sayn-Wittgenstein and, 3:290, 417, 420,
        422
    Schubert and, 3:85, 105, 277–78, 457,
        697, 698
    Schumann (Robert) and, 3:309, 432, 683
    Serov and, 3:439, 446
    Smetana and, 3:444, 445–46
    style hongrois and, 4:371
    symphonic music preemption and, 3:675
    symphonic poem and, 3:419–20,
        422–27, 429–30, 627–28
    thematic transformation and, 3:284–85,
        336, 420, 425, 433–35, 777
    tonal practice of, 3:543–47
    as virtuoso, 3:261–73
    Wagner and, 3:418, 482, 483, 487
    Weimar court appointment of,
        3:417–20
    womanizer reputation of, 3:268, 385–86
    works of
        Années de pèlerinage, 3:432; 4:112
        Bagatelle ohne Tonart, 3:362, 363, 438,
            447
        Ce qu'on entend sur la montagne
            ("Mountain Symphony"),
            3:429–30, 546, 699
        "Diabelli Variation," 3:262, 263
        Don Sanche, ou Le château d'amour,
            3:262
        E flat-major Concerto, 3:287, 336
        Étude en douze exercices, 3:262

        Études d'exécution transcendante d'après
            Paganini, 3:266–68
        Faust-Symphonie, 3:435–37, 546
        Galop chromatique, 3:273
        Grande fantaisie de bravoure sur La
            Clochette de Paganini, 3:264, 265
        Hamlet, 3:446
        Hungarian Coronation Mass, 4:371, 372
        Hungarian Fantasia, 4:371
        Hungarian Historical Portraits, 4:371
        "Hungarian Rhapsodies," 3:433, 449;
            4:626, 632
        Hunnenschlacht, 3:446
        Lorelei, Die, 3:543
        Orpheus (Symphonic Poem No. 4),
            3:627–28
        Piano Concerto no. 1, 3:277–85, 698
        Préludes, Les, 3:422–27, 435, 776
        Quatre élémens, Les, 3:425, 426
        Réminiscences de Don Juan, 3:268–72,
            273, 347
        Sonata in B minor for piano,
            3:432–35, 446
        Sursum corda, 3:432
        Totentanz, 3:339
        Valses oubliées, 3:362
Liszt at the Piano (Danhauser), 3:75–77, 76
"Litanei," 4:315
litanies, 1:58
literacy, 3.63, 3.289. *See also* written music
literalism, 3:66
literary music, 1:710–51
    Berlioz and, 3:320
    Counter Reformation liturgical style
        and, 1:773, 777–79
    definitions of, 1:721–22
    madrigalism and, 1:723–41
    Schumann (Robert) and, 3:294–305,
        309, 312, 317–18
    sixteenth-century movement in,
        1:722–51
    Tuscan dialect and, 1:723
    See also poetry; vernacular
literate tradition. *See* written music
literati. See elite culture
literature
    artistic sensibility origins in, 2:410, 416
    essentialist notion of, 2:82
    home reading of, 3:63
    music viewed as, 3:294
    novel as operatic source, 2:445–46, 450
    Renaissance, 1:382
    romantic, 3:570
    Slavic, 3:345
    Sturm und Drang and, 2:416, 528–29
    trecento, 1:365–66
    verismo movement, 3:658–59
    vernacular, 1:351, 383
    See also poetry
Lithuania, 1:347
Litolff, Henry, 3:277
"little Modernsky," 4:678, 691

Little Opera Theater of Leningrad, The,
    4:790
"Little Sacred Concertos" (Schütz),
    2:66–69
liturgical day, 1:11–12
liturgical drama, 1:52, 93–95, 131, 138
    Musica and, 1:495–96
    sacred play with music and, 1:834
liturgical music, 1:10–29
    Anglican Reformation and, 1:402,
        672–73, 675, 677–78
    antimusical screeds and, 1:311, 645–47
    antiphoner and, 1:6, 7
    Avignon papacy and, 1:310–14
    Bach (J. S.) and, 2:255–57, 340–90,
        363–83, 389
    Beethoven and, 2:721
    Byrd and, 1:678–89
    Byzantine chant and, 1:33–35
    Calvinist rejection of, 1:754–55; 2:44,
        125
    cantata and, 2:341–90
    castrati and, 2:16
    choral, 1:314
    choral hymnody and, 2:49–50, 53–54
    Christian origins of, 1:7–8
    church calendar and, 1:12, 37–39
    church plays and, 1:93–94
    church sonata and, 2:177–84, 187–92
    Clemens and, 1:593–99
    concerted style and, 1:666
    concerto grosso and, 2:178
    congregational singing and, 1:27–28, 47,
        58, 758, 765
    Council of Trent and, 1:649–50, 653,
        655, 656, 672, 789
    Counter Reformation and, 1:771–96
    "Credo I" and, 1:34–35
    Dies irae and, 1:88–90
    divine service and, 1:65
    earliest surviving artifact of, 1:33
    in England, 1:1–5, 7, 27, 513–18
    English fifteenth-century influence on,
        1:423
    English sixteenth-century, 1:612–13
    Frankish hymns, 1:41–43, 47–49
    Frankish modal theory and, 1:72–104
    Frankish reorganization of, 1:5, 37–67
    Frescobaldi and, 2:35, 43
    Gabrielis and, 1:780, 782–83
    "intelligibility" movement and, 1:647,
        649–53, 672, 769, 771
    Josquin's exemplary, 1:565–72
    Lutheranism and, 1:758–69; 2:49–55,
        255, 341–42
    Machaut and, 1:307–10
    Mass ordo standardization, 1:60,
        62(table)
    medieval vernacular song similarities
        with, 1:111–12, 131
    modern esthetics and, 1:496–97
    monastic day and, 1:10–12

Monteverdi and, 2:5, 10, 18–20
motet and, 1:217, 219, 277–85, 311, 501–46
motet-ricercare and, 1:607
Neoplatonist Musica ideas and, 1:37–40
Notre Dame composers and, 1:171–72
oral tradition ande, 1:11–35
organ and, 2:35–44, 48, 49, 255–57
organist improvisation and, 1:437, 607, 617
Palestrina and, 1:630–67
Passion settings and, 1:775–77
polyphony and, 1:155–68, 310–14
Protestant Reformation effects on, 1:753, 754
Roman Catholic reform and, 1:645–53, 672
Schütz and, 2:59, 66–73
Second Vatican Council and, 1:278
secular music's blurred line with, 1:105–6, 128, 131, 136, 311, 532–34
stile antico and, 1:667, 669
Sweelinck and, 2:44, 48
See also chant; cyclic Mass Ordinaries; Gregorian chant; hymns and hymnody; Marian antiphons; Mass; Ordinary; psalms and psalmody
Litweiler, John, 5:335
Lives of the Artists (Vasari), 1:641; 3:264
"Living Room Music" (Cage), 5:55
Livre d'orgue (Messiaen), 5:26
Ljubav i zloba (Lisinsky), 3:447–48
Lobgesang (Fanny Mendelssohn), 3:184
Lobkowitz, Joseph Franz Maximilian von, Prince, 2:671; 3:131
Locatelli, Pietro, 2:296, 299; 3:252
Lochamer Liederbuch, 1:701
Locke, Matthew, 2:126, 127, 132, 134
Locke, Ralph P., 3:405–6
Lockwood, Lewis, 1:559
Locle, Camille du, 3:595
"loco" Masses. See *motetti missales*
locus classicus, emulation of, 3:47, 55
Lodoïska (Cherubini), 3:2–3
Lodoïska (Kreutzer), 3:2
Loewe, Carl,
ballad and, 3:155, 158
oratorio and, 3:164–65
Wunderhorn poems and, 4:21
works of
Erlkönig, 3:155, 158–59, 367
Gutenberg, 3:164
Johann Hus, 3:164
Palestrina, 3:164
Zerstörung Jerusalems, Die, 3:164
"Loge" leitmotif (Wagner), 3:506, 515
Logische Aufbau der Welt, Der (treatise, Carnap), 5:155
Lohengrin (Wagner), 1:138; 3:418, 421, 480, 483, 486–87, 565
costume design, 3:486

Elsa's bridal song, 3:487
preludes, 3:486, 487
premiere performance of, 3:479, 487
Verdi's *La traviata* and, 3:580
Lomax, Alan, 4:659; 5:334
American Ballads and Folksongs, 4:659, 660
Lomax, John A., 4:659, 662, 672
American Ballads and Folksongs, 4:659, 660
Cowboy Songs and Other Frontier Ballads, 4:659
"Git Along, Little Dogies," 4:663, 666
Lombardi alla prima crociata, I (Verdi), 3:568, 573–74
Lombards, 1:2, 3, 696
lombards (short-long rhythms), 2:134, 407
Lombardy, 2:2, 504
London
Artaserses pasticcio version performed in, 2:158, 168–69
Bach (J. C.) in, 2:419, 606
Handel in, 2:237–39, 306, 307–40, 401, 419
Haydn's tours in, 2:555–88, 589, 607, 633, 652, 695
intermezzo hit in, 2:435
Liszt in, 3:262, 288
Mozart in, 2:464, 601
music criticism in, 3:290
music publishing in, 2:177
nineteenth-century symphonic music in, 3:678, 680
Paganini concerts in, 3:253
public concert series in, 2:419, 499, 555, 571, 577, 639
Purcell and, 2:128–38
theater, 2:125–28
Verdi commissions from, 3:568
London Daily Post, 2:315
London Symphony in D major, no. 104 (Haydn), 2:578–88; 3:16, 691; 4:19
development section, 2:581–88
finale, 3:692
historical importance of first movement of, 2:584
opening theme of, 2:581–82, 584, 588
slow introduction, 2:579–81, 583
Lonesome Cowboy, The (White-Shackley), 4:662, 663
Lonesome Train (Robinson), 4:669
Long, Michael P., 1:352, 356, 368, 383, 5:328
longa triplex. See three-tempura length
longa ultra mensuram. See three-tempora length
Longfellow, Henry Wadsworth, 3:123, 158, 657, 760, 763, 765
longissima melodia, 1:157
Longo, Alessandro, 2:392
Longueval, Antoine de, 1:776–77
Lönnrot, Elias, 3:123, 763
Lorca, Federico Garcia
Ancient Voices of Children, 5:422
George Crumb and, 5:422, 423, 442

Night of Four Moons, 5:422
Night Music, 5:422
Songs, Drones, and Refrains of Death, 5:422
"Lord Nelson Mass" (Haydn), 2:577, 633
Lord's Prayer (Josquin polyphonic setting), 1:563, 564
Lord's Prayer (Lutheran), 2:365
Lord's Supper (Lutheran Mass), 1:755, 769. See also Eucharist
Lorelei (mythical Rhine mermaid), 3:127
Lorelei, Die (Liszt), 3:543
Lorentz, Pare, 4:660
The Plow That Broke the Plains, 4:660, 661
Lorenzo Masini, 1:366
A poste messe, 1:366
Non so qual i' mi voglia, 1:366, 367
Loriod, Yvonne, 4:240
Loris, Heinrich. See Glareanus, Henricus
Lortzing, Albert, 3:753
Los Angeles Festival of the Arts, *The Death of Klinghoffer* and, 5:522
Los Angeles Philharmonic, 5:75
"lost generation," 4:589, 598
Louis I (Louis the Pious), King of the Franks, 1:37
Louis IX, King of France, 1:120
Louis X, King of France, 1:258
Louis XI, King of France, 1:455, 458
Louis XII, King of France, 1:554, 555, 558, 559, 563, 574, 589; 2:538–39
Louis XIV, King of France, 2:89, 109, 111, 125; 3:208; 4:478
Couperin and, 2:277
court opera and, 2:87, 88, 90, 155, 454, 465
Lully's compositions and, 2:89, 94, 97
musical patronage and, 2:89, 99
musical taste and, 2:85
Louis XV, King of France, 2:89, 91, 92–93, 442, 461; 3:11
Louis XVI, King of France, 2:459; 3:211
execution of, 3:331
Louis XVIII, King of France, 3:11, 211
"Louisiana trilogy" (Gottschalk variation sets), 3:377–78, 386
Louis Philippe, King of France, 3:214, 215, 348
Louisville Orchestra, 5:295
loure, in suite format, 2:263, 271, 276–74
Louvre (Paris), 1:117; 3:349
love
as music theme, 3:295
as *opera buffa* theme, 2:447
See also love songs
Love for Three Oranges, The (Meyerhold), 5:11
Lovejoy, Arthur, 3:320
Lovers Made Men (Jonson), 2:114
love songs, 1:526–34
ballata and, 1:367
bergerette and, 1:526–34
cantigas and, 1:128–29

love songs (*continued*)
  Gesualdo madrigal and, **1:**738
  monodic madrigal and, **1:**813, 815
  sacred devotional, **1:**270–73, 275–76,
    316, 429–33, 501, 532–33
  by Schumann (Robert), **3:**295–305
  troubadour genres, **1:**107–9, 110–13, 115
  trouvère examples, **1:**118–19
  See also courtly love poetry and song;
    eroticism
Low, Jackson Mac, **5:** 91
"low dance," **1:**621–22
Lower Rhine Music Festival, **3:**173, 685
  Mendelssohn (Felix) and, **3:**166, 172
  oratorio and, **3:**165
Lowinsky, Edward, **1:**577–78, 579, 580,
    584; **2:**397
low style, **1:**459–60, 549, 715
  middle-style convergence with,
    1:528–29
  motetti missales and, **1:**519–26, 584
Lübeck, **2:**241
Lucas (composer), **2:**158
Lucchesini, Laura (Laura Guidiccioni),
    1:823
Lucia di Lammermoor (Donizetti), **3:**46–59,
    46, 144; **4:**45, 437
  "Chi mi frena," **3:**49–51, 587
  mad scene, **3:**46–48, 52–59, 73, 655
  sextet, **3:**49–51, 273
Lucio Silla (J. C.Bach), **2:**507
Lucretius, **5:**303
  De Rerum Natura, **5:**302
Lucrezia Borgia (Donizetti), **3:**45
Ludus Danielis. See Play of Daniel
Ludus tonalis (Hindemith), **4:**768
Ludwig II, King of Bavaria, **3:**498
Ludwig, Friedrich, **1:**266
Luening, Otto, **5:**192, 199, 211
  Incantation, **5:**198
  "King Lear Suite," **5:**214
  Rhapsodic Variations, **5:**198
Luke, Gospel according to, **1:**775; **2:**73
Lulli, Giovanni Battista. *See* Lully,
    Jean-Baptiste
Lully, Jean-Baptiste, **2:***85*, 86, 89–106,
    108–9, 126, 132, 133, 460, 506;
    3:208, 703; **4:**131
  as autocratic disciplinarian, **2:**99, 111
  background of, **2:**89
  court opera and, **2:**89–106, 108–9
  French royal monopoly of, **2:**89
  as German musical influence, **2:**259
  incidental music to *Le bourgeois
    gentilhomme*, **3:**386
  librettist of, **2:**90, 94, 97, 478; **3:**37
  passacaille and, **2:**94–96
  "patter chorus" of, **2:**102
  Rameau's style compared with, **2:**109,
    110, 441
  tragédie lyrique and, **2:**89–106, 108–9,
    454, 459

works of
  Alceste, **2:**90, *90*
  Armide, **2:**94–96
  Atys, **2:**91–92, 97–106, 110
  Cadmus et Hermione, **2:**86
  Isis, **2:**102
  Lulu (Berg), **4:**714
  "Lumír's song" (Smetana), **3:**454
Lunacharsky, Anatoly, **4:**776, 777,
    779
Luscinius, Othmar, **1:**383–84
Lust hab ich ghabt zuer Musica (Sennfl),
    1:704–6
lute, **1:**373, 671, 691, 698, 829; **2:**198, 263
  ayres, **2:**120; **3:**119
  Bach (J. S.) suite and, **2:**262, 265
  chitarrone, **1:**804–5, 809
  Dowland and, **1:**742
  English dances and, **2:**114
  Galilei and, **1:**799
  medieval, **1:**108, *108*
  monody and, **1:**802
  "preludizing" style of, **2:**249–50, 251
  ricercari for, **1:**606, 607, 620; **2:**624
  as song accompaniment, **1:**741–42
  Spanish divisions, **2:**47
  tablatures, **1:**606, 626
Luther, Martin, **1:**552, 772; **2:**50, 302, 353,
    356, 389; **3:**726
  chorale sponsorship by, **3:**165
  compositions by, **1:**756, 758, 759–60
  Feste Burg, Ein', **1:**760, *761*; **3:**167–68, 232
  hymns by, **3:**171
  musical interests of, **1:**754–56, 758,
    760–61, 762, 763
  ninety-five theses of, **1:**753, *754*
Lutheran chorale. *See* chorale
Lutheran Church, **1:**550, 596; **3:**165, 167
  Augsburg Confession and, **2:**353, 402
  Bach (J. S.) and, **2:**50, 240, 241, 255,
    302–3, 341, 363–64, 365, 370–74,
    389, 402
  Bach (W. F.) and, **2:**353, 402
  ban on women church vocalists by, **2:**352
  cantata form and, **2:**341–90
  chorale form and. *See* chorale
  congregational singing and, **1:**758, 765
  Enlightenment vs., **2:**368
  liturgical music and, **1:**755–69
  liturgical organ use by, **2:**49, 50
  musical asceticism of, **2:**68, 363, 370–72
  operatic forms of, **2:**341, 342
  oratorio form and, **2:**341–42
  Reformationsfest and, **2:**353
  sacred music reforms and, **2:**341
  Scheidt and, **2:**49
  Schütz and, **2:**57–59, 69–73
  social ideology and, **2:**302
  worldview of, **2:**363–64
Lutosławski, Witold, **3:**256
luxuriant style, **1:**301–5, 318, 325, 612;
    2:59–66, 67

Luzzaschi, Luzzasco, **2:**5
Lvov, Nikolai, **3:**233
  Yamshchiki na podstave, **3:**236
Lyadov, Anatoliy, **4:**60
Lydian mode, **1:**479, 509, 554; **2:**687
  symbolism of, **1:**831
Lydian scale, **1:**99
Lyons, **1:**706
Lyotard, Jean-François, **5:**413
lyre, **1:**29, 31, 32, *32*, 697, *697*, 802, 803, 804,
    809; **3:**120
  continuo and, **1:**829, 830
lyre de braccio, **1:**804
Lyrical Ballads (Wordsworth), **3:**64
lyric poetry, **1:**125–26; **3:**63–64
  German Romanticism and, **3:**124–26
  lied genre and, **3:**119
Lyric Suite (Berg), **4:**523, 710, 711, 712–13,
    714, 719, 721
Lyrischen Gedichte (Reichardt), **3:**124, 126,
    129
lyrisches intermezzo, **4:**18–20
Lyrisches Intermezzo (Heine), **3:**296
Lyubov' k tryom apel'sinam (Prokofieff).
    See*Love for Three Oranges, The*

M

Ma bouche rit et ma pensée pleure
    (Ockeghem), **1:**526–28, 529–30
Ma (codice), **1:**183
Ma, Yo-Yo, **5:**524
macaronic texts, **1:**113
Macaulay, Thomas, **2:**124
Macbeth (Shakespeare), **3:**576
Macbeth (Verdi), **3:**568, 576, 611
Macbeth a čarodějnice (Smetana), **3:**446–47,
    457
McCarthy, Joseph, U. S.Senator, **5:**107
  Permanent Subcommittee on
    Investigations, **5:**107
McCartney, Paul, **5:**317, 318, 319, 321, 328,
    332
  "Not a Second Time," **5:**318
McClary, Susan, **2:**21, 301, 302; **3:**117, 406;
    5:492, 493
  John Zorn and, **5:**507–8
McClymonds, Marita, **2:**151, 175
McCrae, John, "In Flanders Fields," **4:**291
Macdonald, Hugh, **3:**227, 320–21
MacDonald, Ian, **5:**321
MacDowell, Edward, **3:**767–68, *767*
  "Eroica," op. 50, **3:**768
  "Indian Suite," **3:**768
  "Keltic," op. 59, **3:**768
  "Norse," op. 57, **3:**768
  "To a Wild Rose," **3:**768
  "Tragica," op. 45, **3:**768
Mace, Thomas, **2:**118
Machaut, Guillaume de, **1:**270–73,
    289–307, *289*, 317–36, 368, 563,
    5:409–10; **5:**43

artistic cleverness and, 1:327–36
autobiographical poems of, 1:290, 297
ballade and, 1:302–5, 371
beliefs of, 1:272–73
career of, 1:289–90
cathedral epitaph and will of, 1:317
chace (canon) and, 1:332–36
legacy of, 1:289–98, 336–42, 343, 495
luxuriant style and, 1:301–5, 318
"Machaut manuscripts," 1:289
Mass setting by, 1:307, 316, 317–26, 460
top-down composition by, 1:296–98, 311
unaccompanied melody and, 1:298
virelai and, 1:292–97, 298, 299–301,
    349, 366
works of
    DAVID melisma, 1:291–92
    De toutes flours, 1:303–7, 308–9, 371,
        373
    Douce dame jolie, 1:295, 298
    En mon cuer, 1:296–97, 298, 299
    Felix virgo/Inviolata/AD TE
        SUSPIRAMUS, 1:270–73, 291, 301,
        302
    Lai de confort, 1:332
    Lai de la fonteinne, 1:332–36
    Lasse/se j'aime/POURQUOY, 1:292,
        293–94, 298
    Ma fin est mon commencement,
        1:327–30, 328
    Messe de Nostre Dame, La, 1:307,
        317–26
    Remède de Fortune, Le, 1:290, 297, 299
    Rose, liz, printemps, 1:302, 303
    Très bonne et belle, 1:301–1
    Voir Dit, Le, 1:297, 299
Machiavelli, Niccolò, 1:208
machinery
    English semi-opera and, 2:127
    French opera and, 2:88, 106, 127
    French tragedy and, 2:87
machismo, 3:77
Machover, Tod, "electronic glove" and,
    5:509
Maciunas, George, 5:91
    Fluxus, 5:91
Mackerras, Charles, 4:444
McKinley, William, 4:262
MacLise, Angus, 5:362
    Theatre of Eternal Music, 5:362
McNamara, Mark, "interactive sound
    installations" and, 5:514
McPhee, Colin, 5:255–56
Mac the Knife, Die Dreigroschenoper and,
    4:537
    carol, 1:420
    motet, 1:233–36
Mädchenlied, op. 6, no. 3 (Schoenberg),
    4:314–15, 324
Maderna, Bruno, 5:22, 94, 193, 463
    Musica su due dimensioni, 5:211
    Richard Maxfield and, 5:94

Ritratta di città, 5:193
madrigal, 1:352–64, 352, 367, 374, 722–41;
    2:74, 229, 254, 258, 316, 321, 336,
    341, 643; 3:455, 703, 704
    ballata culture vs., 1:368
    cantata as solo successor to, 2:75, 142
    characteristics of, 1:813
    chromaticism in, 1:724–25, 729–30,
        732, 734, 738, 739, 751, 785; 3:428
    consort repertory effects of, 2:121
    as Counter-Reformation musical
        influence, 1:773, 777, 800
    culture of, 1:354–56, 368
    distinctive poetic style of, 1:724
    duetto and, 2:331
    echo pieces, 1:792
    emotional expression of, 1:723–24
    England and, 1:742, 744, 746–51
    experimentation and, 1:725–26
    French-Italian genre fusion and, 1:374
    Galilei's critique of, 1:800–801
    Gesualdo and, 1:738–41
    intermedii and, 1:804
    as international craze, 1:723
    Italian-born composers of, 1:728–41,
        740
    Italian-English differences in, 1:750, 751
    mimesis and, 1:802
    monody and, 1:813–22, 823; 3:119
    Monteverdi and, 1:733–38, 749, 750; 2:11,
        2–10, 11, 229; 3:455
    motet-style, 1:374–77, 380
    "northern," 1:723, 724–33
    notational visual puns and, 1:778
    Palestrina and, 1:632, 642, 746
    poetic style of, 1:724
    polyphony and, 1:354, 356, 364,
        800–801, 816, 817, 818
    Schütz and, 2:57, 58
    sensuality of, 1:738, 772
    sixteenth-century revival of, 1:722–51
    structure of, 1:352, 374, 724, 813
    Sweelinck and, 2:44
    trecento-style example of, 1:356–59
    two types of, 1:817
    ultimate stage of, 1:738–41
    Vivaldi mimesis and, 2:229–30
    "wild bird" songs and, 1:359–64
    women singers/composers of, 2:80
Madrigali guerrieri, et amorosi (Monteverdi),
    2:6–7
madrigalism, 4:195
madrigali spirituali, 1:632
Madrigals to Five Voices: Selected out of the best
    approved Italian authors (Morley),
    1:746
mad scenes, 2:106–7
    Lucia di Lammermoor, 3:46–48, 52–59,
        73, 655
    Madama Butterfly (Puccini), 3:667–72;
        4:444
    "Un bel dí," 3:668–72

Maelzel, Johann Nepomuk, 2:654, 672–43
    Panharmonicon and, 5:177
    pendulum metronome and, 5:177
maestro. See conductor
Maeterlinck, Count Maurice, 4:86, 88, 89,
    92, 106, 126
    Pelléas et Mélisande, 4:308
    Princesse Maleine, La, 4:126
Ma fin est mon commencement (Machaut),
    1:327–30, 328
Magee, Bryan, 3:505, 539, 558–59, 774
Magic Bullet, The. See Freischütz, Der
Magic Flute, The (Mozart), 2:479–85, 480,
    481, 643, 676; 3:188–91; 4:449
    Act II finale, 3:190
    armonica's use in, 3:737–66
    Papageno's aria, 3:189
magic opera, 3:73, 188
magic plays, 3:188
"Magic Toy Shop, The," 3:12
magnetophone, 5:175
Magnificat, 1:11, 686
    organ settings of, 2:49
Magnificat (Bach), 3:711
magnus (Tinctoris genre ranking), 1:459,
    460
Magnus, Saint, 1:393
Magnus Liber (Leonin attrib.), 1:183, 184
    revision of, 1:186
Magyar népdalok (Bartok-Kadaly), 4:375,
    377
magyar nota, 4:367–68, 369, 373, 374, 375,
    377
Magyars, 4:365
Maharajah of Mysore, Medtner and, 4:555
Maharishi Mahesh Yogi, transcendental
    meditation and, 5:408
Mahler, Gustav, 3:216; 4:1, 2, 3, 4, 6–29, 55,
    59, 67, 104, 105, 106, 153, 208, 303,
    305, 306, 319, 320, 339, 347, 360, 374,
    420, 422, 457, 473, 498, 520, 549,
    714, 752, 772; 5:37, 326, 348, 415,
    433, 436, 437
    anti-Semitism and, 4:7
    background, 4:6–9
    Beethovenian tradition and, 4:13
    as conductor, 4:6–7
    death of, 4:20
    Des Knaben Wunderhorn and, 4:20, 21, 22
    dissonance and, 4:14
    as "hypermodern conductor," 4:7, 7
    maximalism and, 4:6–9
    moderism and, 4:4
    opera and, 4:8
    "retransition" and, 4:13–14, 23
    Schreckensfanfare chord and, 4:14
    symphonic maximalism and, 4:9
    symphony and, 4:8
    "tendency tones" and, 4:28
    unfinished symphonies and, 4:6
    Verdi's Il trovatore and, 4:6
    Vienna court opera and, 4:7

Mahler, Gustav (continued)
   works of
      Das Lied von der Erde, **4:**717; **5:**318, 319
      Die drei Pintos, **4:**10
      Lieder eines fahrenden Gesellen, **4:**13
      Second Symphony, **4:**315
      "Song of the Earth," **4:**283
      Symphony no. 1, **4:**9; **5:**343
      Symphony no. 2, **4:**9, 12, 15, 18, 19, 20, 21, 22, 23, 26, 48, 192, 208, 374; **5:**347
      Symphony no. 3, **4:**11, 20, 23
      Symphony no. 4, **4:**20, 23
      Symphony no. 6, **4:**20
      Symphony no. 7, **4:**20, 692
      Symphony no. 8 ("Symphony on a Thousand"), **4:**23, 344
      Symphony no. 10, Adagio, **4:**23, 24–29, 192, 319
      Todtenfeier, **4:**9, 14, 15, 16, 17, 18–19, 20, 21, 22, 26, 374
      Urlicht, **4:**21
Mähler, Josef Willibrord, **3:**79
Mahu, Stephan, **1:**762, 765
   Ein' feste Burg ist unser Gott, **1:**762, 764
Maiden's Blush, The (Gottschalk), **3:**380
"Maidens Came, The" (Stravinsky), **5:**118
Maintenon, Mme de, **2:**97
Maitres musiciens de la Renaissance, Les (Expert), **4:**67
Ma joie premeraine (Guyot), **1:**135
Majorana, Cristoforo, **1:**454
Majorano, Gaetano. See Caffarelli
major-minor tonal system, **1:**99, 101, 394, 596; **2:**539
   Glareanus and, **1:**553–54
   ground bass and, **1:**627
   signs for, **1:**253
   See also minor mode
major scale, **1:**101
major second, **1:**495
Makropoulos Affair, The (Janáček), **4:**425
Malatesta family, **1:**281
"Malédictions de Pétrouchka" ("Petrushka's curses"), **4:**165, 166
Malevich, Kazimir, **4:**776
Malipiero, Gian Francesco, **2:**217
   La favola del figlio cambiato, **4:**749
Mallarmé, Stéphane, **3:**368; , **4:**86, 91, 111; **5:**65
Mal un muta per effecto (Cara), **1:**695–96, 697, 699
Malvezzi, Cristofano, **1:**804
Mamelles de Tirésias, Les (Poulenc), **4:**578, 578, 580–81
   Apollinaire and, **4:**578, 578, 580–81
   "drame surréaliste" and, **4:**578, 578, 580–81
"Man at Arms." See Homme Armé, L'
mandolin, Vivaldi concerto for, **2:**217
Manetti, Giannozzo, **1:**285, 286
Manfredini, Vincenzo, **3:**235

manger plays, **1:**52
Manicheism, **1:**116
Mann, Thomas, **3:**479, 480, 482, 495
   Death in Venice, **5:**225
   Doktor Faustus, **4:**774
Mann, William, **3:**503–4; **5:**318, 319, 324, 326, 327
   "Beatles Revive Hopes of Progress in Pop Music, The" (article), **5:**324
Männerchor, **3:**162–63, 202
   American barbershop quartets and, **3:**382
   Schubert choruses and, **3:**83, 84, 162
mannered style (later ars subtilior), **1:**338, 342, 356
Männergesangvereine, **3:**84
mannerism, **1:**733; **2:**122
Mannheim
   Bach (J. C.) commissions from, **2:**419
   musical establishment of, **2:**505–7, 525
Mannheim orchestra, **2:**505–6, 507, 603–4
"Mannheim rocket," **2:**506, 507, 603, 698
Mannheim School, **2:**400
Manon (Massenet), **3:**640–41, 673; **4:**89
Mantua, **1:**696, 722, 733, 823
   Monteverdi and, **2:**1–11, 14, 18
   musical tales, **1:**827
Mantua, Duke of, **1.**713. See also Gonzaga, Francesco; Gonzaga, Vincenzo
manuscripts. See written music
Manuscrit du Roi, **1:**120, 131, 133, 219, 220–21, 294
Manzoni, Alessandro, **3:**569–70, 576, 595
Mao Tse-tung, **5:**14, 84, 86
   Long March, **5:**14
Marais, Marin, **2:**321
Marcabru (troubadour), **1:**113
Marcello, Alessandro, **2:**192, 193–95
   Concerto a cinque in D minor, **2:**192
   Oboe Concerto in D minor, **2:**193–95, 215, 285
Marcello, Benedetto, **2:**192
Marcellus II, Pope, **1:**647, 649; **3:**164
Marcha solemne brasileira (Gottschalk), **3:**383
Marche funèbre, **3:**366
Märchenbilder (Schumann), **4:**556
Märchenerzählungen (Schumann), **4:**556
Marchetto of Padua, **1:**354, 355, 356
"Marchin through Georgia" (Work), **4:**275
"March to the Scaffold" (Berlioz), **3:**322, 331; **4:**191, 751
March to Tonality (Del Tredici), **5:**444
Marcia funebre in C minor (Beethoven), **2:**685, 702; **4:**13
Marcus, Greil, **5:**333, 334
   Mystery Train: Images of America in Rock 'n' Roll Music, **5:**333
   recordings editor at Rolling Stone, **5:**333
Mare au Diable, La; Bois de Chanteloup (Dudevant), **3:**349
Marenzio, Luca, **1:**728–33, 746, 773, 804; **2:**5

Solo e pensoso, **1:**728–33
Maria Barbara, Queen Consort of Spain, **2:**79, 390
Marian Alleluia, **1:**209
Marian antiphons, **1:**11–12, 94–99, 109, 389, 407, 441, 501, 513, 535
   Alma Redemptoris Mater, **1:**99, 461, 462
   Anglican rejection of, **1:**672, 675
   Dunstable and, **1:**429–33
   English High Church style and, **1:**517–18
   Josquin's Ave Maria . . . Virgo motet and, **1:**565–72
   motet and, **1:**270–73, 275–76, 501–26, 565–72
   Sancta Maria virgo, intercede, **1:**407
   seasonal round of, **1:**96
   stock epithets of, **1:**520
Marian chant sequence, **1:**134
Marian conductus, **1:**403, 406
Marian trope, **1:**410
Marian worship. See Virgin Mary
Maria Pawlowna, Grand Duchess of Saxe-Weimar, **3:**418
Maria Theresa, dowager Empress and Co-Regent of Austria, **2:**90, 156–57, 171, 462
   Haydn and, **2:**517, 526
Marie Antoinette, Queen of France, **1:**349; **2:**459; **3:**65, 66
Marienkirche (Lübeck), **2:**241
Marienleben, Das (Hindemith), **4:**769, 770–71
Marie of Champagne, **1:**118, 119
Mariés de la tour Eiffel, Les (Cocteau), **4:**589; **5:**56
Marignano, battle of (1515), **1:**711, 787
Marinetti, Emilio, futuristi and, **4:**299
Marinetti, Filippo, **5:**179
   Futurist Manifesto of 1909, **5:**178
   sintesi radiofonici and, **5:**188
Marinetti manifesto of 1909. See Futurist Manifesto of 1909
Marino, Giovanni Battista, **1:**819; **2:**37
Mariolatry. See Marian antiphons; Virgin Mary
Marissen, Michael, **2:**302, 303
Maritain, Jacques, **5:**281
   Art and Scholasticism, **5:**221
Marito giocatore e la maglie bacchettona, Il (Orlandini), **2:**435, 436, 439, 441
Mariyinsky Theater (St. Petersburg), **4:**139, 144, 750
Mark, Gospel According to, **1:**775
Marmontel, Jean François, **2:**460
Marot, Clément, **1:**706, 708, 754
Marriage (Gogol), **3:**619
Marriage (Musorgsky), **3:**619–21, 623
   opening speech, **3:**619–20
Marriage of Figaro, The (Beaumarchais), **3:**16
Marriage of Figaro, The (Mozart), **2:**478, 493, 622, 684; **3:**16, 22, 220

Mars (mythology), **2**:93

Marschalk, Max, **4**:8, 9, 10

Marschner, Heinrich August, **3**:194

"Marseillaise, La" (French national anthem), **3**:130; **4**:291

"Pour cette cause sainte" compared with, **3**:223

Marsh, Simon B., **4**:269

Marshak, Samuil, **5**:12

Marteau sans Maitre, Le (Boulez), **5**:451, 452, 463

Martenot, Ginette, **4**:24

Martenot, Maurice, **4**:240

ondes martenot and, **5**:183

Martignac, Vicomte de, **3**:209, 211

Martin, George, **5**:318, 322

Beatles and, **5**:318, 391

Martinella, La (Martini), **1**:544–45

Martinengo, Giulio Cesare, **2**:6

Martini, Giovanni Battista ("Padre Martini"), **2**:419; **3**:235

Martini, Johannes, **1**:523, 539, 544, 547, 574

J'ay pris amours, **1**:538, 539

Martino, David, **5**:164

Martín y Soler, Vincente, **2**:476, 493; **3**:235

Martucci, Giuseppe, **3**:745

Marwick, Arthur, **5**:327

Marx, Adolf Bernhard, **2**:694; **3**:287, 502

Marx, Karl, **3**:480, 488, 559; **4**:745, 746, 775; **5**:86, 88

Communist Manifesto, The, **4**:745; **5**:89

Das Kapital, **4**:745

Marxism, **3**:417, 480

Mary, mother of Jesus. *See* Virgin Mary

Mary I ("Bloody Mary"), Queen of England, **1**:675

Mary of Burgundy, **1**:455, 457

Mary Stuart (Mary Queen of Scots), **1**:675

Masaniello. *See* Aniello, Tommaso

Mascagni, Pietro, **3**:659–64; **4**:423

Cavalleria rusticana, **3**:659–61, 663

Maschera, Florentio, **1**:787

Masnadieri, I (Verdi), **3**:568

masochism, von Krafft-Ebing and, **4**:30

Mason, Daniel Gregory, **3**:769; **4**:621–22, 636, 666

Columbia University and, **4**:621

"Lincoln Symphony," **4**:621

"String Quartet on Negro Themes," **4**:621

Tune In, America: A Study of Our Coming Musical Independence (book), **4**:622

Masons. *See* Freemasons

masque, **2**:113–14

Handel and, **2**:313–14

oratorio relationship with, **2**:314

Purcell and, **2**:130–31, 132, 134

Restoration theater and, **2**:126, 127, 137

Masque of Four Seasons, **2**:130

Masque of Sleep (Purcell), **2**:130

Masque of the Drunken Poet (Purcell), **2**:131

Mass, **1**:8, 10, 12–16, 53–60, 171

Anglican, **1**:672–73

antiphons, 1.12, 1.40. *See also* as separate listing

Avignon-style, **1**:310–14, 316

Bach (J. S.) setting of, **1**:54; **2**:289, 375–77, 383

Beethoven setting of, **1**:54; **2**:376, 671, 674–75, 682, 686, 721; **3**:14

Byrd settings of, **1**:679–89

components of, 1.53–60. *See also* as separate listings

concerted, **1**:780, 788–90

concerto grosso and, **2**:178

Council of Trent mandates for, **1**:789

cyclic Ordinaries. *See* cyclic Mass Ordinaries

Du Fay setting of, **1**:434–35, 511–12

English vs. continental styles in, **1**:518

fifteenth-century characteristic cantus firmus for, **1**:486–90

fifteenth-century lofty setting of, **1**:460–500

Frankish mode theory and, **1**:86

Frankish standardization of, **1**:53–60

French-Cypriot settings of, **1**:345–49

Frescobaldi organ compositions and, **2**:43–44

as functional music, **1**:324

Haydn setting of, **2**:577, 633

"intelligibility" movement and, **1**:647, 649–53, 672

Josquin settings of, **1**:499, 555–57, 560

jubilated singing and, **1**:39, 317–26

Lutheranism and, **1**:755, 763, 769

Machaut setting of, **1**:307, 316, 317–26, 460

Monteverdi setting of, **2**:5, 10

Ockeghem setting of, **1**:473–81

"oratorio-style," **2**:375–76, 377

Ordinary. *See* Ordinary

organ works for, **2**:49

origins of, **1**:13

Palestrina settings of, **1**:632, 633–63, 724

Parisian music books and, **1**:171

parody works, **1**:574–76, 593, 641–44, 710, 788–89

Passion settings, **1**:775–77, 778, 779

polychoral, **1**:780

polyphonic elaborations and, **1**:162, 307, 310–16, 588–89

Power setting of, **1**:462

psalmody and, **1**:23–25

Requiem, **1**:88–90

Rhau setting of, **1**:763

sequence and, **1**:42

standard of, **1**:60, 61(table)

substitute motets for, **1**:518–26

Taverner setting of, **1**:612–14, 680; **2**:115–16

tropes and, **1**:50–53

unity of, **1**:495

votive, **1**:314–26, 429, 460

votive motet substitutions in, **1**:518–26, 584

See also specific compositions

Massarelli, Angelo, **1**:649, 652

"Massa's in de Cold, Cold Ground" (Foster), **4**:1075

mass culture, **3**:743

Massenet, Jules, **3**:642; **4**:454

orientalism and, **3**:390

suites caractéristiques for orchestra, **4**:454

works of

Cid, Le, **5**:493

Elegy, **5**:181

Manon, **3**:640–41, 673; **4**:89

Roi de Lahore, Le, **3**:390

Sarabande di XVIe siecle, **4**:454

Scènes alsaciennes, **4**:454

Scènes hongroises, **4**:454

Scènes napolitaines, **4**:454

Werther, **3**:640

Mass in B Minor (J. S. Bach), **2**:110, 289, 375–77, 383

Mass in D major (Beethoven), **2**:671, 674–75, 682, 686, 721; **3**:14

Mass in E-flat major (Schubert), **3**:82, 155, 428

Sanctus, **3**:101, 103, 284

Mass in Five Parts (Byrd), **1**:682–86

Mass in Four Parts (Byrd), **1**:681–82

"Mass In Time of War" (Haydn), **2**:577, 633

Mass of Our Lady (Machaut). *See Messe de Nostre Dame, La*

Mass of the Catechumens, **1**:13

Mass of the Faithful, **1**:13

Mass of the Time Signatures (Ockeghem), **1**:477–79

Mass of Toulouse, **1**:315, 316

Mass of Tournai, **1**:316, 317, 321, 590

Mass Ordinary. *See* Ordinary

Mass Ordinary cycle. *See* cyclic Mass Ordinaries

Massine, Leonid, Ballets Russes and, **4**:561, 566

Massnahme, Die (Eisler), **4**:541, 542–43, 544

"Master Array of Interval Cycles" (Perle), **4**:523

"master array," *Wozzeck* and, **4**:524

Masterpieces of the Twentieth Century, **5**:294

masterwork, concept of, **1**:139; **2**:639

symphonic music and, **3**:681

Matelots, Les (Auric), **4**:569

mathematical sublime (Kant concept), **2**:646, 732

mathematics, music and, **1**:248–50, 252–53, 410, 495, 587

senaria theory and, **1**:587–88

Mathews, Max V., **5**:498, 499

"transducer" and, **5**:495–96

Mathis der Maler (Hindemith), **4**:767, 768

Matinées musicales (Britten/Rossini arrang.), 3:13
matins, 1:11, 33, 37, 171
　Easter responsory, 1:631–32
　Liturgical drama and, 1:93, 94
Matona mi cara (Lasso), 1:714–17
Ma towu oholecho Jaakow (Lewandowski), 3:175–76
Matrimonio segreto, Il (Cimarosa), 3:34
Mattheson, Johann, 2:48, 329–30; 3:290
Matthew, Gospel According to, 1:775; 2:73, 375, 389
Matthews, Lora, 1:558, 559
Matthias, Holy Roman Emperor, 2:58
Maugars, André, 2:36–37
Maundy Thursday, 1:465
Mausefalle, Die (Wolpe), 5:13
Má vlast (Smetana), 3:452–54, 459–63, 755
Mavra (Stravinsky), 4:675
Max, Peter, 5:319
Maxfield, Richard, 5:92, 94
　Baker's Biographical Dictionary of
　　Musicians, entry in, 5:94
　Bruno Maderna and, 5:94
　Fulbright Fellowship, 5:94
　Luigi Dallapiccola and, 5:94
　Milton Babbitt and, 5:94
　Princeton, 5:94
　Roger Sessions and, 5:94
　suicide, 5:94
　works of
　　"Concert Suite from *Dromenon,*" 5:92
maximalism, 4:5–6, 191–97, 456–57
　Ballets Russes and, 4:159
　demise of, 4:345
　failure of, 4:22–29
　hysteria and, 4:56–58
　intertextual reference and, 4:11–12
maximas, 1:217
Maximinus, Saint, 1:91
Maxmilian I, Holy Roman Emperor, 1:455, 457, 544, 572, 759
Maxwell, James, Clerk, 5:472
Maxwell-Boltzmann law, 5:79
Maxwell Davies, Peter
　Eight Songs for a Mad King, 5:426–29
　L'homme armé, 5:427
　Revelation and Fall, 5:427
　Vesali icones, 5:427, 429
May, Der (Oswald), 1:143
May Day, 4:654
Mayr, Simon, 3:3
Mazarin, Jules Cardinal, 2:87, 88, 89
Mazeppa (Scheel), 3:431
mazurek, 3:357
Mazurek Dąbrowskiego (Dombrowski), 3:357
mazurka, Chopin and, 3:350, 357–60, 363, 364–65
Mazurka, op. 17 (Chopin), 3:357–60
Mazurka in F-sharp minor, op. 6, no. 1 (Chopin), 3:363, *363*
Mazurs, 3:357

Mazzini, Giuseppe, 3:567, 570
Mead, Andrew, 5:147, 148
　pupil of Milton Babbitt, 5:147
meaning. *See* interpretation; semiotics
measure
　indication of beats in, 1:251
　Notre Dame polyphony and, 1:180, 184
　Petronian "division points" and, 1:251
Measure for Measure (Shakespeare), 2:137; 3:481
measurement systems, 1:252–53
Meck, Nadezhda von, 3:791, 792, 793, 795, 796; 4:70, 142; 5:223
Medée (Charpentier), 2:89
mediant (mediatio), 1:20
media-synthesis, 3:306
Medici, Antonio de', 1:832
Medici, Cosimo I de', 1:803
Medici, Ferdinando de', 1:803, *803*
Medici, Lorenzo de' (the Magnificent), 1:531, 538, 622, 798
　SS. Giovanni e Paolo, 1:823, 834
Medici, Lorenzo de', Duke of Urbino (grandson), 1:803
Medici, Maria de', 1:812
Medici family, 1:531, 538, 803–4, 813, 818, 826, 831; 2:15, 80, 81
Medici library (Florence), 1:177
Medici Press, 1:631, 632
medieval period. *See* Middle Ages
Medinaceli, Duke of, 2:141
mediocris (Tinctoris genre ranking), 1:459, 460
Medium, The (Menotti), 5:226
Medtner, Nikolai, 4:555–58; 5:53
　Maharajah of Mysore, 4:555
　Skazki, 4:556, 557, 558
　"Medtner Society," 4:555
Meegeren, Hans van, 5:436
Mefistofele (Boito), 3:596
Méhul, Étienne-Nicolas, 3:2
Mei, Girolamo, 1:798, 799, 800, 822
Meienzit (anon. "Pseudo-Neidhardt"), 1:137
Meilhac, Henri, 3:648
Meine Seufzer, meine Tränen, BWV 13 (Bach), 2:364–65
Mein Leben (Wagner), 3:482–83, 487
Meissen. *See* Heinrich von Meissen
Meistergesang, 1:140, 141, 142
Meisterlied (master-song), 1:139–40
Meistersinger, 1:118, 139–44, 760
Meistersinger von Nürnberg, Die (Wagner), 1:139, 141; 3:28, 29, 559–60, *560,* 611, 729
Meisterstück (master-piece), 1:139
melisma, 1:11, 28, 37
　Ambrosian chant, 1:27
　Blumen, 1:140
　Caput, 1:465, 466, 468, 469
　contrapuntal voice and, 1:156, *156,* 159
　embellishments, 1:28
　English, 1:614

Gregorian, 1:28, 228–29
　Handel and, 2:331, 437
　"In seculum," 1:222–24, 227–33, 228, 229
　jubilation, 1:24, 26, 98
　Kyrie, 1:58–59
　ligatures and, 1:199, 200
　madrigal, 1:356, 364, 733, 749, 818, 819
　neuma triplex, 1:37–39
　Notre Dame school and, 1:177, 178–79, 186, 196, 199–200, 212, 214
　onomatopoetic, 1:733, 749
　proliferation of, 1:172
　prosulation and, 1:39–41
　repetition and, 1:26, 41
　sequences, 1:41–43
　word additions, 1:39–41
　See also discant
melismatic organum, 1:156–57, 159, 171, 180
Melissa's *petit air* (Lully), 2:104
Mellan, Claude, 2:35
Mellers, Wilfrid, 4:236
melodic elaboration, 2:212–13, 235
melodic motif in *Erwartung,* 4:334–35
melodic recitative, 3:625–26
melodic shape, Bach (W. F.)
　unpredictability of, 2:405, 409
melodic sixths, Chaikovsky's use of, 3:633, 636–38
mélodies, Fauré and, 4:97, 100
Mélodies orientales, 3:387
melodramma eroico. *See* opera seria
melody
　Adam of St. Victor and, 1:89–90
　Bellini and, 3:42
　cantilena and, 1:298–99
　chant and, 1:28, 34, 35, 298
　contrafactum and, 1:48, 52, 90
　Dorian, 1:83, 99, 136, 137, 270–71
　early Greek, 1:32, 33
　elaboration of, 1:149–53
　　See also ornamentation; polyphony
　Frankish hymn, 1:49, 83–86
　Frankish mode theory and, 1:81
　Hildegard of Bingen and, 1:90–91
　interval exemplifier, 1:100–104
　leisurely flow of, 1:603, 610, 634–35
　in lieder, 3:120
　Marian antiphon, 1:96–99
　motivicity and, 1:555
　oral/aural transmission of, 1:17
　pitch and, 1:33, 34–35
　repetition scheme of, 1:26, 39, 41
　rondellus technique and, 1:403
　Rossini and, 3:21
　round and, 1:331
　sequence, 1:39, 41–47
　staff notation and, 1:16
　strophic form, 1:68
　trecento characteristic, 1:363, 371
　troubadour/chant affinities and, 1:111
　Wagner and, 3:501

See also melisma

Meltzer, Richard, 5:332

"Aesthetics of Rock, The," 5:332

Allan Kaprow and, 5:332

Melville, Herman

Billy Budd and, 5:1005

Rochberg's *The Confidence Man* and, 5:436

Mémoires sur la revolution de Naples de 1647 (Moirmoiron), 3:208

Memor esto verbi tui servo tuo (Josquin), 1:554, 555, 556, 557–58

memory

basic notation and, 1:47, 60

chant transmission and, 1:26, 28, 39

mnemonic devices, 1:39, 60, 78, 102–4, 103, 162, 185–86

modal theory and, 1:78, 185

musical patterns as aid to, 1:162

nonnotated music and, 1:17, 23

Notre Dame vocal performance from, 1:184, 186

repetition and, 1:64

for staff notes, 1:102–3

See also oral tradition

Mendel, Arthus, 4:639; 5:330

Joshua Rifkin and, 5:330

Mendelssohn, Abraham, 3:166–67

Mendelssohn, Arnold, 3:174

Mendelssohn, Fanny, 3:184–86, 184, 770

Gounod and, 3:185–86, 676

lack of career support for, 3:185, 292

works of

Hiob, 3:184

Lobgesang, 3:184

Oratorium nach den Bildern der Bibel, 3:184

Trio, 3:185

Verlust, op. 9, no. 10, 3:18

Mendelssohn, Felix, 3:139, 166–86, 167, 173, 712; 4:549

Bach (J. S.) revival and, 2:381; 3:163–64, 172, 178, 179, 180, 346, 347

backlash against, 3:174, 177–79, 186

on Berlioz, 3:323

career appointments of, 3:172–73, 294

Chopin and, 3:364

concerto and, 3:275–77

concert overture and, 3:183, 419

as conductor, 3:163, 166, 172, 173, 317

death of, 3:174, 177

"elfin" style of, 3:179–81

Gounod and, 3:676

improvisation by, 3:287–88

Leipzig monument to, 3:177, 177

Lieder ohne Worte and, 3:184, 368

nationalism and, 3:166–77

oratorio and, 3:163–64, 166–74, 178, 657

press appreciation of, 3:174

as prodigy, 3:179–84

Romanticism and, 3:181–82

St. Matthew Passion performance by, 3:163–64, 167, 172

Schumann on, 3:174, 230

sister Fanny and, 3:184–85, 287, 676

in symphonic music repertoire, 3:679, 680

symphonies, 3:183, 745

teaching by, 2:736

Wagner and, 3:177–79, 227, 482

Wunderhorn poems and, 4:21

works of

Elijah, 3:173–74

Ferne, op. 9, no. 9, 3:185

Hebriden, Die, 3:183

Midsummer Night's Dream, op. 21, 3:179–80, 183, 419

Octet in E-flat major for strings, op. 20, 3:179, 180, 182–83

Paulus, 3:166–72, 177–78, 184, 230, 292, 675

Piano Concerto in D minor, op. 40, 3:275

Piano Concerto in G minor, op. 25, 3:275

Rondo capriccioso, op. 14, 3:180

Symphony No. 2, 3:184

Symphony No. 3 in A minor, 3:183

Symphony No. 4 in A major, 3:183

Symphony no. 5 (*Reformation* Symphony), 3:167, 675

Violin Concerto in E minor, op. 64, 3:181, 275–76, 277, 287, 316

Mendelssohn, Moses, 3:166

Mengelberg, Willem, 4:626, 627

Mennin, Peter, 4:649

Menotti, Gian Carlo, 5:226–27

Amahl and the Night Visitors, 5:226

Amelia al ballo, 5:226

Consul, The, 5:226

Festival of Two Worlds and, 5:226–27

Help, Help, the Globolinks!, 5:226

Last Savage, The, 5:226

Medium, The, 5:226

Pulitzer prizes and, 5:226

Saint of Bleecker Street, The, 5:226

Telephone, The (film) and, 5:226

Wedding, The, 5:226

mensural notation

Ars Nova, 1:248–87, 254

Franconiann, 1:212–17, 234–35, 238, 248

"In seculum" instrumental motets, 1:229–33, 229

invention of, 1:214, 248

modern vs., 1:253

trecento, 1:354

mensuration canon, 1:477–78

mental disintegration, as Romantic theme, 3:153

Menzel, Adolf Friedrich Erdmann von, 2:411

Merbecke, John, 1:672, 673

mercantile economy, 1:143, 630; 2:14, 237; 3:664, 682

England and, 1:678

Florence and, 1:367, 368

music publishing and, 1:691, 694, 713, 746, 782

as Protestant Reformation underlying factor, 1:753–54, 765

Mercury, Freddie, 5:328

Meredith, Burgess, 5:186

Mérimée, Prosper, 3:405, 641

meritocracy, 1:121

Merkley, Paul, 1:558, 559

Merriam, Alan, 5:381

"Merry Kate, black-browed Kate" (round-dance tune), 3:472

Merry Wives of Windsor (Shakespeare), 3:611

Merulo, Claudio, 1:787; 2:41

Mertens, Wim, *Amerikaanse repetitieve muzick*, 5:397

Mescalin Mix (Riley), 5:362–63

Mesmer, Franz Anton, 3:71, 73

mesmerism, 3:71–73

Messa della Domenica (Frescobaldi), 2:44

Messa della Madonna (Frescobaldi), 2:43–44

Messager, André, 4:62

Messe de Nostre Dame, La (Machaut), 1:307, 317–26

reconstructed "original" version of, 1:325

Messenger (*Orfeo*), 2:22–24

Messiaen, Olivier, 3:351; 4:229–42; 5:22–30, 35–37, 44, 45, 166, 189, 301

"chromatic scales," 5:26

"divisions," 5:24–25

Église de la Saine-Trinité (Paris) and, 4:230

French sixth chord and, 4:231

maximalism and, 4:229–30, 234

"modes of limited tranposition" and, 4:230–32

"motivic consistency," 5:26

"O" matrix, 5:29, 30

octatonic scale and, 4:231, 232

Pierre Boulez and, 5:1, 19, 26, 27, 37, 269

rhythmic palindromes and, 4:237–38, 239

Technique de mon language musical, 4:229, 234–35, 237

whole-tone scale and, 4:231, 232

works of

Catalogue d'oiseaux, 4:239–40

Corps glorieux, Les 4:232

Eaux de la grace, Les 4:232, 233

Livre d'orgue, 5:26

Mode de valeurs et d'intensités, 5:22–27, 29, 35, 44, 45, 153

Nativité du Seigneur, La, 4:230

Quatuor pour la fin du temps, 4:237, 238–39

"Soixante-quatre durées," 5:26

Messiaen, Olivier (*continued*)
　　Turangalila-symphonie, **4**:240–42,
　　　　5:183
Messiah (Handel), **2**:316, 325–27, 331–40,
　　377; **3**:174
　　Hallelujah Chorus, **3**:180
　　Handel's revision of, **2**:459
　　Handel's self-borrowings from,
　　　　2:331–40
　　Mozart's modernized score of, **2**:399
　　performance history of, **2**:325, 336, 340
　　unbroken performances in standard
　　　　repertory of, **2**:326
　　yearly "revivals" of, **2**:326
Metallica, plunderphonics compact disc
　　and, **5**:504
Metamorphoses (Ovid), **1**:812, 824
metaphor, musical, **1**:733–34
　　fantasia as, **2**:634–35
　　symphony and, **2**:720
metaphorical description, **2**:634, 637, 720
metaphysics, **3**:440, 610–11
Metastasio (Pietro Antonio Trapassi),
　　　　2:152–72, 172, 174, 175, 438, 476;
　　　　3:207, 611
　　aria types and, **2**:153–54, 161, 164–65
　　ban on comic elements by, **2**:434
　　Calzabigi rivalry with, **2**:455
　　death of, **2**:476
　　Demofoonte libretto and, **3**:235
　　Farinelli friendship with, **2**:172
　　Gluck *opera seria* reforms and, **2**:452, 453,
　　　　455
　　libretto style of, **2**:153–54
　　most frequently reused libretto of, **2**:158
　　Mozart's *La Clemenza di Tito* and, **2**:481
　　works by
　　　　Artaserse, **2**:153, 158–71, 419
　　　　Attilio Regolo, **2**:155–58
　　　　Didone abbandonata, **2**:154–55
　　　　Metastasis (Xenakis), **5**:78, 79, 80
　　　　*Meta-Variations: Studies in the
　　　　　　Foundations of Musical Thought*
　　　　　　(Boretz), **5**:160
　　　　Meteor Farm (Brant), **5**:422
meter, **1**:37
　　Ars Nova concept of, **1**:251–55
　　classification systems, **1**:176, 197, 355–56
　　hymn, **1**:47
　　modern concept of, **1**:251
　　Notre Dame polyphony and, **1**:175–83,
　　　　187, 197
　　quantitative, **1**:175–76
　　trecento madrigal, **1**:356, 359, 363
　　troubadour songs, **1**:114–15
　　versus, **1**:86–92
method books, instrumental, **1**:620–21
*Method of Transferring the Pitch Organization
　　of a Twelve Tone Set through All
　　Layers of a Composition, A, a Method
　　of Transforming Rhythmic Content
　　through Operations Analogous to*

Those of the Pitch Domain (essay,
　　Weinberg), **5**:160
metonymy, **3**:549
　　orientalism and, **3**:392, 410
metrical modulation, **5**:275, 279
　　in "Music and the Time Screen," **5**:279
metrical psalms
　　Clemens and, **1**:597–99
　　first English-language collection of,
　　　　1:672
　　Geneva Psalter and, **1**:754–55
metric foot, **1**:180, 191
metric system, **1**:252–53
metronome, **2**:673
Metropolitan Museum of Art, **5**:265
Metropolitan Opera House (New York
　　City), **2**:466; **3**:206, 755; **4**:7, 327,
　　423, 506, 613, 626, 751
　　Peter Grimes and, **5**:225
Metropolitan Opera Orchestra, **5**:336
Metternich, Klemens von, Prince, **3**:14, 445
Metzmacher, E., **3**:319
Mexico, **2**:261
Meyer, Leonard B., **3**:471, 599; **5**:412,
　　450–51, 471, 472
　　"Future Tense: Music, Ideology, and
　　　　Culture," **5**:411
　　"Seven, Plus or Minus Two" rule and,
　　　　5:450–51
　　organicism and, **5**:413
　　Romanticism and, **5**:412, 413
Meyerbeer, Giacomo, **3**:215, 253; **4**:8
　　background of, **3**:215–16
　　Chopin and, **3**:349
　　criticism of, **3**:227–30
　　grand opéra and, **3**:207, 215–23
　　orientalism and, **3**:389–90
　　Rossini and, **3**:216
　　Schumann (Robert) on, **3**:229, 230
　　Wagner and, **3**:227–29
　　Weber and, **3**:216
　　works of
　　　　Africaine, L', **3**:219, 389–90
　　　　Crociato in Egitto, Il, **3**:216
　　　　Huguenots, Les, **3**:215, 218–32, 286, 292
　　　　Prophète, Le, **3**:218–19
　　　　Robert le diable, **3**:217
Meyer-Eppler, Werner, **5**:52
Meyerhold, Vsevolod, **4**:498–99, 534;
　　　　5:10–11
　　Love for Three Oranges, and, **4**:498–99;
　　　　5:11
mezz'aria (half-aria), **2**:349, 351
mezzo-soprano voice, **3**:36
Michael Kohlhaas, (Klenau), **4**:774
Michelangelo, **1**:719, *719*; **4**:478
Michel de Toulouze, *1*:621
Michelet, Jules, **1**:382
Mickiewicz, Adam, **3**:345, 350, 367–68,
　　375; **4**:9, 10, 19
　　Dziady, **4**:9, 10
Micrologus (Guido), **1**:16, 153–54, 155, 185

microtonality, Carrillo and, **4**:292
Middle Ages, **1**:583
　　ballad origins in, **3**:126
　　British monasticism and, **1**:387–88
　　choral music and, **3**:162
　　church plays, **1**:52, 93–94
　　flagellant movement and, **1**:134
　　French urbanization and, **1**:120
　　Gregorian chant and, **1**:21
　　hymns and, **1**:47–49
　　literate secular repertory and, **1**:105–45
　　modal theory, **1**:29–35, 72–104
　　motet and, **1**:208–45
　　musical notation and, **1**:11
　　musical space and, **1**:577
　　music treatises and, **1**:254
　　notation and, **1**:60
　　Notre Dame school and, **1**:171–205
　　Renaissance outlook vs., **1**:382, 383, 586,
　　　　614–15
　　sacred parodies and, **1**:48
　　stanza-and-refrain poetry and, **3**:124
　　tropes and, **1**:50–53
Middle C, **1**:101, 102
middle-class values
　　English taste for Old Testament
　　　　oratorios and, **2**:315
　　Enlightenment and, **2**:302
　　grand opéra and, **3**:210–11
　　importance of nineteenth-century music
　　　　to, **2**:736
　　individualism and self-expression as
　　　　paramount, **2**:737
　　national consciousness and, **3**:63
　　opera buffa and, **2**:447, 450
　　personal liberation ideal and, **1**:579–80
　　Romanticism and, **2**:670
　　salon culture and, **3**:78–79
　　"self-made" aspirations and, **3**:63
　　as Victorian norm, **3**:36
　　See also bourgeoisie
middle style, **1**:459–60, 461, 462
　　low-style convergence with, **1**:528–29
　　motet as, **1**:501–46
MIDI, **5**:508
Midi, Le (Haydn), **2**:528
"MIDI revolution," **5**:501–2
Midsummer Night's Dream, A, op. 21
　　　　(Mendelssohn), **3**:179–80, 183, 419
Midsummer Night's Dream, A, op. 64,
　　　　(Britten), **5**:225, 250
Midsummer Night's Dream, A (Reinhardt),
　　　　4:551
Midsummer's Night Dream, A (Shakespeare),
　　　　Purcell's adaptation as semi-opera,
　　　　2:127, 130–31
Miel de Narbonne (Poulenc), **4**:575–76
Mielichy, Hans, **1**:714
"Mighty Fortress Is Our God, A" (Luther),
　　　　1:760, *761*; **2**:353, 356
　　Huguenots, Les, and, **3**:229–32
Mignon (Thomas), **3**:640; **4**:452, 454

Mikado, The (Gilbert and Sullivan), **3**:40
Mikhail Fyodorovich, Emperor of Russia, **3**:241, 242
Mikolaj z Radomia. *See* Nicolaus de Radom
Milan, **3**:570, 573
  archdiocesen liturgical chant. *See* Ambrosian rite
  Austrian control of, **2**:504
  Bach (J. C.) in, **2**:419
  court chapel, **1**:459
  French conquest of, **1**:708, 711
  Josquin and, **1**:558, 583–84
  libroni and, **1**:519
  madrigalists and, **1**:352
  motet and, **1**:518–26, 528, 530–31, 583–84
  Sforza rulers of, **1**:518, 522–23, 558, 584
  symphonic development and, **2**:500–504
Milan Cathedral, **1**:518, 519, *519*, 558, 584; **2**:419
Milanese rite. *See* Ambrosian rite
Milan studio, **5**:193, 195, 197
Milhaud, Darius, **4**:570, 573, 581, 587, 607, 615, 625, 628, 666
  American jazz and, **4**:602–5
  jazz fugue and, **4**:603–6
  Les Six group and, **4**:588
  "minute stylizations" and, **4**:609–10
  polytonality and, **4**:580–82
  riff figure in *La creation du monde*, **4**:603, 605
  surrealism and, **4**:579–80
  works of
    Création du monde, La, **4**:603, 609–10, 630
    Ipanema, **4**:582
    L'homme et son desir, **4**:582
    Saudades do Brasil, **4**:582–83
    Sérénade, **4**:585
    String Quartet no. 4, **4**:583, 584
    Symphony no. 3, **4**:585, 586–87
    Train bleu, Le, **4**:569
"Militant" (Copland), **4**:654
military bands
  percussion instruments, **2**:558
  Turkish Janissary, **2**:470–71
Military Polonaise, op. 40, no. 1 (Chopin), **3**:796
"Military Symphony" in G major, no. 100 (Haydn), **2**:558, 577
Miller, Arthur, *View from the Bridge, A*, **5**:515
Miller, Glenn, **4**:628
Miller, Henry, **5**:186
  Air-Conditioned Nightmare, The, **5**:186
  "With Edgar Varèse in the Gobi Desert," **5**:186
Miller, Robert, **5**:212
Millington, Barry, **3**:485, 492
Milsom, John, **4**:234
Milt Jackson Quartet (MJQ), **5**:337
  John Lewis and, **5**:337

Milton, John, **2**:633
Milyukova, Antonina, **3**:795
mime characters, opera and, **3**:209
mimesis (imitation), **3**:618
  Berlioz on, **3**:332–35
  definition of, **1**:474
  emulation vs., **1**:474–75
  as extroversive symbolism, **2**:539, 680, 682
  Handel's musical, **2**:317, 318–21
  Monteverdi's lexical signification vs., **2**:10, 229
  motet and, **2**:357
  of nature, **1**:331–32, 333, 349, 700–701, 711–12, 727, 728, 733–34, 747, 749; **2**:227–31, 316, 317–21, 539; **3**:277, 324, 333, 618
  polyphony and, **1**:330–36, 337
  radical humanists and, **1**:786, 802
  Scarlatti (Domenico) sonatas' lack of, **2**:392
  sigh-figure and, **1**:363
  structural, **1**:528–29, 535–36
  Vivaldi's musical and, **2**:227–31, 316, 317
mind-matter dualism, **1**:797
Minerva (mythology), **1**:550
Ming Cho Lee, **3**:624
minima, **1**:253, 354
Minimalism, **5**:351–410
  Ad Reinhardt, **5**:353–55, 361
  Angus MacLise, **5**:362
  Barnett Newman, **5**:353
  Brian Eno, **5**:351, 352, 362, 387–88
  "disco" music, **5**:367
  Edward Strickland, **5**:359
  ethnomusicology, **5**:382
  etic versus *emic*, **5**:382
  John Blacking, **5**:380–83
  Keith Potter, **5**:371
  La Monte Young, **5**:355–63
  Lou Reed, **5**:362
  Mark Rothko, **5**:353
  Michael Nyman, **5**:355
  Mies van der Rohe, **5**:353
  "mood" music, **5**:367
  Morton Feldman, **5**:351, 359
  "New Age" music, **5**:367
  Philip Glass, **5**:388–96
  Pran Nath, **5**:359, 360
  Richard Wollheim, **5**:353
  Steve Reich, **5**:351, 352, 368–88
  Terry Riley, **5**:362–68, 370
  Theatre of Eternal Music, **5**:359, 360, 361, 362
minimalist music, **5**:411, 413
minim-stems, **1**:260, 341, 355
Minkus, Ludwig, **4**:140
  Bayadère, La **4**:139
  Don Quixote, **4**:139
Minnelieder, **1**:134–39, 143
Minnesang, **1**:134–39, 142
Minnesinger, **1**:135–44, *141*, 701, 704; **3**:486

Tannhäuser as, **3**:485
three main genres of, **1**:136–37
minorities
  folklore and, **3**:122
  politics of art and, **2**:82, 112
minor mode, **1**:99, 253, 553
  chamber music rarity of, **2**:695
  as Dorian signature, **2**:120
  harmonic minor and, **1**:277
  Haydn and, **2**:695
  Mozart and, **2**:695
  See also C-minor moods
Minsky's Burlesque, **4**:617
minstrels, **1**:109–10, 129, 130, 294, 295, 299
  instrumentalists, **1**:131–317, 296
minuet
  in Abel accompanied sonata, **2**:432
  in Bach's (J. C.) Sonata in D, **2**:427
  in divertimento, **2**:547
  in Haydn's "Farewell" Symphony, **2**:532–33, *534*, 537
  in Haydn's "Joke" Quartet, **2**:547, *548*
  in Haydn's late symphonies, **2**:549, 557
  in Mozart's *Don Giovanni*, **2**:490, *491*
  Rossini and, **3**:25
  as symphony movement, **2**:506, 520
"minute stylizations," **4**:609, 613
Mirabile mysterium (Gallus), **1**:772–75
"Miracle Symphony" in D major, no. 96 (Haydn), **2**:556
Miraculous Mandarin, The (Bartók), **4**:749
"Miraculous Transport of Mount Parnassus, The" (Schütz), **2**:58
Mirate, Raffaele, **3**:585
Mir iskusstva (The world of art), **4**:149, 151, 152
Miro, Joan, **5**:52
"Miserere supplicant Dufay" (Du Fay), **1**:510–12
Misfortune on Account of a Coach (Pashkevich), **3**:235–36
misogyny, **2**:478–79, 495
  Puccini's operas and, **4**:57
Miss 1917 (Herbert-Kern), **4**:624
Missa ad imitationem style, **1**:574–75
Missa Alma Redemptoris Mater (Power), **1**:462–65
Missa Ave Regina Coelorum (Du Fay), **1**:574
Missa Caput (anon.), **1**:465–71, 472, 473, 475, 481, 489
  composer's identity and, **1**:475–77
Missa Caput (Obrecht), **1**:473, 481–83
Missa Caput (Ockeghem), **1**:458, 473–77, 482, 483
Missa cuiusvis toni (Ockeghem), **1**:479–80
Missae Josquin, **1**:520, 529
Missae Quatuor concinate ad ritum Concili Mediolani (Ruffo), **1**:650, 651
Missa Gloria Tibi Trinitas (Taverner), **1**:612–13, 614, 672; **2**:115–16
Missa Graecorum (Obrecht), **4**:722

Missa Hercules Dux Ferrariae (Josquin), **1**:560–63, 696

Missa L'Homme Armé, **2**:118

Missa L'Homme Armé (Basiron), **1**:493, 494, 501

Missa L'Homme Armé (Busnoys), **1**:486–93, 494, 495, 497–98, 499, 500, 501

Missa L'Homme Armé (Du Fay), **1**:497–99; **5**:285, 286–87

Missa L'Homme Armé (Faugues), **1**:493

Missa L'Homme Armé (Morales), **1**:634

Missa L'Homme Armé (Obrecht), **1**:493

Missa L'Homme Armé (Tinctoris), **1**:484

Missa L'Homme Armé super voces musicales (Josquin), **1**:499–500, 520, 529, 530–34, 634

Missa O magnum mysterium (Palestrina), **1**:643–49

Missa Pange lingua (Josquin), **1**:555–57, 566, 641

Missa Papae Marcelli (Palestrina), **1**:649, 650, 653–63, 673, 680, 684–85, 724; **2**:110, 111

polychoral arrangement of, **1**:782

Missa parodia. See *Missa ad imitationem* style

Missa Prolationum (Ockeghem), **1**:477–78, 480, 529, 641

Missa pro Victoria (Victoria), **1**:788–90

Missa Quant j'ay au cuer (Isaac), **1**:543–44, 545

Missa Repleatur os meum laude (Palestrina), **1**:636–41

Missarum liber primus (Palestrina), **1**:633, 634

Missarum liber secunds (Palestrina), **1**:633, 634, 649

Missarum liber tertius (Palestrina), **1**:635–37, 653

Missa Sancti Jacobi (Du Fay), **1**:434–35, 436, 437

Missa Se la face ay pale (Du Fay), **1**:532

Missa solemnis (Beethoven), **2**:671, 674–75, 682, 686, 721; **3**:14; **4**:371

Missa super Ave Maria (Févin), **1**:574–76

Missa super La Spagna (Isaac), **1**:623–25

Missa super L'Homme Armé (Palestrina), **1**:634, 635, 635–37

Missa super Ut re mi fa sol la (Palestrina), **1**:634, 635, 653

Missionary Chant, The (Ye Christian Heralds) (Zeuner), **4**:269, 271

mistaken identity device, **2**:446, 448

Mistral, Gabriela
  *Nino, El,*and, **5**:524
  Sun of the Incas, The, (Denisov) and, **5**:463

"Mit Bockstriller" (Wagner)

Mitchell, Danlee, Harry Partch and, **5**:484–85

Mitchell, Donald, **4**:680

Mitchell, Joni, **5**:315, 334

Mittheilung an meine Freunde, Eine (Wagner), **3**:493, 496, 498–501, 504

"Mit Tränen säen, Die" (Schein), **3**:704–7

mixed mode (*modus mixtus*), definition of, **1**:83

Mixolydian mode, **1**:89, 479, 509, 627

Mixolydian scale, **1**:99

mnemonic (mnemotechnic) devices, **1**:39, 60, 162
  Guidonian hand as, **1**:102–3, *103*, 104
  modal theory origination as, **1**:78, 185–86

Mo. See Montpellier Codex

mock debate. See tenso

mock-naive style
  rondeau and, **1**:122, 220
  virelai and, **1**:349–50

mock-popular genres, troubadour, **1**:113–14

modal discant counterpoint, **1**:179, 472

modal meter, **1**:176–83, 215

modal mixture, Schubert and, **3**:87, 92–94, 113, 135

modal rhythm, **1**:176, 177, 179, 180–205, 235
  Ars Nova and, **1**:260–73
  changes in, **1**:245, 249
  chief shortcoming of, **1**:199
  dactylic foot and, **1**:191–92
  Garlandia classification, **1**:197
  as mnemonic device, **1**:78, 184–86
  theoretical descriptions of, **1**:186

modal theory, **1**:105
  change to tonal, **1**:471–72, 628, 666
  chromaticism and, **1**:273–76
  Glareanus and, **1**:553–54
  Mei treatise on, **1**:799
  See also Frankish modal theory; Greek (Hellenistic) music theory

mode
  as composition guide, **1**:80–86
  concepts of, **1**:28–29, 76–86, 99–104, 111
  eight medieval, **1**:73–76
  Frankish classification of, **1**:74–75, 78–80
  Frankish numbering of, **1**:77
  Garlandia six-mode scheme and, **1**:197–98
  Greek nomenclature for, **1**:74–75, 77, 800, 801, 802
  octave species and, **1**:74
  scale and, **1**:28–29, 75–76, 100–104

"Modern Art and Its Philosophy" (Hulme), **4**:467–68, 474–75

Mode de valeurs et d'intensités (Messsiaen), **5**:22–27, 153

modern architecture, **5**:412–13

modernism, **2**:173
  historicist theory and, **3**:416
  Mozart's worldview and, **2**:600, 606
  music appreciation and, **3**:782, 783
  nationhood and, **3**:63
  origins of, **3**:599
  reactions to Beethoven and, **2**:693, 706

modern music, **3**:682

Rimsky-Korsakov on, **3**:105, 107

modern repertory. See standard reperty

modern style. See *stile moderno*

Moderwell, Hiram K., **4**:622
  ragtime and, **4**:281–82

"Modo di cantar sonetti" (song), **1**:698

Modo di fugir le cadenze, Il (Zarlino), **1**:604–5

modulation, **1**:471; **2**:539
  Bach (J. C.) and, **2**:370, 424
  Berlioz's use of, **3**:327
  flat submediant and, **3**:69
  Mozartean concerto first movement and, **2**:606, 609
  Scarlatti (Domenico) and, **2**:393–94

modus mixtus (mixed mode), definition of, **1**:83

modus ultra mensuram, **1**:191

Moengal (monk), **1**:71

moguchaya kuchka ("mighty little bunch"), **3**:397, 468, 474, 617, 625, 786
  See also New Russian School

Moirmoiron, Raimond de, **3**:208

Moldau, The (Smetana), **3**:452, 454–57, 459–60, 462, 463, 538

Molière, Jean-Baptiste, **2**:436; **3**:386
  Bourgeois gentilhomme, Le, **4**:453

mollis (re mode), **1**:102

Moment musical no. 6 (Schubert), **3**:90–94, 95, 96

moments musicaux, Schubert and, **3**:89–94, 110, 111, 295, 303; **4**:347

momentum, **1**:253

monarchism
  as anti-Freemasons, **2**:479
  Beethoven choral tribute to, **2**:722–24
  divine right belief and, **2**:88, 92, 124, 125
  English Civil War and Restoration of, **2**:124–27
  English nationalism and, **1**:405–6
  English Protestant Reformation and, **1**:670–73, 753
  Enlightenment thought and, **2**:462
  neoclassical operatic representation of, **2**:151–52
  underground criticism of, **2**:441–42, 443
  See also absolutism; *specific monarchs*

monasteries, **1**:7, 9–10, 219
  Benedictine rules and, **1**:10–12
  British musical manuscript and, **1**:387, 403, 408
  British suppression of, **1**:671, 672, 675
  chant transmission and, **1**:17
  Cluniac reform and, **1**:50
  decline as learning centers of, **1**:148, 169
  development of, **1**:9–10
  Frankish music theory and, **1**:17, 71–76, 76–78
  law code (973) of, **1**:93
  liturgical day in, **1**:10–12
  liturgical music studies in, **1**:39–40
  map of early Christian centers, **1**:9

offices of. *See* Office

polyphonic manuscripts and, **1**:156–62, 166

psalmody and, **1**:8–10

tropers (manuscripts) and, **1**:51

troubadour songs and, **1**:111, 790

votive antiphons and, **1**:94

women composers from, **2**:79

Mondestrunken (Schoenberg), **4**:461, 463–64

Mondfleck, Der (Schoenberg), **4**:462, 465, 466 *Mater, Patris Filia* (Gaspar), **1**:520–21, 528, 583

Mondo, Dominique, *Dictionnaire de musique,* **4**:68

Mondonville, Jean-Joseph Cassanéa de, **2**:427, 427

Pièces de clavecin en sonates avec accompagnement de violon in C major, op. 3, no. 4, **2**:428, 429

Monet, Claude, **4**:76–78, 77, 79, 97

Mongols, **1**:143; **3**:234

Moniot d'Arras, **1**:120–21

Ce fut en mai, **1**:120–21, 131

Moniuszko, Stanis3aw, **3**:448

Halka, **3**:447

Monk, Meredith, **5**:487–91, 493, 494, 508, 513

American Music Theater Festival and, **5**:490

Atlas, **5**:490–91, 490

Boosey and Hawkes contract, **5**:491

Dolmen Music, **5**:489

Houston Grand Opera and, **5**:490, 490

"oral" ideal and, **5**:490

monochord, **1**:30, 70, 73, 100, 103

monodia. See monody

monody, **1**:699, 802–3, 806–34; **2**:66, 74, 75; **3**:119

embellishment and, **1**:816–17

hermit songs and, **1**:818, 821

madrigals and, **1**:813–22, 823; **3**:11

Monteverdi and, **2**:1, 6

monophony, **1**:10, 143

ancient Greek **1**:799

ballata and **1**:364, 366, 371

British carol **1**:420–21

British conductus and **1**:387

conductus and **1**:198–99, 201, 203, 204, 204

French motet and **1**:220, 221, 255

Gregorian chant and **1**:47, 130, 148

Mass Ordinaries and **1**:315

medieval songs and **1**:130, 131

polyphony and **1**:148

rondeau and **1**:123

virelai and **1**:294, 295, 297, 298, 349, 366

Monsigny, Pierre-Alexandre, **3**:187

Monte Cassino abbey, **1**:100

Montéclair, Michel Pignolet de, **2**:90–91, 93

Monteux, Pierre, **4**:186

Monteverdi, Claudio, **1**:831; **2**:1–34, 1, 83, 94, 113, 291, 548; **3**:485, 488, 615, 626; **4**:18, 70, 453, 556; **5**:326, 436

career of, **1**:733; **2**:2–6

ciaccona and, **2**:37, 38

declaration of musical principles of, **2**:4–5

ground bass and, **2**:10, 35

laments of, **2**:10, 104

lexical signification of, **2**:10

librettists for, **2**:10, 14, 15, 18, 21, 23, 26–27

liturgical music of, **2**:5, 10, 18–20

madrigal and, **1**:733–38, 749, 750; **2**:1, 2–10, 11, 229; **3**:455

musical historiography and, **2**:12–13

opera and, **1**:826; **2**:1–2, 12, 13, 14, 16, 18–33

Orpheus legend and, **3**:645

parody Mass of, **1**:593

recitative convention and, **2**:21, 25

as Schütz influence, **2**:59, 66, 67, 68, 69

seconda prattica manifesto of, **2**:4, 59, 67, 254

stile concitato and, **2**:8–9

toccata as term and, **2**:41

works of

Arianna, **2**:104

A un giro sol, **1**:733–34, 735, 736, 747, 756–58; **2**:229

Combattimento di Trancredi e Clorinda, **2**:7–9, 110

Cruda Amarilli, **1**:735–38

Gloria, **2**:10

Incenerite spoglie, **2**:6, 7

Incoronazione di Poppea, L', **2**:1–2, 13, 26–33, 35, 87–88, 140, 146, 148; **3**:611

Lagrime d'amante al sepolcro dell'amata, **2**:6

Lamento d'Arianna, **2**:104

Lamento della Ninfa, **2**:10, 11

Lettera amorosa, **2**:6, 8

Madrigali guerrieri, et amorosi., **2**:6–7

Orfeo, **2**:1–2, 3, 13, 14, 16, 18–25, 26, 27, 33, 41, 87, 88, 151, 454, 455, 464

Possente spirto

Pur ti miro (attrib.), **2**:30, 32–33

Ritorno d'Ulisse in patria, Il, **2**:26

Selva morale at spirituale, **2**:10, 376

Vespers (1610), **2**:5, 10, 18–20

Vespro della beata virgine, **2**:19–20

Vi ricorda o bosch'ombrosi, **2**:22

Zefiro torna, **2**:37, 38

Monteverdi, Julius Caesar, **2**:4, 5

Monteverdi, Creator of Modern Music (Schrade), **2**:13

Montmartre, **4**:63, 70

Montpellier Codex, **1**:235–45, 406

British motet and, **1**:402, 403

Friedrich study of, **1**:266

macaronic motet and, **1**:235–36

Petronian motet and, **1**:236–45

Montpensier, Mme de, **2**:89

"mood music," **5**:367

"Moonlight" Sonata in C-sharp minor no. 14, op. 27 (Beethoven), **3**:273

Moonrise on an Empty Shore (Friedrich), **2**:611

"Moon Shone at Midnight, The" (Verstovsky), **3**:236

Moore, Douglas, **5**:198

Moore, Julia, **2**:607, 608

Moore, Macdonald Smith, **3**:772–73

Moore, Thomas, **3**:389

Moore, Thomas, *Irish Melodies,* **4**:97

Moorman, Charlotte, **5**:93–94

Opéra sextronique, performance of, **5**:93

Tonight Show appearance, **5**:94

Moors, **1**:63, 130

Morales, Cristóbal de, **1**:634, 634

morality

music and (or as), **2**:496

popular art and, **3**:673

Victorian middle-class, **3**:36, 117

morality play, oldest extant example of, **1**:93

Moran, Michael, **4**:244

"Moravian Duets" (Dvořák), **3**:753

morceaux de concert, **4**:452, 453

morceaux d'ensemble, in grand opéra, **3**:222, 223

mordant, **2**:277

Mörder, Hoffnung der Frauen (Hindemith), **4**:528

More, Sir Thomas, **1**:629, 671

Moreau, Gustave, **4**:57

Morgan, Robert, **4**:330

Morgan, Robert P., *Twentieth-Century Music,* **5**:455

Morgante maggiore (Pulci), **1**:697

Moritz, Landgrave of Hessen, **2**:76

Morlacchi, Francesco, **3**:483

Tebaldo ed Isolina, **3**:308

Morley, Thomas, **1**:423, 694, 743–44, 746; **2**:113, 115

madrigal books and, **1**:746

"Now is the month of Maying," **1**:746, 747–48

"Morning by a Lake" (Schoenberg), **4**:339

Moro, lasso (Gesualdo), **1**:739, 740

morphemes, **3**:633

Morpheus (mythology), **2**:100, 102

Morrison, Simon, **4**:217, 227

Morte! (Gottschalk), **3**:380, 383

Morzin, Karl Joseph Franz von, Count, **2**:519–20

Morzin, Wenzel von, **2**:225

Moscheles, Ignaz, **3**:351

Moscow Conservatory, **3**:632, 786; **4**:777–78

Moscow Religious Philosophical Society, Scriabin and, **4**:201

Mosè (Rossini), **3**:258

Moses und Aron (Schoenberg), 5:44, 129
Mosonyi, Mihály (né Michael Brand),
    4:369, 371
motet, 1:207–45, 247–87, 742
    Adam de la Halle and, 1:122, 220–21
    Ars nova and, 1:255–87
    ars perfecta and, 1:607
    Brahms and, 3:704, 711
    Busnoys and, 1:456–57, 456, 500
    Byrd and, 1:677–79, 686–89
    in caccia style, 1:378–80
    changed audience for, 1:236
    changed style of, 1:461, 501–46
    chanson and. See under chanson
    Clemens and, 1:593–97
    color and, 1:232, 262, 265–66, 270–71
    concerted, 1:780, 789
    Concert Spirituel (Paris) and, 2:499
    contrafactum and, 1:217–21, 227–28
    contratenor (fourth voice) and,
        1:270–73, 298–99
    as Dante metaphor, 1:286
    declamation, 1:429–33, 566, 567, 577,
        603
    definition of, 1:209
    double notation of, 1:210, 210–13
    ducal, 1:519–26
    Du Fay and, 1:282–85, 429, 441, 495,
        507–12
    English model of, 1:399–403, 405,
        406–7, 408–11, 423–33, 460, 462,
        512–18
    fancy as textless form of, 2:120
    fifteenth-century transformation of,
        1:280–87, 399–433, 461, 501–26,
        530–34
    fourteenth-century growth of, 1:232,
        236, 255–87, 311, 461
    French model of, 1:219–21, 222, 229–36,
        229, 233, 255–77, 286, 555
    Gabrieli (Giovanni) and, 1:782–86
    Gombert and, 1:590–93; 2:5
    gospel-style, 1:595
    heterogeneity of, 1:226, 272–73
    as hybrid genre, 1:221, 228, 236
    instrumental accompaniment and, 1:780
    isorhythmic, 1:266–67, 272, 278–85,
        291, 316, 378, 461, 495
    Italian model of, 1:277–87
    "Johannes Carmen" and, 1:378–80
    Josquin and, 1:530–34, 554–55, 565–72,
        577–84, 601–2, 604
    Josquin parodies and, 1:572–76
    Landini madrigal in style of, 1:374–76,
        380
    Latin texted, 1:219, 311
    Lutheran continuation of, 2:357
    Luther-Sennfl settings comparison,
        1:756–58
    macaronic, 1:233–36
    Machaut and, 1:270–73, 291–92, 298,
        301, 326, 495

madrigal, 1:366, 374–77, 380
    Marian antiphon and, 1:270–73,
        275–76, 501–26, 535
    Mass Ordinary and, 1:311, 316, 318, 632,
        636–37, 642–43
    mélange artistry of, 1:233–36
    as middle style, 1:501–46
    Milanese style of, 1:518–26, 528, 530–31,
        583–84
    Monteverdi and, 2:2, 5, 10
    Mouton and, 1:589
    notation, 1:209–11, 213–26
    occultism and, 1:271–72, 278
    origin elements of, 1:219–21, 354
    Palestrina and, 1:632, 663–66
    paraphrase, 1:501, 503, 506, 507, 556–57,
        566–67, 641
    patterning of, 1:261–67
    performance specification for, 1:783
    personal aspect of, 1:507–9, 517
    Petronian, 1:236–45, 251, 259
    Petrucci publication volume, 1:555,
        557–58, 559, 565, 579
    Phrygian polyphony and, 1:529
    as political and propaganda vehicle,
        1:277–81, 423–24
    polyphony and, 1:122, 221–36, 255, 259
    polytextuality and, 1:212, 226, 286–87
    Praetorius and, 2:54–56, 57
    ricercare and, 1:608; 2:40
    Schütz and, 2:58–59
    sixteenth-century polyphony and,
        1:588–89, 595–97
    sixteenth-century texts and, 1:595–96,
        632
    social theory and, 1:207–8
    songlike, 1:262
    Sweelinck and, 2:44
    tablatures of, 1:606
    Tallis and, 1:673, 677
    technical innovation and, 1:226–27, 255
    tenor voice's importance in, 1:259
    thirteenth-century, 1:207–45
    thirteenth-century vs.
        fourteenth-century, 1:258–67
    Tinctoris's ranking of, 1:460
    top-down composition of, 1:296–98
    trecento, 1:354
    trobar clus and, 1:226–28
    trouvère poetry and, 1:218–19, 218, 221,
        224–26, 236, 238
    Vitry and, 1:256–59, 261–65, 298–99,
        337, 378
    Willaert and, 1:601–4
motet enté, 1:221, 226–27, 234
Motetti A numero cinquanta (Petrucci
    publication), 1:559
Motetti della corona (Petrucci publication),
    1:555, 557
motetti missales, 1:518–26, 530–31, 583, 584
"Mother Goose," 4:104
Mother of Us All, The (Thomson), 5:225–26

motivic development, 1:555, 614
    Bach (J. S.) and, 2:266
    Bach (W. F.) and, 2:405–6
    Beethoven and, 3:424, 466–67
    Brahms and, 3:693–95, 699, 726,
        732–35, 739, 741
    Dvořák and, 3:756, 759
    Franck and, 3:776–77, 781
    Glinka and, 3:466–67
    Haydn and, 2:542, 545–47, 572,
        584–88, 589
    Italian keyboard sonatas and, 2:433
    Liszt and, 3:424–25
    sign system and, 2:539
    Wagner and, 500, 502–4, 735. See also
        leitmotives
    See also reminiscence motives
Mottl, Felix, 3:747
motto, 1:535, 572
    melody, 3:2
    paraphrase, 1:501, 503
"Mountain Symphony" (Liszt), 3:429–30,
    546, 699; 4:117
Mout me fu grief/Robin m'aime (French
    motet), 1:233
Mouton, Jean, 1:555, 589, 602, 603, 632,
    786; 2:5
Movements for piano and orchestra
    (Stravinsky), 5:124, 129
movie industry
    grand opéra compared with, 3:214–15
    popular entertainment and, 3:674
movies (silent), 4:562
Mozarabic chant, 1:63–64
Mozart, Constanze Weber (wife), 2:475;
    3:191
Mozart, Leopold (father), 2:463, 464, 465,
    589, 590, 608, 621, 633; 3:179
Mozart's letters to, 2:471–72, 476–77, 505,
    591
Mozart, Maria Anna ("Nannerl") (sister),
    2:463, 613, 621
Mozart, Wolfgang Amadeus, 2:462–96,
    463, 499, 589–639, 621, 651, 653,
    660, 737; 3:155, 287, 363, 440, 599,
    688, 735; 4:19, 124, 142, 145, 264,
    309, 311, 449, 454, 470; 549, 630,
    632; 5:261, 305, 326, 515, 415
    absolute music and, 2:646
    autonomous artistic creation and,
        2:589–90, 599–600
    Bach (C. P. E.) as musical father to,
        2:399, 410, 601, 606
    Bach (J. C.) as model for, 2:399, 420,
        464, 601–2, 606
    Bach (J. S.) works and, 2:399
    balance of spontaneity and calculation in
        works of, 2:591
    Beethoven's *Eroica* Symphony and,
        2:656–58
    Beethoven's use of C-minor and, 2:692,
        696, 698, 702

biographical interest in, 2:464, 474–75, 620

body portraiture of, 3:324, 638

Brendel's view of, 3:414

cadenza and, 2:609–10, 613, 614–15

canonization of, 2:399, 400, 401, 463, 464, 481, 638, 646, 738

Chaikovsky and, 3:796, 798

character portrayal by, 2:474, 475

as child prodigy, 2:463–64, 601, 607; 3:179

Classical period and, 2:16, 646–47, 739

C-minor works of, 2:692, 702

concerto and, 2:476, 601–25, 696; 3:179, 273–75, 287–88

dance music and, 3:35, 114, 796, 798

Da Ponte collaboration with, 2:476–79

death of, 2:463

earliest surviving composition of, 2:463

Enlightenment thought and, 2:463, 470, 472, 475, 479–80, 482, 494, 495, 621

esthetic debate concerning, 3:115–16

fantasia and, 2:611, 613, 624–34; 3:312, 314, 542

financial problems of, 2:607, 608, 620

as freelance artist, 2:465, 476, 589–90, 599, 600, 607–8, 620, 639

fugal sonata movements and, 2:726–27

Gluck's operatic reforms and, 2:465–66

Handel's works and, 2:399

Haydn's interrelationship with, 2:589, 590, 601, 607–8, 631, 633–39, 634, 637

as iconic figure, 2:463, 464

improvisational skills of, 2:610–11, 624, 625–31, 650; 3:287

instrumental style of, 2:589, 646

keyboard fantasias of, 2:611–13, 624–34

Köchel catalogue of works of, 2:463

last composition of, 2:463

late symphonies of, 2:590, 591–99, 641

letters of, 2:471–72, 476–77, 505, 591, 612–13

librettists of, 2:465, 466, 476–79, 481, 485; 3:16, 23, 37, 599

lieder and, 3:130–31

listener's bond with, 2:464, 474, 475, 486, 495, 590–91, 599, 611–13

Liszt and, 3:287–88

lyrical profusion of, 2:591

on Mannheim musical establishment, 2:505, 506, 603–4

marriage of, 2:474–75

Mass setting of, 1:54; 2:376

musical breakthroughs by, 2:472–75

musical inner portraiture by, 2:599

"music as pleasing" statement of, 2:471–72, 494, 655, 678

music's emotional iconicity and, 2:464, 474, 475, 486, 495, 590–91

myths about, 2:464, 606

nineteenth-century progeny of, 2:637–39

nocturnes, 3:64

operatic genres of, 2:464–96, 507, 620, 622

performance improvisation by, 2:610

performance skills of, 2:519, 590, 600, 601, 607, 610

piano concerto and, 2:476, 602–25, 696; 3:273–75, 287–88

piano trio and, 2:695

psychological studies of, 2:464, 599

Romantic esthetic and, 2:479, 486, 590, 591, 599, 622, 641, 643–45, 646, 647, 648, 655

Rossini compared with, 3:10, 13, 15, 27

Salieri legend and, 2:464, 477

Sarti and, 3:235

Schubert and, 3:113–15

singspiel and, 2:470–76, 479–85, 602; 3:188

spontaneous audience reaction to, 2:613, 651

standard repertory and, 2:94, 399

string quartet and, 2:589, 590, 631–33

subjective emotional expression and, 2:590–600

sublime breakthrough of, 2:643–44

subscription concerts sponsored by, 2:607–8

in symphonic music repertoire, 3:679, 680

symphonies concertante and, 3:277

symphony and, 2:589, 590–600

Turkish mode and, 2:470–76, 602; 3:193, 386

unbroken performing tradition of works by, 2:464

unique genius of, 2:643

unwritten ornaments and, 3:591

versatility of, 3:656–57

violin concerto and, 2:601, 602–7; 3:179

on Vogler, 3:192

whimsical fugalism used by, 2:721

whole-tone scale and, 3:101

works of

    Andante pour le clavecin, 2:463

    Bastien und Bastienne, 2:656–58

    Clemenza di Tito, La, 2:481–82

    C-minor Concerto, K. 491, 3:273–74

    C-minor Fantasy, K. 475, 3:314, 356

    Così fan tutte, 2:478–79

    Divertimento in F, K. 22 ("A Musical Joke"), 2:549

    D-minor concerto, K. 466, 3:287

    Don Giovanni, 2:478, 485–86, 492, 573, 631, 637, 645; 3:16, 23, 25, 34, 197, 235, 268 72, 347, 612; 5:117, 280

    Eine Kleine Nachtmusik, 3:64

    Entführung aus dem Serail, Die (Abduction from the Seraglio), 2:470–76, 479, 602, 678; 3:193, 386, 638

    Fantasia in C minor, K. 475, 2:625–31, 634, 637, 692

    Fantasia in D minor, K. 397, 2:624–26

    Finta semplice, La, 2:464–65

    Idomeneo, re di Creta, 2:90, 465–70, 474, 645

    Magic Flute, The (Die Zauberflöte), 2:479–85, 480, 481, 643, 676

    "Musical Joke" serenade, 3:101

    Nozze di Figaro, Le (The Marriage of Figaro), 2:478, 493, 622, 684; 3:16, 22, 220

    Piano Concerto no. 5 in D major, K. 175, 2:602

    Piano Concerto no. 11 in F major, K. 413, 2:607

    Piano Concerto no. 17 in G major, K. 453, 2:608–10, 613–25; 3:115

    Piano Concerto no. 20 in D minor, K. 466

    Piano Concerto no. 24 in C minor, K. 491, 2:696, 698, 702

    Piano Concerto no. 26 in D, K. 537 ("Coronation"), 2:610–11, 612

    Piano Concerto no. 27 in B-flat minor, K. 595, 2:607

    Requiem, 2:463

    "Rondo alla Turca," 2:471, 602

    Schauspieldirektor, Der (The Impressario), 2:481

    String Quartet in C major ("Dissonance"), K. 465, 2:631–33, 634

    String Quartet in E-flat major, K.171, 2:631

    String Quartet in G major, K. 387 (Mozart), 2:721

    Symphony no. 31 in D major, K. 297 ("Paris"), 2:612–13, 651

    Symphony no. 35 in D major ("Haffner"), K. 385, 2:589

    Symphony no. 39 in E-flat major, K. 543, 2:590, 591–99; 3:113, 742

    Symphony no. 40 in G minor, K. 550, 2:590, 591; 3:109, 798

    Symphony no. 41 in C major, K. 551 ("Jupiter"), 2:590, 646

    Veilchen, Das, 3:130–31

    Violin Concerto no. 3 in G major, K. 216, 2:602

    Violin Concerto no. 4 in D major, K. 218, 2:602

    Violin Concerto no. 5 in A major, K. 219 ("Turkish"), 2:602–5

    Zauberflöte, Die (The Magic Flute), 2:479–85, 480, 481, 643; 3:73, 188–91

"Mozart and Salieri" (Pushkin), **2**:464

Mozartiana (Chaikovsky), **4**:454, 455

Mozart-Verzeichnis (Köchel), **3**:83

Mr. Josias Priest's Boarding School (London), **2**:132

Mravinsky, Yevgeniy, **4**:795

MTV. *See* "Music Television",

Much Ado About Nothing (Shakespeare), **3**:320

Muette de Portici, La (Auber), **3**:207, 208–14, 216, 219

"Amour sacré de la patrie," **3**:212, 213

Muezzin's call (David), **3**:388–89, 397

Muffat, Georg, **2**:259

Muffat, Gottlieb, **2**:327, 329

Muhammad II (the Conquerer), Ottoman Sultan, **1**:484

Mühlhausen, **2**:239

"Můj drahý národ český neskoná!" (Smetana), **3**:462

Müller, Wilhelm, **3**:140

Müller und der Bach, Der (Schubert), **3**:143–45

Mullin, John, **5**:176

Multiple Order Functions in Twelve-Tone Music (essay, Batstone), **5**:160

mummery, **2**:113

Munich, **1**:572; **3**:227

Lasso in, **1**:713, *714*, *717*

Mozart in, **2**:90, 465

municipal music, **2**:287

Municipal Orchestra of Turin, **4**:751

Municipal Theater of Hamburg, **4**:7

Munkacsi, Kurt, Philip Glass and, **5**:391

Muradeli, Vano, **5**:9

works of

Velikaya druzhba, **5**:9

Murail, Tristan, *musique spectrale* and, **5**:499

Murger, Henri, **3**:666

Musae Jovis (Gombert), **1**:589

Musae sioniae (Praetorius), **1**:765–66, 767–68

Muse and Fashion (Medtner) (book), **4**:555–56

Musée Condé (Chantilly), **1**:342

Musen Siziliens (Henze), **5**:344–45, 346

Muses, **1**:804

Musette, **4**:696

museum culture, **2**:639, 650

symphonic music and, **3**:676–82

Musica, **1**:69–76, 148, 248, 552

cosmology of, **1**:70–71, *71*

illuminated manuscript, **1**:71, *71*

late classical texts on, **1**:69–72

Missa L'Homme Armé unity and, **1**:495–96

music differentiated from, **1**:71, 495–96

music academies, 2.504. *See also* academies, Florentine

musica cum littera, 1.199–205. *See also* motet

Musica dei donum (Clemens), **1**:709, 710

Musica disciplina (Aurelian), **1**:76

Musica enchiriadis (Frankish treatise), **1**:*17*, 44, 45, 46, 47

polyphony and, **1**:148, 149, 151–52, 153, 154, 435

musica falsa *See* musica ficta

musica ficta, **1**:273–76, 291, 293, 343, 512, 596, 597, 628

See also chromaticism

Musica (Hermann), **1**:99

musica humana, **1**:70, 71

musica instrumentalis (audible music), **1**:70, 71

musical Americanism, Copland and, **4**:662

Musical Angels (d'Alessandro), **1**:267

musical composition. *See* composition

musical content, Hanslick's definition of, **3**:441

musical depiction. *See* musical expression

Musical Dictionary (Koch), **2**:622

musical entertainments, *See also* concert

musical entrepreneurs, **3**:252

musical expression, **2**:336, 409–10, 416, 427, 720

affective style and, **1**:738

in Beethoven's late quarters, **2**:684–88

as beyond translation of intent, **2**:680

Chaikovsky's emotional channeling and, **3**:632

classical purpose of, **2**:642–43, 649

concerto soloist-orchestra interaction and, **2**:619–20

depiction theory and, **3**:332–35

as "great" music, **2**:649–50, 655

instrumental vs. vocal, **2**:222, 539

literary music and, **3**:296

madrigal and, **1**:724–51, 815, 816, 821; **3**:428

Mozart and, **2**:464, 474, 475, 486, 495, 590–600, 606, 613, 619, 621

obscurity and, **2**:670

principle of "objective," **1**:798

representational style and, **2**:643

rhetorical embellishment and, **1**:816–17, 821

Romantic purpose of, **2**:486, 599, 641, 648–49, 659, 720

sacralization of, **2**:650

as speech representation, **1**:827, 829, 830

virtuosity and, **3**:254–55

See also introspection; semiotics; signification; subjectivity

musical foot. *See* metric foot; *pes*

Musical Form as Process (Asafyev), **3**:632–33

Musical Instrument Digital Interface. *See* MIDI

Musicalisches Blumen-Büschlein, op. 2 (Fischer), **2**:260

Musicalische Vorstellung einiger biblischer Historien, **3**:65

Musicalis Sciencia/Sciencie Laudabili (anon.), **1**:267, 268–70

Musica (Listenius), **1**:550–51

"Musical Joke, A" (Divertimento in F major, K. 522) (Mozart), **2**:549

Musical Joke, K. 522 ("The Village Musicians") (Mozart), **4**:275

musical jokes. *See* joke, musical

musical journalism, **2**:692; **3**:289–90

musical nationalism. *See* nationalism

musical notation, obsolescence of, **5**:177

Musical Offering, The (J. S. Bach), **2**:306, 384–85; **4**:361, 465

musical perfection. *See* ars perfecta

Musical Quarterly (journal), **4**:621, 627, 640; **5**:40

musical rhetoricians, **1**:550

musical semiosis. *See* semiotics

musical sociology, **1**:207, 219, 453

musical sound

beautiful vs. unsettling, **2**:363–73, 471–72, 493–94, 645, 677–78

Counter Reformation Mass reform and, **1**:650

Counter Reformation music and, **1**:772

extroversive symbolism and, **1**:642–43

fifteenth-century courtly art and, **1**:448, 452

hearing habit changes and, **1**:471–72, 739

introversive semiotics and, **2**:539–41, 591

number ratios and, **1**:70

onomatopoeia and, **1**:331–32, 333, 349, 364, 711, 717, 733, 749; **3**:25–27

pictorialisms and, **1**:749, 750

pitch and, **1**:35

radical humanism and, **1**:802–3

recording of, **1**:65

See also literary music; musical expression

musical space, **1**:577, 579

musical style

development of affective, **1**:738

evolution theories of, **1**:580

fourteenth-century technical progress and, **1**:247–48, 266

See also specific styles

musical tales. *See* favole in musica

musical taste, **2**:87, 173

allemande/gavotte contrast and, **2**:274–75

beauty of sound and, **2**:363, 368

democratization of, **3**:251, 292

displacement of patronage in forming, **2**:639

Enlightenment and, **2**:363, 470

German, **2**:259

grand opéra courting of, **3**:211

professional reviewers' influence on, **2**:571, 639

for symphonies, **2**:498

musical theater. *See* opera; theater

musical tradition, **3**:287

as innovation enabler, **3**:723–24, 726

musica mundana, 1.38, 1.271. *See also* cosmic harmony
music analysis
  earliest instances of, 1:40
  Hoffmann and, 2:705–6
  See also criticism; musicology; theory
Music and Society (pamphlet) (Siegmeister), 4:658
"Music and the Time Screen" (Carter), 5:277
  metrical modulation in, 5:279
Musica Nova (ricercari collection), 1:588, 607, 617
musica poetica, meaning of, 1:551, 553
music appreciation, 3:442, 782–83, 785, 786
  courses in, 2:540, 738
  musica practica, 1:248, 551
musica recta, 1:275
"Music as a Gradual Process" (Reich), 5:371, 374, 375
Musica son (Landini), 1:355
musica speculativa (music of reason). *See* Musica
Musica stricta (Volkonsky), 5:461–62
Musica su due dimensioni (Maderna), 5:211
musica theoretica (rules and generalization), 1:551, 552, 553
Musica Transalpina (Yonge anthology), 1:744, 746
music audience. *See* audience
Musica Viva, 4:772
music criticism. *See* criticism
music drama, Wagner and, 3:7, 488, 521, 547, 567
"Music Discomposed" (Cavell), 5:42
music education
  academies and, 1:798–801, 818; 2:504
  Carolingian, 1:5
  classical music and, 2:650, 738
  conservatories and, 2:149, 650, 756; 3:286–88, 468, 617
  counterpoint texts and, 1:669–70
  Czerny textbooks and, 2:606
  ear training and, 1:99, 100–104
  Hanslick's impact on, 3:442
  Lutheran songbook and, 1:760–61
  nineteenth-century importance of, 2:736
  Notre Dame/University of Paris and, 1:171–72, 196–98
  oral examples and, 1:18
  Palestrina's music used in, 1:666
  Paris Conservatory and, 2:736; 3:262, 287, 385, 676, 774
  polyphony and, 1:148, 168
  quadrivium and, 1:4–5, 6, 69
  singing texts and, 1:550–51
  sonata form and, 2:584
  standard repertory as basis of, 2:234
  twelfth-century shift in, 1:148
  universities and, 3:769, 783
music festival, German, 2:385

Music for 18 Musicians (Reich), 5:383–88
Music for Piano (Cage), 5:65
Music for Radio (Copland), 4:661
Music for Strings, Percussion and Celesta (Bartók), 4:394, 398, 399, 401, 402, 421
Music for the Magic Theater (Rochberg), 5:411, 415–18, 420, 423
Music for the Theatre (Copland), 4:615–16, 617–19, 620, 621, 627, 629; 5:3
"Music from across the Alps" (Yonge anthology), 1:744, 746
Music from Mathematics (record), 5:496
musiche, 1:813–18, 823–26
music historiography
  anachronism and, 1:143–44, 792
  assumption of progression in, 1:738–39
  Bach's (J. S.) elevated status in, 2:235
  on Bach's (J. S.) musical transgressions, 2:301–2
  as biography, 2:12–13
  Burney's history and, 1:388–89
  change and, 1:812
  context and, 1:689, 739; 2:234–35, 389–90
  Darwinian view of, 2:396–97
  earliest emergence of "artful" music and, 1:267–70
  English nationalism and, 1:405–6
  English style and, 1:423, 429
  era concepts and, 1:281, 380–85, 429, 471, 483, 547, 583
  false assumptions in, 2:399
  fifteenth-century harmonic changes and, 1:472
  first general survey of Western music and, 1:388
  Harley (978) manuscript and, 1:387, 388
  historicism and, 3:415, 665–66
  interpretation and, 2:682
  Josquin's *Ave Maria... Virgo serena* dating and, 1:477–79
  Josquin's rediscovery by, 1:560
  lack of "usable past" view and, 1:383–84
  Mendelssohn's place in, 3:179
  mid-eighteenth-century gaps in, 2:400, 432, 434–35
  misleading artifacts and, 1:129–31
  modern vs. contemporary context and, 1:739, 741
  nationalism and, 3:8
  new periodization of music (1840) and, 2:646
  nineteenth-century birth of, 2:235, 736
  Notre Dame school and
  opera buffa's significance in, 2:434–35
  philosophy of, 1:144–45
  Quantz mid-eighteenth century encyclopedia, 2:218
  Renaissance periodization and, 1:281, 380–85, 471, 483
  retrospective advantage in, 1:689, 739

  Smetana's portrayal in, 3:447
  stylistic evolution and, 1:245
  Sumer is icumen in significance in, 1:387–88, 388, 389
  tonality and, 1:471
  women's underrepresentation in, 2:78–82
  written music's importance to, 1:1
Music in the Moment (Levinson), 5:511–14
  "concatenationism" and, 5:511, 512
Music in Western Civilization (Lang), 2:738; 3:229
musicisti futuristi, 5:178
music journalism
  nineteenth-century birth of, 2:706, 736, 737
  See also criticism
music lovers, earliest literate, 1:542
music notation. *See* notation
musico. See trousers role
Music of Changes (Cage), 5:64, 66
"Music of the Beatles, The" (Rorem), 5:325
"Music of the Present and the Holistic Art of the Future, The" (Brendel), 3:422
musicology, 1:173; 3:7, 442
  British twentieth-century, 1:403
  as by-product of German nationalism, 2:388, 389
  feminist, 2:78, 82, 619–20
  Garlandia classification and, 1:197
  genetic fallacy and, 1:221
  Grocheio's social theory and, 1:207–8
  nineteenth-century birth of, 2:388, 736
  pre-thirteenth-century verse-music rhythmic style and, 1:114
  trecento repertory rediscovery and, 1:383
  See also music analysis; music historiography
music publishing, 1:691–94
  Bach (J. C.) and, 2:419
  Beethoven and, 2:674, 675, 682, 736
  as bibliophile novely, 1:693
  canzona and, 1:787
  Christmas carols and, 1:420
  commodification of music through, 1:542, 691, 694, 713, 746, 754, 782; 2:736
  Corelli and, 2:177, 178
  cross-fertilization and, 1:65, 550–51, 694
  early keyboard work and, 2:48
  in England, 1:678, 679, 692, 694, 741, 746
  in France, 1:692, 694, 706, 708, 710
  Frescobaldi and, 2:36, 37–38, 39
  in Germany, 1:550–51, 691–92, 701, 760, 762, 765
  Handel and, 2:306
  Haydn's quartets as written for, 2:541
  instrumental method books and, 1:620–21

music publishing (*continued*)
  in Italy, **1:**499–500, 542–43, 544, 691,
    693, 722, 781, 790–92
  Josquin and, **1:**499, 500, 542, 549, 550,
    559, 560–61
  Lasso and, **1:**713–14, 717
  Lutheran chorales and, **1:**760, 762, 763,
    765–66
  madrigals and, **1:**723, 724, 728, 733, 741,
    744, 746, 817–18
  meterical psalms and, **1:**597–98
  monodic "revolution" and, **1:**809,
    812–22
  movable music type's impact on,
    1:692–93, 692
  as nineteenth-century big business,
    2:736
  "nuove musiche" and, **1:**812–22
  organ bass books and, **1:**780, 781–82
  organ chanson arrangements and,
    1:786–87
  partbooks as earliest products of, **1:**542
  Passion text setting and, **1:**776
  Petrucci and, **1:**499–500, 520, 529,
    542–43, 544, 555, 557–58, 559,
    560–61, 563, 565, 574, 579, 606,
    666, 691–95, 697, 698, 699
  salon music and, **3:**78, 79
  Scarlatti (D.) and, **2:**392, 396
  secular music and, **1:**689
  sheet music, **1:**420, 606; **3:**212, 633
  Strozzi and, **2:**75–76
  of textless, instrumental chamber music,
    1:542–46
  vernacular songbooks and, **1:**693–94
  Willaert and, **1:**600–601
  women's compositions and, **2:**78–83
music scholarship. *See* musicology
"Music Television," **5:**506, 511
music theory. *See* theory
music trance, **3:**329, 646
  Bellini's "Casta diva" aria and, **3:**71
  darkened theaters and, **3:**564
  Field's creation of, **3:**71
  Romanticism and, **3:**71–73, 77, 86–87,
    94
musika, **3:**234
Musikalisches Opfer (J. S. Bach), **2:**306,
  384–85
Musique concrete, **5:**187–88
musique D'ameublement, **4:**570
musique de l'avenir, la, **3:**421
Musique en Russie, La (Cui), **3:**786
musique mesurée a l'antique, **4:**449
musique naturele (poetry) vs. *musique artificiele*
  (music), **1:**337
Musique pour les soupers du Roi Ubu
  (Zimmerman), **5:**419
Muslims. *See* Islam
Musorgsky, Modest, **3:**617–31, 617, 644
  on beauty, **3:**440
  Chaikovsky on, **3:**441

nationalism and, **3:**617
New Russian School and, **3:**397, 468,
  474, 617
orientalism and, **3:**397
realism and, **3:**617, 618, 622, 624, 625,
  629, 631–32
Teatr-buff and, **3:**647
works of
  Boris Godunov, **3:**544–45, 623–32,
    624, 638, 754
  Marriage, **3:**619–21, 623
Musorgsky, Petrovich, **4:**66, 70, 89, 151, 153,
  181, 207, 428, 440
Musset, Alfred de, **3:**76, 322
Mussolini, Benito, **4:**476, 477, 478,
  746–47, 751, 752, 753
  Stravinsky and, **4:**478
Mustel, Auguste, **4:**145
Mustonen, Andres, Hortus Musicus and,
  5:401
Musurgia universalis (Kircher), **2:**75
Muti, Riccardo, **3:**579, 591
Muxfeldt, Kristina, **3:**116
muzïka, **3:**234, 235
My Home (Dvořák), **3:**755
Myaskovsky, Naxos, **5:**9
Myaskovsky, Nikolai Yakovlevich, **4:**777,
  778, 795
Myrick, Julian, **4:**254
Mysliveček, Josef, **2:**158
Mysterium (Scriabin), **4:**192, 224–27, 283,
  345; **5:**186; 347, 359
*Mystery Train: Images of America in Rock 'n'
  Roll Music* (Marcus), **5:**333
"mystic chord," Scriabin and, **4:**216, 217, 219
"mystical symbolism," Scriabin and, **4:**201,
  205
mysticism, **1:**11, 12, 91
  Counter Reformation and, **1:**771,
    772–75
  Lasso *Prophetiae Sibyllarum* and,
    1:720–21, 722
  motet and, **1:**285
  nature and, **3:**158, 200, 202
myth of perfection, **2:**235
mythology
  English masques and, **2:**113
  French court opera and, **2:**91, 92–93, 94,
    97–108
  Germanic, **3:**127, 492
  German Romanticism and, **3:**127
  neoclassical opera and, **2:**151–52
  Russian nationalism and, **3:**241
  as Wagner theme source, **3:**480, 492
  See also folklore; Greek mythology

N

Nabokov, Nicolas, **5:**293, 294
  Congress for Cultural Freedom and, **5:**21
Nabokov, Vladimir, **3:**20; **5:**293
Nabucco (Verdi), **3:**570–73

Va, pensiero, sull'ali dorate, **3:**570–73
Nach dich, Herr, verlanget mich (Bach), **3:**729
Nadar, Félix, **3:**215, 319
Nägeli, Hans Georg, **3:**163
Name of the Rose, The (Eco), **5:**434–35
Namier, Sir Lewis, **3:**375, 376
Nanino, Giovanni Maria, **3:**102–4
Naples, **2:**140–50, 153, 158, 419
  Farinelli and, **2:**166, 167, 172
  first opera house and, **2:**140
  Metastasio and, **2:**154–55
  opera seria audience behavior at, **2:**174
  Pergolesi and, **2:**438
  Rossini and, **3:**11
  Scarlatti (Alessandro) and, **2:**141–250,
    186
  Scarlatti (Domenico) and, **2:**390
  Tinctoris in, **1:**453, 536
Napoleon I, Emperor of France, **2:**12, 671,
  673; **3:**22, 121, 252, 357
  Beethoven and, **2:**655–56, 659, 672, 673,
    689, 722
  Code Napoléon and, **3:**15
  defeat of, **3:**163, 198, 211
  Egyptian campaigns of, **3:**387
  Patriotic War of 1812 and, **3:**242
  Vienna occupation by, **3:**3
Napoleonic Wars, **2:**388, 645, 655, 672,
  736; **3:**206
  Congress of Vienna and, **2:**673, 673–74,
    722, 724
  Haydn Masses and, **2:**577
  Russia and, **3:**242
Nápravnik, Eduard, **3:**458
narodnïye pesni, **3:**233
narodnost', **3:**237–41
narrative poetry, **3:**124, 126–27
  cantiga and, **1:**129
  Machaut and, **1:**290, 297, 332
  trouvère songs and, **1:**119–21
Narváez, Luis de, **2:**47
Nath, Pran, **5:**359, 360
national anthems, **1:**18
  Austria, **3:**130
  England, **3:**130
  France, **3:**130, 223
  Germany, **3:**130
  Israel, **3:**456
  Poland, **3:**357
  United States, **3:**120, 381
National Archaeological Museum
  (Delphi), **1:**32
"national character" concept, **2:**670; **3:**62
National Conservatory of Music (New
  York City), **3:**755, 760, 765, 768; ,
  4:246
National Endowment for the Arts (U.S.),
  3:385
  Final Alice and, **5:**442–43
national identity. *See* nationalism
nationalism, **3:**8
  Bach (J. S.) and, **2:**385, 388, 390

Beethoven and, 2:689
Blut und Boden and, 3:178
Brahms and, 3:703–4, 710–12, 719
change in nature of, 3:62–63
Chopin and, 3:344–47, 357–58, 367, 375–76, 753
classical music and, 2:388
as cosmopolitanism response, 3:745
Czech, 3:67, 445, 451–56, 463
Dvořák and, 3:753
English, 1:389, 405–6, 409, 670, 746; 2:306, 313
English oratorio and, 2:238, 315, 321, 385, 633
English seventeenth-century opera and, 2:133, 138
ethnicity and race and, 3:62–63, 178, 480
ethnocentricity and, 2:739
exoticism and, 3:192–93, 347–48, 386, 393
folklore and, 3:122
French, 3:205–6, 567, 775–76
German, 1:138, 141; 2:235, 259, 385, 388, 389, 670, 689, 739; 3:8, 14, 62, 121, 123–24, 129, 158, 160–68, 171, 177, 194–97, 205, 345, 417, 422, 704, 710–12, 719
Handel and, 2:238, 385
Herder's philosophy and, 3:121
historical opera and, 3:205–6
Hungarian, 3:1–2
"I" and "We" outlook and, 3:61–63, 124, 163
idealism and, 3:14
Italian, 1:666; 3:62, 567, 660
Mendelssohn and, 3:166–77
Minnesinger art and, 1:138, 139, 141
musical profundity and, 2:235
music as vehicle for, 2:385, 388, 390
nineteenth-century composers and, 2:736
nineteenth-century development of, 2:385, 388
oratorio rebirth and, 3:163–66
orientalism and, 3:192–93, 393
patriotism and, 3:178, 346, 386
Polish, 3:344, 375–76
pre-modern absence of, 1:141–42
Protestantism and, 1:754, 765
rescue opera and, 3:249
Romantic, 3:62, 63, 155, 158, 162–63
Russian, 3:230–33, 237–42, 241, 242, 249–50, 468, 471, 478, 617, 786–88
Schumann and, 3:344–46
as separate superiority, 2:321
in seventeenth-century Europe, 2:139
Smetana and, 3:443, 445–59, 462
stereotyping and, 3:33
tourist, 3:347, 753
Wagner and, 3:479, 490, 491, 559–61, 566
National Library (Madrid), 1:183

National Library of Turin, 1:345; 2:217
national opera, 3:250, 760, 763
in Slavic lands, 3:447–48
Smetana and, 3:447–51
for United States, 3:760, 763, 764
Weber's *Der Freischütz* as, 3:194–97, 763
"National Music" (Schoenberg) (essay), 4:703
National Organization for Women (NOW), 5:307
National Socialism. *See* Nazi Germany
National Socialist (Nazi) Party, 4:747–48
National Symphony Orchestra, 5:107
National Theatre (Pest), 3:1
National Training School (England), 3:651
"nation" concept, 3:62–63
Native Americans, 3:767, 768
Dvořák's *Hiawatha* and, 3:764–66
Nativitas Alleluia, 1:291
Nativité du Seigneur, La (Messiaen), 4:230
Nativity, 1:54, 209, 566
natural harmonic series, 1:30, 588
naturalism, 3:673
eighteenth-century stylistic changes and, 2:432–34, 437
verismo and, 3:440, 641, 658, 660, 661
natural language, 1:801
natural music. *See* poetry
natural philosophy, 1:586–87, 588
natural speech, 3:619–21, 624
natural supernaturalism, 3:73
nature, 1:332
art as imitation of, 2:643; 3:277, 324, 333, 618
Berlioz and imitation of, 3:324
faux-naïve virelai and, 1:349–50
in Germanic mythology, 3:127
horn evocation of, 3:158, 200, 202
lied genre and, 3:144, 155, 158
musical embodiment of, 3:619
musical homologies with, 1:801–3
musical imitations of, 1:331–32, 333, 349, 700–701, 711–12, 727, 728, 733–34, 747, 749; 2:227–31, 316, 317–21, 539; 3:277, 324, 333, 618
"true" representation of, 3:36
See also pastorals
nature mysticism, 3:158, 200, 202
Naumann, Emil, 3:676, 681, 785
nawba (*nuba*), 1:108
Na zarye tï eyo ne budi (Varlamov), 3:634
Nazi Germany, 2:369; 3:177, 462–63; 4:550
art glorifying, 2:111
Carmina burana and, 1:138
NBC Symphony, 5:8
Neapolitan harmony, 2:142, 144, 146, 634
Bach (J. S.) and, 2:213, 215–16
Beethoven and, 2:697, 698
Carissimi and, 2:74
Haydn and, 2:584
Mozart and, 2:631
Romantic introspection and, 3:96

Schubert and, 3:88–89, 93–94, 96, 100, 112
nebular hypothesis, 2:634
nega (desire), 3:399, 401–4, 407
Negro Episode (Gilbert), 4:613
"Negro Fantasy" (Harris) 4:672
Negro music, 4:612–13
Negro Rhapsody (Goldmark) and, 4:614
Neidhardt von Reuenthal, 1:136–38
Neinsager, Der (Brecht), 4:547
neoclassicism, 1:797–834; 2:15, 150–65, 434; 5:353
classicism vs., 2:151–52
Enlightenment and, 2:706
Gluck and, 2:452, 453, 457–58, 465–66
Metastasio librettos and, 2:152–65
Musorgsky and, 3:618
Wagner and, 3:611
"neo-exoticism," 4:609
neonationalism, 3:504; 4:161, 175, 378, 609, 610, 658, 664, 666
Neoplatonism, 1:172; 3:557
beliefs of, 1:69–72, 271
humanism and, 1:615, 616
neoprimitivism, 4:21, 159, 188
neorealism, 3:674
"neotonalists," 5:454
Ne poy, krasavitsa (Balakirev), 3:394–97, 398, 474
Ne poy, krasavitsa (Glinka), 3:393–95
Ne poy, krasavitsa (Pushkin), 3:393–99
Ne poy, krasavitsa (Rachmaninoff), 3:395–99, 400, 401
Nero, Emperor of Rome, 2:1, 27, 30, 88
Nerone, Il (adapt. from Monteverdi), 2:140
Netherlanders, 2:45, 48
Netherlands, 2:259; 3:212
Clemens and, 1:593–99
English composers in, 2:45, 47
organ music, 2:44, 56
See also Belgium
Netherlands Opera, *Nixon in China* and, 5:518
"Neue Bahnen" (Schumann), 3:683, 685
Neue Klassizismus, Der (Schoenberg), 4:678
Neue Sachlichkeit, 4:527, 533, 540, 541, 545, 549, 550, 692, 768, 871
Neue Zeitschrift für Musik (journal), 3:421, 439
Brendel and, 3:416–17, 683, 685
Judenthum in der Musik, Das article, 3:177–79, 227–28
music criticism and, 3:291, 292
Schumann and, 3:174, 291, 292, 340, 416, 683–84
"Neuf mélodies" (Berlioz), 4:4:97
neuma triplex, 1:37–39
prosulae to, 1:40
Neumeister, Erdmann, 2:341, *341*, 342, 348, 351, 354, 377
neumes, 1:13–16, *15*, 16, 17, 22, 37, 60, 214
definition of, 1:13–14

neumes (continued)
  Frankish, 1:14–16, 17–18, 62, 76
  modal meter and, 1:159
  ornamental, 1:24, 48, 57, 105
  on ruled staff, 1:16, 62, 99–100
  shapes of, 1:22–23, 60, 176, 177
  staffless, 1:60, 93, 105, 138, 155
  stroke ("fold") added to, 1:181
  See also ligatures
neurohypnotism, 3:71
Neverov, Yanuariy, 3:237–39, 241
"Nevsky Pickwickians," 4:146, 149
New Age meditation, 1:66
"New Age" music, 5:367, 408
"new art of music." See Ars Nova
Newcomb, Anthony, 2:80; 3:202, 205, 311
"New Complexity," 5:475–76
"New Deal," 4:647
Newe deudsche geistliche Gesenge (sacred song
    collection), 1:762, 765
New England Conservatory (Boston),
    3:769
New England Idyls (MacDowell), 3:768
New England Transcendentalism, 4:243,
    267
New German School, 3:416–22, 426, 427,
    547, 564, 594; 4:3, 16, 195, 263, 341,
    353, 358, 363, 371, 552, 579, 639, 687,
    702; 5:16, 159, 222, 437
  absolute music and, 3:698
  art and truth debate and, 3:438–41
  Beethoven and, 3:439, 440, 464
  Beethoven's Ninth Symphony and,
    3:719–20
  Berlioz and, 3:421–22, 685
  Brahms and, 3:418, 684, 685, 692, 719,
    727
  Chaikovsky and, 3:799
  chamber music and, 3:731
  Liszt and, 3:417–22, 426, 428–38, 676,
    685, 692
  opposition to, 3:418, 441, 531
  Schumann and, 3:482, 683
  Smetana and, 3:443, 446, 449, 451, 476
  symphonic music's preemption by, 3:675
  Wagner and, 3:418, 421, 483, 531, 676,
    729
"New Grand Overture" (Haydn). See
    "Oxford" Symphony
New Grove Dictionary of American Music, The
  Elvis Presley in, 5:314
  John Cage in, 5:76
New Grove Dictionary of Music and Musicians,
    The, 1:549, 579, 832; 2:240; 4:256;
    5:301, 381, 382
  John Zorn in, 5:504
New Grove Dictionary of Opera, The, 4:423
New Harvard Dictionary of Music, 3:351
Newlin, Dika, 5:170
  Arnold Schoenberg and, 5:170
Newman, Barnett, 5:353
  Ornament 1, 5:353

Stations of the Cross, 5:353
Newman, William S., 2:427–28
New Masses, The, 4:654, 655
Newmarch, Rosa, 3:788
"new music" (nuove musiche). See monody
New Music Edition, 5:153
New Music Hall (Dublin), 2:326
New Oxford History of Music, 3:8
New Republic, The, 5:335
New Russian School, 3:393, 395–97, 431,
    468, 474, 617, 625, 786, 787–88
"New Sa-Hoo, The" (Farnaby), 2:48
New School, 5:93
newspapers. See press
New Testament. See Gospels; specific books
New Testament oratorio, Messiah as,
    2:325–40
New World Symphony in E minor, op. 95
    (Dvořák), 3:754, 755–66, 770, 772,
    773, 774
New York City
  Carnegie Hall, 3:679, 755
  Dvořák in, 3:753, 755, 760, 765, 768
  Metropolitan Opera House, 3:206
  music criticism in, 3:290
  nineteenth-century symphonic music,
    3:679
New York City Ballet, 5:122
New York Herald Tribune, 3:290
New York Metropolitan Opera, 1980 and
    1990 opera commissions, 5:515
New York Museum of Modern Art, 5:58
New York Philharmonic Orchestra, 3:679,
    755, 783
New York Philharmonic Society, 3:679
New York Philharmonic-Symphony, 5:75,
    88, 96, 113, 346
New York Pro Musica ensemble, 1:93, 94
New York Review of Books, 5:305
New York Times, 3:290
Neyts, J. F., 1:77
Nibelungenlied (epic), 3:492, 501
"Nice Dilemma, A" (Gilbert and Sullivan),
    3:652
Nicene Creed, 1:34
Nicholas, Saint, 1:93, 378
Nicholas of Clémanges, 1:378
Nicolaus de Radom, 1:346–49
Nicolaus Geraldi de Radom, 1:348
Nicole d'Oresme, Bishop of Lisieux, 1:248
Nicolini (Nicolo Grimaldi), 2:155
Nicomachus, 1:29, 70
Nidaros, archbishop of, 1:392–93
Niecks, Frederick, 3:371, 374
Niederrheinisches Musikfest. See Lower Rhine
    Music Festival
Nietzsche, Friedrich, 2:732; 3:478, 558,
    732; 4:53, 310; 5:415
  on beauty, 3:440, 561
  on Bizet's Carmen, 3:642–43
  decadence and, 4:30
  Wagnerian dualism and, 5:77

Nightingale, The (Stravinsky), 4:204, 675
Night Music, Lorca and, 5:422
Night Office. See matins
Night of the Four Moons (Crumb), 5:422, 423
Night of the Four Moons, Lorca and, 5:422
Nijinsky, Vaslav, 4:170, 188
  Jeux and, 4:567
  Petrushka and, 4:169
Nikisch, Arthur, 3:747
Nikkal (goddess), 1:31
Nikolai I, Emperor of Russia, 3:240, 241,
    242, 249, 344, 348, 418; 4:779
  Paganini performance before, 3:253
  Wagner hymn honoring, 3:481
Nikolai II, Emperor of Russia, 4:151
Nikolais, Alwin, 5:482
Nikolaus Joseph, Prince Esterházy. See
    Esterházy, Nicolaus Joseph
Nikolsky, Vladimir, 3:623
Nimm von uns, Herr, Du treuer Gott, BWV
    101 (J. S. Bach), 2:365–68
Nineteenth Amendment, passage of, 4:259
nineteenth century
  absolute music and, 1:541, 542
  audience decorum in, 2:223–24, 613
  Bach (J. S.) revival in, 1:584; 2:234, 235,
    364, 368, 375, 381, 383, 388, 389, 390,
    399, 464
  Beethoven as musical symbol of, 2:639,
    686
  "classical music" as invention of, 2:639
  "double-exposition" terminology and,
    2:607
  free market concert life and, 2:571
  Gregorian chant restoration project,
    1:22
  Haydn and Mozart as musical forebears
    of, 2:637–39
  measures of artistic greatness in, 1:792
  middle-class ideals and, 1:579–80
  as music century, 2:735–39
  music historiography in, 2:235, 736
  nationalism and, 2:385, 388
  notion of sublime vs beautiful in, 2:644
  rediscovery of Purcell's Dido and Aeneas
    in, 2:137–38
  standard repertory's crystallization in,
    2:233, 233–34, 289
  See also Romanticism
Ninety-five Theses (Luther), 2:353
Ninth Symphony in D minor, op. 125
    (Beethoven), 2:675–82, 718, 721,
    729; 3:14, 108, 482; 5:3, 71, 347
  Brahms and, 3:688, 690, 715, 720–23,
    726, 776
  Brendel and, 3:415
  Bruckner and, 3:747, 749–51, 776
  Bülow and, 3:729
  choral theme, 3:184
  critics of, 2:677
  as David's Le Désert influence, 3:387
  Franck and, 3:776

German Romanticism and
imagery and symbolism and, 2:678, 680
musical dominance of, 2:677
New German School and, 3:719–20
"Ode to Joy," 2:655, 677, 678, 680, 731
opening tremolos in, 2:732
Schreckensfanfaren, 2:677–78
Schubert and, 3:109, 110, 778
Vienna concert premier of, 2:676–77,
683, 689
Wagner and, 3:483, 485, 675, 719
Ninth Symphony (Shostakovich), 5:10,
12–13
"Niun mi tema" (Verdi), 3:606, 608
Nixon, Richard M., 5:521–22
"No. 16" (Weill) 4:535
Nobilis, humilis (Nordic hymn), 1:393–94,
393
Noblet, Lise, 3:209, 209
Noblitt, Thomas, 1:578–79, 583, 584
Noces villageoises, Les (Stravinsky), 4:447,
448f, 756, 762
Nochlin, Linda, 4:124–25
"Why Have There Been No Great
Women Artists?" (article), 4:124
nocturne
Chopin and, 3:348, 367
as Romantic genre, 3:64–65
as salon music, 3:77, 78
"Nocturne" (Copland), 4:652
Nocturne no. 4 in A major (Field), 3:71–74
Nocturnes (Debussy), 4:78 79
No, di voi non vo'fidarmi (Handel), 2:331,
332–33
Nohant, France, 3:349, 349
Nomos, op. 19 (Hauer), 4:681, 682, 685, 686,
688, 692
twelve pitch-classes and, 4:681
Nomos technique
Dubinsky and, 4:681
Hauer and, 4:681
Webern and, 4:719–20
Non avrà ma' pietà (Landini), 1:368–71,
373–74
nonconformity, 2:620
nondiatonic modes (ancient Greek), 1:730,
732
Nonesuch Records, 5:497
Non havea febo (Monteverdi), 2:10, 11
Nono, Luigi, 5:88–90, 217, 460, 463
Italian Communist Party and, 5:88
Maurizio Pollini and, 89
Nuria Schoenberg, marriage to, 5:89
works of
Ein Gespenst geht um in der Welt,
5:89–90
Non so qual i' mi voglia (Lorenzo), 1:366, 367
Non vos relinquam (Byrd), 1:686–87, 688
Nordau, Max, *Entartung* (treatise),
4:754–55
Nordica, Lillian, 3:539
Norma (Bellini), 3:37–44, 40, 41

"Casta diva," 3:39–44, 49, 71
scene e cavatina, 3:38
Norman Conquest (1066), 1:6, 397, 397, 419
Normandy, 1:421
Normans, 1:6, 41, 50, 106, 397, 419
Norn's ballad refrain (Wagner), 3:506, 515
Norsemen. See Vikings
North, Sir Dudley, 2:114, 115
North, Sir Roger, 2:114–15, 118, 198
North Atlantic Treaty Organization
(NATO), 5:7, 8
Northcott, Bayan, 5:301
on Elliott Carter, 5:301
Northumbria, 1:392–94
*Norton/Grove Dictionary of Women
Composers*, 2:77
Norway, 1:392–93
Norwegian Dances (Grieg), 4:632
Norwich, Bishop of, 1:423
Norworth, Jack, 1:19
Nose, The (Shostakovich), 4:782–86; 5:185
Nos qui vivimus (sequence), polyphonic
setting of, 1:149
"Not a Second Time"
(Lennon/McCartney), 5:318
nota simplex (free-standing note), 1:187, 192,
197, 199, 212, 217
notation
alphabetic, 1:17, 17, 33, 45, 99–100
Ars Nova breakthrough in, 1:248–87,
355
ars subtilior complexity, 1:338, 339–42,
345, 355–56
Babylonian, 1:31–32
basso continuo, 1:809, 811
of beats, 1:251
chant, 1:1–2, 214
choral music, 3:162
of coloration, 1:266, 269
of conductus, 1:199–205
of counterpoint, 1:163, 165
Daseian, 1:47
double, 1:60, 210
Ex semine clausula, 1:209, 210, 211, 212
as following practice, 1:1–1, 184–85
Franconian, 1:212–17, 234–35, 355
Frankish pitch, 1:47
Frankish polyphonic, 1:45
instrumental tour de force and,
1:538–39
Italian-style, 1:341
Italian vernacular song and, 1:351–52,
356–59
Italian vs. French systems of, 1:355–56
key system and, 1:75–76
Machaut and, 1:327–28, 328
modal meter and, 1:176–77, 204, 215
modern staff, 1:74, 105
modern vs. mensural, 1:253
of motet, 1:209–11, 214–17
neume antecedents of, 1:14
Notre Dame school, 1:184, 186, 212, 214

oldest extant, 1:76
oral/aural learning vs., 1:17
orchestration and, 1:782–86
Philippus treatise on, 1:337–42, 341
pitch and, 1:16–17, 76
polyphonic, 1:122, 157, 158, 159, 166
quadratic, 1:22, 23, 114, 214
Regule de proportionibus on, 1:536
rhythm fixture and, 1:114, 131, 133,
185–86, 204–5, 214
shapes and, 1:176, 177
staff invention and, 1:16, 102, 105
syllabic, 1:39, 41, 60
of syncopation, 1:266
tabulature and, 1:606
trecento, 1:354–59
universal European system of, 1:62
visual effects of, 1:778–79, 801
Vitry and, 1:262, 265, 337
Western Christian, 1:1–2, 5–7
written shape use in. *See* mensural
notation
See also measure; syllabic notation
Notations (Cage), 5:95
note shapes. *See* notation
notes inégales (unequal notes), 1:261
Notitia artis musicae. See *Ars novae musicae*
Notker Balbulus (Notker the Stammerer),
1:5, 41, 42–43, 42, 51, 71, 90
Notre Dame, collegiate church of
(Condé-sur-l'Escaut), 1:563
Notre Dame Cathedral (Antwerp), 1:454
Notre Dame codices, 1:171–86, 209,
209–11, 210, 211, 212, 217
Notre Dame de Paris, 1:169–205
Albertus as cantor of, 1:165, 172
construction of, 1:120, 169
interior of, 1:170
liturgical music composition and, 1:89,
171–86, 646, 679
Mass setting for, 1:310
Ockeghem as cantor of, 1:455
University of Paris and, 1:170, 172, 174,
175, 196
Notre Dame school, 1:171–205, 212, 214,
217, 291, 347
conductus settings of, 1:173–74,
198–205
English motet and, 1:513–14
English students and, 1:397, 403
first measured Western music from,
1:184
four codices of, 1:177, 179, 180, 181–83,
184, 186
Perotin vs. Leonin generation and,
1:186–87
polyphonic *organum cum alio* and,
1:186–205
polyphonic *organum duplum* and,
1:171–86
rhythmic practices of, 1:175–86, 214, 215
Nottebohm, Gustav, 3:703

notturno, 3:64
definition of, 2:498
noumenal music, 1:827
phenomenal music vs., 2:21, 22, 720
Nourrit, Adolphe, 3:225, 227
Nouveaux des amoureus, Les (Machaut), 1:289
nouveaux riches
salons and, 3:74
See also self-made man
Nouvelle revue française, La (journal), 4:188, 468
Nouvelles méditations poétiques (Lamartine), 3:422–23
"Nov. 2, 1920" (a.k.a. "An Election") (Ives), 4:257, 258–59
Novak, Josef Ludwig, 3:683
Novalis, 3:166
Nova, nova, ave fit ex Eva (carol), 1:420
novels, operas based on, 2:445–46, 450; 3:46–48
Noverre, Jean-Georges, 4:132–33
ballet d'action and, 4:132
"Now is the month of Maying" (Morley), 1:746, 747–48
Now It Can Be Told (Gibbs), 4:472–73
"now-opera," 4:527, 529; 5:519
"Now there arose new king" (Handel), 2:316
Noyers, Jean de. *See* Tapisier
Noye's Fludde (op. 59) (Britten), 5:225
Nozze di Figaro, Le (Mozart), 2:478, 493, 622, 684; 3:16, 22, 220
Nuages (Debussy), 4:79, 80, 81, 82, 83, 204
nuba (*nawba*), 1:108
Nude Paper Sermon, The (Salzman), 5:95
Nu is du Betfart so here (Geisslerlied), 1:134
Nuit des tropiques, La (Gottschalk), 3:380
Nuits d'été, Les (Gautier), 4:97
"numberless" continuity, 3:210–11
Numbers, Book of, 1:399
number-sound relationship, 1:38, 41–42
number symbolism, 1:284–85
Nun komm, der Heiden Heiland, BWV 61 (J. S. Bach), 2:342–43, 348–53, 354, 356
Nuova Rivista Musicale Italiana, 5:328
Nuovo musiche, Le (Caccini), 1:812–13, 816, 821, 823; 2:15
preface to, 1:816–17
Nuper rosarum flores (Du Fay), 1:282–85, 429, 441, 507
Nuremberg, 1:728, 765
Lochamer Liederbuch and, 1:701
master singers, 1:139
municipal music and, 2:287
Nuremberg trials, 5:19
Nutcracker, The (Chaikovsky), 3:406; 4:139, 145
Nyman, Michael, 5:355
Cornelius Cardew and, 5:355

O
"Oath of the Three Cantons" (Deshayes), 3:11
obbligato
for accompanied keyboard sonata, 2:428
Bach (J. S.) and, 2:300–301, 402, 428
oberek, 3:357
Oberon (Weber), 3:193
Oberto (Verdi), 3:567
objectivity
artwork and, 3:315–16
musical representation and, 1:798
in playing style, 3:364
verismo and, 3:658
objets de féerie, 4:144, 145, 152
"Oblivion" leitmotif (Wagner), 3:507, 517, 519, 520, 526, 528
oboe, 2:217
Oboe Concerto in D minor (Marcello), 2:193–95, 215
Bach (J. S.) keyboard arrangement, 2:287
Obouhov, Nikolai, 4:228, 229, 681
Berceuse d'un bienheureux, 4:228
Obrecht, Jacobus, 1:459, 492, 493, 499, 544, 547, 574, 776
J'ay pris amours, 1:539
Missa Caput, 1:473, 481–83
Missa Graecorum, 4:722
Missa L'Homme Armé, 1:493
obscure music, 2:670
Observations on the Florid Song (Tosi), 2:165, 166
Occitan. *See* Provençal
occultism, 1:271–72, 285, 615–16
occult knowledge, 4:84, 192, 227
occursus, 1:152, 154, 155, 168, 276, 356
fifth relations vs., 1:471
Oceanflug, Der (Brecht), 4:541
O che nuovo miracolo (Cavalieri), 1:804
Ockeghem, Jan van, 2:5
Ockeghem, Johannes, 1:454–55, 455, 459, 499, 547, 574, 667
Bartoli on, 1:641
bergerette classic by, 1:526–28
Busnoys motet and, 1:456–57, 500
cyclic Mass Ordinaries and, 1:460, 473–81, 482, 483
historical reputation of, 1:480–81
Josquin and, 1:500, 529–30, 531
Phyrgian polyphony and, 1:529
veneration of, 1:457, 458, 500
works of
Ma bouche rit et ma pensée pleure, 1:526–28, 529–30
Missa Caput, 1:458, 473–77, 482, 483, 493
Missa cuiusvis toni, 1:479–80
Missa Prolationum, 1:477–78, 480, 529, 531, 641
"O clemens, O pia, O dulcis," 1:505–6
Salve Regina, 1:504–6, 517

Ut heremita solus, 1:457, 500
O'Connell, Charles, 3:781–82, 783; 4:269
octatonic-diatonic interaction, 4:110
octatonicism, *Petrushka* and, 4:164, 192
octatonic scale, 3:701
equivalency, 1:77, 151
leap, 1:447, 448
Liszt and, 3:429–30
paralleling of, 1:150
as "perfect" interval, 1:149
plus fifth, 1:166, 168
seven distinct species, 1:74
syllabic representation, 1:101
whole-tone scale and, 3:102
See also scale
octave, 1:102, 187, 495
Octavia, Empress of Rome, 2:27, 28
Octet for Winds (Stravinsky), 4:447, 448, 449, 451, 471, 478
"pastiche" element and, 4:449, 451
Octet in E-flat major for strings, op. 20 (Mendelssohn), 3:179, 180, 182–83
Octet in F major (Schubert), 3:84, 103, 105
"October Revolution" (Russia), 4:743
octonaria meter, 1:355, 364
ode, 1:34, 118
definition of, 3:120
Ode for St. Cecilia's Day (Dryden), 2:327
Ode for St. Cecilia's Day (Handel), 2:330
Oden mit Melodien (lieder collection), 3:120
"Ode on a Grecian Urn" (Keats), 3:440
Ode-Symphony, 3:387
"Ode to Joy" (Beethoven), 2:655, 677–78, 680, 681, 731; 3:726; 4:14
"Ode to Joy" (Schiller), 2:675, 678, 680, 731
Ode to Napoleon Bonaparte (Schoenberg), 4:462
Odets, Clifford, 5:106
Aaron Copland and, 5:106
Odhecaton (Petrucci music book), 1:543, 544, 559
Odington, Walter, 1:402, 403
Odo. *See* Eudes
O Domine, adjuva me (Byrd), 1:679
Odoyevsky, Vladimir, Prince, 3:34–35, 46, 239, 245–46
Odyssey (Homer), 2:26; 3:127, 481; 4:525
Oedipus complex, Freud and, 4:124, 676
Oedipus (mythology)., 4:676
Oedipus Rex (Stravinsky), 4:675–78
Oedipus tyrannis (Sophocles), 1:780
Offenbach, Jacques, 3:644
death of, 3:657
operetta and, 3:644–47
works of
Belle Hélène, La, 3:644, 645, 648
Contes d'Hoffmann, Les, 3:657
Deux avegules, Les, 3:654
Grand Duchess of Gérolstein, The, 3:644
Orphée aux enfers, 3:644, 645–47
Périchole, La, 3:651
Offertory, 1:13, 34; 2:44, 178

antiphon, **1:**24–25, 35, 79
in Mass ordo, **1:**61(table)
Palestrina cycle of, **1:**632, 663–66, 667
tropes and, **1:**50
Office, **1:**20–23, 48, 72, 99, 310
Hucbald antiphons, **1:**100
polyphonic elaborations, **1:**162
versus and, **1:**89
votive antiphons and, **1:**94–99
Office of Martyrs, **1:**23
Öglin, Erhard, **1:**691
Ogny, Count d' (Claude-François-Marie
Rigoley), **2:**557
Ohren des Consumenten, **3:**439, 441, 451
"O Jesu Christe, wahres Licht"
(Mendelssohn), **3:**170
"O King" (Berio), **5:**348, 350
oktoechos (eight-mode cycle), **1:**28, 73
"O là o che bon eccho" (Lasso), **1:**792
Old Hall manuscript, **1:**409–18, 429, 461,
513
Old Roman chant, **1:**62, 63
old style. *See stile antico*
Old Testament oratorios, **2:**314–21
"Old Way of Singing," **1:**25
oltremontani madrigalists, **1:**723, 724–33
"Omaggio a Joyce" (Berio), **5:**193
O magnum mysterium (Palestrina),
1:642–44, 667
O magnum mysterium (Sartori), **1:**667,
668–69
"O" matrix, **5:**29, 30
"Omen" leitmotif (Wagner), **3:**507, 516
"omnibus progression," *Sleeping Beauty* and,
4:145, 146
On a parole/A Paris/Frese nouvele (motet),
1:237–38, 239
isorhythm and, **1:**266
O nata lux de lumine (Tallis), **1:**673–74, 678
Oñate, Count d' (Spanish viceroy), **2:**140
"On Baptism" (Augustine), **1:**70
Onda dal mar divisa, L' (Hasse), **2:**168
Onda dal mar divisa, L' (Vinci), **2:**161–65
ondes martenot ("Martenot Waves"),
4:240;**5:**183, 185
ondes musicales ("musical waves"), **5:**183
"One Hundred Metronomes" (Cone),
5:162
One Hundred Russian Folk Songs
(Rimsky-Korsakov), **4:**153, 183
O'Neill, Eugene, **3:**59
On Springfield Mountain (or, *The Pesky
Sarpent*), **4:**668
On the Sensations of Tone (Helmholtz),
4:287
1,000 Years: A Musical Picture (Balakirev),
3:477
Ono, Yoko, Tavener's *The Whale* and,
5:408
onomatopoeia, **1:**331–32, 333, 349, 364, 711,
712, 716, 717, 733, 749; **3:**25–27

Onta irrita lo sdegno a la vendetta', L'
(Monteverdi), **2:**9
"On the Invention and Use of Music"
(Tinctoris), **1:**453–54, 536
"On the Musically Beautiful" (Hanslick),
3:441
"On the Term 'Music Drama'" (Wagner),
3:521
ontogeny, **4:**358–61
Opella nova (Schein), **2:**53–54
"open and closed" cadence, **2:**432
opera
aria and, **2:**75, 146; **3:**219–20
Bach's (J. S.) cantatas and, **2:**341, 342, 345
Bach's (J. S.) St. John Passion and, **2:**378
ballet included in, **3:**12, 208
Baroque, **1:**797
Beethoven and, **3:**1–7, 567
beginnings of, **1:**127, 812, 824, 826–27,
832–33, 834; **3:**557, 566, 618
bel canto, **3:**36–46, 48
Bellini and, **3:**37–44, 45, 49, 71, 93, 565,
567
between-acts instrumental performance.
See intermezzo
birth of (1600), **2:**16
Brendel's view of, **3:**414
castrati and, **2:**16–17
censorship of, **2:**18, 88
Code Rossini and, **3:**14–22, 27, 239, 568
comedization of, **3:**611–15, 617, 640, 658
continuous revisions and versions of,
2:33–34
controversial disputes about, **2:**34
court. *See* court opera
Czech, **3:**447, 448–51, 463
darkened theaters and, **3:**564
death of, **4:**547–49
development of, **2:**13–18, 445–96
diagrammatic representations in,
2:151–52
disruptive quality of, **2:**18
divided world of, **2:**34
dramatic and musical value
reconciliation in, **3:**35
durability of, **2:**34
eighteenth-century reforms of,
2:445–96
empfindsamer Stil and, **2:**418, 434
English seventeenth-century, **2:**113, 114,
126–27, 131, 132–38
English eighteenth-century, **2:**237,
307–13
ensemble pieces and, **3:**35, 46, 48
exotic locales and, **3:**667
as *favole in musica,* **2:**11, 13–14, 15, 21, 23,
27
festive mood of, **3:**20
first German text for, **2:**58
folk songs and, **3:**187, 194, 448–51
French. *See* French opera
French reception to, **2:**87

gender roles and, **3**.36. *See also* trousers
role
German. *See* German opera
Gluck reforms and, **2:**452–59, 465–66
government support of, **3:**206
happy endings (*lieto fine*) in, **2:**151
Haydn and, **2:**464, 526
historical, **3:**205–6, 621–31
as instrumental style influence, **2:**281, 433
intermission plays. *See* intermezzo
Italian. *See* Italian opera
librettists and *See* librettists; libretto
literal meaning of word, **2:**1
mime characters in, **3:**209
monodies and ayres and, **3:**119
Monteverdi and, **2:**1–2, 11, 12, 13, 14, 16,
18–33
Mozart in standard repertory of, **2:**94,
464–96
musical transmission of unexpressed
thoughts in, **2:**590–91; **3:**59
music vs. words and, **1:**827
national, **3:**194–97, 250, 447–51
neoclassical, **2:**151–52
nineteenth-century reforms and, **3:**210,
498, 567
nineteenth-century voice categories and,
3:36, 77, 578–79
noumenal and phenomenal music in,
1:827
oratorio as form of, **2:**314–15
orientalism and, **3:**389–92, 397,
400–406
overture and, **2:**146
"painful" music in, **2:**645
performance practice and, **2:**172–76
political/social content and, **2:**17–18, 34,
110, 111
presages of, **1:**780, 826
querelles concerning, **2:**34, 110, 445
realism and, **3:**35–36, 41, 45, 204–5, 591
recitative vs. aria time in, **2:**154
representational style and, **2:**418, 643
"rescue," **3:**2–3, 239, 249
Rossini and, **3:**21, 27
Russian, **3:**230–50, 621–31
Scarlatti's (Alessandro) standardizations
of, **2:**141, 146, 152
singers and, **2:**16–18, 86–87
Slavic, **3:**447–48
social customs and, **2:**175
soprano/mezzo-soprano duets and, **3:**36
as source of accompanied keyboard
sonata, **2:**433
stage action and, **3:**41
stage music in, **2:**490–91, 492–93, 631
staging of, **3:**206, 215
stylistic impact of instrumental music of,
2:418
symphony's relationship with, **2:**497,
498, 499, 507, 515, 589
tragic, **3:**20, 35, 216

opera (continued)
  two political strains of, 2:34
  Verdi and, 3:563–615
  verismo, 3:440, 641, 658–64
  Wagner and, 1:138, 139, 141, 142
  women divas and, 2:17
  See also comic opera; grand opéra; opera
    buffa; opera seria; singing
Opera As Drama (Kerman) 3:664
opéra bouffe. See opera buffa
opera buffa, 2:446–52; 3:644, 645
  antecedents of, 2:17
  comic opera and, 3:22, 187
  ensemble finales in, 2:247–48, 451, 622;
    3:24–27
  fluidity of texts of, 2:172–73
  Galuppi's importance to, 2:433
  Goldoni as chief librettist of, 2:433
  imbroglio and, 2:451
  kinetic sections in, 2:486–87, 488, 492,
    494
  Mozart and, 2:464–65, 470–76,
    478–79, 485–96, 620, 622; 3:22
  musical significance of, 2:434
  as music of eighteenth century, 2:434
  Paisiello and, 2:476, 477
  patter songs and, 3:655
  Pergolesis and, 2:438–41
  Piccinni and, 2:445–52
  plot and musical complexity of,
    2:450–51
  political subtext of, 2:110, 620–21
  Rossini and, 2:670; 3:24–27
  second-act finale convention of,
    2:487–88
  serious opera borrowings from, 3:48
  stock ending of, 2:447
  stock types of, 2:478, 488
  Verdi and, 3:10
  War of the Buffoons and, 2:110
  See also comic opera
opéra comique, 3:208, 644
  Meyerbeer and, 3:217
  "rescue" theme and, 3:2–3
  in Russia, 3:235–36
Opéra Comique (Paris), 3:216–17, 335
Opéra de Lyon (France), The Death of
    Klinghoffer and, 5:522
opéra fantastique, 3:657
opera houses
  concert halls as competitors to, 3:677
  design and mechanical innovations of,
    3:206–7
  first Neopolitan, 2:140
  Lenten closure of, 2:313, 470, 499, 608
  Western world's first (Venice), 2:12
  See also specific opera houses
opéra lyrique, 3:639–43, 653
Opera of the Nobility (London), 2:237, 311,
    313
opera reggia, 2:1
opera seria, 2:141–76, 234, 399–400; 4:453

Araja and, 3:235
aria and, 2:308, 311, 341
Artaserse as exemplifier of, 2:159–65
artifice of, 2:17
audience behavior and, 2:153–54,
    173–75, 174, 223
Bach (J. C.) and, 2:240, 419, 507
ballroom dance rhythms and, 3:35
bel canto, 3:37
British rejection of, 2:313
casting of, 2:153, 155, 156, 159, 166–67
castrati and, 2:153–56, 173–76, 307, 308
class values and, 2:175, 447
comic elements banned from, 2:434
comic opera imports to, 3:48
concerto's kinship with, 2:222, 231, 308
design symmetry of, 2:159
deus ex machina and, 3:197
Dido-and-Aeneas theme, 3:219
end of, 2:485
ensemble pieces in, 3:35, 46, 48
"exit opera" nickname and, 3:48
Farinelli's influence on, 2:172
fundamental values of, 2:173, 433–34,
    447
Gluck reforms and, 2:452–59
Handel and, 2:109, 236–37, 238–39,
    306–12, 313, 351
intermezzos (intermission plays) and,
    2:434–37
Italian singers of, 2:158
Joseph II's dislike of, 2:470
leading singers and, 3:578
mad scene in, 3:46–48, 52–59
Metastasio librettos and, 2:152, 155–65,
    438, 453, 476
modern counterpart of, 2:174, 175
Mozart and, 2:465–70, 474, 481–82
nature and function of, 3:20
opera buffa in relationswhip with,
    2:433–34, 447, 455
oratorio as biblical form of, 2:314
parody of, 2:155
patter songs and, 3:655
performance practice of, 2:172–76
Pergolesi and, 2:438
realism and, 3:35–36
"remainder" characters in, 2:153–54
Romanticism and, 3:27
Rossini and, 3:11, 27–35, 596
Scarlatti (Alessandro) and, 2:141, 148
Scarlatti (Domenico) and, 2:390
self-sacrifice as classic culmination of,
    2:447, 454
social system and, 2:174–75
subject matter of, 2:174
three acts in, 2:155, 434
unity of affect of, 2:439
Verdi and, 3:611
Vinci and, 2:161–65
Opera sextronique (Paik), 5:93
operetta, 3:644–57

Gilbert and Sullivan and, 3:651–56
Offenbach and, 3:644–48
patter songs and, 3:655
Strauss (Johann) and, 3:647–51
opérettes, 3:644, 645
Oper und Drama (Wagner), 3:488, 496, 497
Opitz, Martin, 2:15
Oppenheimer, J. Robert, 5:2
opuscoli in genere rappresentativo, 2:10–11
Opus musicum (Gallus), 1:772
Opus musicum (Handl), 1:679
O quam tu pulchra es (Schütz), 2:59, 60–66
  refrain of, 2:64–66
Oracle (London newspaper), 2:569
oral tradition, 1:11–35, 583; 5:480–81
  appropriation from. See contrafactum
  ballata and, 1:364, 366, 374
  British, 1:387–88, 399, 403, 407
  chromatic adjustments and, 1:275
  current popular tunes and, 1:18
  denigration of, 2:639
  diatonic pitch set and, 1:30, 31
  Gregorian chant and, 1:6–12, 13, 17–20,
    26–29, 157
  harmonizing and, 1:168, 437, 472
  imitative pieces, 1:336
  improvisation and, 1:17–18, 666–67
  Landini and, 1:374
  literacy beginnings from, 1:11
  Minnesingers and, 1:137–38
  mnemonic devices and, 1:39, 162
  mode extraction from, 1:76–86
  modern church music and, 1:27
  monodic revolution and, 1:816–17, 821
  Notre Dame polyphony and, 1:184, 186
  Old Roman chant and, 1:62
  organ accompaniment and, 1:437, 607,
    617, 781, 782; 2:35–39, 49
  ornamentation and, 1:697, 783, 816–17;
    2:174, 278–79
  polyphony and, 1:46–47, 161–62, 168,
    178, 185, 392
  "Reading Rota" and, 1:392
  sixteenth-century performance practices
    and, 1:617–21
  staff notation and, 1:185
  troubadour art as, 1:108, 109, 110
  unwritten conventions and, 1:46, 261
  vernacular song and, 1:696–97
  vocal harmony and, 1:392, 394
  women's creativity and, 2:79, 81
  written examples as cream of, 2:35, 44
  See also folk music; improvisation
oratorio
  Bach (J. S.) Passions and, 2:377–81, 383
  Beethoven and, 2:675, 722
  biblical themes of, 3:163, 164
  Carissimi and, 2:73–75, 90
  chorus's role in, 2:315
  English, 2:314–40
  English nationalism and, 2:315, 633
  German concert movement amd, 2:385

Handelian specific concept of, **2**:316

Haydn and, **2**:385, 388, 633–37

Italian, **2**:73–345, 237, 313, 314

Lutheran style of, **2**:341–42

Masses styled like, **2**:375–76, 377

nationalism and rebirth of, **3**:163–66

origins of, **1**:834

Schütz and, **2**:73

Oratorio del Crocifisso, **1**:809

Oratorio del Santissimo Crocifisso (Rome), **2**:73

Oratorium nach den Bildern der Bibel (Fanny Mendelssohn), **3**:184

orchestra

for Berlioz's *Symphonie fantastique*, **3**:323, 324

for Bruckner's Seventh Symphony, **3**:748–49

conductor's control of, **2**:111–12, 291

first examples of, **1**:791

first violin leadership of, **2**:291

Italian court spectacle and, **2**:15

for oratorio, **2**:314

seventeenth-century innovations and, **1**:798

as social microcosm, **2**:290–91, 301

soloist performance with, **3**:173, 274–75

tragédie lyrique and, **2**:106

vingt-quatre violons du Roi, **2**:94

virtuoso, **2**:234

in Wagner's works, **3**:512

orchestral music. *See* instrumental music

orchestral portamento, Korngold and, **4**:550

orchestral suite. *See* suite

Orchestral Suite, no. 3 (Bach), overture, **2**:286–87, 288

orchestral symphony. *See* symphony

Orchestral Symphony, first (C. P. E. Bach), **2**:510–16

orchestration

Bach (C. P. E.) and, **2**:510

Bach's (J. S.) Brandenburg Concertos and, **2**:290

Berlioz and, **3**:323–24, 339

Gabrieli (Giovanni) and, **1**:792

Haydn's *Creation* and, **2**:637

Liszt and, **3**:419

Meyerbeer's *Les Huguenots* and, **3**:225

Mozart and, **2**:753

opera seria and, **2**:166

origins of, **1**:782–86

Rossini and, **3**:21

Weber's *Der Freischützr* and, **3**:202, 203

Orchestra Trio in C minor, op. 4, no. 3 (Stamitz), **2**:506–7, 519, 718, 719

Order of the Golden Fleece, **1**:484, 485, 495

Ordinary, **1**:53–60, 58, 60–63, 310, 322, 324, 460

Avignon settings of, **1**:310–14, 331

Byrd's settings of, **1**:679–89

components of, **1**:53–54

earliest setting of, **1**:307

English Old Hall manuscript, **1**:409

fifteenth-century cyclic organization of, 460. *See also* cyclic Mass Ordinaries

Frankish standardization of, **1**:53–60

French-Cypriot settings of, **1**:345–49

instrumental music extracted from, **1**:543–44

Isaac and, **1**:622–24

Kyriale (chant book), **1**:58, 322

Machaut setting of, **1**:307, 317–26

Nicolaus de Radom and, **1**:348

ordo, **1**:61(table)

paired settings of, **1**:311–12, 460–61

Palestrina's 104 settings of, **1**:632, 633

performance practice of, **1**:310

polyphonic, **1**:54, 307, 308–14, 324, 325–26, 512

standard settings of, **1**:488

Taverner setting of, **1**:612–14

votive Masses and, **1**:314–26, 460

votive motet substitutions in, **1**:518–26

ordo, representation of, **1**:176

Ordo victutum (Hildegard), **1**:93

Orestes (mythology), **4**:49, 57

Orfeo (Monteverdi), **2**:1–2, 3, 13, 14, 16, 26, 464

deus ex machina in, **2**:151

discussion of, **2**:18–25

first performance of, **2**:14

Gluck's *Orpheus and Eurydice* contrasted with, **2**:454, 455

Incoronazione di Poppea contrasted with, **2**:27, 33

Rossi's *Orfeo* and, **2**:87, 88

toccata and, **2**:41

Orfeo (Rossi), **2**:87–88

austere elements of, **2**:455, 457

French readaptation of, **2**:458, 459–60

Orff, Carl, **4**:756–65, 757, 772; **5**:344

Carmina burana, **1**:138–39; **4**:756, 757–62, 764

Catulli carmina, **4**:760, 764

"organicism," **4**:639

"organized sound," **5**:205, 207

organ music, **2**:35–55, 242–43

Bach family and, **2**:208, 241, 247, 402, 419

basso continuo and, **1**:780–81

Bruckner and, **3**:746–47, 749

canzona adaptations as, **1**:787–96

chanson arrangements as, **1**:786

as choral accompaniment, **1**:780–81

chorale and, **2**:255

earliest extant manuscript of, **1**:306

English Reformation and, **1**:672

faburden bass lines and, **1**:437

famous blind line of, **1**:374

form and, **2**:301, 701, 706, 714

Franck and, **3**:774

Frescobaldi and, **1**:821; **2**:35–44

Handel and, **2**:305

Landini and, **1**:366, 368, 371, 374

Mass Ordinary and, **1**:324

organist improvisation and, **1**:437, 607, 617, 781; **2**:37, 43, 44

pedal point in, **2**:202, 208, 211–12, 216

Praetorius and, **2**:52

prelude-and-fugue form and, **2**:247

printed accompaniments for, **1**:781–82, 783

Purcell and, **2**:127

ricercari, **1**:588, 606–7, 607, 616, 617, 617–19, 618–19, 619, 786

Scheidt and, **2**:48–49

Schein and, **2**:52–54

Sweelinck and, **2**:44–46

unity concept and, **3**:284, 299

organ musicetto, **1**:363

Organ Piece (Brecht), **5**:91

"Organ" Symphony, no. 3 in C minor (Saint-Saëns), **3**:783–85, 799

organum, **1**:167, 219, 296

Grocheio's social theory and, **1**:208, 233

melismatic, **1**:156–57, 159, 171, 178–79

Notre Dame settings, **1**:171, 173, 177–79, 186

patchwork, **1**:184

Viderunt omnes, **1**:173, 177–78, 177, 178, 179–80

See also motet

organum cum alio, Notre Dame school and, **1**:186–98

organum duplum, **1**:171, 177–78, 184, 186, 187, 211, 298

See also motet

organum per se, **1**:187

organum purum, **1**:179

organum quadruplum, **1**:174, 187–91, 199–201, 199

hocket and, **1**:233

organum triplum, **1**:173, 187, 190, 397

Alleluia Nativitas, **1**:191–96

Ex Semine clausula, **1**:210–11, 212, 217, 222

modal rhythm and, **1**:245

Musicalis Sciencia/Sciencie Laudabili, **1**:267, 268–70

Thomas gemma Cantuariae/Thomas caesus in Doveria, **1**:408–9, 411–12

See also motet

Orgelbüchlein (J. S. Bach), **2**:255–56, 258

Orientales, Les (Hugo), **3**:387

orientalism, **3**:386–92

Balakirev and, **3**:395–97, 409

Beethoven and, **3**:1, 386

biblical, **3**:391–92

Bizet and, **3**:390, 641

Borodin and, **3**:397, 400–405, 786, 789

Chaikovsky and, **3**:406–10

Cui and, **3**:397

David and, **3**:387–89

female portrayals and, **3**:405–6

France and, **3**:387–91, 393

orientalism (*continued*)
   Hugo and, 3:387
   Massenet and, 3:390
   Meyerbeer and, 3:389–90
   Mozart and, 2:470–76, 602; 3:193, 386
   Musorgsky and, 3:397
   nationalism and, 3:192–93, 393
   otherness and, 3:386, 390, 392, 393, 398, 405–10
   Puccini and, 3:667–68
   Rachmaninoff and, 3:395–99
   Rimsky-Korsakov and, 3:397
   Rubinstein and, 3:391–92
   Russia and, 3:392–405, 786–87, 789
   Saint-Saëns and, 3:390–91
   Serov and, 3:391–92
   Thomas and, 3:390
   verismo and, 3:660
   Weber and, 3:192–93
   See also Turkish mode
"original genius" concept. *See* genius, Romantic notion of
Origin of Species, The (Darwin), 2:396
Orkney Islands, 1:392–93
Orlandini, Giuseppe Maria, 2:435–36, 437
   Marito giocatore e la maglie bacchettona, Il, 2:435, 436, 439, 441
Orlando de Lassus. *See* Lasso, Orlando di
Orleans, Anne-Marie-Louise d' ("Grande Mademoiselle"), 2:89
Orléans, Duke of, 3:214
ornamental neumes, 1:24, 48, 57
   loss of, 1:105
ornamentation (embellishment), 2:106
   Bach (J. S.) and, 2:281–82
   Baroque and, 1:699
   concerto cadenza and, 2:609, 610
   Couperin and, 2:277–79, 281
   da capo aria and, 2:144, 171–72
   Farinelli's arias and, 2:167–69
   German theories on, 2:59
   Italian opera and, 2:279, 281, 282
   Italian vs. French conventions of, 2:281
   Landini cadential, 1:368, 369–71
   luxuriant style dissonances as, 2:59
   Machaut and, 1:307, 325
   melismatic, 1:28, 39
   musico-rhetorical, 1:816–17, 819, 821
   Praetorius written, 2:55, 739
   Scarlatti (Domenico) and, 2:392–93
   unwritten, 2:174, 278–46
   unwritten recitative, 3:591
   vernacular song and, 1:697
   vocal cadenza and, 2:171–72
   written out, 1:783
Ornament 1 (Newman), 5:353
Ornstein, Leo, 4:299
   Danse sauvage, 4:299, 300
   Suicide in an Airplane, 4:299, 300–301
   Wild Men's Dance, 4:299
Orphée aux enfers (Offenbach), 3:644, 645–47

Orphée et Eurydice (Gluck), 2:459–60
Orphée (Henry), 5:188
Orpheus legend, 1:10, 456, 804
   Gluck and, 2:454, 455–59
   Monteverdi and, 2:21–25, 454, 455
   Offenbach and, 3:645
   Peri and, 1:811–12, 823, 829–31, 832; 2:454, 455
   Restoration drama and, 2:126
   Rossi and, 2:88
   Schütz and, 2:15, 58
Orpheus (Symphonic Poem No. 4; Liszt), 3:627–28
Or sus, vous dormez trop (anon.), 1:349, 350
Ortega y Gasset, José, 1:326–27; 4:60, 69, 72, 90, 294, 465, 467, 476, 477, 495, 518, 523–24, 534, 550, 692
   "art for artists" and, 4:294, 295
   "ban on all pathos," 4:472
   "dehumanization," modern art and, 4:474, 476, 527
   "Dehumanization of Art, The," 4:476
   "Few Drops of Phenomenology, A" (essay), 4:519
   seven points and, 4:69, 71
   Revolt of the Masses, The, 4:476
Orthodox Church. *See* Greek Orthodox (Byzantine) Church
Ortiz, Diego, 1:620–21, 622, 625–28
   Recercada segunda, 1:627–28
   Trattado de glosas
Osborne, Nigel, Introduction to *Musical Thought at IRCAM,* 5:473
Osborne, Richard, 3:15
Oselleto salvagio (Jacopo), 1:359–64
Osiander, Lucas, 1:765
   Christ lag in Todesbanden, 1:766–67
"O signore, dal tetto natio" (Verdi), 3:574
Osmin's rage aria (Mozart), 2:471–72, 602, 678
Osmond-Smith, David, 5:348
   Playing on Words: A Guide to Luciano Berio's "Sinfonia", 5:348
"Osservazioni critiche sopra un quartetto di Mozart" (Sarti), 2:631–32
Ossian, 3:772
ostinato, 1:388
Ostrovsky, Alexander, 4:423
   The Storm, 4:423, 430
Oswald, John
   Elektrax and, 5:504
   "plunderphonics" and, 5:504
Oswald von Wolkenstein, 1:142–43, 142, 701
   Der May, 1:143
Otello (Rossini), 3:596, 600, 606
Otello (Verdi), 3:596–611, 596, 615, 660; 4:133
   Act I, 3:597–604, 610
   Act IV, 3:604–10
Othello (Dvořák), 3:755

Othello (Shakespeare), 3:596, 597, 600, 605, 606, 608
otherness, 3:405–10
   orientalism and, 3:386, 390, 392, 393, 398, 405–10
O Tod (Brahms), 4:356, 357–58, 360
Ottavia ristituita al trona (D. Scarlatti), 2:390
Ottoboni, Pietro Cardinal, 2:150–51, 152, 177
ottocento, 3:594
Otto IV, Holy Roman Emperor, 1:112
Ottoman (Turkey) Empire, 1:141–42, 779; 2:114, 139; 3:234, 386, 392
   fall of Constantinople to, 1:484
   Vienna and, 2:470, 525
ottonario (trochaic pattern), 1:696–97
Ottonelli, Giovan Domenico, 2:17
Oude Kerk (Amsterdam), 2:44
Our Gal Sunday (soap opera), 2:446
ouverture. See overture
"Ouvertures," 4:132
"Over-Soul, The" (Emerson), 4:243
Overton, Hall, 5:368
   Steve Reich and, 5:368
   Vincent Persichetti and, 5:368
overtone series. *See* natural harmonic series
overture
   Bach (J. S.) and, 2:286–87, 288, 348–49
   Beethoven and, 2:702; 3:197
   English theatrical incidental music and, 2:126
   French *tragédie lyrique* and, 2:91–92, 286
   German orchestral suite and, 2:260
   Handel and, 2:239
   Haydn and, 2:556
   Lully and, 2:91–92, 286
   Mozart and, 2:487–88, 504, 515
   Paisiello and, 3:16–20
   Rossini and, 3:15, 16–20
   Scarlatti (Alessandro) and, 2:146–48, 497
   as term for symphony, 2:497, 498, 499, 500, 507
Overture-Fantasia, 3:406–8
Overture in D minor (Purcell), 2:127–30
Overture on Russian Themes (1857–58; Balakirev), 3:468–71
Overture on Russian Themes (1864; Balakirev), 3:470–78
Overture "1776" (Ives), 4:276
Ovid, 1:811–12, 813, 823, 824, 827, 832; 2:47
Owen, Wilfred, 5:257–58
Owen Wingrave, op. 85 (Britten), 5:225
"O wie ängstlich, o wie feurig" (Mozart), 2:472–75
"Owl and the Pussy-Cat, The" (Lear), 5:128
Oxford, Earl of. *See* Harley, Robert

"Oxford Symphony" in G major, no. 92
(Haydn), 2:556
Oxford University, 1:403
Haydn honorary degree from, 2:556

P

Pachmann, Vladimir de, 3:364
Packard, Vance
Hidden Persuaders, The 5:396
Status Seekers, The, 5:163
Paderewski, Ignacy Jan, 4:558
Padilla y Ramos, Mariano, 3:409
Padovano, Annibale, 1:787
Padua
Ciconia and, 1:277–81
madrigalists, 1:354
university, 1:354
paduana. See pavan
Paepcke, Walter, 5:257
Paer, Ferdinando
Leonora ossia L'amore conjugale, 3:3
Liszt and, 3:262
Paganini and, 3:255, 257
Paganini, Master-Magician (Burmeister
[Lyser]), 3:254, 254, 292
Paganini, Niccolò, 1:617; 3:251–61, 252, 348
background and career of, 3:252–53
Black Romanticism and, 3:255
caprice and, 3:252, 253, 255–57, 266, 292,
340
caricature of, 3:254, 268, 292
concerto and, 3:252, 255, 256–57
death and burial of, 3:253
harmony and, 3:256–57, 264
Liszt and, 3:253, 256, 261, 264, 266–68,
292
physical appearance of, 3:252, 253, 254
Schumann (Robert) and, 3:253, 256, 292
semiretirement of, 3:253
variation sets of, 3:255–61
Vienna debut of, 3:85
works of
Caprice, op. 1, no. 13, 3:255, 256
Caprice, op. 1, no. 17, 3:255–57
Caprice, op. 1, no. 24, 3:256, 257, 340;
4:553
Carmagnole, La, 3:257
Concerto no. 1, 3:255
Concerto no. 2, 3:253, 255, 264
God Save the King, 3:258
Introduction and Variations on "Dal
tuo stellato soglio," 3:258
Palpiti, I, 3:258–61
St. Patrick's Day, 3:257–58
Streghe, Le, 3:255
paganism, 1:10, 11, 12; 2:331
art and 2:649
musical notation and 1:31–32
Page, Christopher, 1:208
Paget, Thomas, Lord, 2:45
Pagliacci, I (Leoncavallo), 3:659–60, 659

"Vesti la giubba," 3:662–63
Paik, Nam June, 5:92–94, 162
Darmstadt refugee, 5:94
Wolfgang Fortner, pupil of, 5:94
works of
Hommage à John Cage, 5:92, 94
Opéra sextronique, 5:93
Paine, John Knowles, 3:769, 774
Paine, Thomas, 2:460, 461
"paired imitation" style, 1:521–22, 555, 556,
589
Paisiello, Giovanni, 2:158, 476, 499, 646
Rossini compared with, 3:15–20, 22–23
in Russia, 3:235
works of
Barbiere di Siviglia, Il, 3:16–20, 22–23,
235
Re Teodoro, Il, 3:34
Paix, Jakob, 1:574; 3:102
Palacky, Frantisek, 3:345
Palais Esterházy (Vienna), 2:526
Palais Royal (France), 2:87
Palästinalied (Walther), 1:135–36
Palatinate, 2:504–7
Palazzo Pitti (Florence), 2:16
Palermo, 2:139
Palestrina (Loewe), 3:164
Palestrina (Pfitzner), 1:652–53, 652, 654, 656
Palestrina, Giovanni Pierluigi da,
1:630–70, 634, 675, 733; 2:237;
3:529, 566
ars perfecta and, 1:630, 632–33, 652, 655,
663, 667, 713
background and career of, 1:630–31,
650–53, 666, 667, 713
Brendel's view of, 3:413
Byrd compared with, 1:678, 680,
684–86
eighteenth-century imitations of, 1:667,
668–69
esthetic ecstasy induction and, 3:528
fame of, 1:632
Italian musical hegemony and, 1:666
Lasso compared with, 1:713
liturgical intelligibility movement and,
1:647, 649–63, 771
Mass settings of, 1:632, 633–63, 724
motet compositions of, 1:632, 663–66
musical emulation by, 1:633–35
musical legend and, 1:650–53
parody Masses of, 1:641–44
post-Tridentine style and, 1:655, 656
prolific output of, 1:632
stile antico and, 2:180
style of, 1:667, 669–70, 773; 2:357
works of
Missa O magnum mysterium, 1:643–49
Missa Papae Marcelli, 1:649, 650, 673,
680, 684–85, 724, 782; 2:110, 111
Missa Repleatur os meum laude,
1:636–41

Missa super L'Homme Armé, 1:634,
635–37, 653
Missa super Ut re mi fa sol la, 1:635, 653
O magnum mysterium, 1:642–44, 667
Tui sunt coeli, 1:663–66
Vestiva i colli, 1:642, 746
palindrome, 1:161; 2:406
Palisca, Claude, 1:826
Palm Sunday, 1:775
Palmer, Carl, 5:328
Palmer, Robert, 5:391
Palpiti, I (Paganini), 3:258–61
Pamela; or, Virtue Rewarded (Richardson),
2:445–46, 450; 3:131
Pange lingua gloriosi (Venantius), 1:47, 48,
83–84, 555
panharmonicon, 2:672–73
pan-isorhythm, 1:266, 325, 345
English motet and, 1:410, 423–24, 427
French-Cypriot Gloria-Credo pairing
and, 1:345, 346–47
Pannini, Giovanni Paolo, 2:36
Panorama de "Musique Concrete," 5:191
pantonality, 4:334, 344
Panufnik, Andrzej, 5:53–54
Papa, Clemens non. See Clemens non Papa
"Papa Bach," 4:679, 691
papacy, 1:9, 170
Anglican repudiation of, 1:671–72
antimusical bull of, 1:311
antipopes and, 1:278, 310, 311, 378
Avignon, 1:249, 307–21, 310, 331, 337,
342, 378
Carolingian Empire and, 1:2–5
choirbooks and, 1:458–59
Great Schism and, 1:310–14, 348,
423–24
Gregorian chant and, 1:5–7, 23
Guelphs and Ghibellines and, 1:286, 354
musical patronage by, 1:278, 281, 559,
754; 2:37
non-Italian popes and, 1:630
Palestrina's musical service with, 1:631,
632, 633, 649, 650–53, 666, 667, 675
Polish court ties with, 1:347–48
See also names of specific popes
Papageno (Zauberflöte), as character type,
3:188–91, 197, 236
Papal Chapel Choir, 1:559, 650
Papal States, 1:2–3; 2:139
Papiermusik, 4:462
Pappenheim, Bertha, 4:326–27
Pappenheim, Marie, 4:326, 327, 344
Pappenheim, Martin, 4:326
Parabosco, Girolamo, 1:605, 607
"Paracelsus" (Browning), 4:259
Parade, Ballets Russes and, 4:561
Parade (Cocteau-Satie), 4:599
Paradise Lost (Milton), 2:633
Paradiso, Il (Dante), 1:286
Parakilas, James, 3:347, 367

Paralèle des Italiens et des Français (Raguenet), 2:85–86
paraliturgical music, 1:128
parallel doubling, 1:47, 149–53, 155, 406
as utopian, 1:152
parallel fifths, 1:406, 819
parallel-imperfect-consonance style, 1:406–9
parallel seconds (Corelli clash), Schütz use of, 2:69
parallel thirds, 1:394, 406
paraphrase Masses. *See* parody Masses
paraphrase motets, 1:501, 503, 506, 507, 556–57, 566–67, 641
Parfum impérissable, Le (Fauré), 4:97, 98–99
"Parigi, o cara" (Verdi), 3:582
Paris
Ars Nova and, 1:254–55
Bach (J. C.) commissions from, 2:419
Chopin in, 3:75, 348–50
Concert Spirituel series in, 2:498–99, 505, 556, 603
concert symphony and, 2:504
English music and, 1:423, 424
English occupation of, 1:421–22, 461
fourteenth-century musical scene in, 1:422
Gluck in, 2:459–60
Gottschalk in, 3:377–78, 385
guilds and, 1:118, 120, 131
Haydn symphonic concert series in, 2:556–57
intermezzos and *opera buffa* in, 2:435, 441
Liszt in, 3:262
Meyerbeer in, 3:216–18
motet and, 1:219–21, 229–36, 229, 233
Mozart in, 2:601, 603, 612
music criticism in, 3:291
music publishing in, 1:692, 694, 706, 708
nineteenth-century symphonic music in, 3:677–78, 680
Notre Dame cathedral and school, 1:89, 169–205
opera house. *See* Académie Royale de Musique
operetta, 3:644–47
Paganini concerts in, 3:253
Rossini in, 3:11, 14
Salle Le Peletier in, 3:206
salons of, 3:75
Sorbonne Mass and, 1:315
symphonies concertante and, 3:277
Théâtre Lyrique in, 3:639
as twelfth- and thirteenth-century intellectual capital, 1:148, 207–8
urban clergy and, 1:207–8
urbanization and, 1:120, 169, 207
Verdi commissions in, 3:568, 594
Wagner in, 3:482, 483
See also University of Paris
Paris Conservatory, 2:736; 4:63, 97, 125, 452
Americanism backlash and, 3:385

Franck and, 3:774
Liszt and, 3:262
symphonic music and, 3:676
textbooks used by, 3:287
Parisian chanson, 1:706–9, 711, 714, 786
Parisian neoclassicism, 4:605
Parisian sequence (Victorine), 1:90, 91
Parisian-style music books, 1:171
Paris Opera. *See* Académie Royale de Musique
"Paris" symphonies, nos. 82–87 (Haydn), 2:557
"Paris" Symphony in D major, no. 31, K. 287 (Mozart), 2:612–13
Paris University. *See* University of Paris
Parker, Horatio, 3:769; 5:198
Parker, Roger, 3:569, 572; , 4:245, 246, 251, 253, 266
Hora novissima, 4:246, 247, 248–49, 251, 252
Parker, Tom ("Colonel"), 5:314
appearance on the *Ed Sullivan Show*, 5:314
contract with RCA Victor, 5:314
parlante
in Bellini's *Norma*, 3:38, 41
in Donizetti's *Lucia di Lammermoor*, 3:48–49, 53–55, 59
in Verdi's *Otello*, 3:597, 606
in Verdi's *Rigoletto*, 3:587, 591
Parliament, British, 2:124
parlor piano, 2:736; 3:64
Parma, Grand Duchess of, 3:253
Parma, Italy, 3:253
Parnasse contemporain, Le, 4:97
Parnassians group (poets), 4:97, 100
decadence and, 4:97
Parnasso confuso, Il (Gluck), 2:454
parodies-opérettes, 3:644
parody (humor), 1:389
Gilbert and Sullivan operettas and, 3:652–55
of *opera seria*, 2:155
parody Masses, 1:572–76, 593, 641–44, 710, 788–89
parody (musical appropriation)
of Josquin motet, 1:572–76, 593
See also contrafactum; parody Masses
parody (polyphony), 1:314, 574
Du Fay and, 1:512
See also contrafactum
Parrenin Quartet, 5:36
Parrish, Carl, 1:157–58
Parsifal (Wagner), 3:480, 499, 611; 4:61, 90, 225, 328
Pärt, Arvo, 5:407, 408, 471, 526
bell imagery and, 5:402
Cantus in memoriam Benjamin Britten, 5:404
Estonia and, 5:400–401, 404
Fratres, 5:404
"Holy minimalism" and, 5:408
minimalism and, 5:400–408

St. John Passion, 5:403–404
Socialist Realism and, 5:401
Symphony no. 3, 5:401
Symphony no. 3, "Landini sixth" and, 5:401
Tabula rasa, 5:404–5
Tabula rasa, II (Silentium), 5:405–6
"tintinnabular" style and, 5:402–3, 404–5
partbooks, 1:539–44, 709, 710
commercial printing of, 1:542, 691–92
Germany and, 1:701
organ accompaniment and, 1:781
Parisian chanson and, 1:709
Vivaldi and, 2:224–25
Partch, Harry, 4:285, 5:481–89, 482, 513
Bitter Music, 5:481, 483, 487
"Corporeal versus Abstract Music," 5:482
Eight Hitchhiker Inscriptions from a Highway Railing at Barstow, California, 5:482, 483–85, 486
"Gate 5" label, 5:485
Genesis of a Music, 5:482
Gesamtkunstwerk and, 5:482, 485
hobo experiences, 5:481–82
instrumentarium, 5:482–83
King Oedipus, 5:481, 485
Letter: A Depression Message from a Hobo Friend, The, 5:482
Revelation in the Courthouse Park, 5:485–87
San Francisco: A Setting of the Cries of Two Newsboys on a Foggy Night in the Twenties, 5:482
"speech-melodies" and, 5:481, 483
tablature notations and, 5:483, 484–85
US Highball: A Musical Account of a Transcontinental Trip, 5:482
Wayward, The, 5:481
partesnoye peniye, 3:234
particell draft, Mahler and, 4:26, 29f
particularism, 3:62, 121
partita, 2:499
Baroque, 2:37
former vs. current meaning of, 2:262
Lutheran chorale and, 2:49–52, 262
See also suite
Partite sopra ciaccona (Frescobaldi), 2:39
Partite sopra passacagli (Frescobald), 2:39
Partito Nazionale Fascista, 4:746
Parton, Dolly, plunderphonics compact disc and, 5:504
"Parto qual pastorello prima che rompa il fume" (Hasse), 2:166, 167, 168, 169
part-song
Dowland and, 1:742
Dunstable and, 1:427, 429
Ganassi treatise and, 1:698
Italian *frottola*, 1:666, 694–95
Italian *laude*, 1:691
printing of, 1:694–95, 698, 699

singing etiquette of, 1:709

party music, 2:427

parvus. See low style

Parzival (Wolfram), 1:138

Paschal Time, 1:24, 686–87

Pas d'acier, Le (Prokokieff-Yakulov), 4:776

pas de deux, 4:135

Pasdeloup, Jules-Étienne, 3:677–78, 679–80

Pashchenko, Andrey, *Simfonicheskaya misteriya,* 5:182

Pashkevich, Vasily, 3:235–36

  Misfortune on Account of a Coach, 3:235–36

Pasquini, Bernardo, 2:150, 151

passacaglia, 2:38, 38–39, 193, 261, 345

Passacaglia in C minor (J. S. Bach), 2:247

Passacaglia (Wolpe), 5:296

passacalle, 2:38, 39

passaggii, 1:817; 2:15–16, 171

passamezzo (ground bass), 1:626

passamezzo antico (ground bass), 1:626

passamezzo moderno (ground bass), 1:626, 627

passepied, 2:96

Passibus ambiguis (Greiter motet), 2:184

passing tones (counterpoint), 1:430

Passio germanica, 3:167

Passion

  Bach (J. S.) oratorios and, 2:375, 377–82, 383, 385, 389–90

  Counter Reformation settings of, 1:775–79, 832

  Handel's *Messiah* and, 2:326

  Lutheran oratorio form and, 2:341

  Schütz setting of, 2:73

Passion Chorale, 2:378, 382

Passover seder, 1:13

passus duriusculus, 2:44, 95, 103, 128, 135, 729; 3:4, 359, 398, 514; 4:18

  Bach (J. S.) and, 2:254, 345

  Handel and, 2:317

  Mozart and, 2:627–28

  Sweelinck *Fantasia chromatica,* 2:44, 46

  Vivaldi and, 2:231

Pasta, Giuditta, 3:41

"Past and Present Concepts of the Nature and Limits of Music" (Babbitt), 5:155

pasticcio, 2:158, 168

"pastiche" element, *Octet for Winds* and, 4:449, 451

Pastorale ad libitum (Corelli), 2:189–92

pastorals, 1:722–73; 2:446

  Cavalieri and, 1:823, 826, 827, 834

  Dante and, 1:351

  eclogue and, 1:811–12; 3:67

  madrigal text and, 1:736–37, 750–51

  rondel and, 1:122

  trecento-style madrical and, 1:356–59, 363

"Pastoral" Symphony no. 6 in F major, op. 68 (Beethoven), 2:655, 680, 682; 3:204, 273

  Berlioz and, 3:322–23, 334

  Chopin and, 3:368, 375

pastorela, 1:113, 348; 2:446

Pastor Fido, Il (Guarini), 1:736–37, 813

pastourelle, 1:119, 120–21, 122, 127, 131; 3:187

  motet, 1:224–26, 234

"patent office modernism," 4:195, 292–95

Pater, Walter, 2:643; 3:59, 101

Pater noster (Josquin), 1:563, 564

Pater noster (van Wilder), 1:676–77

pathetic fallacy, 1:221

"Pathétique" Sonata in C minor, no. 8, op. 13 (Beethoven), 2:727, 728; 3:429

Pathétique Symphony in B minor, op. 74 (Chaikovsky), 3:108, 799–801; 4:19; 5:75

pathos (pathetic style)

  Beethoven's lieder and, 3:132

  B-minor mood and, 3:108

  C-minor mood and, 2:121, 696, 697, 727, 730

  in Dussek pieces, 3:65

  introversive signaling and, 2:588

  Italian opera and, 3:594

  Mozart's G-minor Symphony and, 2:591

  Purcell's Overture in D minor and, 2:128

  Romanticism and, 3:71

  Sweelinck's *Fantasia chromatica* and, 2:46

  See also empfindsamer stil

Path to the New Music, The (Webern), 4:359

patriarchy

  creativity theories and, 2:81

  female composers and, 3:186

  Handel's outlook and, 2:306

  opera seria and, 2:175

"Patriotic Anthology" (Diabelli), 3:262

patriotic songs, 1:18. *See also* national anthems

Patriotic War of 1812, 3:242

patriotism

  English music and, 2:306, 313

  nationalism and, 3:178, 346, 386

patronage

  Bach (C. P. E.) and, 2:462, 509

  Bach (J. C.) and, 2:419

  Bach (J. S.) and, 2:261–62

  Beethoven and, 2:653, 671, 675, 694; 3:443

  Bernart and, 1:109

  Brahms and, 3:690

  Burgundian court and, 1:424, 439, 447, 455, 458, 484–85, 498

  Chopin and, 3:348

  collective, 3:251, 254

  composer-patron symbiosis and, 2:527–28, 553, 555

  composer's emancipation from, 2:737

  composer's need for, 2:519

court opera and, 2:14

cyclic Mass Ordinary and, 1:460

demise of system of, 2:655

Elector Palatine and, 2:505–7, 505

English music and, 2:113, 124, 125

by Esterházy family, 2:525–30, 538

European diminished sources of, 2:607

fifteenth-century elite and, 1:453–54, 455

by Frederick II (the Great) of Prussia, 2:462, 509

by Frederick William of Prussia, 2:509

French political, 2:87–89

by Gaston of Languedoc, 1:342–45

Handel and, 2:237, 306

Haydn and, 2:519–20, 525–28, 538, 607, 655; 3:79, 261

Italian city-states and, 1:277–81

Josquin and, 1:554–55, 558, 559–63, 578, 578, 584, 696, 699; 2:538–39

Lasso and, 1:713

Lully and, 2:89, 99

Machaut and, 1:289, 290

madrigalists and, 1:353

male power of access and, 2:79

by Medicis, 1:531

Metastasio and, 2:171

by middle-class aristocracy, 3:730

by Milanese Sforza family, 1:518–19, 522–23

Mozart and, 2:607, 737

musical taste and, 2:87, 173, 639

by Ottoboni, 2:151

Palestrina and, 1:631, 675

by papacy, 1:278, 281, 754, 1559; 2:37

political power and, 1:277–78

Protestant Reformation effects on, 1:754

public taste vs., 2:639

salons and, 3:75

Schütz and, 2:56, 68

by ticket-buying public, 3:251, 292

of trouvères, 1:118

United States government and, 3:385

Willaert and, 1:600

"pattern and process music," 5:351

patter songs, 3:655

  basso buffo and, 2:439–40

Paul, Apostle and Saint, 1:13; 2:68; 3:166

Paul I, Emperor of Russia, 2:541, 541

Paul III, Pope, 1:649

Paul IV, Pope, 1:633

Paul, Anton, Prince Esterházy. *See* Esterházy, Paul Anton

Paul, David, 5:428

Paul, Jean, *Titan,* 4:9

  chorales, 3:167–70

  Fanny Mendelssohn and, 3:184

  Schumann's (Robert) critique of, 3:230, 292

Paul Sacher Foundation, 298 Paul the Deacon, 1:100–101

Paulus, Stephen, neotonality and, 5:454

pavan, **2:**53, 120, 126
  Dowland ayre and, **1:**742–43
Pavarotti, Luciano, **3:**579
Pavel Petrovich. *See* Paul I, Emperor of
  Russia
Pavolini, Alessandro, **4:**743
Pax! In nomine Domini (Marcabru), **1:**113
Peace Conference, **5:**108
Pearl Fishers, The (Bizet), **3:**390
Pearl Harbor, **4:**668
Pears, Peter, **5:**225, 229, 230, 231, 232, 241,
  243, 248, 258
  homosexuality and, 246–247
peasant revolts, **1:**138
peasants
  in Czech lands, **3:**444
  dances of, **1:**332, 621
  folklore and, **3:**122, 174
  idealization of, **3:**193
  in Romantic opera, **3:**187–205
  in Russia, **3:**232–33, 238, 246, 622
  Slavic languages and, **3:**345
Péchés de vieillesse (Rossini), **3:**12–13, 78
  ballet arrangements of, **3:**13
Pêcheurs de perles, Les (Bizet), **3:**390
Pecht, August Friedrich, **3:**479
Peckham, Morse, **3:**570, 660
"pedal music," **3:**68
pedal part
  Bach (J. S.) and, **2:**258, 361
  organ sonata, **2:**402
pedal point
  Bach Toccata in F and, **2:**208–12, 216
  of fugue, **2:**202
Pederson, Sanna, **3:**293
Pedro II, Emperor of Brazil, **3:**382
Peirol d'Auvergne, **1:**228
Pekenino, Michele, **2:**477
Pelléas et Mélisande (Debussy), **4:**86–96, *87,*
  89, 104, 443, 567
  symbolism and, **4:**86
  synopsis of action, **4:**87–88
Pelléas et Mélisande (Maeterlinck), **4:**508
Pellegrina, La (Bargagli), **1:**803
Penderecki, Krzysztof, **5:**217, 322, 437, 501
  Anaklasis, **5:**217
  De natura sonoris, **5:**217
  Fluorescences, **5:**217
  Polymorphia, **5:**217
  Roman Catholic faith and, **5:**407
  Solidarnosé movement (Poland) and,
    5:437
  St. Luke Passion, **5:**217
  Stabat Mater, **5:**217
  Symphony no. 2, **5:**437–38
  Symphony no. 2, "Christmas at
    Wotan's" and, **5:**437–38
  Symphony no. 2, "Silent Night" and,
    5:437–38
  Threnody, **5:**363
  Tren ofiarom Hiroszimy, **5:**217
Pendle, Karin, **3:**211

pendular harmonic plan
  ("there-and-back"), **2:**267, 606, 660
pendulum metronome, Maelzel and, **5:**177
Pendulum Music (Reich), **5:**372–73, 375
penitents, **1:**133–34
peniye, **3:**234
pentachord (fifth)
  canon and, **1:**331
  in counterpoint, **1:**154
  Diatonic pitch and, **1:**30, *31*
  Dorian, **1:**276–77
  four species of, **1:**73–74
  madrigal and, **1:**356
  octave plus, **1:**166, 168
  parallel doubling of, **1:**150, 151, 152
  as "perfect" interval, **1:**149
  protus final and, **1:**79
  tetrachord and, **1:**74, 83
  See also perfect fifth
pentagonal virginal, **2:**46
pentatonic scale, **1:**30
Pentecost, **1:**12, 49, 436, 686, 758
Pentecostal revival meetings, Partch's
    Revelation and, **5:**485
"People United Will Never Be Defeated!,
    The" (Rzewski), **5:**84, 85
Pepin III (the Short), King of the Franks,
    1:2, 3, 5, 13, 40, 64
Pepusch, Johann, **2:**312, *312*
Peraino, Judith, **1:**220–21
percussion, **2:**558; **3:**21
Peregrinus plays, **1:**93
Peress, Maurice, **4:**629
peremennost' tone, **3:**471, 474, 475
perestroyka, **4:**778, 785
perfect (perfection), **1:**180, 187, 196, 587
  Ars Nova notation and, **1:**249–50, 253,
    254–55
  dactylic foot and, **1:**191
  hocket and, **1:**233
  Zarlino harmonic theory and, **1:**587
  See also measure
perfected art. *See ars perfecta*
perfect fifth, **1:**149, 150, 154, 284
  chromaticism and, **1:**274
  parallel doubling at, **1:**152
perfect fourth, **1:**40, 149, 152, 284
  chromaticism and, **1:**274
perfect/imperfect notion, **1:**341, 417
perfect intervals, **1:**149
perfection. *See ars perfecta*; myth of
    perfection; perfect
perfect long, **1:**180, 181
perfect number, **1:**587
perfect pitch, **1:**76, 434
Perfect Wagnerite, The (Shaw), **3:**492
performance art, women and, v492,
performance practice
  accompanied keyboard sonata and,
    2:428
  artist self-representation and, **3:**64

"authentic" movement and, **1:**782; **2:**233,
    362–63
  Bach's (J. S.) musical demands vs.
    practical considerations of,
    2:369–75
  charismatic effects of, **1:**616–17
  Chopin and, **3:**363–65
  composers and, **1:**65, 299; **2:**519, 600,
    607, 610–14, 653
  composer specifications and, **1:**782–83
  conductor's absolutism and, **2:**111–12
  creative role separated from, **2:**639, 642,
    655
  critical exigesis and, **2:**650, 696, 714
  English singing qualities and, **1:**452
  harmonization and, **1:**392, 394, 406,
    434–39
  historical speculation on, **1:**158–59
  improvisation and, **1:**17, 617–18
  improvised vs. written cadenza and,
    2:171, 609–10, 613, 614–15, 650
  madrigal and, **1:**364
  Mass Ordinary and, **1:**310, 312–13
  medieval vernacular song and, **1:**130–31
  monody and, **1:**817
  musical dramatization and, **1:**786
  notation following, **1:**1–2, 184–85
  opera seria fluidity of, **2:**172–76, 432–36
  polyphonic singing and, **1:**44–47,
    147–48, 149, 157–59, 163
  professionalization of, **1:**786
  ricercari and, **1:**619
  sixteenth-century instrumental,
    1:617–21
  study of, **1:**452
  troubadour's songs and, **1:**109–10
  unwritten conventions and, **1:**46, 452
  Verdi's *Rigoletto* and, **3:**590–91
  written music and, **1:**104, 262, 265
  written supplementary directions for,
    1:262, 265
  See also concerts; domestic
    entertainment; standard repertory
performance repertory. *See* standard
  repertory
Pergolesi, Giovanni Battista, **2:**438, *439;*
    3:27, 33, 655
  Flaminio, Il, **2:**440
  Serva padrona, La, **2:**438–41, 450, 474,
    477
Peri, Jacopo, **1:**804–5, 806, 809, *809,*
    811–12, 823, 826, 829; **2:**1, 5, 6, 58
  Dafne, La, **1:**824, 826, 827–29, 831
  Dunque fra torbid' onde, **1:**810
  Euridice, **1:**811, 812, 813, 823, 824, 829–32;
    2:21, 23, 24, 454
  "Qual nova meraviglia!," **1:**827–28
  recitative convention and
Périchole, La (Offenbach), **3:**651
Perilous Night, The (Cage), **5:**59, 60
Perils of Pauline serials, **4:**563
periodization, **1:**380–85

Perle, George, 4:391, 392, 413, 415, 418, 520, 523, 704, 711, 713; 5:137, 169
  analytical table summarizing "set complex" of Babbitt's *Three Compositions for Piano*, 5:137
  Twelve-Tone Tonality, 5:456
Péronne d'Armentières, 1:297, 299
Perotin, 1:173–75, 186, 187, 191, 192, 198, 209, 347, 397
  organa quadrupla, 5:378
Perrault, Charles, 4:104, 144, 456
Perréal, Jean, 1:548
Persichetti, Vincent, 5:368
  Hall Overton and, 5:368
  Steve Reich and, 5:368
personal computers, music making and, 5:495
personal identity
  narratives and, 3:375
  Schubert and musical constructions of, 3:116–18
personal manager, Liszt's use of, 3:272
Perspectives of New Music (Berger and Boretz), 5:164, 167–72, 303
Perspice, christicola (Latin versus), 1:387
pertichini, 3:28
  in Donizetti's *Lucia di Lammermoor*, 3:53, 55, 59
pes (melodic repetition), 1:118, 129, 388, 389, 392
  British motets and, 1:399–403, 405, 408, 410, 411
  Ockeghem motet and, 1:457
  voice-exchange of, 1:399
Pesaro family, 1:281
pessimism, 2:721, 724
  verismo, 3:659
Petelin, Jacov. *See* Gallus, Jacobus
Peter, Johann Friedrich, 2:519
Peter Grimes (op. 33) (Britten), 5:225
Peter, Paul, and Mary, 5:315, 334
  Paul Stookey and, 5:315
  "Puff, the Magic Dragon," 5:315
Peter, Saint, 1:80
Peter I (the Great), Tsar of Russia, 3:230–31, 234, 248, 478
Peter Schmoll und seine Nachtbarn (Weber), 3:191–92
Petipa, Marius, 4:139–40, 144, 145, 152
  Russian "classical" ballet and, 4:139
Petite messe solennelle (Rossini), 3:13
petite reprise. See coda
Petrarch, 1:116, 310, 352, 723, 724, 728, 747, 818; 2:6, 37; 4:692
Petrarchan revival, 1:722–23
Petrassi, Goffredo, 5:295
Petre family, 1:679
Petronian motet, 1:236–45, 251, 259
  trecento system and, 1:355
Petrucci, Ottaviano, 2:114
  first competitor of, 1:691

publications of, 1:499–500, 520, 529, 542–43, 544, 555, 557–58, 559, 560–61, 563, 565, 574, 579, 606, 666, 691, 693, 694, 695, 697, 698, 699
  typographical method of, 1:692
Petrus Alamire, 1:457
Petrus de Cruce, 1:238–45, 249, 251, 258–67, 355
Petruschka-chord, 4:164, 165, 167, 174, 175, 182, 191, 204
  octatonic derivation of, 4:165
"Petruschka's despair," 4:169
Petrushka (Stravinsky), 4:159–170, 172, 189, 405, 408
"petty I," Ivanov and, 4:206, 208, 213, 227
Pezel (or Petzoldt), Johann, 2:287
Pfitzner, Hans, 1:652–53
  Palestrina, 1:652–53, 652, 654, 656
Phaedo (Plato), 2:416
Phaedrus (Plato), 1:17
Phantasie, op. 17 (Schumann), 3:309–15, 320, 324, 354, 360, 432
  autobiographical aspects of, 3:311–12, 321
  "Ruinen," 3:311, 312–15
Phantasiestücke, op. 12 (Schumann), 3:306–8
phantasmagorias, 3:202–3, 205, 217
Phelps, William Lyon, 4:243, 270, 272
  Music, 4:243
phenomenal music, 1:827
  noumenal music vs., 2:21, 22, 720
  Philadelphia Orchestra, 4:781
Phenomenology of Spirit (Hegel), 5:332
Philby, Kim, 5:7
Philharmonic Society of London, 2:673–74
Philidor, Anne Danican, 2:499
Philidor, François-André, 2:499
Philip I, King of France, 1:93
Philip I (the Handsome), King of Spain, 1:457
Philip II, King of France, 1:170
Philip II, King of Spain, 1:649
Philip II (the Bold), Duke of Burgundy, 1:424, 485
Philip III (the Good), Duke of Burgundy, 1:439, 484–85, 486
Philip IV (the Fair), King of France, 1:258, 310, 559
Philip V, King of Spain, 2:167, 169
Philip Glass Ensemble, 5:390, 391, 392
Philippus (or Philipoctus) de Caserta, 1:337–42, 356
  En remirant, 1:338–39, 341, 341
Philips, Peter, 2:45, 47
Philips Pavilion, 5:77, 79
Philip the Chancellor, 1:174, 184
  Dic, Christi veritas, 1:201–5
Philistines, 3:291, 390–91
philistinism, 3:291–94, 397
Phillips, Wendell, 4:287

Philomel (Babbitt), 5:211
  John Hollander and, 5:201
philosophes, 2:461, 462, 577
philosophical Romanticism. *See* Romanticism
philosophy of history, 1:144–45
Philosophy of New Music, The (Adorno), 4:189, 335; 5:17
phrase symmetry, 2:432
Phrygian mode, 1:76, 79, 83, 479, 555
Phrygian scale, 1:44, 79, 82, 802
  polyphony and, 1:529
phylogeny, 4:358–61
Piange, madonna (d'India), 1:819–20
Pianissimo (Schnittke), 5:463
piano
  Beethoven pieces for, 3:65
  Beethoven's instrument, 2:653
  Beethoven's late compositions for, 2:686
  Beethoven's performance skills and, 2:652, 655
  Charakterstück and, 3:65, 119, 444
  Chopin pieces for, 3:75, 350
  Chopin's performance skills and, 3:343–76
  five-octave, Mozart-era, 2:590
  home entertainment and, 3:63–64
  keys/scale relationship, 1:76
  lied and, 3:119
  Liszt's performance skills and, 3:261–73
  manufacturers of, 3:73, 382
  mass production of, 3:63
  Mélodies orientales, 3:387
  as middle-class furniture, 2:736; 3:64
  Mozart concertos for, 2:476, 601–25, 696
  Mozart fantasias for, 2:611, 613, 624–34
  Mozart's compositions for, 2:590
  Mozart's performance skills and, 2:590
  nocturnes for, 3:65
  "pedal music" for, 3:68
  Romantic music for, 3:68
  salon music for, 3:75, 77, 78
  Schubert duets for, 3:83, 84
  Schubert pieces for, 3:82–84
piano concerto
  genre transformation of, 3:273–85
  Liszt and, 3:277–88, 419
  Mendelssohn (Felix) and, 3:275–77, 287–88
  Mozart and, 3:273–75, 287–88
  Schumann (Robert) and, 3:316
  Piano Concerto no. 1 (Liszt), 3:273–85, 698
  Piano Concerto no. 1 in D minor, op. 15 (Brahms), 3:686–88, 692, 776
  Piano Concerto no. 2 in B-flat major, op. 19 (Beethoven), 2:652
  Piano Concerto no. 3 in C minor, op. 37 (Beethoven), 3:273–74
  Piano Concerto no. 4 in G major, op. 58 (Beethoven), 2:655; 3:275, 276

Piano Concerto no. 5 in D major, K. 175 (Mozart), **2:**602, 612, 614–15

Piano Concerto no. 5 in E-flat major, op. 73 ("Emperor") (Beethoven), **2:**671; **3:**275

Piano Concerto no. 17 in G major, K. 453 (Mozart), **2:**608–10, 613–15; **3:**115

 finale, **2:**622, 623

 first movement cadenzas, **2:**613, 614–15

 first movement themes, **2:**609, 610 (table)

 interpretations of, **2:**619–21

 slow movement, **2:**613–14, 615–22

Piano Concerto no. 24 in C minor, K. 491 (Mozart), opening theme, **2:**696, 698, 702

Piano Concerto no. 26 in D, K. 537 ("Coronation") (Mozart), **2:**610–11, 612

Piano Fantasy (Copland), **5:**112, 114

"piano lyric," **3:**65

Piano Phase (Reich), **5:**373–75

Piano Piece 1962 (Brecht), **5:**91

Piano Piece for David Tudor (Young), **5:**355

Piano Quartet (Copland), **5:**109–13

piano sonata

 Beethoven and, **2:**653, 674, 721

 eighteenth-century accompanied, **2:**695

 Mozart and, **2:**471, 616

Piano Sonata in A flat major, op. 110 (Beethoven), fugal finale, **2:**686, 726

Piano Sonata in A major, op. 101 (Beethoven), fugal finale, **2:**686, 724, 725

Piano Sonata in B-flat major, op. 106 ("Hammerklavier") (Beethoven), **2:**673, 674

 fugal finale, **2:**686, 724, 726

Piano Sonata in C minor, K. 457 (Mozart), **2:**626

Piano Sonata in C minor, no. 8, op. 13 ("Pathetique") (Beethoven), **2:**727, 728

Piano Sonata in C minor, no. 32, op. 111 (Beethoven), **2:**674, 721, 727–35

 second movement variations (*Arietta*), **2:**731

 sublime moments in, **2:**732, 734

 trills, **2:**732, 733

Piano Sonata in F minor, op. 57 ("Appassionata"; Beethoven), **2:**670; **3:**1, 376

Piano Sonata no. 2 (Ives), **4:**262, 263

piano trio

 Beethoven and, **2:**652–53, 655, 694, 695–701

 as French genre, **2:**695

Piano Trio in B-flat major ("Archduke"), op. 97 (Beethoven), **2:**655, 671

Piano Trio in C minor, op. 1, no. 3 (Beethoven), **2:**653, 694, 695–701, 721, 730

 announcement theme, **2:**696–98

 Fifth Symphony opening compared with, **2:**706–7

 finale, **2:**698–701

Piano Trio in F-sharp Minor, op. 1, no. 1 (Franck), **3:**777

Piano Variations (Copland), **4:**652–53, 654

Piano Variations (Webern), **5:**23

Piano Variations (Wolpe), **5:**20

Piatti, Ugo, **5:**179

Piave, Francesco Maria, **3:**575–76, 577, 580, 583, 594

Piazza San Marco (Venice), **2:**12

Picabia, Francis, *Relache* and, **4:**571

Picander (Christian Friedrich Henrici), **2:**378

Picard family, **1:**411

Picardy third, **2:**494

Picasso, Pablo, **4:**563, 566, 567

 Ballets Russes and, **4:**561

 Josephine Baker and, **4:**602

Piccinni, Niccolò, **2:**158, 445–52; **3:**202, 329

 Gluck rivalry with, **2:**441, 445, 452, 455, 459, 460

 Mozart's *La finta semplice* style compared with, **2:**465

 works of

  Buona Figliuola, La, **2:**445–52, 453, 486

  Iphigenia in Tauris, **2:**460

Pickford, Mary, **4:**563

Picker, Tobias, neotonality and, **5:**454

pictorialisms, **1:**749, 750; **3:**181, 183

"Picture of Dorian Gray, The" (Wilde), **4:**30

Pictures at an Exhibition (Musorgsky), **5:**328

Pidgeon, Walter, **5:**107

Pie Jesu (L. Boulanger), **4:**126, 127–28

pièce à machines, **2:**87

pièce bien faite (well-made play), **3:**207

Pièce caractéristique, **3:**65, 119

Piece dans le style ancien (Chaminade), **4:**65

Piece for Four Pianos (Feldman), **5:**99–100

Piece for Tape Recorder (Ussachevsky), **5:**198

Pièces de clavecin (Couperin), **2:**269, 279

Pièces de clavecin en concert (Rameau), **2:**695

Pièces de clavecin en sonates avec accompagnement de violon in C major, op.3, no. 4 (Mondonville), **2:**428, 429

Piero, Maestro, **1:**352, 352

Pierre de la Croix. *See* Petrus de Cruce

Pierre Hosdenck, **1:**174

Pierrot lunaire (Schoenberg), **4:**456, 457, 458, 458, 460, 460, 462, 465, 573, 576, 679, 695, 749,

Pierrot Players

 Eight Songs for a Mad King and, **5:**426–27

 Schoenberg's *Pierrot Lunaire* and, **5:**426

"Pif paf pouf!" (Meyerbeer), **3:**220

pincée. See mordant

Pincherle, Marc, **2:**218

Pindar, **3:**120

Pini di Roma (Respighi), **4:**750, **5:**179

Pio Ospedale della Pietà (Vivaldi), **2:**216, 223

Pirandello, Luigi, **4:**495, 496, 498, 499, 534

 La favola del figlio cambiato and, **4:**749

 works of

  Sei personaggi in cerca d'autore, **4:**495

Pirates of Penzance, The (Gilbert and Sullivan), **3:**652, 653–54, 655

 "Come, friends who plow the sea," **3:**653

 "Poor wand'ring one," **3:**653

Pirrotta, Nino, **2:**1, 2

Pisendel, Johann Georg, **2:**222

Piston, Walter, **4:**648, 649, 666; **5:**21

 Symphony no. 3, **4:**648

pitch, **1:**30, 105; **2:**248

 chant-setting, **1:**50

 color and, **1:**232

 early Greek notation and, **1:**16–17, 17, 45, 732

 fixed, **1:**76

 Frankish notation and, **1:**73, 75–76, 78

 Guidonian scale range of, **1:**101–3

 interval ratios, **1:**38

 key system and, **1:**76

 ligatures and, **1:**176–77

 medieval modal scale and, **1:**101–3

 modal-to-tonal change and, **1:**471–72

 natural harmonic series and, **1:**588

 neumes' staff placement and, **1:**16, 99–100

 oral/aural transmission of, **1:**117

 Pythagorean proportions and, **1:**282, 284

 relationships, **1:**37, 596–97

 tendency tones and, **1:**275–76

"pitch classes," **4:**26, 191

pitch-letter code, **4:**313–14, 316

Pithoprakta (Xenakis), **5:**78

Pitti Palace (Florence), **1:**826, 832

Pius IV, Pope, **1:**650, 652

Pius V, Pope, **1:**675

Pius X, Pope, **3:**13

pivot, **3:**299

Pixis, Theodor, **3:**560

pizzicato technique, **3:**256

plagal harmony, **1:**427

plagal modal form, **1:**74, 75, 76, 83, 554

plagal scales, **1:**74

plagiarism, **1:**746; **2:**327–29

plainchant. *See* chant

Plaine and Easie Introduction to Practicall Musicke (Morley), **1:**694, 743

Plançon, Pol, **3:**640

planctus cigni (song), **1:**111–12, 112

planctus settings, **1:**111–4212

planh (troubadour genre), **1:**107

plantation songs, **3:**765, 766

Platen, Count August von, **3:**116

Plato, 1:17, 70, 281, 615, 831; 2:5, 312, 416; 3:529, 557
  artistic creation and, 1:552
  essences and, 1:37, 827; 2:720
  forms and, 1:69, 71
  harmony of the spheres and, 1:152
  musical modes and, 1:801–2
  social aspect of music and, 1:208
Platonic Academy (Florence), 1:615
Playing on Words: A Guide to Luciano Berio's "Sinfonia" (Osmond-Smith), 5:348
Play of Daniel, 1:93–94, 95–96
Play of Herod, 1:93
Play of Robin and Marion (Adam), 1:127, 128, 233, 349
Pleyel, Ignaz, 2:499, 571
plica, 1:181, 197
Plow That Broke the Plains, The (Lorentz), 4:660, 661
Ployer, Barbara, 2:608, 613
"plunderphonics," John Oswald and, 5:504
Plutarch, 2:702; 4:750
Pocahontas (Carter), 5:268
podium virtuoso, baton conducting and, 3:222
Poe, Edgar Allen Poe, 4:84
  as Baudelaire's mentor, 4:96
Poem in Cycles and Bells, A (Ussachevsky), 5:198
Poème de l'extase, Le (Scriabin), 4:213, 214, 215, 219, 225, 227
  Tristanisms and, 4:213
Poeme électronique (Varese), 5:208, 208, 209, 502
Poeme symphonique (Ligeti), 5:162, 373
poesia per musica (bucolic poetry), 1:351
Poésies barbares (Leconte de Lisle), 4:97
"Poet, The" (Pushkin), 3:633
poète maudit, 4:100
  Chopin as, 3:343
  mythology of, 3:117
  Paganini as, 3:254
  Romanticism and, 3:71
poetic content, 3:428
  Dvořák and, 3:755, 759
  interpretation and, 3:425–27
  in symphonic poems, 3:419, 420, 425–26
Poetics (Aristotle), 1:551
poetics, meaning of, 2:13
poetry
  affective style and, 1:737–38
  aria and, 2:144
  ballads and, 3:126–29, 367
  British laureates, 2:113, 127, 132
  by Christine of Pisane, 1:446–47, 448
  ciaccona and, 2:37
  conductus setting of, 1:198–205
  Deschamps on, 1:337
  difficult vs. accessible, 1:115–16
  English song settings of, 1:742–51
  formes fixes and, 1:125–26
  German, 3:124–29

German folk style, 3:124
goliardic, 1:138
by Hildegard of Bingen, 1:90–92
irony in, 3:142
Italian recitation of, 1:697
Italian settings of, 1:666, 722–23, 736–37
as Lasso sibylline prophecy text, 1:719
lyric, 3:63–64, 119, 124–26
of Machaut, 1:289–90, 297, 307, 332
as madrigal text, 1:354, 356–57, 723–25, 727, 728, 736–37, 739, 742, 749, 802, 813, 816–17, 818, 819; 2:6, 7–10
medieval, 3:124
meters of, 1:5, 175, 191, 197
motet and, 1:218–19, 255–60, 742
music's relationship with, 1:337, 550, 738; 2:642
music's separated from, 1:351
Passion, 2:378
prosodic accents and, 1:14
recitation formulas for, 1:697, 698
rhyme patterns of, 1:43, 89
Romantic, 3:64
roundeau form, 1:122–24
stanza-and-refrain forms of, 3:124
Sturm und Drang and, 2:529
troubadours and trouvères and, 1:98–99, 107–45, 351
vernacular, 1:3, 99, 106–7, 351–85, 459
volkstümlich, 3:126–29, 367
See also courtly love poetry and songs; epics; literary music; lyric poetry; narrative poetry; versification
"Poet Speaks, The" (*Der Dichter spricht*; Schumann), 3:360–61
Pöhlmann, Egert, 1:33, 34
poietic fallacy, definition of, 2:13, 14
point shape (punctum), 1:131, 214
"Pointwise Periodic Homeomorphisms" (Babbitt), 5:172 Poitiers, 1:109, 111
Poitou, Duchy of, 1:106
Poland, 1:728
  ars subtilior and, 1:346–49
  ballad and, 3:367
  Chopin and, 3:343–44, 346, 348, 375–76, 447
  folk dance and, 3:357
  Glinka's *A Life for the Tsar* and, 3:242, 245
  literature and, 3:345
  national anthem of, 3:357
  nationalism and, 3:344, 375–76
  national opera of, 3:447
  partitions of, 1:347; 3:344
Polashek, Timothy, "interactive sound installations" and, 5:514
Policraticus (John of Salisbury), 1:172
Polish Composers Union, 5:216
"Polish renaissance," 5:217

Polish State Publishing House for Music, 5:220
political correctness, 2:112
political thought
  artistic expression and, 1:653, 673
  artistic products in context of, 2:12–16, 111–12, 175–76, 369, 389–90
  artistic style judgments and, 1:145
  artist oppression and, 3:345
  art separated from, 3:62
  Bach's (J. S.) Brandenburg Concerto and, 2:301–3, 369, 619
  Bach's (J. S.) cantatas and, 2:368, 369, 373–64
  Beethoven's works and, 2:655–56, 659, 670, 673, 686, 721–24
  Classic/Romantic dichotomy subtext and, 2:647–48
  composer activism and, 2:736
  covert argumentation and, 2:111–12
  Darwinian historiography and, 2:397
  English Civil War and Restoration and, 1:132; 2:114–15, 124, 125–27, 126, 137
  Enlightenment and, 2:110, 461–62, 724
  Enlightenment backlash and, 2:645
  French press wars and, 2:86, 110
  German lieder and, 3:158, 160–63
  Haydn's works and, 2:577
  Hegelian dialectic and, 3:413, 414
  Liszt's activism and, 3:264–66
  medieval allegiances and, 1:141–42
  minority artistic representation and, 2:82, 112
  motet as satirizing, 1:255–69
  motet as vehicle for, 1:277–81
  Mozart's Piano Concerto no 17 soloist/orchestra interaction and, 2:620
  musical interpretation and, 3:476–78
  music's role in, 3:206, 212–14
  operatic division and, 2:34
  Romanticism and, 2:651, 724
  significance of virtuoso singing and, 2:15–16
  War of the Buffoons and, 2:110–12, 441
  women's rights and, 2:82
  See also absolutism; nationalism
politics of patronage. See patronage
Poliziano, Angelo, 1:823
polka, 3:455, 754
Pollini, Maurizio, 5:89
  Luigi Nono and, 5:89
Pollock, Howard, 4:661, 663, 669
Pollock, Jackson, 5:77, 264, 353
  "Dionysian" art, 5:77
polonaise, 3:35, 49, 579
  Chaikovsky and, 3:796–97
  Chopin and, 3:347, 348, 350, 357, 367, 796
"Polovtsian Dance" (Borodin), 3:401, 402
Polovtsy (Turkish nomads), 3:400

polychoral style, **1:**776–82, 791; **2:**46, 58
"polychord," **4:**191
Polyhymnia caduceatrix et panegyrica
  (Praetorius), **2:**54–55, 57
polymeter, **1:**337–38
Polymorphia (Penderecki), **5:**217
polyp, symbolism of, **2:**437
polyphony, **1:**145, 147–68
  accelerated development of, **1:**148, 149
  Adam de la Halle works and, **1:**122, 123,
    142, 291
  ancient origins of, **1:**147
  Anglican "stripped down," **1:**672
  Aquitanian monastic centers and,
    1:156–62
  Bach (J. S.) and, **2:**241, 428
  Byrd and, **1:**670, 679, 680
  cadential progression and, **1:**276–77
  Calvinist church service ban on, **1:**755;
    2:44
  canon and, **1:**330–36, 364
  cantilena and, **1:**298–301
  chorale settings and, **2:**49–55, 353
  choral performance and, **1:**314
  chromaticism and, **1:**273–76
  Clemens's psalm settings and, **1:**597–99
  closure signal in, **1:**168
  Codex Calixtinus and, **1:**162–68
  Compostela manuscript and, **1:**162, 171
  conductus and, **1:**131, 162, 165, 166–67,
    173–74, 198–205
  Du Fay and, **1:**441–42, 498, 512
  early British, **1:**387–92
  early Christian rejection of, **1:**10
  English High-Church, **1:**518, 526,
    612–14
  English pre-Reformation, **1:**387–99,
    402–11, 419, 423, 434–35, 672
  English Reformation and, **1:**672, 673,
    676
  fauxbourdon and, **1:**435–39, 441, 442
  fourth voice. *See* contratenor; four-part
    polyphony
  Frankish practice of, **1:**44–47, 45
  French style of, **1:**429
  Gabrieli (Giovanni) and, **1:**786
  Garlandia classification of, **1:**196–98
  German courtly songs and, **1:**701
  Glareanus's modal theory and, **1:**554
  Grocheio's social theory and, **1:**208
  Guido of Arezzo and, **1:**153–54, 155, 156
  homorhythmic, **1:**122, 146, 199, 296
  imitative, **1:**330–36, 337, 493, 546, 574,
    577, 579, 580, 589, 596
  improvisational, **1:**392
  isosyllabic performance of, **1:**115, 159
  Italy and, **1:**699
  Josquin and, **1:**529, 538, 563, 566,
    568–70, 572, 578, 579
  Lutheran chorales and, **1:**755, 758,
    760–62, 768
  luxuriant style and, **1:**301–5

  Machaut and, **1:**290–91, 293, 296–314,
    325–36
  madrigal and, **1:**354, 356, 364, 800–801,
    816, 817, 818
  Marian antiphons and, **1:**501, 672
  Mass Ordinary and, **1:**54, 307, 308–16,
    324, 325–26, 512
  metrical, **1:**175–83
  Milanese ducal motets and, **1:**520–26
  as model of tension and release, **2:**486
  Monteverdi and, **2:**6
  motet and, **1:**122, 221–36, 255, 259,
    270–73, 298, 604
  multiple choirs and, **1:**783–84
  Netherlanders and, **2:**45
  neume shapes and, **1:**22
  "northern," **1:**722
  notation of, **1:**185
  Notre Dame school and, **1:**171–205
  old-style. *See* stile antico
  Oswald von Wolkenstein and, **1:**143
  Palestrina and, **1:**635–41, 655–65, 666
  parody and, **1:**314, 512, 574
  partbooks and, **1:**539–40, 542
  Passion text settings, **1:**775–77
  Phrygian, **1:**529
  Poland and, **1:**347–49
  pre-Christian, **1:**31, 147
  quadruplum, **1:**174, 187, 198, 199–201,
    199
  remodeling of. *See* parody
  rhythmic performance of, **1:**114
  Roman Catholic standard and, **1:**666,
    667, 686; **3:**13
  rounds and, **1:**331
  St. Martial-style, **1:**157, 159, 160–61, 162,
    171
  Schütz motets and, **2:**68
  sixteenth-century, **1:**587–89, 596–97,
    747
  Sweelinck's vocal music and, **2:**45
  Tallis and, **1:**673
  Tenorlied and, **1:**701
  trecento, **1:**351, 353–54, 353
  as Western music's norm, **1:**148
  See also clausula; counterpoint; four-part
    polyphony; fugue; organum;
    three-part polyphony; two-part
    polyphony
polytextuality, **1:**212, 226, 286–87
  antiphon motet and, **1:**508
  papal complaint about, **1:**311
polytonality, **1:**150, 152; **4:**46, 54
Pomerium (Marchetto and Syphans), **1:**354
Pompeii, **2:**453
Pompidou, Georges, IRCAM and, **5:**478
Ponchielli, Amilcare, *Gioconda, La*, **3:**669
Ponte, Lorenzo da. *See* Da Ponte, Lorenzo
Pontifici decora speculi ("Johannes Carmen"),
  1:378–80
Pontius Pilate, **2:**378

"Poor wand'ring one" (Gilbert and
  Sullivan), **3:**653
Pope, Alexander
  Dunciad, **5:**302
Pople, Anthony, **4:**231
pop music
  audience interaction and, **1:**617; **2:**223,
    613
  crooning and, **1:**817
  impromptu arrangements of, **1:**131
  improvisation and, **2:**174, 611, 650–51
  nineteenth-century origins, **3:**682
  vamping and, **2:**38, 564
Popovici, *Carul cu boi*, **3:**456
Poppea, Empress of Rome, **2:**1, 27, 31–32,
  88
Popper, Karl, **3:**413
Pop-Pourri (Del Tredici), **5:**442
Poppy Nogood and the Phantom Band (Riley),
  5:366
"pops" concerts, **4:**668
popular art
  high art vs., **1:**115–16, 120
  trouvères and, **1:**120–26, 136, 142
Popular Concerts (London "Pops"), **3:**678,
  680
Popular Front, **4:**657, 658, 659, 661, 662,
  663, 664, 669, 671
popular music. *See* pop music
Porgy and Bess (Gershwin), **4:**628, 636
poriv, Ivanov and, **4:**219, 224
Porpora, Nicola, **2:**158, 169, 173, 518
Porque trobar (canso), **1:**129, 131
Porta, Costanzo, **1:**605
portamenti, **4:**609
"Portare" (tenor melisma), **1:**233
portative organ, **1:**363
Porter, Andrew, **5:**426, 436, 444
  review of Carter's *Symphony for Three
    Orchestras*, **5:**301
  review of Carter's *Third Quartet*, **5:**301
Porter, Cecilia Hopkins, **2:**385
Portugal, **2:**390
positivism, **3:**619
Possente spirto (Monteverdi), **2:**21
postlude, Schumann's use of, **3:**304
postmodernism, **5:**411–72
  architecture and, **5:**412
  "Green" movements and, **5:**414
potpourri overture, **3:**197
Potsdam, **2:**385, 462
Potsdam Conference, **5:**6
Potter, Keith, **5:**371, 378
Potter, Pamela, **4:**756
Poulenc, Francis, **4:**570, 573, 576, 579, 585,
  597; **5:**13, 326, 434
  Dialogues of the Carmelites, **5:**225
  Elegie, **5:**103
  Les Six group and, **4:**588
  Rag mazurka in *Les biches* and, **4:**568
  works of
    Biches, Les, **4:**568

Bonne d'enfant, **4:**575

Cocardes, **4:**575, 576, 577

Enfant de troupe, **4:**575

Mamelles de Tirésias, Les **4:**578, 578, 580–81

Miel de Narbonne, **4:**575–76

*Rapsodie negre,*op. 1, **4:**573

Pound, Ezra, **1:**389; **4:**11, 5, 13, 23, 28

"Pour cette cause sainte" (Meyerbeer), **3:**223

Pour les funérailles d'un soldat (L. Boulanger), **4:**126

Pourquoy me bat mes maris (Machaut), **1:**292–93

Pousseur, Henri, *Scambi,* **5:**195

"Povera Ragazza, Una" (Piccini), **2:**448–49

Power, Leonel, **1:**413, 416, 461

   Missa Alma Redemptoris Mater, **1:**462–65, 499

practical jokes. *See* joke, musical

Praetorius, Michael, **1:**765–66; **2:**54–55, 57

   chorale concerti and, **2:**52

   Christ lag in Todesbanden, **1:**767–68; **2:**55

   Musae Sioniae, **1:**765–66

   productivity of, **2:**54

Prague

   Dvořák and, **3:**753

   Mozart and, **2:**478, 611–12

   Smetana and, **3:**444–45, 447, 457–58

Prague Provisional Theater, **3:**753–54

Prairie Journal (Copland), **4:**661

Pratella, Francesco Balilla,*Inno alla vita,* **5:**178

Pratsch, Johann Gottfried (Jan Bogumir), **3:**233

prebends, **1:**169

precambulum, **2:**40

precentor, **1:**169

"Preclassic" period, **2:**401–2

prefaces. *See* tropes

preface themes

   Beethoven and, **3:**109, 112

   Schubert and, **3:**109, 110, 112, 113

Preis der Tonkunst (Rochlitz), **2:**673

Prejean, Sister Helen, *Dead Man Walking,* **5:**516

prejudice. *See* social prejudice

Prélude a L'apres-midi d'un faune (Debussy), **4:**86

prelude and fugue, **2:**247–51

Prelude in C major, no. 1 (Bach), **2:**249–50, 253

preludes

   Chopin and, **3:**350, 351–56, 438

   suite, **2:**262

   Wagner and, **3:**486, 487

Préludes, Les (Symphonic Poem No. 3; Liszt), **3:**422–27, 435, 776

Preludes, op. 28 (Chopin), **3:**351–56

Preludio a Colón (Carrillo), **4:**292–93, 294, 295

Premier amusement à la mode (Guilleman), **2:**427

Premier coup d'archet, **2:**506, 507

"premodern" world view, Symbolism and, **4:**85

"Preparatory Act" (Scriabin), **4:**227

Presley, Elvis, **1:**617; **5:**313–14, 318, 327, 336

   appearance on the *Ed Sullivan Show,* **5:**314

   "Elvis the Pelvis," **5:**314

   Partch's *Revelation* and, **5:**485

press, music criticism and, **3:**289–90

press wars

   on French vs. Italian opera, **2:**86, 110

   political/social subtexts of, **2:**110–11

   Querelle des Bouffons, **2:**110–11, 441–44

   Querelle des Gluckistes et Piccinistes, **2:**441, 445, 452, 459, 460

   Querelle des Lullistes et Ramistes, **2:**441

Previn, Andre, *Streetcar Named Desire, A* (opera) and, **5:**516

Prévost d'Exiles, Antoine-François (Abbé Prévost), **3:**641

Preys, Alexander, **4:**786

Prez, Josquin des. *See* Josquin des Prez

Price, Curtis, **2:**127

Prigioniero superbo, Il (Pergolesi), **2:**438

Prihody Lisky Bystrousky (Janáček), **4:**424

prima donna, **3:**9, 578

   castrati as, **2:**16–17, 153

   figurative meaning of, **2:**153

   Metastasian libretto and, **2:**153, 161

   Monteverdi roles for, **2:**27

   in Musorgsky's *Boris Godunov,* **3:**623, 629

   women as, **2:**17

Prima parte dei salmi concertati (Giacobbi), **1:**781

Primavera, La (Vivaldi), **2:**225–31, 308

   popularity of, **2:**226, 227

prime number, **1:**495

Primitive (Cage), **5:**59

"primitive music," **4:**4

primitivism, **3:**123

Primo libro de motetti accomodati per cantare e far concerti, Il (Trombetti), **1:**780

Primo libro di musiche (d'India), **1:**819

Primo libro d'intavolatura (Frescobaldi), **2:**41–42

primo uomo, **2:**153, 161, 175

Prince Igor (Borodin), **3:**397, 400–405, 407, 789

   Chorus of Polovtsian Maidens, **3:**401, 402

   costume for, **3:**400

   "Polovtsian Dance," **3:**401, 402

   Princesse de Polignac (née Winnaretta Singer), **3:**572

Prince of the Pagodas, The (op. 57) (Britten), **5:**225

Princesse Maleine, La (Maeterlinck), **4:**126

Princetonian serialism, **5:**136

Princeton Seminar in Advanced Musical Studies, **5:**295

Princeton University, **5:**134–36

Princeton University Library, **1:**408

print culture, **1:**553

Printemps, Le (Debussy), **4:**78

printing. *See* music publishing

Prioritätstreit, **4:**686–87

Prisoner in the Caucasus, A (Cui) **3:**397

private music, Romanticism and, **3:**63–69

Prix de Rome, **3:**326; **4:**70

   women and, **4:**125

Problems of Modern Music, **5:**40

Probst (publishing house), **3:**84

Prochazka, Ludevit, **3:**443

prodigies, **2:**463–64

   Liszt as, **3:**261–62, 264

   Mendelssohn (Fanny) as, **3:**184–86

   Mendelssohn (Felix) as, **3:**179–84

   Meyerbeer as, **3:**215

   Mozart as, **2:**463–64, 601, 607; **3:**179

production-consumption relationship. *See* supply and demand

production numbers. *See* morceaux d'ensemble

professional reviewers. *See* criticism

profundity, **2:**235

programmatic music, **3:**686

   Berlioz and, **3:**321

   Dvořák and, **3:**754–55

   Liszt and, **3:**421

   Romantic values and, **3:**66

   Russian, **3:**471

   Smetana and, **3:**446–47, 454–55

   symphonic music preemption by, **3:**675

programs

   for Berlioz's *Symphonie fantastique,* **3:**321–22, 324, 335, 340–41, 425, 793

   for Chaikovsky's Fourth Symphony, **3:**793, 795

   for Liszt's *Les préludes,* **3:**423, 425, 426

   Liszt support of, **3:**421

progress

   historiographical view of, **1:**580, 738–39

   periodization and, **1:**381, 383

   technical vs. stylistic evolution, **1:**245, 247–48, 252, 580, 738–39

Progressive Era, **4:**253

"progressive" music, **5:**411

progressivism, conservatism vs., **3:**179

Prohibition, **4:**602

Projection I (Feldman), **5:**98–99

Projection II (Feldman), **5:**99

Projections (Feldman), **5:**98

Prokofieff, Serge, **4:**479, 491, 496–506, 497, 548, 553, 555, 619, 620, 628, 691, 696, 776, 795; **5:**9–11, 13, 294,434

   background, **4:**497–98

   neoclassicism and, **4:**496

   response to "Resolution on Music," **5:**11

   works of

      "Classical Symphony," **4:**496

Prokofieff, Serge (*continued*)
    "Classical Symphony" III (Gavotte),
        4:496, 497
    Eighth Sonata for piano, **5:**9
    Love for Three Oranges, **4:**496, 498,
        499, 500, 501, 502, 503, 504
    *Lyubov'k tryom apel'sinam.*See *The Love*
        for Three Oranges
    Na strazhe mira, **5:**12
    "Ode to the End of the War," **5:**12
    Pas d'acier, Le, **4:**776
    Prométhée: Le poeme de feu Scriabin),
        4:216, 217, 227
    Semyon Kotko, **5:**11
    Seventh Sonata for piano, **5:**9
    Sixth Symphony, **5:**9
    Zimniy kostyor, **5:**12
Proksch, Josef, **3:**444
prolation
    four basic combinations of, **1:**251
    lilt, **1:**261, 262
prologue, court opera, **2:**93–94, 113
Promenade (Proms) concerts (London),
    3:678
promesse du bonheur ("promise of
    happiness"), **3:**528, 531
Pro Musica Society (New York), **4:**379
propaganda
    British nationalism and, **1:**405–6
    French court opera as, **2:**88
    motet and, **1:**277–81, 423–24
Proper of the Time, **1:**112
Propers, **1:**679–80
prophecy, **1:**719, 720–21
    artist-prophet myth and, **3:**59, 438, 439
Prophète, Le (Meyerbeer), **3:**218–19
Prophetiae Sibyllarum (Lasso), **1:**717, 719–22,
    773
proportional numbers, **1:**284–85
"Proportion" (rhythm), **1:**521
propositional relationships, **1:**282, 284, 495
Prose della volgar lingua (Bembo), **1:**723
prose text. *See* prosula
proslambanomenois (lowest Greek-system
    note), **1:**77
prosodia daseia, **1:**47
prosody
    accents and, **1:**14
    English musical, **1:**742; **2:**133, 134, 138
    "feminine endings" and, **2:**413
prostitution, **1:**208; **2:**80
prosula, prosulation, **1:**39–43, 57, 59–60,
    60
    Kyries, **1:**307, 310
    motet and, **1:**209–12, 219, 259
    See also sequence
Protagonist, Der (Weill), **4:**540
protean changeability, **2:**437
Protestantism
    Augsburg Confession and, **2:**353–54,
        402

    Counter Reformation musical legacy
        and, **2:**69, 112
    economic factors and, **1:**753–54
    in England, **1:**670–75
    in France, **1:**754
    in Germany, **1:**549; **2:**68; **3:**167
    grace and, **1:**552
    literal textuality and, **1:**553
    liturgical music and, **1:**754–69
    Lutheran esthetic and, **2:**68
    nationalism and, **1:**754, 765
    printing industry and, **1:**754
    reform doctrine of, **1:**765
    Scheidt's *Tabulatura nova* and, **2:**49
    Thirty Years War and, **2:**55–56, 68
    See also Anglican Church; Calvinism;
        Lutheran chorale; Lutheran
        Church; Reformation
Protestant work ethic, **1:**765
Proteus (mythology), **2:**437
proto-tuba, **3:**168, *168*
protus, authentic and plagal, **1:**74, 75, 76,
    79
Protyazhnaya pesnya (Balakirev), **3:**471–72
Proust, Marcel, **2:**693; **4:**22, 79, 99, 595
    In Search of Lost Time, **4:**79; **5:**248
    "La recherche du temps perdu," **4:**22
Prout, Ebenezer, **2:**607
Provençal, **1:**98, 107, 108, 109, 111–13, 116,
    117, 118, 128, 270, 351, 352, 399
Prussia, **2:**68, 385; **3:**710
    Austrian war with, **3:**569
    Enlightenment thought in, **2:**462
    German unification and, **3:**165, 710
    Poland and, **3:**344, 357
Prussian Academy of Arts, **4:**539
"Prussian" sonatas (C. P. E. Bach), **2:**413,
    518
    Sonata no. 1 in F major, **2:**411–13
Przybyszewski, Boleslaw, **4:**778
"Psallite regi" (prefatory trope), **1:**51–52,
    82–83
Psalm 46, **1:**760
Psalm 70, **2:**66–67
Psalm 71, **1:**598–99
Psalm 91, **1:**20, 21, 23
Psalm 117, **1:**26
Psalm 118, **1:**554, 756
Psalm 119, **2:**538
Psalm 138, **1:**51
Psalm 150, **1:**7–8
Psalmen Davids (Schütz), **2:**58, 68
    second edition, **2:**59
Psalmes, sonets and Songs of sadness and pietie
    (Byrd), **1:**741
Psalms, Book of, **2:**316
psalms and psalmody, **1:**8–10, 12, 20–29,
    33, 42; **2:**178
    Anglican liturgy and, **1:**672
    antiphonal, **1:**8, 11, 23, 611
    antiphon pairing with, **1:**20–21, 72–76,
        78, 83

    as art-prose, **1:**39
    Calvinism and, **1:**754–55
    Clemens and, **1:**597–99
    concerted, **1:**789
    Handel and, **2:**314
    hymnody vs., **1:**48, 50
    imagery and, **1:**91
    Mass chants, **1:**13, 23–25, 47
    monastic, **1:**9–12
    Office and, **1:**20–23
    Praetorius motets, **2:**54–56
    pre-Christian Jewish, **1:**7–8
    Schütz and, **2:**58, 59
    tonaries and, **1:**72–76
psalm tones, **1:**20, 21–22, 28, 29
Psalter (Book of Psalms), **1:**7–8, 10, 12
pseudodactyls, **1:**708, 787
pseudomotet style, **1:**326
Pseudo-Neidhardt, **1:**137, 140
psychoanalysis, **2:**597, 599; **3:**155, 293; **4:**307
psychological realism, **3:**153, 619
    Schoenberg and, **4:**326–31
Psychopathia Sexualis (von Krafft-Ebing),
    4:30
Ptolemy, **1:**70, 799
publication. *See* music publishing
public concerts. *See* concerts
public conservatory system. *See*
    conservatories
public instrumental music. *See* concert
publicity, **3:**253, 316
public opinion, **3:**289
public privacy, Romanticism and, **3:**63, 75,
    76, 86, 292
"public sphere" concept, **3:**289
public taste. *See* musical taste
published music. *See* music publishing
Puccini, Giacomo, **3:**641, 664–74, *665*;
    4:423, 526
    historians' treatment of, **3:**665–66
    librettists of, **3:**666
    misogyny and, **4:**57
    orientalism and, **3:**667–68
    Verdi and, **3:**664, 666
    works of
        Bohème, La, **3:**666–67; **4:**751
        Fanciulla del west, La **4:**751
        Madama Butterfly, **3:**667–72
        Tosca, **3:**664, 667
        Turandot, **3:**192, 673–74, *673*
Puclete/Je langui (motet), **1:**236
Pugni, Cesare, **4:**140
    Konyok-gorbunk, **4:**139
Pulci, Luigi, **1:**697
Pulitzer Prizes, "classical" composers and,
    5:454
Punch-and-Judy tradition, **3:**188
punctum (point shape), **1:**131, 214–17
puns, musical, **1:**331, 456, *456*
    Du Fay and, **1:**511, 512
    harmonic, **2:**576
    Haydn and, **2:**576, 634

musical imitations as, 2:104, 321
notational visual, 1:777–79
puppet theater singspiels, 2:526
Purcell, Henry, 2:127–38, 127
    all-round musical genius of, 2:127
    bicentennial of death of, 2:138
    choral music and, 2:314
    English prosody and, 2:133, 134
    fantasia and, 2:196–98, 202
    fugal style and, 2:198–203, 204, 208
    as organist, 2:127
    string ensemble and, 2:195–98
    works of
        Dido and Aeneas, 2:132–38, 155
        Fairy Queen, The, 2:127, 128, 130–31
        "Fantazia 7," 2:196–97
        Overture in D minor, 2:127–30
        "Sonnatas of III Parts: Two Viollins
            and Basse: To the Organ or
            Harpsecord," 2:198, 203
        Sonnatas of III Parts, no. 3 in D
            Minor, 2:198, 199–201, 203
"pure ballet," Russia and, 4:139
Purgatorio (Dante), 1:352
Puritani, I (Bellini), 3:37
Puritans, 2:124–25
"purposeless purposiveness" (Kantian
    concept), 1:541
Pur ti miro (Monteverdi, attrib.), 2:30,
    32–33, 77
Pushkin, Alexander, 2:464; 4:456, 675
    Ne poy, krasavitsa settings, 3:393–99
    operas adapted from
        Boris Godunov, 3:623, 624, 629, 631, 632
        Eugene Onegin, 3:632, 633
        Prisoner in the Caucasus, A, 3:397
        Ruslan and Lyudmila, 3:399
        Stone Guest, The, 3:612
Putnam, Israel, 4:273
"Putnam's Camp" (Three Places in New
    England) (Ives), 4:273, 275,
    276–77, 278–79, 280
Pycard, Jean (alias Vaux), 1:410–11
Pycard's Gloria, 1:409–11, 413–15, 418, 433
Pygmalion (Rousseau), 4:458
Pylades (mythology), 4:57
Pyrker, Johann Ladislau, 3:138
Pythagoras, 1:29, 30, 147
Pythagorean consonances, 1:29–31, 30, 70,
    154, 187, 282, 284, 410, 587
    Busnoys Mass and, 1:485, 495
    Busnoys motet and, 1:456, 457, 495
    deduction of diatonic pitch set from, 1:31
Pythagorean intervals, 2:247–48

Q

quadratic notation, 1:22, 23, 114, 214
Quadrille (Tailleferre), 4:589
quadrivium, 1:4–5, 16, 69, 175, 248, 282,
    424
    music's ranking in, 1:550

quadruplum. See organum quadruplum
"Qual nova meraviglia!" (Peri), 1:827–28
Qual prodigio e ch'io miri (Stradella), 2:327,
    328
Quam pulchra es (Dunstable), 1:429–33, 462
"Quand'ero paggio" (Verdi), 3:614, 615, 660
quantitative meter, 1:175–76
Quant j'ay au cuer (Busnoys), 1:543
Quantz, Johann Joachim, 2:218, 259, 411
quarter rest (soupir), 2:104
quarter tone, 1:33
Quartet for trumpet, saxophone, piano,
    and drums (Wolpe), 5:14, 15
Quartet in C major, K. 465 ("Dissonance")
    (Mozart), 2:631–33, 634
    autograph score of, 2:632
    Fétis rewrite of, 2:632
Quartet in E-flat major, K.171 (Mozart),
    2:631
Quartet in E flat, op. 33, no. 2 ("The Joke")
    (Haydn), 2:542–55, 559, 565
Quartet in G major, K. 387 (Mozart), 2:721
Quartet in G major (Schubert), 3:101–2,
    105–7, 135, 137–38, 429
Quartet no. 1 ("From My Life") (Smetana),
    3:731
Quartet no. 1 in C minor, op. 51 (Brahms),
    3:731–42
Quartet no. 1, op. 7 (Schoenberg), 4:342
Quartet no. 2 (Rochberg), "Duino Elegies"
    and, 5:415
Quartet no. 2 (Schoenberg), 4:315, 354, 359;
    5:425
Quartet no. 3 in C major, 2:721
Quartet no. 4 (Bartók), 4:402, 403–4,
    404–5, 405, 406–8, 409, 410,
    412–13, 416–17, 418, 445
Quartet no. 5 (Bartók), 4:402
Quartet no. 7 (Rochberg), 5:437
Quartet no. 11 in F minor, ("Serioso")
    (Beethoven), 3:1
Quartet no. 12 in E-flat major, op. 127
    (Beethoven), 2:682, 683; 3:778
Quartet no. 13 in B-flat major, op. 130
    (Beethoven), 2:682, 683, 686; 3:69,
    778
    Cavatina, 2:684–85, 726, 731
Quartet no. 14 in C sharp minor, op. 131
    (Beethoven), 2:682
    first movement fugue, 2:726, 727
Quartet no. 15 in A minor, op. 132
    (Beethoven), 2:682, 683
    Heiliger Dankgesang, 2:682, 686–88, 721,
    731
Quartet no. 16 in F major, op. 125
    (Beethoven), 2:682, 683
Quartets, nos. 1–6, op. 18 (Beethoven),
    2:653
Quartets, nos. 7–9, op. 59 ("Razumovsky")
    (Beethoven), 2:670, 683, 721
Quartets, op. 33 ("Russian") (Haydn), 2:541
Quartetto dorico (Respighi), 4:750

quaternaria, 1:176
quatrain, 1:44, 352
Quatre élémens, Les (Liszt), 3:425, 426
Quattro pezzi sacri (Verdi), 4:751
Quattro stagioni, Le (Vivaldi), 2:225–31, 317;
    3:455
    popularity of, 2:216
    Primavera, La, 2:225–31
    in standard repertory, 2:234
Quatuor pour la fin du temps (Messiaen),
    4:237, 238–39
Queen, 5:328
    "Bohemian Rhapsody," 5:328, 329
    Freddie Mercury, 5:328
    Night at the Opera, A, 5:328
"Queen of the Night" aria (Mozart),
    2:480–81, 482–83
Queen's Hall (London), 3:678
Quel prodigio e ch'io miri (Stradella), Handel's
    "borrowings" from, 2:327, 328
Quelques riens (Rossini), 3:12, 78
Quem quaeritis in sepulchro (Easter dialogue
    trope), 1:53, 83
Quem terra pontus aethera (Gaspar),
    1:521–22, 583
Quem vere pia laus (Hucbald trope), 1:80
Querelle des Bouffons. See War of the
    Buffons
Querelle des Gluckistes et Piccinistes, 2:441, 445,
    452, 455, 459, 460
Querelle des Lullistes et Ramistes, 2:441
"Questa o quella" (Verdi), 3:584
Qui consolabatur me recessit a me (Clemens),
    1:594–97, 599
Quiet Flows the Don (Dzerzhinsky), 4:790
Quinault, Philippe, 2:90, 94, 102, 478; 3:37
    Armide libretto, 2:155
    Atys libretto, 2:97
Quine, W. V., 5:332
Quintet in C major (Schubert), 3:82,
    109–10, 138–39, 141, 202, 429
Quintilian, 1:550
quodlibet (grab-bag), 1:233–35, 239
"quotational" methods, 4:671

R

Rabelais, François, 1:711
"Race Values in Aframerican Music"
    (Laubenstein) (article), 4:621
Rachmaninoff, Sergey, 4:151, 216, 491, 497,
    552, 555, 556, 557, 558, 619, 626, 776
    concerto style, Hollywood and, 4:558
    orientalism and, 3:395–99
    Paganini and, 3:256
    preludes, 3:351
    works of
        Ne poy, krasavitsa, 3:395–99, 400, 401
        Piano Concerto no. 2, 4:553
        Rhapsody on a Theme by Paganini,
            3:339–40, 4:553, 554
racial equality, 2:480

Racine, Jean, **2:**106, 459; **3:**333, 576
racism, **3:**767
    nationalism and, **3:**63
    Wagner and, **3:**177–79, 483
    See also anti-Semitism
radical humanism, **1:**689, 797–834; **2:**4, 21
    expressive ideal of, **2:**254
    Galilei and, **1:**799–803
    mimesis and, **1:**786, 802
    nondiatonic modes and, **1:**730–31
    See also favole in musica
radicalism, modernism and, **4:**3
Radio Berlin, **5:**176
Radio Cologne, **5:**189, **5:**211
Radiodifusion française (Paris), **5:**198, 206
Radio Frankfurt, **5:**176
Radio Italiana, **5:**197
Radio Serenade (Copland), **4:**661
Radom (Poland), **1:**346–49
Radziwill, E., **3:**348
Raff, Joachim, **3:***418*, 675–76, 767; **4:**454
    chamber music and, **3:**731
    Liszt and, **3:**418, 419
Rag mazurka, Poulenc's *Les biches* and, **4:**568
rage aria
    Handel and, **2:**308–11, 340, 437
    Metastasio and, **2:**155
    Mozart and, **2:**471–72, 481, 482–85, 602, 678
    Orlandini's vs. Handel's, **2:**437
Raggionamenti accademici (Bartoli), **1:**641
Ragtime, **4:**282, 486, 488, 599
    Gottschalk and, **3:**378, 382
Rag-time pour onze instruments (Stravinsky), **4:**600
Raguenet, François, **2:**86–87
Raimbaut d'Aurenga (Linhaure), **1:**115–16, 226
Raimon de Miraval, **1:**98–99
Rainbow in Curved Air, A (Riley), **5:**366
Raising of Lazarus (verse plays), **1:**93
Rake's Progress, The (Stravinsky), **5:**117–18, 225, 343
Ramberg, Johann Heinrich, **3:**202
Rameau, Jean-Philippe, **2:**91, *91*, 109–10, 286; **3:**561
    Baroque and, **1:**797; **2:**110
    influences on, **2:**109, 428
    Lully's style compared with, **2:**109, 110, 441
    treatise on harmony by, **2:**192
    works of
        Castor et Pollux, **2:**91, *92–93*, 94, 107–8
        Hippolyte et Aricie, **1:**797
        Hyppolite et Aricie, **2:**110
        Indes galantes, Les, **2:**321
        Pièces de clavecin en concert, **2:**695
        Traité de l'Harmonie, **2:**192
Rameau, Pierre, **2:**92
Rameau's Nephew (Diderot), **2:**437, 442, 443
Ramler, Karl Wilhelm, **3:**120

Randall, J. K., computer composition and, **5:**496
range-deployment. *See* tessitura
Raphael (Raffaello Santi), **1:**585, *585*; **3:**264
Rapimento de Cefalo, Il (musical play), **1:**813, 831
RAPM. *See* Russian Association of Proletarian Musicians
Rappresentatione di Anima, et di Corpo (Cavalieri), **1:**809, *811*, 812, 823, 831, 832–34
Rapsodie espagnole (Ravel), **4:**121, 122–23, 160, 164
Rapsodie negre, op. 1 (Poulenc), **4:**573
Raro, Meister (Davidsbund character), **3:***293*
Rasi, Francesco, **2:**21
Rat, **5:**327
rationalism, **1:**614, 615; **3:**528
    Counter Reformation vs., **1:**771
ratios, **1:**69, 70, 284, 410, 587
Raupach, Hermann Friedrich, **2:**601
Rauschenberg, Robert, **5:**77, 91, 354, 361
    John Cage and, **5:**77, 353
Ravel, Maurice, **4:**106–23, *107*, 120, 146, 151, 200, 231, 261, 397, 398, 408, 410, 509, 579, 625, 628, 755; **5:**326, 347
    affinity for Russian music, **4:**107
    "Blues," **4:**606
    blues movement and, **4:**607–9
    Boléro, 424
    eclecticism and, **4:**111
    fantaisie lyrique and, **4:**605
    heritage, **4:**107
    jazz stylizations and, **4:**606
    Jewish culture and, **4:**107–8
    "L'énigme éternelle," **4:**108, 110, 111
    "minute stylizations" and, **4:**609–10, 613
    "neo-exoticism" and, **4:**609, 610
    Yiddish folk songs and, **4:**108
    works of
        "Chanson hébraïque," **4:**107
        Chants polulaires, **4:**107–8
        Concerto in D for piano (left hand), **4:**606
        Concerto in G, **4:**606
        Deux mélodies hébraïques, **4:**107–8
        Fete d'eau, **4:**111
        Grands vents venus d'outremer, Les, **4:**111
        Jeux d'eau, **4:**111, 112–16, 117, 119, 120, 121, 164
        L'enfant et les sortileges, **4:**605
        Rapsodie espagnole, **4:**121, 122–23, 160, 164
        Valse nobles et sentimentales, **4:**112
        Violin Sonata, **4:**606–11
        Violin Sonata, II ("blues"), **4:**607–11
Ravenna, **1:**2, 64
Raw and the Cooked, The (Levi-Strauss), **5:**347
Razumovsky, Count, **2:**670, 683; **3:**625

"Razumovsky" quartets, op. 59 (Beethoven), **2:**670, 683, 721
RCA Mark II music synthesizer, Babbitt and, **5:**198, 478, 497
Read, Herbert, **5:**294
Reading Abbey, **1:**387
"Reading Rota," **1:**388, 391, 392
realism, **3:**592, 638, 673, 686
    beauty and, **3:**622
    Black Romanticism and, **3:**255
    Chaikovsky and, **3:**632
    comedy and, **3:**631
    Meyerbeer's *Les Huguenots* and, **3:**229
    Musorgsky and, **3:**617, 618, 622, 624, 625, 629, 631–32
    operatic, **3:**35–36, 41, 45, 204–5, 591
    operatic comedization and, **3:**611–15, 617, 658
    Paganini and, **3:**253, 255
    psychological, **3:**153, 619
    Renaissance and, **1:**382, 383
    Russian arts and, **3:**464, 622, 632
    tragicomedy and, **3:**576
    truth and, **3:**612, 629, 632
    Verdi and, **3:**564–65, 576, 591–94, 597
    verismo and, **3:**440, 641, 658–61, 663–64
    Wagner and, **3:**565
    Weber's *Der Freischütz* and, **3:**204–5
    See also naturalism
reality, music and, **1:**37; **2:**720
reason
    Bach (J. S.) vs. Enlightenment view of, **2:**369
    as Enlightenment standard, **2:**460, 479, 496, 600
    scholastic tradition and, **1:**90
recalling themes, **3:**239
recapitulation
    Brahms's use of, **3:**724–26
    in Schumann's "Ruinen," **3:**314
    symphonic, **2:**525, 549
"Recent Advances in Musical Thought and Sound" (Blackmut), **5:**39
Recercada segunda (Ortiz), **1:**627–28
recercadas/recercars. *See* ricercare
Recercare de tous biens (composition), **1:**606
"Recherche du temps perdu, La" (Proust), **4:**22
recital, instrumental, **3:**272–73
recitar cantando, **1:**826
recitative, **1:**809, 812, 823
    aria pairing with, **1:**25; **2:**78, 142, 143–44, 154, 341, 342, 348, 349, 351–52, 378
    cantata and, **2:**75, 78, 341, 342, 348
    choral, **3:**242
    Dafne and, **1:**828, 829, 831
    Euridice and, **1:**829, 830
    extended *parlante* and, **3:**48
    Glinka and, **3:**239, 242
    Gluck and, **2:**455–57
    grand opéra and, **3:**208
    Handel's *Israel in Egypt*, **2:**316–17

Haydn's *Creation* and, **2:**637, 638
improvisation of, **2:**174
instrumental, **2:**413, 414
Lully and, **2:**133
melodic, **3:**625–26
Metastasian libretto and, 2:164
Monteverdi and, **2:**21, 25
opera and, **2:**418
Passion and, **2:**378
Purcell and, **2:**133
scena ed aria replacement of, **3:**27
Schubert and, **3:**149
tragédie lyrique and, **2:**106
unwritten ornaments and, **3:**591
recitativo. *See* recitative
Recollection des Fêtes de Notre Dame, La, **1:**566
recorder, **1:**620; **2:**130
recordings, **1:**65; **2:**9; **3:**782
Red Channels: The Reports of Communist Influence in Radio and Television, **5:**106
Aaron Copland's reaction to, **5:**106
redemptive culture, **3:**772–73, 783
Re d'Espagna, Il (bassadanza), **1:**621, 622–25
red-inked notes, **1:**262, 265, 266, 269, 337, 340–41, 341, 410
Reed, Lou, **5:**362
refined love. *See fin' amors*
Reflections on the Revolution in France (Burke), **2:**645
Reformation, **1:**689, 753–69; **3:**167–68
attitudes toward music and, **1:**754–58
in England, **1:**387, 402–3, 502, 513, 518, 670–79, 680, 686, 753
factors leading to, **1:**315
in Germany, **1:**548, 552, 660, 697, 755–69
Meisterlieder and, **1:**140
Roman Catholicism and, **1:**630, 644, 649–50, 753, 771
See also Counter Reformation
underlying factors of, **1:**753–54
vernacular-language psalm settings and, **1:**597–98
See also Anglican Church; Lutheran Church; Protestantism
Reformationsfest (J. S. Bach), **2:**353–63, 364, 402
Reformation Symphony (Mendelssohn), **3:**167, 675
Reformed churches, **1:**754–58
Reformed Judaism, **3:**174
refrain
ballate, **1:**366–67, 368, 397, 694–95
bergerette, **1:**526
carole (carol), **1:**419, 420
falala nonsense, **1:**746
motet and, **1:**220–21, 234
narrative with, **1:**120, 129
rondeau, **1:**122–23, 124, 220–21, 227
Schubert's use of, **3:**152

stanza insertion within, **1:**221
villanella, **1:**716
See also antiphons
Regicide, The (Lucas), **2:**158
Regina caeli, laetare (Marian antiphon), **1:**96–98, 102, 389, 392, 509
Regino of Prüm, **1:**72, 73
Regis, Johannes, **1:**458
"Regnava nel silenzio" (Donizetti), **3:**53, 54
Regnum tuam solidum permanebit in aeternam (trope), **1:**56–57
Regola rubertina (Ganassi), **1:**620, 698
regressive traits, **1:**381
Regulae rhythmicae (Guido), **1:**185
Regula monachorum (Benedict), **1:**10–11
Regularis concordia of 973 (monastic code), **1:**93
Regule de proportionibus (compendium), **1:**536
Regulus, Marcus Atilius, **2:**155–56
Reich, Steve, **5:**351, 352, 368–388, 389, 390, 397, 402, 422, 438, 459, 490, 49
association with San Fransisco Tape Music Center, **5:**369
background, **5:**368
Balinese gamelan, **5:**369
Cave, The, **5:**504
Cornell, **5:**368
Different Trains, **5:**503–4
drumming lessons, **5:**369
education, **5:**352, 368
Hall Overton and, **5:**368
Juilliard School, **5:**368
Mills College, master's degree from, **5:**368, 369
orthodox Judaism and, **5:**407
"phase" procedure and, **5:**390
Piano, Phase, **5:**390
San Fransisco Bay Area, **5:**369
Steve Reich and Musicians, **5:**375
Terry Riley and, **5:**369
Three Tales, **5:**50
timpanist of the New York Philharmonic, **5:**369
West African drumming, **5:**369
William Bergsma, **5:**368
works of
Clapping Music, **5:**374–75, 385, 386, 391
Come Out, **5:**369–37, 374
Drumming, **5:**379–80, 383, 384
Four Organs, **5:**375–79, 384, 386
It's Gonna Rain, **5:**369–70
"Music as a Gradual Process" (essay), **5:**371, 374, 375
Music for 18 Musicians, **5:**383–88
Pendulum Music, **5:**372–73, 375
Piano Phase, **5:**373–75
Reicha, Anton, **2:**736
Berlioz and, **3:**327
Liszt and, **3:**262
textbook by, **3:**287
Reichardt, Gustav, 158–62

Deutschen Vaterland, Des, **3:**158, 160–61, 162
Reichardt, Johann Friedrich, **3:**129, 132, 145
Erlkönig, **3:**126–28, 132, 149, 158, 367
Heidenröslein, **3:**124–26
Reiche, Gottfried, **2:**287, 287
Reichenau abbey (Switzerland), **1:**71, 99
reification, **1:**65
Reign of Terror (France), **3:**61, 211, 214
Reihe, Die **5:**37, 50, 67, 165
Reihenkomposition ("serial composition"), **4:**688, 710
Reims, **1:**289, 316, 317, 325
Reims Cathedral, **1:**317
Reinach, Théodore, **1:**33
Reincken, Johann Adam, **2:**241–42, 241, 249, 255, 261
Hortus musicus, Sonata no. 1, **2:**242, 243–44, 274, 402
Reinecke, Carl, **3:**675–76, 681
Reinhard, Johnny, **4:**283
Reinhardt, Ad (Adolph), **5:**353–55, 361
"Rules for a New Academy," **5:**354
"Six General Canons or Six Noes, The," **5:**354
"Twelve Technical Rules," **5:**354
Reinhardt, Max, **4:**551
A Midsummer Night's Dream, **4:**551
Reinthaler, Karl, **3:**675–76
Reise, Jay, **5:**436
Reis glorios (Guiraut), **1:**110–11
Relache (Satie), **4:**571–72
relativism, **3:**62, 121
religion
English intolerance, **2:**313, 314
nationalism and, **3:**62
tolerance as opera theme, **3:**215
Wagner on, **3:**488–89
See also specific religions
religious awe, romanticism and, **4:**5
religious ecstasy, **1:**772
Remaking the Past: Musical Modernism and the Influence of the Tonal Tradition (Straus), **4:**360
Rembrandt van Rijn (Klenau), **4:**774
Remède de Fortune, Le (Machaut), **1:**290, 297, 299
"Remember Thy word unto Thy servant" (Josquin motet)
Remer, Paul, **4:**314
reminiscence motives
Berlioz and, **3:**324
in Donizetti's *Lucia di Lammermoor,* **3:**53–54
in Puccini's *Madama Butterfly,* **3:**667, 669–72
in Verdi's operas, **3:**581, 587
Wagner and, **3:**485, 502, 504
Réminiscences de Don Juan (Liszt), **3:**268–72, 273, 347
re mode, **1:**102
Renaissance, **1:**551, 576, 696; **4:**449

Renaissance (continued)
    ars perfecta and, 1:585–628, 797
    Brendel's view of, 3:413
    first historiographical use of terms, 1:382
    genius idea and, 1:552
    irony of musical, 1:797
    issue of musical, 1:281, 380–85, 429, 471,
        483, 547
    Josquin and, 1:554, 577–84
    medieval outlook vs., 1:614–15
    metamorphosis to Baroque from,
        2:14–15
    musical space and, 1:577
    radical humanism and, 1:689
    secular-sacred fusion and, 1:533
    trecento and beginnings of, 1:382
    Verdi's musical approach and, 3:610
    visual arts and, 1:382–83, 382, 641
Renan, Ernest, 4:101
Renaud. See Rinaldo
René, King of Sicily and Duke of Anjou,
    1:558
Rentsch, Johann Ernst, 2:238
repertoire. See standard repertory
repetition
    Binchois motet and, 1:456
    Mass Ordinary and, 1:311, 317, 324, 325
    as memory device, 1:26, 39, 41
    monodic madrigal, 1:819
    sequence, 1:41–43
Repin, Ilya, 3:617
Repleatur os meum laude (Jacquet of
        Mantua), 1:637–38
Répons (Boulez), 5:478
representational style, 1:802; 2:418, 643
"Representation of Chaos, The" (Haydn),
    2:633–37
reproduction, imitation as, 1:474
Republic (Plato), 1:801
"Requiem, Bardo, Nirmanakulya" (El Nino)
    5:523–24
Requiem Canticles (Stravinsky), 5:128–35
    first performance of, 5:134
    Lacrimosa, 5:129–32
    Libera me, 5:131, 133
    performance at Princeton University,
        5:134–35
    Postlude, 5:132, 134–35
Requiem for a Young Poet (Zimmermann),
    5:420
    Beatles songs and, 5:420
    Beethoven's Ninth and, 5:420
    Churchill and, 5:420
    Goebbels and, 5:420
    Ribbentrop and, 5:421
    Stalin and, 5:420
Requiem, In paradisum (Fauré), 4:102–3
Requiem Mass, Dies irae, 1:88–90
Requiem Mass (Mozart), 2:463
Requiem Masses (Berlioz, Verdi), 4:11
Requiem, op. 48 (Fauré), 4:101, 126
rescue opera, 3:2–3

Glinka and, 3:239, 249
"Resolution on Music," 5:111
    response to, 5:111
Respighi, Ottorino, 4:750–51, 764
    Gregorian chant and, 4:750
    works of
        Antiche arie e danze per liuto, 4:750
        Boutique fantasque, 3:1
        Church Windows, 4:750
        Concerto gregoriano, 4:750
        Concerto in modo misolidio, 4:750
        Feste romane, 4:750
        Fontane di Roma, 4:750
        Pini di Roma, 4:750; 5:179
        Quartetto dorico, 4:750
        Trittico botticelliano, 4:750
        Vetrate di chiesa, 4:750
responsories, 1:11, 12, 25, 310, 324
    Angelus Domini (Medicean and Solesmes
        versions), 1:631
    Parisian-style music books and, 1:171
    polyphonic, 1:162–68, 178
Restoration (Britain), 2:124, 125–27, 132,
    137
Resurrection oratorio, 2:73, 313
Resurrexi tropes, 1:15, 51–52
Re Teodoro, Il (Paisiello), 3:34
retrospectivism, progressivism vs., 3:179
"Return of Ulysses" (Monteverdi). See
        Ritorno d'Ulisse in patria, Il
Reuter, Ernst, 5:293
"Reveille," 4:275
Revelation and Fall (Davies), 5:427
Revelation in the Courthouse Park (Partch),
    5:485–87
Reverie, op. 9, no. 4 (Strauss), 4:31–32, 33
reviewers. See criticism
"Revival" leitmotif (Wagner), 3:505
Revolt in the Arts (book), 4:628
Revolt of the Masses, The (Ortega), 4:476
revolutionary hymns, 3:162–63
Revolver (Beatles), 5:319, 321
Revue et gazette musicale (magazine), 3:786
Revue Musicale, La (journal), 4:581, 585
Revue musicale (magazine), 3:333
Revue negre, La, Josephine Baker and,
    4:602
Rex caeli Domine, 1:43–47, 45, 99, 153
Rex regum (Notker sequence), 1:42–43, 44
Rhapsodic Variations
        (Luening-Ussachevsky), 5:198
rhapsodies, Tomásek and, 3:67
Rhapsody in Blue (Gershwin), 4:626–36
Rhapsody on a Theme by Paganini
        (Rachmaninoff), 3:339–40; 4:553,
        554
Rhau, Georg, 1:550, 762–63, 765, 765, 776
Rheinberger, Josef, 3:769; 4:245, 253
Rheingold, Das (Wagner), 3:497, 497, 502,
        512, 513, 515–17, 519, 520, 537, 610,
        668, 754
Rheinlied, 3:158, 202

"Rhenish" Symphony (Schumann), 3:788
rhetoric
    musical embellishment and, 1:816–17
    music linked with, 1:550, 551, 572, 679,
        722, 813–14
"Rhine gold" leitmotif (Wagner), 3:507,
        519, 526
"Rhine" leitmotif (Wagner), 3:505, 513
Rhine Palatinate. See Palatinate
rhyme scheme, 1:43, 44, 114
    ottonario, 1:696–97
    ritornello, 1:352
    tercet, 1:89, 352
    See also versus
"Rhyming Rules" (Guido), 1:185
rhythm, 1:5, 37
    Ars Nova notation and, 1:252
    Beethoven's distinctive, 2:696–97, 709,
        711, 713
    English prosodic effects and, 2:134
    faux-naïve imitation and, 1:349
    Gregorian chant indeterminacy of, 1:114,
        115
    hymn and, 1:48
    isorhythm and, 1:266–67, 291, 311
    Italian note-shapes and, 1:355–56
    Machaut repetition and contrast of,
        1:325, 326
    as memory device, 1:185–86
    monodic singing and, 1:817
    motet stratification and, 1:238
    Mozart and, 2:494, 591
    neume shape and, 1:177
    notation of, 1:114, 131, 133, 185–86,
        204–5, 210, 214–17, 234–35, 248
    Notre Dame polyphony and, 1:175–205
    Obrecht's Caput Mass and, 1:483
    Parisian chanson and, 1:708–9
    polyphonic indeterminacy and, 1:157,
        166
    subtilior effects in, 1:339–40
    syncopation and, 1:266
    troubadour verse-song performance and,
        1:114–15
    See also modal rhythm
Ribbentrop, Joachim von, Requiem for a
        Young Poet and, 5:421
"ribbons of scales variation," 4:485
ricercari, 1:588, 606–7, 616, 617, 619, 620,
        625, 643, 783, 787; 2:40, 44, 114,
        250, 384, 624
    first use of term, 1:606
    performance practice, 1:618–19, 786
    See also fugue; toccata
Ricercari di M. Jacques Buus, Organista in
        Santo Marco di Venetia da cantare, &
        sonare d'Organo & altri Stromenti…,
        Libro Primo, a quatro voci (Buus),
        1:608–11, 617
Richard I (Lion-Heart), King of England,
    1:110, 117–18, 117, 345
    Ja nun hons pris, 1:117–18

Richard III (Smetana), 3:446
Richard Coeur-de-Lion (Grétry), 3:2
Richardson, Samuel, 2:445–46, 450; 3:131
Richter, Johann Paul Friedrich. *See* Jean
        Paul
"Ricordati ch'io t'amo" (A. Scarlatti), 2:147
Ricordi, Giulio, 3:564, 565, 596
"Ride" leitmotif (Wagner), 3:538
Rieger, Frantisek, 3:448, 451
Riegger, Wallingford
        (pseud. J.C. Richards), 4:295, 628,
        654; 5:21
Riemann, Hugo, 2:400
Rienzi (Wagner), 3:481, 482, 483
Ries, Ferdinand, 2:667, 694
Rieti, Vittorio, 3:364
Rietz, Julius, 3:675–76, 681
Rifkin, Joshua, 1:555; 2:363; 5:330–32
    Arthur Mendel and, 5:330
    Baroque Beatles Book, The, 5:332
    Darmstadt, 5:330
    Karlheinz Stockhausen and, 5:330
    Lennon Companion, The, 5:330
    "Music of the Beatles, On the" (article),
        5:330–32
    Princeton University, 5:330
Riga, Latvia, 3:345
    Wagner in, 3:481, 482, 503
Rigoletto (Verdi), 3:568, 577, 578, 583–94,
        584, 597, 660, 666
    "Bella figlia dell'amore," 3:587–89
    criticism of, 3:593
    "Donna è mobile, La," 3:585–87, 591,
        593, 606
    last act, 3:590–92
Rigoley, Claude-François-Marie. *See* Ogny,
        Count d'
Rihm, Wolfgang, Four Passions cycle and,
        5:524
Riley, Terry, 5:362–68, 370, 390, 392, 438
    algorithmic composition of, 5:364
    Berkeley degree, 5:362
    echoplex, use of, 5:362
    nomadic existence, 5:367
    premiere performance of, 5:365
    reception of, 5:365
    Yogic meditation and, 5:407
    works of
        In C, 5:363–68, 369, 373, 397
        Mescalin Mix, 5:362–63
        Poppy Nogood and the Phantom
            Band, 5:366
        Rainbow in Curved Air, A, 5:366
Rilke, Rainer Maria, 4:769; 5:415
    "Duino Elegies," 5:314
Rilling, Helmut, 5:524
Rillosi, Giuseppe, 3:47
Rimbaud, Arthur, 4:100
Rimsky-Korsakov, Nikolai, 3:531; 4:32, 71,
        117, 140, 141, 145, 151 152, 153,
        162–163, 164, 171, 175, 179, 200, 205,

208, 231, 408, 410, 479, 481, 620,
        632, 750; 5:216
    Dargomïzhsky's *Stone Guest* and, 3:612
    New Russian School and, 3:397, 468,
        474
    orientalism and, 3:397
    on Schubert, 3:105, 107
    as teacher, 3:474
    on Wagner, 3:520–21
    works of
        Antar, 3:397
        "Bells are Ringing in Yevlashev
            Village, The" 4:183
        Capriccio espagnol, 4:121
        Heaven and Earth, 4:120
        Kaschey the Deathless, 4:153, 154, 160
        One Hundred Russian Folk Songs, 4:153,
            183
        Sheherazade, 3:397; 4:121–22
        Sadko, 4:117, 118, 119, 160
Rinaldo (Brahms), 3:703
Rinaldo (mythology), 2:94, 95
Ring des Nibelungen, Der (Wagner),
        3:491–540, 500, 610, 623, 719, 734,
        735, 759, 764, 776; 4:3, 7, 283, 305,
        326, 765; 5:347
    Chaikovsky on, 3:564
    chronology of, 3:499
    form and content of, 3:496–95
    harmony in, 3:521–28, 531–40
    origins of, 3:491–96
    texture in, 3:505–20
Ringer, Alexander, 5:415, 416
"Ring" leitmotif (Wagner), 3:506, 515, 519,
        538
Rinuccini, Ottavio, 1:804, 809, 827; 2:10,
        15, 21, 23, 37, 58
    Dafne, La, 1:824, 826
    Euridice, 1:811–12, 826
    "Qual nova meraviglia!," 1:827–28
Rio de Janeiro, 3:382–83
ripieno, 2:220, 222, 223, 230, 234, 290–91
"Rire du diable, Le", op. 1, no. 13 (Paganini),
        3:255, 256
Risorgimento (Italy), 3:569–70, 573, 580,
        595, 660
Risset, Jean-Claude, 5:499
    "Fall," from *Music for Little Boy*, 5:499
    IRCAM and, 5:499
Rite-chord, 4:177, 178, 179, 284, 323, 331, 387
Rite of Spring (Stravinsky), 2:110; 4:170–90,
        191, 193, 195, 196, 219, 328, 331, 447,
        468, 471, 485, 562, 602, 627, 776; 5:
        59, 75, 93, 127, 178, 206, 368, 432
ritornello, 1:352, 356, 363, 374, 377, 784–86;
        2:38, 100, 104, 130, 135, 146, 161–62,
        165, 166, 431
    Alleluia as, 1:784–85
    Bach (J. S.) cantata and, 2:351, 364
    concerto and, 2:192, 193–94, 218–20,
        222, 291, 295, 298; 3:273–75
    intermedii and, 1:804, 806–7

Mozartean concerto and, 2:606, 609,
        613, 616
    opera seria aria and, 2:308
    vamping and, 2:38
Ritorno d'Ulisse in patria, Il (Monteverdi),
        2:26
ritournelle. *See* ritornello
Ritratto de citta (Berio-Maderna), 5:193
"Ritual Action of The Ancestors"
        (Stravinsky) (*Rite of Spring*),
        4:176–77, 183
Riviere, Jacques, 4:188, 468, 471, 473
"roaring twenties," 4:637
Robbe-Grillet, Alain, 5:65
Robbers, The (Schiller), 3:568
Robbins Landon, H. C., 2:517
Robert (Robertson), Étienne-Gaspard,
        3:202
Robert de Handlo, 1:394, 784–85
Robert de Sabilone, 1:174
Robert le diable (Meyerbeer), 3:217, 218
Roberts, John H., 2:329, 330
Robertson, Anne Walters, 1:325
Robeson, Paul, 4:662
"Robin and Marion, a play with music"
        (Adam), 1:127, 128, 233, 349
Robin des bois (opera), 3:217
Robins m'aime (Adam), 1:127, 233
Robinson, Earl, 4:657, 658, 659, 662, 669
    Abe Lincoln, 4:658, 669, 670
    "Ballad for Americans," 4:662
    Joe Hill, 4:657, 658
    Lonesome Train, 4:669
Rochberg, George, 5:411–37, 453, 459, 460,
        471
    Confidence Man, The (Rochberg), 5:436
    Duo concertante, 5:414
    *Hexachord and Its Relation to the
        Twelve-Tone Row, The*, 5:414
    In Contra mortem et tempus, 5:415
    Music for the Magic Theater, 5:411, 415–18,
        420, 423
    Quartet no. 7, 5:437
    "Reflections on the Renewal of Music,"
        5:221
    Second Quartet, 5:442
    serial composition and, 5:414
    String Quartet no. 2, 5:415
    String Quartet no. 3, 5:414, 429–30
    "tempo simultaneity" and, 5:415
    Third Quartet, 5:431, 432
    Third Quartet's Adagio, 5:429, 431, 433
    "Transcendental Variations," 5:431
    University of Pennsylvania and, 5:414
Rochlitz, Friedrich, 2:673; 3:291
rock bands, 1:17
    cult of personality and, 3:268
"rocket." *See* "Mannheim rocket",
Rockmore, Clara, 5:182, 333, 426, 493
    All American Music: Composition in
        the Late Twentieth Century, 5:333
    New York Times, The, 5:333

Rockmore, Clara (*continued*)
    Rolling Stone magazine, **5**:393
rococo, **2**:279
rod shape, **1**:214
Rodchenko, Alexander, **4**:776
Rodelinda (Handel), **2**:306–11
Rodeo, "Corral nocturne" (Copland) **4**:663,
    665, 666
Rodin, Auguste, **4**:2
Roerich, Nikolai, **4**:170, 171, 172
Roger, Estienne, **2**:177, 281
Rohe, Mies van der, **5**:353
Roi de Lahore, Le (Massenet), **3**:390
Roi et le fermier, Le (Sedaine), **3**:187–88
Roi Lear, Le (Berlioz), **3**:320
Roi malgré lui, Le (Chabrier), **4**:61, 65
Roi s'amuse six airs de danse le style ancien, Le
    (Delibes), **4**:65
Roland de Lassus. *See* Lasso, Orlando
Roland (Gluck), **2**:460
Roldan, Amadeo, **5**:58
Rolland, Romain, **4**:95
Roller, A., **3**:430
Rolling Stone, **5**:327, 333
    George Martin in, **5**:318
    Nat Hentoff in, **5**:318
Rolling Stones, The, **5**:316, 343, 346
"Rollo Finck," **4**:255–57
Roman architecture, **1**:797
Roman calendar, **1**:12
Roman Catholic Church, **3**:162
    as anti-Freemason, **2**:479
    ars perfecta and, **1**:629, 630, 644–45, 646,
        652, 667, 684, 713, 771, 775
    Bach (J. C.) conversion to, **2**:419
    Bach (J. S.) Mass and, **2**:375–77
    ban on women church vocalists by, **2**:352
    Brendel's view of, **3**:413–14
    Byrd's compositions and, **1**:670
    calendar cycle of, **1**:12, 171, 173, 314, 632,
        642, 679
    Carolingian Empire and, **1**:2–5
    cathedral community and, **1**:169–70,
        208–8
    Council of Constance and, **1**:278, 281,
        310, 423–24
    Council of Trent and, **1**:88, 649–50, 653
    "Credo I" and, **1**:34–35
    Crusades and, **1**:96, 107, 108, 117, 135, 141,
        345, 484
    Eastern schism with, **1**:141
    England's break with, **1**:670–75, 673,
        686
    English recusant members, **1**:670, 675,
        676, 677, 678, 679, 686, 742
    Germany and, **3**:165
    Great Schism and, **1**:249, 277, 278,
        310–14, 423–24
    Gregorian chant and, 1.2–35, 1.148, 3.13.
        See also Gregorian chant *as separate*
        listing
    hierarchy in, **1**:9

intelligible liturgy movement in, **1**:647,
    649–53, 671, 672, 769
    liturgical music style reform and,
        1:645–53, 672
    loss of universality of, **1**:630
    Manicheism heresy and, **1**:116
    Mass ordo standardization and, **1**:60,
        61table, 460
    monophony vs. polyphony and, **1**:148
    motet and, **2**:357
    musical notation and, **1**:1
    Notre Dame composers and, **1**:172
    official chant book of, **1**:23, 87, 177
    Paganini and, **3**:253, 254
    Papal States and, **2**:139
    Protestant Reformation and, **1**:644,
        753–54
        See also Counter Reformation
    Psalter and, **1**:7–8, 10, 12, 33
    Rossini's music banned by, **3**:13
    special occasion Massess of, **1**:314–21,
        630
    stile antico and, **2**:357, 375
    stile antico/stile moderno and, **1**:667, 669
    two musical styles of, **1**:667
    venal abuses of, **1**:753
    See also cyclical Mass Ordinaries;
        liturgical music; Marian antiphons;
        Mass; monasteries; papacy
romance novels, **2**:446
romances, **1**:119
Roman chant, **1**:1–7
    See also Gregorian chant
Roman de Fauvel (Gervais du Bus),
    1:255–60, 286
Romanelli, Giovanni Francesco, **2**:74
Romanesca tenor (ground bass), **1**:626,
    821, 823, 823
Roman history, **1**:798; **2**:1, 27, 30, 88,
    155–56, 158, 702
Romani, Felice, **3**:37, 44, 45
Roman law, **1**:354
Roman measurements, **1**:252–53
Romanov dynasty, **3**:242, 250
Romantic nationalism, **3**:62, 63, 155, 158
    choral music and, **3**:162–63
Romanticism, **2**:641–89; **3**:305; **4**:2, 5, 28,
    29; **5**:75
    alienation and, **2**:600
    art distinguished from entertainment by,
        2:655
    artistic greatness concept and, **2**:81
    art media as mutually reinforcing and,
        1:337
    art of as Christian, **2**:649
    "authentic" performance and, **1**:782
    autonomous art and, **1**:65
    Bach (J. S.) revival and, **2**:383, 390
    Beethoven and, **1**:548; **2**:648–89, 651,
        654–55, 656, 659, 675, 686, 692,
        702, 714, 717, 731, 735, 739; **3**:71, 77,
        273, 288

    Beethoven myth's undesirable side
        effects on, **2**:670–71
    Beethoven vs. Rossini, **2**:670;
        3:7–8, 10, 13–14, 25, 34
    Bellini bel canto and, **3**:42
    Berlioz's musical depiction theory and,
        3:332–35
    Brahms and, **3**:686, 688, 703
    Christian idea of art and, **2**:649
    classicism vs., **2**:642–43, 646–48, 739
    composer's importance under, **2**:173,
        655, 689
    concerto genre transformation and,
        3:273–85
    contemplation of the infinite and,
        2:641–42, 643
    continued influence of, **2**:651
    core meaning of, **2**:641
    creative subjectivity and, **2**:590
    critic's role and, **2**:649
    definition of, **2**:643, 644
    delineation with Classical period of,
        2:646
    difficulty in defining, **2**:641
    domestic, **3**:68
    Donizetti's *Lucia* mad scene and,
        3:46–48, 52–59, 655
    as elitist, **2**:645
    Empfindung and, **2**:409–10, 687
    as Enlightenment rebuke, **2**:390, 460,
        706, 724
    esthetic of, **1**:65, 142, 144, 359; **2**:641, 701,
        714
    folk music and, **1**:703
    in France, **3**:318
    gender and, **2**:81
    German. *See* German Romanticism
    "Gothic impurities" and, **1**:631
    Haydn and, **2**:643, 645–46, 647, 648
    hegemonic claims of, **2**:738
    heroism and, **3**:273, 275
    historicism and, **2**:390; **3**:412, 413, 415
    home entertainment and, **3**:63–64
    individualism and, **2**:12; **3**:15, 62, 63, 273
    infinite and, **2**:641–42, 643–45, 648–49,
        670
    instrumental music and, **2**:591, 642, 646
    intent and interpretation and, **2**:680
    irony as tool of, **3**:143
    in Italy, **3**:570
    Mendelssohn and, **3**:181, 183–84
    Mozart and, **2**:479, 486, 591, 599, 622,
        641, 643–45, 646, 647, 648
    musical expression and, **2**:486, 599, 641,
        648–49, 659, 720
    as music's natural birthright, **2**:735
    music's preeminence with, **2**:659
    music trance and, **3**:71–73
    "national character" concept and, **3**:62
    operatic ensembles and, **3**:35, 48
    organic form and, **2**:701, 706

"original genius" concept of, 2:329, 416, 641, 648–49
philistinism and, 3:291–94
political and philosophical outlook of, 2:724
private music and, 3:63–69
professional critics and, 2:641–42
realism and, 3:35–36, 41, 45, 204–5, 253, 255, 622
in Russia, 3:230–50
sacralization of art by, 2:649–50
salon culture and, 3:73–79
Sturm und Drang and, 2:416, 417, 529
subjectivity and, 2:486, 590, 599, 600, 643, 648; 3:62, 66, 94, 152, 305, 315–16, 363
sublime and, 2:643–46, 648, 656, 692
symphonic music and, 2:599; 3:681
transcendence and, 1:65
Victorian values and, 3:36
virtuosos and, 3:251–61
Wagner and, 3:228
Weber and, 3:193
See also German Romanticism
"Romanticism and Classicism" (Hulme), 4:467
Romantic opera
armonica parts in, 3:73
verismo opera compared with, 3:659, 663, 664
Rome, 3:569
Arcadian Academy, 2:150–52
cantata origins in, 2:75, 80, 81
Cavalieri sacred play and, 1:832, 834
Corelli in, 2:177–80, 204
Handel in, 2:204, 237, 313
Josquin in, 1:559
oratorio in, 2:73–75, 237, 313
Palestrina in, 1:630–31, 633, 645
papacy and, 1:2–4, 310, 348
Piccinni and, 2:445
printed music in, 1:691, 693
Scarlatti (Alessandro) in, 2:142, 150, 177
Romeo and Juliet (Shakespeare), 3:45, 406
Romeo and Juliet concert overture (Chaikovsky), 3:406–9, 663
Romeo and Juliet legend, 3:28, 48
Roméo et Juliette (Berlioz), 3:320, 329, 482, 483, 788
Roméo et Juliette (Gounod), 3:639, 640
"Roméo seul" (Berlioz), 3:329
rondeau (rondel), 1:122–24, 125, 695
bergerette and, 1:526, 695
Binchois and, 1:446
Du Fay and, 1:445–46
example of, 1:126
first written, 1:123
J'ay pris amours, 1:534–42
Machaut and, 1:290, 291, 327–30
motet and, 1:220, 227, 255, 302, 532
Solage and, 1:342–45
rondeaux cinquaines, 1:526

Ronde du sabbat (Berlioz), 3:339
rondellus style, 1:402, 403, 408
"Rondo alla Turca" (Mozart), 2:471, 602
Rondo all'ongarese (Haydn), 4:367, 368
Rondo capriccioso, op. 14 (Mendelssohn), 3:180
"rondo-gavotte" (Thomas), 4:452, 454
Rongier, Jeanne, 3:774; 4:266
Ronsard, Pierre de, 1:589, 713
Ronteix, Eugène. *See* Toreinx, F.R. de
Ronzen, Antonio, 1:310
Roosevelt, Franklin D., 4:647, 660
root extractions, 2:192
Rore, Cipriano de, 1:605, 725–26, 727
Dalle belle contrade d'oriente, 1:726–27, 728–29, 802
Rorem, Ned, 5:325–26, 344, 431, 516
dismissal of Nat Hentoff, 5:325
"Distortion of Genius," 5:325
"Music of the Beatles, The" (essay), 5:325
tribute to the Beatles, 5:431
Rorschach, Dr. Hermann, 5:95
Rosand, Ellen, 2:10, 12, 16, 80; 3:109
rosary recitation, 1:524
Roseingrave, Thomas, 2:392
Rose, liz, printemps (Machaut), 1:302, 303
Roselli, John, 2:16
Rosen, Charles, 2:720; 3:152, 268, 311–12, 314, 346; 4:334, 465; 5:265, 268, 5:305–6
Classical Style, The, 5:305
Rosenberg, Harold, 5:49
Rosenberg, Julius and Ethel, 5:7
Rosenfeld, Monroe, Tin Pan Alley and, 4:624
Rosenkavalier, Der, Hofmannsthal and, 4:49, 453
Rosenkavalier, Der (Strauss), 4:49, 49, 453, 550
Rosenman, Leonard
The Cobweb (movie), 4:560
twelve-tone movie score and, 4:560
Rosetta stone, 3:387
Ross, Alex, 3:82, Alex, 5:522
Rossellini, Roberto, 3:674
Rossignol en amour, Le (Couperin), 2:277–81, 282, 428
Rossi, Luigi, 2:81, 87, 89
Orfeo, 2:87–88
Rossi, Michelangelo, 2:42–43
Toccata settima, (Toccata VII), 2:42–43
Rossini, Gioacchino, 2:675; 3:7–35, 7, 567, 648, 798; 4:266; 5:343
antecedents of, 3:15–16
aria style and, 3:15, 27–35
background and career of, 3:8–12
Beethoven and, 3:7–8, 10, 13–14, 25, 34
bel canto and, 3:578
on Bellini bel canto opera, 3:37–40, 43, 45–46
Berlioz and, 3:77

buffa finale of, 3:24–27
clarity of, 3:33
comic finales and, 3:49
comic opera and, 2:670
crescendos of, 3:18, 20, 21, 22
critics of, 3:21–22
in Danhauser's painting, 3:77
death of, 3:595
early retirement of, 3:11, 12, 595
ensemble finales of, 3:22–27
fame and popularity of, 3:14
formulas (Code Rossini) of, 3:14–22, 27, 239, 568
French opera and, 3:11, 775
Meyerbeer and, 3:216
Mozart and, 3:10, 13, 15, 27
Neapolitan period of, 3:11–12
opera and, 3:9–35
orientalism and, 3:386
overture and, 3:15, 16–20
Romani and, 3:37
Russian craze for, 3:14
sacred music and, 3:13
as salon host, 3:12, 74, 77, 78
Schubert and, 3:80, 84, 109–10
songs and piano pieces of, 3:12–13
tenori di forza and, 3:13, 578, 579
texture as specialty of, 3:109
Verdi and, 3:10, 571
works of
Aureliano in Palmira, 3:20
Barbiere di Siviglia, Il, 3:9, 10, 16–20, 20, 22–24, 34, 109, 110, 240; 5:515
Guillaume Tell, 3:11–12, 11, 18, 273, 578, 579
Italiana in Algeri, L', 3:10, 11, 20, 25–27, 386
Mosè, 3:258
Otello, 3:596, 600, 606
Péchés de vieillesse (Sins of Old Age), 3:12–13, 78
Petite messe solennelle, 3:13
Quelques riens, 3:12, 78
Semiramide, 3:14, 30
Signor Bruschino, Il, 3:21
Stabat mater, 3:13
Tancredi, 3:11, 20, 28–35, 41, 258
Torvaldo e Dorliska, 3:9
Turco in Italia, Il, 3:21
Viaggio a Reims, Il, 3:11
"Rossini crescendo," 2:669–70
Rossiter, Frank R., 4:253, 254
Rosula primula (hymn text), 1:394
"rotation" technique, 5:123–24
Rothko, Mark, 5:353
Rothschild family, 3:348
rotrouenge, 1:118
rotulus, 1:267, 267
Roubillac, Louis François, 2:306
roulades, 2:106; 3:43
round (song), 1:331
Sumer is icumen in, 1:388, 388, 389, 399

round (song) *(continued)*
    See also canon
rounded bar, **1:**136
Rouse, Christopher, neotonality and, **5:**454
Rousseau, Jean-Jacques, **2:**442, 555; **3:**61,
        62, 66, 192, *193*, 788; **4:**2, 68, 132,
        458
    Confessions, **2:**443, 641
    Dictionnaire de musique, **4:**68
    Enlightenment thought and, **2:**442–43,
        461, 470
    Gluck and, **2:**459
    gymnopédie and, **4:**68
    Herder's philosophy and, **3:**121
    on instrumental music, **2:**642
    on Italian commercial vs. French court
        opera, **2:**110
    one-act opera by, **2:**110, 442
    Pergolesi and, **3:**33
    primitivism and, **3:**123
    Pygmalion, **4:**458
    Romantic ideal and, **2:**641
    Social Contract, **5:**82, 177
    tragédie lyrique and, **2:**442
    Vivaldi's *Primavera* arrangement by,
        2:227
    War of the Buffoons and, **2:**442–43, 459
Rouvroy, Claude-Henri de (Comte de
        Saint-Simon), **3:**264
"Row, row, row your boat" (round), **1:**331,
        399
Royal Albert Hall (London), **3:**678
Royal Chapel (England). *See* Chapel Royal
Royal College of Music (England), **3:**651
Royal Court Theater of Saxony (Dresden),
        3:483
"Royal Fireworks Music" (Handel), **2:**306,
        362
Royal Library (Kraków), **1:**539
Royal Opera at Budapest, **4:**7
Royal Opera House (London). *See* Covent
        Garden
Royal Society of London, **2:**464
"Roy Henry" (King Henry of England),
        1:413, 417
    Deo gratias Anglia ("Agincourt Carol"),
        1:418–21
    Sanctus, **1:**417–18
Rózsa, Miklós, *Spellbound*, and, **5:**183
rubato. *See* tempo rubato
Rübezahl (Mahler), **4:**8
Rubinstein, Anton, **2:**736; **3:**467–69, *468*,
        470, 475, 755, 786; **4:**453–54
    nationalism and, **3:**467–68
    nineteenth-century symphonic music
        and, **3:**675, 679, 680–81
    orientalism and, **3:**391–92
    Suite for piano, op. 38, **4:**453
    Tower of Babel, The, **3:**392
Rubinstein, Arthur, **3:**364
Rubinstein, Nikolai, **3:**468, 786
rubrics, **1:**52, 262, 265

canon and, **1:**331
    Machaut rondeau and, **1:**327–28, 330
Rückert, Friedrich, **3:**135
Ruddigore (Gilbert and Sullivan), **3:**655
    Act II, "Matter" trio, **3:**656
Rudhyar, Dane, **4:**295
Rudolph, Archduke of Austria (later
        Archbishop), **2:**671, 674–75, 682
Rufer, Joseph, **4:**70, 705, 707
Ruffo, Vincenzo, **1:**650, 653, 666; **2:**2
    *Missae Quatuor concinate ad ritum Concili
        Mediolani*, **1:**650, 651
ruggiero (ground bass), **1:**626–27
Ruggles, Carl, **4:**295; **5:**268
    Sun-treader, **4:**297, 298
Ruinen von Athen, Die (*Ruins of Athens, The*)
        (Beethoven), **3:**1, 386
Ruines: Fantasie pour le Pianoforte
        (Schumann), **3:**309
rule of closeness, **1:**276–77
"Rules for a New Academy" (Reinhardt),
        5:354
    "Six General Canons or Six Noes," **5:**354
    "Twelve Technical Rules," **5:**354
Rupertsberg convent (Trier), **1:**90, 91
Rupp, Ladislaus, **3:**571
Rurik, Prince, **3:**477
Rus' (Balakirev), **3:**477–78
Rusalka (Dvořák), **3:**754
"rush to the patent office," modernism,
        4:193–97, 686
Ruslan and Lyudmila (Glinka), **3:**73, 399,
        400, 457; **4:**443
    costume sketch, **3:**430
    overture, **3:**430–31
Russia
    art criticism in, **3:**439
    autocracy in, **3:**478, 622–23, 647
    Ballets Russes and, **3:**786–87
    censorship in, **3:**227, 249, 478, 622, 623
    comic opera in, **3:**235
    Communist revolution, **3:**679
    conservatories in, **2:**736; **3:**468, 617, 786
    Crimean War and, **3:**476, 622
    Enlightenment thought and, **2:**462
    Field and, **3:**73–75
    "first Russian opera," **3:**234–36, 238–39,
        241
    folk idiom of, **3:**233, 236, 237–38,
        241–46, 397, 463–76, 624–25
    historical operas and, **3:**621–31
    imperialism and, **3:**392, 457, 459
    Italian opera and, **3:**14, 233–35, 239, 240,
        617
    musical Westernization of, **3:**230–35,
        467–68
    music journalism and, **2:**737
    nationalism and, **3:**230–33, 237–42,
        249–50, 468, 471, 478, 617, 786–88
    nineteenth-century musical
        establishment in, **3:**617–18

nineteenth-century symphonic music in,
        3:467, 679, 745, 786–801
    octatonic and whole-tone scale use in,
        3:430
    Official Nationalism doctrine of, **3:**241,
        242
    operetta in, **3:**647
    orientalism and, **3:**392–405, 786–87,
        789
    Patriotic War of 1812 and, **3:**242
    Poland and, **3:**344, 357
    political unrest in, **3:**476–77
    Romantic opera in, **3:**230–50
    Rossini craze in, **3:**14
    salons and, **3:**74, 75, 241, 273
    serfdom in, **1:**143
    singspiel genre and, **3:**236, 242
    Slavic language speakers in, **3:**345
    Stravinsky and, **2:**397
    Verdi and, **3:**594
    See also St. Petersburg; Soviet Union
Russian Association of Proletarian
        Musicians (RAPM), **4:**656, 657,
        777
Russian ballet, **1:**127; **4:**138–140
"Russian Composers" (Rubinstein),
        3:467–68
Russian History for Purposes of Upbringing
        (S. Glinka), **3:**242
Russian Imperial Ballet, **4:**149
Russian Imperial, Theaters, **3:**249; **4:**139
Russian language, **1:**102
Russian minor, **3:**471, 472
Russian Musical Society, **3:**467, 679
"Russian" Quartets, op. 33 (Haydn),
        2:541–42, 589
Russian Revolution (1917), **3:**61; **4:**227
Russian school of symphony, **4:**6
"Russian season" in Paris, ballet and, **4:**151
Russian Union of Soviet Composers, **4:**651
Russolo, Luigi, **5:**178–79
    concerti futuristichi and, **5:**179
    futuristi and, **4:**299
    Il risveglio di una citta, **5:**179, *180*
    L'arte dei rumori, **5:**179
rustic parody. *See* faux-naïveté
Ryom, Peter, **2:**218
Rzewski, Frederic, **5:**82–84, 89
    works of
        "People United Will Never Be
            Defeated!, The," **5:**84, 85

S

Sabaneyeff, Leonid, **4:**215, 216
Sabina, Karel, **3:**448
Sabor, Rudolph, **3:**509, 520
"Sabre Dance" (Khachaturian), **5:**9
Sacchetti, Liberio, **1:**127
Sacher, Paul, **4:**394
Sacher-Masoch, Leopold von, masochism
        and, **4:**30
Sachs, Curt, **4:**765

Sachs, Hans, 1:139, 140, 141, 142, 143; 3:559

Sacrae symphoniae (G. Gabrieli), 1:782–86, 790–92

Sacrae symphoniae (Schütz). See *Symphoniae sacrae*

sacra rappresentazione (sacred play), 1:832–34

See also liturgical drama

Sacrati, Francesco, 2:33, 37

"Sacred Harp" singing, 4:659

sacred music. See liturgical music; oratorio

Sacred Service, The (Bloch), 4:749

Sacre du printemps, Le. See *Rite of Spring, The*

sacrifice of child, theme of, 2:73–74, 90, 91, 465

"Sacrificial Dance," 4:177, 182, 184, 185, 191

sadistic representation, 3:671, 673

Sadko (Rimsky-Korsakov), 4:117, 118, 119, 160

"Sad Pavan for These Distracted Times, A" (Tomkins), 2:122–24

Saga of the Prairie (Copland), 4:661, 672

Said, Edward, 3:390

St. Armand abbey, 1:71, 77

St. Bartholomew's (Naples), 2:390

St. Benoit abbey, 1:93

St. Blasius Church (Mühlhausen), 2:239

St. Boniface Church (Arnstadt), 2:239

St. Cecilia's Day, 2:314, 327, 330

Saint-Denis abbey and basilica, 1:2, 169

Sainte Chapelle (Dijon), 1:485

Sainte en son auréole, Une (Fauré) (poem), 4:100, 101

Sainte Gudule Church (Brussels), 1:548

Saint-Evremond, Seigneur de (Charles de Marguetel de Saint-Denis), 2:87, 106, 108

St. Florian's monastery (Linz), 3:746

St. Gallen abbey, 1:15, 17, 41, 42, 42, 51, 52, 71

St. Gallen troper, 1:17, 51, 52

St. Geneviève collegiate church, 1:170

St. James Hall (London), 3:678, 680

St. Jean de Réôme abbey (Burgundy), 1:76

St. John Passion (Gallus), 1:775, 776, 777–79, 801

St. John Passion (J. S. Bach), 2:377–81

anti-Semitism and, 2:389–90

Saint-Léon, Arthur, 4:139

Konyok-gorbunok, and, 4:139

St. Luke Passion (Penderecki), 5:217

Saint Madeleine Church, 1:310

St. Mark's Cathedral (Venice), 1:600, 600, 605, 606, 607, 611, 620, 786; 2:5, 6, 11, 59, 75

concerted music and, 1:789–90, 795

Gabrielis and, 1:779–80, 784, 787, 790–96

interior view of, 1:611

organ lofts, 1:611

polychoral style and, 1:779–81

St. Martial abbey (Limoges), 1:51, 52, 111

polyphony manuscripts, 1:157, 159, 160–61, 162, 171

St. Martial troper, 1:51, 52

St. Martin abbey, 1:71

St. Martin of Tours Church (Loire valley), 1:455

St. Matthew Passion (J. S. Bach), 2:377–78, 381, 382, 389

as Bach revival vehicle, 2:381, 383; 3:163–64, 167, 172

Bach's autograph manuscript of, 2:377, 381

St. Nicolai Church (Leipzig), 2:238

Saint of Bleecker Street, The (Menotti), 5:226

St. Patrick's Day (Paganini variation set), 3:257–58

St. Paul's Church (Leipzig), 2:238

St. Peter's basilica (Rome)

Frescobaldi and, 2:35

interior of, 2:36

St. Petersburg, 2:631, 683

Adam's *Jeu de Robin et de Marion* revival in, 1:127, 128

Beethoven's *Missa solemnis* premier in, 2:675

censorship of Meyerbeer's *Les Huguenots* in, 3:227

first professional orchestra in, 3:467, 679

Liszt recitals in, 3:272–73

opera in, 2:158, 477; 3:14, 16, 230–31, 235

Paisiello opera debut performance in, 3:16, 235

Rossini opera performances in, 3:14

Teatr-buff and, 3:647

Verdi commissions in, 3:594

Westernization of music in, 3:230–35

St. Petersburg Conservatory, 3:467, 476, 675, 786

St. Peter's Church (Rome), 1:3, 6

saints

feast days, 1:12, 23, 24, 25, 26, 37, 38, 42

votive antiphons to, 1:94

Saint-Saëns, Camille, 3:564, 784; 4:66, 97, 102, 691, 755

Liszt and, 3:784

orientalism and, 3:390–91

Société Nationale de Musique and, 3:775–76, 783

symphony and, 3:657, 676, 679

on Wagner, 3:561

works of

Danse macabre, 3:203, 339

"Gavotte en final," 4:65

Samson et Dalila, 3:390–91, 397

Septet for trumpet, string quartet, and piano, 4:65

Symphony no. 3 in C minor ("Organ Symphony"), 3:783–85, 799

Swan, The, 5:181

Saint-Simonians, 3:264

St. Stephen's Cathedral (Vienna), 2:517, 518, 652

St. Stephen's Church (Venice), 1:607

St. Swithin abbey (Winchester), 1:155

St. Thomas Church and School (Leipzig), 1:763, 768; 2:53, 238, 239, 239, 363; 3:177, 481

St. Victor abbey (Paris), 1:89, 170, 175

"Saison Musicʾl Iall" (Paris), 4:611, 612

Salammbô (Flaubert), 3:397, 631

Salieri, Antonio, 2:476, 477, 652

as Gluck's pupil, 2:454, 464

Liszt and, 3:262

Meyerbeer and, 3:216

Mozart poisoning legend and, 2:464

Schubert and, 3:79

Salimbeni, Ventura, 1:803

Salisbury Cathedral, 1:465, 466, 672

Salle Le Peletier (Paris), 3:206

Salomé (Strauss), 4:36–48, 50, 57, 328, 388

biblical basis for, 4:36–37

Salomé (Wilde), 4:36, 38, 57, 467

Salomon, Johann Peter, 2:555–56, 555, 577, 607, 633, 646; 3:65

"Salomon" Symphonies (Haydn). See London symphonies

salons, 3:73–79

attitudes toward, 3:77–79

Chopin and, 3:75, 78, 348

Field and, 3:74, 75, 78

Liszt and, 3:75–77, 273

Rossini and, 3:12, 74, 77, 78

in Russia, 3:74, 75, 241, 273

Schubert and, 3:81, 85

Salvator mundi Domine (contrafact), 1:436, 437, 439, 441

Salve Regina (Adhémar attrib.), 1:96, 97–98, 99, 102, 103–4, 110–11, 118, 501, 502, 533

Machaut motet and, 1:270–73

Salve Regina (Basiron), 1:501–4

Salve Regina (Cornysh), 1:513–18

Salve Regina (Ockeghem), 1:504–6, 517

Salve scema/Salve salus (Dunstable), 1:424–25, 427–29

Salzburg Festival, 5:343

Salzburg, Mozart and, 2:463, 464, 465, 602, 737

Salzman, Eric, 5:95–96

Darmstadt, 5:95

works of

Nude Paper Sermon, The, 5:95–96

same-rhythm. See isorhythm

Sammartini, Giovanni Battista, 2:455, 500, 506

Sinfonia in G, 2:500–504

Samson et Dalila (Saint-Saëns), 3:390–91, 397

Samson (Handel), 2:75, 315, 339

Sancta Maria virgo, intercede (Marian antiphon), 1:407

Sancta Susanna (Hindemith), 4:528

Sanctus, 1:54, 310, 311, 313, 314, 646–47; 2:115–16

Sanctus (continued)
  Agnus Dei pairing with, 1:461, 758
  Bach (J. S.) and, 2:375
  Caput Mass and, 1:470, 482, 493
  chorale replacement for, 1:758
  in Mass ordo, 1:61(table)
  Missus L'Homme Armé and, 1:493, 494, 495
  Palestrina Missa O magnum mysterium and, 1:647–48
  Palestrina Missa Papae Marcelli and, 1:656–57
  Power and, 1:463, 464–65
  "Roy Henry," 1:417–18
  Taverner Mass and, 1:612–13, 614
  text and settings of, 1:54, 55, 56
  Victoria Missa pro Victoria and, 1:789–90
  votive Mass and, 1:316, 317, 318
Sand, George (Baroness Dudevant)
  Chopin and, 3:76, 349, 355, 368, 375, 376, 385–86, 420
  in Danhauser's painting, 3:76
  on grand opéra, 3:218
  salon culture and, 3:76, 77, 78
Sandburg, Carl, 4:670
  American Songbag, The, 4:659
  biography of Lincoln, 4:659
Sands, Carl (Charles Seeger pseud.), 4:651, 654
Sandwich, Earl of, 3:680
San Francisco: A Setting of the Cries of Two Newsboys on a Foggy Night in the Twenties (Partch), 5:482
San Francisco Opera
  1990 commissions, 5:516
  Death of Klinghoffer, The and, 5:522
San Francisco Symphony, El Nino and, 5:523
Sangaride (mythology), 2:97, 98, 102, 103
Sangarus (mythology), 2:103
San Giacomo Maggiore Church (Bologna), 1:435
San Lorenzo Church (Florence), 1:818
San Martini. See Sammartini, Giovanni Battista
San Petronio Cathedral (Bologna), 1:551, 780, 781; 2:193
Sanskrit, 4:307
Sans Souci (Potsdam), 2:411, 462
Santacroce, Francesco, 1:611
Santa Maria del Fiore Cathedral (Florence), 1:282, 285, 818
Santa Maria della Victoria church (Rome), 1:772
Santi, Giovanni, 1:585
Santi, Raffaello. See Raphael
Santiago de Compostela Cathedral, 1:162
Sappho, 3:120
sarabande, 2:96, 104, 105, 428
  history of, 2:261
  in suite format, 2:261, 262, 263, 270–71

Sarabhai, Gita, 5:61
  John Cage and, 5:61
Saracini, Claudio, 1:818–19
  Da te parto, 1:821, 821, 822
Sarastro's rage aria (Mozart), 2:481, 484–85
Sardanapale (Berlioz), 3:326
Sardou, Victorien, 3:667
Sárka (Smetana), 3:452
Sárka (Janáček), 4:427
Sarnoff, David, 4:752
Sarti, Giuseppe, 2:158, 493, 631–32; 3:235; 4:453
Sartori, Balthasar, 1:667
  O magnum mysterium, 1:667, 668–69
Sartori, Claudio, 1:558–59
Sartre, Jean-Paul, 5:2, 19
  works of
    L'existentialisme, 5:3
Sarum rite, 1:466, 672
SATB (soprano-alto-tenor-bass), 1:468, 783
Satie, Erik, 4:63–70, 63, 71, 89, 102, 126, 457, 506, 561–67, 572, 573, 576, 588, 590, 592, 755
  Ballets Russes and, 4:561
  bohemian life in Montmartre, 4:63
  caricature of Beethoven's Fifth, "De podophthalma," 4:502, 505
  Embryons desséchées, 4:502
  gymnopédie and, 4:68
  works of
    Carrelage phonique, 4:570
    first Sarabande, 4:64, 65
    Parade, 4:572, 589
    Relache, 4:571–72
    Socrate, 4:572, 573, 574–75
    Tapisserie en fer forgé, 4:570
    Tenture de cabinet préfectoral, 4:570
    Trois gymnopédies, 4:67–69
    Trois sarabandes, 4:63, 65–67, 70
    Vexations, 4:570, 571
satire,
  "fourth wall" and, 4:495
  musical, 1:255–58, 270
satyr plays, 3:644
Saudades do Brasil Milhaud), 4:582–83
Saul. See Paul, Apostle and Saint
Saul (Handel), 2:314–15, 316
Saul, Saul was verfolgst du mich (Schütz), 2:68–72, 74
Saunders, Frances Stonor, 5:295, 304
Sauveur, Joseph, 4:285
Savage, Robert, 5:38
Savane, La, ballade créole, op. 3 (Gottschalk), 3:377, 378
Savoy (London), 3:652
"Savoy operas," 3:652, 654, 655
Sax, Adolphe, 3:512
Saxony. See Weimar
Saxony, Elector of, 2:57, 58, 68

Sayn-Wittgenstein, Princess Carolyne, 3:290, 417, 417, 420, 421, 422; 4:371
  Liszt and, 4:210
Sbornik russkikh narodnïkh pesen (Balakirev), 3:471
Scala, Mastino della, 1:353
Scala family, 1:352, 353
scale, 1:100–104
  alphabet letter note names for, 1:75
  authentic, 1:74
  chromatic, 1:32, 729
  conjunct/disjunct tetrachords, 1:78, 151
  conjunct tetrachords, 1:151–52
  degrees in, 1:73
  disjunct/conjunct tetrachord, 1:78, 151
  disjunct tetrachords, 1:151
  fifth equivalency, 1:151
  five-note, 1:30
  Frankish, 1:72–76
  full range of pitches, 1:101–3
  Greek Greater Perfect System, 1:70
  interval exemplifier, 1:100–101
  key signature and, 1:76
  major-minor tonality and, 1:99, 101, 394, 553–54; 2:247
  medieval modal, 1:74–76
  middle C and, 1:101, 102
  mode concept and, 1:28–29, 76, 553–54
  modern tonal system and, 1:628
  octatonic, 3:429–30, 701
  perfect parallel counterpoint and, 1:151–52
  transposition of, 1:76; 2:248
  See also whole-tone scale
Scambi (Pousseur), 5:195
Scandinavia,
  ballads, 3:126, 367
  as British musical influence, 1:392–94, 403
  Kalevala epic and, 3:123, 126, 763
  nineteenth-century symphonic music and, 3:745
  Thirty Years War and, 2:55–56
  twinsong and, 1:392
  See also Denmark; Norway; Sweden; Vikings
Scandinavian school of symphony, 4:6
scapigliati, 3:567, 596
Scarlatti, Alessandro (father), 2:109, 141–50, 141, 158, 175, 213, 237, 392
  brass instrumentation and, 2:166
  career of, 2:141–42, 150, 151, 177
  chamber cantata and, 2:141, 142–47, 331
  da capo aria and, 2:144, 146
  diatonic tonality and, 2:186, 188
  ground bass and, 2:186–87, 189
  Handel's "borrowings" from, 2:327, 330, 336, 392
  legacy of, 2:141, 147, 152
  overture and, 2:146–48, 497
  siciliana and, 2:146, 274
  works of

Aldimoro, L', 2:186–87
Andate, oh miei sospiri, 2:142, 143–47
Caduta de' decemviri, La, 2:148–50
Eraclea, L', 2:146, 147
"Ricordati ch'io t'amo," 2:147
Scipione nelle Spagne, 2:152
"S'empia man," 2:186–87
"Sinfonia avanti L'Opera," 2:148–50
Tutto il mal non vien per nuocere, 2:148
Scarlatti, Domenico (son), 2:390–96, 407, 429, 504, 620
    canonization of, 2:233, 235, 390
    career of, 2:390–91
    Enlightenment esthetic and, 2:390
    Handel's "borrowings" from, 2:327, 331
    keyboard music of, 2:234, 390–97
    Kirkpatric numbering system for, 2:392
    late musical development of, 2:396
    local color use by, 2:391–92, 393
    as miniaturist, 2:391
    returning theme of, 2:394–95, 407
    significance of, 2:396, 397
    significant birth year of, 2:233
    standard repertory inclusions of, 2:234
    works of
        Berenice, regina d'Egitto, ovvero le gare da amore e di politica, 2:390
        Essercizi per gravicembalo, 2:396
        Ottavia ristituita al trona, 2:390
        Sonata in C major, K. 159, 2:395–96
        Sonata in E major, K. 264, 2:393–94
        Sonata in F minor, K. 481, 2:394–96
        Sonata in G major, K. 105, 2:392–93
Scarlatti, Giuseppe, 2:158
"scat" singing, 2:174
scena ed aria, 3:27
scenario-symphony, 3:323
scene popolari, 3:660
Scènes de la vie de bohème (Murger), 3:666
Schadenfreude, 3:302, 671, 711–12
Schaeffer, Pierre, 5:206
    Concert de bruits, 5:188
    Étude aux casseroles, 5:188
    Étude aux chemins de fer, 5:188
    Étude noire, 5:188
    Étude violette, 5:188
    Groupe de Recherche de Musique Concrete and, 5:188
    musique concrete and, 5:188, *188*
Schauffler, Robert, 1:579; 2:671
Schauspieldirektor, Der (Mozart), 2:481
Scheel, Boris (Baron Vietinghoff), 3:447
    Mazeppa, 3:431
Scheidt, Samuel, 2:48–52, *48*
    Christ lag in Todesbanden, 2:50–52
    Tabulatura nova, 2:48–49, *48*, 50
Schein, Johann Hermann, 2:52–54, *53*; 3:704–7
    Christ lag in Todesbanden, 2:52–54
Schenker, Heinrich, 2:711–12; 3:138, 548

Scheper-Hughes, Nancy, *Death without Weeping, The Violence of Everyday Life in Brazil*, 5:450
Scherchen, Hermann, 4:362; 5:206
scherzando, definition of, 2:498
Scherzi musicale a tre voci di Claudio Monteverde, raccolti da Giulio Cesare Monteverde suo fratello, con la dichiaratione di una lettera che si ritrova stampata nel quinto libro de suoi madrigali (Monteverdi), 2:3, 4, 22
Scherzi musicali: O rosetta (Monteverdi), 2:3–4, 22
scherzo,
    Haydn and, 2:547–50, 551
    Tomásek and, 3:71
    See also divertimento
"scherzoids," Ives, and, 4:272, 273, 282
Schicksalslied (Brahms), 3:714–16, *714*, 719, 781
Schiff, David, 4:254, 599, 680; 5:268, 280, 293, 298, 300, 303, 454, 475
Schikaneder, Emanuel, 2:479, *480*; 3:188, 191
Schiller, Friedrich, 5:67
Schiller, Johann Christoph Friedrich von, 2:479, 675, 678, 680, 731; 3:192, 688
    on beholder's role, 3:305, 315
    musical works adapted from, 3:11, 446, 568, 594
Schilling, Gustav, 2:643, 645, 649
Schillinger, Joseph, 4:340, 341, 628, 636
Schillinger System of Musical Composition, The, 4:628
Schlegel, August Wilhelm von, 3:309, 310
Schlegel, Friedrich von, 3:310, *310*, 314, 315
Schlegel, Joseph, 3:167
Schliesse mir die Augenbeide (Berg), 4:710, 711
Schloezer, Boris de, 4:227, 469, 471, 573
Schloezer, Tatyana, 4:210, 227
Schmeller, Johann Joseph, 3:*167*
Schnittke, Alfred, 5:463–71
    Chaikovsky's *1812* Overture, Concerto for Piano and Strings and, 5:467–68
    Concerto for Piano and Strings, 5:467–70
    Concerto Grosso No. 1 5:465–66
    Concerto Grosso No. 1, postmodernist collage and, 5:466
    Darmstadt serialism and, 5:466
    Franz Kafka and, 5:463
    Konzert zu 3 5:467
    Pianissimo, 5:463
    "polystylistics" and, 5:465, 466
    postmodernism and, 5:466
    Shostakovich and, 5:466
    Symphony no. 1 5:465, 466, 471
    Symphony no. 1, Dostoevsky and, 5:465
    Symphony no. 1, modernism and, 5:465
    Symphony no. 1, orchestra and, 5:465

    Symphony no. 1, single performance in Gorky (Nizhniy Novgorod), 5:465
    Symphony no. 3 5:367
    "Thanksgiving Hymn" and, 5:467
    tone clusters and, 5:466
Schmitz, E. Robert, 4:286, 379
Schneider, Xavier, 2:721
Schober, Franz von, 3:140
Schoenberg, Arnold, 3:422, 528, 735; 4:3, 30, 33, 37, 38, 105, 106, 120, 192, 193, 195, 197, 198, 215–16, 303–61, 303, 379, 380, 385, 387, 391, 420, 421, 444, 473, 477, 523, 526, 539, 543, 545, 549, 550, 553, 560, 576, 581, 628, 645–710, 710, 719, 721, 732, 739, 741, 748, 764, 765, 766, 768, 773, 774; 5:16, 17, 18, 20, 44–45, 49, 51, 56, 74, 89, 118, 126, 136, 137, 144, 170, 189, 331, 347, 372, 414
    "aggregate compositions" and, 4:681
    Alexander von Zemlinsky and, 4:304
    artistic isolation and, 4:306
    "atonal" music and, 4:312
    atonality and, 4:506
    BACH cipher and, 4:313–14, 734–35
    Brahms and, 3:725
    Chamber Symphony, op. 9 5:416
    "comprehensibility" and, 4:308
    consonance and dissonance and, 4:309–10
    contextuality and, 4:313–16
    Craft of Musical Composition, The, 5:103
    definition of "expressionism," 4:307
    Der neue Klassizismus, 4:678
    Die glückliche Hand, compared with *Erwartung*, 4:679–80
    Dika Newlin and, 5:170
    emotional/marital upheavals and, 4:309
    Eschberg set and, 4:316
    expressionism and, 4:337
    expressionistic idiom and, 4:319
    "Farben," 4:339
    "fluctuating tonality," and, 4:312
    German romantic attitude and, 4:306
    Grundgestalt and, 2:701; 5:156
    John Cage and, 5:55, 73
    madwoman theme and, 4:326–28
    maximalism and, 4:330, 339, 457
    melodrama and, 4:458–61
    metamorphosis of style and, 4:305–6
    moderism and, 4:4
    Mozart and, 4:311
    "National Music" (essay), 4:703
    neoclassicism and, 4:677
    "New Geman" tradition of composition and, 4:304
    pantonality and, 4:312, 313, 334, 344
    Pierrot lunaire, 5:426
    principle of "developing variation," 4:640
    Prioritätstreit and, 4:686–87
    psychological realism and, 4:326–3
    Quartet no. 2 5:425

Schoenberg, Arnold (*continued*)
  Reihenkomposition and, 4:688
  "representation of inner occurrences"
    and, 4:306–7
  Rochberg and, 5:437
  Romantic legacy of, 4:337–38
  as self-taught musician 4:303–4
  sensuality and, 4:33–34
  serial technique, 5:157
  social alienation and, 4:3
  "sprechstimme" technique, 5:42
  Stravinsky's *Oedipus* and, 4:675, 677
  "suspended tonality," and, 4:312
  Tonreige and, 4:688
  tradition of Brahms and, 4:304
  transcendental maxmimalism and, 4:303
  twelve-note series and, 4:687
  twelve-tone system and, 4:774
  twelve-tone technique and, 4:704–5
  Wagner and, 3:566
  World War I and, 4:679
  works of
    Am Wegrand, 4:335, 336, 337
    Angsttraum, 4:326
    Chamber Symphony, op. 9, 4:386
    Das Buch der hängenden Gärten, op. 15,
      4:354
    Erwartung, 4:33, 34–35, 303, 328,
      329–32, 333, 334, 336, 337, 342, 353,
      414
    Five Orchestral Pieces, op. 16, 4:307, 339
    Glückliche Hand, Die, op. 18, 4:679
    Gurrelieder, 4:305, 306, 344, 347, 460
    Harmonielehre, 4:309–10, 311, 331, 339,
      386
    Jakobsleiter, Die, 4:192, 344, 345, 346,
      347; 5:347
    Klavierstück, op. 33a and 33b, 4:707,
      708–10
    Kleine Klavierstücke, op. 19, 4:347, 348,
      363
    Mädchenlied, op. 6, no. 3, 4:314–15, 324
    Mondestrunken, 4:461, 463–64
    Mondfleck, Der, 4:462, 465, 466
    "Morning by a Lake," 4:339
    Moses und Aron, 5:44, 129
    Ode to Napoleon Bonaparte, 4:462
    op. 21. See *Pierrot lunaire*
    op. 22, 4:679
    op. 23, 4:679, 683
    op. 23, no. 5 (Walzer), 4:681, 683–84,
      686
    op. 23, no. 1 (Sehr langsam), 4:687
    op. 24 (Tanzschritte), 4:692
    Pierrot lunaire, 4:453–64, 466, 467
    Quartet no. 1, op. 7, 4:342
    Quartet no. 2, 4:315–16, 342, 354, 359
    Quartet no. 2 (*Entrücking*), 4:320, 321
    Quartet no. 4, 5:153
    Sechs kleine Klavierstücke, op. 19, 4:321,
      322–23, 325, 355

    Serenade, op. 24 (*Sonnet No. 217 von
      Petrarch*), 4:692, 693
    Suite, op. 23, 5:356
    Suite, op. 25, 4:692, 4:694; 5:138
    Suite, op. 25, Gavotte, 4:700
    Suite, op. 25, Gigue, 4:692, 694
    Suite, op. 25, Menuette, 4:697–99,
      710–11
    Suite, op. 25, Musette, 4:696
    Suite, op. 25, Präludium, 4:697
    Suite, op. 25, Trio, 4:695
    Suite, op. 25, twelve-tone row
      technique and, 4:689–702, 710
    Suite, op. 29, 5:122
    Three Satires, op. 28, 4:678
    *Über schwebende und aufgehobene
      Tonalität*, 4:311
    Variations for Orchestra, op. 31,
      4:700–702, 703, 704, 706, 707, 734
    Verklärte Nacht, op. 4, 4:304
    Vielseitigkeit, 4:678
    "Vorgefühle," 4:342, 343
    Wanderer, Der, op. 6, 4:310, 314
    Wind Quartet, 5:17
"Schoenberg est mort" (Boulez), 5:18, 27,
  37, 154
Schöffer, Peter, 1:691, 701
schola, 1:58
scholasticism, 1:90, 196–98, 459, 753
Scholia enchiriadis, 5:44
*Schönberg et son École: L'État contempoaine du
  la ngage musical* (Leibowitz),
  5:15–16
Schönbrun Palace (Vienna), 2:454
Schöne Galathee, Die (Suppé), 3:648
Schöne Müllerin, Die (Schubert), 3:81, 140,
  143, 295
Schönfelder, Jörg, 1:701
  Von edler Art, 1:702, 703, 704
"school opera," 4:541, 543, 661
Schopenhauer, Arthur, 1:653; 2:720–21;
  3:530, 530, 531; 4:59; 5:68
  on Beethoven, 3:6
  on "the Will," 3:546, 551
  Wagner and, 3:7, 497, 521, 546–47, 549
Schöpfung, Die (Haydn). See *Creation, The*
schottische, 3:35
Schrade, Leo, 2:13; 5:21
Schreckensfanfare chord, Mahler and, 4:14
Schreckensfanfaren, 2:677–78; 4:21
Schröder-Devrient, Wilhelmine, 3:151
Schubart, Christian Friedrich, 2:506
Schubert, Ferdinand, 3:83
Schubert, Franz, 2:674, 686; 3:79–118, 79,
  82, 85, 524, 646, 677; 4:16, 19, 29,
  110, 112, 117, 200, 205, 306, 454, 699;
  5:326
  ballad and, 3:148–49
  Beethoven and, 3:80, 84, 93, 98, 103,
  108–10
  B-minor mood and, 3:107–13
  Brahms and, 3:697–99, 703

  chamber works of, 3:83, 84, 86, 731, 754
  Chopin and, 3:346
  choral settings and, 3:83, 84, 162
  conjectured homosexuality of, 3:116–18
  dances and, 3:83, 84
  Dvořák and, 3:87, 754, 755
  early compositions of, 3:79–80
  early life of, 3:79
  Field and, 3:87, 88
  as freelance composer, 3:81
  Gebüsche, Die setting by, 3:310
  Goethe and, 3:129, 151
  harmonic cycle and, 3:99–105
  harmonics and, 3:89, 92–94, 96,
    99–107, 115, 117, 428–30, 436, 550
  illnesses and death of, 3:81–82, 116–17
  irony in works of, 3:142–47, 149
  lied and, 3:135–55, 189
  Liszt and, 3:85, 105, 277–78, 457, 697,
    699
  Mass settings and, 3:83
  Moments musicaux and, 3:89–94, 110, 111,
    295, 303
  Mozart and, 3:113–15
  number of published works of, 3:83–84
  overture and, 3:81
  on Paganini, 3:252–53
  piano pieces of, 3:82–84
  preface themes of, 3:109, 110, 112, 113
  Rimsky-Korsakov on, 3:105, 107
  Rossini and, 3:80, 84, 109–10
  salons and, 3:81, 85
  Schumann (Robert) and, 3:81, 294–95,
    310, 703
  singspiel and, 3:79, 81, 84
  sonata and, 3:82, 84, 86, 96–100, 368,
    427
  song cycles and, 3:81, 142–43, 295
  songs and, 3:81, 82–83, 116
  symphony and, 3:84–87
  Tomásek and, 3:87, 88
  works of
    Alfonso and Estrella, 3:84
    Allmacht, Die, 3:138, 140
    Am Meer, 3:138, 139
    Doppelgänger, Der, 3:153–57
    Erlkönig, 3:80, 81, 145–46, 148–52,
      155, 158, 367, 371, 372
    Fantasie in F-minor, 3:82
    Fierabras, 3:140
    Freunde von Salamanka, Die, 3:84
    Gretchen am Spinnrade, 3:80, 81, 151–54
    Heidenröslein, 3:145–48, 189
    Impromptu in A-flat major, op. 142,
      no. 2, 3:110–11
    Impromptu in E flat, op. 90, no. 2,
      3:87–89, 92, 100, 101
    Lachen und Weinen, 3:135–36, 144
    Mass in A-flat major, 3:81
    Mass in E-flat major, 3:82, 101, 103,
      155, 284, 428
    Moment musical no. 6, 3:90–94, 95, 96

Müller und der Bach, Der, **3:**143–45
Octet in F major, **3:**84, 103, 105
Piano Quintet in A major ("The Trout"), **3:**81
Psalm 92 choral setting, **3:**174
Rosamunde incidental music, **3:**108
Schöne Müllerin, Die, **3:**81, 140, 143, 295
Sei mir gegrüsst, **3:**85
Sonata in B-flat, D. 960, **3:**96–100
Spiegelritter, Der, **3:**84
String Quartet in D minor ("Death and the Maiden"), **3:**81
String Quartet in G major, **3:**101–2, 105–7, 135, 137–38, 429
String Quintet in C major, **3:**82, 109–10, 138–39, 141, 202, 429
Symphony no. 4 in C minor ("Tragic"), **3:**80, 85
Symphony no. 5 in B-flat major, **3:**80
Symphony no. 6 in C major ("Little"), **3:**81, 82
Symphony no. 7 in E major, **3:**108
Symphony no. 8 in B minor ("Unfinished"), **3:**81, 85, 108–17, 675, 697
Symphony no. 9 in C major ("Great"), **3:**82, 85, 94–96, 94, 101, 108, 173, 697
Trio in E-flat major, op. 100, **3:**84, 85, 108, 777–78
Wanderer, Der, **3:**101
Wanderer Fantasy, op. 15, **3:**81, 85, 101, 277–78, 282, 457, 698
Wasserfluth, Die, **3:**142–43
Winterreise, Die, **3:**82, 142–43
Zwillingsbrüder, Die, **3:**84
"Schubert circle," **4:**306
Schubertiade, **3:**85, 86, 731
Schubring, Julius, **3:**166
Schuetz, Carl, **2:**471
Schuller, Gunther, **5:**336
Metropolitan Opera Orchestra, **5:**336
Third Stream, **5:**336–40, 368
Transformation, **5:**337, 338–40
Schuloper, **4:**545. See also "school opera",
Schulz, Johann Abraham Peter, **3:**129
Schuman, William, **4:**647–48, 649; **5:**164
"Conversation" A, **5:**473
Symphony no. 3, **4:**648
Schumann, Clara Wieck, **3:**293, 302, 411, 770
Brahms and, **3:**684–85, 692–93, 697, 698, 720
courtship and marriage of, **3:**292, 295, 296, 311–12
as performer, **3:**317
Wagner and, **3:**557–58
Schumann, Robert, **3:**291–318, 291, 293, 302, 483; **4:**8, 198; **5:**347
Beethoven and, **3:**294, 309–15, 324, 346
on Beethoven's Fifth Symphony, **2:**692
Berlioz and, **3:**683

on Berlioz's *Symphonie fantastique,* **3:**340–41, 420–21
Brahms and, **3:**683–88, 691, 694, 703
Brendel and, **3:**416, 482, 685
chamber music and, **3:**731
Chopin and, **3:**343–47, 354, 365–67, 368, 683
Davidsbündler and, **3:**293, 294, 309, 316, 343
on folk songs, **3:**345
hand injury of, **3:**292
historicism and, **3:**683
later career and, **3:**316–18
Liszt and, **3:**309, 432, 683
literary music and, **3:**294–305, 309, 312, 317–18
on Mendelssohn (Felix), **3:**174, 230
mental illness of, **3:**292, 318, 684, 686
on Meyerbeer's *Les Huguenots,* **3:**229, 230, 292
as music critic, **3:**291–94, 336, 340–41, 343, 346
music journalism and, **2:**692, 706, 737
nationalism and, **3:**344–46
Neue Zeitschrift für Musik and, **3:**174, 291, 292, 340, 416, 683–84
New German School and, **3:**482, 683
Paganini and, **3:**253, 256, 292
piano concerto and, **3:**316
piano sonata abd, **3:**309
Schubert and, **3:**81, 294–95, 310, 703
song cycles and, **3:**295–305
suicide attempt of, **3:**318, 318, 686
symphony and, **3:**675, 679, 745
syphilis of, **3:**292
titling of works of, **3:**306–12, 321
Wagner and, **3:**482, 557
wife of (Clara Wieck), **3:**292, 295, 296, 311–12
works of
Alten, bösen Lieder, Die, **3:**304–5
Am leuchtenden sommermorgen, **3:**303–4
Aus meinen thranen, **3:**299–300
Bride of Messina, The, **3:**409–10
Concert sans orchestre, **3:**309
Dichterliebe, op. 48, **3:**295–306
Fantaisie in A minor for Piano and Orchestra, **3:**316–17, 336, 419
Genoveva, **3:**418
Ich grolle nicht, **3:**301–3
Im wunderschönen Monat Mai, **3:**296–99
Kinderscenen, op. 15, **3:**360–61
Phantasie, op. 17, **3:**309–15, 320, 321, 324, 354, 360, 432
Phantasiestücke, op. 12, **3:**306–8
Symphony no. 2, **3:**688
Symphony no. 3 ("The Rhenish"), **3:**788
Symphony no. 4, **3:**688–90
Warum?, **3:**306–8
Schuppanzigh, Ignaz, **2:**683; **3:**83, 103

Schuré, Edouard, **4:**85, 86, 89
Schütz, Heinrich, **2:**56–73, 57, 79, 83, 341, 345; **3:**91, 166, 168–69, 703, 711
background of, **2:**56–57
luxuriant style and, **2:**59–66, 67
oratorio and, **2:**73, 74
Thirty Years War effect on, **2:**58–59, 66, 67
Venetian style and, **2:**57, 59, 66, 68, 69, 74, 259
works of
Dafne, **2:**15, 58
Eile mich, Gott, zu erretten, **2:**66–68
Geistliche Chor-Music, **2:**59, 68
Historia der freuden und gradenreichen Geburth Gottes and Marien Sohnes, Jesu Christi, unsers einigen Mitlers, Erlösers und Seeligmachers, **2:**73
Kleine geistliche Concerte, **2:**66–69
O quam tu pulchra es, **2:**59, 60–66
Saul, Saul was verfolgst du mich, **2:**68–72, 74
Symphoniae sacrae, **2:**59, 60–66, 68–72, 497
Schwanengesang (Schubert), **3:**83, 138
Schwantner, Joseph, neotonality and, **5:**454
Schwartzkopf, Elisabeth, **5:**176
Schwarz, Boris, **3:**251
Schwarz, Hans, **1:**572
Schwarz, K. Robert, "additive and subtractive" structure and, **5:**390
"Schweig nur, taumelnde Vernunft" (J. S. Bach), **2:**368–69
Schweigsame Frau, Die (Strauss), **4:**37f
Schwerdgeburth, C. A., **3:**191
Schwer gefasste Entschluss, Der, op. 135 (Beethoven), **3:**424, 776
Schwind, Moritz von, **3:**2, 82, 82, 86, 129
science,
Galilean, **1:**797
sixteenth century, **1:**586–87
scientific empiricism, **3:**619
Scipione nelle Spagne (A. Scarlatti), **2:**152
Scipione nelle Spagne (Zeno), **2:**152
Scivias (Hildegard), **1:**91
Scolica enchiriadis (commentary), **1:**149, 150, 152, 154, 185, 782–83
scordatura violin, **3:**258
score,
Beethoven's vs. Rossini's view of, **3:**10
first use of, **1:**578
as inviolable text, **3:**288
Score, The, **5:**153
Scotch snaps (short-long rhythms), **2:**134
Scotland, **1:**393; **3:**47
Scott, Sir Walter, **3:**46–48, 658
Scotto brothers, **1:**600–601
"Scottsboro boys" trial, **4:**653, 662
Scratch Music (Cardew), **5:**85, 87, 355
Scratch Orchestra, **5:**84, 85, 88, 99
"Scratch Orchestral Piece with Gramophone," **5:**86

Scribe, Eugène, **3:**207–10, 215, 219, 220, 223, 225

Scriabin, Alexander Nikolayevich, **3:**351; **4:**151, 195, 197–229, *197*, 231, 234, 236, 240, 284, 295, 339, 345, 473, 498, 550, 681, 754, 776; **5:**192
  ad hoc" chord and, **4:**210; **5:**37
  aggregate harmony and, **4:**225–26
  atonality and, **4:**218–24
  Chopin and, **4:**197–98, 208
  "chord of the pleroma" and, **4:**216
  death of, **4:**225, 227
  "maximal maximalism" and, **4:**283
  Moscow Religious Philosophical Society and, **4:**201
  Mysterium, **5:**186, 347, 359
  "mystic chord" and, **4:**216, 217, 219
  "mystical symbolism" and, **4:**201, 205
  six-tone extended dominant chord and, **4:**213
  theosophy and, **4:**201, 203
  "tritone link" and, **4:**200, 204, 207, 211
  twelve-tone chord and, **4:**225, 226
  "Wagnerian" dominants and, **4:**211
  "White Mass, The" and, **4:**219
  whole-tone scale and, **4:**212, 213–14
  works of
    Acte préalable, **4:**224, 225, 226, 345
    Désir, **4:**215
    Divin poème, Le,(The Divine Poem), **4:** :208, 209, 211, 213, 214
    Four Preludes, op. 74, **4:**198, 200
    Mysterium, **4:**192, 224–27, 283, 345
    Poème de l'extase, Le **4:**213, 214, 215, 219, 225, 227
    Prelude in C major, op. 48, no. 4, **4:**98, 199, 206, 211
    Prelude, op. 74, **4:**204, 206, 208, 217, 225
    Prométhée: Le poème de feu, **4:**216, 218, 219
    Sonata no. 4, **4:**208
    Sonata no. 6, **4:**208
    Sonata no. 7, **4:**219
    Symphony no. 1, **4:**208
    Symphony no. 3, **4:**208
    Symphony no. 4, op. 54, **4:**213
    Symphony no. 5, 216. See also *Prométhée: Le poeme de feu*
    Vers la flamme, **4:**219, 220, 221, 222, 223, 224, 226

Scriabin "double dominant," **4:**211
"Scriabin sixth," **4:**210, 211, 212
  vs. German sixth, **4:**209, 210
Scriven, Michael, **5:**155–56
Sea Pieces (MacDowell), **3:**768
Searle, Humphrey, **3:**418
Seasons, The (Haydn), **2:**385, 388, 633; **4:**449
Sebbers, Julius Ludwig, **3:**412
*Sechs Bagatellen,*op. 9, no. 5 (Webern), **4:**347, 348, 349

Sechs kleine Klavierstücke, op., 19, **4:**321, 322–23, 325, 355
Second Annual American Workers' Music Olympiad, **4:**654
seconda prattica, **1:**831; **2:**76, 78, 121, 418
  luxuriant style and, **2:**59, 67
  Monteverdi as spokesman of, **2:**2, 59, 254
Second Berlin School, **3:**126, 129
Seconde Musiche (Saracini), **1:**821, *821*
Second Hurricane, The (Copland), **4:**661
Second International Congress of Composers and Music Critics, **5:**11
Secondo libro di recercari, Il (Buus), **1:**618–19
"Second Overture on the Themes of Russian Folk Songs" (Balakirev), **4:**9
Second Piano Sonata (Boulez), **5:**63
Second String Quartet (Carter), **5:**295–300, 328
  commission of, **5:**295
  metronomic plan for, **5:**297
Second String Quartet (Feldman), **5:**101
  first performance of, **5:**101
Second Symphony in B minor (Borodin), **3:**789–91
  scherzo, **3:**789, 790
Second Symphony in D major, op. 36 (Beethoven), **3:**690, 691, 692, 800
  scherzo trio, **3:**692
Second Symphony (Mahler), **5:**347
"second theme",
  Chaikovsky and, **4:**19, 20
  Todtenfeier and, **4:**17, *18*–20
Second Vatican Council, **1:**63, 278; **2:**326
"Second Viennese School," **4:**309
Second Yankee School (Boston School), **3:**769
Secrecy's song (Purcell), **2:**130, 131
Secret Doctrine, The (Blavatsky), **4:**216
Secret Marriage, The (Paisiello), **3:**34
secularism,
  Bach (J. S.) and, **2:**374, 385, 388
  chamber music and, **2:**114, 261–80
  Early Modern period and, **1:**797–98
  Enlightenment and, **2:**302
  Handel and, **2:**303, 305, 321, 340
  Handel's *Messiah* and, **2:**325, 327, 335, 336
  instrumental music and, **2:**204
  liturgical music and, **1:**66–67, 99, 111–12
  printing industry and, **1:**754
  Renaissance, **1:**382
  universities and, **1:**148
secular music, **1:**689
  blurred line with sacred music of, **1:**105–6, 128, 131, 136, 311, 532–34
  cantilena and, **1:**298–301, 311
  composer attribution for, **1:**172
  earliest literate, **1:**105–45
  Grocheio's social theory and, **1:**208
  Lasso and, **1:**713, 714–21
  Lutheran chorale adaptations of, **1:**759
  Machaut and, **1:**289–307

  as Mass cantus firmus basis, **1:**483–97
  motet and, **1:**236, 259
  trecento and, **1:**351, 383
  vernacular song and, **1:**99, 108–45, 351, 694–709
  See also instrumental music; madrigal; opera
Sedaine, Michel-Jean, **3:**187
Sederunt principes et adversum me loquebantur (Pérotin), **1:**173
"Sedlák, sedlák" (Erben), **3:**463
Seeger, Charles, **5:**651, 652–53, 654, 655, 657, 658; **5:**315
Seeger, Pete, **4:**658; **5:**315, 334
Seeger, Ruth Crawford, **4:**295, *295*; **5:**268
Segni, Julio, **1:**607, 611–12
"Segreto comunicato e raccomandato da Paganini al suo caro amico L. G.Germi: Armonici a doppie corde di terza", **3:**257, 258, 259, 261
Seidl, Anton, **3:**755, 770
Sei mir gegrüsst (Schubert), **3:**85
Sei personaggi in cerca d'autore (Pirandello), **4:**495
Se j'ai ame (French motet), **1:**218–19, *218*
Se je chant mains (canon), **1:**331–33, 364
Se la face ay pale (Du Fay), **1:**498
Seldes, Gilbert, **4:**621
self
  hypnotism and, **3:**73
  orientalism and, **3:**393
  otherness and, **3:**405–10
  Romanticism and, **3:**193
  separation from others of, **2:**321
self-accompaniment, **1:**132
self-analysis, **1:**383
self-borrowing, **2:**327–40
self-conscious theory, **3:**415–16
self-expression, **2:**590, 591, 737
  Romantic purpose of, **2:**641
  See also subjectivity
self-interest, **1:**765
self-made man
  Bach (J. C.) as, **2:**419
  chamber music and, **2:**114, 124
  comic opera and, **2:**450
  English Civil War and, **2:**124
  English identification with, **2:**114, 237, 450
  Florentine elite as, **1:**383
  Handel as, **2:**237, 240, 313, 340, 419
  Haydn as, **2:**517, 525, 538
  nineteenth-century idealization of, **2:**737
  Romanticism and, **3:**63, 77
  salons and, **3:**74
  See also bourgeoisie; middle-class values
"Self-Portrait with Reich and Riley (and Chopin in the Background)" (Ligeti), **5:**438
self-realization, **2:**641
"Self-Reliance" (Emerson), **4:**243
self-sacrifice theme, **2:**155, 156, 447, 454, 459

"Selig sind, die da Lied tragen" (Brahms), 3:704
Sellars, Peter, 5:523
    Don Giovanni and, 5:517
    El Nino and, 5:523–27
    Marriage of Figaro and, 5:517
Selva di varia ricreatione (Vecchi), 1:746
Selva morale et spirituale (Monteverdi), 2:110, 376
semantics. *See* words-music relationship
semibreve, 1:217, 231–32, 233, 235, 236, 237–38, 239, 244, 251, 260
    beat and, 1:251–52
    Giovanni madrigal grouping of, 1:363, 364
    rationalization of, 1:249
    red notes and, 1:266, 340–41, 410
    subdivision of, 1:260–61, 355, 364
semicrome (sixteenth note), 1:785
semiminims (sixteenth notes), 1:515
semi-opera (English mixed genre), 2:126–27
    Purcell and, 2:128, 130–31
semiotics, 2:539–42, 550, 591, 680, 718
    Dvořák and, 3:756
    introversive, 1:643
    Meyerbeer and, 3:229
    orientalism and, 3:390
    Russia and, 3:233
    Wagner and, 3:541
    See also extroversive semiotics; introversive semiotics
Semiramide (Rossini), 3:14, 30
semiseria opera, 2:447–48
    See also opera buffa
semitone, 1:74, 99; 4:17–18
    clashes, 2:368
    constant parallel distance between, 2:364
    diatonic vs. chromatic, 1:729
    early Greek, 1:32–33
    equalizing of, 2:247–48
    See also chromaticism
"semitone composers," 4:28
"Semper Fidelis" (Sousa), 4:275
"S'empia man" (A. Scarlatti), 2:186–87
"Sempre libera" (Verdi), 3:581
senaria perfecta (meter), 1:363
senaria theory, 1:587–88, 603
Sender, Ramon, 5:362
    development of echoplex, 5:362
Seneca, 2:27
Senesino, 2:307, 308
Senfl, Ludwig, 1:545, 572–73, 572, 704, 762
    Isaac's *Choralis Constantinus* and, 1:679
    Luther's relationship with, 1:756, 758
    Tenorlied and, 1:704–6
    works of
        A un giro sol setting, 1:757, 758
        Ave Maria. . . Virgo serena, 1:572–73, 588, 704
        Lust hab ich ghabt zuer Musica, 1:704–6

sensibility, 2:409–18, 737
    reform opera and, 2:452
    See also empfindsamer Stil
sensuality,
    Counter Reformation music and, 1:772–77, 785
    German Romanticism's contempt for, 3:146
    modernism and, 4:5
    orientalist representations and, 3:390, 398–405, 407
    salon culture and, 3:78
    spirituality vs., 3:13, 22
sentimentality
    barbershop quartets and, 3:382
    in Beethoven's works, 3:132
    Gottschalk's parlor-piano compositions and, 3:380
    opera buffa and, 2:445–52
    See also Empfindsamkeit
sentimental romance idiom, 3:245
Septet for trumpet, string quartet, and piano (Saint-Saëns), 4:65
Septet for Winds and Strings, op. 20 (Beethoven), 2:653
sequence, 1:39, 41–47, 50, 86, 99, 131, 171
    British motet and, 1:399–402
    double-entry, 1:60
    madrigal descending seconds and, 1:363
    paired vesicles of, 1:98, 604
    planctus settings and, 1:112–13
    polyphonic setting and, 1:149
    rhymed metrical, 1:86–92
    rhythmic performance speculation and, 1:114
    See also melody
sequence-and-cadence model, 2:189–98, 212
sequentia melisma, 1:41, 42, 42–43
sequentia vocalise, 1:39
Séraphita (Balzac), 4:338–39, 344
Sérénade (Milhaud), 4:585
Sérénade en la (Stravinsky), 4:491–93, 585
Serenade no. 1 in D major, op. 11 (Brahms), 3:690–92
serenata, 2:142; 3:64
    definition of, 2:498
serfdom, 1:107, 143; 2:462
Sgt. Pepper's Lonely Hearts Club Band (Beatles), 5:319, 321, 324, 327
Series of Old American Songs (Foster), 4:659, 661
"Serioso" Quartet (Beethoven). *See* Quartet in F minor, no. 11, op., 95
Sermisy. *See* Claudin de Sermisy
Serov, Alexander, 2:737; 3:438–39, 438, 440, 772
    on Glinka's *A Life of the Tsar*, 3:248–49
    Judith, 3:391–92
    Liszt and, 3:439, 446
    as music critic, 3:290
    orientalism and, 3:391–92

serpent proto-tuba, 3:168, *168*
Serpina's aria (Pergolesi), 2:439, 440
Serva padrona, La (Pergolesi), 2:438–41, 450, 474, 477; 3:27
services, liturgical day, 1:11–12
sesquitertia, 1:341
Sessions, Roger, 4:522–23, 525, 649; 5:94, 160, 163
    Richard Maxfield and, 5:94
sestina, 1:352; 2:6, 7
    derivation of term, 2:6
Sestina (Krenek), 5:39, 40–41, 140
Settle, Elkanah, 2:126
Seufzer (sighs or groans), 2:254; 3:91
Seufzern. See sigh-figures,
Seven Last Words, 1:777
    Schütz setting of, 2:73
seventeenth century
    academies, 1:798–99
    birth of opera in, 2:16–34
    compositional "borrowings" in, 2:327
    designations for, 1:797–98
    English music in, 2:113–38, 196–97
    European borders and nationalities in, 2:139
    French music in, 2:85–110
    French vs. Italian music in, 2:86, 110
    ground bass and, 2:10, 35, 94, 138
    Italian string music in, 2:177–231, 234
    key system and, 1:44
    luxuriant style and, 2:59–66, 67
    madrigal types and, 1:817
    meaning of "symphony" in, 2:497
    minor keys with flats and, 2:120
    monodic revolution and, 1:699, 806–34
    musical significance of year 1685 and, 2:233–35
    "nuove musiche" publications in, 1:812–22
    organ music in, 2:35–55
    Thirty Years War devastation during, 2:55–56
    tonality and, 2:181–203
    women musicians and, 2:80
Seventh Book of Madrigals (Monteverdi), 2:6, 8–9
Seventh Sonata for piano (Prokofieff), 5:9
Seventh Symphony in A major (Beethoven), 3:16, 331
Seventh Symphony in E major (Bruckner), 3:747–51, 755
Seventh Symphony (Shostakovich), 5:8
sexism, *Don Giovanni* and, 2:495–96
Sexta hora, counterpoint to, 1:154
sextolets, English, 2:47, 48
sexual behavior, 3:36
sexual identity
    castrati and, 2:86–87
    See also gender; homosexuality
sexuality
    musical representation of, 3:558

sexuality (*continued*)
  orientalist representations and, **3**:390,
    398, 400–405
  salon music disrepute and, **3**:78
  Victorian views on, **3**:117
  See also eroticism
Sforza, Ascanio Maria Cardinal **1**:518, 552,
    558, 578, *578*, 584, 699
Sforza, Galeazzo Maria, Duke of Milan,
    1:459, 518, 519, 522–23, 558, 584
Sforza family, **1**:518
Sgambati, Giovanni, **3**:745
Shackley, George
  "Git Along, Little Dogies," **4**:663
  Lonesome Cowboy, The, **4**:662, *663*
Shadwell, Thomas, **2**:126
Shaffer, Peter, **2**:464
Shakespeare, William, **1**:819; **2**:27, 137, 434,
    649
  Beethoven compared with, **2**:706
  Berlioz and, **3**:320
  German Romantics' worship of, **2**:416,
    706
  history plays of, **1**:420; **3**:623
  iambic pentameter and, **1**:742
  incidental music and, **2**:113
  Mozart on, **2**:645
  musical works adapted from, **3**:45, 406,
    446–47
  Musorgsky and, **3**:623–24, 631
  opera adaptations of, **3**:481, 596–610,
    639, 640
  semi-opera adaptations of, **2**:127, 130–31
  sonnet form of, **1**:352
  as *Sturm und Drang* hero, **2**:416, 417
  Verdi and, **3**:576, 582–83, 594, 596–610,
    611, 623
  vocal fantasia and, **2**:416, 417
  works of
    Coriolanus, **2**:702
    Hamlet, **2**:416, 417, 645; **3**:320, 558
    Henry IV, **3**:623
    Henry V, **1**:420
    King Lear, **3**:576–77, 591
    Macbeth, **3**:576
    Measure for Measure, **2**:137; **3**:481
    Merry Wives of Windsor, **3**:611
    Midsummer's Night Dream, A, **2**:127,
      130–31
    Much Ado About Nothing, **3**:320
    Othello, **3**:596, 597, 600, 605, 606, 608
    Romeo and Juliet, **3**:45, 406
    Tempest, The, **2**:127
shamanism, **1**:616
Shankar, Ravi, **5**:389, *389*
Shaporin, Yuri, Andrey Volkonsky and,
    5:461
shared solitude, Romanticism and, **3**:75,
    77, 85, 86–87
Sharngadeva, **4**:237
Shaw, George Bernard, **5**:261
  Back to Methuselah, **5**:198

on *Dido and Aeneas,* **2**:138
on Liszt's "Don Juan Fantasy," **3**:271
as music critic, **3**:271, 290
on Sarasate's aria, **2**:481
on Sullivan's *Ivanhoe,* **3**:658
on Wagner, **3**:492
sheet music
  Christmas carols and, **1**:420
  household romance songs and, **3**:633
  of operas, **3**:212
  tabulatures, **1**:606
Sheherazade (Rimsky-Korsakov), **3**:397;
    4:121–22
Shelley, Mary, **3**:194
Shelley, Percy Bysshe, **3**:416
Sheppard, W. Anthony, **5**:256, 486
sherbet aria, **2**:154, 174
Sherr, Richard, **1**:558
Shestakova, Lyudmila, **3**:458
Shevchenko, Taras, **3**:345
Shifrin, Seymour, **5**:359
  composition seminar at Berkeley and,
    5:438
  La Monte Young and, **5**:359
"shipwreck aria" (Farinelli), **2**:168–72
Shirley, Wayne, **4**:263, 662
Sholokhov, Mikhail, **4**:790
"Short but Most Necessary Draft for a
    Well-Appointed Church Music;
    Together with Certain Modest
    Reflections on the Decline of
    Same" (J. S. Bach memorandum),
    2:362, 376
short trill, **2**:277
Shostakovich, Dmitriy Dmitriyevich,
    4:227, 661, 780–96, *781*; **5**:9–13,
    104, 294, 305, 434, 438
  Alfred Schnittke and, **5**:466
  Edison Denisov and, **5**:463
  "formalism" of, **5**:10
  Moscow Conservatory and, **5**:12
  Testimony, "The Memoirs of Dmitry
    Shostakovich as Related to and
    Edited by Solomon Volkov," **5**:471
  works of
    *Lady Macbeth of the Mtsensk District,
      The,* **5**:230–31, **5**:241, **5**:243
    Nad rodinoy nashey solntse siyayet, **5**:12
    Nose, The, **4**:782–86; **5**:185
    Pesn' o lesakh, **5**:12
    preludes, **3**:351
    Symphony no. 1, **4**:780, 782
    Symphony no. 4, **4**:791
    Symphony no. 5, **4**:791–92, 793–94,
      795
    Symphony no. 7, **5**:8
    Symphony no. 8, **5**:8, 10
    Symphony no. 9, **5**:10, 12–13
    Symphony no. 15, **3**:514; **5**:422
    Twelfth Quartet, **5**:104, 105
Sibelius, Jean, **4**:641–42, 643, 647; **5**:429
  Symphony no. 7 **4**:641

Sibylline Prophecies, **1**:719, *719*, 773
siciliana, **2**:144–46, 274
Sicily, **1**:351; **2**:139
"Sidewalks of New York, The," **4**:654
Sidney, Henry, **4**:281
Siege of Chester (1645), **2**:124
Siegfried's horn call (Wagner), **3**:508, 520,
    527
Siegfrieds Rheinfahrt (Wagner), **3**:522
Siegfrieds Tod (Wagner), **3**:491, 492–95,
    497, 501, 502, 505, 511
  Norn's refrain and first Norn's speech,
    3:494–95
Siegfried (Wagner), **3**:510–12, 513, 516, 537,
    539, 610
  Brahms studying score of, **3**:697
Siegmeister, Elie, **4**:651, 659, 661, 671
  Music and Society (pamphlet), **4**:658
  "Strange Funeral in Braddock," **4**:656,
    658
Siehe zu, dass Deine Gottesfurcht, BWV 179
    (J. S. Bach), **2**:370–72
Siemirdzki, Hendrik, **3**:344
sigh-figure, **1**:363, 371, 372–73; **2**:364, 368;
    4:17, 18, 21, 319, 320, 348
Sight of Faburdon, The (treatise), **1**:436, 437,
    438
sight-singing, **1**:47, 76
  choral, **1**:617
  fauxbourdon and faburden, **1**:435–39
  harmonization and, **1**:434, 436, 437, 438
  mnemonic device and, **1**:104
  modal breakthrough and, **1**:99, 100–104,
    153
  printed partbooks and, **1**:694
  See also ear training
Sigismund, Holy Roman Emperor, **1**:282
signature,
  clef, **1**:99–100
  major and minor prolation, **1**:253
  neumes and, **1**:13–16
  time, **1**:252–53, 254
signification, **2**:10, 133, 539–55
  Beethoven and, **2**:680, 686
  interpretation and, **2**:680
  ornamentation, **2**:278–79, *279*
  See also semiotics
"sign of congruence," **1**:378
Signor Bruschino, Il (Rossini), **3**:21
Silberweise (Sachs), **1**:140
silent movies, **4**:562
Silvana (Weber), **3**:209
Silver Apples of the Moon (Subotnick), **5**:497
Silvestrov, Valentin, Third Symphony
    ("Eschatophony"), **5**:463
Simfonia-Poema (Khachaturian), **5**:12
Simfonicheskaya misteriya (Pashchenko),
    5:182
simile aria, **2**:161, 168–69, 231, 308, 340
  See also rage aria
Simon, Paul, Philip Glass and, **5**:391
Simon Boccanegra (Verdi), **3**:596

Simpson, Christopher, **2:**120

Simrock, Nikolaus, **2:**736

"simultaneous conception" (Aaron concept), **1:**577, 579

simultaneous style. *See* homorhythmic counterpoint

Sinatra, Frank, **1:**617, 817; **5:**312, 313

    Partch's *Revelation* and, **5:**485

sincerity, artistic, **3:**64, 69

sinfonia. *See* overture; symphony

sinfonia avanti l'opera, **2:**497, 498, 507, 508, 520

    A. Scarlatti and, **2:**148–50

Sinfonia (Berio), **5:**348, 349

    collage technique and, **5:**417–18

sinfonia caratteristica, **2:**680; **3:**322–23

Sinfonia dramatica: China kämpft (Hartmann), **4:**772

Sinfonia in B flat major, op. 18 no 2 (J. C. Bach)4943, **2:**507–11

Sinfonia in G (Sammartini), **2:**500–504

Sinfonia Sacra (Weill), **4:**539

Sinfonietta (Janáček), **4:**424

Sinfonietta, op. 5 (Korngold), **4:**549

Sing Out Sweet Land, **4:**659

Singakademie (Berlin), **2:**381

singing,

    a cappella, **1:**666–67, 780; **2:**6, 73; **3:**234

    accompanied, **1:**131–33, 296, 298–99, 352, 363

    basso buffo rapid-patter effect, **2:**439–40

    bel canto, **3:**36–46, 48, 578

    castrato, **2:**16–17, 86–87, 97, 153, 166–69, 173, 174

    chromatic adjustment and, **1:**274

    congregational, **1:**27–28, 47, 58, 758, 765

    countertenor, **2:**130

    crooning, **1:**817; **2:**15

    ear training, **1:**75, 99–104

    English qualities of, **1:**452

    etiquette books, **1:**694, 709

    falsetto, **2:**98, 130; **3:**578

    of familiar tunes, **1:**598

    fauxbourdon technique and, **1:**435–39

    florid, **1:**356

    four-part voice nomenclature, **1:**468

    gorgia (throat-music), **1:**816–17, *816,* 821; **2:**15

    gradual elaboration of, **1:**163

    Guidonian hand mnemonic device for, **1:**102–4

    harmonizing, **1:**168, 392, 394, 406, 434–35, 452, 472

    haute-contre, **2:**98, 100, 130, 459

    imitative rounds, **1:**331

    jubilated, **1:**11, 24, 26, 38–39

    Mass ordo, **1:**61(table)

    melismatic, **1:**11, 24

    monodic style of, **1:**817

    new medieval tonal system and, **1:**77–78

    Nuove musiche instructions in, **1:**813

    opera seria's dominance of, **2:**158, 173–74

ornamental neumes and, **1:**24

ornamentation and, **1:**816–17

partbooks for, **1:**539–60

polyphonic, **1:**44–47, 147–68

printed music texts for, **1:**550–51

rhetorical embellishment and, **1:**816–17

scale intervals and, **1:**100–101

sight transposition and, **1:**76

sweetness of, **1:**452

trope rubrics for, **1:**52

unison. *See* monophony

vocal expression and, **1:**816–17

See also aria; choral music; madrigal; opera; prima donna; virtuosity; vocal music; voice types; specific song and voice types

singing-society movement, **3:**163

singspiel, **1:**127

    Haydn and, **2:**518, 526

    Mozart and, **2:**470–76, 479–85, 602; **3:**188

    opera origins and, **3:**566

    Romantic opera origins and, **3:**187, 188

    Russia and, **3:**236, 242

    Schubert and, **3:**79, 81, 84

    Weber and, **3:**191–92, 193, 567

Sinnlichkeit, **3:**22, 239

    Rossini and, **3:**13

Sins of Old Age (Rossini), **3:**12–13, 78

    ballet arrangements of, **3:**13

sintesi radiofonici and, **5:**188

siren songs, **3:**127

"Si ridesti il Leon di Castiglia" (Verdi), **3:**574–75

si (scale-singing syllable), **1:**101

Sisman, Elaine, **2:**645, 695

Sistine Chapel, **1:**459, 460, 486, 496, 498, 555, 632, 634, 649, 652, 666, 667

    a cappella rule of, **1:**666–67

    Michelangelo ceiling, **1:**719, *719*

Sitwell, Dame Edith, *Petrushka* and, **4:**170

Six, Les, *See* Group des Six, Le

six-as-perfect-number (*senaria*) theory, **1:**587–88, 603

"Six characters in search of an author." See *Sei personaggi in cerca d'autore*

"Six Grand Overtures" (J. C. Bach), **2:**507

Six morceaux caractéristiques (Smetana), **3:**444

Six Sonatas for the Harpsichord with Accompaniments for a Violin or German Flute and Violoncello, op. 2 (Abel), **2:**429

Six sonates en quators ou conversations galantes et amusantes (Guilleman), **2:**427

Six Studies for Four Timpani (Carter), **5:**269

six-tone extended dominant chord, Scriabin and, **4:**213

sixteenth century

    ars perfecta and, **1:**585–628, 629–30, 722

    Byrd and, **1:**670–89

    cyclic Mass Ordinaries and, **1:**459–500

emulative composition and, **1:**474–75

English music and, **1:**423

imitative polyphony and, **1:**546

instrumental genres in, **1:**606, 617–28

international style and, **1:**453–59

Josquin and, **1:**549–84, 601

Lasso and, **1:**678, 712–22

madrigal revival in, **1:**723–51

Palestrina and, **1:**630–70

Passion text polyphonic settings and, **1:**776

Protestant Reformation and, **1:**753–69

representative style in, **2:**643

vocal chamber music in, **1:**540

sixteenth notes, **1:**262, 515, 785

Sixth Book of Madrigals (Monteverdi), **2:**6, 7

sixth degree harmonization, **3:**649–51

sixth mode, **1:**80

6/3 position, **1:**406, 409

sixths,

    augmented, **2:**364

    Chaikovsky's melodic, **3:**633, 636–38

    Landini, **1:**368, 383, 441, 470

Sixth Symphony (Chaikovsky), **4:**19

Sixth Symphony in C major (Schubert), **3:**81

Sixth Symphony, no. 6 in F major, op. 68 (Beethoven). *See* "Pastoral" Symphony

Sixth Symphony (Prokofieff), **5:**9

Sixtus IV, Pope, **1:**458–59, 486, 496

Sixties, The, **5:**30750

    Altamont Festival, **5:**311

    annus horribilis, **5:**310

    Beatles, **5:**316–33

    Betty Friedan, **5:**307

    Bing Crosby, **5:**312

    Bob Dylan, **5:**315

    "bourgeois," **5:**309

    Chicago Eight, **5:**310

    Civil Rights Act, **5:**307

    "Colonel" Tom Parker, **5:**314

    "counterculture of," **5:**309, 310, 327

    cultural miscenenation, **5:**314

    Daniel Bell, **5:**312

    Democratic National Convention, **5:**310

    drug culture of, **5:**309

    Ed Sullivan Show, **5:**314

    Elvis Presley, **5:**313–14, 318, 327, 336

    Feminine Mystique, The, **5:**307

    folk music, **5:**314–16

    Frank Sinatra, **5:**312, 313

    Gustav Mahler, **5:**326, 348

    Haight-Ashbury, **5:**309

    "hippies," **5:**309

    James Brown, **5:**313

    Joan Baez, **5:**315

    Joe, 310–311

    John F. Kennedy (President), **5:**310

        assassination of, 310

    Johnson, Lyndon (President), **5:**309

Sixties, The (continued)
  Joni Mitchell, 5:315
  Judy Collins, 5:315
  Kent State University, 5:310
    shootings at, 5:310, 311
  Kingston Trio, 5:315
  Martin Luther King Jr., 5:309, 310, 349,
    350
    assassination of, 310
  National Organization for Women
    (NOW), 5:307
  Ohio State Militia, 5:310
  Ray Charles, 5:313
  Robert Allen Zimmerman, 5:315
  Robert F. Kennedy, 5:310
    assassination of, 5:310
  rock 'n' roll, 5:312–13
  Rolling Stones, The, 5:316, 343, 346
  Stonewall riots, 5:307–8
  Strom Thurmond, 5:309
  Students for a Democratic Society, 5:310
  "Summer of Love," 5:309
  Todd Gitlin, 5:312
  Vietnam War, 5:308–9
  Weavers, The, 5:315
  Who, The, 5:316, 327–28, 332
  Woodstock, 5:311
  Wozzeck, 5:312
Skazki, (Medtner), 4:556, 557, 558
Sketch (Lewis), 5:337, 341–42
Sketch of a New Aesthetic of Music (Busoni),
    5:177, 182, 184
Skinner, B.F., behavioral psychology and,
    5:446, 448, 449
"Skip to My Lou, My Darling," 3:378
Skroup, Frantisek, 3:448
Slater, Montagu, 5:228, 234, 240
Slaughter of the Holy Innocents, 1:93, 177
Slava (Russian folk melody), 3:625
slavery, 3:385
slave songs, 3:378
Slavic languages, 3:345, 448
Slavic peoples
  opera and, 3:447–48
  Smetana and, 3:443–63
"Slavonic Dances" (Dvořák), 3:753; 4:632
Slav'sya theme (Glinka), 3:248–50
Sleep (mythology), 2:100, 102
Sleeping Beauty, The, 4:144, 145, 146, 147–48
  "omnibus progression" and, 4:145, 146
"sleep scene",
  Lully and, 2:100–102
  Purcell and, 2:130
"Slïkhal li vï" (Chaikovsky), 3:634–36
Slonimsky, Nicolas, 4:302, 339, 621; 5:185
Slovakia, 3:345
Slovenia, 3:447–48
"smallest link," Erwartung and, 4:303
Smetana, Bedřich, 3:443–63, 444, 752, 754;
    4:426, 427
  background of, 3:443
  Balakirev and, 3:457–58

chamber music and, 3:731
illness of, 3:447
Liszt and, 3:444, 445–46
nationalism and, 3:443, 445–59, 462
New German School and, 3:443, 446,
    449, 451, 476
opera and, 3:447, 448–50, 458–59,
    461–63
symphonic poems and, 3:446–47,
    451–54, 457
as teacher, 3:444, 445, 447
works of
  Bartered Bride, The, 3:458–59, 458,
    463, 464
  Blaník, 3:452, 459–62
  Braniboři v Čechách, 3:448–50, 463
  Hakon Jarl, 3:446, 452
  Jubel-Ouvertüre in D major, op. 4,
    3:445
  Libuše, 3:461–63
  Macbeth a čarodějnice, 3:446–47, 457
  Má vlast, 3:452–54, 459–63, 755
  Richard III, 3:446
  Šárka, 3:452
  Six morceaux caractéristiques, 3:444
  String Quartet no. 1 ("From My
    Life"), 3:731
  Tabór, 3:452
  Triumph-Symphonie mit Benützung der
    österreichischer in E major, op. 6,
    3:445
  Vltava ("The Moldau"), 3:452,
    454–57, 459–60, 462, 463, 538
  Vyšehrad, 3:452–54
  Wallensteins Lager, 3:446
  Z mého zivota, 3:446–47
Smijers, Albert, 1:565
Smith, David Stanley, 3:769
Smith, John Stafford, 1:409
Smith, Ruth, 2:315
Smithson, Harriet, 3:320–21, 320, 322, 326
soap operas, 2:446
So ben mi c'ha bon tempo (Vecchi), 1:746, 748
Sobinin, Bogdan, 3:241
sociability music, 2:426–32
social class
  artistic creation and, 2:14
  Beaumarchais's Figaro plays and,
    2:477–78
  cathedral clerical hierarchy and, 1:169,
    213–18
  chamber music and, 2:114
  commercial (comic) opera and, 2:17
  court vs. commercial opera and, 2:34
  dance style and, 1:621
  English Civil War and, 2:124
  English self-made men and, 2:114, 124,
    237
  Enlightenment ideal and, 2:302, 461,
    477, 577
  feudal hierarchy and, 1:107, 143
  Florentine ballata and, 1:367–68

French urbanization and, 1:120, 142, 143,
    169, 207–8, 219, 226–28
Haydn and, 2:577, 607
high art and, 1:116; 2:112
international musical style and,
    1:453–57
madrigal and, 1:354–56, 368
Meistersinger and, 1:139, 141
minstrels and, 1:109–10
mobility and, 1:579–80, 694; 2:446
motet and, 1:226–28, 236, 237–38, 239
nineteenth-century music and, 2:736,
    737
opera buffa and, 2:110
opera haters and, 2:106
opera seria and, 2:174–75
pastorelas and, 2:446
salons and, 3:75, 78–79
thirteenth-century musical treatise and,
    1:207, 219
troubadours and, 1:108–9
trouvères and, 1:121
view of virtuosity and, 2:15–16
women's musical accomplishments and,
    2:79, 80, 81
  See also aristocracy; bourgeoisie; elite
    culture; middle-class values
Social Contract (Rousseau), 2:461; 3:61, 123;
    5:82, 177
social elite. See aristocracy; elite culture
Socialist Realism, 4:778–79, 796
  Arvo Pärt and, 5:401
"socialist realist" art, 4:671
social mobility, 1:579–80, 694; 2:446
social prejudice
  against artists, 3:385–86
  female composers and, 3:186, 292
  See also ethnocentrism
Société des Concerts du Conservatoire
    (Paris), 3:677
Société des Jeunes Artistes du
    Conservatoire (Paris), 3:677–78,
    679
Société Nationale de Musique (France),
    3:775–76, 782, 783; 4:102, 138
  Ars Gallica, and, 4:59, 61
Society for Jewish Folk Music, 4:108
Society for Private Musical Performances,
    4:351–53
Society for the Promotion of Church
    Music (Moravia), 4:423
Society of Jesus. See Jesuits
Society of St. Gregory of America, 3:13
sociology. See musical sociology
"Sociology of Baroque Music, The"
    (Bukofzer), 2:14–17
Socrates, 1:802; 2:416
Socrate (Satie), 4:572, 573, 574–75
soggetto cavato dalle vocali, 1:560–61, 563
Sohr, Martin. See Agricola, Martin
Soir, Le (Haydn symphony), 2:528

Soirées musicales (Britten/Rossini arrang.), **3**:13

"Soixante-quatre durees" (Messiaen), **5**:26

Solage, **1**:342–45

Soldaten, Die (Zimmerman), **5**:418

Soldier's Tale, The (Stravinsky), **4**:600, 603

Solera, Temistocle, **3**:571, 573, 576

Solesmes abbey, **1**:22, 23, 631, 632; **4**:101

Solidarnosc movement (Poland), **5**:437

solita forma, **3**:594

solitude,
    artistic, **3**:64
    shared, **3**:75, 77, 85, 86–87

Sollberger, Harvey, **5**:164, 212, 213

solo concerto. *See* concerto; *specific instrumental types*

Solo e pensoso (de Wert), **1**:733, 734

Solo e pensoso (Marenzio), **1**:728–33, 818

soloists, **3**:173, 272–76

Solomon (Handel), **2**:315

Solomon, Maynard, **2**:464, 672, 678, 680; **3**:116; **4**:264

Solomon's Temple (Jerusalem), **1**:285

Solti, Sir Georg, *Final Alice* and, **5**:443

Solzhenitsyn, Alexander, **5**:469

Sombrero de tres picos, El (Falla), **4**:502

"Some Aspects of Twelve-Tone Composition" (article, Babbitt), **5**:153–54

Somfai, Lászlo, **4**:402

Somma, Antonio, **3**:583

sommeil (sleep scene), **2**:100–102, *100*, 130

sonata,
    accompanied keyboard, **2**:427–32, 695
    Bach (C. P. E.) and, **2**:411–13
    Bach (J. C.) and, **2**:421–26
    Bach (J. S.) and, **2**:300, 402
    Bach (W. F.) and, **2**:402–9
    biblical, **3**:65
    Corelli genres of, **2**:177, 178
    fugue genre vs., **2**:726–27
    geneaology of, **1**:791–96
    Handel and, **2**:305
    meaning of, **1**:791
    Mozart and, **2**:471, 601
    Scarlatti (Domenico) and, **2**:391–97
    See also chamber sonata; church sonata; piano sonata; sonata form; trio sonata

sonata-allegro form. *See* sonata form

Sonata auf Concertenart, **2**:301

sonata da camera. See chamber sonata

Sonata da camera in G minor, op. 4, no. 2 (Corelli), **2**:179–81, 189

sonata da chiesa. See church sonata

Sonata da chiesa, op. 3, no. 11 (Corelli)
    compared with *Sonata da camera*, **2**:179–81
    presto, **2**:187–89
    second movement, **2**:182–84

sonata form, **3**:16, 52
    Beach and, **3**:772

Beethoven and, **2**:660; **3**:197

beginnings of, **3**:286–87

Brahms and, **3**:723–24

Chaikovsky and, **3**:792

first academic description of, **2**:736

Haydnesque features of, **2**:520–25, 549, 557, 660

Haydn's breaching of, **2**:531–33, 540, 304

later academic descriptions of, **2**:584

Mozartean concerto and, **2**:606

Schubert and, **3**:94–95, 427

Schumann and, **3**:309, 316–17

symphonic elaboration of, **2**:524–25

thematic dualism and, **2**:395, 514

Weber and, **3**:197

Sonata in B flat, D. 960 (Schubert), **3**:96–100

Sonata in B-flat major, op. 2, no. 4 (Abel), **2**:429–32
    phrase symmetry demonstrated in, **2**:432

Sonata in B-flat minor, op. 35 (Chopin), **3**:365–67

Sonata in B minor for piano (Liszt), **3**:432–35, 446

Sonata in C major, K. 159 (D. Scarlatti), **2**:395–96

Sonata in C major, op. 1, no. 3 (Alberti), **2**:432–33

Sonata in D major, op. 5, no. 1 (Corelli), **2**:282–85

Sonata in D major, op. 5, no. 2 (J. C. Bach), **2**:420–26

Sonata in E major, K. 264 (D. Scarlatti), **2**:393–94

Sonata in F minor, K. 481 (D. Scarlatti), **2**:394–96

Sonata in G major, K. 105 (D. Scarlatti), **2**:392–93

Sonata no. 2 (Galuppi), **2**:432–33

Sonata no. 7 (Scriabin), **4**:219

Sonata for solo viola, op. 25, no. 1 (Hindemith), **4**:528, 529

Sonata per tre violini (G. Gabrieli), **1**:795–96

Sonata pian'e forte (G. Gabrieli), **1**:791–94

Sonatas and Interludes (Cage), **5**:59

song
    English incidental music, **2**:126
    round, **1**:331, 388, 389, 399
    Shakespearean texts, **2**:113, 130
    See also chanson; lied; madrigal; singing; vocal music

"Songbook from Glogau," **1**:539, 540

songbooks, **1**:555, 691, 693–94, 724, 741
    canzona printed in, **1**:787
    Lutheran, **1**:760–61, 762–63

song competitions, **1**:139, 141, 208
    madrigalists, **1**:352–53, 364, 367, 701, 737

song cycles
    Beethoven and, **3**:131–36
    Schubert and, **3**:81, 142–43, 295
    Schumann (Robert) and, **3**:295–305

Song of Hiawatha, The (Longfellow), **3**:123, 760, 763, 764

Song of Igor's Campaign, The (Russian epic), **3**:400

"Song of Myself" (Whitman), **4**:243

Song of Songs, **1**:91, 429, 432, 632; **2**:59

"Song of Thanksgiving" (Beethoven), **2**:686–88, 721, 731

"Song of the Earth" (Mahler), **4**:283

"Song of the Prairies" (Copland), **4**:672

song-poem, Italian trecento. *See* madrigal

Songs, Drones, and Refrains of Death, Crumb and, **5**:422, 423

Songs, Drones, and Refrains of Death, Lorca and, **5**:422

Songs of sundrie natures, some of gravitie, and others of myrth, fit for all companies and voyces (Byrd), **1**:741

Songs That Changed the World (Whitman), **4**:659

"Songs with Music, Chosen from Several Books Printed by the Above-Named, All in One Book" (Sermisy), **1**:692

"Songs Without Words," piano pieces as, **3**:64

"song without words," **1**:543–46

sonic homomorphism, **3**:697–98

Son imbrogliato io già (Pergolesi), **2**:439–40, 441

Sonnambula, La (Bellini), **3**:37

Sonnatas of III Parts, no. 3 in D Minor (Purcell), **2**:198, 199–201, 203

sonnet form, **1**:352

Sonnleithner, Joseph von, **3**:2, 3

"Son qual nave ch'agitata" (Broschi), **2**:168–72

Sontag, Susan, **5**:325
    Against Interpretation, **5**:325

Sophie Elisabeth, Duchess of Brunswick, **2**:79

Sophocles, **1**:780; **3**:576; **4**:49, 676

soprano,
    castrato paired with, **3**:578
    choirboy cantata arias, **2**:352, 370–71
    etymology of word, **1**:468
    gender identification and, **3**:36
    as intermezzo character, **2**:434, 438
    tenor paired with, **3**:578

Sorbon, Robert de, **1**:170

Sorbonne, **5**:347
    riots at, **5**:347
    See also University of Paris

Sorbonne Mass, **1**:315

Sorcerer, The (Gilbert and Sullivan), **3**:652

"Sorcerer's Apprentice, The." *See L'apprenti sorcier*

soul-loss, **1**:616

soul-magnetism, **3**:71

sound. *See* musical sound

"sound designers," **5**:514

Sounds of New Music, **5**:192

soupir (quarter rest), **2**:104
Sousa, John Philip, **4**:275
Souterliedekens (Clemens), **1**:597–99,
    754–55
South America, **3**:382–83
Southern Baptist hymnody, **4**:659
Southern Syncopated Orchestra, **4**:602,
    612, 616
Southwest German Radio (Baden-Baden),
    5:217
souvenir books, **1**:804
"Souvenir de Porto Rico, Marche des
    Gibaros" (Gottschalk), **3**:378,
    380–81, 382
Souvenirs de Munich (Chabrier), **4**:61–62, 63
Souvtchinsky, Pierre, **5**:277
Sovetskaya musika (Soviet music), **4**:654,
    778, 791, 792
Soviet music, demise of, **5**:460–64
Soviet Union, **3**:392, 477
    art glorifying, **2**:111
    See also Russia
Soviet Writers' Union, **4**:793
space. *See* musical space
Spagna, La. (bassadanza), **1**:621, 622–25
Spain,
    Christian reconquest of, **1**:64
    Codex Calixtinus and, **1**:162
    dance forms of, **2**:37, 38, 261
    Granados and, **2**:391–92
    Ma codice and, **1**:183
    Moorish invasion of, **1**:63
    Mozarabic chant, **1**:63–64
    Scarlatti (Domenico) in, **2**:390–92, 393
    song variations and, **2**:47
    Thirty Years War and, **2**:56
    troubadour influence in, **1**:116, 128
    vernacular song of, **1**:128–33, 724
    villancico
Spanish Armada (1588), **1**:743
Spanish Civil War, **4**:659
"Spargi d'amaro pianto" (Donizetti),
    3:57–59
Spataro, Giovanni, **1**:551–52
Spaun, Josef von, **3**:79, 80, 86
Spaziergänge eines Einsamen, op. 78 (Heller),
    3:361, 363
"speakeasies," **4**:602, 617
Specht, Richard, **4**:2
Spectator (journal), **3**:290
"spectral" music, **5**:499–501
spectralism, **5**:499–501
Speculum musicae (Jacobus), **1**:254
speech,
    natural, **3**:619–21
    operatic representation of, **1**:827
    See also language; prosody; word-music
        relationship
Speech Songs (Dodge), **5**:498–99
Spellbound (Hitchcock), **5**:183
Spellbound, Rózsa and, **5**:183
Spem in alium (Tallis), **1**:673

Spengler, Oswald, **4**:530
    Untergang des Abendlandes, Der, **4**:530
Spiegelman, Joel, Kiev composers and,
    5:463
Spiegelritter, Der (Schubert), **3**:84
Spielleute, **1**:141
Spielmusik, **4**:528
Spike Jones and His City Slickers, **5**:505
    Fuehrer's Face, Der, **5**:505
Spinacino, Francesco, **1**:606, 620
spinning out. *See* Fortspinnung
Spiritual Exercises (Ignatius), **1**:771
spiritualism, **1**:616
spirituality,
    Beethoven and, **3**:14
    Romantic, **2**:642, 643, 649; **3**:18, 21
    sensuality vs., **3**:13, 22
spirituals, **3**:765
Spiritus et alme orphanorum (Marian trope),
    1:410, 411
Spitta, Philipp, **3**:703, 716
Spitzer, Leo, **1**:383
split choirs, **1**:611, 776, 780, 782–83, 787,
    792
Spohr, Louis, **3**:252, 253
    critique of Beethoven's Fifth and Ninth
        symphonies by, **2**:677, 678, 692
spoken theater. *See* acting; theater
spondaic meter, **1**:197, 198, 201, 202, 217,
    403
    French motet and, **1**:221, 232
Sprechstimme technique, **4**:460, 462; **5**:424
sprezzatura, **2**:15
"Spring Auguries," **4**:177
Spring (Vivaldi), **2**:225–31, 308
Spruchdichtung, **1**:140
Sputnik, **5**:157
Spyaschaya krasavitsa (Chaikovsky), **4**:456
Squarcialupi Codex, **1**:353, *353*, *354*, *355*, 363
square notation. *See* quadratic notation
Srb-Debrnov, Josef, **3**:448
SS. *Giovanni e Paolo* (Isaac/Medici), **1**:823,
    827, 834
Stabat juxta Christi crucem, **1**:394, 396
Stabat Mater (Penderecki), **5**:217
Stabat mater (Rossini), **3**:13
Stabat mater dolorosa (chant sequence),
    1:134, 394
Stabreim, Wagner and, **3**:501, 504, 509
Stadtkonvikt (Vienna), **3**:80
Stadtpfeifer, **2**:287, 353, 357; **3**:711
staff,
    intervals, **1**:29–30, 35, 73
    invention implications, **1**:105
    invention of, **1**:16, 102, 105, 153
    letter names of, **1**:75
    medieval modal scale and, **1**:75–76
    mnemonic device and, **1**:102–3
    modern notation and, **1**:74
    neume arrangement on, **1**:16, 62, 99–100
    notation prior to, **1**:60, 93, 115

stage machinery. *See* machinery
stage managers, opera and, **3**:206
"Stairway to Parnassus" (Fux), **1**:667,
    669
Stalin, Joseph, **4**:657, 775, 790
    death of, **5**:216
    Requiem for a Young Poet and, **5**:420
Stalingrad, German defeat at, **4**:671
Stamic, Jan Václav. *See* Stamitz, Johann
    Wenzel
Stamitz, Carl (son), **2**:505; **3**:735
Stamitz, Johann Wenzel (father), **2**:505–7
    Orchestra Trio in C minor, op. 4, no. 3,
        2:506–7, 519, 718, 719
stamping songs (estampie), **1**:294
standard of perfection. *See* ars perfecta
standard repertory, **3**:657
    Bach and Handel revivals and,
        2:234–35, 375, 399, 464
    Bach's (J. S.) Brandenburg Concertos in,
        2:289, 306
    Bach's (J. S.) cantatas' musical demands
        and, **2**:374
    basis of, **2**:234–35
    Beethoven's *Fidelio* in, **3**:3
    Beethoven's unshakeable presence in,
        2:691, 738
    Beethoven's works in, **3**:3., 131, 679, 680
    as canon, **2**:577, 638, 646
    canon vs., **3**:665–66, 682
    Carmina burana and, **1**:138–39
    Chaikovsky's *Romeo and Juliet* in,
        3:406–9, 663
    Donizetti operas in, **3**:46
    emergence of, **2**:399, 464, 638–39, 738
    Handel's oratorios as earliest perpetually
        performed works in, **2**:305, 326,
        464
    Haydn's continuous place in, **2**:399, 464,
        578, 646; **3**:679, 680
    later additions to, **3**:674
    Liszt's *Les préludes* in, **3**:422
    Monteverdi operas in, **2**:1–2, 21
    Mozart's continuous place in, **2**:464,
        578, 646
    Mozart's late operas in, **2**:94
    music appreciation and, **2**:540, 738;
        3:782
    nineteenth-century symphonic music in,
        3:675, 679–82, 686
    Puccini in, **3**:664, 665, 666, 674
    romantic bel canto and, **3**:37
    Rossini vs. Beethoven in, **3**:14
    Serva padrona as earliest comic opera in,
        2:438
    textual sanctity of, **2**:650–51
    three earliest composers in, **2**:233–34
    Verdi in, **3**:566, 568
    Vivaldi's *Four Seasons* in, **2**:226
    year 1685's significance to, **2**:233–34
    See also canonization
Stanley, Glenn, **3**:166

Stanley Quartet of the University of Michigan, 5:295

stanza
  Ambrosian, 1:49
  bar form and, 1:118
  bergerette and, 1:526
  canso/ballade structure of, 1:349, 694–95
  lai and, 1:119
  madrigal's single, 1:352, 724, 813
  refrain insertion of, 1:221
  repetition of, 1:813
Star of Bethlehem, 1:399
Starr, Ringo, 5:317
"Star-Spangled Banner, The" (American national anthem), 1:409; 3:120, 667; 4:275, 653
  Gottschalk's arrangement of, 3:381
Starzer, Joseph, 4:133
Stasov, Vladimir, 3:288, 439, 468, 477, 631
  Borodin and, 3:403
  on Liszt, 3:272–73
  New Russian School and, 3:393, 395, 397, 468, 786
  orientalism and, 3:393
Statements for Orchestra (Copland), 4:654
Stations of the Cross (Newman), 5:353
Statira, La (A. Scarlatti), 2:151
Status Seekers, The (Packard), 5:163
Steffani, Agostino, 2:331
Stein, Erwin, 4:739
Stein, Gertrude, 4:589, 590, 591–93, 594, 597
  Four Saints in Three Acts, 4:589, 595, 595; 5:394
Stein, Leonard, 5:94
  La Monte Young and, 5:94, 356
Stein, Werner, 3:177
Steinberg, Maximilian, 4:164
Steinecke, Wolfgang, 5:20
Steiner, George, 3:576, 582–83, 783
Steiner, Max, "underscoring" techniques and, 4:551
"Stella by Starlight," 5:415
stems, note, 1:260–61
Stendahl (Marie-Henri Beyle), 3:32–34, 528
Stephan, Rudolf, 3:440; 4:6
Stephen, Saint, 3:178
Stephen II, Pope, 1:2, 38
Stephens, Henry Louis, 3:377
Steppenwolf (Hesse), 5:415–16
stereotypes,
  conventions vs., 3:49
  national, 3:33
  orientalism and, 3:386, 390, 392, 398
  women's musical creativity and, 2:78, 79, 81
  See also otherness
Stern, Daniel. *See* d'Agoult, Countess Marie
Stevens, Jane R., 2:621

Stevens, John, 1:420
Steve Reich and Musicians, 5:375, 387
sticherons, 1:33–34
stichic principle, 1:12, 20, 23, 24, 48
stile antico, 1:667, 669–70, 687; 2:43, 120, 165, 241; 4:556, 558
  ars perfecta as, 1:831
  Bach's (J. S.) *Christ lag in Todeshanden, BWV* 4 as, 2:345
  Bach's (J. S.) Mass and, 2:375
  Beethoven and, 2:686
  Carissimi and, 2:74
  Fux rules of, 1:667, 669; 2:180, 518
  Monteverdi and, 2:5
  Palestrina and, 2:180
  Roman Catholic composers and, 2:357
  See also counterpoint
stile concitato, 2:8–9, 69, 308
stile da cappella. See stile antico
stile moderno, 1:667, 669, 687
stile rappresentativo, 1:802, 826; 2:418, 643
  earliest surviving example of, 1:827, 831
stile recitativo, 2:6
  first practice of, 1:823, 826
Stiller, Andrew, 5:487
Stimmen der Völker in Liedern (Herder), 3:123, 126
Stimmungsbilder ("mood pictures"), 4:31
Stockhausen, Karlheinz, 5: 8, 22, 37, 40, 44–49, 52, 54, 63, 64, 65, 84, 165, 189, 220, 319, 321, 396, 463, 474
  Catholic upbringing, 5:44
  Cologne Musikhochschule, 5:44
  Elektronische Studie II, 5:190
  Gesang der Jünglinge, 5:191
  Gruppen for four orchestras, 5:421
  Gyorgy Ligeti and, 5:49
  Hymnen, 5:191, 420
  "intermodulation" and, 5:191–92
  Kontakte, 5:191
  Momentform and, 5:611
  "mosaic of sound," 5:25
  Summer Courses at Darmstadt, 5:44
  works of
    Klavierst‚ck X, 5:83
    Klavierst‚ck XI, 5:54, 64, 82
    Kreuzspiel, 5:44, 45–48, 153
Stockhausen Serves Imperialism (Cardew), 5:88
  Rochberg's Music for the Magic Theater, and, 5:415
  Studien, 5:189
  Telemusik, 5:420
  World Trade Center terror attack and, 5:474
Stoeber, Franz, 2:689
Stokowski, Leopold, 4:781, 5:54, 193
Stone, Kurt, 5:497
Stone Guest, The (Dargomïzhsky), 3:612–15, 618, 619, 623
  Don Juan's Arioso, 3:612–14
Stonewall Bar, 5:307

riot at, 5:307–8
Stookey, Paul, 5:315
Stoppard, Tom
  Travesties, 5:162
Stork Club (New York), Josephine Baker and, 4:611–12
Storm, The (Ostrovsky), 4:423, 430
Storm, Theodor, 4:710
"Storm and stress." *See* Sturm und Drang
Stow, Randolph, *Eight Songs for a Mad King* and, 5:427
Stradella, Alessandro
  Handel's alleged "borrowings" from, 2:327, 328–29
  Qual prodigio e ch'io miri, 2:327, 328
Stradivari, Antonio, 2:2
Stradivarius violins, 3:255
Straeten, Edmund vander, 1:559
Strand, Marl, Charles Dodge and, 5:498
"Strange Funeral in Braddock" (Siegmeister), 4:656, 658
Strange Interlude (O'Neill), 3:59
"Stranger in Paradise" (song), 3:401, 402
strategic harmonic delays, 3:528
Strauss, Johann II, 3:647–51
  waltz and, 3:648
  works of
    An der schönen, blauen Donau, op. 325, 3:648
    Fledermaus, Die, 3:648–51
    Geschichten aus dem Wienerwald, op. 325, 3:648
Straus, Joseph, *Remaking the Past: Musical Modernism and the Influence of the Tonal Tradition*, 4:360
Strauss, Richard, 3:323–24; 4:3, 30, 36–58, 37, 59, 67, 94, 95, 153, 208, 303, 304, 305, 306, 320, 326, 327, 349, 391, 422, 467, 473, 508, 549, 580, 621, 724, 750, 754, 755; 5:437
  death of, 4:49
  lieder and, 4:31
  maximalism and, 4:50
  modernism and, 4:49–50
  Tondichtung ("tone poem") and, 4:31
  works of
    Ein Heldenleben, 4:374
    Elektra, 4:48–58, 164, 453
    Enoch Arden, 4:459
    Reverie, op. 9, no. 4, 4:31–32, 33
    Rosenkavalier, Der, 4:49, 49, 453
    Salomé, 4:36–48, 257, 328, 388, 580, 756
    Schweigsame Frau, Die, 4:37
Stravaganza, La (Vivaldi), 2:225
Stravinsky, Igor, 1:152; 3:13, 364; 4:21, 152–90, 192, 200, 212, 221, 231, 261, 327, 367, 378, 382, 387, 397, 398, 408, 410, 420, 422, 454, 456, 473, 475, 477–78, 496, 497, 502, 506, 508, 522, 525, 526, 545, 553, 573, 609, 615, 619, 620, 621, 627, 628, 650,

Stravinsky, Igor (*continued*)
    662, 666, 675, 675, 680, 690, 691,
    699, 724, 741, 747, 754, 755,
    765–66, 776; 5:49, 116–35, 172,
    216, 246, 261, 265, 268, 294, 295,
    301, 326, 347, 431
  "Bachy" style and, 4:485, 488
  on Beethoven's music, 2:693
  Chronicles of My Life (autobiography),
    4:469
  Darwinian view of music historiography
    and, 2:397
  denunciation of *War Requiem*, 5:261
  Firebird, piano roll, 4:155f, 156
  Gesualdo madrigals and, 1:738, 739
  "Great Sacrifice, The," 4:170
  Harvard lectures and, 4:475, 676, 677
  "Konzerstrück" in *Petrushka*, "Danse
    Russe," 4:161, 162–63, 166–67, 168
  "major-minor triad," 5:125
  meeting with Khrushchev, 5:460–61
  "minute stylizations" and, 4:609–10
  Mussolini and, 4:478
  neoclassicism and, 4:447–93, 592, 677
  plunderphonics compact disc and, 5:504
  Petrushka, "Dance Russe," 4:160, 161
  "ragtime" and, 4:599
  Rake's Progress, The, 5:225
  Rite of Spring, The, 5:178, 206
    "Dance of the Adolescent Girls,"
      4:177
    "Glorification of the Chosen One,"
      4:178, 182,
    "Ritual of Abduction," 4:173–75
    "Sacrificial Dance," 4:177
  Robert Craft and, 5:117–18, 126,
    128–29, 134
  "Russian" period and, 4:488
  serialism and, 5: 414
  "Slavic soul" and, 4:468
  "Some Ideas About My Octuor" (essay),
    4:488, 490, 491
  Studies in Counterpoint, use of, 5:122–23
  "verticals" technique, 5:125
  "zero pitch," 5:132–33
  works of
    Agon, 5:122
    Cantata, 5:118–22
    Canticum Sacrum, 5:122
    Concerto for Piano and Winds,
      4:491, 555
    Firebird, 4:152, 154–59, 160, 447, 555;
      5:127, 134
    Histoire du soldat, 4:486, 600
    In Memoriam Dylan Thomas, 5:122
    Les noces villageoises, 4:447, 448, 756,
      762
    "Maidens Came, The," 5:118
    Mavra, 4:675
    Movements for piano and orchestra,
      5:124, 129
    Nightingale, The, 4:204, 675

    Octet for Winds, 4:447, 448, 449, 451,
      456, 467, 468, 469, 478–93,
      526–27
    Oedipus Rex, 4:675–678
    Petrushka, 4:498, 561, 580
    Poetics of Music, 5:277
    Ragtime, 4:486
    Rag-time pour onze instruments, 4:600
    Rake's Progress, The, 5:117–18, 343
    Requiem Canticles, 5:128–35
    Rite of Spring, The, 1:349; 2:110; 4:203,
      204, 278, 297, 323, 447, 468, 469,
      486, 488, 556, 776; 5:59, 75, 93, 127,
      368
    Sérenade en la, 4:491–93, 585
    Soldier's Tale, The, 4:600, 603
    Sonate, 4:491, 492, 749
    Souvenir d'un marche boche, 4:502, 504
    Svadebka, 4:447, 448
    Symphonies d'instruments a vent, 4:469,
      470, 471
    Symphony of Psalms, 4:637
    Three Songs from William Shakespeare,
      5:122
    Threni, 5:122, 124
    "Tomorrow Shall Be My Dancing
      Day," 5:118, 119, 122
    Variations for orchestra, 5:124–25,
      127–28
Streetcar Named Desire, A (opera), 5:516
"Street in a Frontier Town" (Copland),
    4:662
street music, opera as, 3:212
"Streets of Laredo, The" (Thomson) 4:660
Streghe, Le (Paganini), 3:255
strepitosissimo, 3:52
stretto, 2:45, 48, 202; 3:49, 50, 52, 105
Strickland, Edward, 5:359
Striggio, Alessandro (father), 2:14
Striggio, Alessandro (son), 2:14, 18, 21
string music
    Italianate, 2:177–231, 234
    Purcell and, 2:196–98
string quartet
    Beethoven and, 2:653, 682–88, 694, 721,
      726
    Brahms and, 3:731–42
    Dvořák and, 3:754
    eighteenth-century nomenclature for,
      2:541
    Haydn and, 2:518–19, 526, 541, 578, 589,
      600, 721
    Mozart and, 2:589, 590, 631–33, 721
    public and private
    Schubert and, 2:137–39; 3:101–2,
      105–109–10
    See also listings under "Q" of specific
      quartets
String Quartet no. 1 (Carter), 5:415
String Quartet no. 2 (Ferneyhough), 5:476
String Quartet no. 2 (Rochberg), 5:415

String Quartet no. 3 (Rochberg), 5:414,
    429–30
String Quartet (Webern), 5:23
string trio. *See* trio
String Trio (Young), 5:356–59
Strobel, Heinrich, 5:217, 345
Strohm, Reinhard, 2:384
Strone, Varl, 2:504
strophe (stanza), 1:13, 366, 374, 827
    bergerette, 1:526
    as Nuova musiche song type, 1:813
    repetition and, 1:813
strophic aria, 2:33, 144
strophic form. *See* couplet
strophic office hymn, 1:47–49
Strozzi, Barbara, 2:75–78, 75, 80–82, 142
    Diporti di Euterpe, 2:75–78
    Lagrime mie, 2:75–78, 81
Strozzi, Bernardo, 2:75
Strozzi, Giulio, 2:75
Strozzi, Piero, 1:800
Strozzi, Ruberto, 1:620
structural imitation, 1:528–29, 535–36
Structures (Boulez), 5:27–36, 38, 39, 41, 47,
    49, 50, 64, 69, 140, 153, 165, 166
struggle-to-victory paradigm, 2:654–55,
    658–59, 694
    undesirable effects of, 2:670–71
Stuart dynasty, 1:675; 2:113–14
Stuckenschmidt, Hans Heinz, 4:686, 5:345
    "Henze Turns the Clock Back," 5:345
    Schoenberg's biographer, 5:345
    Technical University of Berlin, 5:345
Students for a Democratic Society, 5:310
Studien (Stockhausen), 2:189
Studies in Counterpoint, 5:122–23
Studio di Fonologia Musicale, 5:193
Studnikow, A., 3:752
Stuessy, Joe, 5:393
Sturm und Drang, 3:121
    Empfindsamkeit and, 2:416, 417, 529
    Haydn's "Farewell" Symphony and,
      2:528–29, 530
Stutterheim, Baron von, 2:682
Styka, Jan, 3:343
style brillant, 3:277
    Liszt and, 3:262, 264, 273
    Paganini and, 3:255
style brisé, 2:249–50, 251, 260, 265, 274
"style chef-d'oeuvre, le," 3:732
style dépouillé, 4:468, 545, 573
style galant, 2:263
style hongrois, 4:367–69, 371, 373, 374, 376
Style of Palestrina and the Dissonance, The
    (Jeppesen), 1:670
stylistic consciousness, 1:267, 270
stylistic evolution, meaning of, 1:245,
    247–48, 580
stylus gravus, 2:59
stylus luxurians. *See* luxuriant style
stylus oratorius, 2:66–67
subjectivity, 2:590–600

Beethoven's late quartets and, 2:684
of the beholder, 3:305, 315–16
bond between composer's and listener's,
2:475, 486, 590–91
eighteenth-century instrumental style
and, 2:588, 589, 599
Mozart's instrumental works and,
2:599–600, 606, 613
music trance and, 3:71
as Romantic ideal, 2:486, 590, 599, 600,
643, 648; 3:62, 66, 94, 152, 305,
315–16, 363
Sturm und Drang and, 2:416
of truth, 3:62, 71
See also introspection; introversive
semiotics
subject of fugue, 2:198, 201, 202
Germanic length of, 2:241–42
sublime,
awe and, 1:287
beauty differentiated from, 2:643–46,
649
Beethoven's works and, 2:648–51, 656,
692, 724, 732, 734
Brendel's view of, 3:413, 440
Chopin and, 3:365–67
context as determinant of, 3:22
Haydn's Creation and, 2:645–46
Mozart's works and, 2:643–45, 646, 648
Palestrina and, 3:414
Romanticism and, 2:643–46, 648–51,
732
Schubert and, 3:101, 138
Wagner and, 3:548
Subotnick, Morton, Silver Apples of the
Moon, 5:497
Subotnik, Rose Rosengard, 2:600; 3:354
subscription seasons, 3:173, 677
subscription symphony (genre), 2:556, 557,
558, 579, 588
as democratization of high art, 2:577
priorities of, 2:566, 576
See also concerts; symphony
subsemitonium modi, 1:274, 275, 276, 293,
298
subtilitas (subtlety), 1:327–49, 342
notation and, 1:339–42, 341
subtle art, 1:327–36
subtonium modi, 1:79, 274, 368, 469
successive composition, 1:301
Suez Canal, opening of, 3:565
Sufferings of the Queen of France, The, no. 9
(Dussek), 3:65, 67–68
Suicide in an Airplane (Ornstein), 4:299,
300–301
suite
Bach (J. S.) and, 2:260, 261–77,
286–89, 306
Froberger model of, 2:260–61, 262, 263
Handel and, 2:234, 306
internal/external distinctions and,
2:274–77

Schein and, 2:53
Suite in D major (Bach), 3:711, 714
Suite, op. 23 (Schoenberg), 5:356
Suite, op. 25 (Schoenberg), 5:138
Suite, op. 29 (Schoenberg), 5:122
Suleiman the Magnificent, Ottoman
Sultan, 2:525
Sullivan, Arthur
death of, 3:658
Ivanhoe, 3:658
oratorios of, 3:657
See also Gilbert (William S.) and
Sullivan (Arthur)
Sullivan, J. W. N., 2:671
Sulzer, Johann Georg, 3:73
Sulzer, Solomon, 3:174
Sumarokov, Alexander, 3:235
Sumer Canon, 1:387–92, 388, 394, 397,
399, 408, 419, 457, 565
Sumerian language, 1:31
Sumer is icumen in/Lhude sing cuccu!,
1:387–88, 1.388. See also Sumer
Canon
Summa artis rithimici vulgaris dictaminis
(Antonio), 1:723
Summer, Donna, Love to Love You Baby,
5:393
"Summer of Love," 5:309
sung verse play. See liturgical drama
Sun King. See Louis XIV, King of France
Sun of the Incas, The (Denisov), 5:463
Sun-treader (Ruggles), 4:297, 298
super librum singing, 1:438–39
supernatural, 3:73, 701
forest-horn music and, 3:158, 202
Gothic romance and, 3:47
Loewe's representation of, 3:158
magic play portrayals of, 3:188
phantasmagorias and, 3:203
siren songs and, 3:127
in Verdi's Macbeth, 3:576, 611
Suppé, Franz von, 3:647
Dichter und Bauer overture, 3:647
Leichte Kavallerie, 3:648
Schöne Galathee, Die, 3:648
Supplimenti musicali (Zarlino), 1:800
supply and demand, aristocratic patronage
and, 2:527–28, 553, 555
supra librum (improvised polyphony),
1:758
Supremum est mortalibus bonum (Du Fay),
1:282
"surge songs," 1:27
Sur incises (Ades), 5:474
surnaturalisme, 4:567
"Surprise" Symphony in G major, no. 94
(Haydn), 2:557–77, 557, 584
andante, 2:566–73, 577
"Big Bang" in, 2:562, 563, 566, 567–68,
576, 577
finale, 2:573–77
minuet, 2:573–77

slow introduction of, 2:557, 558–59
story behind sobriquet for, 2:568–69
surprises in, 2:566, 568–71, 573, 576, 577
as symbol for all of Haydn's music, 2:577
surrealism, 4:599
surréalisme, 4:567
"Surrealist Manifesto" (Breton) 4:590
Sursum corda (Liszt), 3:438
Sur toutes flours (ballade), ars subtilior
puzzle-notation, 1:345
Susanin, Ivan, 3:241–42
Susato, Tylman, 1:589, 593, 597, 598, 709,
712, 714
Suschitzky, Anya, 4:106
Susie Asado (Thomson), 4:590–91, 596
suspension
Frescobaldi and, 2:44
Schubert and, 3:94
Schumann and, 3:297–98
suspension chain, 2:188–92
Chopin and, 3:356, 359
Süssmayr, Franz Xaver, 2:485; 3:255
Suzuki, Daisetz, 5:62
Svadebka (Stravinsky), 4:447, 448; 5:212
Swafford, Jan, 4:273, 276
Swanee (Gershwin), 4:624
"Swanee River" (song), 1:18
Swan Lake (Chaikovsky), 3:108; 4:141,
142–43, 449
Sweden, 3:445–46, 447, 455
Thirty Years War and, 2:55–56
Swedenborg, Emanuel, 4:338, 338
Sweelinck, Jan Pieterszoon, 2:44–50, 53,
208
Fantasia chromatica, 2:44, 46
pupils of, 2:48, 241
Sweetness and Light, culture of, 3:773
Swieten, Gottfried van, Baron, 4:141,
142–43, 399, 499. 509, 633
Swift, L. E. (Elie Siegmeister pseud.),
4:651, 654
Swingle, Ward, 5:346
"Bach's Greatest Hits," 5:347
Swingle Singers, 5:346–47
"Swing Low, Sweet Chariot" (spiritual),
3:765
Swiss German reformed church, 1:755
"Sword" leitmotif (Wagner), 3:507, 520
Sy dolce non sonò con lir' Orfeo (Landini),
1:374–78, 380, 384
syllabic notation, 1:39, 41, 60
conductus and, 1:201
motet and, 1:210, 214–17
voces musicales and, 1:499
syllabic performance, 1:115
Kyrie, 1:58–59, 101
syllabic text
conductus and, 1:199–205, 209, 211
discant and, 1:209
Gloria and Credo and, 1:311
syllable,
declamation and, 1:566, 567

syllable (*continued*)
line length and, **1:**44, 175
meter classification and, **1:**175, 197
scale singing and, **1:**101
sequence melody and, **1:**41–43, 50, 57
Sylvia (Delibes), **4:**136, 138, 141
Sylvia (nymph), **2:**22–24
symbolism,
chace (canon) and, **1:**333–34
cognitive, **3:**528, 531, 540
cyclic Mass Ordinary and, **1:**461
declamation motet and, **1:**432, 433
extroversive, **3:**528, 756, 759
extroversive and introversive. *See* extroversive semiotics; introversive semiotics
Missa L'Homme Armé and, **1:**495
motet and, **1:**226, 229, 236, 255, 282, 284–85, 286, 429
musical iconic representation and, **1:**363
tragédie lyrique and, **2:**89–94, 95, 96
See also allegory; semiotics
symphonia. *See* symphony
Symphoniae jucundae (schoolbook), Luther preface to, **1:**755
Symphoniae sacrae (Gabrieli), **2:**59, 60–66, 497
Symphoniae sacrae (Schütz), **2:**59, 68–72, 497
symphonia of the diapente, **1:**150, 151
symphonic binary form. *See* sonata form
"symphonic jazz," **4:**614, 629, 637
symphonic maximalism, Mahler and, **4:**9
Symphonic Metamorphoses on Themes by Carl Maria von Weber (Hindemith), **3:**192, 193
symphonic poem
Balakirev and, **3:**477, 478
Dvořák and, **3:**755
Franck and, **3:**776
Liszt and, **3:**419–20, 422–27, 429–30, 627–28
poetic content in, **3:**419, 420, 425–26
Smetana and, **3:**446–47, 451–54, 457
"Symphonic poem in five movements" (Mahler), **4:**9
Symphonic Variations (Dvořák), **3:**755
symphonie concertante (sinfonia concertante), **3:**277
Symphonie fantastique (Berlioz), **3:**320–32, 335–40, 368; **4:**79, 191, 431, 751
autobiographical aspects of, **3:**320, 321, 322, 326
critiques of, **3:**333, 340–41, 482
"Dream of the Witches' Sabbath," **3:**203, 322, 335–39
idée fixe and, **3:**321, 324, 326–31, 336, 425, 502
Liszt's transcription of, **3:**324, 325–26, 340
"March to the Scaffold," **3:**322, 331
poetic content in, **3:**419

program for, **3:**321–22, 324, 335, 340–41, 425, 793
Ronde du sabbat, **3:**339
Schumann (Robert) on, **3:**340–41, 420–21
sequel to, **3:**387
symphonies concertantes, definition of, **2:**505
Symphonies d'instruments a vent (Stravinsky), **4:**469, 470, 471
symphony, **2:**497–588
Bach sons and, **2:**507–9
ballroom dance inclusions in, **2:**573
Beethoven and, **2:**653, 702, 705–20
concert development and, **2:**498–99
concerto in relationship with, **2:**606–7
cyclic Mass Ordinary compared with, **1:**496–97
definition of, **2:**498
as drama, **2:**599
eighteenth-century production and demand for, **2:**497–588
four movement form and sequence of, **2:**520
Germany and, **3:**376, 566
Haydn's development of, **1:**632; **2:**515–40, 542, 549, 717
Haydn's later developments in, **2:**556–88
Haydn's transformation of style and status of, **2:**577, 588, 601
as instrumental drama, **2:**515
international development of, **3:**745–801
Mannheim as spawning ground of, **2:**505–7
metaphorical description and, **2:**720
movements as connecting narrative of, **2:**533
Mozart and, **2:**589, 590, 590–600, 641
museum culture and, **3:**676–82
music appreciation and, **3:**782, 785, 786
nineteenth-century decline and revival of, **3:**675–743, 745
operatic precedents for, **2:**497, 498, 499, 507, 515, 589
overtures and, **2:**497, 498, 499, 500, 507, 515
public audience for, **2:**498
Romantics' elevated status of, **2:**599; **3:**681
seriatim performance of, **3:**173
sonata form development in, **2:**520–25, 549, 557
Stamitz and, **2:**718
subscription genre, **2:**556, 557, 558, 576, 579, 588
as symphonia, **1:**149–53, 154, 187
terms and genres associated with, **2:**497–98, 507
thematic structure of, **2:**520–25
women composers of, **3:**769–73
symphony concert. *See* concerts
Symphony for Three Orchestras (Carter), **5:**301

Andrew Porter's review of, **5:**301
Symphony Hall (Boston), **3:**679
Symphony in C Major (Bizet), **3:**657
Symphony in D minor (Franck), **3:**774–81, 784
thematic conspectus, **3:**777
Symphony no. 1 in C major (Beethoven), **2:**653
Symphony no. 1 in C minor, op. 68 (Brahms), **3:**685–86, 692–702, 716, 719–29, 730, 742
Symphony no. 1 in E-flat major (Borodin), **3:**788–89
cello theme, **3:**789
Symphony no. 4 (Schumann), **3:**688–90
Lebhaft theme, **3:**690
slow introduction, **3:**689
Symphony no. 4 in B-flat major (Beethoven), **3:**16
Symphony no. 4 in C minor ("Tragic") (Schubert), **3:**80, 85
Symphony no. 4 in E minor (Brahms), **3:**724, 729, 745
Symphony no. 4 in F minor (Chaikovsky), **3:**791–99
Symphony no. 8 in B minor ("Unfinished") (Schubert), **3:**81, 85, 108–17, 675, 697
Symphony no. 9 in C major ("Great") (Schubert), **3:**82, 85, 94–96, 94, 101, 108, 173, 697
Symphony no. 9 ("New World") in E minor, op. 95 (Dvořák), **3:**754, 755–66, 770, 772, 773, 774
Symphony no. 39 in E-flat major, K. 543 (Mozart), **3:**113, 742
Symphony no. 40 in G minor, K. 550 (Mozart), **3:**109, 798
Synaxis, **1:**25, 313
Synchronisms (Davidovsky), **5:**211, 212
syncopation, **1:**266, 269, 295, 305, 345
Du Fay's *Missa L'Homme Armé* and, **1:**497, 498
fifteenth-century counterpoint and, **1:**368
Machaut and, **1:**325, 326
Obrecht Caput Mass and, **1:**482
precadential, **1:**368
stile antico and, **1:**667
subtilior notation of, **1:**339
trecento madrigal and, **1:**363
syncretism,
Beethoven and, **3:**14–15
Chopin and, **3:**357
Synergy (Brown), **5:**95
synesthesia, **4:**84
Synge, J. M., **4:**613
Syntagma musicum (Praetorius), **2:**54
synthesis, **3:**424, 567, 746, 751
Hegelian dialectic and, **3:**412, 414

"syntonistic" music, 4:297

Syphans de Ferrara, 1:354

Syriac Christian Church, 1:33

Syzgy (Del Tredici), 5:438–42

Szymanowska, Maria Agata, 3:74

Szymanowski, Karol, 4:569–70

T

ta'amim (ecophonetic neumes), 1:16

tablature, 1:606, 626

Tabór (Smetana), 3:452

tabula compositoria, 1:578, 579

Tabulatura nova (Scheidt organ
    collection), 2:48–49, 48, 50

Tabulaturen (Meistersinger codes),
    1:139–40, 143

Tacitus, 2:26, 27

tactus. See beat

Tafelmusik, 2:53

tag. See refrain

Tagelied (daybreak song), 3:549

Tailleferre, Germaine
    Les Six group and, 4:588
    Quadrille, 4:589

"Tailors' Chorus" (Wagner)

"Take Me Out to the Ballgame" (song),
    1:18; 5:481
    original sheet music, 1:19

"Tale of Bygone Years," 4:171

talea, 1:232, 234, 265, 266, 269, 270, 311, 378
    English motet and, 1:424–25, 427
    French-Cypriot Gloria-Credo, 1:345
    Machaut DAVID melisma, 1:292
    Machaut dismissal response, 1:326

"Tale of Joan of Arc, The" (Christine de
    Pisane), 1:447

Tales from the Vienna Woods (J. Strauss),
    3:648

Tales of Hoffmann, The (Offenbach), 3:657

Tales of Olden Times (Perrault), 4:104

Talich, Václav, 4:444

"talkies," 4:628

Talking Heads, 5:328
    Philip Glass and, 5:391

Tallis, Thomas, 1:673–75, 673, 677
    music printing monopoly of, 1:678, 741
    O nata lux de lumine, 1:673–74, 678
    Spem in alium, 1:673

Talma, François-Joseph, 3:333

Talvela, Martti, 3:624

Tamara (Balakirev), 3:397

Tamberlik, Enrico, 3:579

Tan, Margaret Leng, 5:76

Tancred, 2:7–9

Tancredi (Rossini), 3:11, 20, 28–35, 41
    Paganini's variation set on, 3:258

Tan Dun
    Four Passions cycle and, 5:524
    Symphony 1997 (Heaven Earth Mankind),
        5:524

Taneyev, Sergey Ivanovich, 3:799; 4:141,
    555

Tanglewood (Massachusetts), 5:211

Tanner, Michael, 3:654

Tannhäuser (historical poet-singer), 1:137,
    138; 3:485, 486

Tannhäuser und der Sängerkrieg auf Wartburg
    (Wagner), 1:137, 138, 139, 141;
    3:483, 485, 487, 488, 696; 4:83, 133,
    186

Tansillo, Luigi, 1:818

Tant que vivray (Claudin), 1:706–7, 708,
    709, 711, 712

Tanzsuite (Hartmann), 4:770

tape recorder, advent of, 5:175–76, 187
    Ampex Company and, 5:176

Tapisserie en fer forgé (Satie), 4:570

Tapissier (Jean de Noyers), 1:422, 423–24
    Eya dulcis/Vale placens, 1:423–24,
        425–26, 429

"Taps," 4:668

Tarquin, legendary King of Rome, 1:719

Tasso, Torquato, 2:7–9, 94, 95; 3:164, 326,
    703

tastar de corde, 2:40

taste. See musical taste

Tate, Nahum, 2:132, 155

Tauber, V., 3:240

Tausig, Carl, 3:431, 447

Tavener, John, 5:408–10, 526
    Ikon of Light, 5:409
    ma fin est mon commencement, 5:409
    nomine Jesu, 5:408
    Russian Orthodox faith and, 5:408
    Whale, The, 5:408

Taverner, John, 1:612–14, 672, 673, 680,
    692
    Missa Gloria Tibi Trinitas, 1:612–13, 614,
        672; 2:115–16

"Taxman" (Harrison), 5:319

Taylor, Deems, 3:783; 4:626, 666
    Fanfare for Russia, 4:670

Taylor, Sedley, 2:327

Tchaikovsky. See Chaikovsky, Pyotr Ilich

Tcherepnin, Alexander, 4:784

Teatr-buff (St. Petersburg), 3:647

Teatro alla Scala (Milan). See La Scala

Teatro di San Bartolomeo (Naples), 2:140,
    146, 148
    interior of, 2:141

Teatro La Fenice, 5:117

Teatro San Bartolomeo (Venice), 2:174,
    438

Teatro San Cassiano (Venice), 2:12, 16, 26

Teatro San Moisè (Venice), 3:8

Teatro SS. Giovanni e Paolo (Venice),
    2:26

Tebaldo ed Isolina (Morlacchi), 3:308

Tecchinardi-Persiani, Fanny, 3:46

technical progress, 1:226–27, 245, 247–48,
    252

technique,
    academic music and, 1:608–11
    conservatory training in, 3:288

style vs., 1:248–8

subtilitas and, 1:327–42

virtuosity and, 1:330, 337

voice training and, 3:38–40

Technique de mon language musical
    (Messiaen), 4:229, 234–35, 237

Te Deum laudamus, 1:94

Teitsch, ?1191, 573

Te Joseph celebrent (Gregorian hymn),
    1:136

Telbarmonium, 5:177

Telegraphone, 5:175

Telemann, Georg Philipp, 2:240, 286, 342;
    4:132
    obbligato writing and, 2:300
    prolificity of, 2:260
    teleological history, 1:144, 381, 383,
        738–39; 2:396

Telemusik (Stockhausen), 5:420

Telephone, The (Menotti), 5:226

television set, 2:175

Tema con variazon (*Octet for Winds*), 4:479,
    481

tempered tuning, 1:730

Temperley, Nicholas, 1:27

Tempest, The (Shakespeare), 2:127

Tempesta del mar, La (Vivaldi), 2:230

Temple of the People, 4:297

temporale, 1:12

tempo rubato, 4:475
    Beethoven and, 3:132, 222
    Chopin and, 3:363–65
    Romantic performing style and, 3:132,
        363

"tempo simultaneity",
    Ives and, 5:415
    Rochberg and, 5:415

tempus, 1:197, 217, 251
    division of, 1:253
    four basic combinations of, 1:251
    notational coloration and, 1:266

tempus perfectum, 1:441

ten-based system. See decimal system

"tendency tones," 1:275–76
    J'ay pris amours settings, 1:540–41
    Mahler and, 4:28

ten-five open-spaced triad, 1:409

Tenney, James, Noise Study, 5: 5:496

Tennyson, Alfred Lord, 4:459
    Enoch Arden, 4:459

tenor,
    caccia, 1:364
    Caput Mass and, 1:466, 468, 473, 474,
        475, 477
    coloration and, 1:266
    conductus and, 1:198–99, 403
    discant and, 1:209, 276
    evolved meaning of, 1:468, 474
    ground bass and, 1:625–28
    "In seculum" and, 1:228
    Machaut composition and, 1:292,
        297–305, 307, 324–25, 326, 328, 328

tenor (continued)
  madrigal and, 1:374
  Mass cycle section unification based on, 1:461
  motet and, 1:212, 219, 228–33, 234, 238–39, 259, 262, 265–66, 267, 271, 282, 296, 378, 399
  motet fourth voice and, 1:270–73
  paraphrase motet and, 1:503
  See also tenor voice
tenore di forza (tenore robusto), 3:13, 578–79, 584, 600, 660
Tenorlied, 1:701–6, 717
  Lutheranism and, 1:756, 758, 760
tenor tacet pieces, 1:543, 544
tenor voice
  bel canto tessitura and, 3:578
  falsetto, 2:98
  French haute-contre, 2:98, 100, 459
  Italian "sobbing" and, 2:77
  in SATB voice-part range, 1:468
  soprano paired with, 3:578
Ten Plagues of Egypt, 2:315, 316, 321, 327
tenso (debate-song), 1:115–16
  jeu-parti equivalent, 1:121
  motet and, 1:226
Tenture de cabinet préfectoral (Satie), 4:570
tercet,
  madrigal, 1:352, 356, 359, 360–61, 363, 374, 377
  rhymed, 1:89
Teresa of Avila, Saint, 4:772
Termen, Lev Sergeyevich, 5:180–81, 180. See also Theremin, Leon
  "etherphone" and, 5:181
Termenvox, 5:181
termination (terminatio), 1:20
ternaria, 1:176, 177, 187, 197, 217
Terpsichore (Praetorius), 2:54
terzetti, 1:363
tessitura, 1:76; 3:578
Testimony, "The Memoirs of Dmitry Shostakovich as Related to and Edited by Solomon Volkov," 5:471
tetrachord (fourth), 1:70, 74, 75, 77–78, 79, 83
  augmented, 1:40, 152
  disjunct/conjunct, 1:78, 151
  as dissonance, 1:153
  equivalence, 1:495
  hexachord and, 1:99
  parallel doubling at, 1:152
  as "perfect" interval, 1:149
  See also diminished fourth; perfect fourth
text. See syllabic text; words-music relationship
texted Agnus Dei, 1:520
texted discant. See motet
texted Kyrie, 1:58, 59
texture
  ballata and, 1:368

Janequin's chansons and, 1:711–12
Machaut luxuriant style and, 1:318, 325
madrigal and, 1:356, 374
Missa Caput and, 1:466
musical space and, 1:577, 579
Notre Dame polyphonic integration and, 1:171–205
in Rossini's works, 3:109
Tenorlied and, 1:758
top-down cantilena and, 1:312–13
in Wagner's Ring cycle, 3:505–20
Thalberg, Sigismond, 2:677; 3:37
"Thanksgiving Hymn," Schnittke and, 5:467
That Mysterious Rag (Berlin), 4:563, 566
"thaw" decade, Soviet Bloc and, 5:216, 460
theater
  Beethoven's incidental music for, 3:1–2
  Caccini musical spectacles and, 1:812–13, 831, 832–34
  darkening of, 3:564
  design and mechanical innovations for, 3:206–7
  English and French tradition of, 2:87, 113
  English incidental music for, 2:113, 126, 127
  English Puritan closure of, 2:125
  English Restoration, 2:125–27, 132, 137
  English semi-opera and, 2:126–27, 128, 130–31
  five-act plays and, 3:323
  French court and, 2:96–97, 106
  gendered casting and, 2:153
  intermedii and, 1:803–12, 823, 826
  Italian music for, 3:109
  monodists and, 1:822–34
  sacred play and, 1:832–34
  seventeenth-century prominence of, 1:798
  stage illusions and, 3:564, 565
  See also acting; drama; opera; tragedy
Theater an der Wien, 3:647
Theater auf der Wieden, 2:479
Théâtre de la Monnaie (Brussels), 3:213
Théâtre des Champs-Elysées (Paris), 4:602, 612; 5:206
Théâtre du Chatelet (Paris), 4:561
  El Nino and, 5:523
Théâtre-Italien (Paris), 3:11
Théâtre Lyrique (Paris), 3:639
Théâtre of Eternal Music, 5:359, 360, 361, 362
Théâtre National de l'Opéra Comique, 3:641
Théâtre Royale de la Monnaie (Brussels), The Death of Klinghoffer and, 5:522
"Their land brought forth frogs" (Handel), 2:317, 318
Thema (Berio), 5:193
thematic development, 3:369
  Beethoven's Ninth Symphony and and, 2:680–81

Beethoven's struggle-to-victory paradigm and, 2:654–55, 658–59, 662, 694
in Berlioz's Symphonie fantastique, 3:327, 328
in Mozartean concerto and, 2:606, 609–10, 613
Rossini's lack of, 3:21–22
symphonic, 2:520–25, 557, 572–73, 578–79, 583
traits of, 2:572
variations and, 2:571–72
See also double return; signification
thematic transformation
  Liszt and, 3:284–85, 336, 420, 425, 433–35, 777
  Saint-Saëns and, 3:784, 785
thematische Arbeit ("thematic process"), 2:520, 572, 583, 584; 3:732
Thematischer Leitfaden durch die Musik zu Richard Wagners Festspiel 'Der Ring des Nibelungen' (Wolzogen), 3:502, 503
theme and variations, 2:571–72, 602
Theocritus, 1:356
Theodal, 1:100
theorbo (hurdy-gurdy), 1:805
theory,
  Aaron as first "Renaissance" writer of, 1:576–77
  ancient Greek, 1:29–35, 32–33, 32, 799
  ars perfecta and, 1:586–89
  Frankish organization of, 1:117, 72–104
  Glareanus and, 1:553–54, 581, 587, 592
  Guido's Micrologus, 1:154
  mathematics and, 1:248–50, 248–55, 252–53, 410, 495, 587–88
  Mei treatises on, 1:799
theosophy
  Scriabin and, 4:201, 203, 205–8
  Temple of the People colony and, 4:297
Theremin, Leon, 5:180, 181. See also Termen, Lev Sergeyevichtheremin, 5: 181, 183
"Thereminists," 5:181
Theresa, Saint, 2:44; 4:594
Thespis; or, the Gods Grown Old (Gilbert and Sullivan), 3:651
"They loathed to drink of the river" (Handel), 2:317–18, 364
Thibaut IV, Count of Champagne and King of Navarre, 1:118, 120
  De bone amour vient seance et bonté, 1:118–19
Third Communist International Organization, 4:651
Third Crusade, 1:117, 345
third mode. See dactylic meter
Third Partition, 3:344
Third Piano Sonata (Boulez), 5: 65
Third Quartet (Carter), 5:300–301
Third Reich. See Nazi Germany

Third Stream, 5: 336–40, 368

Third Symphony (Copland), 5:3–5, 105

Third Symphony (Harris), 5:3

thirds
British preference for, 1:394, 395, 397
as consonances, 1:153, 394, 397
harmonic succession by, 1:475
triads and, 1:587

Third Symphony, no. 3, op. 55
(Beethoven). See Eroica Symphony

Third Symphony in C minor ("Organ
Symphony"; Saint-Saëns),
3:783–85, 799
thematic resume, 3:785

Third Symphony in D minor (Bruckner),
3:747, 776

thirteenth century
British monastic music manuscript and,
1:387
British musical nationalism and,
1:405–6, 409
mensural notation and, 1:248
motet and, 1:207–45, 258–67
Paris as intellectual capital in,
1:169–205, 399
polyphonic genres, 1:296
troubadours and trouvères, 1:107–26,
139, 142, 144, 351
urbanization, 1:120
Worcester fragments, 1:403

Thirty-ninth Sympony in E-flat major, K.
543 (Mozart), 2:590, 591–99
slow movement, 2:591–99

32-bar chorus, 3:572

Thirty Years War, 2:15, 55–56
musical effects of, 2:58–59, 66, 67
political effects of, 2:56, 68

Thomas, Ambroise, 4:63, 452, 496, 691
morceaux de concert and, 4:453
orientalism and, 3:390
works of
Caïd, Le, 3:390
Hamlet, 3:640
Mignon, 3:640; 4:452, 454

Thomas, Duke of Clarence, 1:409

Thomas à Becket (Saint Thomas of
Canterbury), 1:172, 408, 408

Thomas Aquinas, Saint, 1:48, 89–70;
4:230

Thomas de la Hale, 1:408

Thomas gemma Cantuariae / Thomas caesus in
Doveria (motet), 1:408–9, 411–12

Thomas, Michael Tilson, 5:378–79
Boston Symphony and, 5:378–79

Thomson, James, 2:633

Thomson, Virgil, 3:290; 4:553, 588,
591–93, 599, 614, 615, 636, 647, 648,
666; 5:227; 5:3, 268, 289
John Cage and, 5:70
review of Carter's First String Quartet,
5:292
works of

Capital Capitals, 4:592, 593, 594–95
Four Saints in Three Acts, 4:589, 595,
595 596–97, 598, 660; 5:394
"Git Along Little Dogies," 4:660, 662
"Houlihan" (a.k.a. "I Ride an Old
Paint"), 4:660
Mother of Us All, The, 5:225–26
"Streets of Laredo, The," 4:660
Susie Asado, 4:590–91, 596
Symphony on a Hymn Tune,
4:659–60

Thoreau, Henry David, 4:244, 267, 270;
5:74
Walden; or Life in the Woods, 4:244

Thoscanello de la musica (Aaron), 1:576–77

Thought on the Imitation of Greek Works
(Winckelmann), 2:453

"Three B's, the," 3:729

Three Choirs Festival (England), 4:246

Three Compositions for Piano (Babbitt),
5:137–39, 141, 153
Perle's analysis of, 5:137

Three Little Pieces for Cello and Piano, op. 11
(Webern), 5:356

three-note ligature. See ternaria

three-part polyphony, 1:165–67, 168, 171,
187
cantilena-style, 1:298–99, 311
Clemens's psalm settings in, 1:597–99
conductus and, 1:198
English technique and, 1:419, 434, 435
Landini ballata and, 1:368
West-country style and, 1:403

Threepenny opera, The, 4:649. See also Die
Dreigroschenoper

Three Pieces for Two Pianos (Ligeti), 5:438

Three Places in New England (Ives), 4:262,
265, 273; 5:268, 272

Three Quarter-Tone Pieces (Ives), 4:286,
288–89, 290, 291

Three Satires, op. 28 (Schoenberg), 4:678

Three Songs from William Shakespeare
(Stravinsky), 5:122

Three Telephone Events (Brecht), 5:91

three-tempora length, 1:180, 249

"Three Tenors," 3:579

"Three Who Made a Revolution" (Wolfe),
2:397

Threni (Stravinsky), 5: 122, 124

Threnody (Penderecki), 5:363

"Threnody for the Victims of Hiroshima"
(Penderecki), 5: 217–20

throat-music. See gorgia

through-composed settings, 3:146, 152
Dargomïzhsky's Stone Guest and, 3:612,
615

through-composed song, 1:813

Thurber, Jeannette M., 3:755, 760, 764, 768

Thurmond, Strom, 5:309

Tides of Manaunaun, The (Cowell), 4:298,
302

tierce de picardie. See Picardy third

Tikvatenu (Imber), 3:456

Tilbury, John, 5:86

Timaeus (Plato), 1:70

timbre, 3:187, 203

time
audience's experience of, 3:69
Augenblick and, 3:91–92, 110
opic chronotope, 3:513
suspension of, 3:91, 94
in Wagner's works, 3:510, 513

timelessness, musical evocation of, 3:158

time-measurement. See meter

time signatures, 1:252–53
Ars Nova notation of, 1:260–61
four standard, 1:253
Frescobaldi changes in, 2:42
Ockeghem Mass and, 1:477–78
Philippus supplementations to, 1:338,
341

timpani glissando technique, 4:394

Tin Pan Alley, 4:563, 623–24, 625, 629,
632, 633
"jazz" and, 4:625
Max Dreyfus and, 4:624
T.B. Harms & Co. and, 4:624

Tinctoris, Johannes, 1:384, 423, 424, 429,
453–54, 454, 551, 577, 585, 620
background and career of, 1:453
De inventione et usu musicae, 1:453–54,
536
on English style, 1:514, 517
musical honor roll of, 1:454–59, 465,
472, 484, 501
musical style rankings by, 1:459–60,
486, 501, 526

tinta, Verdi and, 3:568–71, 573, 581, 592,
604

Tintoretto (Jacobo Rubusti), 1:741

Tippett, Michael, 5:224, 232

ti (scale-singing syllable), 1:101

Tischbein, Johann Heinrich, 2:659

"Tis the Gift to Be Simple" (Shaker hymn),
4:666

Titan (Paul), 4:9

Titian (Tiziano Vecellio), 1:741

"To Anacreon in Heaven" (drinking song),
3:120

"To Anacreon in Heaven" (Smith), 1:409

"To a Wild Rose" (MacDowell), 3:768

To Catch a Thief (Hitchcock), 5:198

toccata, 2:37, 40–44
Bach (J. S.) and, 2:208–16, 247, 300
Frescobaldi and, 2:37, 40–44
fugue paired with, 2:247
Merulo and, 2:41
term's earliest recorded use, 2:40
term's variety of uses, 2:41–42

toccata di durezze e ligature (toccata
chromatica), 2:44

Toccata in F major, BWV 540 (J. S. Bach),
2:208–16, 247, 295

Toccata nona (Toccata IX) (Frescobaldi), 2:41–42

Toccata settima (Toccata VII) (Rossi), 2:42–43

toccate di durezze e ligature, 2:43

Toccate d'intavolatura di cembalo et organo, partite di diverse arie, e correnti, balletti, ciaccone, passacagli (Frescobaldi), 2:37

Toch, Ernst, 5:181, 182

"Today" show, Dave Garroway and, 5:198

todesca, 1:716

Todtenfeier (Mahler), 4:9, 10, 14, 15, 17, 18–19, 20, 21, 22, 26, 374
  maximalism and, 4:10–11
  "second theme" and, 4:17, 18–20

"To Josquin, his Companion, Ascanio's musician" (Serafino), 1:552

Toledo, 1:64, 130

Toledo Cathedral, 1:64, 183

Tolstoy, Leo, 4:476, 779; 5:380
  War and Peace, 5:461
  What Is Art?, 4:779

Tomášek, Václav Jan, 2:653; 3:67–71
  dithyrambs and, 3:67, 69, 70, 71
  eclogues and, 3:67–69, 71, 92
  Schubert and, 3:87, 88
  works of
    Dithyramb, op. 65, no. 2, 3:69, 70
    Eclogue, op. 35, 3:68–69

tombeau, 2:265

Tombeau de M. Blancheroche (Froberger), 3:65–66

Tomkins, Calvin, 5:92

Tomkins, Thomas, 1:746; 2:128
  "Sad Pavan for These Distracted Times, A," 2:122–24

Tomlinson, Gary, 1:272, 615

Tommasini, Anthony, 5:514

Tommy (The Who), 5:327–28

"Tomorrow Never Knows" (Beatles), 5:319–20

"Tomorrow Shall Be My Dancing Day" (Stravinsky), 5:118, 119, 122

tonality, 1:40–44, 471; 2:181–203; 3:529–30, 540, 542; 4:311, 4:312
  atonality and, 1:472
  Bach's (J. S.) uses of, 2:208–16, 234, 242, 247, 249, 251, 253–54, 267, 271, 357, 361, 368, 381
  ballade and, 1:305
  basis of progressions and, 2:189
  Beethoven and, 3:5–7
  binary dance and, 2:261
  change from modal concept to, 1:471–72, 505, 628, 666
  circles of fifths and, 2:185–89, 202, 212, 213, 216, 220
  deviant behavior metaphor and, 2:620
  eight-tone system and, 1:22, 74, 76
  emergence of, 2:187–88, 195, 234
  English descant and, 1:423, 424

English style of, 1:425, 447, 448
  Frankish innovations and, 1:28–29, 48, 72–104
  Frescobaldi and, 2:39
  Gregorian chant range and, 1:99
  ground bass and, 1:627
  harmonic dissolution and, 3:362
  harmonic minor and, 1:277
  harmonic rhythm and, 1:628
  Haydn's *Creation* and, 2:634–35
  hierarchies and, 1:471
  Italian frottole and, 1:666
  Liszt and, 3:543–47
  major-minor, 1:99, 101
  modulation and, 1:471
  musical logic and, 2:195
  Musorgsky and, 3:544–45
  Palestrina and, 1:666–67, 669
  scale degrees as basis of, 1:73
  Schubert and, 3:96, 152, 522
  semitone and. *See* semitone
  sequence-and-cadence model of, 2:192–98, 212
  tonic and, 1:76, 77
  Wagner and, 3:543–48
  See also signification

Tonality and Atonality in Sixteenth-Century Music (Lowinsky), 2:397

"tonal music," 4:312, 313

"tonal navigation," 4:5

"tonal revolution," 1:628

tonal vs. atonal, 4:312, 313, 315, 316–21

tonaries, 1:72–76, 78–180, 83

Tondichtung ("tone poem"), 4:31

tone, 1:137
  diatonic pitch set and, 1:29, 42
  equivalence, 1:495
  in Greek nomenclature, 1:74–75
  psalm, 1:20, 21–22, 28, 29, 83
  semantic connotations by, 1:724

Töne (song formulas), 1:139–40

"tone clusters," 4:298

tone painting, 1:56–57

tone poem, 1:599

Tonreige, 4:688

Tone Roads, 5:93, 94

"tone row," 4:688. *See also* dominant-tonic relationship

"Tonwille, der" (the "tone's will"), 3:548

Toop, Richard, 5:52
  "The New Complexity" and, 5:475–76

top-down composition, 1:296–98, 311, 312–13, 435
  caccia and, 1:364

Torah, 1:16

Toreinx, F. R.de (Eugène Ronteix), 2:646

Torelli, Giuseppe, 2:193

Torgau, 2:15

Torkem Michael, neotonality and, 5:454

Torrefranca, Fausto, 2:400

Tortoise, His Dreams and Journeys, The (Young), 5:361

Torvaldo e Dorliska (Rossini), 3:9

Tosca (Puccini), 3:664, 667

Toscanini, Arturo, 3:572, 665; 4:476, 751–53, 756; 5:18, 73
  La Scala and, 4:751, 752
  Municipal Orchestra of Turin and, 4:751, 752
  New York Philharmonic Orchestra and, 4:752

Tosi, Pier Francesco, 2:165, 166, 171–72

Tosto che l'alba (Gherardello), 1:365, 371

totalitarianism, 3:514; 4:476. *See also* absolutism

total serialism, 5:36, 37, 38, 39, 41, 42, 48, 78

Totem Ancestor (Cage), 5:59

Totentanz (Liszt), 3:339

Tote Stadt, Die (Korngold), 4:550

Toulouse Mass, 1:315, 316

tour-de-force genres
  academic style and, 1:608
  ars subtilior and, 1:338–49, 341
  canon and, 1:331
  compositional, 1:536, 538–39
  Josquin Agnus Dei II and, 1:529
  motet and, 1:226–27, 232
  Ockeghem Masses and, 1:477, 480, 481

tourist nationalism, 3:347, 753

Tournai, 1:590
  Mass Ordinary, 1:316, 317, 321, 590

Tours, 1:455

Tovey, Donald Francis, 2:592, 622, 633–34; 3:691

"Toward a Theory That Is the Twelve-Note-Class System," 5:160

Tower, Joan, neotonality and, 5:454, 455

tower music (Turmmusik), 2:287

Tower of Babel, The (Rubinstein), 3:392

town pipers (Stadtpfeiferei), 2:287

Townshend, Pete, 5:327, 332

town song. *See* villanella

Tract, 1:28

Tractatus de diversis figuris (Philippus)

tractus, 1:180

"Tradition and Innovation in Recent European Music" (Copland), 5:116

Traetta, Tommaso, 3:235

Tragedia, La, 1:832

tragedia giapponese, 3:667

tragédie en musique. See tragédie lyrique

tragédie lyrique, 2:88–110; 3:208
  allegory and, 2:89–94, 95, 96
  ballet and, 4:131
  Campra Idoménée as, 2:90, 465, 465–70
  contemporary dress in, 2:96
  conventions of, 2:91–97, 100, 106–7
  dramatic realism vs. vocal display in, 2:96–97, 98, 99, 113, 437
  egalitarianism vs., 2:111
  English semi-opera as adaptation of, 2:127

Gluck and conventions of, **2:**454, 455, 459–60

Lully and, **2:**89–106, 454, 460

political content of, **2:**91–94, 96, 97

Rameau and, **2:**91

Rousseau and, **2:**442

themes of, **2:**90, 96, 97

War of the Buffoons and, **2:**442, 443

tragedy,

Aristotelian principles of, **2:**151, 435, 706

C-minor mode and, **2:**121, 696, 697, 701, 702, 721, 730

French declamatory style and, **2:**99, 106

French theatrical tradition and, **2:**87, 106

Italian neoclassic opera librettos, **2:**151–52

as voyeurism, **3:**670–71, 673

Wagner and, **3:**611

See also Greek drama; opera seria

tragicomedy, Verdi operas and, **3:**575–83

tragic opera

conventions, **3:**216

dramatic and musical value reconciliation, **3:**35

Rossini and, **3:**20

"Tragic Overture" (Brahms), **3:**752

"Tragic" Symphony (Symphony no. 4 in C minor) (Schubert), **3:**80, 85

Train bleu, Le (Milhaud), **4:**569

Traité de haute composition musicale (Reicha), **3:**287

Traité de l'harmonie (Koechlin), **4:**195–96

Traité de l'harmonie (Rameau), **2:**192

trance. *See* music trance

transcendence, **2:**65; **3:**272

Beethoven and, **2:**655, 656, 706, 714

musical expression and, **2:**720

Neoplatonism and, **1:**69, 70, 71

Schopenhauer and, **2:**721

Transcendentalism, **4:**243

transcendental maximalism, **4:**295

Transcendental meditation, Maharishi Mahesh Yogi and, **5:**408

"Transcendental Variations" (Rochberg), **5:**431

Beethoven and, **5:**431

Concord Quartet and, **5:**431

Transformation (Schuller), **5:**337, 338–40

transition, Wagner's use of, **3:**512–13, 517, 542, 547

transposition, **1:**76, 149, 434, 436, 475, 482, 560, 628

of finals, **1:**554

Trapassi, Pietro Antonio. *See* Metastasio

Trattado de glosas (Ortiz), **1:**620–21

Trattnerhof Theater (Vienna), **2:**608

Trauerspiel, connotation of, **2:**702

Träume (Wagner), **3:**549

Träumerie, See Reverie (Strauss)

trautonium, **5:**183–84

Trautwein, Friedrich, trautonium and, **5:**183–84

Travesties (Stoppard), **5:**162

travesty role. *See* trousers role

Traviata, La (Verdi), **3:**565, 568, 580–83, 580, 641, 660, 666

"Addio del passato," **3:**582

"Ah, quell'amor," **3:**581

"Parigi, o cara," **3:**582

"Sempre libera," **3:**581

Treasury of American Song (Siegmeister), **4:**659

Treatise of Good Taste in the Art of Musick (Geminiani), **2:**392

Treatises on the Art of Poetry (La Harpe), **3:**33

"Treaty" leitmotif (Wagner), **3:**506, 515, 516

Trebor (Jehan Robert), **1:**342

trecento, **1:**351–85, 697

ballata and, **1:**366–74

basic musical treatise of, **1:**354

characteristic melodic feature of, **1:**363, 371

Decameron as prose classic of, **1:**365–66

discant style and, **1:**356–59

historiographic views of, **1:**383–84

madrigal and, **1:**352–64

proto-Renaissance indicators and, **1:**382, 383, 384

Zarlino and, **1:**586–89, 597, 601, 603, 604–5, 699, 736, 800

Tregian, Francis, **2:**45

Treib, Marc, **5:**208

Treitler, Leo, **1:**158–59, 161; **2:**594; **4:**415, 418

tremblement. *See* short trill

tremolando, **4:**16, 351

tremolo

in Berlioz's Symphonie fantastique, **3:**329, 330–31

as timelessness evocation, **3:**158

Weber's use of, **3:**202, 203

Tren ofiarom Hiroszimy (Penderecki), **5:**217

Tres bonne et belle (Machaut), **1:**301–1

Tres dous compains, levez vous (canon), **1:**332

Trés riches heures du duc de Berry, **1:**342, 343

Treviso, **1:**611

Treybenreif, Peter (Petrus Tritonius), **1:**691

triad, **1:**168, 470, 627, 687, 776

English chains of, **1:**433, 447

in "first inversion," **1:**813

Hegelian dialectic and, **3:**412

monodic harmony and, **1:**813–14, 819

sixteenth-century theory and, **1:**587–88, 597

Willaert and, **1:**603

Trial by Jury (Gilbert and Sullivan), **3:**651–52

tribrachic meter, **1:**198

Tribum/Quoniam/MERITO (Vitry), **1:**256–58, 258, 259, 261, 337

tricinium, **1:**550, 769

trill (trillo), **1:**816, 817

short, **2:**277

signification of, **2:**279

Trinitarian symbolism, **1:**333, 334

Trinity of Essays, A (Kassler), **5:**160

Trinity Sunday, **1:**461; **2:**116

trio

as chamber piece, **2:**695

style of Haydn's and Mozart's vs. Beethoven's, **2:**695–96

in symphonic minuet movement, **2:**506, 516

See also piano trio

Trio for Violin, Horn, and Piano (Ligeti), **5:**438

Trio, op. 1, no. 3 (Beethoven), **3:**14, 108–9, 112

trio sonata, **2:**402, 432

Corelli and, **2:**177, 178–81, 178, 192, 196, 198

Handel and, **2:**305

Purcell and, **2:**198–99

Reincken and, **2:**241

tripla, **2:**53

triplet, **1:**359; **2:**42, 291, 346

triplum. *See* organum triplum

Tristan-chord, **3:**543; **4:**2, 71, 90, 155, 164, 209, 210

Mozart *Fantasia* theme and, **3:**542

Verdi's use of compared with Wagner's, **3:**604–5

Wagner and, **3:**540–42, 543, 546, 552, 557

Tristanisms, *Le poème de l'extase* (Scriabin) and, **4:**213

"Tristan ninth," **4:**221

Tristan und Isolde (Wagner), **3:**485, 498, 539–58, 611, 628, 729, 732;), **4:**3, 33, 37, 61, 66, 88, 89, 90, 161, 206, 209, 211, 213, 240, 305, 312, 390, 528, 599, 619

Act II Love Duet, **3:**550–55, 558

Brahms's First Symphony and, **3:**695–96, 698

Franck and, **3:**778

Isolde's Verklärung, **3:**555–57

Prelude, **3:**540–44, 546–52, 695–96

Prelude Lisztian variant, **3:**543, 544, 546

quotation, **4:**711, 712

Schumann (Clara) on, **3:**557–58

Verdi and, **3:**563, 566, 602–4

See also Tristan-chord, "Tristan ninth"

Tristitia et anxietas (Byrd), **1:**679

tritone link, Scriabin and, **4:**200, 204, 207

tritones, **1:**149–50; **4:**167, 690

Scriabin and, **4:**206–7

Trittico botticelliano (Respighi), **4:**750

Triumphes of Oriana, The (Morley), **1:**746

Triumphlied (Brahms), **3::**708–14

trivium, **1:**4, 37

trobairitz (female troubadours), **1:**110

trobar clus vs. trobar clar debate, **1:**115–16

trobar clus vs. trobar clar debate (continued)
  Ars Nova and, 1:326
  creative virtuosity and, 1:330, 342, 352
  French motet and, 1:226–28
  trouvères and, 1:120, 228, 352
  See also high art
trochaic meter, 1:47, 176–77, 179, 187, 191, 192, 197, 198, 200, 201
  British conductus and, 1:403
  French motet and, 1:221, 232
  in Longfellow's Hiawatha, 3:763–64
  notation of, 1:214, 260, 261
  ottonario and, 1:696
Trois gymnopédies (Satie), 4:7–69
Trois sarabandes (Satie), 4:63, 65–67, 70
Trojan War, 2:90, 132; 4:48
Trombetti, Ascanio, 1:780
Tromboncino, Bartolomeo, 1:696, 699
trombone, 1:424, 783; 2:314
Trondheim, 1:393
troparion, 1:33
tropers, 1:51, 93
  polyphonic collection, 1:155
tropes, 1:7, 50–53, 55
  Balaam motet and, 1:401
  church plays and, 1:52, 93
  cyclic Mass Ordinary organization and, 1:461
  to Easter Introit, 1:51–52
  English votive antiphons and, 1:517, 518
  expectations of, 1:64–65
  Gloria, 1:80
  regular features of, 1:81
troubadours, 1:107–16, 120, 139, 142, 144, 352; 2:6; 3:126
  courtly love and, 1:98–99, 108–9, 128, 351, 367
  duration of art of, 1:116, 142
  genres of, 1:107, 110–15, 121, 224, 290, 349, 397, 501
  high (Latinate) style of, 1:110–13, 114, 131
  influence of, 1:128–42, 351
  instrumentalists and, 1:131
  last of, 1:116
  Latinate style of, 1:110–13, 298
  as Machaut antecedents, 1:290
  madrigalists compared with, 1:352–54
  metrical rhythmic performance and, 1:114–15
  minstrel performers and, 1:109–10
  in northern Italian courts, 1:116, 133–34, 351
  pastorelas of, 2:446
  secular repertory of, 1:107
  sestina and, 1:352
  as trecento influence, 1:351, 352, 383
  trobar clus and, 1:115–16, 120, 228, 236, 326
  trouvère successors, 1:116–26, 208
  as vernacular poets, 1:107, 351, 459
  women as, 1:110; 2:79
  writen documentation of, 1:109–10, 353

trousers role, 3:30, 36
  in Fledermaus, Die, 3:648
  in Huguenots, Les, 3:220
  Nozze di Figaro and, 2:478
  soprano pairing with, 3:578
  in Tancredi, 3:28
trouvères, 1:116–26, 142
  Eleanor of Aquitaine descendants and, 1:117, 118
  Grocheio's social theory and, 1:208
  influence of, 1:128, 134–35, 139, 142
  as Machaut antecedents, 1:270–73, 290
  motet and, 1:218–19, 218, 220, 221, 224–26, 233, 236, 238
  popularization and, 1:120–26, 136, 142, 219, 290–91
  troubadour vs., 1:119–26
Trovador, Il (García Gutiérrez), 3:577
Trovatore, Il (Verdi), 2:110; 3:568, 577–80, 591, 660, 666; 4:6
  anvil chorus, 3:653
  Di quella pira, 3:579–80, 581, 654
  Gilbert and Sullivan parody of, 3:652, 653
Truax, Barry, 5:476
"true style" (Gluck partisans), 2:453, 457–58
Truman, Harry, 5:309
trumpet, 1:485, 792; 2:287
Trumpet (clarino) Concerto in E-flat major (Haydn), 2:611
Truppe 31, Die, 5:13–14
"Trust" (Tye), 2:116, 117
truth,
  absolute, 1:629
  art as, 3:59
  artistic, 3:64, 77, 229–30, 397
  beauty's relationship with, 2:363; 3:62, 440
  comedy and, 2:437
  different concepts of, 3:61
  Enlightenment and, 3:61, 122
  metaphysical, 3:440
  Musorgsky's commitment to, 3:618
  New German School views on, 3:438–41
  primitivism and, 3:123
  realism and, 3:612, 629, 632
  Romanticism and, 3:61–62, 66, 69, 71
  verisimilitude and, 3:229–30, 397
Tschudi, Aegidius, 1:555
Tsefal i Prokris (Araja), 3:235
T-S-T tetrachord, 1:78
Tuba sacre/In Arboris/VIRGO SUM (Vitry), 1:261–65, 262, 311, 337
Tuba Sonata (Hindemith), 5:104
tubas, Wagner and, 3:512, 748
"Tu che accendi" (Rossini), 3:30–31
Tucker, Richard, 3:579
Tudor dynasty, 1:513, 517–18, 614
Tui sunt coeli (Palestrina), 1:663–66
"Tu l'as dit!" (Meyerbeer), 3:225–27

Tudor, David, 5:65
  John Cage and, 5:65
Tune In, America: A Study of Our Coming Musical Independencce (Mason) (book), 4:622
tuning system, 1:5, 730, 732; 2:247–48
Tuotilo (monk), 1:51, 71
Turandot (Puccini), 3:192, 673–74, 673
Turandot, Prinzessin von China (Gozzi), 3:192, 193
  Weber's incidental music to, 3:192, 193, 386
Turco in Italia, Il (Rossini), 3:21
Turiddu's arioso (Mascagni), 3:660–61
Turkey. See Ottoman (Turkey) Empire
Turk in Italy, The (Rossini), 3:21
"Turkish March" (Beethoven), 3:11
Turkish mode, 2:470–71, 602, 675, 678, 679; 3:192
  Mozart and, 2:470–76, 602; 3:193, 386
  operas and, 3:386
"Turkish Rondo" (Mozart), 2:471
"Turkish" Violin Concerto in A major, no. 5, K. 219 (Mozart), 2:602–7
Turmmusik (tower music), 2:287
Turn of the Screw, The (James), 5:225
Turn of the Screw, The, op. 54 (Britten), 5:225, 226, 250
Tuscan dialect, 1:723, 799
Tuscany, 1:367, 803–5
"Tu se' morta" (Orfeo's recitative), 2:25
"Tu solus altissimus" (Busnoy Gloria), 1:490–92
tutti
  Divine words represented in, 2:69
  multiple choir, 1: 1:785
Tutto il mal non vien per nuocere (A. Scarlatti), 2:148
twelfth century
  polyphony and, 1:149–68, 296
  university origins in, 1:148, 169–72
Twelfth Night (Shakespeare), 2:113
Twelfth Quartet (Shostakovich), 5:104, 105
"Twelfth Street Rag" (Bowman), 4:605
twelve-based system. See duodecimal system
twelve-mode theory, 1:553–54
twelve pitch-classes, 4:681
twelve-note series, Schoenberg and, 4:687
"Twelve-Stringed Lyre, The" (Glareanus), 1:553
twelve-tone chord, 4:192, 196, 225
  Scriabin and, 4:225, 226
twelve-tone music, Eimert and, 5:189
twelve-tone principle, 5:63
"Twelve-tone Rhythmic Structure and the Electronic Medium" (Babbitt), 5:167, 172
twelve tone row, 4:196
"twelve-tone technique," 4:688; 5:415. See also Zwölftontechnik
Twelve-Tone Tonality (Perle), 5:456

twentieth century
  atonal music and, **1:**472
  audience etiquette instructions in, **2:**651
  commercialization of music and, **1:**65
  critics of Beethoven in, **2:**692
  early music revival and, **2:**233
  standard repertory in, **2:**234
  trecento repertory rediscovery in, **1:**383
Twentieth-Century Music (Morgan), **5:**455
twenty-first century, standard repertory
  and, **2:**234
"Twenty-Five Years of Russian Art"
  (Stasov), **3:**393
24 Caprices (Paganini), **3:**252
24 Präludien, op. 67 (Hummel), **3:**351
twinned voices, **1:**408–9, 410
Twinning, Thomas, **2:**392
twinsong, **1:**392, 394–96, 408, 517
Two Pages for Steve Reich (Glass), **5:**391
two-part polyphony, **1:**156, 157, 159–60,
  171, 177–78, 296
  canon and, **1:**330–36
  conductus and, **1:**198
  Machaut and, **1:**296, 297
  madrigal and, **1:**356, 746
  Northumbrian style and, **1:**392–93
  Notre Dame school organum duplum
    and, **1:**171, 177–78, 184, 186
  three-part derivation from, **1:**435
  See also discant
two-tempora breve, **1:**249
Tye, Christopher
  In Nomine fancies, **2:**116–18
typography, **1:**692–93, 692
Tyrrell, John, **3:**448; **4:**427, 434

U
"Über das Dichten und Komponieren"
  (Wagner), **3:**729
Über das Dirigiren (Wagner), **3:**719
Über das Geistige in der Kunst (Kandinsky),
  4:338
*Über den gegenwärtigen Zustand der Musik
  besonders in Deutschland und wie er
  geworden* (Wendt), **2:**739
Über den Ursprung der Sprache (Herder),
  3:121
Übermensch concept, **3:**439
Über Paganinis Kunst die Violine zu spielen
  (Guhr), **3:**261
Über schwebende und aufgehobene Tonalität
  (Schoenberg), **4:**311
Uberto's aria (Pergolesi), **2:**439–40, 441
Uffenbach, Johann Friedrich Armand von,
  2:217
Ugarit, **1:**31, 32
"Ukelele Serenade" (Copland), **4:**652, 653
Ukraine, **3:**345
"Ulibischeff gegen Beethoven" (Serov),
  3:439
"Ulibischeff und Seroff. Kritik der Kritik"
  (Liszt), **3:**439

Ulman, Eric, **5:**476
Ulybyshev, Alexander, **3:**439
"Ulysses" (Joyce), **4:**525; **5:**193
Ulysses' Return to His Homeland
  (Monteverdi), **2:**26
*Umfang, Methode und Ziel der
  Musikwissenschaft* (Adler), **4:**4
Umlauf, Michael, **2:**677
unaccented passing tones, **1:**430
unaccompanied melody, **1:**298
  ballade performance as, **1:**452
  carol tunes as, **1:**420
unaccompanied voice. *See* a cappella
Unanswered Question, The (Ives), **5:**290, 300
uncia. *See* tempus
Uncle Remus (Gilbert), **4:**613
unconscious, art and **4:**307–8
"underscoring" techniques, Steiner and,
  4:551
under-third cadence (Landini), **1:**368,
  369–71
"Underwater Valse" (Ussachevsky), **5:**192
unendliche Melodie ("endless melody"),
  3:486, 521, 547, 751
unequal notes (*notes inégales*), **1:**261
"Unfinished" Symphony (Symphony no. 8
  in B minor) (Schubert), **3:**81, 85,
  108–17, 675, 697
Unger, Karoline, **2:**677
Union (Gottschalk), **3:**381–83
"Union" leitmotif (Wagner), **3:**531, 532
Union of Soviet Composers, **4:**654, 657
Union of Soviet Socialist Republics. *See*
  Soviet Union
*Union Thematic Catalogue of
  Eighteenth-Century Symphonies*
  (LaRue, ed.), **2:**497, 528
uniqueness, **2:**641
unison, **1:**151, 152, 356
  chant, **1:**47, 130
  see also monphony
United Kingdom. *See* Great Britain
United States, **3:**618, 764
  Americanism backlash and, **3:**384–85
  arts support in, **3:**206, 385
  barbershop quartets and, **3:**382
  Boston School in, **3:**768–69, 774
  centrisms and, **2:**739
  church musical oral tradition and, **1:**27,
    28
  Dvořák and, **3:**755–67
  egalitarian ideals of, **2:**111
  Enlightenement principles and, **2:**111,
    302, 461–62
  first chamber composition in, **2:**519
  Gottschalk in, **3:**379–82, 385
  Hiawatha as national epic of, **3:**123, 763,
    764
  high culture and, **3:**377, 379, 380, 384
  music appreciation initiatives in, **3:**783
  national anthem of, **3:**120, 381
  national opera and, **3:**760, 763, 764–66

  nineteenth-century popular culture in,
    3:385
  nineteenth-century symphonic music in,
    3:679, 745, 766–73
  operetta in, **3:**652–53
  public conservatory system in, **2:**736
  social stigma against artists in, **3:**385
  United States' bicentennial, *Final Alice*
    and, **5:**442–43
unity of affect, **2:**439, 706
universality, **1:**580, 713, 722, 724; **3:**491
  as Enlightenment ideal, **2:**302, 460, 495,
    496, 600, 738; **3:**61, 121, 188
  ethnocentricity vs., **2:**739
  German musical claims to, **2:**258–59,
    389, 738–39
  German Romanticism and, **3:**21
  modern critical worldview vs., **2:**600
  Romantic particularism vs., **2:**645; **3:**62
  See also subjectivity
"Universe in Tones" (Ives), **4:**282, 284, 285
Universe symphony (Ives), **4:**192, 331, 345;
  5:359
university,
  music forms, **1:**122, 149, 354, 364
  quadrivium, **1:**4–5, 6, 37, 175, 282, 424,
    550
  twelfth-century origins of, **1:**148–49,
    169–72
  urban clerical class and, **1:**207–8
University of Berlin, **3:**413
University of Bologna, **1:**170, 354
University of Breslau, **3:**729
University of California, Berkeley, **1:**31
University of Cambridge, **1:**166, 513
University of Freiburg im Briesgau, **1:**553
University of Orléans, **1:**453
University of Oxford, **1:**403
  Haydn honorary degree from, **2:**556
University of Padua, **1:**354
University of Paris (Sorbonne), **1:**120, 170,
    170, 207, 214–15, 378
  Ars Nova and, **1:**248
  clerical intellectuals and, **1:**207–8, 254
  English students at, **1:**172–73, 397, 399
  music curriculum of, **1:**196–98
  Notre Dame alliance with, **1:**170, 172,
    174, 175, 196
University of Salzburg, **2:**464
University of Uppsala, **1:**392
University of Vienna, **3:**442
Unnamable, The (Beckett), **5:**347
Untergang des Abendlandes, Der (Spengler),
  4:530
Unterhaltungsmusik ("U-Musik"), **5:**15
unwritten conventions, **1:**17, 261
Upon a Bank (Ward), **1:**747, 749–50
Upper Palatinate, **2:**505
urbanization, **1:**120, 142, 143, 169; **3:**63, 289,
    676
  ballata and, **1:**367, 368
  clerical class and, **1:**207–8, 219

urbanization (continued)
  cosmopolitanism and, 3:228
  English chamber music and, 2:124
  Florentine elite and, 1:367, 368, 383
  motet and, 1:226, 236
  psychological realism of, 3:153
  trouvère art and, 1:120, 142, 290–91
Urban VIII, Pope, 2:37
Urbino, Duke of, 1:585
Urlicht (Mahler), 4:21
Urpflanze ("primal plant"), 3:277
Urwüchsigkeit concept, 3:146, 191
US Highball: A Musical Account of a
      Transcontinental Trip (Partch),
      5:482
Ussachecsky, Vladimir, 5:192, 199, 207, 211,
      497; 5:362
  Concerted Piece for Tape Recorder and
      Orchestra, 5:198
  Incantation, 5:198
  "King Lear Suite," 5:214
  Linear Contrasts, 5:198
  Piece for Tape Recorder, 5:198
  Poem in Cycles and Bells, A, 5:198
  Rhapsodic Variations, 5:198
  "Underwater Valse," 5:192
Ut heremita solus (Ockeghem), 1:457, 500
utilitarianism, 1:765
ut mode, 1:102
Utopia (More), 1:629, 671
utopianism, 3:59
  artist-prophet myth and, 3:59, 438
  Herder's view on, 3:345
  Wagner and, 3:483, 491
Ut queant laxis (hymn tune), 1:100–101
Uvarov, Count Sergey, 3:240–41

V
Valenti, Fernando, 2:396
"Valhalla" leitmotif (Wagner), 3:506, 515,
      516, 524
Valkyries Song (Wagner), 3:532, 537
Valli profonde (Gagliano), 1:818–19
Valois dynasty, 1:480
valse. See waltz
Valse nobles et sentimentales (Ravel), 4:112
Valses oubliées, 3:362
value-free periodization, 1:381
values
  culture wars and, 3:22
  German Kultur and, 3:123–24, 228
  popular art and, 3:673
vamp, eighteenth-century use of term, 2:38,
      564
  gymnopédies and, 4:68
Vampyr, Der (Marschner), 3:194
Van, Guillaume de, 5:43
Vannini, Ottavio, 1:531
Va, pensiero, sull'ali dorate (Verdi), 3:570–73
Varèse, Edgar (Edgard)
  Amériques, 5:184

Dance for Burgess, 5:196
Densité 21.5, 5:186
Déserts, 5:207, 208, 211, 214, 415
Ecuatorial, 5:186, 5:209
Étude pour Espace, 5:186
Hyperprism, 5:185
Intégrales, 5:185
Ionisation, 5:185, 5:209
"Liberation of Sounds, The," 5:184, 187
Poème électronique, 5:208, 208, 209, 502
Rochberg's Music for the Magic Theater,
      and, 5:415
twelve-tone technique and, 5:415
Varian, John, 4:297, 298, 299
variation, development technique in,
      3:734–42
variations,
  Bach (J. S.) "Goldberg," 2:383–84
  Beethoven's Diabelli, 2:674
  chorale, 2:49–55, 257
  English keyboard, 2:47, 53
  over ground bass, 2:38–39, 193
  Haydn's "Suprise" Symphony second
      movement and, 2:571–72
  passacaglia and, 2:39
  Schein and, 2:53
  Sweelinck and, 2:45, 47–48
  See also theme and variations
variation sets
  Gottschalk's "Louisiana trilogy,"
      3:377–78, 386
  Paganini and, 3:255–61
Variations for orchestra (Stravinsky),
      5:124–25, 127–28
Variations for Orchestra, op. 30 (Webern),
      4:773
Variations for Orchestra, op. 31
      (Schoenberg), 4:700–702, 703,
      704, 707, 734
Variations for Orchestra on a Theme by
      Joseph Haydn (Brahms),
      3:716–19, 720
Variations for Piano, op. 27 (Webern),
      4:722, 723, 724, 725, 726, 727, 728,
      732, 738
Variations (Haydn), 4:18
Variazioni per orchestra (Crumb), 5:423
  Berg's Lyric Suite and, 5:423
Varlamov, Alexander, 3:633–34
Vasari, Giorgio, 1:641; 3:264
Vasilyev, Fyodor, 3:787
Vaterlandslied, 3:158
"Vater unser im Himmelreich" (Lutheran
      Lord's Prayer), 2:365
Vatican II. See Second Vatican Council
Vatican City, 1:3
Vatican library, 1:458, 459
vaudeville, origin of term, 3:188
vaudevilles-opérettes, 3:644
Vautier, Ben, 5:92
  Audience Pieces, 5:92

Vec Makropoulos (Janáček), 424. See also
      Makropoulos Affair, The
Vecchi, Orazio, 1:746
  So ben mi c'ha bon tempo, 1:746, 748
"Veil of Orpheus, The" (Henry), 5:188
Veit, Philipp, 3:310
Velvet Underground, 5:328, 362
  Lou Reed, 5:362
Venantius Fortunatus. See Fortunatus,
      Venantius
Venetia, 2:504
vengeance aria. See rage aria
Venice, 1:278; 3:37, 569, 574
  cantata and, 2:75
  carnival season, 2:12, 12
  concerted cathedral music in, 1:789–90,
      795
  Cyprus and, 1:345
  Gabrielis and, 1:605, 779–80, 782–95;
      2:5
  instrumental music in, 2:114
  intermezzos in, 2:434–35, 438
  Marcello brothers and, 2:192
  Monteverdi and, 2:1, 2, 5–12, 59
  musical heritage of, 2:57
  musicians, 1:792
  opera in, 2:12, 16, 126, 139, 434
  operatic reform in, 2:152
  organ ricercari in, 1:607
  polychoral style and, 1:779–81
  power and status of, 2:139
  printed music and, 1:542, 559, 600, 606,
      607, 691, 722, 781, 781, 787, 790–92
  Schütz and, 2:57, 59, 66, 68, 69, 73, 259
  Strozzi and, 2:75–78, 80
  Vivaldi and, 2:193, 216–31
  Willaert and, 2:600, 605–6, 611, 620
Veni creator spiritus, 4:23
Veni creator spiritus (Binchois), 1:439–41
Veni creator spiritus (Frankish hymn), 1:49,
      83, 436, 758
Veni creator spiritus (hymn)
Veni redemptor gentium (hymn), 1:758; 2:342
Venit ad Petrum (antiphon), 1:465
Venus (mythology), 2:93
Venus and Adonis (Blow), 2:132
Venusberg music, 4:133
Vêpres siciliennes, Les (Verdi), 3:594
Veracini, Francesco Maria, 2:298
Verbonnet. See Ghiselin, Johannes
Verbum patris humanatur (conductus),
      1:166, 167, 168
Verdelot, Philippe, 1:711–12, 723
Verdi, Giuseppe, 2:16; 3:208, 563–615, 564,
      573, 595, 657, 660, 798; 4:11, 101;
      5:224, 237, 343
  on Barbiere di Siviglia, 3:10
  on bel canto, 3:40
  choral set pieces and, 3:570–75
  early career of, 3:568–69

librettists of, **3:**571, 573, 575–76,
  577–78, 580, 583, 594, 595, 596,
  599, 600, 606, 611, 639
on Palestrina, **1:**666
Puccini and, **3:**664, 666
retirement of, **3:**594, 595–96
source materials used by, **3:**564–65
tinta and, **3:**568–71, 573, 581, 592, 604
tragicomedy and, **3:**575–83
Wagner and, **3:**563, 565–66, 567, 576,
  583, 594, 595, 597, 599, 602, 610–11
works of
  Aida, **3:**565, 595, 643
  Don Carlos, **3:**594, 595, 596, 643
  Ernani, **3:**569, 574–75, 583
  Falstaff, **3:**599, 611, 611, 614, 615, 660
  Forza del destino, La, **3:**594, 595
  Jérusalem, **3:**568
  Lombardi alla prima crociata, I, **3:**568,
    573–74
  Macbeth, **3:**568, 576, 611
  Masnadieri, I, **3:**568
  Nabucco, **3:**570–73
  Oberto, **3:**568
  Otello, **3:**596–611, 596, 615, 660;. **4:**133
  Quattro pezzi sacri, **4:**75
  Requiem Mass, **3:**595
  Rigoletto, **3:**568, 577, 578, 583–94, 584,
    597, 606, 660, 666
  Simon Boccanegra, **3:**596
  Traviata, La, **3:**565, 568, 580–83, 580,
    641, 660, 666
  Trovatore, Il, **2:**110; **3:**568, 577–81, 591,
    652, 653, 660, 666
  Vêpres siciliennes, Les, **3:**594
"Verein für musikalische
  Privataufführungen." _See_ Society
  for Private Musical Performances
Verfremdung, **4:**534
Verga, Giovanni, **3:**658–59
Veris ad imperia (conductus), **1:**397–99
verisimilitude,
  artistic truth and, **3:**229–30, 397
  orientalist representations and, **3:**390,
    397
verismo,
  neorealism and, **3:**674
  opera and, **3:**440, 641, 658–64
Verklärte Nacht, op. 4 (Schoenberg), **4:**304,
  315
  criticism of, **4:**304
  risque subject matter in, **4:**304
Verkündigungslied, **1:**760
Verlaine, Paul, **4:**100, 111
Verlust, op. 9, no. 10 (Mendelssohn), **3:**186
Vermeer, Jan, **5:**436
vernacular, **1:**3, 99, 106–45, 351, 459,
  694–709
  England and, **1:**387–95, 419–20, 741–51
  first major music theory written in, **1:**576
  France and, **1:**106–7, 706–13
  Germany and, **1:**134–42, 701–6, 717

Handel oratorios in, **2:**237
Haydn _Creation_ and, **2:**633
instrumental accompaniment for poetry
  in, **1:**131–33
Italian poetry and, **1:**722–23
Italy and, **1:**133–34, 350, 351–52,
  694–701
macaronic texts, **1:**112, 222–24, 430
"metrical psalms" published in,
  1:597–99
music printers and, **1:**691–92, 693–94,
  710
Palestrina motet texts and, **1:**632
as psalm settings, **1:**754–55
Rabelesian genre of, **1:**711
singspiel and, **2:**470
song types. _See_ ballata; chanson; frottola;
  madrigal; virelai
  Spain and, **1:**116, 128–33, 724
  Tinctoris's ranking of, **1:**460, 526
Véron, Louis, **3:**207, 208
Verona, madrigalists, **1:**352, 353, 738
Veronese (Paolo Caliari), **1:**741
"Verrano a te" (Donizetti), **3:**54
Versailles, **1:**349; **2:**90
"Versailles" style, **4:**456
verse-music. _See_ troubadours
verse play. _See_ liturgical drama
verse sequences. _See_ versus
versification,
  as mnemonic device, **1:**185–86
  as natural music, **1:**337
  See also poetry
Vers la flamme, op. 72 (Scriabin), **4:**219, 220,
  221, 222, 223, 224, 226
Verstovsky, Alexey Nikolayevich,
  3:236–38, 244
  Askold's Grave, **3:**236, 238
Versuch einer Anleitung zur Composition
  (Koch), **2:**622
_Versuch über die wahre Art das Clavier zu
  spielen_ (C. P. E. Bach), **2:**410–11,
  414, 418
versus (musical form), **1:**86–92, 93, 94, 111,
  171, 387
  end of tradition of, **1:**174
  goliards and, **1:**138
  harmony and, **1:**122
  liturgical drama and, **1:**93–95
  polyphonic settings of, **1:**156, 157, 159,
    160, 162
  rhythmic performance of, **1:**114
  subgenres of, **1:**111–12
  troubadour parallels with, **1:**111–12
  verticalization, **4:**181, **4:**387
Vesali icones (Davies), **5:**427, 429
Vesalius Andreas, _Vesali icones_ and, **5:**427
Vesper Psalms (Viadana collection), **1:**782
Vesper Psalms (Willaert), **1:**611–12
Vespers, **1:**11, 23, 94; **2:**115–16
  antiphonal psalm-singing and, **1:**611–12
  Byrd antiphon and, **1:**686–88

concerto grosso and, **2:**178
Eton Choirbook and, **1:**513
Monteverdi and, **2:**5, 10, 18–20
organ works for, **2:**49
Palestrina hymns for, **1:**632
tonaries and, **1:**72
Vivaldi's Venetian program for, **2:**216–17
Vespro della beata virgine (Monteverdi),
  2:19–20
Veste nuptiali (monophonic conductus),
  1:204, 204
"Vesti la giubba" (Leoncavallo), **3:**662–63
Vestiva i colli (Palestrina), **1:**642, 746
Vetrate di chiesa (Respighi), **4:**750
Vetus abit littera (conductus), **1:**199–201,
  199
Vexations (Satie), **4:**570, 571
Viadana, Lodovico, **1:**780, 781, 782, 783,
  812; **2:**52
  _Cento concerti ecclesiastici, a una, a due,
    a tre & a quattro voci_, **1:**780, 812.
    2:52, 53
Viaggio a Reims, Il (Rossini), **3:**11
Vicentino, Nicola, **1:**605, 730, 732, 732;
  4:285
Victimae paschali laudes (Easter sequence),
  1:86–88, 758, 759
Victor Book of the Symphony (O'Connell),
  3:781–82, 785
Victor Emmanuel, King of Italy, **3:**569,
  572, 573
Victoria, Queen of Great Britain, **3:**173,
  213, 657, 658
Victoria, Tomás Luis de, **1:**788
  Missa pro Victoria, **1:**788–90
Victorianism,
  Gilbert and Sullivan and, **3:**655
  impact on Romanticism of, **3:**36
  middle-class morality and, **3:**36
  salon culture and, **3:**78
  sexual roles and, **3:**36, 117
Victorine sequence, **1:**90, 91
Victor Talking Machine Company, **3:**782
victory music, Beethoven and, **3:**1, 2
Vida (Teresa of Avila), **1:**772
Viderunt omnes fines terrae (Perotin, attrib.),
  1:173, 177–78, 177, 178, 179–80,
  180, 183
  first syllable of setting, **1:**189–90
  as organum quadruplum, **1:**188, 191
Vieille prière bouddhique (L. Boulanger),
  4:126
Vielseitigkeit (Schoenberg), **4:**678
Vienna,
  Beethoven and, **2:**652–56, 671, 675–76,
    689, 694, 721, 722, 723; **3:**3
  Brahms and, **3:**703
  Bruckner and, **3:**746
  Chopin and, **3:**347, 348
  concert program, **2:**499–500, 500, 509
  Congress of Vienna celebration, **2:**722
  Gluck and, **2:**454, 455, 459

Vienna (continued)
    Haydn and, 2:517–20, 555, 607, 633
    Huguenots censorship by, 3:227
    Liszt and, 3:262
    magic opera and, 3:188
    Mozart and, 2:462–63, 465, 470–71, 476, 478, 479, 589, 590, 607–8, 620, 626, 633; 3:10
    nineteenth-century symphonic music in, 3:677, 680, 745–51
    northern Italian musical developments and, 2:504
    operetta in, 3:644, 647–51
    Ottoman siege of (1683), 2:139, 525
    Paganini concerts in, 3:252–53
    Rossini and, 2:675; 3:14, 80
    Schubert and, 3:79–81, 84, 85
    subscription chamber concerts in, 2:683
    symphony and, 2:591
    Turkish vogue in, 2:470, 525
Vienna Conservatory, Mahler and, 4:6
Vienna Court Opera, 4:549
    Mahler and, 4:7
Vienna Gesellschaft der Musikfreunde, 3:85, 677, 716
Vienna Musicians' Club, 4:304
Vienna Musikverein, 3:677, 678
Vienna Opera, 4:423
Vienna Philharmonic, 3:677
Vienna Schoenberg circle, 4:444
Vienna Singakademie, 3:703
Vienna State Opera, 4:2f
Viennese atonalists, 4:540
Viennese classicism, 2:542
Viennese waltz, 1:261
Vietnam war, 5:308–10
Vietinghoff, Baron. See Scheel, Boris
Vigil, 1:33, 47
Vikings, 1:41, 50, 392–93, 399
Vilar-Paya, Maria Luisa, 4:699
Village Soothsayer, The (Rousseau intermezzo), 2:110, 442
villancico, 1:129, 133, 724
villanella, 1:716
Villani, Filippo, 1:353
Villedieu, Alexandre de, 1:197
Vinci, Leonardo (composer), 2:165
    Artaserse, 2:158, 161–65
    Didone abbandonata, 2:330
    Handel "borrowings" from, 2:330–31
    style of, 2:161–62, 311
vingt-quatre violons du Roi, les, 2:94
Vinogradova, Dunyasha, 4:183
Vintage Alice (Del Tredici), 5:442
viol, 1:741, 741, 742, 795; 2:53
    accompanied sonata and, 2:428
    chest of, 2:118, 120
    consorts, 2:114, 118, 120
    In Nomines for, 2:118
    string ensemble and, 2:196
viola, 1:783
    Bach's (J. S.) writing for, 2:290–91

Mozart and, 2:473, 589
    orchestral role of, 2:291
viola da gamba, 2:241, 291, 419, 527
    Bach (J. S.) sonatas for, 2:300–301
    method book, 1:620, 625, 698
viola paradon. See baryton
violin, 1:783, 791, 792
    Bach's Sixth Brandenburg Concerto and, 2:290
    birdsong imitations by, 2:227–28
    concerto-quality, 3:255
    Corelli and, 2:177, 178, 193
    famous makers of, 2:2; 3:255
    "first" and "second" player positions, 2:291
    Haydn concertos for, 2:600–601
    keyboard sonata obbligato of, 2:428
    Mozart's writing for, 2:601, 602–7
    orchestra leadership by, 2:291
    Paganini and, 3:252–61
    in piano trio, 2:695
    pizzicato technique, 3:256
    scordatura (mistuned), 3:258
    virtuosos, 3:251–61
    Vivaldi and, 2:216, 217, 222–23, 231, 234
    See also fiddlers
violin concerto
    Mendelssohn and, 3:181, 275–76, 277, 287, 316
    Mozart and, 2:602–5; 3:179
    Paganini and, 3:252, 255, 256–57
Violin Concerto in E minor, op. 64 (Mendelssohn), 3:181, 275–76, 277, 287, 316
Violin Concerto no. 3 in G major, K. 216 (Mozart), 2:602
Violin Concerto no. 4 in D major, K. 218 (Mozart), 2:602
Violin Concerto no. 5 in A major, K. 219 (Mozart), 2:602–5
Violin Sonata, II ("blues") (Ravel), 4:607–11
violino, 1:784
virelai, 1:125–26, 127, 129, 233, 694; 3:126
    antecedents of, 1:349
    as ballata influence, 1:364, 366, 368
    bergerette and, 1:526
    birdsong, 1:349, 711
    laude and, 1:134
    Machaut and, 1:292–97, 298, 299–301, 349, 366
    rustic parodies, 1:349–50
virga (rod shape), 1:214–17
Virgil, 1:356, 383; 2:90, 132, 155; 3:67, 320
virginal (English harpsichord), 1:671; 2:45, 47, 53, 260
    name origin of, 2:45
    pentagonal, 1:46
Virgin Mary
    Anglican Mariolatry rejection and, 1:672
    Annunciation carol and, 1:420
    antiphon motet and, 1:270–73

    antiphons to. See Marian antiphons
    conductus to, 1:403, 406
    cult of, 1:94, 109
    devotional songs to, 1:98, 99, 128, 140, 270–73, 275–76, 333, 532–33
    "Ex Semine" clausula to, 1:196, 209–11, 210, 211
    feasts of, 1:112, 191–92, 291, 565, 566
    Florence cathedral dedication to, 1:282, 285
    Gloria tropes and, 1:55
    Machaut Mass Ordinary to, 1:307, 316
    Magnificat and, 1:111
    Notre Dame Cathedral dedication to, 1:169
    numerical symbol of, 1:285
    offices to, 1:48
    Stabat mater dolorosa sequence and, 1:134
    stock votive epithets for, 1:520
    votive Masses to, 1:307, 314, 316, 317–26, 595
    votive motets to, 1:501–26, 532, 565–72
Vi ricorda o bosch'ombrosi (Monteverdi), 2:22
"Virtues of Tobacco, The" (masque), 2:113
virtuosity, 2:234
    audience effects of, 1:616–67
    Bach's organ Toccata in F and, 2:208–16
    ban on, 2:15
    cadenza and, 2:171–72, 609–10
    Chopin and, 3:343–76
    compositional, 1:330, 339, 342, 349
    concerto genre transformation and, 3:273, 275, 277
    Corelli's "La Folia" and, 2:193
    Counter Reformation music and, 1:785, 786
    division viol and, 2:120
    Dussek and, 3:65
    etymology of word, 2:174
    improvisational, 1:536–41
    Liszt and, 3:261–73
    motet composition and, 1:233–36
    musical expressivity and, 3:254–55
    orchestral special effects and, 2:506, 507, 508–9
    Paganini and, 3:251–61
    political implications of, 2:96–97
    Romantic interest in, 3:251
    Romantic rejection of, 2:642
    Rossini orchestration and, 3:21
    Scarlatti (Domenico) and, 2:391, 392
    sestina and, 1:352
    style brillant and, 3:255, 262, 273, 277
    Sweelinck and, 2:44–46
    toccata and, 2:41
    as trobar clus principle, 1:330, 352
    Vivaldi and, 2:222–26
virtuoso singing, 3:222–23
    castrati and, 2:174
    commercial theater and, 2:16
    as "common," 2:15–16

court limits on, 2:15
da capo aria and, 2:144, 171–72
fermatas and, 2:171
French tragédie lyrique prejudice
    against, 2:96–97, 98, 106, 107, 113
madrigalist, 1:356, 363, 364
Metastasian librettos and, 2:154
Notre Dame polyphony and, 1:178
operatic, 2:116; 3:223
ornamentation and, 1:816–17
Rossini arias and, 3:27–35
unwritten ornamentation and, 2:174
women and, 2:80
See also bel canto; coloratura
Vischer, Antoinette, 5:74
Visconti family, 1:352
Vishnevskaya, Galina, 5:258
Vision and Prayer (Babbitt), 5:210–11
visitatio sepulchri, 1:52
Vitalian, Pope, 1:62
vitalism, 4:474, 476, 520, 523
"Vitalist" fallacy, 4:496
"Vitebsk" trio, 4:652
Vitellozzi, Cardinal, 1:650
Vitry, Philippe de (later Bishop of Meaux),
    1:248, 249, 256–58, 259, 261, 267,
    281, 286; 5:285
    contratenor addition and, 1:298–99
    Landini musical tribute to, 1:378, 384
    Machaut's legacy compared with, 1:289
    on musica ficta, 1:273
    notational innovations of, 1:262, 265, 337
    works of
        Ars nova, 1:248, 258, 273, 337
        Tribum/Quoniam/MERITO,
            1:256–58, 258, 259, 261, 337
        Tuba sacre/In Arboris/VIRGO
            SUM, 1:261–65, 262, 311, 337
Vittoria, battle of (1813), 2:672
Vivaldi, Antonio, 2:1, 193, 216–31
    concerto and, 2:193, 216–31, 609
    excessive atypical works of, 2:222–26,
        281
    musical mimesis of, 2:227–31, 316, 317
    numbering of works of, 2:218
    partbooks of, 2:224–25
    post–World War II revived interest in,
        2:217
    prolificity of, 2:217
    standard repertory and, 2:234
    works of
        Concerti per l'orchestra di Dresda
        Concerto for Bassoon in C major, F
            VIII/13, 2:217–24
        Concerto for Four Violins in B minor,
            op. 3, no. 10, 2:222–26, 282, 287
        Primavera, La op. 8 no. 1, 2:225–31
        Quattro stagioni, Le (Four Seasons),
            2:225–31, 234, 317; 3:455; 5:75
        "Sinfonia al Santo Sepolcro" in B
            minor, 2:222–23
        Tempesta del mar, La, 2:230

Vivats, 3:248
VIVA V.E.R.D.I.! (engraving), 3:573
Vive le roy (Josquin), 1:563, 563
Vivi, tiranno! (Handel), 2:308–11, 340, 437
Vltava ("The Moldau") (Smetana), 3:452,
    454–57, 459–60, 462, 463, 538
"Vniz po matushke po Volge" (song),
    3:242, 244
vocal music
    Augustine's reaction to, 1:66
    Bach (C. P. E.) on, 2:418
    Bach (J. S.) and, 2:340–90
    ballata as, 1:364–74
    barbershop quartets as, 3:382
    Beethoven and, 2:686
    bel canto, 3:36–46, 48, 578
    Brendel's view of, 3:415
    cantata as, 2:75–77, 341–90
    canzona as, 1:788–89
    chamber works as, 1:539–40, 542
    chorale concerto as, 2:52–55
    as domestic entertainment, 3:63–64
    earliest written-down secular, 1:106
    empfindsamer instrumentale music
        borrowing from, 2:416, 418
    English, 1:387–96, 452
    Frankish polyphonic, 1:44–47
    ground bass and, 1:812
    Handel and, 2:305
    instrumental accompaniment to,
        1:131–33, 296, 307, 741–42, 780–81
    Italy and, 3:566–67
    Josquin and, 2:539
    lied genre, 3:119, 142
    Monteverdi's seconda prattica and, 2:254
    Nuove musiche and, 1:813–22
    oral tradition and, 1:17–18, 19
    ornamentation and, 2:281
    partbooks, 1:539–40
    printed organ accompaniment,
        1:781–82
    rhetorical embellishments of, 1:816–17,
        821
    Romantic elevation of instrumental
        music over, 2:642
    sight-singing and, 1:47, 76, 104, 617
    song competitions and, 1:139, 141, 208,
        352–53, 364, 367, 701, 737
    standard forms of, 2:234
    Sweelinck and, 2:44–45, 47–49
    unaccompanied, 1:666–67, 732
    women performers of, 2:80
    See also aria; chanson; chant; choral
        music; madrigal; opera; singing
voces, 1:101–2, 103–4
voces musicales, 1:101
    Josquin and, 1:499–500, 560, 634
    Palestrina and, 1:634
Vogelstein, Carl Christian Vogel von, 3:191
Vogelweide. *See* Walther von der
        Vogelweide
Vogl, Johann Michael, 3:85, 85

Vogler, Georg Joseph (Abbé Vogler)
    Meyerbeer and, 3:216
    Weber and, 3:192
voice-exchange, 1:394–95, 397, 399, 402,
    407, 413
    Du Fay and, 1:441–42
    Taverner and, 1:613
Voice of Lir (Cowell), 4:299
voice parts (SATB)
    orchestration of, 1:783
    range of, 1:468
voice-throwing, 3:236–37
voice training, 3:38–40
voice types, 3:36, 77, 578–79
    bass, 2:434, 438
    etymology of nomenclature, 1:468, 474
    mezzo-soprano, 3:36
    soprano, 2:434, 438
    tenor, 2:98, 100
    See also coloratura; singing
Voiles (Debussy), 4:73–74, 75–76, 313
Voir Dit, Le (Machaut), 1:297, 299
Volker (Raff), 3:731
Volkmann, Robert, 3:675–76
Volkonsky, Andrey, 5:461–63, 471
    Concerto for Orchestra, 5:461
    expulsion from Moscow Conservatory,
        5:461
    Lamentations of Shchaza, The, 5:463
    Musica stricta, 5:461–462
    Nadia Boulanger and, 5:461
    twelve-tone composition and,
        5:461–462
    Union of Soviet Composers and, 5:461
    War and Peace and, 5:461
Volkov, Solomon, *Testimony*, 4:795–96
Volkslied,
    Herder's coining of term, 3:123, 233
    opera and, 3:194
"Volkslied" (Weber), 3:194–96
Volkstümlich style
    Beethoven and, 3:132
    Glinka and, 3:238, 464–67
    lieder and, 3:120, 125, 132, 135, 145, 155, 158
    in Mendelssohn's (Felix) works, 3:174,
        183
    Mozart and, 3:188
    oratorios and, 3:164, 165
    poetry and, 3:124
    as Romantic ideal, 3:187
    in Russia, 3:236, 463–70
    Schumann (Robert) and, 3:303
    Smetana and, 3:449, 462–63
Volkstümlichkeit, 4:20
Völlner, Johann Anton, 3:291, 293
Volsungasaga (Icelandic epic), 3:492
Voltaire (François Marie Arouet), 2:462,
    470, 479; 3:11, 28, 229
    on Atys, 2:97
voluptuous music, 1:429–33
Vom dem Worte und dem Kirchenliede
    (Arndt), 3:165

Von der musikalischen Poesie (Krause), **3**:120

Von edler Art (Brahms), **1**:703–4

Von edler Art (Schönfelder), **1**:702, 703, 704

Von Tilzer, Albert, **1**:19

Von zwei Kulturen der Musik (Halm), **2**:726

"Vorgefühle" (Schoenberg), **4**:342, 343

vorimitation, **1**:758, 761; **2**:50, 53

Voříšek, Jan Vaclav, **3**:87

Vormärz period, **3**:177

Vos qui secuti estis me (Du Fay), **1**:434–35

Vostellung des Chaos (Haydn), **2**:633–37

votive antiphon, **1**:94–99

   English, **1**:512–18

   Milanese substitution of Ordinary texts with, **1**:518–19

   See also Marian antiphons

votive Masses, **1**:314–26, 460

   as composite compositions, **1**:316, 317

   Machaut's Messe de Nostre Dame as, **1**:317, 317–26, 460

votive occasions, **1**:12

Vox populi, vox Dei, Beethoven's disclaimer of, **2**:724

vox principalis/vox organalis, **1**:150, 152–53, 154, 155, 156, 159, 163

Voyage in Lower and Upper Egypt (Denon), **3**:387

voyeurism,

   tragedy as, **3**:670–71, 673

   verismo opera and, **3**:660

Vsevolozhsky, Ivan, **4**:144, 146, 149

Vuillermoz, Émile, **4**:101, 102

Vulgate, **1**:20, 606

Vultum Tuum deprecabuntur cycle (Josquin), **1**:531–34

Vylet pana Broucka do XV. stoleti (Janáček), **4**:423

Vyšehrad Motive, **3**:459

Vyšehrad (Smetana), **3**:452–54

W

W1 codice, **1**:180, 183, 184

W2 codice, **1**:180, 183, 186, 187, 209, 210, 211, 212, 217, 219

"Wachet auf, ruft uns die Stimme" (Mendelssohn), **3**:168

Wachet auf, ruft uns die Stimme, BWV 104 (J. S. Bach), **2**:375

Wackenroder, Wilhelm, **2**:599

Wagner, Cosima Liszt, **3**:77, 262, 418, 558, 567, 729

Wagner, Minna, **3**:549

Wagner, Peter, **1**:28

Wagner, Richard, **2**:16; **3**:139, 208, 479–562, 479, 565, 596, 643, 657, 673; **4**:5, 8, 12, 13, 16, 29, 60–63, 85, 90, 142, 150, 153, 198, 207, 209, 210, 213, 224, 225, 262, 266, 281, 304, 305, 326, 331, 341, 354, 506, 508, 570, 677, 714, 751; **5**:223, 68, 223, 261, 368

   atonality and. 312

   "absolute music" definition by, **2**:714; **3**:502

   anti-Semitism of, **3**::177–79, 227–29, 480, 559, 560

   on art of transition, **1**:600

   autobiography of, **3**:482–83, 487

   background and early career of, **3**:481–83

   Baudelaire and, **4**:83, 84

   Bayreuth festival and, **3**:498, 498, 499, 500, 502, 512, 564, 719

   Beethoven and, **3**:7, 178, 480, 483, 485, 547, 558, 675, 719, 729

   on Beethoven's fanfares, **2**:677

   on Beethoven's musical authority, **2**:738

   Berlioz and, **3**:482, 483, 485

   bigotry of, **3**:559

   Brahms and, **3**:695–96, 699, 719, 729, 743

   Bruckner and, **3**:746, 747

   Chaikovsky and, **3**:798

   chromaticism and, **1**:738, 739

   composing activity hiatus of, **3**:487–88

   as conductor, **3**:481, 483

   controversies concerning, **3**:557–62

   criticism of, **3**:520–21, 557–58, 774

   Dvořák and, **3**:753, 754

   extramarital relationships of, **3**:549, 558

   folklore and, **3**:485, 501, 504

   Franck and, **3**:778

   future-istic methods and, **4**:3

   Gesualdo compared with, **1**:738, 739

   harmony used by, **3**:521–28, 531–54, 702

   "horror fanfares" and, **4**:14

   invisible orchestra and, **3**:563, 564

   as *Judenthum in der Musik, Das* author, **3**:177–79, 227–28

   leitmotives of, **3**:503–28, 530–38, 540, 541, 557, 560, 565, 734, 735, 759

   librettos of, **1**:337; **3**:487, 492, 576

   Liszt and, **3**:418, 482, 483, 487

   Meistersinger art and, **1**:137, 141

   Mendelssohn and, **3**:177–79, 227, 482

   Meyerbeer and, **3**:227–29

   moderism and, **4**:4

   on Muette de Portici, **3**:210, 219

   music drama and, **3**:7, 488, 521, 547, 567

   nationalism and, **1**:142; **3**:479, 490, 491, 559–61, 566

   New German School and, **3**:418, 421, 483, 531, 676, 729

   nostalgic vision and, **4**:3

   phrase structure fluidity of, **3**:547–48

   preludes pf, **3**:486, 487

   on religion, **3**:488–89

   Schumann (Clara) and, **3**:557–58

   Schumann (Robert) and, **3**:482, 557

   self-mythologizing by, **3**:483, 487, 565

   sensuality and, **4**:33–34

   tonal music and, **3**:529–30, 540, 542

   Verdi and, **3**:563, 565–66, 567, 576, 583, 594, 595, 597, 599, 602, 610–11

   on Weber's *Der Freischütz*, **3**:194–97, 208, 479

   Weber's influence on, **3**:199, 481

   widespread influence of, **3**:479–81, 543, 557, 563–68

   writings by, **3**:488–90

   works of

      Capitulation, **3**:560

      Feen, Die, **3**:481

      Fliegende Holländer, Der, **3**:483–85, 484, 487, 501, 504

      Götterdämmerung, **3**:495, 497, 503–8, 511–40, 543, 610, 643, 759; **4**:13, 20

      Liebesverbot, Das, **3**:481

      Lohengrin, **1**:138; **3**:418, 421, 479, 480, 483, 486–87, 486, 565, 580

      Meistersinger von Nürnberg, Die, **1**:139, 141, 142; **3**:28, 29, 559–60, 560, 611, 729

      Parsifal, **3**:480, 499, 611; **4**:90, 328, 329–30

      Rheingold, Das, **3**:497, 497, 502, 512, 513, 515–17, 519, 520, 537, 610, 668, 754

      Rienzi, **3**:481, 482, 483

      Ring cycle **3**:491–540, 499, 500, 564, 610, 623, 719, 734, 735, 759, 764, 776; **4**:13, 7, 283, 305, 326, 765; **5**:347

      Siegfried, **3**:510–12, 513, 516, 537, 539, 610, 697

      Siegfrieds Tod, **3**:491, 492–95, 497, 501, 502, 505, 511

      Tannhäuser, **1**:137, 138, 139, 141; **3**:483, 485, 487, 488, 696;, **4**:83, 133, 186

      Traüme, **3**:549

      Tristan und Isolde, **3**:485, 498, 539–58, 563, 566, 602–4, 611, 628, 695–96, 729, 732, 778; **4**:305, 360, 390, 619

      Walküre, Die, **3**:496, 497, 502, 513, 514, 516, 517, 520, 532, 536, 610, 746, 776

"Wagnerian" dominants, Scriabin and, **4**:211

"Wagnerian revolution," **4**:677

Wagnerian tradition, **4**:4

Wagnerism, **3**:480, 565–66, 667

Wagner satire genre, **4**:60–63

Wakefield Mystery Plays, *El Nino* and, **5**:524

Walcha, Helmut, **1**:374

Walden; or Life in the Woods (Thoreau), **4**:244, 267

Walden Quartet of the University of Illinois, **5**:293, 295

Waldhörner, **3**:158, 199–202

Waldmüller, Ferdinand Georg, **3**:85

Waldstein, Count, **2**:694; **3**:443

"Waldstein" Sonata, op. 53 (Beethoven), **2**:670

Wales, **1**:392, 394, 410, 438

Walker, Alan, **3**:262

Walker, Keith, **2:**125

Walküre, Die (Wagner), **3:**496, 497, 502, 513, 514, 516, 517, 520, 532, 536, 610, 746, 776

  Shostakovich's Fifteenth Symphony and, **5:**422

Wallenstein, Albrecht Wenzel Eusebius von, **3:**446

Wallensteins Lager (Smetana), **3:**446

Walpole, Robert, **2:**237

Walser, Robert, **4:**602

Walsh, John, **2:**177, 432

Walsh, Michael, **5:**392

Walter, Bruno, **4:**749, 765, 780–81

Walther, Johann, **1:**760–61, 765

  Christ lag in Todesbanden, **1:**761–62

  Geystliches gesangk Buchelyn, **1:**760–61

Walther von der Vogelweide, **1:**135–36, 138, 139

"Walzer" (op. 23, no. 5) (Schoenberg), **4:**681, 683–84

waltz, **3:**357

  Austrian origins of, **2:**573

  Chaikovsky and, **3:**791–93, 796, 797

  Chopin and, **3:**350

  in operettas, **3:**648

  Strauss (Johann) and, **3:**648

  in Verdi's *La traviata,* **3:**581, 582

  Viennese lilt, **1:**261

Walzer, **2:**573

Wanderer, Der (Schubert), **3:**101

Wanderer, Der, op. 6, no. 8 (Schoenberg), **4:**310, 314, 323

Wanderer Fantasy, op. 15 (Schubert), **3:**81, 85, 101, 277–78, 282, 457, 698

Wangenheim, Gustav von, **5:**13, 14

War and Peace, Andrey Volkonsky and, **5:**461

Ward, John, **1:** 746–47, 749–50, 751

  Upon a Bank, **1:**747, 749–50

Warhol, Andy, **5:**332

War of the Austrian Succession, **2:**306

War of the Buffoons, **2:**110–11, 441–44, 459, 460

  Enlightenment thought and, **2:**443

War of the Polish Succession, **2:**93

War of the Spanish Succession, **2:**505

War Requiem, op. 66 (Britten), **5:**257, 261, 422

Warsaw, **3:**348, 357

  Italian opera performance in, **2:**80

Warsaw Autumn Festival, **5:**217, 463

Warsaw Concerto (Addinsell), **4:**559

Warsaw Pact, **5:**7

Warum? (Schumann), **3:**306–8

Warwick, Earl of, **1:**423

Was ist Aufklärung? (Kant), **2:**461

Was ist des Deutschen Vaterland? (Arndt), **3:**158, 165

Wasserfluth, Die (Schubert), **3:**142–43

Waste Land, The (Eliot), **4:**473

Waterhouse, John C.G., **2:**750

"Water Music" (Handel), **2:**306

Watson, Thomas, **1:**746

Waverley novels (Scott), **3:**47

Wayward, The (Partch), **5:**481

Weavers, The, **5:**315

  Pete Seeger, **5:**315

Weber, Aloysis, **2:**474, 475

Weber, Carl Maria von, **3:**191, 253

  background of, **3:**191–92

  Beethoven and, **3:**197–99

  Meyerbeer and, **3:**216

  orientalism and, **3:**192–93

  singspiel and, **3:**191–92, 193, 567

  standard repertory and, **3:**680

  tonal practice of, **3:**543–44

  as Wagner influence, **3:**199, 481

  Wunderhorn poems and, **4:**21

  works of

    Abu Hassan, **3:**193, 386; **5:**176

    Drei Pintos, Die, **3:**193, 216

    Euryanthe, **3:**193, 544

    Freischütz, Der, **3:**191–205, 202, 208, 217, 236, 335, 419, 447, 455, 763; **4:**135

    "Invitation to the Dance," **3:**208

    Konzertstück in F minor for piano and orchestra, **3:**275

    Oberon, **3:**193

    Peter Schmoll und seine Nachbarn, **3:**191–92

    Silvana, **3:**209

    Turandot, Prinzessin von China incidental music, **3:**192, 193, 386

Weber, Constanze. See Mozart, Constanze Weber

Weber, Marion von, **4:**10

Weber, William, **3:**680, 681

Webern, Anton von, **4:**309, 313, 330, 339, 341, 349, 359, 361, 380, 391, 457, 523, 543, 681, 690, 710, 719–41, 719f, 772–73, 774; **5:**16, 17–18, 20, 22, 23, 51, 126, 140, 144, 159, 356

  BACH cipher and, **4:**313–14, 734–35; **5:**189, 415

  Path to the New Music, The, **4:**359

  "pointillism" and, **4:**361–62

  refinement of Schoenberg's twelve-tone methods, **5:**62

  "Sator Arepo" diagram, **5:**28

  symmetrical row structures, **5:**123

  twelve-tone row technique and, **4:**710, 719–41

  works of

    Bagatelles for string quartet, **4:**347

    Bagatelle no. 4, **4:**388

    Concerto, op, 24, **4:**724, 735, 737, 738, 739; **5:**143, 153

    Five Pieces for Orchestra, op. 10, **4:**347, 351, 692

    Fünf Stücke, op. 10, no. 4, **4:**350

    Kinderstück, **4:**720

    Piano Variations, **5:**23

    Quartet, op, 28, **4:**723, 735

    Sechs Bagetellen, **4:**347, 348, 349

    String Quartet, op. 28, **4:**734, 735, 736, 739; **5:**23

    Symphony, op. 21, **4:**723, 729–30, 732–34

    Three Little Pieces for Cello and Piano, op. 11, **5:**356

    Variations for Orchestra, op. 30, **4:**773

    Variations for Piano, op. 27, **4:**722, 723, 724, 725, 726, 727, 728, 732, 738

"Webern cult," **5:**18

Webernian palindromes, **5:**29

Webster, James, **2:**532, 540

Wedding at Cana, The (Veronese), **1:**741

Wedding March (Mendelssohn), **3:**183

Wedding of Ferdinand de' Medici and Christine of Lorraine (Salimbeni), **1:**803

"Wedding Song and a Dance Song, A" (Glinka). See Kamarinskaya

Weelkes, Thomas, **1:**746–47, 751

Weerbeke. See Gaspar van Weerbeke

"Weg! Weg!" (J. S. Bach), **2:**378, 379–81, 389

Wehinger, Rainer, **5:**52

Weill, Kurt, **4:**533–47, 548, 555, 649, 748, 765

  "gestic character" of music, **4:**535, 536

  neoclassicism and, **4:**539–40

  works of

    Der Jasager, **4:**543

    Der Protagonist, **4:**540

    "No. 16," **4:**535

    Sinfonia Sacra, **4:**539

Weimar, **2:**66, 68, 222; **3:**417–20, 445–46, 479, 487; **4:**532, 543, 547, 548, 550, 600, 763

  Bach (J. S.) and, **2:**208, 235, 239, 241, 247, 261, 262

  See also Leipzig

Weinberg, Henry, **5:**164

  A Method of Transferring the Pitch Organization of a Twelve Tone Set, etc.(essay), **5:**160

Wein, Der (Berg), **4:**749

Weingartner, Felix, **3:**222

Weiniger, Otto, *Geschlecht und Charakter,* **4:**680

Weisgall, Hugo, **5:**516

Weiss, Adolph, **5:**55

Weiss, Piero, **1:**806; **2:**435; **3:**576–77, 583, 593

Welles, Orson, King Lear, and, **5:**198

Wellesz, Egon, **4:**37, 38, 460, 467, 680–81, 685

Wellington, Duke of (Arthur Wellesley), **2:**672; **3:**198

Wellington's Victory (Beethoven), **2:**672–73

Well-Tempered Clavier, The (J. S. Bach),
    2:247–51, 253, 262, 291, 383; 3:155,
    346, 347, 351; 4:486, 768
Well-Tuned Piano, The (Young), 5:360
Weltanschauung, 2:721
Weltanschauungsmusik, 3:440; 4:6, 8, 53,
    283, 339
Weltgenie (world-genius) concept, 3:439,
    451, 456
Weltschmerz, 2:693
Wenceslaus, King of Bohemia, 1:289
Wendt, Amadeus (Johann Gottlieb
    Wendt), 1:3, 286; 2:739; 3:12
Werckmeister, Andreas, 2:248
Werner, Gregor Joseph, 2:526
Wert, Giaches (Jacques) de, 1:733; 2:5
    Solo e pensoso, 1:733, 734
Werther (Massenet), 3:640
Wesendonck, Mathilde, 3:549, 549, 558
Wesendonck, Otto, 3:549, 558
Wessel, David, 5:480
Wessex dialect, 1:387
West, Martin L., 1:33, 34
West-country style (England), 1:394, 402,
    403
Westergaard, Peter, 5:164, 168–69
Western-American folklore, 4:660, 668
Western Christianity. *See* Roman Catholic
    Church
"Western Cowboy" (Harris), 4:672
Western Roman Empire. *See* Holy Roman
    Empire
West Franks. *See* France
Westley, Ozzie, 3:384
Westminster Abbey (England), 2:132
    Handel oratorio festivals, 2:578, 633
    Purcell as organist at, 2:127
Westphalia, Peace of (1648), 2:68
What Is Post-Modernism? (Jencks), 5:411
"When Johnny Comes Marching Home
    Again" (Harris) 4:671–72
"When You're Lying Awake" (Gilbert and
    Sullivan), 3:655
White, John I.,
    "Git Along, Little Dogies," 4:663
    Lonesome Cowboy, The, 4:662, 663
White, Pearl, 4:563
    Perils of Pauline and, 4:563
Whiteman, Paul, 4:625–27
"White Mass, The," Scriabin and, 4:219
"white noise," 5:190
White Spirituals in the Southern Uplands
    (Jackson), 4:659
Whitman, Walt
    Leaves of Grass, 4:243
    "Song of Myself," 4:243
Whitman, Wanda, *Songs That Changed the
    World*, 4:659
Whitsunday, 1:686–87
Who, The, 5:316, 327–28, 332
    Pete Townshend, 5:327–28
    Tommy, 5:327

"Who Cares If You Listen?" (Babbitt),
    5:157–58, 170, 449, 454
whole-tone scale, 3:101–5, 701; 4:313
    Debussy's "Voiles" and, 4:313
    Glinka and, 3:430–31, 447
    Liszt and, 3:429–32
    Mozart and, 3:101
    Schubert and, 3:101, 103, 105, 42930
    Scriabin and, 4:212, 213–14
    Smetana and, 3:447
"Whoopee" in *Lonesome Cowboy*, 4:663
"Why Have There Been No Great Women
    Artists?" (Nochlin) (article), 4:124
Widor, Charles-Marie, 3:781–82
Wieck, Clara. *See* Clara Schumann Wieck
Wieck, Friedrich, 3:293, 294
    Brendel and, 3:411, 416
Wieland, Christoph Martin, 2:416
Wiener Klassik (Viennese classicism),
    2:542
Wiener Tonkünstlerverein, 4:304
Wiggins, Ella May, 4:656
Wilbye, John, 1:746–47
"wild bird" songs, 1:359–64
Wilde, Oscar, 3:352, 799–800; 4:30, 31, 36,
    756
    decadence and, 4::36
    homosexuality and, 5:246
    Salomé, 4:38, 57, 467
Wilder, Philip van, 1:676–77
    Pater noster, 1:676–77
Wild Men's Dance (Ornstein), 4:299
Wilhelm, Duke of Bavaria, 1:572
Wilhelm, Friedrich, 2:409
Wilhelmina, Princess of Prussia, 2:79
Wilhelmj, August, 4:510
Wilhelm Meisters Lehrjahre (Goethe),
    3:640
Will (Schopenhauer concept), 2:720, 721;
    3:548
    music and, 3:546–47, 551
Willaert, Adrian, 1:555, 588, 589, 593,
    599–606, 613, 615, 617, 620, 629,
    635; 2:5
    Benedicta es, coelorum regina, 1:601–4
    career of, 1:589, 600–661
    declamation and, 1:612, 646
    influence of, 1:786
    madrigal and, 1:724
    pupils of, 1:605–6, 607, 699, 725–26
    ricercari and, 1:588, 607
    split choirs and, 1:611
    stylistic moderation of, 1:601
    technical preeminence of, 1:600–601
    Vespers Psalms, 1:611–12
William I (the Conqueror), King of
    England, 1:397
William (Guillaume) I (the Pious), Duke
    of Aquitaine and Count of
    Toulouse, 1:50

William (Guillaume) IX, Duke of
    Aquitaine and Count of Poitiers,
    1:78, 106–7, 112, 113, 117
William (Guillaume) of Amiens, 1:123
William and Mary, Co-Regents of Great
    Britain, 2:132
Williams, Christopher, 4:195
Williams, Paul, 5:332
    Crawdaddy!, 5:332
    "How Rock Communicates," 5:332
    Swarthmore College, 5:332
Williams, Tennessee, *A Streetcar Named
    Desire*, 5:516
Williams, William Carlos, 4:195
Williams Mix (Cage), 5:196, 197
William Tell (Rossini), 3:11–12, 11, 18, 273,
    578, 579
    Shostakovich's Fifteenth Symphony
    and, 5:422
"willing suspension of disbelief," 3:287
Willow Song (Verdi), 3:605, 608
Wilson, A. N., 5:350
Wilson, Edmund, 5:242, 243
Wilson, Random, 5:395
Wilson, Robert
    De Materie and, 5:399
    Einstein on the Beach and, 5:388, 393
    "knee plays" and, 5:393
    Life and Times of Joseph Stalin, The and,
    5:393
Wilson, Woodrow, 4:257, 472
Winchester Cathedral, 1:93
Winchester Tropers, 1:93, 155, 402
Winckelmann, Johann Joachim, 2:453–54,
    457
wind ensembles
    eighteenth-century, 2:505, 509
    Handel suite and, 2:306
wind instruments, 3:168
    canzona for, 1:787
    concerted style and, 1:780, 787
    method book, 1:620
Wind Quartet (Schoenberg), 5:17
Winham, Godfrey, 5:159–60
    Composition with Arrays (essay), 5:159–60
    computer music technology course
    (Princeton), 5:201, 496, 501
Winterfeld, Carl von, 1:792
Winterreise, Die (Schubert), 3:82, 142–43
Wipo (monk), 1:86
wir arme Leut, 4:508, 537
"Wir arme Leut" leitmotif (Berg), 4:511
"Wir glauben all' an einen Gott" (hymn),
    3:171
Wirrwarr, Die (Klinger), 2:528, 530
Wise and Foolish Virgins (verse play), 1:93
wit, musical. *See* joke, musica; puns,
    musicall
"With Edgar Varèse in the Gobi Desert"
    (Miller) 5:186
Wittenberg, 1:753, 760, 762

Wo Gott der Herr nicht bei uns hält, BWV 178 (J. S. Bach), 2:369–9

Wohltemperirte Clavier, Das (J. S. Bach), 2:247–51, 253, 291

"Wolcum yole!" (Britten), 1:391

Wolf, Hugo, 3:290

Wolfe, Bertram D., 2:397

Wolfe, Tom, 5:248

Wolfenbüttel codices, 1:180

Wolff, Christian, 5:63, 64, 82–83, 88
    Duo for Pianists II, 5:82

Wolff, Christoph, 2:383–84

Wolff, Pierre, 3:264

Wolfram von Eschenbach, 1:138; 3:486

"Wolf's Glen" scene (Weber), 3:198, 202–5, 202, 217, 225, 335

Wolkenstein. *See* Oswald von Wolkenstein

Wollheim, Richard, 5:353

Wolpe, Stefan, 5:13–15, 21, 105, 296
    appearance in New York Composers Collective's *Workers Song Book No. 2*, 5:13
    Morton Feldman and, 5:98
    Palestine Conservatory, 5:13
    United States, 5:13
    Vienna, 5:13
    works of
        Die Mausefalle, 5:13
        Kampflieder, 5:13, 14
        "Ours Is the Future," 5:13
        Passacaglia, 5:296
        Piano Variations, 5:20
        Quartet for trumpet, saxophone, piano, and drums, 5:14, 15

Wolzogen, Hans von, 3:502, 503, 514, 515, 517, 519, 520, 527, 537

women in music, 2:78–81
    Bach (J. S.) cantatas and, 2:352, 375
    Beach, Amy Marcy, 3:769–73, 769, 783
    Beethovenian ideal's negative effects on, 2:670
    Caccini, Francesca, 2:80, 81, 82
    Christine de Pisane, 1:447, 448
    Copland on, 2:78
    female otherness and, 3:406
    Hildegard of Bingen, 1:90–93
    mainstreaming of, 2:81
    Mendelssohn (Fanny) and, 3:184–86, 292, 770
    opera divas and, 2:17
    operatic voice casting and, 3:36, 578
    orientalist portrayals and, 3:405–6
    patriarchal mores and, 3:185, 186, 292
    performance ban on, 2:16, 21, 153, 352
    performance stigma and, 2:80
    power of access and, 2:79
    as prima donnas, 2:17
    reasons for underrepresentation of, 2:78–82
    salons and, 3:74, 77–78
    Schumann (Clara) and, 3:317

social prejudice toward, 3:186, 292
    Strozzi, Barbara, 2:75–78, 80–81
    symphonic compositions by, 3:769–73
    as troubadours, 1:110, 113
    victim portrayals and, 3:673, 674
    Vivaldi's Pietà students, 2:216–17
    See also gender; Schumann, Clara

women's rights, 3:76

Woodland Sketches (MacDowell), 3:768

Woodstock Music and Arts Fair, 4:659; 5:311

woodwinds,
    in Dvořák's Eighth Symphony, 3:766
    Rossini and, 3:21

Woolf, Virginia, "Mr. Bennett and Mrs. Brown," 4:359

Worcester, 1:402

Worcester, Earl of, 1:677, 678

Worcester Cathedral, 1:403

Worcester Festival, 3:657

Worcester fragments, 1:402–3, 406–7

words-music relationship
    artistic synthesis of, 1:337
    Byrd's Masses and, 1:680
    Caccini vocal tricks and, 1:816–17
    embellishment and, 1:816–17
    English prosody and, 2:133, 134
    English semi-opera and, 2:127
    English vs. continental approach to, 1:613–14
    expressiveness and, 2:539
    Gluck and, 2:458–59
    Josquin's Ave Maria . . . Virgo motet and, 1:565–66
    madrigal text and, 1:724–25, 727, 736–37, 739, 749, 802, 813, 816–17
    monody and, 1:802–3, 816–17
    Monteverdi and, 2:4, 10
    "musical tales" and, 1:826
    opera and, 1:827
    Orlandini compared with Handel and, 2:437
    papal Mass "intelligibility" movement and, 1:647, 649–53, 672
    representational style and, 2:418, 643
    Romantic esthetic on, 2:479, 486, 642, 645–46
    tragédie lyrique and, 2:96–97
    See also literary music

Wordsworth, William, 3:64, 138; 4:244

Work, Henry Clay, "Marchin through Georgia," 4:275

Workers Music League, 4:651

Workers' Songbook, Composers Collective and, 4:651, 654, 655

Works Progress Administration (WPA), 4:647, 650, 660. *See also* WPA School

World as Will and Representation, The (Schopenhauer), 2:721

World Exposition (Paris), 4:71

world-genius (Weltgenie) concept, 3:439, 451, 456

world's oldest song, 5:451, 452

"World Spirit" (Hegelian concept), 2:670

World War I, 1:652; 3:445
    Beethoven critics following, 2:692
    Poland and, 3:344, 357

World War II, 3:480, 678; 4:237, 262, 541, 624, 666, 670
    postwar Vivaldi boom, 2:217

Worringer, Wilhelm, Abstraktion und Einfühlung, 4:474

worship music. *See* liturgical music

Woyzeck (Büchner), 4:506, 507

Wozzeck (Berg), 4:506–26, 507, 508, 539, 559, 710, 711, 714, 719, 749, 789; 5:241, 312, 343
    compared with *Die Dreigroschenoper*, 4:536–37
    Invention über eine Tonart and, 4:520
    "leitharmony" in, 4:517
    leitmotifs and, 4:508, 510
    Peter Grimnes and, 5:230

WPA School, 4:648, 660

Wright, Craig, 1:175, 184, 285

written music, 1:11–35
    Adam de la Halle's works, 1:127
    Ambrosian chant, 1:63
    ancient world, 1:31–33
    antiphon grouping, 1:40–44
    autonomy of music and, 1:65, 104
    Beneventan chant, 1:64
    breakthrough in, 1:99–100
    British pre-Reformation, 1:387–409, 409–18, 672
    as business, 1:542
    Busnoy autograph manuscript, 1:456, 456
    cadenza, 2:613, 614–15, 650
    cantiga manuscript miniatures, 1:130
    Caput Mass and, 1:458, 476
    chansonnier, 1:109–10
    Chigi Codex, 1:457–58, 458, 473
    choirbooks, 1:458–59
    classical canon's sanctity of, 2:650–51
    Codex Calixtinus and, 1:162–68
    commodification of music and, 1:542, 549
    composer's improvisation on, 2:610–11, 624, 650
    court vs. commercial opera and, 2:33–34, 174
    as cream of improvisatory practice, 1:161–62, 163; 2:35, 44
    cyclic Mass Ordinaries and, 1:460, 496
    diatonic pitch set, 1:29–31, 32
    earliest British manuscript, 1:387–88, 388
    earliest Christian, 1:33
    earliest extant keyboard composition, 1:305–7

written music (*continued*)
  earliest in European tradition. *See*
    Gregorian chant
  earliest vernacular repertories, 1:105–45
  exigetical interpretation of, 2:650, 706,
    714
  first score, 1:578
  Florence manuscripts. *See* Florence
    Codex
  Frankish Gregorian chant unity and,
    1:62
  Frankish Mass Ordinary, 1:53–60
  as historical record, 1:617
  importance of, 1:11
  instrumental dances, 1:621–28
  Italian vocabulary used for, 2:158–59,
    203
  lutenists and, 1:373
  Machaut collected editions, 1:290,
    327–28, 328, 333
  Mass Ordinaries, 1:315–21
  misleading evidence in, 1:130–31
  motet manuscript layouts, 1:214
  motet rotuli, 1:267
  Mozarabic chant, 1:64
  neumated, 1:13–16, 15
  notational importance and, 1:778–79
  Notre Dame codices, 1:171–86, 209
  Notre Dame polyphonic gap in, 1:184,
    186
  Old Hall manuscript, 1:409–18, 429,
    461, 513
  opera seria performance practice vs.,
    2:173
  partbooks, 1:539–40
  performance vs., 1:452
  polyphonic chant settings, 1:149–63
  Praetorius decoration and, 2:55, 739
  score and, 1:578; 3:10, 288
  staffed notation and, 1:16, 102, 105
  surviving British eleventh-to-fifteenth
    century leaves, 1:402–3
  thirteenth-century treatise, 1:30
  timelessness and, 1:65
  "tonal revolution" and, 1:628
  tonaries, 1:72–76
  trecento song, 1:353
  tropers and, 1:51, 93, 155
  trouvère song survival and, 1:120, 131, 133,
    219
  value placed on, 2:79
  virtuoso reading skills and, 1:536–37, 538
  Vivaldi concerto manuscripts, 2:217
  as whole entity, 1:18, 20
  women's creative underrepresentation
    and, 2:78–83
  See also music publishing; notation
Wulfstan (monk), 1:155
Wunder der Heliane, Das (Korngold), 4:550,
  551, 756
Wunderhorn poems
  Brahms and, 4:21

  Loewe and, 4:21
  Mahler and, 4:20, 21, 22
  Mendelssohn and, 4:21
  Schumann and, 4:21
  Weber and, 4:21
*Wunderlich Translocation des . . . Berges
  Parnassu* (Schütz), 2:58
Wuorinen, Charles, 5:164, 165, 353
Wuppertal, 3:165
Wyclif, John, 1:753
Wylkynson, Robert, 1:513
Wyschnegradsky, Ivan, 4:228, 229, 286

X

Xenakis, Iannis, 5:77–81, 89, 184, 189
  Diamorphoses, 5:189
  Le Corbusier and, 5:77
  "stochastic music," 5:78
  works of
    Metastasis, 5:78, 79, 80
    Pithoprakta, 5:78, 219
X tetrachords, 4:414
XX. Songes (music book), 1:741

Y

Yakulov, Georgiy Bogdanovich, 4:776
  Le pas d'acier, 4:776
Yale-Princeton Game, A (Ives), 4:273
Yale University, 3:769
Yamshchiki na podstave (Fomin and Lvov),
  3:236, 237
"Yankee Doodle," 3:381; 4:275
Yasser, Joseph, 4:285
Yavorsky, Boleslav, 4:208
Yeats, W. B., 3:311; 4:613
  Partch's *King Oedipus* and, 5:485
Yellin, Victor Fell, 4:145
Yezhov, Nikolai, 4:795
Yonge, Nicholas, 1:744, 746
"You Don't Know the Half of It, Dearie"
  (Gershwin), 4:625
Young Hegelians, 3:416–17, 422, 497
Young, La Monte, 4:285; 5:355, 366, 409
  Darmstadt refugee, 5:94
  Fluxus, 5:355
  John Cale and, 5:362
  Leonard Stein, pupil of, 5:94, 365
  Marian Zazeela (wife), 5:359, 360, 361
  Pran Nath and, 5:359
  religious lifestyle, 5:359
    Buddhism, 5:360
    Hinduism, 5:360
  Seymour Shifrin and, 5:359
  Theatre of Eternal Music, 5:359, 360,
    361, 362
  Yogic meditation and, 5:407
  works of
    "Black LP," 5:360–61
    *23 VIII 64 2:50:45–3:11 am the Volga
      Delta*, 5:361
    31 VII 69 10:26–10:49 pm, 5:361

    Compositions 1960, 5:92, 355, 359
    Four Dreams of China, The, 5:359
    *Map of 49's Dream The Two Systems of
      Eleven Sets of Galactic Intervals
      Ornamental Lightyears Tracery*, 5:361
    Piano Piece for David Tudor #1, 5:355
    String Trio, 5:356–59
    Tortoise, His Dreams and Journeys, The,
      5:361
    Well-Tuned Piano, The, 5:360
Yradier, Sebastián, 3:641
Yrieux, Saint, 1:39–40
Y-tetrachords, 4:414

Z

Zabarelle, Francesco, 1:277, 278, 280, 281,
  424
Zacharias, Pope, 1:2
Zachow, Friedrich Wilhelm, 2:236, 402
Zahortsev, Volodymyr, 5:463
zajal (verse structure), 1:129
Zakharov, Vladimir, 5:9, 10
Zal dvoryanskogo sobraniya
  (St. Petersburg), 3:679
Zamboni, Leopoldo, 3:240
Zamboni, Luigi, 3:34, 240
Zápisník zmizelého (Janáček), 4:424
Zappa, Frank, 5:328
zarabanda. *See* sarabande
Zarlino, Gioseffe, 1:500, 560, 586, 599, 608,
  615, 629, 630, 735, 779; 2:5
  Galilei as student of, 1:799–800
  Modo di fugir le cadenze, 1:604–5
  music theory of, 1:586–89, 597, 601–5,
    699, 735, 736, 800
Zar und Zimmermann (Lortzing), 3:753
Zaslaw, Neal, 2:88
Zauberflöte, Die (Mozart), 2:479–85, 480,
  481, 643; 3:188–91
  Act II finale, 3:190
  armonica's use in, 3:73
  Papageno's aria, 3:189
Zauberoper, 3:188
Zauberschlafe, 3:517
Zauberspiel, 3:188
Zazeela, Marian, 5:359, 360, 361
  La Monte Young (husband), 5:359
Zefiro torna (Monteverdi), 2:37, 38
Zefiro torna (Petrarch), 2:37
Zehme, Albertine, 4:460, 462
Zeitgeist, 1:381, 385, 577, 580, 583, 614–15
zeitoper, 4:527, 529, 530, 755
Zeitopern, 5:519
Zelter, Carl Friedrich, 2:368, 381
  on *Freischütz, Der*, 3:205
  lied genre and, 3:129
  Mendelssohn (Fanny) and, 3:184
  Mendelssohn (Felix) and, 3:163, 174, 180
  Meyerbeer and, 3:216
Zemlinsky, Alexander von, 4:304, 326, 342,
  549, 714
Zeno, 3:94

Zeno, Apostolo, 2:152

"zero hour," 5:14–18, 55, 64

Zerstörung Jerusalems, Die (Loewe), 3:164

Zetkin, Clara, 4:777

Zeuner, Charles, 4:269

   The Missionary Chant (Ye Christian Heralds), 4:269

Zhdanov conference, 5:13

Zhdanov, Andrey Alexandrovich, 4:775, 779, 790; 5:9, 10, 19, 156, 163, 172

"Zhdanovite" movement, 5:49

Zhdanovshchina, 5:11, 14, 21

Zhitomirsky, Alexander, 4:108, 110

Zhukovsky, Vasily, 4:241, 247

Zillig, Winfried, 4:774

Zimbalist, Efrem, 4:626

Zimmermann, Bernd Alois, 5:418–21, 422, 423, 424, 426

collage technique and, 5:418–21

suicide of, 5:420

works of

   Die Soldaten, 5:418

   Requiem for a Young Poet, 5:420

Zimmermann, Pierre, 3:385

Zimmerman, Robert Allen, 5:315

Z mého života (Smetana), 3:446–47

Z mrtvého domu (Janáček), 4:424

"Z nového světa" (Dvořák). *See* "New World" Symphony

Zoilo, Annibale, 1:631

Zorn, John, 5:504–8

   Asian-American women and, 5:506–7

   cartoon soundtracks and, 5:505

   Cat o' Nine Tails, 5:506

   in conversation with Cole Gagne, 5:473

   "Forbidden Fruit," 5:507

   Spillane and, 5:505

   Torture Garden, 5:507

Z-tetrachord, 4:387, 394, 406, 408, 410, 415, 418

Zukofsky, Paul, 5:393

Zukunftsmusik, 3:421, 425, 436, 438, 439, 480, 682

Zukunftism (future-ism), 4:3

Zweck, 5:68–69

Zweckmässigkeit ohne Zweck (Kantian concept), 1:541

Zwilich, Ellen Taaffe, neotonality and, 5:454

Zwillingsbrüder, Die (Schubert), 3:84

Zwingli, Ulrich, 1:755

Zwölf Lieder (Mendelssohn), 3:185

Zwölftontechnik, 4:688